The Milwaukee Project

The Milwaukee Project

PREVENTING MENTAL RETARDATION IN CHILDREN AT RISK

BY

HOWARD L. GARBER
University of Wisconsin—Madison

MICHAEL J. BEGAB
Editor, AAMR Special Publications

AMERICAN ASSOCIATION ON MENTAL RETARDATION

Research supported in part by funds from the National Institute of Handicapped Research Grant No. G008300148, U.S. Department of Education, Washington, D.C. 20202.

Published by
American Association on Mental Retardation
1719 Kalorama Road, NW
Washington, D.C. 20009

Library of Congress Cataloging-in-Publication Data

Garber, Howard L.
  The Milwaukee project.

  Bibliography: p.
  1. Mental retardation—prevention. 2. Socially handicapped children—Mental health. 3. Socially handicapped children–Testing. 4. Mothers–Mental health. I. Begab, Michael J. II. American Association on Mental Retardation. III. Title. IV. Title: Preventing mental retardation in children at risk. [DNLM: 1. Child Development Disorders–prevention & control. 2. Mental Retardation–prevention & control. 3. Probability. WS 107 G213m]
  RC570.G37 1987 618.92'8588 87-26970
  ISBN 0-940898-16-0

Printed in the United States of America

This report is dedicated

to those children whose

needs might deprive them

of opportunity to make

their contribution

to society.

We hope this report helps

in understanding how

each to the best

of his or her ability

can have that opportunity

to accomplish.

Contents

Figures

xiii

Tables

Foreword

It is clear, as stated in the first paragraph of the introduction to the complex but clarifying pair of investigations described in this book by Howard Garber, that its impetus was concern with the new subclass of "cultural familial mental retardation." This subclass was so called because it occurs without evidence of pathology of the central nervous system. It is identified almost exclusively by IQ test performance, although it is more commonly found in low SES population subgroups. The extent to which nonorganic mental retardation is identified among disadvantaged populations touches upon one of the most difficult and complex issues in the social sciences, namely the nature of the interactive process which influences intellectual development.

Concern with the special importance of early experience in development goes back to the classical writing of Plato. Belief in the dominating influence of heredity is also of long standing, and it was greatly strengthened by Charles Darwin's conception of heredity as the source of the great variation among living organisms observed during his participation in the voyage of the Beagle. The tendency to emphasize the importance of either nurture or nature is misguided, however, for the process of development is an ongoing interaction between these influences and should be the focus of concern.

A substantial number of investigations have focused on the general nature of the developmental process. They have demonstrated that development consists of acquiring the ability to recognize the demands of situations encountered and, once the demands have been recognized, coping with them or receiving help with the process if it goes beyond the individual's existing skills. Such investigations have revealed a great deal about what is essentially important in early experience for the development of infants and young children. This book, on the other hand, focuses on manipulations of rearing conditions to test whether it is feasible to prevent mental retardation resulting from defects in the rearing conditions that are known to put children at risk for it. Howard Garber has described two investigations which are mutually reinforcing in their logic. The first has examined a seriously disadvantaged population in a census tract showing a high incidence of low IQs in the mentally retarded range. This investigation demonstrated that the tendency to lump people in a population with a low average IQ into a homogeneous group is wrong, for 80% of those children who entered school at age 6 with IQs below 80 had come from a select portion of poverty families in which the mothers had IQs below 80. Although this evidence has been employed by Arthur Jensen (1969) to support his contention that it is heredity that is chiefly responsible for such low IQs, the second study contains evidence that the low IQs found in the children of mothers with IQs of 80 or below need not occur.

The second investigation demonstrated that providing children of low IQ mothers with a tutelage program designed to improve their ability to cope with the kinds of problems that poverty generates and combining that tutelage with home management instruction can enable such children to achieve IQs averaging over 110. Ordinarily, such children would be the ones most likely to have IQs that decline and average in the 70s. The consequence of the logic of these two studies taken together is that they provide evidence against Jensen's contention that children of mothers with phenotypic IQs of less than 80 are doomed to have IQs under 80.

This evidence reported by Garber does not stand alone and becomes even more convincing when considered in conjunction with evidence reported by Wayne Dennis' (1973) study of the children of Creche. The children when first assessed had attained an average IQ of 50. After they were adopted, their IQs increased. However, it is important to note that in spite of the marked improvement in IQ performance, the children continued to show the months of retardation evident at the time they were adopted (albeit to a lesser degree in the IQ measure). To my mind, there is convincing evidence that hampering experiences cause depressed IQ performance, and the earlier infants are removed from hampering rearing conditions, the less evident is that effect.

Garber's evidence should also be considered in conjunction with the finding that mean ages of attaining steps on the Piaget-inspired, ordinal scale of Uzgiris and Hunt (1966, 1975) decrease substantially as the quality of the rearing conditions improves. For instance, among the children being reared at the Municipal Orphanage of Athens, Greece, where the infant-caregiver ratio was 30-to-3, the average age of those who attained the top step on the scale of object permanence was nearly 4 years (45.5 months), and only seven of the 20 attained it in that time (Paraskevopoulos & Hunt, 1971). Compare this with the fact that eight infants of families from the poverty sector of Mt. Carmel, Illinois, who had the advantage of educational day care in which they were shown, among other things, how to put a ping-pong ball through the round hole in the top of a shape box when they were first able to sit up. They attained the top step on the scale of object permanence when they were only 16.86 months old, only a little over a third of the age of attainment by those children at the Municipal Orphanage of Athens (Hunt, Paraskevopoulos, Schickedanz, & Uzgiris, 1975).

For another example, the controls of our research at the Tehran orphanage showed approximately the same degree of retardation as did those of the Municipal Orphanage in Athens, but the fifth wave of 11 foundlings reared by four caregivers, who were taught to respond promptly to their signs of distress and to encourage vocal imitation as a means of facilitating language acquisition, attained the top steps on all seven of the ordinal scales, and they did it on an average of 7 years younger than that required by 12 home-reared children of predominantly middle-class families in Worcester, Massachusetts, whose mean IQ was ultimately 110.

This assemblage of evidence indicates that not only is having the experience of high development-fostering quality of special importance during the early sensorimotor portion of childhood, but attaining all of an individual's genetic potential demands providing the experience of high development-fostering quality at an early age and maintaining it continuously.

While it is obvious that genes operate to define the potential directions in an organism's development and perhaps to set certain limits upon what abilities can become outstanding in a person, the wherewithal to solve problems does not come automatically with the maturation of brain and body. Such skills do not develop simply from varied stimulation from the environment, but rather require opportunities for appropriate interaction with it. It is with this important understanding that the Milwaukee Project has addressed the investigation of early intellectual development of children with the unique experience of being born into an environment of poverty to low functioning mothers. By restricting the treated group to a closely qualified sample of families, the project was able to study the effects of manipulated experience on a relatively controlled phenotypic base. Though the genes may set limits on an individual's potential for intellectual development, a mother's phenotypic level of intelligence as it is commonly measured does not fix her offspring's genotypic potential, even though her low level of functioning may limit her ability to cope with the conditions of poverty and to interact constructively with her infants and young children.

As Garber argues, there is considerable and continuing lack of appreciation of the extent of individual differences in demographically defined samples and a comparable lack of understanding of the implications of that variation for delays in intellectual performance. This lack of understanding is an integral reason for the difficulty in explaining fully the origins of mildly retarded performance and therefore the inability to prevent or satisfactorily ameliorate such poor intellectual performance.

Questions such as those concerning the relative proportion of the variance in intelligence attributable to heredity and to environment are unfortunate because of their unimportance in understanding what controls children's development. Much more pertinent are specific questions relevant to either problems of education and welfare practice or to the theory of human intelligence and its development. Howard Garber has done a commendable job of interpreting the issues and relating the evidence to other evidence in the relevant literature with respect to an important problem.

J. McVicker Hunt

REFERENCES

Dennis, W. (1973). *Children of the Creche*. New York: Appleton-Century-Crofts.
Hunt, J. JcV., Paraskevopoulos, J., Schickedanz, D., & Uzgiris, I. C. (1975). Variations in the mean ages of achieving object permanence under diverse conditions of rearing. In B. Z. Friedlander, G. Sterritt, & G. E. Kirk (Eds.), *Exceptional infant: Vol. 3. Assessment and intervention* (pp. 247–262). New York: Brunner/Mazel.
Jensen, A. (1969). How much can we boost IQ and scholastic achievement? *Harvard Educational Review, 39*, 1–124.
Paraskevopoulos, J., & Hunt, J. McV. (1971). Object construction and imitation under differing conditions of rearing. *Journal of Genetic Psychology, 119*, 301–321.
Uzgiris, I. C., & Hunt, J. McV. (1966). An instrument for assessing infant psychological development. Mimeographed paper, Psychological Development Laboratory, University of Illinois at Urbana-Champaign.
Uzgiris, I. C., & Hunt, J. McV. (1975). *Assessment in infancy: Ordinal scales of psychological development*. Urbana: University of Illinois Press.

Preface

Over the past 30 years, no issue in the field has generated more intense or bitter controversy than that concerning the etiology of *cultural-familial* mental retardation, a mild form of retardation currently referred to as psychosocial (Grossman, 1983). Nationwide interest in this question began with and continues to be based in public and professional recognition that this kind of retardation is almost exclusively found among economically depressed population subgroups. Minority groups, who are disproportionately represented in disadvantaged populations for a variety of reasons, show a particularly high prevalence of this form of retardation. Because the largest proportion of all individuals labeled mentally retarded are categorized as cultural-familial, it is of the utmost educational and social concern to ascertain more precisely the etiology of this form of retardation. The major influence in beginning this project was the perceived need for a more adequate understanding of the epidemiologic factors that might hold clues to the early origins of cultural-familial mental retardation.

Particular interest in this form of mild mental retardation is created by the fact that it is the only form of mental retardation that must be identified by exclusion because it is not accompanied by central nervous system pathology and because it shows uneven epidemiologic characteristics — including, especially, a disproportionate distribution among low SES and minority groups of the general population.

Children identified as cultural-familial mentally retarded not only do not show any pathology to accompany their low IQ performance, but most often are identified only after failed performance in school. Without clear clinical symptoms and with little information regarding the true nature of their early developmental experience, disadvantaged children are often regarded for the trappings of their poverty or their nonmainstream cultural group. At issue therefore is whether the etiology of their low IQ performance (the primary criterion for identifying mental retardation) is their obvious and presumed deprived early developmental experiences or is the nonobvious but presumed inadequate endowment for intelligence requisite to success and a higher SES. On one side of the issue, the nurture side, lowered performance was thought to be depressed by experience and therefore could be compensated for by experience; while on the other side, the nature side, the primary influence on intellectual performance was considered genetic and therefore was thought to be essentially unalterable. Evidence has been marshalled for both sides of this argument. Studies have demonstrated that children who suffer from extremely deprived environments and exhibit severe withdrawal and developmental delays can be restored with treatment (Clarke & Clarke, 1976; Hunt, 1961), while studies of twin intellect or even parent-child problem solving resemblance have been offered as arguments for the primacy of the genetic base to intelligence (Jensen, 1980).

There remain, however, some difficult problems to resolve for both sides of the argument that seem to ensure that both influences are critically involved but not enough to determine how the phenomenon of intellect develops. By far the major dependent measure in this issue has been the IQ score, a measure whose instruments presume a typical if not optimum environment. In the case of the severely disadvantaged, this point of view is probably not tenable. The range of variation within population subgroups is underestimated and even obscured by discussion of the epidemiologic correlates of the IQ score. Even when the largest estimates of heritability for intelligence are used, the rate of cognitive development may still be significantly influenced by natural variations in experience (Jensen, 1969, 1980, 1981; McCall, Appelbaum, & Hogarty, 1973). Unfortunately, social scientists have not had a clear understanding of the process by which variations in experience influence the rate of cognitive development. There is no satisfactorily clear distinction between variables that are simply statistically associated with development. It can be referred to as a confounding of etiologic and epidemiologic relationships.

The Milwaukee Project was part of a larger investigation attempting to understand the complex of influences that interfere with normal intellectual development. It was the test of a hypothesis that a primary etiologic agent for cultural-familial mental retardation is the developmental experience created for her normal newborn child by the mentally retarded mother of a family living in poverty. That hypothesis was derived from an investigation of a seriously disadvantaged population for which there was a disproportionate prevalence of low IQ scores. This investigation indicated that the source of the excess prevalence was not the low SES community in a general sense, but rather it could be targeted to families where the maternal IQ was low and in the retarded range.

Acknowledgments

This report spans nearly two decades since the inception of the research program. It has benefited from both the wisdom and courage of several people who withstood hardships both typical and unusual for such an effort. That it began at all and how it was protected during the early stages are tributes to Dr. Rick Heber. His inspiration and guidance created and developed the program.

Several others including Dr. Richard Dever at Indiana University and Dr. John Rynders at the University of Minnesota not only were involved in its inception but have remained as advisors and friends throughout the program's growth. A number of people provided insightful criticism on content and chapter structure, especially Harvey Stevens, University of Wisconsin–Madison, Dr. Ed Meyers at the University of California–Los Angeles, and Dr. Marcia Heiman, Boston College. Their help was of considerable value.

I am most grateful to Dr. Mike Begab, whose editorial expertise and personal encouragement were essential to the final report.

A special note of thanks is due to a federal agency with considerable heart: the National Institute of Handicapped Research's Special Centers Program, which supported this research. This program is a reflection of the character of two of its key administrators, Dr. Joe Fenton and Emily Cromar. They provided fundamental support and endured, especially when we needed them most.

Many people at the University of Wisconsin–Madison participated in this research over the years. Caroline Hoffman and Susan Harrington, who developed and implemented the curriculum and managed the preschool program during some of the toughest years that our big cities have undergone, deserve special commendations, along with a special thanks to Erma Sims, Program Supervisor, and all of the teachers who devoted so many hours of their time to the program.

The graduate assistants who worked on this study are a very special group of people, whose mettle has been especially tested over the last few years this report was being prepared, and little more could have been asked of them in the way of academic and technical commitment. I have depended on them for many years: They include Dr. Carol Falender and her work on mother-child observations; Elena Reyes' superb work with the language program; Dr. Maurice McInerney's total commitment and insightful contributions to the learning program; Dr. Raja Velu, who masterfully developed the elaborate statistical program for these data; and Karin Shepard, whose tenacity and sensitivity helped Elena Reyes develop the individual family portraits.

In addition, special thanks is given to Pat Williams, who untiringly followed each of the families in this study as though they were her own. And, of course, the families, who trusted us and submitted to this long process, have made a contribution to the lives of hundreds of such families and to whom "thanks" hardly does justice.

In the production of the early report drafts and manuscripts, Breta Gilchrist provided unceasing and invaluable aid. A number of people helped in the assembly of the final manuscript, but a special thanks is extended to June Melder who helped most when we needed help.

Above all, three people in particular have committed themselves to helping me complete this report and have given me considerable personal support. I owe them very much — they are Helen Hartwig and Dr. James Hodge. They were great. The third person is my wife, Elfi — she sure put up with a lot for a long, long time.

But for this whole group and more, this report would not otherwise have been completed.

1
Introduction to the Problem

In 1959 the American Association on Mental Retardation (AAMR) (then the American Association on Mental Deficiency) provided the first official classification of a form of mental retardation for which there was neither clinical evidence of central nervous system disease nor any obvious pathology. It announced the subclassification of *cultural-familial mental retardation*. By doing so, it was officially recognized for the first time that mental retardation is not a fixed, unalterable characteristic and that individuals might be only statistically at risk to be identified as mentally retarded or, having been so identified, would not necessarily be retarded for life. In addition it gave strength to the arguments that environmental or experiential factors were crucial and necessary agents in the process of intellectual development. In effect, this statement helped to fuel interest in issues of the primacy of nature or nurture in intellectual development.

The current study was born out of concerns related to the 1959 AAMR definition of cultural-familial mental retardation and the questions presented regarding the permanence of mental retardation and the underlying nature of retarded functioning in the mild or borderline range. This form of retardation essentially derives its definition from the epidemiologic excess of low IQs in low socioeconomic status (SES) population subgroups and provides few clues to the etiology of the delay or retardation in intellectual performance. The study reported here represents an effort undertaken by the University of Wisconsin Rehabilitation Research and Training Center to resolve part of the complex of possible influences on early intellectual development, in those born into seriously disadvantaged environments, that could account for the increased risk for certain children to be identified as mentally retarded.

The lack of a longitudinal empirical base on individual growth processes together with the fact that the mildly mentally retarded as a group do not present obvious pathologic features associated with their handicap leaves considerable room for speculation as to the source of their problem. Several

1

etiological hypotheses for low intellectual performance have been subsumed under the rubric of the *nature-nurture controversy*, a term that refers to the various historical arguments about the source of intellectual development. One side of the argument uses available evidence to show the predominance of genetically inherited influences ("nature") on the development of intellectual behavior; the other uses basically the same evidence to support the predominance of environmental experiences ("nurture") as the shaper of intelligent behavior. All admit to interaction, accepting that there is an interplay of both sources to some degree.

The fact that there are so many potential influences, many of which cannot be directly measured, has caused major problems for the resolution of this controversy. For example, a piece of evidence often cited in this controversy is the excessively large number of low IQ scores associated with low SES and minority group populations. The nature argument has used this fact to generate support for the prepotence of poor genetic heritability as the cause for the inability of an impoverished person to upgrade his/her socioeconomic status. In effect, proponents of this position say that inherited factors cause achievement deficits, which in turn perpetuate intergenerational poverty. On the other side of the argument, nurture theorists point to the depressed environment as the source of the problem. They suggest that the conditions of an impoverished environment and the experiences associated with those conditions induce low intellectual functioning. This controversy remains for the most part unresolved because there continues to be a confusion of epidemiologic correlations as to etiology and because there has been little direct experimental investigation of the origins of mild retardation in general and even less of the specific etiology of the more restricted cultural-familial retardation.

The epidemiologic relationship between poverty and retardation is complex. In fact, the vast majority of individuals who are considered poor function well within normal intellectual levels, and yet they remain poor. Although low levels of intellectual functioning may exacerbate an individual's problems, improvement in this one factor alone may not provide the ability to improve his/her station in life. The interaction of an organism with its environment involves a complex constellation of factors that does not readily yield to most attempts to unravel it. Factors to consider include basic biological variations that interact with different opportunity levels, various levels of intellectual stimulation events, language models, nutrition, health care, and the insidious influence of a low level of expectations, subtly transferred by caregivers and others in the environment (Hess, 1970; Lewis, 1966). Only as these factors are accounted for can the etiologic influences of development be understood.

With the advent of social concern for the country's poor and those minority groups comprising large portions of that population, there has also been increasing, uncritical acceptance of the view that the high frequency of mental retardation found among the poor is directly attributable to deprivation of opportunities. Such a social-deprivation hypothesis now underlies most research in the area of mild retardation. This view of the etiology of cultural-familial mental retardation has little research evidence to support it. In fact, it is based largely on casual observations of presumed deprivation of learning opportunities and on statistics that show that the average intelligence test scores of slum-dwelling children decline as they grow older. Statistics demonstrating a high incidence of prematurity and delivery among economically disadvantaged population subgroups cannot account for their substantially greater prevalence of mental retardation.

If the nature of interaction among the possible sources of environmental and genetic influence were better understood, we would be increasingly able to predict individual differences in cognitive behavior outcome. In general, it is a lack of appreciation for the extent of individual differences among the mentally retarded and the lack of understanding of the implications of that variation for cognitive performance that have contributed to the inability to explain fully the origins of mildly retarded performance and to provide properly for either its prevention or amelioration. The definition of mild mental retardation suggests generally that the impairment originates in early development and is later associated with deficiencies in adaptive behavior, but this is a definition that has relied on epidemiologic data. Hypotheses such as nature-nurture, social deprivation, and/or critical periods have been evoked as etiologic explanations, but in point of fact, these hypotheses are without sufficient substantive empirical bases and often confuse epidemiologic association as etiologic causation.

Epidemiologic predictors are based on the correlation between certain population characteristics and the incidence of low IQs. There are many such predictors available, but our current knowledge concerning the effects of the environment, as well as the effects of genetic inheritance on growth and development, is limited. Much of what we "know" of the relationship between specific variables and behavior is actually only correlational. Although we can be confident that these variables will show a consistent and substantial statistical association with variations in intellectual performance, we fall far short of understanding the mechanisms by which these variables influence intellectual behavior. We are not even sure that they actually do influence behavior. No one has yet been able to satisfactorily explain the differential effects of the same environment on different individuals.

One attempt by researchers to delineate the importance of certain agents in the process of intellectual development and to specify the extent of detrimental influence on intellectual development is embodied in the notion of *risk*, which refers to the probability of a certain event occurring. A child born with a birthweight below 1,500 grams presents an example of a biomedical risk factor that along with other signs predicts difficulties in the development of this child. Several authors (e.g., Birch, Richardson, Baird, Horobin, & Illsley, 1970; Brain, Heimer, Wortis, & Freedman, 1966; Williams & Scarr, 1971) have shown that infants with organic impairments born to impoverished mothers are at least doubly disadvantaged. In particular, biological vulnerability will interact with inadequate social circumstances and improper developmental stimulation to increase pernicious maturational pressures on the infant's later intellectual functioning. A low IQ score is a comparable risk factor in the psychological realm. IQ is an estimate of current functioning, but one that should also suggest that the child is not adequately processing information that would enable future normal growth.

Risk, however, is not a condemnation but a caution. It can only alert us to possible problems at some time in the future, as Clarke and Clarke (1976) point out. Risk reflects the dual notion that disposing conditions are operating that could work against proper development and that there are important individual differences in the effect these conditions can and will have across individuals and individual families.

Among homes exhibiting all the signs and evidence of severe disadvantagement, circumstances vary greatly. Parental attitudes, anxieties, and skills differ; children's needs change from home to home; a family's goals, resources, commitment, and communication are unique to that family. We can appreciate the fact, then, that no one set of familial circumstances will have the same effect across all people, all children, and/or all adults. Nevertheless, there is a special concern for the case of children from certain disadvantaged families in which a nonsupportive or negative psychosocial environment can act to change behavior in ways that interfere with ability. A constellation of possible influences must be delineated and tested to determine its importance as a source of declining IQ performance and the excess of low intellectual performance among severely disadvantaged subgroups in our population. An investigation of these influences would have a twofold purpose: to identify those influences that, if manipulated to the advantage of the individual, can enhance intellectual behavior and to determine which influences interfere with intellectual development, prevent them from exerting a detrimental influence, and allow normal intellectual development.

But, as was noted, a major reason for the intractability of the problem of cultural-familial retardation has been the difficulty of its detection. The mildness of cultural-familial mental retardation has obscured its origins. The nature of the early environment and related experiences serves to conceal the very growth process it is acting to compromise. The mildly retarded individual is usually first discovered upon failing to meet the challenge of the formal school system (Birch et al., 1970) and often not until several years into school. Thus, the only children diagnosed early in life as mentally retarded are those who have demonstrated conspicuous abnormal functioning. The milder deficits in intellectual growth remain undetected. By the time the problems are revealed, they may well have become quite resistant to traditional remedial measures. Of prime importance, therefore, are the early identification of cultural-familial mental retardation and the development of a process to discover its causes. The Milwaukee Project began this task with an investigation of a disadvantaged population reported to have an excessively high frequency of mental retardation.

The results of an extensive investigation of a seriously disadvantaged community, which indicated that low IQ was not a general phenomenon of a low SES community, led to a research focus emphasizing the immediate family and home environment as influences more important to a child's intellectual development than the general poverty environment. The Milwaukee Project was a longitudinal study concerned with understanding the influence of family and/or home environments on the intellectual development of normal newborns for whom the survey data indicated high risk of declining intelligence test performance and who were therefore increasingly likely to be identified as mentally retarded by school age.

The Milwaukee Project began during the 1960s, when our nation's consciousness of the plight of the disadvantaged was reawakened. That interest in the plight of disadvantaged children spawned different lines of research. In general the research was bolstered by recently gathered evidence (Bloom, 1964; Hunt, 1961) that pointed to the effects of both experiential deprivation and experiential enrichment and their importance in the early development of children. One line of research responded mainly to social and political concerns for the discrepancy between poor children's school performance and that of their more advantaged peers. Using a *social deprivation hypothesis*, a number of studies were initiated to prepare disadvantaged children through a compensatory preschool educational program just prior to school entry (Lazar, Darlington, Murray, Royce, & Snipper, 1982). For these studies, children were typically selected by general poverty indicators and/or already reduced IQ test performance.

Another line of research was concerned more expressly with the nature of the early developmental experiences of such children in an attempt to determine the source or sources of influence that negatively affect social and cognitive processes in intellectual development. In this line of research, children were more closely qualified for selection by using a family characteristic such as parent education rather than a general population demographic such as socioeconomic status. In these studies data were gathered by extensive observation strategies and elaborate interviews, but with few actual treatment programs. The Milwaukee Project both closely qualified children for selection (seriously disadvantaged families with very low maternal IQ) and entered them into an intervention program as a test of whether compensating for the immediate environment of high risk children could prevent declining intellectual development. The Milwaukee Project also attempted to minimize the statistical effect of heredity by limiting the IQ range of the mentally retarded mothers and thereby providing a longitudinal test of the relationship between the experience of being reared by a retarded mother living in poverty and the rate of intellectual development.

INTELLECTUAL DEVELOPMENT AND
RETARDATION

Intelligence tests have been the primary instrument used to assess intellectual performance and to characterize intellectual development. Such tests obtain a limited sample of behavior for comparison with a standardized estimate for the individual child's appropriate rate of intellectual development in terms of mental age relative to chronologically age matched peers. A significant delay in the rate of cognitive development is signaled by a low test score that, if low enough, defines mental retardation. The reasons for performance-defined retardation have been attributed to several sources (Grossman, 1983; Heber, 1961). In clinically defined retardation, there is evidence of significant central nervous system damage attributable to trauma or disease or to genetic anomaly. Such retardation is usually severe but accounts for only approximately 25% of the retarded population. These individuals are fairly evenly distributed throughout all SES categories. In the absence of clinical evidence, performance exclusively defines retardation as delays in intellectual development for the remaining 70 to 80% of those individuals identified as mentally retarded. Because such retardation is without clinically obvious pathology, it can only be attributed to an unspecifiable relationship between polygenic and environmental influences that govern development and even then may fall within what may be considered the normal range (Zigler, 1967; Zigler, Balla, & Hodapp, 1984). Unlike those whose retardation is attributable to biological factors, individuals with mild retardation or delays are disproportionately represented within low SES and minority groups.

The American Association on Mental Retardation (AAMR) (Heber, 1961) first designated this form of mild retardation as cultural-familial retardation simply to reflect the statistical association between low IQ and low socioeconomic class membership and the high probability that one or both parents and siblings within the individual's family were also retarded. The original emphasis was on the familial history of intellectual subnormality within low SES populations, and there was "no intent to specify either the independent action or the relationship between genetic and cultural factors in the etiology of cultural-familial retardation" (Heber, 1961, p. 40). As a result, an important question remained as to which experiences interact with any given genetic makeup and operate within its reaction range to either facilitate or depress what are considered normal rates of development (Hunt, 1961, 1968; Jensen, 1968).

The opportunity to examine this question came from Hunt's (1961) synthesized findings from several areas of research that brought into question the traditional notion of fixed intelligence and predetermined development. His argument for the importance of experience, particularly early experience, was based in part on Piaget's destinational model of intellectual development

(Hunt, 1969). In destinational models of development, the order of acquisition of increasingly complex mediational processes is believed to be species specific and highly influenced by genetics, while the timing and range of developmental behaviors is influenced more by variations in experience (Cole, Gay, Glick, & Sharp, 1974; de Lacy, 1970, 1971a, 1971b; DeLemons, 1969; Gollin, 1981; Hyde, 1969; Price-Williams, 1961). While recognizing that the reaction range for the rate of development was a product of inheritance, Hunt viewed differences in the time between landmarks of cognitive growth as the result of experience. In essence, Hunt was suggesting that such differences were the inverse indications of the capacity that various interactions between children and their environment had to differentially influence intellectual development.

During the early 1960s, the increased social and political interest in the plight of minority groups and the economically poor together with Hunt's findings provided the impetus for many programs aimed at helping young disadvantaged children. Unfortunately, the emphasis on the global and obvious environmental differences of low SES groups in their standard of living and other measures of deprivation were also considered *explanations* for differences in measured intelligence. Considerable evidence of variability within SES groups and the overlap of characteristics across groups tended to be overlooked when attempts were made to ameliorate deficiencies (Condry, 1983), and they were increasingly attributed to undifferentiated social deprivation (Heber, Dever, & Conry, 1968; Hunt, 1968).

DEFINITION IN MENTAL RETARDATION

Mental retardation is a concept that is defined as a function of societal demands, which are in turn related to differences in technological sophistication and in social philosophy. The definition therefore varies over time as a function of variations in these factors within and between given societies. The difficulty in achieving consensus concerning an adequate definition that is both objective and measurable is highlighted by Clarke and Clarke's (1974) overview of the many attempts made through the years.

Although efforts by the AAMR continue to meet with criticism (Clausen, 1967; Mercer, 1973), they have been particularly helpful in promoting definitional consensus. The AAMR committees formed for this purpose (Grossman, 1973; Heber, 1961) have suggested definitions for various forms of mental handicap that place a dual emphasis on intellectual and adaptive behavior. This requires that a person's relative inability to adapt his/her behavior to society's standards be established before s/he is classified as retarded. In addition, because adaptive behavior is culturally relative (Tizard, 1974), the criteria for the definition require that the appropriateness of each person's behavior be judged in relationship to his/her age and the requirements of the local community in which s/he resides. Because life situations and behavioral expectations vary across the life span, classification of a person as retarded must be viewed within a temporal framework and must provide for change as circumstances change. The most current AAMR definition states:

> Mental retardation refers to significantly subaverage general intellectual functioning existing concurrently with deficits in adaptive behavior, and manifested during the developmental period (Grossman, 1983, p. 1).

This definition is basically the same as the definition developed by the AAMR committee in 1959 (see Heber, 1961) except that the "significant subaverage" IQ level was dropped from 1 to 2 standard deviations to minimize the negative effects of labeling individuals with borderline mental handicaps for which there is no clinical evidence of organic involvement and mental handicaps for which there are no evident symptoms of pathology. There are literally scores of specific diseases and conditions known to produce damage to the brain and that often lead to mental retardation. But estimates are that no more than 20% of the total population of individuals labeled mentally retarded present demonstrable pathology in the structure or functioning of the central nervous system.

Mental retardation in which pathology of the central nervous system is a presenting feature is fairly evenly distributed throughout the various socio-economic, ethnic, and racial population subgroupings. Furthermore, this type of mental retardation is generally, although not always, associated with measured intelligence more than 3 standard deviations below the mean (IQ less than 55 or so on the major tests) (Zigler, 1967). Affected persons tend to be placed in self-contained programs in school and often demonstrate severely impaired adaptive behavior in adult life. They are also likely to demonstrate physical disabilities and/or special health problems.

By contrast, 80% of all individuals considered mentally retarded do not present obvious gross pathology of the central nervous system and they function within the mild range of retardation. The AAMR subcategory for mild mental retardation is described as follows:

> Criteria for inclusion under this category require that there be evidence of subnormal functioning in at least one of the parents and in one or more siblings, where there are such. These cases are usually from impoverished environments involving poor housing, inadequate diets, and inadequate medical care. There may be prematurity, low birthweight, or history of infectious diseases, but no single entity appears to have contributed to the slow or retarded development (Grossman, 1977, pp. 67–68).

A small number from this group may be labeled retarded because of longstanding emotional or psychotic disorders of childhood that interfere with learning. A few may be called retarded because a specific disability, such as impaired vision, impaired hearing, or cerebral palsy, has resulted in a restriction of learning opportunities. There are probably some individuals with organic involvement so mild that it goes undetected, yet contributes to their lowered performance. For example, inadequate prenatal and postnatal care factors among mothers in low socioeconomic groups often result in high rates of prematurity, which may be associated with central nervous system damage. Additional factors that have been suggested include genetically transmitted intellectual limitations and inadequate infant health supervision. Both of the latter are often present in high risk groups and may be related to mild central nervous system insults.

The greatest proportion of this group, however, is comprised of persons who seem quite normal in the physical sense; they simply function as mentally retarded. It is this group that is designated as the cultural-familial mentally retarded. If there is an underlying causal factor for this type of retardation, it has not yet been specifically identified. Most of the factors presumed to be causative have been implicated epidemiologically because they are not detectable with present methods of examination. Individuals within this group have mild degrees of retardation, falling within the IQ range of 50 to 75, and they may demonstrate mild or moderate impairments in adaptive behavior, although adaptive behavior is not always clinically assessed (Clausen, 1967). This form of retardation is almost exclusively found among economically depressed urban and rural population subgroups. Although there is some evidence to suggest that deprivation of social and cognitive stimulation essential to normal intellectual development may be a contributing etiological factor in this group, the specific mechanisms of this relationship have not been identified.

The label *cultural-familial* therefore cannot imply etiological factors because it accurately reflects only epidemiological factors, that is, the statistical association between mental retardation and certain subgroups in the general population, the high probability that more than one other member of the cultural-familial family can also be labeled retarded, and a lack of evidence of biological factors or organic conditions that could account for the intellectual deficit.

PREVALENCE OF CULTURAL-FAMILIAL MENTAL RETARDATION

A major reason for the intractability of the problem of cultural-familial mental retardation is the difficulty of detection. The mildness of the intellectual and adaptive deficits obscures not only the origins of the disorder, but also the extent of the disorder within the population. Hypotheses about etiological factors responsible for cultural-familial mental retardation have relied on the relationship among epidemiological factors. However, epidemiologic survey reveals statistical, not causal, associations and, given the variation in methodology in such surveys, the reliability of these data can be suspect and can limit the conclusions drawn. Perhaps the most vexing problem is the degree of reported variation in prevalence of low IQ scores as a function of both racial and ethnic grouping. Most of these epidemiological studies have used a statistical definition of abnormality (e.g., the use of army inductee rejection rates) to provide estimates of mild retardation. Mercer (1972) argued that such a statistical model tends to define cultural subgroups as deviant. In support of this argument, she estimated that community agencies label two and a half times more persons from minority groups as retarded as would be expected under the normal curve. This high prevalence occurs despite the fact that these agencies identify only half as many persons as they might under a strict clinical definition of retardation.

Stein, Susser, and Saenger (1976) suggest: that surveys based on "use of agencies" infer lower rates than population studies; that this "use of agencies" procedure samples only a selected few from among many who are functioning at similar levels; and that the particular IQ test or definition used to define the cases further skews the interpretation of cultural-familial mental retardation prevalence estimates. Other authors (Adams, 1973; Adams, McIntosh, & Weade, 1973; Sattler, 1973) have discussed the need for test instruments that would avoid ethnic and racial biases and that would quantify pertinent sociocultural and environmental factors in order to make valid across-group comparisons. Additionally, several studies (Kushlick, 1961, 1964; Tarjan, Wright, Eyman, & Keeran, 1973) report a consistent decrease in the number of mildly retarded individuals served by hospitals and by special education classes in Great Britain and the United States over the past 30 years. Yet, published figures on the number of exceptional education needs students being served by special education classes in both countries have shown a consistent increase over this same period. Modifications in the legal definition of mental deficiency, liberalization of institutional or custodial regimes, increases in exceptional education funding, and even such social forces as unemployment, inflation, and changes in political administrations are confounding factors that can help explain variations in statistical trends.

Therefore, a major problem in establishing prevalence rates is that the yield of cases will vary greatly with the method of assessment, depending on whether we use population surveys, diagnostic criteria, or clinical evaluations (Appelbaum & McCall, 1983). As a result, attempts to make definitions of mental retardation more precise and objective will continue to be undercut by the practices of clinical labeling and educational classification (MacMillan, Meyers, & Morrison, 1980). Definition may require that both intellectual and adaptive skill levels be ascertained, but in practice the fact remains that low IQ typically precedes any observed behavior impairment, and it is the low IQ score that causes the label of mentally retarded to be applied.

The vast majority of cases of mental retardation are diagnosed during the school years, with the school being the principal labeling agent (Birch et al., 1970; Robbins, Mercer, & Meyers, 1967). This practice has resulted in reports of relatively low prevalence rates for both the preschool years and for the age periods after school, but an extremely high prevalence rate for those years during which school attendance is compulsory. These prevalence figures are traditionally interpreted to mean that mildly retarded children do not meet the academic requirements of school and that failure to learn in school results in the mentally retarded label. This explanation produces the "6-hour retarded" child (i.e., a youngster who is retarded only during the 6 hours spent in the classroom).

One of the more plausible explanations for the observed shifts in prevalence would be that it is the greater availability of school aged children for testing that results in apparently increased prevalence rates for school aged populations (Birch et al., 1970; Heber, 1970). Lemkau and Imre (1966) sampled every household within a rural county in southeastern Maryland. These authors found neither a sharp increase in prevalence from preschool to school age populations nor a significant decrease in prevalence from school to postschool age. Rather, they found a developmental continuum in which increasing numbers of individuals are unable to meet the performance requirements first of the school system and then of the community at large. The U.S. Office of Education, for example, reports that a large percentage of the handicapped are unemployed, dependent on welfare, and/or under total care (Comptroller General of the United States, 1976).

A tragic social byproduct of flawed methodologies is that all similar-appearing members of population subgroupings for whom an excess prevalence of low IQs has been found are assumed to be low functioning. The result is that many individuals are labeled mentally retarded who should not be. The stigma of being labeled retarded or being placed in a special class can induce a unique personality development that may significantly alter the way of life in a manner nearly impossible to undo. The simple act of applying the label *mentally retarded* often results in the child being exposed to a succession of experiences that inhibit both social and academic growth because of the notion that society should expect less of such children. Given these conditions, we may be artificially increasing the number of children who are actually retarded and in need of services.

Definitions provide convenient categories, but also avoid recognition of individual variation within categories and the social consequences such labels tend to precipitate. Therefore, it is clearly necessary to refine our understanding of the epidemiologic factors of poverty in general and of the group of individuals labeled *mildly mentally retarded*, specifically. The important task is to study individual variation within these groups, which have been viewed in the past as homogeneous.

2
The Course of Early
Intellectual Development

STUDYING INTELLECTUAL GROWTH

The intellectual growth of children has been intensely studied for the better part of this century, but not until the middle 1960s were any programmatic efforts made to manipulate this developmental process longitudinally. The major impetus for the most recent efforts has been a national concern for the significant discrepancy observed between advantaged and disadvantaged children's early entering school performance. Earlier longitudinal studies of development provided considerable information about general growth (Berkeley Growth Study [Jones, Bayley, MacFarlane, & Honzik, 1971], Fels Longitudinal Study [Kagan & Moss, 1962]). The major exception was Terman et al.'s (1925) longitudinal study of the gifted, which focused on intellect. More recent studies in this same realm include Werner's Kauai Study (Werner, Bierman, & French, 1971). Large cohorts selected for date of birth were observed for their development.

The current effort is directed toward a concern for the advantaged and disadvantaged and, at least for purposes of discussion, is considered as a test of a social deprivation hypothesis. This hypothesis argues that school performance deficits are the result of a deprived or impoverished early environment and that compensatory preschooling offsets the negative effects of that experience and lifts the low performance for disadvantaged children by the time they attain school age. These studies generally selected poor and/or essentially normal nonorganically involved low IQ scoring children (1 or 2 standard deviations below the mean) and focused on raising IQ scores. The recent summary report of a number of such studies by Lazar et al. (1982) has interpreted this effort as successful. Success was indicated mainly by lower rates of special

13

class placements for treated children and, as Schweinhart and Weikart (1981) pointed out, with increased cost-benefit effectiveness. Studies of compensatory preschooling and general longitudinal observations of development may be distinguished from other studies of the development of children by the subjects being specified as organically involved (e.g., children with Down's Syndrome as in Hayden & Haring, 1976); that is to say, a clinical etiologic referent for impaired development has been obtained as a criterion. For the compensatory preschool subjects, the primary selection criterion was poverty.

Poverty, low SES, or even serious disadvantage are broad demographic descriptors that have generally been accepted as indicators of risk for low IQ performance, primarily because of the excess prevalence of low IQs among disadvantaged ethnic minorities and low SES population subgroups. Membership in such subgroups has long been recognized as a fairly reliable predictor of low intellectual functioning and poor academic achievement (Davis, 1947; Havighurst & Janke, 1944; Hieronymous, 1951; Jones, 1954; Kennedy, Van de Riet, & White, 1963; Lavin, 1965; Milner, 1951; Terrell, Durkin, & Wiesley, 1959; Zigler & de Labry, 1962). In addition, losses in IQ score for children have been found to be widespread and consistent enough in low SES circumstances to be considered normative (Asher, 1935; Deutsch & Brown, 1964; Gordon, 1923; Klaus & Gray, 1968; Sherman & Key, 1932; Skeels & Fillmore, 1937).

Unfortunately, the close association between low and declining intellectual performance and a broad demographic variable such as poverty can lead to some confusion between epidemiology and etiology. The fact is that only a small percentage of the poor are mentally retarded. For that matter, the extent of individual variation within the low SES population is effectively concealed by a global index of poverty such as low SES. Gross demographic characterizations of population subgroups together with estimates of intellectual functioning for those population groups extrapolated from incidence figures of low IQ scores mislead efforts to resolve the etiology of this form of mental retardation. This confusion is epitomized by the cultural deprivation hypothesis (Deutsch, 1966; Tulkin, 1968), which became popular in the late 1950s and early 1960s. Low SES environments were considered culturally deprived or disadvantaged and were believed to depress or retard intellectual development and academic achievement. This resulted in what has been termed *progressive retardation* (Klaus & Gray, 1968) or *cumulative deficits* (Ausubel, 1964; Deutsch, 1966), an oft-noted phenomenon for the disadvantaged, that is, a slow but steady decline in IQ performance over time. Cumulative deficit conveniently embraces both aspects of the issue — on the one hand it suggests that the decline results from an increasing inability to successfully challenge performance demands, while on the other hand, it suggests that for some the increasing dissipation of skills and motivation is caused by the press of poverty's ills.

The *curve of cumulative deficits*, although regarded as an adequate description of intellectual growth for the disadvantaged, obscures individual differences in rate of performance. This problem results from the population sampling procedure that uses poverty or some other global population demographic and then assumes an adequate population base rate to make presumptions about individual intellectual performance. In other words, even though epidemiologic data can suggest a greater likelihood for a low IQ score to occur in a low SES population, that likelihood ratio is still only a gross estimate and will require additional careful delineation of individual characteristics to qualify likelihood estimates more accurately. The resolution of this conflict can have important social implications, but still more important are the psychoeducational implications that may be derived from ascertaining the source of the excess prevalence of low IQ scores among the disadvantaged of our society and understanding the nature of the course of intellectual development that occurs with increasing age for children from seriously disadvantaged families.

Earlier views of intelligence as an intrinsic, fixed, and predetermined characteristic suggested that the major influence of environmental factors was on test-taking behavior and the understanding of content rather than on intelligence per se (Deutsch, 1973). The basic assumption was that cultural biases in the tests and negative influences in the environment prevented children in low SES groups from demonstrating their full intellectual capabilities (Davis & Eells, 1953; Eells, Davis, Havighurst, Herrick, & Tyler, 1951). Hunt recognized that genes set limits on an individual's potential for intellectual development, but he suggested that intellectual behavior is made up of hierarchically arranged central mechanisms that operate within these limits and emphasized the crucial role of life experiences in their development (Hunt, 1961, 1964). He urged, therefore, that the question of what proportion of variance in intelligence is related to either genetics or environmental influence be considered less important than the question of how the environment interacts with a given genetic makeup and operates within its limits to depress intellectual development.

Although Hunt's (1961) synthesis of research included considerable discussion of the basic nature of intelligence, early intervention efforts based on his theories were more interested in the extent to which environmental influences on performance could be manipulated to prepare disadvantaged children to enter public school on a level comparable with that of middle class children (Horowitz & Paden, 1973). The basic nature of intelligence was not considered, and *intellectual performance*, or a score on an IQ test, was simply used as an exemplar or criterion variable in these investigations (Deutsch, 1973).

ATTEMPTS TO UNDERSTAND LOWERED INTELLECTUAL PERFORMANCE

There is continued controversy about the underlying nature of retarded functioning (for a review, see Zigler & Balla, 1982). The developmental delay theory of retardation outlined by Zigler (1969) proposes that the only differences between the cultural-familial retarded and nonretarded children are their rate of development and their upper limits, a difference related to polygenetic factors rather than to specific neurologic defects. This theory is contrasted to several difference theories that postulate underlying cognitive process deficits central to all retarded functioning, regardless of specific etiology. Weisz, Yeates, and Zigler (1982) reviewed Piagetian work relevant to retarded functioning and found consistent support for the hypothesis that retarded children progress through a sequence of developmental stages similar to the sequence for normal children, but at a slower rate. They also found somewhat equivocal support for the hypothesis that similar processes are demonstrated at each level of development defined by mental age.

Ellis and Cavalier (1982) cautioned that explaining a difference in behavior by simply invoking the retarded child's slower rate of development does not specify the reason for that slower rate of development. The cross-sectional studies of mental age (MA) matched retarded and nonretarded subjects used to support the developmental delay theory can never be used to separate experiential from maturational determinants of behavior because experience is also a contributor to MA or cognitive development level. Causal relationships between experience and delays in development, regardless of whether they reflect specific process defects or a general delay across all developmental behaviors, can only be demonstrated by controlling developmental variation caused by genetic influences and systematically varying environmental influences over extended periods. A longitudinal investigation of processes and behaviors that have known developmental patterns is necessary to identify the etiology of developmental delays for children identified as at significant risk for cultural-familial retardation.

ATTEMPTS TO MANIPULATE THE ENVIRONMENT

Although early attempts to improve intellectual performance (Skeels & Dye, 1939; Skeels, Updegraff, Wellman, & Williams, 1938; Skodak, 1938; Wellman, 1938, 1940; Wooley, 1925) were largely successful, the results were received with skepticism because of the prevailing view of intelligence as a fixed characteristic, and because the methodology in these studies was open to criticism (McNemar, 1940; Wellman, Skeels, & Skodak, 1940). With the exception of Peters and McElwee's (1944) study, there is little in the literature on further attempts to influence intellectual development until Rheingold (1956) and Kirk (1958) reported positive effects from environmental enrichment programs.

By the late 1950s and early 1960s, participation in our increasingly technological society demanded higher levels of intellectual competency, and major class differences and the resistant conditions of poverty in the United States became even more evident. The extensive examination of our education system that followed Russia's launch of Sputnik reemphasized consistent differences in achievement levels and dropout rates between middle and low SES groups (Conant, 1961). Although free, compulsory, public education had long been used to correct social inequities (Keniston, 1977; Lazerson, 1972), children living in poverty were found to be functioning substantially below middle class children when they entered school, and schools were typically unsuccessful in attempts to improve their performance levels (Schaefer, 1975).

A number of authors (Bloom, 1964; Denenberg, 1964; Hunt, 1961, 1964; Lavin, 1965; Moltz, 1960; Rosenzweig, 1966) suggested that intellectual delays associated with low SES could be optimally affected by intervening before children entered school. When the war on poverty began in 1964, one of the major weapons was a series of early intervention and preschool programs designed to raise the IQ scores and performance levels of children in severely deprived areas to prepare them for the school experience.

It was assumed that providing children from low income families with an intensified curriculum in the form of the "middle class experience" during the preschool years would result in long-term improvements in their general level of academic performance (Deutsch, 1973; Golden & Birns, 1976; Horowitz & Paden, 1973; Snow, 1972). A wide range of early stimulation efforts were undertaken to prepare low SES children to enter school on a level comparable with their middle class peers. In addition to Project Head Start, an official component of the war on poverty under the Office of Economic Opportunity, there were a number of smaller, more rigorously experimental interventions, some of which began prior to 1964. Notable because of their emphasis on research issues were programs by Bereiter and Engelmann (Bereiter, 1972; Bereiter & Engelmann, 1966; Bereiter, Osborne, Engelmann, & Reidford, 1966), Gray (Gray & Klaus, 1965, 1970; Klaus & Gray, 1968), Karnes (Karnes, 1972; Karnes, Hodgins, Stoneburner, Studley, & Teska, 1968; Karnes, Studley, Wright, & Hodgins, 1968; Karnes, Teska, Wollersheim, Stoneburner, & Hodgins, 1968), and Weikart (Weikart, 1971, 1972; Weikart, Bond, & McNeil, 1978; Weikart & Lambie, 1968, 1970; Weikart & Wiegerink, 1968).

Comprehensive reviews of Head Start and other intervention programs can be found in Bronfenbrenner (1975), Caruso, Taylor, and Detterman (1982), Cicirelli (1969), Horowitz and Paden (1973), Jensen (1969), Ramey, Sparling, Bryant, and Wasik (1982), Zigler and Trickett (1978), and Zigler and Valentine (1979). In general, these interventions produced IQ score gains of 8 to 10 points for experimental children, while control children's scores continued to drop. However, within a year or two after intervention ceased, the experimental children were no longer superior to the control children. The effects of intervention on achievement scores were less pronounced and faded even faster.

Comparisons of the relative effectiveness of different intervention approaches and curricula indicated that children benefited the most from highly structured programs, but otherwise there were no substantial differences (Ramey et al., 1982; Weikart & Lambie, 1970). More recently, the outcome of intervention programs has been evaluated in terms of global measures of performance and adjustment. A collaborative follow-up of the original subjects in 12 independent preschool programs found long-lasting effects when, in addition to standardized intelligence and achievement tests, molar indicators of children's school performance were used to assess outcome (Lazar et al., 1982).

These stimulation efforts were primarily conpensatory education programs, not studies of intelligence or child development. Although these programs differed in many aspects, they all shared the major purpose of developing the social-emotional and cognitive aptitudes presumed requisite for success in public school as a means toward ultimately interrupting the cycle of poverty. Most investigators did not bother to question the origins of deficiencies, but were mainly concerned with developing experiences that would ameliorate them (Hunt, 1968). Although measures of intelligence played a central role in this research, IQ scores were simply used as intermediate criteria for success because they predicted achievement (Deutsch, 1973; Golden & Birns, 1976; Horowitz & Paden, 1973).

Hunt's (1961) argument that intelligence is plastic is usually considered to be the major theoretical basis for early stimulation programs, but many programs seem to have been based on what Gollin (1981) referred to as more cumulative models of development, which attribute all individual differences to experience. It was generally taken for granted that differences in intellectual levels for children from middle class and lower class families were completely explained by the deprived conditions of low SES homes (Deutsch, 1966; Vernon, 1979). Emphasis on general differences between middle class and lower class standards of living and other measures of deprivation supported the myth that early environmental action was essentially global in nature (Wachs, 1984), that is, the assumption that children were at significant risk for delays in intellectual development simply because they came from low income or minority group homes. In turn, this led to the expectation that large amounts of varied stimulation with heterogeneous groups of children could improve intelligence for all poor children.

The usefulness of data from these early intervention efforts for developing a clear understanding of the etiology of cultural-familial retardation is limited. While some later investigations took a preventive approach and intervened when the children were infants (for a review, see Ramey et al., 1982), a majority of the programs were compensatory and attempted to determine the degree to which environmental variables could be manipulated to remediate existing intellectual deficits for 3- or 4-year-old children. No effort was made in any of these investigations to account for or experimentally control the possible genetic influences on intellectual development. Many programs used stimulation substantially outside the range of experiences that naturally differentiate middle class and lower class environments. These data, then, should actually be qualified as being more limited than generally perceived in their value for our attempts to establish causal relationships or to identify the processes through which the environment depresses or retards intellectual development.

MATERNAL INFLUENCES ON DEVELOPMENT

Intelligence tests mainly measure individual differences between persons, which cannot be immediately attributed to either socioeconomic or ethnic background (Jensen, 1980). While the mean IQ level for middle class white populations may be significantly higher than the mean IQ for lower class black populations, such global comparisons fail to take into account the individual differences in IQ within these populations. It has been estimated that SES and ethnic subgroup membership together account for less than 20% of the total variability in IQ scores, with the remaining variability being attributable to between-family differences within subgroups, differences between members of the same family, and measurement error.

In addition, the global view of low SES and minority subgroup environments as generally detrimental to normal rates of cognitive development fails to take into account the range of variability in environmental conditions that can and does exist within these subgroups. SES measures provide a gross and often erroneous picture of the child's actual living conditions (Bradley & Caldwell, 1984). The important question is what experiences are provided or not provided in the home environments of children who differ in rates of cognitive development (Henderson, 1981). Considerable research has been conducted recently in an attempt to identify the pattern of correlations between proximal home variables and measures of cognitive development within different populations (for a review of this research, see Gottfried, 1984).

Not only is having a mentally retarded parent one of the primary criteria for diagnosis of cultural-familial mental retardation, but parental intelligence is also the most reliable predictor of a child's later intelligence (Reed & Reed, 1965). The intellectual level of a child's parents is not a defining characteristic of SES level, but because of the economic importance of intelligence in our society, low parental intelligence occurs more frequently within the lower SES levels. Mothers not only provide a genetic contribution for low intelligence, but may also influence their children's intellectual development by inadequately mediating early experiences for them. Brown (1958) suggested that parents transfer their own cognitive structures to their children as they talk and interact with them and, in early studies of mother-child interactions, Bernstein (1960), Bing (1963), and Hess and Shipman (1965) identified significant class differences in the quality of language and teaching strategies used by mothers, which are related to later cognitive functioning. However, the summarizing nature of SES undoubtedly conceals a considerable range of variation in maternal language skills and teaching styles and care should be taken not to equate disadvantagement with poor family functioning.

Retarded mothers by definition have less sophisticated verbal skills and poorer problem solving skills, which may be passed on to their children through interactions. Disadvantaged retarded mothers may create an emotional and psychological microenvironment that not only differs from that found in middle class homes, but may also differ from the learning microenvironments created by higher functioning mothers living in the same economically depressed area.

The Milwaukee Project and the Carolina Abecedarian Project (Ramey, Collier, Sparling, Loda, Campbell, Ingram, & Finkelstein, 1976), which began several years later and is often compared with the Milwaukee Project, attempted to evaluate the role of the social environment by controlling its effects in prospective investigations. These were therefore attempts to demonstrate the possibility of preventing the progressive delays in cognitive development that characterize cultural-familial retardation. More importantly, these investigations attempted to determine which children within the low SES population were actually at risk for delays in cognitive development *before beginning their intervention*, rather than stimulating children simply on the basis of low SES group membership.

It should be noted, however, that although they were procedurally similar, the purposes of these two projects were different. The Abecedarian Project was actually more similar to the amelioration programs that selected their sample by the global index of poverty and designed the intervention program for the major purpose of promoting normal intellectual and social growth in order to prevent school failure (Ramey & Haskins, 1981). Poor families were entered into the program where the mothers often had low IQs, but no attempt was made to restrict the selection process by imposing a limiting criterion IQ performance level. A parallel research program was conducted to develop an understanding of the conditions that shape the development of high risk children, but the emphasis was on curriculum content and the conditions that influence responses to intervention. Infants in the Abecedarian investigation were subsequently qualified for risk on the basis of low maternal IQ level, which had been identified as a significant risk factor in the Milwaukee survey study, plus family income, parental education, intactness of the family, and seven other factors that were weighted and combined to yield a single score called High Risk Index (Ramey & Smith, 1977). An attempt has been made more recently to define risk within the framework of general systems theory through analysis of interactive outcome at various levels (MacPhee, Ramey, & Yeates, 1984). This is similar to the attempts to identify patterns of correlations between proximal home variables and measures of cognitive development mentioned earlier (Gottfried, 1984).

In contrast to efforts to prevent school failure for low SES children, the Milwaukee Project was designed more specifically to test possible etiologic factors responsible in whole or part for the progressive delays in intellectual development that characterize cultural-familial retardation. The AAMR definition (Heber, 1961) of this mild form of retardation suggested that there may be a familial basis for the delays in development and retarded performance in measured intelligence. The initial phase of this study was the establishment of a high risk population laboratory in a carefully selected, economically depressed inner city area of Milwaukee, Wisconsin, in order to study more closely the characteristics of a seriously disadvantaged population in which there was a disproportionate prevalence of low IQ test scores. A cross-sectional investigation was conducted that ultimately determined that certain families within the low SES sample contributed to the disproportionate excess in low IQ scores. The findings of this investigation established a basis for sampling strategy that would ensure that the infants selected for a longitudinal investigation were likely to be identified as mentally retarded and/or evidence significant delays in cognitive development.

THE HIGH RISK POPULATION LABORATORY

A survey of an economically disadvantaged urban area was undertaken prior to initiation of the longitudinal study. This survey was intended to provide information about the distribution of mental retardation in a high prevalence area beyond the often-found epidemiologic association of low SES and low IQ. The area was located in the city of Milwaukee (pop. 620,000) and consisted of nine contiguous census tracts in the city's inner core that comprised what was termed the *High Risk Population Laboratory*. Statistics from the 1960 U.S. Census had characterized this area as having the city's lowest median family income, greatest rate of dilapidated housing, greatest population density per living unit, and highest rate of unemployment.

In the past, it has been difficult to study the cultural-familial mentally retarded in the natural settings of their own families or neighborhoods largely because such mildly handicapped individuals do not generally present a degree of pathology that would precipitate agency contact. Nor do they use the special diagnostic clinics that may be available. In fact, even failure in school has not always brought the appropriate special help to these individuals and their families. Rather, they have come to the attention of public agencies only after repeated failures in adult life have brought them into legal and social conflict with the community. The establishment of the High Risk Population Laboratory and the surveys of the community it represented ultimately led to the opportunity for a prospective research effort in a natural environment characterized by high prevalence rates of mental retardation. The specific objectives were:

1. To evaluate the epidemiologic relationship of a seriously disadvantaged population and the excess prevalence of low IQ scores in order to establish the features of sociocultural and psychosocial risk.
2. To study the development of the intellect of children whose family history indicates a predisposition to cultural-familial retardation.
3. To determine the age at which deviations in development occur and become manifest in this population group.
4. To identify the environmental stimulation essential to normal intellectual development.

5. To determine the extent to which mental retardation in children without demonstrable organic pathology, who are being reared under adverse environmental conditions, may be minimized or prevented through techniques of environmental stimulation, through modification of parental attitudes and practices, and/or through various other educational procedures.

The first of the surveys selected families of 88 consecutive births (selected from monitored newspaper birth announcements) in which the mothers also had at least one 6-year-old child. This selection procedure drew large families into the sample: These 88 mothers had a total of 586 children. The mean IQ of this group of children (excluding the newborns) was 86.3 and the prevalence of IQs of 80 or below was 22%. However, when the IQ of each child was plotted as a function of the mother's IQ, we found that 45.4% of the mothers with IQs below 80 accounted for the 78.2% of the children with IQs below 80 (Table 2-1).

Table 2-1   Distribution of Child IQs as a Function of Maternal Intelligence

Mother IQ	% of Mothers	Child IQ		
		% > 90	% 80-90	% < 80
> 80	54.6	65.8	47.3	21.8
< 80	45.4	34.2	52.7	78.2

This relationship held even more strongly for children over chronological age (CA) 6 than for the younger children, as can be seen in Table 2-2.

Table 2-2   Distribution of IQs of Children 6 Years of Age and Older as a Function of Maternal Intelligence

Mother IQ	% of Mothers	Child IQ		
		% > 90	% 80-90	% < 80
> 80	54.6	68.0	51.6	19.2
< 80	45.4	32.0	48.4	80.8

The survey data from the High Risk Population Laboratory in Milwaukee illustrated another point with respect to the distribution within socioeconomic class groupings: Figure 2-1 shows the distribution of children's IQs, according to ages, for the two groups of mothers. The first or upper curve shows the mean IQ of the survey children whose mothers have IQs above 80 and the second or lower curve shows the mean IQ of those whose mothers have IQs below 80.

Note that on the early infant intelligence scale, both groups scored about equally well. After the infancy period, however (from about CA 36 months), the children whose mothers had IQs greater than 80 continued to maintain a

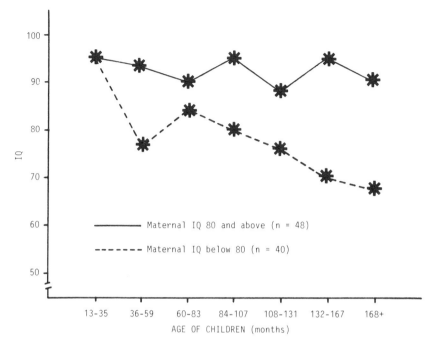

Figure 2-1.   Mean IQs of 586 Children of 88 Mothers as a Function of Age of Children

fairly steady level in the normal range, while the children whose mothers had IQs less than 80 exhibited a marked, progressive decline in measured IQ. In other words, the generally acknowledged statement that slum-dwelling children score lower on intelligence tests as they become older held true only for the offspring of mothers whose IQs were below 80.

Moreover, the survey data showed that the lower the mother's IQ the greater the probability of her child's scoring low on intelligence tests. For example, the mother with an IQ below 67 was 14 times as likely to have a 6-year-old child who tested below IQ 75 as the mother whose IQ fell within the average range (Table 2-3).

Table 2-3   Probability of Child IQ Falling Within
IQ Ranges as a Function of Maternal IQ

Child's IQ	Mother's IQ			
	100	99-84	83-68	67-52
100	1	.98	.67	.25
84-99	1	1.02	.95	.93
68-83	1	1.57	1.24	2.20
52-67	1	2.30	3.70	14.20

For us, these data represented a major breakthrough, for they showed that it was not simply families of low socioeconomic status but families of low socioeconomic status with a very low maternal IQ who contributed so heavily to the ranks of the mentally retarded. This was a key to the development of a detection procedure that would make accessible to us those individuals who were not yet retarded, but were at very high risk for retardation.

In a second survey, the families of over 500 consecutive newborns in our study area were interviewed extensively. In these families, the mothers and fathers and all children over the age of 2 were given the Peabody Picture Vocabulary Test (PPVT). The results of this survey added to our knowledge of the distribution of intellectual functioning within a slum population. A most striking finding was the congruence of maternal and paternal PQ (Peabody Quotient) (Figure 2-2). Sixty-two percent of mothers with scores below 70 had

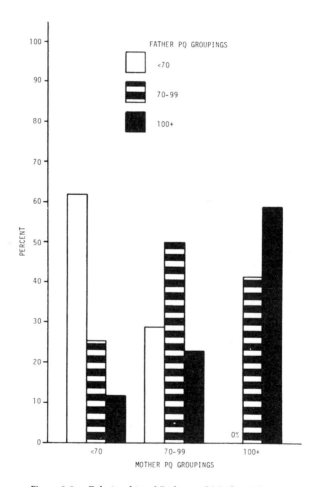

Figure 2-2.   Relationship of Father and Mother PQ Levels

husbands who also scored below 70, and only 12% had husbands who scored above 100. In contrast, none of the mothers scoring above 100 had a husband who scored below 80. Figure 2-2 graphically shows the intragroup concordance. Another interesting observation was that the percentage of absent fathers remained approximately the same in the three maternal PQ groups (Table 2-4).

Table 2-4   Mean Maternal Age and Percentage of Absent
Fathers as a Function of Maternal IQ

| | Maternal IQ | | |
	<70	70-99	100+
% Fathers Absent	34.5	38.6	35.0
Mean Maternal Age	25.4	25.8	25.1
n	100	280	120

Table 2-4 also shows that the average age of mothers of newborns was comparable in all three PQ groups; however, as is shown in Table 2-5, a substantially greater number of mothers with PQs below 70—nearly twice that of mothers with PQs above 100—fell within the high risk age categories of under CA 20 and over CA 35. This difference between family groupings is reflected in the greater number of offspring in families where both mother and father tested below 70. Table 2-6 shows an average difference of 1.2 children between

Table 2-5   Percentage of Mothers of Newborns in Various Age
Groups as a Function of Peabody Quotient

| | Maternal Age | |
| | High Risk | Low Risk |
Maternal PQ	<20, >35	20-34
<70	.32	.68
70-99	.23	.77
100+	.18	.82

Table 2-6   Mean Number of Offspring

| | Father PQ | | | | |
Mother PQ	<70	70-99	100+	None	Mean
<70	4.63	2.95	1.50	4.24	3.41
70-99	3.42	3.39	3.21	3.65	3.50
100+	.00	3.06[a]	3.43	3.05	3.20
Mean	4.02	3.25	3.14	3.64	

[a]No fathers between PQ 70-79.

these families and those where the mother and father tested above 100. Considering that some of those families are perhaps about halfway through their child-rearing years, the total difference in the number of offspring in completed families might be on the order of two and one-half.

In general, the population survey data convinced us that the relatively high incidence of mental retardation associated with slum conditions in America was not randomly distributed within the population subgroup considered poor, but was strikingly concentrated among families who could be more specifically identified on the basis of low maternal intelligence. Although the conditions of poverty may exacerbate the problem, maternal IQ levels were the best indicators of which children were at risk of being labeled retarded by 6 years of age.

Furthermore, the fact that mean IQ level for children in the 36- through 59-month age range who had mothers with IQ scores below 80 was substantially lower than the mean IQ level for their siblings in the 13- through 35-month age range indicated that children whose mothers had relatively low IQ scores were at greater risk for progressive delays in cognitive development with increasing age. This difference across age categories mirrored the 20-point difference between 1- and 3-year-old black lower SES children identified by Kennedy, Van de Riet, and White (1963).

In summary, the cross-sectional study indicated that the intellectual level of mothers accounted for a significant portion of the individual differences in measured intelligence for children in these disadvantaged families, and the lower the level of maternal IQ, the greater the delay with increasing age. At first glance, these data seemed to support the genetic hypothesis of etiology for cultural-familial mental retardation, but they did not add to our understanding of why intellectual performance decreases across age for children from these families. Environmental influences notwithstanding, retarded mothers not only may have relatively less bright children, but they also may provide their children with intellectually impoverished or low quality home environments (Scarr-Salapatek, 1971). This interpretation was supported by the study by Reed and Reed (1965) in which children reared by their retarded mothers but with normal IQ fathers had two and one-half times the rate of retardation identified among children with equally retarded fathers and normal IQ mothers.

As primary caregivers, particularly during infancy, mothers provide an indirect influence on the rate of cognitive development for their children as they structure and mediate the environment for them (Scarr, 1981). The experiences a mother provides are determined by the level of sophistication in cognitive style, which is in turn partially determined by her own innate ability. By definition, retarded mothers lack sophistication in those mental processes that define abstract and conceptual intelligence and therefore may not be capable of effectively mediating the environment for their children. We hypothesized that, in addition to whatever genetic endowment for low IQ functioning these mothers passed on to their children, while mediating the environment for their children they also passed on learning and problem-solving styles that were antagonistic to cognitive development.

To test this hypothesis it was necessary to design an intervention program that could demonstrate that the declines in IQ performance could be prevented by intervening very early in the child's life and continuing until the child entered formal schooling. In addition to preventing declines in IQ levels, a longitudinal study of this nature would also allow further investigation of the developmental acquisition of learning and problem-solving skills in young children as well as differences in mother-child interaction styles that may be related to cognitive development.

Therefore, our surveys provided cross-sectional data that more specifically defined the relationship between the tendency for declining intelligence by the age of 6 and membership in particular types of families within the larger population of individuals considered poor or deprived. The identification of children at risk for mental retardation on the basis of maternal intelligence levels would allow experimental testing of the significance of the relationship between these two variables.

3
Design and Method

The cross-sectional study of the distribution of intelligence in severely disadvantaged neighborhoods of Milwaukee revealed that measures of maternal intelligence accounted for a significant proportion of the variance in children's IQ scores. In fact, it was found that the disproportionate excess of children with low and declining intellectual development among the low SES population could be more specifically targeted within these neighborhoods to families who had a mentally retarded mother. Considering the polygenetic theory of intelligence, the measure of maternal intelligence provided an estimate of the mother's genotype, which is responsible for both the psychosocial and intellectual microenvironment she creates within the home and the more direct influence of inheritance she contributes to her child's organismic capacity for cognitive development. These two influences, the effects of inheritance and experience, are in turn confounded in the MA scores or DQ (developmental quotient) or IQ scores used to estimate individual differences in the rate of intellectual development for children as they are reared at home by their natural parents.

However, although measures of maternal intelligence provide only a limited estimate of organismic capacity because, for example, the father's genotype is not considered, an attempt was made to experimentally control the genetic contribution to individual differences by matching experimental and control groups selected by maternal IQ levels. In effect then, assuming that hereditary factors were controlled, the early life experiences of a group of infants with retarded mothers could then be systematically varied and compared with a control group of infants who remained naturally with their retarded mothers.

The primary question could now be addressed by a longitudinal experimental investigation: To what extent does the experience of being reared by a primary caregiver who is retarded influence the rate of cognitive development for such children? The Milwaukee Project was undertaken to determine the extent to which, by controlling variations in the intellectual level of primary

29

caregivers and minimizing the potential confounding effect of heredity, experience influenced the rate of cognitive development for children from disadvantaged homes.

DESIGN CONSIDERATIONS

A longitudinal multifactorial treatment design in which the subject constituency remains the same is perhaps the most appropriate experimental design to test causal relationships. Retrospective designs are based in memory or records of important facts that are often inaccurate or incomplete. Cross-sectional designs are limited because they can be based on inappropriate or erroneous assumptions about the criteria for matching participants (Baltes & Nesselroade, 1973). They also must assume that developmental processes are sufficiently stable to allow analysis of different cross-sections to yield the same results (Coleman, 1968), an assumption that can be rather tenuous. Rogosa (1979) notes that these designs falsely assume that interindividual differences identified between age groups can be interpreted as changes that each individual would undergo in a similar fashion with increasing age. But the performance of different individuals matures over time in different ways, and this variability is reflected within observed interindividual differences between age groups (Huston-Stein & Baltes, 1976). Longitudinal factorial designs promote efficiency and comprehensiveness in their use of observations because information regarding both main effects and interaction can be generated (Fisher, 1949).

Subject Selection

Every effort must be made to make groups being studied representative of the general population of interest and to establish equality between the groups being compared before treatment is introduced. Census tracts in the inner city of Milwaukee contiguous to those used for the cross-sectional study were selected for screening families with normal newborn infants between 3 and 6 months of age. The 1960 census indicated that blacks were the most predominant and least mobile of the ethnic groups residing in this most disadvantaged area of the city. Initial screening was limited to black families to control for cultural and ethnic differences and further limited to families in which English was the only or major language used in the home to control for language differences. Mothers with newborn infants visiting Well-Baby Clinics were screened by researchers employed by the University of Wisconsin Survey Research Center using the vocabulary subscale of the Wechsler Adult Intelligence Scale (WAIS) (Wechsler, 1955). Mothers who had scaled scores of 6 or lower were administered the remainder of the test in their homes by a trained psychometrist. Additional information was collected using a home inventory checklist.

Infants whose mothers had WAIS Full Scale IQ scores of 75 or lower were considered for participation in the longitudinal investigation if the infants demonstrated no gross pathology during the first months of life. This selection procedure ensured that the infants were at significant risk for deficiencies in cognitive development and declines in DQ and IQ scores.

Subject Assignment

Selection of comparable samples is fundamentally related to the internal validity of an experiment and allows for causal inference. Random assignment reduces the number of assumptions that must be accepted for causal inference and increases their plausibility. Strict randomization procedures call for three basic steps: A basic list of potential experimental units must be prepared or made available in the form of a register, each unit that agrees to participate in the study must be given a set of pretests that evaluate the initial screening level, and participants must be assigned to groups by randomization procedures (Cook & Campbell, 1979).

It is not always possible to follow strict randomization procedures in field settings (Cook & Campbell, 1979; Goldstein, 1979). In this investigation, black mothers with newborn infants were screened for low vocabulary scores and pretested and selected on the basis of low IQ scores. The infants who were considered potential subjects because their mothers had low IQ scores were further screened on the important requirement that they be healthy and not demonstrate any gross pathology in the first months of life. However, it was not possible to identify enough infants meeting these criteria who were between 3 and 6 months of age at a single point in time to form a register for random assignment to experimental and control conditions. Family selection had to be carried out on a continuous basis. This selection process occurred over a 24-month period between 1966 and 1968.

Although a total of 82 infants meeting criteria were identified during this 24-month screening period, 27 could not be assigned: Three families moved before assignment could be made, three families refused to participate at the first follow-up contact, two mothers were identified as predominantly Spanish-speaking, one mother was living with a family previously assigned to a group, one mother was identified as being too young for the WAIS, a physical pathology was identified for one infant, and during the period between the time the mothers were tested and the time their families could be assigned, 16 infants passed the 6-month age criterion. Over the 24-month screening period, a total of 55 families met the basic criteria and were considered for assignment in the project before their infants reached 6 months of age.

Since it was logistically impossible to accumulate a pool of subjects meeting screening criteria from which to make random assignments to treatment at one time, the three or four families identified each month were assigned as cohorts on an alternating basis to the experimental and control conditions. A total of

28 experimental and 27 control families were assigned over the 24-month period and no family was allowed to change groups.

During the screening process, nine mothers living in the same disadvantaged area of the city were identified who had vocabulary scores on the WAIS of 10 and above, compared with scores of 6 and below for the mothers in high risk families. At follow-up interviews, these mothers were tested and found to have WAIS Full Scale IQ scores above 100. Based on the original survey results, infants from these families would not be expected to demonstrate declines in cognitive performance although they lived in the same general poverty environment. These infants were assigned to a low risk contrast group and followed for the duration of the intervention study. This group was small, but as a low risk contrast it allowed for conservative but meaningful comparisons with the children living in the same disadvantaged neighborhoods who formed the high risk experimental and control groups.

Attrition

Several subjects were lost before they could begin participation in the study or shortly thereafter. In the experimental group, one family moved from the city just as they were about to begin participation, one dropped out because of marital problems that disrupted the home, one mother experienced a severe illness that precluded her family's participation, three refused to allow continued testing of their children, and two dropped out shortly after their infants began participating in the center based program (one after 2 weeks and the other after 4 months). In the control group, one family refused to participate almost immediately after assignment, two moved away from the city before testing began with their infants, and four were dropped for refusing to allow continued testing of their infants.

The 20 experimental and 20 control infants who remained were the only ones considered to have begun participation in the program. Three of the experimental families moved when their children were 42 months, 48 months, and 54 months old, respectively. Two of the control families moved from the city within 1 year of assignment. The remaining cohorts of 17 experimental and 18 control infants comprised the groups on which all tests related to the effectiveness of the intervention program were made.

COMPARABILITY OF GROUPS

Strict random assignment procedures were not used in this investigation, but an assessment was made of the comparability of groups before intervention began on the basis of assignment criteria. It should be noted that, even with random assignment, comparability or equivalence are only probabilistic and cannot be guaranteed.

Screening and Assignment Criteria

Table 3-1 summarizes descriptive statistics for the measures used in screening and identification of target families: maternal scores on the WAIS vocabulary subtest obtained in screening and the WAIS full scale IQ scores. Three statistical comparisons (t tests) of experimental and control families were made: for the full sample of families originally assigned, for the more limited sample of families who began participation in the program, and for the final 17 experimental and 18 control families who were followed across the full course of the investigation. No significant differences between the experimental and control families were identified among these screening and assignment criteria nor did it seem that attrition significantly affected group means for these variables.

Table 3-1   Comparison of Maternal Screening and Assignment Variables for Full and Limited Experimental, Control, and Low Risk Contrast Families

	Originally Assigned			Lost Before Initiation			Enrolled In Program			Lost During Program			Completed Program			Low Risk Contrast		
	M	SD	n	M	SD	n	M	SD	n	M	SD	n	M	SD	n	M	SD	n
Vocabulary Score																		
Exp	2.92	1.98	28	2.13	2.03	8	3.25	1.92	20	2.00	2.65	3	3.47	1.77	17			
Con	3.22	1.99	27	2.86	2.12	7	3.35	1.98	20	4.50	0.71	2	3.22	2.05	18			
LRC																12.57	0.98	8
Full Scale WAIS IQ																		
Exp	67.29	6.35	28	66.25	7.46	8	67.70	6.02	20	65.33	3.06	3	68.12	6.37	17			
Con	66.30	6.35	27	65.71	5.15	7	66.50	6.83	20	71.50	0.71	2	65.94	6.99	18			
LRC																111.29	3.99	8

Family Characteristics

Most of the mothers and fathers in the experimental and control groups were born in the South and had lived in Milwaukee about 5 years (only two mothers and two fathers reported being born in the Milwaukee area). Mothers came from families with an average of 9.3 children while fathers came from families with an average of 6.9 children. Fathers were on the average about 5 years older than their wives and were 31.3 years of age when the target children were born. The fathers' average educational level was about the ninth grade, and the majority had manual labor jobs, including foundry, construction, and maintenance jobs. Annual household incomes ranged from $2,000 to slightly over $9,000 with an average of $4,000. In general, these families must be considered substantially disadvantaged. The percentage of households reporting fathers or father figures present decreased substantially across the preschool years for both the experimental group (from 88% to 41%) and the control group (94% to 39%). This increased the need for social welfare services as the years passed.

Table 3-2 summarizes descriptive statistics and statistical comparisons on maternal and family characteristics not considered for assignment purposes. These characteristics have been implicated as factors in individual differences in cognitive development (e.g., Henderson, 1981; Nichols, 1981; Schaefer, 1965). These data were gathered during initial interviews with the 35 families who were followed across the full course of the program and in follow-up assessments approximately 8 to 10 years later. Information on the mother's age, the target child's birth order, and the number of children and average spacing provides some indication of the environmental conditions within the home in terms of "crowding" and "competition for mother's attention." No significant differences were identified between the experimental and control groups for any of these factors.

Maternal education level and maternal literacy level provide information on important correlates of IQ levels for the mothers; there were no significant differences between the two groups on these factors. The second assessment of maternal intelligence, made almost 8 years after the initial assessment for assignment purposes, provided a means of evaluating whether the two groups remained comparable on this major risk factor over time. Experimental and control mothers gained an average of 5 IQ points on the follow-up assessment, while the low risk contrast mothers, who originally scored well above 100, demonstrated a slight decrease in IQ level. This change over time is most reasonably attributed to the principle of regression to the mean and did not affect the comparability of groups identified in the original assessments.

Infant Characteristics

The 20 experimental and 20 control families selected for study each contributed nine girls and eleven boys to the investigation. After attrition, there were eight girls and nine boys in the experimental group and eight girls and ten boys in the control group. The original low risk contrast group consisted of four girls and five boys, and one girl was lost early in the study. Sex differences in cognitive development should be fairly evenly represented in experimental and control comparisons.

The average birth order for the target infants was 4.05, and the average age of the mothers at the birth of the target infant was 26.25 years. The average education level of the mothers was 9.48 years. In contrast, the average birth order of low risk children was 3.86, their mothers were an average of 26 years old when their infants were born, and their average educational level was 12.86 years. No significant differences were identified between the experimental and control groups for any of these factors.

Birth records for the infants who actually began participation in the project were reviewed to determine whether there were differences in the incidence of

	Enrolled in Program			Lost During Program			Completed Program			Low Risk Contrast		
	M	SD	n	M	SD	n	M	SD	n	M	SD	n
Maternal Education Level												
Experimental	9.95	1.32	20	8.67	0.58	3	10.18	1.29	17			
Control	9.00[a]	2.71	20	8.50	0.71	2	9.06[a]	2.86	18			
Low Risk										12.86	1.07	8
Maternal Age – First Child												
Experimental	18.55	1.99	20	18.67	2.08	3	18.53	2.03	17			
Control	19.00	3.89	20	17.00	0.00	2	19.22	4.05	18			
Low Risk										21.43	3.05	8
Target Child Birth Order												
Experimental	4.40	2.66	20	4.33	3.21	3	4.41	2.67	17			
Control	3.70	1.98	20	3.50	2.12	2	3.72	2.02	18			
Low Risk										3.86	4.99	8
Maternal IQ Reassessment												
Experimental							72.62	7.85	17			
Control							71.22	7.54	18			
Low Risk										108.29	4.99	8
# Children at 10-Year Follow-up												
Experimental							5.71	2.57	17			
Control							4.44	2.12	18			
Low Risk										4.14	2.71	8
Average Spacing[b]												
Experimental							30.60	15.00	17			
Control							24.29	8.32	18			
Low Risk												
WRAT Literacy at 10-Year Follow-up												
Experimental							4.22	1.78	17			
Control							3.62	1.89	18			
Low Risk										12.20[c]	2.70	8

[a] The educational level for one control mother was not recorded. Control means for mothers enrolled in treatment and mothers completing the program are based on samples of $n = 19$ and $n = 17$, respectively. [b] Target children in one experimental and one control family were only children. Average spacing of children was calculated only for families with more than one child, which occurred in 16 experimental and 17 control families. [c] Only four low risk contrast mothers were given the WRAT.

cesarean delivery, use of forceps, or other conditions that would have obvious implications for deleterious effects on cognitive development. Reports of such conditions were rare and comparable for all groups, and there was no indication or suspicion of neurologic difficulties for any of the infants. Table 3-3 summarizes descriptive statistics and t-test comparisons for weight and length data collected from birth records for the experimental, control, and low risk contrast infants who began participation in the program and for the more limited groups that completed the program. There were no significant differences among the groups for either weight or length measures.

Table 3-3   Mean Weight and Length Comparisons for Children Enrolled in the Program and Children Completing the Program

	Weight (pounds)				Length (inches)			
	M	SD	Range	n	M	SD	Range	n
Children Enrolled								
In Program								
Experimental	6.91	0.97	4.84-8.50	20	19.32	1.28	17.00-21.50	20
Control	7.10	1.09	4.38-9.09	20	19.96	1.23	17.00-21.50	20
Low Risk Contrast	6.58	1.65	2.88-8.00	9	18.13	1.66	15.00-20.50	8[a]
Children Lost								
During Program								
Experimental	6.86	1.78	4.84-8.19	3	19.67	1.04	18.50-20.50	3
Control	7.38	0.53	7.00-7.75	2	20.50	0.71	20.00-21.00	2
Low Risk Contrast	8.00			1	18.00			1
Children Completing								
Program								
Experimental	6.92	0.85	5.44-8.50	17	19.26	1.34	17.00-21.50	17
Control	7.07	1.14	4.38-9.09	18	19.90	1.28	17.00-21.50	18
Low Risk Contrast	6.40	1.68	2.88-7.63	8	18.14	1.80	15.00-20.50	7[a]

[a]Length data were unavailable for one low risk contrast child.

Two complete physical examinations of all children were conducted at the Milwaukee Children's Hospital, one at the average age of 4 and another just prior to the time the children entered first grade. Both series of examinations failed to identify any significant physical differences between the groups for Stuart Growth Chart percentiles (see Watson & Lowry, 1967, for norm tables). Blood serum analyses for evidence of the adverse environmental influences that are commonly reported in poverty areas (e.g., malnourishment, lead absorption) found slightly elevated blood lead levels but no significant differences between the two groups of children (Platt & Blodgett, 1973).

EXPERIMENTAL INTERVENTION

The intervention had two major components: infant/early childhood stimulation and family/maternal rehabilitation. The control and low risk contrast children participated equally in the preschool assessment program conducted at the Infant Stimulation Center and in assessments conducted during follow-up after the children entered school. However, the control and low risk contrast children did not participate in any intervention activities and, although their mothers were visited at home intermittently, they received no services from the program.

As families were assigned to the experimental group, a paraprofessional infant caregiver went into each home to work with the mother and the infant in preparation for bringing the child daily to the infant center. In order to facilitate removal of the infants from their homes for large portions of each day, it was necessary to establish rapport and a sense of trust with both the infants and their mothers. The infant caregivers had been trained to provide basic information on child care techniques, preventive medical care, nutrition, money management, and community related social issues. Visits 3 days per week for 3 to 5 hours per day established a personal relationship between each mother and an individual caregiver. The mothers were also prepared to begin a formal family/maternal rehabilitation program designed to develop skills that would enable them to be more effective in gaining better employment as well as improve their home management and increase responsible participation in the community. Both mothers and infants were taken to the Infant Stimulation Center for short visits. When the mothers were ready to begin their rehabilitation program, the infants began participation in the stimulation program 5 days per week for 7 hours per day with the infant caregivers.

The intervention program for the experimental infants was carried out in a three story duplex in the heart of the high risk neighborhood, rented and refurbished as an Infant Stimulation Center expressly for this program. The infant caregivers began to bring the infants to the center for visits between 2 weeks and 2 months after they started visiting the homes, depending on how long it required for them to gain the family's confidence. All children began attending the center for extended periods each day by 6 months of age.

The formal rehabilitation program for mothers began when their infants were transferred to the infant center and lasted approximately 18 months. This program included on-the-job training in two private nursing homes during the day and adult education classes in the evening. At the end of their training the mothers were provided job counseling and general parent support services by a family specialist.

Family/Maternal Rehabilitation

All of the mothers were retarded (mean IQ = 67.7) and had relatively low educational levels (mean grade in school = 9.95). They also had poor or nonexistent work histories and there was no stable income producing father in most families. The major purpose of the rehabilitation program was therefore to develop skills that would enable these mothers to better provide an income for their families. A parent supervisor was responsible for organizing and supervising the rehabilitation program and for serving as liaison between the infant stimulation program and the parents.

Each mother was paid $1.40 per hour for participating in the rehabilitation program. Child care was also provided for children under 6 years of age who were not in the infant stimulation program to facilitate participation.

The rehabilitation program began with basic academic preparation for job adjustment. This included refresher courses in functional reading, writing, and mathematics skills, which are considered prerequisites for on-the-job training. Sessions were held 4 days per week for 4 weeks. During this time, discussions were also held on mothering, child care, and home management; motivational re-education (life skills and attitudes); general remedial education; vocational information and counseling; and occupational training in areas such as laundry service, patient care, food preparation, and janitorial service. The curriculum also included discussions on community responsibility, social skills, interpersonal relations, medical needs, and personal hygiene.

On-the-job training took place in two large private nursing homes in Milwaukee. The nursing homes were chosen as the training sites mainly for the job skill areas represented in this type of facility and the availability of a professional staff with an understanding of rehabilitation problems. The rationale for determining the appropriateness of this job situation was suggested in part by the personal needs and abilities of the mothers and in part by existing employment opportunities in these job areas. The choice of private business settings for training was dictated by the mothers' strong resistance to involvement with community agencies.

The mothers received 26 weeks (3 days per week) of paid, on-the-job vocational training. Each mother was paired with an experienced employee of the nursing home. When a mother encountered difficulties that her workmate could not resolve, she was temporarily removed from the work area and given special help. On the 2 days of the week that they were not in training, the mothers continued remedial classes.

An interesting development was the obvious improvement in the attitude of the mothers when the on-the-job training program began. Even the mothers who were doing only moderately well in the academic phase renewed their interest and enthusiasm in the program. As the mothers realized the application of academic skills in such activities as reading and following a bus schedule, calling in sick, and being on time, their spirits rose considerably. The mothers also began to form a support group for one another. This support and encouragement helped individual mothers to continue with the program. Their common problems and the positive interactions among the mothers created strong peer pressure to complete the 22 to 26 week job training program.

The vocational training involved four different areas of health services: laundry, housekeeping, food service, and nursing. These jobs are outlined in Table 3-4.

Each mother was allowed to progress according to her individual learning rate and group counseling sessions were held at the end of each day of training. After the training program was completed, each mother was evaluated by her training site supervisor on the Workshop Scale of the Revised Scale of

Table 3-4   Overview of Vocational Training Program
for High Risk Mothers

Vocational Training Area	Time Devoted to Training	Examples of Some of the Tasks in the Area
Laundry	5 Weeks	1. Feeding linens into the mangle 2. Folding garments as they are ironed 3. Sorting clothes 4. Operating laundry machinery 5. Mending by hand and machine
Housekeeping	3 1/2 Weeks	1. Preparation of cleaning materials cart 2. Learning serial order for room cleaning (e.g., sweeping before mopping, etc.) 3. Performing all cleaning tasks with speed and thoroughness
Food Service	9 Weeks	1. Stocking and inventory of food items 2. Preparing food for the cook (e.g., peeling, chopping, cleaning, etc.) 3. Cleaning utensils 4. Preparing salads and desserts 5. Operating food preparation equipment (e.g., blender, peeler), etc. 6. Preparing special diet trays
Nursing	9 Weeks	1. Helping patients (e.g., feeding, dressing, bathing, shaving, and transporting them) 2. Taking temperature and counting pulse 3. Caring for the incontinent patient

Employability for Handicapped Persons. This instrument was adapted from an employability scale developed by the Chicago Jewish Vocational Service for the purpose of assessing the potential employability of mentally, physically, and emotionally handicapped persons.

As the job training program came to an end, attention was given to helping the mothers find employment. Not all mothers who completed the vocational training program sought the jobs for which they were specifically trained. For example, one mother who had been taught the skills of a nursing assistant decided she preferred sewing and found a job as a seamstress. "I want to try something I have never done before," she told the others. This woman subsequently moved her family into a better home and neighborhood. Another mother specialized in cooking and became the cook for a large nursing home.

With the end of the vocational training program and the employment of many of the mothers, the focus of the maternal program shifted to evening sessions centered around the remedial reading and math activities. The fathers were also invited to attend these sessions, which were organized and taught by the parent coordinator. She monitored each parent individually by using prepared worksheets and taught a curriculum based on skills adapted from *How to Prepare for the High School Equivalency Examination* (Rockwitz, 1968). When parents asked for more formal instruction in order to improve their reading skills, Science Research Associates' *The Kaleidoscope Readers* (Bamman, 1969) was used. This series developed skills in word attack, comprehension, vocabulary, and rate of reading.

In actuality, however, most of the classes were structured to deal with problems in daily life that might be encountered at home or at work. For example: If you bought some groceries for $1.75 and gave the clerk $5.00, how much change should you get? How would you fill out tax forms and how would you balance a checkbook? Whom should be contacted if you can't go to work or whom should be asked if you need help at work? How do you pay the telephone bill and the gas and electric bill? When you go for a job interview, what information should you bring with you and how would you actually apply for a job?

Within a few months after the job training program ended, the formal adult evening classes were discontinued. Employed parents could not easily attend classes at night, and interest slackened as satisfactory and/or satisfying levels of academic success and knowledge were achieved. However, the maternal rehabilitation program continued, with the parent coordinator providing direct support to individual families.

When the remedial academic classes were no longer practical and the night program had ended, attention was directed in a more personal way toward the families. One of the infant caregivers who had been with the program since the beginning and was familiar with all the families took over the responsibilities of parent coordinator. She was well known and respected by the parents and was able to provide parent support, counseling, and crisis intervention for each family according to its needs. She continued to speak with the parents about nutrition, health concerns (viz., preventive medicine – inoculations, eye and ear check-ups, hygiene, care of injuries, contagious diseases), medical insurance, money management, child management, and methods of dealing with legal and social agencies. She also advised them on finding and maintaining employment. At a mother's request, the parent coordinator attended public school conferences, talked to landlords and social service workers, and even appeared as a character witness in court. The parents knew that she was always available as an information resource and for emotional support. In addition, it was the parent coordinator's responsibility to maintain contact and rapport with the control families, and she would often chauffeur both control mother and control child to testing sessions at the Center.

As the contact person between the Center and the home, the parent coordinator was invaluable. For instance, after the children had been tested for lead poisoning, she explained to each family the dangers of ingesting lead. When one experimental child required an operation for eye muscle correction, the parent coordinator, after much contact, convinced the parent of the need for medical attention. She also provided the parents with frequent feedback about their children's performance and behavior at the Center. She arranged staff-parent conferences and the open house reception held twice each year for family, relatives, staff, and friends.

Throughout the program, the parent coordinator was the liaison between parents and staff and even between parents and their children. For example, one of the children, a 4-year-old, had told his mother he could read. She asked him to show her by reading from her Bible. Because he could only read a few words by sight, he was unable to read the book. The mother then accused him of lying. When he related this the next day at school, the parent coordinator called the mother and explained to her how a child learns to read with a few initial sight words and how she could help him develop his reading skills further.

In another situation, a single parent with three children thought her child had behavior problems. She worked all day and was exhausted when she returned home at night. What she wanted was to prepare and serve dinner and then sit quietly and enjoy television. Her 3-year-old son, who was in the experimental program, had different needs. As part of the program, all of the children were being encouraged to use language and express themselves. At night, when she wanted quiet, he wanted to talk about school. Because he talked so much, she called the school and asked what was wrong with him. The parent coordinator worked with her to explain the program's goals. As it turned out, the child himself helped to resolve the problem by understanding how and when to gain the attention and time from his mother.

The parent coordinator worked full time during the remainder of the program after the job training phase and continued contact with the families after the children had entered public school in order to keep track of their locations, monitor the general health of the families, and, especially, to keep informed on the progress of the target children in the public school. The parents continued to call for advice and help of different kinds. For example, at the parents' request, the parent coordinator attended parent-teacher conferences, counseled a mother whose children had been removed to a foster home, and served the very important function of minimizing the effects of conflicts that arose between public school staff and the parents.

Infant/Early Childhood Stimulation Program

The goal of the stimulation program was to prevent what were presumed to be delays in cognitive development that are characteristically evidenced as deficiencies in measured intelligence before 3 years of age. It was hypothesized that retarded mothers create psychosocial and intellectual microenvironments in the home that are inadequate for stimulating normal rates of cognitive development. Paraprofessionals were employed to serve as substitute caregivers in order to supplement the intellectual stimulation being provided within the home.

PROGRAM STAFF AND TRAINING

When a family was assigned to the experimental group, a paraprofessional caregiver began visiting the home 3 days a week for 3 to 5 hours each day to develop rapport and trust with the mother. During these visits, the mother came to trust the caregiver and the infant became comfortable in her presence and came to rely on her as well as his/her parents. The caregiver became acquainted with the needs and expectations of both parents and infant. When the mother began her rehabilitation program, the caregiver transferred the infant to the Infant Stimulation Center and became responsible for his/her total daytime care.

A program supervisor was responsible for monitoring the activities of the paraprofessional caregivers, the transfer of infants out of the home, and the activities carried out at the Infant Stimulation Center. Both black and white women were employed as caregivers. All but one were paraprofessionals with educational backgrounds ranging from 10th grade through 1 year of technical college and none of these women had formal training in child development or the education of young children. The caregiver staff remained relatively stable throughout the program, with a core group of nine caregivers working for more than 5 years.

The caregivers were responsible for the total daytime care of the infants at the Center, including feeding and bathing, monitoring, recording, and reporting general health signs, organizing activities, and stimulating the infant within the parameters of the program. As the program changed from infant stimulation to early childhood stimulation and then to preschool stimulation, the duties of the caregivers changed substantially. An ongoing training program that included group meetings, on-the-job training, and annual seminars was implemented by the curriculum supervisor to ensure that caregivers were well prepared to meet the changing demands of the program.

For purposes of presentation, each group meeting was divided into two sections. The first part was devoted to discussions of specific topics:

1. Knowledge of child development with an emphasis on the first 6 years of life.
2. Knowledge of approaches to early childhood education and related philosophies.
3. Developing an understanding of the overall stimulation goals.
4. Understanding methods of motivating and interacting with groups of children.
5. Developing an awareness of children's needs by being a sensitive observer and interpreter.
6. Understanding the importance of all aspects of the environment: physical, social, emotional, organizational.
7. Understanding and utilizing evaluation techniques.
8. Understanding health needs in the Center.
9. Understanding appropriate methods and purposes for discipline in the Center.

The second portion of the group meetings centered around the personal needs of the caregivers and sensitizing the caregivers to the needs of the children. Because of the stability of the staff, these group discussions were on a more personal level than would have been possible with a more transient group. Discussions emphasized personal attitudes toward specific children, education, school, authority, discipline, specific behavior, etc. The discussions were aimed at increased self-awareness and fostering caregiver commitment by involving them in program planning.

It was strongly felt that the caregiver's greatest responsibility was to provide a supportive emotional environment for the child. The goal was to sensitize the caregivers continually to their own feelings and those of the children. Through open communication, the staff could honestly discuss their feelings toward individual children. This enabled placement of each child with a caregiver who felt positive about him/her. Techniques derived from sociometry were also used at group meetings to further our understanding of the dynamics of interpersonal relationships. For example, each caregiver was asked to write two single-word descriptions of each child. By reviewing the comments, the caregivers were able to see whether the overall group attitude toward that child was positive or negative. Did only one caregiver see the child in a negative way? Why? Were all the caregivers reacting to the same negative behavior of the child? Did some caregivers see a behavior as positive while others saw it as negative?

A behavior rating scale (Bower & Lambert, 1962) that places children on a curve with extremes of "least like" and "most like" was also useful in promoting open discussion. Some of the criteria were:

1. This pupil gets into fights or quarrels with other pupils, more often than others.
2. This pupil is unhappy or depressed. He or she may cry easily, be inattentive, or daydream (Bower & Lambert, 1962).

Some children were consistently seen more negatively than other children. Using the "Class Pictures," each child and caregiver were shown 12 picture cards with children engaged in different behaviors. Half of the behaviors would be considered negative, while half were positive or neutral types of behavior. Each child was asked a question such as, "Who could this be having fun on the swings, fighting with this other boy, being told by the teacher not to do something" (Bower & Lambert, 1962). Each child was also asked to identify the caregivers in the picture cards. The concrete results and the discussions generated by such insights enabled the staff to be more sensitive to their own attitudes toward particular children and to the children's attitudes toward each other and the caregivers. In addition, it helped the caregivers to adjust their programs to meet the needs of those children experiencing difficulty.

Group staff discussions were also furthered by questionnaires that sampled attitudes on room arrangement, equipment, scheduling, children's behavior, discipline, reading skills, art materials, reading stories, etc.

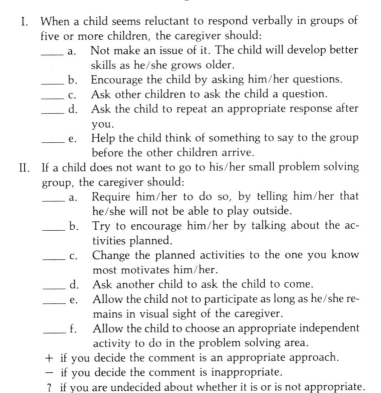

I. When a child seems reluctant to respond verbally in groups of five or more children, the caregiver should:
_____ a.   Not make an issue of it. The child will develop better skills as he/she grows older.
_____ b.   Encourage the child by asking him/her questions.
_____ c.   Ask other children to ask the child a question.
_____ d.   Ask the child to repeat an appropriate response after you.
_____ e.   Help the child think of something to say to the group before the other children arrive.

II. If a child does not want to go to his/her small problem solving group, the caregiver should:
_____ a.   Require him/her to do so, by telling him/her that he/she will not be able to play outside.
_____ b.   Try to encourage him/her by talking about the activities planned.
_____ c.   Change the planned activities to the one you know most motivates him/her.
_____ d.   Ask another child to ask the child to come.
_____ e.   Allow the child not to participate as long as he/she remains in visual sight of the caregiver.
_____ f.   Allow the child to choose an appropriate independent activity to do in the problem solving area.

+ if you decide the comment is an appropriate approach.
− if you decide the comment is inappropriate.
? if you are undecided about whether it is or is not appropriate.

These questionnaires were not only useful in stimulating discussion, but also indicated to the curriculum coordinator and caregiver supervisor areas of differences among the staff or between the staff and supervisors. More extensive inservice was then planned around these areas of difference.

A vital aspect of the caregiver training program was the on-the-job training. Each caregiver was observed and evaluated by the curriculum coordinator and caregiver supervisor. From these observations, the caregiver was given help in planning her instructional units, choosing appropriate equipment, and motivating the children. Small group caregiver meetings were held to discuss a particular child or a peer group of children. The curriculum coordinator advised each caregiver on the goals and content of the intervention program. Frequently, the curriculum coordinator prepared curriculum sheets with activity suggestions or lists of types of activities specifically prepared for a single group of children.

To a limited extent, other methods of training, such as self-evaluation and observation of each other's interactions with children followed by discussion, were also utilized.

Each year, the school was closed for 3 days for a seminar that provided an opportunity to expand information and experience, visit other programs, hear guest speakers, participate in workshops, and hold intensive staffing sessions during which each child's progress in the Center was considered and specific planning for the following year was discussed. The content of the annual seminars was determined by caregiver requests as well as needs identified by the supervisory staff. In addition, the caregivers were encouraged to participate when educational workshops or conventions were held in the Milwaukee area.

At the completion of the early intervention program, each caregiver received certification stating that she had been involved in the program and had had a minimum of 3 years of supervised early childhood training and experience. In addition the caregiver received credit for the Child Care I course offered by the state vocational school system for daycare personnel.

ANECDOTAL REPORT

Explanations of the specifics of scheduling and curriculum content do little to give the reader a feeling of what transpired on a daily basis. The following anecdotal report of a typical day for a preschool child is included to give the reader an idea of how the logistics, content, and procedures were translated into a relevant, responsive, and exciting experience for the children.

An Instructional Day: Preschool

Kim waits at the window of her home for the "brown van" to pick her up. It is 8:30 a.m. Kim sees the van round the corner and begins to put her coat on. By the time Gerry, the driver, who is also Kim's Reading teacher, honks the horn, Kim is out the door. Already in the van are Gerry, Betty (a teacher of the younger children), Danny, and Kisha. As she gets in the van, Kim notices that John is absent. She asks Gerry where he is. Gerry explains that John has a sore throat and his mother is keeping him home today. As more children are picked up, the ones already in the van shout out a greeting. Curtis tells everyone about a movie he saw on television the night before. Soon everyone joins in with stories of the previous night. Danny mentions that he got to stay up till 1:00 a.m. Gerry makes a mental note to talk to Danny's mother about the importance of his getting sufficient sleep.

By 9:00, the van pulls up to the school parking lot and the children run into the building. They hang up their coats and go to the dining room for breakfast. Today's breakfast includes orange juice, scrambled eggs and bacon, toast, and milk. While Kim is sitting down, the second van load of children has arrived. Patricia, Kim's special friend, runs up to show Kim her new dress. Patricia sits next to Kim and they happily talk through breakfast. Florine, their Language teacher, joins them. As the children finish breakfast, they bring their dishes and utensils into the kitchen. From the kitchen they go to the Free Flowing Room.

They are greeted at the door by Marge, one of the two Free Flowing Room teachers. She tells them that the clay figurines they had made yesterday are dry and that those who want to can paint them. David, Patricia, and Curtis ask if they can paint. While Marge helps them on with their smocks, the other children, with the help of Mamie, a teacher, become involved with other things in the room. Kim decides that she wants to wait to paint until later, because she knows that soon Gerry will come to get her for a small group activity. For now, Kim chooses to put together one of her favorite puzzles, the circus wagon.

As Kim finishes the puzzle, she sees Gerry at the door. Gerry calls for Kim, Kisha, and Charles to come with her to the small group Reading area. At the same time, Becky asks Betsy, Jessica, and Danny to go with her to the small group Math/Problem Solving area. The instructional day has begun.

While Gerry and Becky teach their small groups, Florine, the Language teacher, and the two Free Flowing Room teachers are in the Free Flowing Room. Florine has noticed that Tony is having trouble choosing an activity. Because this is unusual for him, she goes over to talk to him. She asks him if anything is worrying him. They begin to talk about a lot of different things. Eventually she learns that he is upset because he heard an argument that his parents had the night before. Florine tries to help him understand the fight and to explain that sometimes adults yell at each other when they are angry.

In the Reading area, as Kim sits down, she sees the letter book she began the day before is at the table. Kim smiles because cutting and pasting are some of her favorite activities. Magazines are also laid out on the table and Kim and the other children look through them for words that start with the letter "B." As they find pictures, they check with Gerry and then paste them in their books. When Kim, Kisha, and Charles seem to be losing interest in the activity, Gerry takes some homemade alphabet cards from the shelf. Because all three children have the verbal label for the letters of the alphabet, Gerry plays a memory game with them. All of the alphabet cards are placed face down. The children in turn pick up one card and then another, trying to match them. As in the game Concentration, the children have to remember where each card is. Gerry helps them to remember and to make associations with the letter name.

When the game is finished, Kim asks Gerry if they can play the rhyming game. Gerry takes out the game and the four of them throw dice and rhyme words that are on the board.

It is a little after 10:00 and it is time for Kim and the others to return to the Free Flowing Room. Teachers Gerry and Becky take two more groups of children. Florine also has a small group in the Language area. In the Free Flowing Room Kim goes to the art table where Marge helps her to put on her smock. After painting her figurine, Kim washes her hands and walks over to the block area. Danny and Jessica are there building a castle with a road around it. Kim joins them, but soon Danny leaves because a game of house in the Dramatic Play area interests him more. Other children are playing with pegboards, working puzzles, or looking in the aquarium with a magnifying glass. Kim and Jessica are still involved in the castle when Kim hears Becky call her name. Marge promises to keep the castle intact while Kim is out of the room in Becky's Math/Problem Solving class.

In Becky's area, Kim, Kisha, and David notice that a lot of small objects are on the table. Becky gives them each a large piece of string tied in a circle. She asks Kim to put in her circle everything that can carry people, Kisha to find things we can eat, and David to find things that can hold water. Kim notices a cup near her, so she gives it to David. Once all the sorting is completed, Becky asks the children for the objects back. "Who has something that is glass?" "Who has something that has four wheels and travels on roads?" "Who has something that is round and red?" When all the objects are back in the box, Becky asks the children to try to remember some of the objects. She pulls them out of the box as the children say the label. Becky encourages the children to help each other and provides them with clues when they are stuck. Once all the objects are put away again, Becky takes out a game of number dominoes. She helps the children match the numerals with the number of objects pictured. Soon the domino cards are laid out throughout Becky's area. She helps the children to clean up the cards and asks them if there is something special they would like to do. Kisha says she wants to play color and shape bingo, three cards at once. David and Kim quickly agree. Becky is excited that Kisha thought of a way to make the game harder. She gives each child three bingo cards to play with. Instead of showing them the card she picks from the pile, Becky makes the game harder by telling the children the color and shape. Becky notices that Kim is having trouble manipulating two attributes at once. Although able to remember the stated color, she cannot remember the second attribute, shape. Becky decides to work with Kim a little in the afternoon to help her.

It is soon 11:15 and Kim, Kisha, and David go with Florine to the Language area. Florine has been doing a unit on family relationships. First, she reads them a book about an older brother, then she helps them to make a graph representing their own family relationships. David begins to talk about the things his older siblings do to make him angry. Kisha and Kim join in. A lively discussion ensues. By now it is 11:45 and Florine tells the children they can either watch Sesame Street or go back to the Free Flowing Room. Kisha and David go to see Sesame Street, but Kim returns to the Free Flowing Room to check on her castle. Marge has kept her promise, it is still intact. Kim decides she does not want to play with it any more, she checks with Jessica, and they both knock it down and put the blocks away.

It is after 12:00. All of the children go to the bathroom and then to the dining room. Lunch today is chicken, green beans, mashed potatoes, milk, and chocolate pudding for dessert. As the children finish their meal, they put their dishes away and go into one of the classrooms where their cots are laid out. Kim is one of the last children finished. By the time she reaches her cot most of the other children are asleep. Those who are not sleeping are lying quietly on their cots. Today, Louise, a teacher, stays with the children during their nap. The Math/Problem Solving and Reading teachers are meeting with the curriculum coordinator. The other teachers are relaxing over lunch.

By 1:45 Louise wakes up everyone except Curtis, who did not feel well in the morning, and sends them to the bathroom. After a snack of milk and cookies the children return to the Free Flowing Room. Kim is in the first Peabody group, so she and five of the other children join Florine in the Language area. Kim loves P. Mooney and is glad to see him. The Peabody lesson for today revolves around animals. The children imitate animal sounds, label animal pictures, and hear the story of "The Elephant That Did Not Know How To Listen." After the story Florine asks them to name the animals that were in the story. She helps them to pantomime the story. Jessica reminds everyone of their last trip to the zoo and all the children become involved in relating what they saw at the zoo. Because they are excited about the topic, Florine takes out a large sheet of paper with crayons and has them draw pictures of what they saw. A lot of conversation is exchanged as the children discuss where they are going to place different animals. When the picture is finished, Florine helps them hang it up. Kim and the others then return to the Free Flowing Room.

Mamie has taken out the rhythm instruments and passes them out to those children who are interested. Kim, Kisha, Patricia, and Danny go to the gym with Mamie to play and march with their instruments. Other children soon join them. After Mamie has put the instruments away, Kim and Patricia go over to the art table where Marge has put out some Play-Doh. Kim says she would rather draw, so Marge clears a space for her at the table. When Kim is finished, she takes her name card off the shelf to copy her name and then places the drawing in her cubby so she will remember to take it home. She joins Kisha at the Fine Motor area. Together they disassemble a take-apart car and put it back together again.

When Kim is finished, Becky asks her to come to the Math/Problem Solving area. During the morning class, Becky noticed that Kim was having trouble with remembering two attributes. In the Math/Problem Solving area, Becky and Kim play games using two attributes. This tutoring session lasts only a short time, because it is now 3:30. Kim grabs her coat as Marge announces it is time to go outside. Curtis and two other children choose to stay in the Free Flowing Room. Kim, Kisha, and Danny grab the jumprope. They have been practicing jumping double dutch and are anxious to show the others. Soon most of the children are gathered around them taking turns at jumping.

Gerry calls that it is almost time to leave. Kim runs back to the Free Flowing Room to get her drawing and then joins the other children in the van. On the way home Gerry sings "There Was An Old Woman." Kim knows almost all the words and sings along with her. Gerry pulls up in front of Kim's house and Kim runs in to show her mother her drawing.

Medical/Health Concerns

The intervention program included provisions for routine care, health screening and follow-up, sick and emergency care, and parent education.

ROUTINE CARE

Safe and sanitary procedures were established for diapering, bathing, feeding, and laundry. Each infant had a daily health check that included monitoring temperature, food intake, and bowel and bladder function and checking the body for rashes. In addition records were kept on sleeping habits and irritability. The infants' growth was checked on a routine basis by doctors at Milwaukee Children's Hospital and appropriate immunizations were administered. A Milwaukee County Visiting Nurse came every other week for routine check-ups and she was also available at other times as needed. She checked each child, provided advice, answered questions, and responded to the concerns of the staff. In addition, each child was provided with two well balanced meals a day. This was considered to be a preventive medical measure.

HEALTH SCREENING AND FOLLOW-UP

The Milwaukee Children's Hospital Preschool Vision Clinic screened each of the children twice before they were 6 years old. The Marquette University Dental Clinic saw each child every 6 months for a check-up from age 4 on. When needed, the children were taken to the clinic for filling cavities or other dental work. Marquette University's Audiology Department screened all of the children for hearing problems. As part of a thorough medical examination given to the whole sample, the children were tested for lead poisoning. In those children with high lead levels, Milwaukee County worked directly with the families to find the source of the lead. The lead levels of these children were monitored by Milwaukee Children's Hospital.

As with any preschool program, we had the usual bouts with colds, flu, and contagious childhood diseases. When a child arrived at the Center sick, we contacted the parents and together assessed the best course of action. If the parents were working or unable to provide care at home, a sick area was set up in the school office. When possible, the child was taken home. For some children whose parents were unable to consistently and accurately administer medication, the Center staff administered the medicine.

In emergency care situations the child was taken to Milwaukee Children's Hospital. Emergency care was provided for the accidents that occurred at school and for injuries that occurred at home but had not been given proper medical attention.

The parent coordinator and infant stimulation program supervisor worked with each family on medical concerns and the parents were involved with all follow-up medical care given to their children. Often the parent coordinator became the liaison between the doctor and the parents. Parents were given advice on nutrition, first aid for cuts and bruises, care of sick children (e.g., avoidance of dehydration), and preventive actions (e.g., substituting water for orange juice when given in a bottle to put the baby to sleep to help prevent tooth decay). The caregivers also contacted the parents frequently to discuss concerns they had.

STIMULATION EDUCATION PROGRAM OVERVIEW

The intervention program curriculum was designed by Susan Harrington and Caroline Hoffman. The curriculum was designed to provide an environment and a set of experiences appropriate to each individual's needs at different ages. The program conceptually attempted to duplicate the quality of adult-child interaction styles that had been identified as differentiating middle class from lower class families and that are traditionally associated with adequate cognitive development. Three areas of development were addressed: social-emotional, perceptual-motor, and cognitive-language. During the different age phases of the intervention program, different emphasis was placed on the area of development appropriate to the children's ages.

During the infancy phase of the program (3 months to 10 months), the adult:child ratio was 1:1 and the major emphasis was on establishing a relationship between the caregiver and the child that encouraged independence and curiosity. During the toddler phase (10 months to 24 months of age), the children were encouraged to develop an interest in persons other than the primary caregiver. Depending on the readiness of each individual, the caregiver:child ratio changed gradually from 1:1 to 2:2 to 1:3. When the children were approximately 18 to 24 months of age, they were grouped together in a transition program in which the caregiver:child ratio was 1:3.

Infant and toddler stimulation centered around activities that middle class parents naturally engage in to teach their children and was individualized as much as possible to meet the needs of each child. Structure was provided in the form of daily activity schedules and activity sequences listed in a curriculum guide. This format provided basic guidelines for the caregivers, but did not require them to teach tasks according to formally specified content or procedure.

The early childhood phase of the intervention began when the children were about 24 months old, lasted until about 4 years of age, and was structured around small group activities, although the program remained highly individualized. A wide range of activities including art, music, storytelling, physical training, field trips, and special events was used to address the children's overall development. Intervention during this phase was designed to emphasize reasoning and the use of receptive and expressive language in problem solving.

As the children grew older, more emphasis was placed on the cognitive and language skills that underlie school readiness. At approximately 4 years of age, prereading and premath components were introduced and taught by two certified teachers. This was the most formal phase of the intervention and the one most similar to other well structured preschool programs (e.g., Karnes, 1973; Weikart, 1972). Spontaneity and creativity were encouraged, and self-directed behavior and the taking of responsibility for task completion were reinforced. These factors have all been associated with an *achievement press* that differentiates families with high functioning children from families in which children experience difficulty (Henderson, 1981; Werner & Smith, 1977).

Early Infancy Program

During the infancy phase of the program (3 to 10 months), the major emphasis was on establishing a close relationship between each infant and one caregiver. This began when the caregiver visited the home, watched the mother care for the infant, and then worked with the infant at the home. When the infant was transferred to the Infant Stimulation Center, this same caregiver remained with the infant and provided for the infant's needs on a 1:1 basis. Care was also taken to establish a relationship between the infant and at least one other adult at the Center to ensure the child's emotional needs could be met appropriately if the primary caregiver became ill or left the program.

All infants entered the program when they were between 3 and 6 months of age and were attending the Center on a full-time basis by 6 months of age. The stimulation program was totally individualized at this point to ensure that each infant's needs, moods, and interests were cared for. The day was planned according to the individual infant's eat-sleep cycle, which required each caregiver to develop appropriate activities so that her infant could acquire new skills and practice those skills that had been attained.

An infant's organization and interpretation of his/her perceptions change as a result of maturation and experience. The development of perceptual skills is enhanced, or may be limited, by environmental factors outside the control of the infant. One of the major roles of the primary caregivers was to provide a variety of sensory experiences and to present materials in such a way that the child had the opportunity to make comparisons (i.e., to allow discrimination between increasingly similar stimuli).

The six perceptual areas are kinesthetic, auditory, visual, tactile, gustatory, and olfactory. In refining the ability to discriminate between stimuli, the following variables were manipulated by the caregiver:

1. *Kinesthetic*: Vary the child's direction and speed of motion. Vary his/her position in space. Vary the stress placed on different muscles.
2. *Auditory*: Vary the sounds presented in pitch, volume, location, duration, tone, and rhythm. Pair sounds with objects, sounds with animals, words with objects.
3. *Visual*: Vary objects by size, color, shape, position, distance, movement, and direction.
4. *Tactile*: Vary play objects by texture, temperature, flexibility, and weight.
5. *Gustatory*: Vary flavors, temperature, and consistency of foods.
6. *Olfactory*: Provide the opportunity to experience various odors.

Motor skills develop concurrently with perceptual skills. Motor control starts with the head and proceeds in downward and outward directions: cephalocaudal (growth from head to foot), proximodistal (growth from the central body to the periphery), and growth from large muscles to smaller muscles. Although the process of learning to walk may take more than a year, development of the fundamental skills required for this complex motor movement can be observed much earlier. As the child develops more complex motor skills, he/she is better able to explore him/herself and the environment to help refine perceptions and understanding of the world. Caregivers provided their infants with opportunities for practice in using various muscles and muscle groups as they gradually came under control.

Special emphasis was placed on verbal interactions with infants, even before they began to talk. All activities with infants were accompanied by positive vocalizations by the caregivers. Infants were encouraged to make sounds. The following guidelines were used to ensure that the environment was supportive for language development:

1. Describe your actions to the infant during physical care (bathing, feeding) and perceptual-motor activities.
2. Label objects important to the infant.
3. Emphasize the pairing of specific words and actions ("up"—picking the child up).
4. Listen to and respond enthusiastically to the child's utterances by touching, smiling, or talking to him/her.
5. Echo the child's babbling and sounds.
6. Expand the child's vocalization (ball, big ball, Tony's ball).
7. Respond to the child's vocalizations, so that he/she learns the communication aspect of language (ball; Where is Tony's ball?).

In infancy, the child's understanding of his/her surroundings develops through physical interaction with his/her environment. Rapidly developing motor abilities, perceptual discriminations, and comprehension of language contribute to this growing understanding. Through this interaction with the environment, the infant determines that specific objects have names, classes of objects have names (toy, book), objects have certain properties (red, big, smooth), and actions result in reactions from both people and objects. The extent or exact nature of the information a child draws from experiences is unknown. However, it can be assumed that his/her attempts at understanding the environment can be enhanced or limited by the availability and quality of the experiences themselves. The quality of the experience was enhanced by pairing activities that involved active exploration and manipulation of the environment by the infant with relevant language expressed by the caregiver, for example:

1. A wide variety of manipulation problem solving toys were available and accessible within the environment.
2. Caregivers learned to view any situation, such as a ball rolling under or behind a chair, as a potential problem solving experience.
3. Caregivers contrived problem solving situations.
4. Naturally developing motor skills were used to expand the child's experiences.
5. Because every activity is a learning experience for the child, routine activities were viewed as potential learning situations.
6. The environment itself was organized to introduce a variety of interrelated concepts.

Toddler Phase

When the infants were about 12 months old, two caregivers began to work together and share the responsibility for their two infants because of the growing interest of toddlers in persons other than the primary caregiver. By the age of 15 months two children shared one caregiver. Between approximately 18 and 24 months all children were grouped together in a transition program where the caregiver:infant ratio was 1:3. The purpose of this transition period was to gradually orient both the children and their caregivers to group routines as opposed to the individual routines of the infancy phase of the program. Such routines as one mid-day nap, sitting next to other children at the table at lunch, playing next to other children, sharing a caregiver's time, and group activities in a small space were introduced.

Increased mobility and contact with other children gave rise to conflicts with peers over toys and laps to sit on. Numerous inservice training sessions were devoted to helping the caregivers understand the social development of the children. Positive strategies were developed for dealing with the adult-child and child-child conflicts typical of the toddler period. The caregivers provided redirection, substitution, and choice as alternatives acceptable to both toddlers and caregivers. This approach was accompanied by verbal explanation, an important component.

The environment was structured so that restrictions ("no-no's") could be kept to a minimum; potentially dangerous materials (thermometers, scissors, glass dishes) were put in safe places, gates limited a child's access to stairways and trash cans, cribs were moved to a new room to provide more space for exploration, and tall metal bookcases were exchanged for two-tier shelving.

The major emphasis of the stimulation program gradually shifted from social-emotional development to perceptual-motor development. The use of perceptual-motor skills can be observed when a child navigates through a room of furniture, toys, and people. In order to cross the room successfully, children must have an awareness of their own bodies, a realization of the position in space they occupy, an understanding of the spatial relationships between their own bodies and the things surrounding them, and the gross and fine motor ability required to complete the journey.

The perceptual-motor program for toddlers emphasized body awareness, gross motor development, and fine motor development. The overall goal of the program was to ensure that perceptual and motoric skills were practiced and mastered so that they could be used by the children to explore their world.

1. *Body Awareness*
   a. Body image
      (1) Experiences seeing own image/image recognition
         (a) Mirrors
         (b) Photographs
         (c) Slides
      (2) Imitates actions with body parts
      (3) Points out parts of body (receptive)
      (4) Labels some body parts (expressive)
   b. Body concepts
      (1) Generalizes names of body parts (hair, eyes, nose, and mouth) to other people, animals, and dolls

(2) Associates clothing or utensils (socks, mittens, brush, comb, and spoon) with appropriate body parts

c. Body movement/position in space plus spatial relations
  (1) Experiences moving within different environments
  (2) Navigates obstacle course
  (3) Is introduced to position words (in, on, under, over, up, down, next to, by). Caregiver gives child verbal feedback of his/her position.

2. *Gross Motor Experiences*
  a. Muscle strength and control
    (1) Grasping, carrying, and releasing large materials: balls, blocks, cartons, and balloons
    (2) Climbing stairs, furniture, hills, and pillows
    (3) Walking and running: forward, backward, changing directions, changing speed, and stop-start
  b. Coordination
    (1) Balancing coordination of crawling, walking, climbing, squatting with reaching, grasping, carrying, releasing, and changing hands
    (2) Coordinating body movement with position in space
      (a) Negotiating obstacle courses, new environments, environmental changes (furniture rearranged)
      (b) Chasing bubbles, balls, and people
    (3) Adapting body to physical resistance: circle games, teeter-totter, "jolly jumper," pulling on plain and stretch ropes, pull toys of various weights and resistance, pushing cartons and furniture, climbing or crawling up and down inclines

3. *Fine Motor Experiences*
  a. Muscle strength, muscle control
    (1) Grasping: large pegs, crayons, pencils, chalk, paint brush, spoons, small balls, Play-Doh, sticks in sand or clay
    (2) Squeezing (strength in fist and finger grasp): Play-Doh, shaking toys, hammer and pounding board, small noisemaking squeeze toys
    (3) Finger opposition: finger foods, pegs in boards or clay, puzzles with knobs, small objects
    (4) Hand-wrist action: pouring and spooning water, macaroni, sand out of containers, pounding bench, musical instruments (drum, triangle, tambourine), screw-top plastic containers
  b. Coordination
    (1) Putting together (hands brought to center of body): stringing beads, large pop beads, cymbals, finger plays, Play-Doh
    (2) Replacing parts in stationary objects: form boards, puzzles, pegs and pegboard, pegs and clay, shape discrimination box, shape mailbox, objects in containers, lacing large boot
    (3) Stacking: table blocks, boxes, paper and plastic cups, stacking rings

(4) Opening and closing: hinged containers, flip-top lid boxes, place-on lid boxes

(5) Banging action: hammering toys, drum, spoons, and bowls

By far, a child's most impressive accomplishment in the second year of life is the development of language. Speech appears, vocabulary grows, and language becomes a tool for acquiring information as well as for meeting needs. The toddler's interest in imitation, his/her memory and new pleasure in words result in much labeling. Listening to the speech of toddlers provides valuable information about what they comprehend and are trying to understand. "More," "that mine," "what that," "big one," and "doing?" are phrases that reveal the toddler as a person beginning to deal with abstractions and able to use language to assert him/herself, acquire information, and even classify things in the world.

The caregiver-child interaction within the environment supported language growth. Caregivers continued to follow the guidelines described in the infancy section. They translated the child's actions into words, labeled objects in the environment, changed the materials in the environment to increase language opportunities, provided children with a language model, used functional words frequently and appropriately ("up," "bye-bye," and "more"), and, more importantly, listened and responded to the children's language.

In addition to the role verbal interaction played in routine activities, caregivers planned two formal language sessions daily. Expressive and receptive vocabulary development were the goals of these sessions. The children participated in activities designed to develop skill in imitation, memory, concept formation, and labeling.

1. *Imitation*: Caregivers imitate the actions and sounds of the children, choose actions and sounds for the child to imitate that are already in the child's behavioral repertoire, and serve as models for the development of speech and language.

   a. Caregiver imitates child's actions or verbalizations as she interacts with him/her during play activities.

   b. Caregiver chooses an action or verbalization the child performs well (crawling, banging, "mama") and encourages the child to imitate her action.

   c. Caregiver chooses actions similar to those already performed by the child and encourages the child to imitate her action.

   d. Child imitates caregiver's body movements, facial expressions, sounds, words, events (e.g., talking on phone).

   e. Child imitates another child's actions.

   f. Child participates in action rhymes, action games ("ring-around-a-rosy," "follow the leader").

2. *Memory*: Memory, both short term and long term, plays an important role in all aspects of learning, including language learning. The toddler, with his/her growing understanding of object permanence, is able to retain more and more information. The structure of the environment and the activities in which the child participates facilitate that growth.

a. The child participates in games in which he/she locates objects hidden within sight. The complexity of the activity is varied by the number of objects hidden, the number and type of objects used to hide the desired object, and the elapsed time between the time the object is hidden and the time of the search.

b. Memory is facilitated by the repetition of pictures, books, songs, games, finger plays, and toys used to stimulate expressive and receptive language. Verbal sequences were repeated as long as the toddlers enjoyed the repetition and indicated more was desired. During repetitive sequences, the caregivers omitted the last word or line so that the toddlers would fill it in.

c. The arrangement of the environment, clean-up activities, and established schedules and routines were used to facilitate development of memory skills.

3. *Vocabulary Development*: Vocabulary development, both receptive and expressive, is a major concern of the education program for toddlers.

   a. Receptive
      (1) Children point to objects and pictures asked for by the caregiver.
      (2) Children follow simple directions.
   b. Expressive
      (1) The child is given time to familiarize him/herself with the objects to be labeled before he/she can be expected to be interested in its label. Children handle (touch, roll, bite, and squeeze) objects while the caregiver casually labels those objects the child likes to handle and things and people which may have special meaning for him/her (e.g., his/her clothes, food, mother, and caregiver).
      (2) The child is provided with objects, then objects and pictures, then pictures to label. The experiences are repetitive; that is, many of the same objects and pictures are used daily, but the activity format is changed enough to maintain interest.
      (3) Children hear caregivers use the question format "What's that?" or "What is he/she/it doing?" often, so they can model their own language questions.
      (4) Children and caregivers converse. That is, activities are never so structured that the caregiver is limited to a set pattern of responding.

4. *Concept Formation*: Concept formation is, essentially, dealing with abstractions. Toddlers are capable of formulating concepts and giving some of these concepts appropriate verbal labels. Caregivers provide the children with the experiences they need to extend their developing concepts and the labels they need to describe them.

5. *Predictive Labeling*: Predictive labeling is the ability to predict an object's verbal label on the basis of previous experience with similar objects. It is

this skill that allows the older toddler, familiar with the word "shoe," to label a moccasin as a "shoe" and immediately associate it with his/her foot. Four areas relate to this language/problem solving skill.

  a. Predictive Labeling
- (1) Visual discrimination of people, objects, and pictures.
- (2) Comprehension and/or expression of verbal labels.
- (3) Experience with the concept that a number of objects can share the same verbal label (shoes, caps, cups, books).
- (4) Opportunity to come in contact with new objects that fit into a known category.

  b. Position Concepts: Up, down, in, out, open, shut . . .
  c. Attribute Concepts: Big, little, heavy . . .
  d. Quantity Concepts: One, more, all gone, two, all . . .

With the toddler's developing language, ability to remember, and curiosity, he/she is a serious student when it comes to understanding his/her world. The toddler is a master of exploration: he/she observes, attends, investigates, and discovers. He/she is able to keep a goal in mind and attempt a variety of purposeful techniques to meet that goal. The toddler is able to remember an action and the result of that action and can repeat the action. He/she is an explorer and a problem solver.

In addition to routine learning experiences, formal learning sessions were planned to give the child things to explore, things to remember, problems to solve, and things to compare.

1. *Children were given "things to explore."* What's in it? What does it do? How does it work? What happens if . . .? These were the questions answered by children through exploration of many objects including music boxes, weighted rolling toys, pull toys, funnels, pots and pans, balls, bubbles, and balloons.

2. *Children were given "things to remember."* Simple directions or guiding statements ("Can you find the ball? Get the ball.") were things to remember for the toddler. By presenting the children with the same problem or a similar problem with some regularity, they learned that solutions that had worked the previous day usually remained valid. Children learned and remembered principles that could be applied time after time, usually with positive results, for example, if you remove the rubber band from a container, it can be opened. Memory was also required when children were given tasks that required a series of steps toward successful completion. For a toddler this could mean problem solving experiences such as the one below:

Step 1: Child puts ball on top of a ramp.
Step 2: Child releases ball.
Step 3: Child follows ball visually and motorically.
Step 4: Child retrieves ball.
Step 5: Child puts ball on top of ramp.
Step 6: Child repeats the action.

3. *Children were given "problems to solve."* Once a child was familiar with a strategy for a particular problem, the problem to be solved was altered. For example, a toddler familiar with the Playschool Postal Station shape discrimination toy could remove the yellow cylinders and/or the red squares from the assortment of eight shapes stored in the bin and place them in the appropriate circle and square slots. (He/she could not yet use the triangle or the disc.) The familiar solution of removing the appropriate pieces, closing the bin door, placing the pieces in the slots, and retrieving them again was altered slightly resulting in a new problem to solve. The following are alterations of original problems:

    a.   The colors of the cube and cylinder were reversed.

    b.   The shapes other than the cylinder and cube were changed.

    c.   Small objects, some of which could fit through the slots, were substituted for the shapes in the bin.

    d.   Small rubber balls replaced or were used in addition to the wooden cylinders.

4. *Children were given "things to compare."* An adult watching a toddler pick out the Life Saver from the Cheerios will not question the child's ability to make discriminations. Discrimination and association are problem solving skills relevant to the toddler. For example, with help, toddlers matched objects to a model when they found the other shoe, sock, and boot, and when they put the crayons in the crayon container and the table blocks in the appropriate can. Children also demonstrated their growing understanding of association by attempting to place clothing on the appropriate parts of their bodies and by bringing together the wooden hammer on the floor and the pounding board on the shelf. Objects were presented in groups to further the formation of associations (farm animals, fire truck and station, different kinds of cars, etc.).

Early Childhood Phase

As the first 10 children approached 24 months of age, they were grouped together in one room with three caregivers. As new infants were added to the program and the total group of 20 were enrolled, the duplex in which the program was housed became too small to meet its needs. Until other accommodations could be found, space was rented in a Salvation Army center for the oldest group of children. Finally, the first floor of a school building owned by a neighborhood church was rented. The facility had classroom space, a well equipped kitchen, a gymnasium, and office space, and was located within the children's neighborhood.

As the children passed from infancy into early childhood, the emphasis of the stimulation program gradually shifted from social-emotional development to perceptual-motor development and then to cognitive-language development. The program became more formal and complex and the role of the caregiver became more like a teacher than a mother figure. Caregivers had to develop strategies for handling children in small and large groups. They also had to develop activities that were caregiver directed and child directed and address the children's needs in the areas of cognitive and language development.

As the stimulation program became more structured, the daily schedule became similar for all infants. Although there were several modifications of the schedule and caregiver assignments over the years, some general time considerations guided the time breakdown of the day. Breakfast, lunch, snack, and nap consumed 2 1/2 hours of the 7-hour day. The remaining 4 1/2 hours were divided into small group caregiver directed or child directed/caregiver supervised learning periods and free choice periods.

Each child participated in three small group sessions designed to promote cognitive or language development and large group sessions for gross and fine motor development, art, music, and free choice activities. The small group cognitive-language sessions were generally part of the morning program, while the afternoon sessions were more flexible and often included more large group activities. A large group session was developed to use activities adapted from the Peabody Language Development Kit (Levels P and II).

Three caregivers were assigned to each classroom where the children were approximately the same age and at approximately the same developmental level. Each caregiver was trained in all areas of the curriculum but specialized in one cognitive-language area and was responsible for planning and operating one learning center within the classroom. The children rotated among learning centers within each classroom in groups of two, three, or four and visited each of the three caregivers each day. Caregivers either rotated or shared responsibilities for planning large group sessions and special events.

The caregivers were comfortable and competent in understanding and implementing the cognitive-language curriculum, in managing the learning environment, and in meeting the needs of groups of children. They recognized the limitations of the established system and were ready to explore new strategies.

In response to the needs for more flexibility in programming, for vertical groupings, and for more opportunity for child directed activities, a Free Flowing Room was added to the Stimulation Center. One classroom contained the structured learning centers, while the Free Flowing Room was designed to accommodate all of the children at once. The room was subdivided into a block area (blocks, cars, garage, animals, and people), a dramatic play area (puppets, housekeeping materials, and dolls), a manipulative area (objects to take apart, puzzles, games, and pegboards), a science table (shells, magnets, rocks, magnifying glass, and plants), an art area (easel, scissors, clay, and crayons), and a reading area (books, records).

The addition of the Free Flowing Room allowed for flexible scheduling. Because the room was large enough to accommodate all of the children at once, those caregivers assigned to one of the cognitive learning areas could vary the grouping of children and the length of time according to the concepts and activities presented. Every morning all of the children went to the Free Flowing Room following breakfast. Because this Room was child directed, each child chose what activity he/she would like to do, for how long, and in what way. The caregivers assigned to the Free Flowing Room were available to listen, converse, read, and guide children in choosing an activity. The other caregivers saw each child every morning, either individually or in a group, picking them up and returning them to the Free Flowing Room.

The addition of the Free Flowing Room created the needed balance of caregiver directed and child directed activities, provided further opportunity for observation and evaluation of the children's ability to utilize concepts, and increased the flexibility of the structure of the program to the benefit of each child while remaining oriented toward a cognitive-language curriculum.

While the emphasis of the early childhood stimulation program was on the areas of language and cognitive development, social-emotional and perceptual-motor development were also addressed. A supportive environment was created to facilitate social-emotional development in terms of a positive self-concept, self-help skills, and interpersonal skills. Staff discussions centered around the patterns of normal social-emotional development so that activities could be structured to promote growth. The environment was structured to be flexible enough to meet the range of emotional needs evidenced by all children while retaining the structure required to provide the sense of security children need. Caregivers recognized the importance of engaging children in discussions about feelings, fears, responsibility, death, birth, losing and winning, peer problems, siblings, adults, family problems, etc. Social-emotional problems were identified early and addressed in a preventive manner. Knowledge of individual child differences from birth aided in developing flexibility in the program to meet individual needs. Frequent interactions with parents kept the staff aware of problems at home that could affect the child's development and adjustment.

A child develops a picture of him/herself through interactions with others and the effect of his/her actions on the environment. The self-concepts of the children were addressed by considering the following needs:

1. *A child needs to feel important.*
   a. People listen to what he/she says.
   b. People choose to be with him/her.
   c. He/she is an important member of the school.
2. *A child needs to feel competent.*
   a. He/she is successful at a majority of the attempted tasks.
   b. People notice what he/she does well.
   c. Other children and adults use him/her as a resource.
3. *A child needs to feel liked.*
   a. The adults around him/her like him/her.
   b. The children around him/her like him/her.

The feelings of accomplishment derived from being able to do things for oneself is yet another building block in the establishment of a positive self-concept.

The self-help skills of feeding, toileting, and dressing are basic to the development of the young child. As a child developed the higher level self-help skills of dealing with rules, protecting oneself (safety), and decisionmaking, the adults responded by allowing him/her more opportunity for independent action.

Being sensitive to all of the clues and nuances that are involved in learning to get along with others in social interaction begins in early childhood and continues throughout one's life. For most children, interpersonal skills are learned through trial and error as they approach peers and adults. Opportunities were provided for frequent peer interaction to occur. The children had been together since infancy and they grew up together using more and more sophisticated forms of interaction. A few of the children did have trouble. Generally, this was in the form of the exclusion of one child by a peer group. When this occurred, the staff attempted to determine the cause. The child was then helped to relate to small groups by being paired with another child for a special activity and by giving or telling the child something special to share with the group. The interpersonal skills focused upon were:

1. The ability to join a group of children
2. The ability to initiate an activity
3. The ability to follow another child who is leading
4. The ability to respect the property and territory of others
5. The ability to share objects and activities
6. The ability to understand the effects of one's speech or action on another child
7. The ability to stand up for one's rights
8. The ability to learn appropriate ways to settle disputes
9. The ability to learn appropriate ways to express anger, frustration, and disappointment
10. The ability to wait one's turn
11. The ability to seek out others for playmates

The perceptual-motor program focused on gross motor, fine motor, and visual motor skills. No child in the program was assessed as having a delay in the development of fine or gross motor skills. The stimulation program, through an appropriately equipped environment, time, and space in which the children practiced emerging skills and through frequent evaluation of their ability levels, simply ensured that perceptual-motor skills were developing at a normal rate.

Verbal interaction among adults and children is probably the single most critical factor in the development of the child's facility with language. The stimulation program was designed to support language growth. The caregivers encouraged communication for companionship, mutual problem solving, and pursuing interests. There were things to talk about: projects, objects, events. The following guidelines helped caregivers to develop an environment that facilitated language production, verbal interaction among children, and communication between children and adults:

1. *Being a good listener encourages children to talk.*
   a. Respond to what children are saying.
   b. Encourage children to complete their verbal messages. (Wait for children to express their needs verbally rather than anticipating them and, by doing so, cutting down on their language production. Let children complete their own thoughts rather than filling in the last words.)
   c. Remember new words or phrases the child uses so that you can incorporate them into other parts of the program or bring up their use another way.
2. *Speak to the children frequently and relevantly.*
   a. Engage *each* child in conversation *every* day.
   b. Use language for conversation as well as for instruction and guidance.
   c. Extend children's ideas and language by conversing about related topics and events.
   d. Take cues for conversations from the child rather than always having the caregiver control and direct the topic. (Even if you have talked about monster movies for a week, there are always new things to say about any topic.)
   e. Stimulate language by providing things and ideas to talk about.
   f. Explain actions and events that occur in the school. ("We can't leave for the zoo because we can't find the keys to the van. That's why everyone is looking through coat pockets and bags.")
   g. Explore topics of interest to children. (Familiarize yourself with TV programs, toys, children's games. Take cues from the children about topics of interest, i.e., circus, fire trucks, birthday parties, monsters, prehistoric animals, cooking, babies, hospitals.)
   h. Know enough about each child to be able to personalize conversations. (Know about siblings, parents, relatives, pets, clothing, family events and problems, neighborhood, friends, favorite toys, and possessions.)
   i. Extend children's interests and thereby topics of conversation through field trips, films, books, objects, and new people.
3. *Demonstrate to the children that language is a resource through which you can gain information, share ideas, and obtain help.* ("Our clock is broken today so I don't know if it is time for lunch yet. John, will you go to the kitchen and ask if it is lunch time yet?")
   a. Encourage children to initiate conversations. ("Ask Freddy what we made out of those cartons yesterday." "Mary, you and Lisa decide what story we should read today.")
   b. Teach the children to use each other as resources. ("Ask John to show you how that puzzle fits together.")
   c. Encourage children to resolve conflicts verbally.

4. *Help each child to feel that he/she is competent in expressing him/herself through language.*
   a. Make each child feel that what he/she has to say is important and that you value speaking to him/her. (Stop what you are doing, make eye contact, get to his/her level, ask follow-up questions, look interested.)
   b. Make yourself available to the child who wants to talk.
   c. Make the time to answer each question posed to you.
   d. Respond to what a child says rather than how it is said; communication is more important than choice of words or articulation.
5. *Encourage conversations among children.*
   a. Provide opportunities for the children to talk.
   b. Learn when not to interfere with child-to-child interactions.

In addition to the creation of a general classroom climate that encouraged children to use language and provided opportunities for the growth of language skills, sections of the day were allocated for specific types of language activities. In the language learning center, caregivers emphasized listening skills, conversing skills, vocabulary development, basic knowledge, and the use of language to solve problems:

1. *Listening skills*
   a. Children hear and repeat songs, poems, finger plays, parts of stories, phrases, messages.
   b. Children follow directions in action songs, treasure hunts, and "Simon Says," and in art, music, movement, or other activities.
   c. Children listen to, retell, illustrate, answer questions about, and act out stories.
2. *Conversing skills*
   a. Children describe objects in sight: talking about their properties, where they belong, what they are used for, and who plays with them.
   b. Children relate personal experiences about a common topic (bedtime, breakfast, siblings).
   c. Children answer questions about a given topic.
   d. Children ask others questions about a given topic.
   e. Children lead discussions about pictures and objects.
   f. Children organize a group to work on a project: block building, making snacks, producing *Goldilocks and the Three Bears* play.
   g. Children create stories (teacher provides a central character or event and the children generate a story about it).
3. *Vocabulary skills:* Children were exposed to a variety of activities that focused their attention on:
   a. Description words (fast, round, blue, skinny).
   b. Action words (jump, roll, wiggle, tell, find).
   c. Prepositions (in, on, under, near, over, on top of, between, behind).

d. Conjunctions (and, or).
e. Concepts (fruits, vehicles, silly things, manufacturing).
f. Synonyms (cap/hat, large/big, pants/jeans/slacks, car/ automobile).
g. Homonyms (hi/high, bear/bare, wait/weight, male/mail, sea/see, flour/flower).
h. New words (monstrous, gigantic, astronaut, dinosaur).
i. Idioms (wall-to-wall carpeting, jumping for joy, tickled pink).

4. *Basic knowledge skills:* Caregivers used a unit approach to information in which children considered a variety of details about a given topic (family, health, traffic signs, transportation, clothing, weather, Thanksgiving). Through the unit approach, children gained information through discussions, stories, films, and concrete experiences. The related vocabulary was stressed. Children were given the opportunity to use the newly acquired information and vocabulary in activities such as sorting, storytelling, building related objects, and art projects.

5. *Verbal problem solving skills*
   a. Critical thinking questions:
      (1) Why does a dog bark?
      (2) What do you think will happen next? What will happen first?
      (3) What belongs to the mailman? To the teacher? In a grocery?
      (4) What do we use a telephone for? A bag? A box?
      (5) What would you do if you lived in a tree?
      (6) How could you reach the other side of the lake? A box on top of a shelf?
      (7) What can we jump over? What can you hide under your bed?
      (8) Describe a dog, a bicycle, an envelope.
      (9) Where could you see an elephant? A fire truck?
      (10) What do you do before you go outside to play in the winter?
      (11) What makes rain?
      (12) What would you play with if you were a fish?
   b. Sentence completion:
      (1) I sleep in a _____. I live in a _____.
      (2) Steve left the house and went to _____.
      (3) A little girl can _____.
   c. Pretending games: Let's pretend that you are going to the zoo today. What will you bring with you? What will you see? What sounds will you hear? What colors will you see?
   d. Guessing games:
      (1) I'm thinking of something that is red, has wheels and hoses. What is it?
      (2) I'm thinking of something that you can eat . . . that is a dessert . . . that is brown.
      (3) Is it something to eat? Is it small enough to fit in my hand?

e. Describing games:
    (1) Show the child an abstract design or an object without a label
         (e.g., piece of machinery) and ask him/her to describe it.
    (2) Have one child act out an animal or a movement and ask the
         other children to describe what they see.
    (3) Can you describe the largest animal you have ever seen?
f. Predicting outcomes:
    (1) Let the children guess and discuss the outcome of stories.
    (2) Show the children pictures and ask them to guess what could
         happen next.
    (3) If I have some crayons, paper, glue, and scissors, what is it
         that I am going to make?
    (4) If my mother gives me a quarter and I go out of the front
         door, down the block, and into a store, what do you think I
         am going to do?

Each day the children also participated in a large group (six to ten children)
language activity. Most of the activities were based on the Peabody Language
Development Kit Level P or II. The Peabody is an oral language program that
is especially useful for paraprofessional teachers because of the comprehensive
manual, interesting materials, and motivating sequenced lessons. The
Peabody was incorporated as an integral part of the stimulation program, with
minor adaptation, when the children were 2 1/2 years old.

The Peabody program stressed overall oral language development. The
manual included 180 daily lessons made up of some 700 activities. These activities dealt with such things as naming, describing, matching, remembering,
sequencing, sentence building, rhyming, listening, storytelling, and problem
solving. Although Level P also emphasized teaching patterns of syntax and
simple grammar, we did not emphasize this aspect of the program because we
chose to program for *comprehension* of standard English but not necessarily
expression in standard English.

Cognitive development was addressed through the following problem solving areas:

1. *Organizational skills*: the ability to acquire, arrange, and store information
2. *Problem solving skills*: the ability to apply the organizational skills in
   order to solve problems
3. *Preschool math skills*: the ability to understand and apply the concept of
   numbers

Basic to the successful implementation of the problem solving program was
the concurrent growth of the children's perceptual-motor skills and expressive
language ability. The increased mobility of the preschool child allows him/her
to acquire information from the active exploration and manipulation of the environment, from trial and error problem solving strategies, and from activities
involving relational concepts. ("My hand is too little for this mitten, but too

big for that one.") The developing expressive language skills permit the child to ask for more information about things not understood and, in fact, to demand from adults concept expansion ("But why?").

Children progress through developmental stages that are defined by how the child organizes his/her knowledge. Learning within a developmental period is directly related to the quality, quantity, and interrelationships of the child's experiences. Within the problem solving program, the children were presented with experiences involving a variety of concepts and processes. The processes, as Piaget emphasized, are the inquiry skills or methods of operation through which a child gains information. Within this context, the concepts are the content, the specific information through which the child organizes, defines, and differentiates among conditions in his/her environment. The specific goal of the curriculum was to expose the children to a variety of concepts in order to maximize their ability to solve problems.

The organizational skills focused on the processes the child uses to solve problems, the type of problems solved, and the information obtained. The processes a child develops to organize information about his/her world are:

1. *Evaluation comparison*: matching, comparing, contrasting
2. *Association*: establishing connections between how to move objects, events, concepts
3. *Classification*: the systematic arrangement of objects and concepts into groups or categories according to a common property or properties
4. *Seriation by pattern, property, time*: the process of ordering or arranging a group of objects, events, or elements according to a continuum

The concepts usually acquired by young children fall into the following categories:

1. *Basic knowledge*: family relationships, transportation, food, animals, clothing, weather
2. *Color*: red, blue, green, yellow, black, white, brown
3. *Shape*: circle, square, triangle, round, flat, "sort of round," line, point, curve
4. *Size*: little/big, small/large, tall/short (taller, tallest, shorter, shortest), long, wide, narrow, thin, thick, fat, deep, shallow, medium, huge, tremendous, tiny
5. *Position*: high/low, top/bottom, middle, above/below, up/down, on/off, between, beside, behind, in front of, under/over, next to, first, last, before, after, left/right, near/far, close/far, beneath, ahead of, center, bottom, around, here/there, beginning/end, outside, in(side)/out(side), on (top of), under(neath), toward, away, open/shut, through, next, by, forward/backward, farther, farthest
6. *Amount* (quantity): all, some, none, full, empty, more, most, less, least, many, few, same, part, whole, half, much, fewer, fewest, a lot, a little, all gone, cupful, truckful, spoonful, everyone, each, no one, (just) enough, too much, too few, big enough, quarter, alike, pair
7. *Weight and density*: heavy/light, thick/thin
8. *Properties* (attribute common to all members of a class): boat-float, birds-fly, drink-liquid

9. *Other contrasting or opposing conditions*: same/different, fast/slow, hot/cold (lukewarm), smooth/rough, hard/soft, wet/dry, happy/sad, night/day, light/dark, with/without, old/new, loud/soft, girl/boy
10. *Function* (relation of objects/usage of objects): lives at, has, belongs to, is wearing
11. *Time*: early/late, tomorrow, yesterday, today, now, later, soon, younger/older, noon, lunch time, night/day, morning, evening, before, often, nap time, time to go outside, on time, a short time, a long time, next, days of the week, seasons
12. *Number*: ordinal numbers, cardinal numbers

Instead of planning the curriculum around either the developing methods of organization or speech content, it was felt that the curriculum should be organized with both goals in mind so that the children would be presented with an array of experiences that would further their abilities both to organize and to describe their environment. By beginning with a process such as classification and coordinating it with the concepts, one could have activities that include grouping objects by color, sorting pictures by shape, making charts of the children grouped by sex (basic knowledge), or solving abstract problems involving classification ("Would you see a cow at the zoo or at a farm?"). The application of the organization skills needed to solve problems requires that the child:

1. Be cognizant of the problem
2. Be motivated to solve the problem
3. Be able to organize and retrieve previously learned information
4. Be able to compare and contrast this problem (object, event, action) with others he/she has experienced
5. Be able to generalize from one situation to another
6. Be able to draw and act on conclusions
7. Be able to evaluate the effectiveness of the solution

Within the problem solving program, the children were provided with both formal and informal manipulative and verbal problems. The children were encouraged to discover all they could about objects and to talk about their discoveries.

The caregiver's role was to present related problems both in the small group learning period and throughout the day. Her goal was to help the children identify relevant cues, formulate strategies, and generalize the information. Initially, all problem solving activities included motoric and verbal components. As the children's language and cognitive skills developed, the emphasis shifted to include activities involving abstract reasoning.

School Readiness Component

In the beginning there was no intention to teach the children to read or prepare them for school in the area of mathematics. However, it became apparent that many of the children were interested in learning to read and developing math skills at around 4 years of age. At this point two certified teachers were employed and a more formal school readiness component was added to the program. This component built upon the language and problem solving skills that had been the basis of the earlier part of the program.

A variety of strategies had been used throughout the program to develop positive attitudes toward reading. In infancy, books meant caregivers' laps and rocking chairs or, said another way, love and approval. Books were a social experience for toddlers and preschoolers, as a caregiver and one or more children could go off by themselves to read. Books were an acceptable alternative to organized group activities and were given as gifts on birthdays and at Christmas. Books gave clues to special activities like trips to The Ranch, zoo, park, beach, airport, or museum. Caregivers and children made books to record events, to relate fantasies, or to give as gifts. Stories using the children themselves as characters were made into books with accompanying photographs.

Throughout the program, emphasis was placed upon auditory discrimination, visual discrimination, and the concepts of symbols, decoding skills that are required for reading. Figure 3-1 represents the development of these skills from infancy through approximately 6 years of age.

Auditory skills begin to develop in infancy when a child hears and attends to a variety of sounds, picking out (discriminating) those that are particularly meaningful to him/her: mother's voice, footsteps on the stairs, the sound of his/her own name, the words "bye-bye." The toddler begins to associate words and objects, listens closely to sounds in words, imitates sounds and words, develops a vocabulary, and communicates. He/she associates people, animals, and machines with the sounds they make. The preschool child continues to experiment with words — real words, nonsense words, very long words, rhyming words.

The stimulation program provided exposure to activities and experiences designed to facilitate the growth of auditory discrimination and auditory memory. Caregivers planned activities in which children focused on particular sounds (cymbal, drum, ticking), associated sounds with the things that produced them (cow mooing, water running, car honking), and replicated pitch, volume, and pattern of sounds and words heard. Children listened for sound-alike rhyming words and completed rhymes and played games with rhymes. They focused on similar sounding words (pen/pan), listening to hear if they were exactly the same. The children heard the caregiver say familiar words in drawn-out syllable fashion (el-e-phant) and then put the word back together. They listened for certain words in rhymes and stories and then focused upon specific letter sounds.

Auditory memory was facilitated by learning songs and finger plays and by playing games requiring children to remember increasingly complex sets of directions. Children duplicated rhythmic patterns thumped out on the table, knees, or drums, and whispered messages to one another.

In order to see and compare complex visual stimuli, a child must call upon a number of specific skills. First, he/she must be able to discriminate the

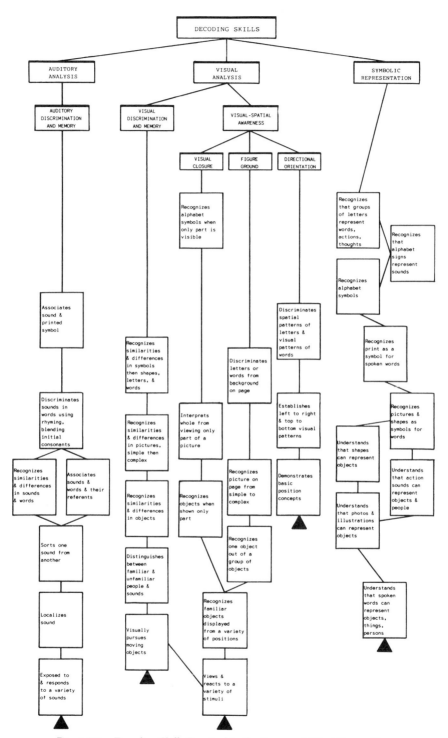

Figure 3-1. Decoding Skills Required in the Process of Word Recognition

material to be focused upon from a background of nonrelevant stimuli (figure-ground perception). Second, he/she must use concepts of orientation in space (direction) as a basis for assessing sameness or differences. Third, he/she must be able to look at symbols and perceive them globally (visual-closure) in order to facilitate the rapid visual discrimination and sight word development associated with the reading process. The visual analysis skills in the stimulation program were visual discrimination, visual memory, and visual-spatial skills.

The emergence of symbolic representation is evident when children point out a shoe in a picture book when requested, get a ball from the shelf after seeing one in a book, or put an inverted funnel or pan on their heads for a hat. The stimulation program guided and fostered the development of this skill from the concrete to the relatively abstract by presenting a variety of activities that used objects, role playing, photographs, slides, realistic illustrations, line drawings, blocks, shapes, and letters to represent people, objects, actions, events, sounds, and words. Caregiver made story boards as well as child directed stories were used extensively to develop the concept that "print is talk written down."

When the children were 2 1/2 to 3 1/2, their interest in letters was sparked by the television program Sesame Street, which most of the children chose to watch daily. The stimulation program picked up on the children's interest by using letter symbols for matching and sorting games. Name cards with each child's first name and photograph were introduced at that time, along with an assortment of alphabet puzzles and books. As a result of this early introduction to letters, all of the children identified letter names before being introduced to the sounds associated with the letters. When letter sounds were paired with letter names, the children accepted the sound the letter made as one of its attributes, much as they understood that a cube could be referred to as red or large or as a house or a block. Once a child expressed interest in learning to read and demonstrated competency in the skills listed below, a formal reading program was begun:

1. Visually discriminating between letters and groups of letters
2. Identifying and discriminating sounds in words
3. Identifying and naming at least half of the letters of the alphabet
4. Associating a few select sounds with the corresponding letter
5. Using sound-letter association coupled with context clues to guess the meaning of a few printed words
6. Recognizing own name in print and distinguishing it from others
7. Having small sight vocabulary
8. Demonstrating interest in learning to read, asking what words said, asking how to write words

The majority of the children expressed an interest and had developed the appropriate skills by about the time they turned 5, although one child began at 3 and a few were interested by 4 1/2. The transition from reading readiness to reading was a natural one. The use of story charts was expanded to encompass a modified version of a language approach to reading as described by Stauffer (1970).

Thus, the reading program began with a language experience approach. The language experience approach was used to introduce the concept that reading is "talk written down," to give the child a meaningful reading vocabulary, and to provide a medium through which the child could develop a sight vocabulary and learn word attack skills. The story charts aided the children in understanding the concept of the symbols, in introducing them to written words, and in teaching them to organize their thoughts into a whole. The following are samples of the stories, dictated by the children in the program individually or in groups, that were used in teaching reading:

> MY FAMILY (told by a 5-year-old)
> My mother put on her new dress and her
> lipstick and get her green purse and
> then she go downtown.
> My father eat some pancakes before he
> go out to town.
> MY BABY BROTHER (told by a 5-year-
> old)
> My baby brother can move in his walker.
> He can move backwards and he can move
> forwards.
> He laughs at me and he play with me all
> the time on my mama's bed.
> He play with his toy keys.

Over the years the focus of the reading program changed. All the children focused on decoding skills and language experience stories. For the oldest children, the emphasis on decoding skills was tangential to the language experience activities, and very little was done with word attack skills out of the context of the language experience approach. As we gained some experience with the teaching of reading to the children and monitored the children's progress, we placed more and more emphasis upon word attack (phonics) skills. The staff used Stauffer's (1970) discussion of word recognition, Durrell and Murphy's (1964) *Speech to Print Phonics*, Ginn's *Pre-Reading Skills Program* (Wisconsin Research and Development Center for Cognitive Learning, 1970), and the teacher's guide to the *Bank Street Reading Series* (Simonton, 1967) as a basis for the development of the phonic decoding program.

When the children had established a sight vocabulary and took books off the shelf to look at words (not just pictures), we introduced the *Bank Street Reading Series*. A basal series was chosen because of the usefulness of a comprehensive teacher's guide to paraprofessional teachers and the extensive use of such basal series in the Milwaukee public schools. The specific basal series was chosen because of its initial use of language experience charts (which interfaced

	NUMBER WORDS AND SYMBOLS	CLASSIFICATION (GROUPING)
EXPOSURE TO NUMBER CONCEPTS	1. **Related Vocabulary** a. Quantity and amount vocabulary (especially more, same, less) b. Relevant cardinal and ordinal number words (First put on your socks, you can have 2 cookies) c. Relevant numerals (telephone dial, TV)	1. **Matching Activities:** matching to a model 2. **Sorting Activities:** putting objects into piles 3. **Related Vocabulary:** same as, is like, not the same, different
ACQUISITION OF NUMBER CONCEPTS	2. **Rote Counting:** memorization of counting sequence in its proper order 3. **Functional Counting:** correspondence of each number in the counting sequence with one object until all the objects are counted 4. **Numeral Recognition:** discrimination and association of the written symbol of a number with its corresponding number word 5. **Association of Numeral (symbol) and Number (concept):** child is able to count the number of objects presented and choose the appropriate numeral to represent concrete number experiences	4. **Classification:** making sets or grouping objects by abstracting the common property a. Concrete familiar objects that are perceptually very different (balls and dolls) b. Pictures and objects increasing in similarity c. Grouping by function or use (chairs and beds) d. Disarranging and reconstructing sets e. Rearranging items into new sets (red and blue cars and balls: sort by color and then by function) 5. **Describing Quantity In A Set:** more than, less than, same as 6. **Using Number As A Property Of A Set:** each member of a set has the same number
UTILIZATION OF NUMBER CONCEPTS	6. **Pictorial Representation:** child is able to use charts and graphs to represent concrete and abstract experiences 7. **Counting With Lasting Equivalence:** after functionally counting, child understands that if no items have been added or subtracted, the number remains the same (conservation of number)	7. **Relations Between Sets** a. Disjoint (sets sharing no elements) b. Intersecting sets (sets sharing some elements) c. Inclusion (sets sharing all members) d. Addition: combining sets e. Subtracting: making subsets 8. **Comparison of Sets** (determined by 1:1 correspondence) a. making equal sets (sets with exactly same members) b. making equivalent sets (sets with the same number of members)

Figure 3-2.   Overview of Preschool Math Program

CORRESPONDENCE	SERIATION (ORDERING)	CONSERVATION
(Matching each member of one set with one and only one member of another set) 1. Exposure to 1:1 **Correspondence** in naturally occurring activities (1 coat for each child) 2. **Provoked Correspondence:** physical association of two groups of objects for which the child always has an association (milk container-straw, shoes-feet) 3. **Related Vocabulary:** enough, one each, too few, one more, more than, less than, too many	1. **Manipulation of Graduated Objects:** nesting cups, stacking rings 2. **Related Vocabulary:** first, next, second, last, middle	1. Experience with arranging, disarranging, rearranging objects, liquids, and moldable materials
4. **Spontaneous Correspondence:** physical association of two groups of objects which have no apparent relationship other than that they were brought together at the same time (a set of cups and a set of pegs) a. Constructing equivalent sets b. Disarranging and rearranging objects into 1:1 correspondence c. Reestablishing equivalence when an object is added or removed d. Constructing many-to-one correspondence e. Establishing mental equivalence	3. **Multiple Comparisons:** making comparisons between two objects or objects in a series 4. **Seriation** or ordering of objects or events by property, pattern or time 5. Application of **Ordinal Numbers** according to position in a series of objects or events (What color is the first crayon?)	2. **Teaching Planned Experiences** with arranging, disarranging and rearranging objects. The teacher combines manipulation of objects with verbal discussion of the objects' properties. 3. **Specific Experiences** designed to graphically represent conservation of number (counting out 5 objects, making different designs with them, recounting them)
5. **Using 1:1 Correspondence** to compare sets and to determine the relative value of numbers (more straws than cups)	6. **Seriation** of objects by quantity 7. **Describing Seriation Relations** using number concepts 8. **Number Value:** understanding that numbers are ordered by increasing value	4. **Conservation of Quantity:** understanding that amount can stay the same when appearance is altered 5. **Conservation of Number:** understanding that number is an invariant property and that physical arrangement does not affect number

with our existing program), colorful illustrations, urban settings, and multi-racial characters.

The preschool math readiness component built upon the problem solving concepts taught during the earlier part of the stimulation program. These skills facilitated the development of number concepts. Figure 3-2 illustrates the manner in which the concepts that underlie mathematics develop for young children. The formal math readiness program was developed to provide children with experience through which they could utilize and apply their knowledge of these concepts in problem solving.

4
Assessment of Intellectual Development

The unique nature of the Milwaukee Project, in contrast to previous longitudinal studies, is reflected in the research design. Specifically, the Milwaukee Project attempted to coordinate subject selection and a prescribed treatment to allow the development of a particular group of children to be evaluated longitudinally in response to that treatment and in comparison to a control group.

The investigation's concern with prevention gave emphasis to those aspects of cultural-familial or sociocultural mental retardation associated with development. The assessment protocol was designed to achieve two major goals: to evaluate the effects of altered experience upon the intellectual and cognitive development of the experimental group by comparison with the control group and to study development as a continuous process through a variety of measures. Our particular concern was with the child's developing awareness about and organization of his/her environment. Therefore, we centered evaluation around cognitive and social development in terms of the effectiveness of information processing and interactions with the environment.

The specific measures selected were within four areas: standardized measures of intelligence (i.e., IQ) (also used in maternal selection), a series of learning measures of patterns and strategies utilized by the children in discrete learning situations, language measures of comprehension and production ability, and social and personality measures of the child in social interaction with his/her mother.

ASSESSMENT

Standardized assessments of cognitive development were conducted for each child at regular age intervals from infancy through early childhood. Control and low risk contrast children were transported to the Infant Stimulation Center for testing on a schedule identical to that used for testing experimental children.

The standardized testing of neuropsychological and intellectual development during the intervention phase of the project was conducted primarily by a single project examiner who was not involved in any aspect of the educational program. To assess possible examiner bias, examiners having no other contact with the children or any other part of the study were brought in during the latter part of the intervention program and when the children were in school to test the children "blind," en masse, in a neutral setting. These psychologists had no prior relationship with the program and were recruited from private practice and the school systems of Milwaukee and Chicago. The experimental and standardized tests of language comprehension and production, measures of problem solving and learning strategies, and measures of mother-child interaction were made at regular intervals from 18 months through 120 months of age by specially trained research staff. In all cases, scores for the groups were cumulated according to a *birthday formula*, that is, an individual's test score closest to the reporting age for the group was used so that each mean performance data point reported represented essentially age-equal children.

Assessment During Intervention

The Gesell Developmental Schedules (Gesell & Amatruda, 1947) were administered to each infant every 4 months from 6 through 22 months of age. The Stanford-Binet Test of Intelligence, Form L-M (Terman & Merrill, 1960) was administered at 3 to 6 month intervals from 24 through 72 months of age. The Wechsler Preschool and Primary Scale of Intelligence (WPPSI) (Wechsler, 1967) was administered at approximately 48, 60, and 72 months of age, allowing comparison of intelligence scores derived from two different instruments. It also allowed separate analyses of verbal and performance components of intellectual development in the later stage of intervention. In the summer just prior to entering first grade, each experimental, control, and low risk contrast child was given the Metropolitan Readiness Battery, Form A (Hildreth, Griffiths, & McGauvran, 1969) to assess school readiness at the end of intervention.

Follow-up Period

Assessments of the intellectual development of children were made each year through the first 4 years of school and three additional assessments were made by the time the children finished eighth grade. Qualified examiners were hired each year to administer the Wechsler Intelligence Scale for Children (WISC) (Wechsler, 1949) to all experimental, control, and low risk contrast children at neutral sites. Examiners were given only the child's first name and an identification number to maintain anonymity in terms of group membership. An informal assessment of general academic and personal adjustment to school was gained from school records of the number of children who repeated a grade, the number who received special and exceptional educational assistance each year, and conduct reports. Standardized assessments of achievement were conducted each spring using the Primary I Battery (Grade 1), Primary II Battery (Grade 2), or the Elementary Battery (Grades 3 and 4) of the Metropolitan Achievement Test (Durost, Bixler, Wrightstone, Prescott, & Balow, 1970) administered individually by project staff. Scores for those tests administered on a group basis by the schools were collected from their school records and used for missing data and for data beyond the fourth grade.

ANALYSIS PROCEDURES

Estimates of the level of sophistication in cognitive skills for experimental and control children were made at various points between early infancy and school age in terms of their MA. The Gesell Developmental Schedules used to assess neuropsychologic maturity during infancy provided MA scores in four different areas of functioning. Scores from the four schedules were averaged to provide a performance mean MA for infants at each assessment. MA levels for Stanford-Binet, WPPSI, and WISC assessments were estimated using the equation: $MA = (CA \times IQ)/100$ (Jensen, 1982). The MA level for control children could then be compared to the MA level for the experimental children as a measure of developmental delay (Zigler, 1969).

Gesell MA scores were converted into DQs to provide a measure of the rate of cognitive development comparable to IQ scores from the Stanford-Binet, WPPSI, and WISC by dividing the performance mean by the child's chronological age and multiplying by 100 (Knobloch & Pasamanick, 1974). Statistical analyses concentrated on differences in the patterns of DQ and IQ scores for experimental and control children across time rather than single point or pre-post comparisons. Data collected for low risk contrast children are reported but were not included in analyses because of the small sample size ($n = 8$). A two sample multivariate regression or profile analysis procedure based on the model outlined by Timm (1975) and by Morrison (1976) provided tests of three hypotheses: parallelism — a test of no interaction between groups and assessments across time, time — a test of differences between assessments across time for the combined experimental-control groups, and groups — a test of differences between the profiles of performance for the two groups across time. When the parallelism hypothesis was rejected, the time hypothesis was analyzed separately for each group using a one sample profile analysis procedure. Major emphasis was placed on comparisons of group profiles of performance across time, but Bonferroni-Dunn multivariate confidence intervals were constructed as a conservative test for group differences at individual assessment points when such comparisons seemed informative.

Morrison (1976) cautions that tests of the time and groups hypotheses "have no meaning" (p. 154) when there is a group assessment interaction. However, the meaningfulness of such hypotheses is dependent upon the nature of the data set rather than statistical limitations. For data sets in this investigation, the time hypothesis was tested separately for each group when parallelism was not found as suggested by both Morrison (1976) and Timm (1975). The groups hypothesis was tested using a multivariate procedure as outlined by Timm (p. 242).

In order to use the profile analysis statistical package (Dixon, 1983), it was necessary to substitute for missing data. Estimates of missing values were based on the average or general score (G-score) for a particular data set or on the average deviation of an individual's scores from group means at other assessment points when the G-score was inappropriate.

A number of different instruments were used to assess the level of sophistication in cognitive skills in this longitudinal investigation. Although scores from different tests used to assess intellectual development may be expected to be similar, caution must be used in making inferences about the comparability of performance levels across instruments (Flynn, 1984; Hilton & Patrick, 1970; Jensen, 1982; Sattler, 1982). While scores from different standardized intelligence tests tend to represent the same construct and are generally correlated within the range from .67 to .77, it is possible for absolute IQ levels for individuals on different tests to vary considerably. Correlation coefficients are independent of the means of the distributions entering into their computation. They reflect the stability of an individual's standing within a group on two tests, not the stability of absolute score levels (Jensen, 1982; McCall, 1976). Performance level discrepancies across tests may represent differences in content or in standardization samples and procedures rather than differences in ability levels. Separate analyses were therefore performed for the profiles of multiple assessments made with each instrument.

The only appropriate comparisons of absolute IQ levels are those among experimental, control, and low risk contrast children in this investigation. Caution must be used when comparing the results in this report with scores for middle class children or children in other preschool intervention programs. The 1960 norms for the Stanford-Binet (L-M) and the 1949 WISC were used in this investigation, and scores reported are not directly comparable with scores derived from the revised 1972 Stanford-Binet norms or 1974 WISC-R norms. Flynn (1984) noted that the absolute levels of IQ scores from the more recently standardized tests are substantially lower than those derived from older versions of the tests. It is possible to rescore the Stanford-Binet data using the 1972 norms, but this was purposefully not done to emphasize the necessity of concentrating on the magnitude of differences between the matched groups within this investigation.

GESELL DEVELOPMENTAL SCHEDULES

In the first 24 months of life, the measurement schedule was largely restricted to data gathered on the Gesell Developmental Schedules (Gesell & Amatruda, 1947) and emerging vocalizations. The number of children tested at 6 months of age was less than half of each group and the results were not included in the analysis of the comparisons between groups. An attempt was made to administer the Gesell Developmental Schedules to each infant in the project within 1 week (plus or minus) of the time they reached the ages of 6, 10, 14, 18, and 22 months. However, assessment of infants, particularly in the early months of the project, was not easily completed for a number of reasons: Some infants were uncooperative in testing situations and were deemed untestable until sufficient rapport could be developed; infants often experienced illnesses that interfered with or precluded testing on the relatively strict schedule; and contact with control and low risk contrast families was less consistent than with experimental families, as families in these neighborhoods often moved without providing forwarding addresses.

The children's Gesell scores were submitted to a multivariate profile analysis computer (BMD 11 V) program. The design format is a $(p \times q)$ factorial in which p = groups = 2 and q = CA test intervals = 4. No data were collected for one subject from the control group at any time point so the analysis was limited to experimental = 17 and control = 17 subjects who participated throughout the preschool intervention. Column means were substituted for missing data points on the four Gesell Schedules to complete the data set for computer analysis and these are also reflected in the data for DQs. We have analyzed four and not five Gesell Schedule time points because the statistical requirement that observations per column equal at least nine for both the experimental and control groups was not met for the 6-month Gesell data. We tested the null hypotheses that: the segments of the experimental and control regression curves are parallel, there is equality of conditions, and the group means are similar.

Gesell Developmental Quotient

An overview or summary of performances across the first 2 years of the intevention program was gained from a comparison of the DQs between groups. The Gesell DQ (Gesell & Amatruda, 1947) uses the Performance Mean as an MA equivalent. This also provided a measure that would be continuous with the Stanford-Binet IQ assessed after the Gesell. The Performance Mean is a child's average of performance on each of the four separate schedules that make up the Gesell test of development. Table 4-1 presents the mean DQ performance for the experimental and control children between 10 and 22 months of age derived from the Performance Mean of the Gesell Schedules.

Profile analysis of these data identified a significant group × age interaction, $F(3, 30) = 7.46$, $p < .001$, for DQ scores. Separate analysis of DQ scores

Table 4-1 Mean Gesell DQ and Stanford-Binet IQ Scores for Experimental, Control, and Low Risk Contrast Children from 10 Months Through 72 Months of Age

Age in Months	Experimental				Control				Low Risk Contrast			
	M	SD	Range	n	M	SD	Range	n	M	SD	Range	n
Gesell DQ												
10	117.28	7.41	102.50-135.00	17	112.48	20.46	67.50-138.75	11	111.46	16.57	90.00-133.75	6
14	119.41	11.36	102.68-139.29	12	109.96	20.65	66.07-150.00	13	113.14	12.61	96.43-133.93	7
18	118.29	11.99	95.14-150.00	15	100.58	11.08	77.78-112.50	12	118.97	18.96	93.75-150.00	7
22	123.55	14.18	102.27-150.00	16	98.09	12.63	68.18-112.50	14	115.34	23.76	98.86-160.23	6
Stanford-Binet IQ												
24	124.60	11.73	91.00-139.00	15	96.18	10.21	64.00-109.00	17	109.29	19.04	80.00-138.00	7
30	123.59	11.19	96.00-137.00	17	94.39	9.38	75.00-117.00	18	113.13	20.73	80.00-149.00	8
36	126.18	9.38	107.00-137.00	17	93.67	10.00	76.00-120.00	18	112.13	19.74	80.00-149.00	8
42	125.29	7.14	105.00-135.00	17	95.17	9.43	80.00-122.00	18	113.25	18.11	87.00-147.00	8
48	126.00	5.92	113.00-136.00	17	95.72	11.13	80.00-123.00	18	118.29	27.13	86.00-170.00	7
54	121.47	8.54	105.00-144.00	17	93.39	10.07	79.00-119.00	18	107.00	13.08	86.00-120.00	6
60	117.94	7.47	107.00-135.00	17	92.67	11.83	75.00-118.00	18	107.63	16.45	81.00-128.00	8
66	120.82	9.72	107.00-139.00	17	91.56	11.08	76.00-112.00	18	108.43	23.34	87.00-141.00	7
72	119.24	9.40	103.00-142.00	17	86.89	12.54	69.00-112.00	18	108.75	14.87	94.00-132.00	8

for experimental children indicated there was no change in their rate of development across the infancy period, but the decreasing rate of development for control children evidenced by a decline in DQ scores from 10 through 22 months of age was significant, F (3, 14)=8.35, p < .001. Bonferroni-Dunn confidence intervals indicated the difference in rate of development for these two groups of children became statistically significant (-6.72< >25.62, p < .05) at 14 months of age. By 22 months of age, the mean difference in developmental level was 26.8 points, which suggests that control children were developing psychoneurologically at approximately three-fourths the rate of experimental children.

The differential in the course of early development between the experimental and control groups can be seen more clearly when the Performance Mean at each of the monthly testing sessions is plotted as a deviation in months from the monthly norms. In Figure 4-1 it can be seen that development for the experimental and control groups is reasonably comparable at 10 months, where

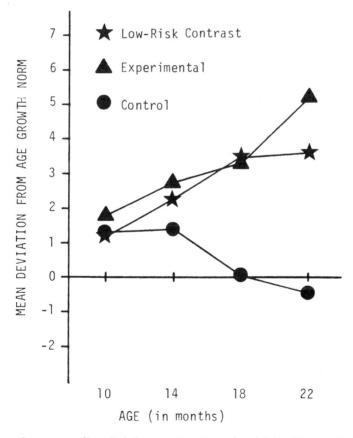

Figure 4-1.   Comparison of Low Risk Contrast, Experimental, and Control Groups' Performance Mean Deviation from Norm Scores on the Gesell Developmental Schedules

both groups perform about 1 1/2 months above the norm. But by 14 months, the experimental group's performance continues to improve, especially in comparison to the control group's performance. After 14 months, the experimental group continues to increase and gains nearly twice as many Gesell Schedule developmental months between 18 and 22 months as they did between 10 and 14 and between 14 and 18 months. After 14 months, the performance of the control group falls away and at 18 months their mean group performance is normal (0 deviation). At 22 months, the experimental group is 5.18 months ahead of the developmental norm while the control group is 0.42 months below the norm.

In the following table (Table 4-2), the mean performance data for the experimental, control, and low risk contrast groups are presented for each schedule, including the Performance Mean. The Performance Mean was used to calculate the mean DQs for each group presented in the table and to derive the deviation in normative performance illustrated in Figure 4-1 as the average deviation from the normative age group for the experimental, control, and low risk contrast groups.

The human organism was regarded by Gesell as a complicated action system that demonstrates different aspects of growth as it matures. The Gesell Developmental Schedules are tests of infant neuropsychologic maturity. An infant's behavior is assessed in four basic areas and the pattern of responses is compared with a normative sample's patterns:

1. Motor capacities of infants constitute the natural starting point for estimates of their maturity and include both gross bodily control and the fine motor coordinations. Tests of motor behavior assess the infant's postural reactions, head balance, sitting, standing, creeping, walking, prehensory approach on an object, and grasp and manipulation of the object and compares them with normative patterns.

2. A child's growth in resourcefulness in relationship to normative patterns is measured through assessment of adaptive behaviors represented by the fine sensorimotor adjustments to objects and situations. These include coordination of eyes and hands in reaching and manipulating, the ability to utilize motor capacities appropriately to solve practical problems, and the ability to adjust responses to simple problem situations.

3. Language behavior for infants centers first on the inarticulate vocalizations and vocal signs that precede words, and then on the use of words, phrases, or sentences as the child matures. Language behavior is broadly defined to cover all visible and audible forms of communication, whether by facial expression, gesture, postural movements, or simple vocalizations and includes mimicry and comprehension of the communication of others.

4. Personal-social behavior reflects the infant's reactions to the culture in which he/she lives. However, the patterning of this behavior is fundamentally determined by intrinsic growth factors. This aspect of growth is subject to the most individual variation, but basic neuromotor

Table 4-2 Mean Performance on the Gesell Developmental Schedules for the Experimental, Control, and Low Risk Contrast Group Children

	6 Months		10 Months		14 Months		18 Months		22 Months	
	Mean	SD	Mean	SD	Mean	SD	Mean	SD	Mean	SD
Motor										
Experimental	7.48	0.69	12.19	0.97	17.21	1.68	22.70	2.65	27.53	3.76
Control	6.41	0.30	12.48	1.64	15.22	2.32	18.12	2.15	22.56	3.47
Low Risk	8.33	1.93	11.59	1.86	15.86	2.10	22.40	4.78	26.26	5.18
Adaptive										
Experimental	6.58	0.72	11.96	0.88	17.03	1.73	21.50	1.96	26.41	3.44
Control	5.61	0.44	11.22	1.71	15.03	2.54	17.53	1.95	20.77	2.75
Low Risk	7.48	1.75	10.91	1.18	14.86	0.95	20.91	2.59	25.00	3.37
Language										
Experimental	7.40	0.91	10.62	1.63	15.72	1.34	19.97	3.22	26.98	3.87
Control	6.90	1.04	9.98	1.83	14.92	2.79	16.68	2.04	20.08	2.34
Low Risk	7.28	0.98	10.26	1.25	16.33	2.25	19.93	3.28	22.00	3.82
Personal-social										
Experimental	7.20	0.95	12.13	1.10	16.89	1.74	21.00	2.05	27.81	3.94
Control	5.89	2.03	11.32	2.10	16.39	3.43	20.09	2.16	22.92	3.15
Low Risk	8.70	1.47	11.83	1.64	17.26	1.92	22.41	3.39	28.26	6.53
Perform. Mean										
Experimental	7.17	0.83	11.73	1.18	16.71	1.63	21.29	2.52	27.18	3.76
Control	6.20	0.78	11.25	1.83	15.39	2.80	18.11	2.08	21.58	2.96
Low Risk	7.94	1.58	11.15	1.51	16.25	1.79	21.43	3.60	25.60	4.88
Sample Size										
Experimental	8		17		12		15		16	
Control	5		11		13		12		14	
Low Risk	4		6		7		7		6	

development will determine the limits within which normal cultural influences and social conventions will be reflected in the child's behavior. Performance on each of the schedules was compared among groups and submitted to separate profile analysis.

Gesell Motor Schedule

The profile analysis for Gesell Motor scores indicated that the null hypothesis should be rejected because the experimental and control regression curves are not parallel, $F(3, 30) = 9.86$, $p < .01$, and there is a (group × age) interaction. When the experimental and control scores were considered together, there was a significant change over time, $F(6, 60) = 34.30$, $p < .01$. The Hotelling T^2 statistic reveals that, overall, the experimental and control means are different ($p < .001$). However, t-test results show that experimental versus control differences do not begin until 14 months and continue at the 18- and 22-month test intervals.

Gesell Adaptive Schedule

This analysis revealed that for the Gesell Adaptive Schedules there is a (group $\times$ age) interaction in that the experimental and control regression curves are not parallel, $F(3, 30) = 9.19$, $p < .01$. The multivariate across time Ho (hypothesis) was rejected, $F(6, 60) = 39.28$, $p < .01$. When the four time points are considered overall, experimental and control mean scores are different (Hotelling T^2: $p < .001$). This experimental versus control difference results from performance at 14-, 18-, and 22-month test intervals for which univariate t-test results were significant ($p < .01$).

Gesell Language Schedule

The experimental and control regression curves for the Language Schedules are not parallel, $F(3, 30) = 10.04$, $p < .01$, a finding indicating that there is a (group $\times$ age) interaction. When the experimental and control scores are considered together, there is significant change over time, $F(6, 60) = 48.04$, $p < .01$. The experimental and control means, overall, are different (Hotelling T^2: $p < .001$). Univariate t-test results show that significant ($p < .001$) experimental versus control differences exist at 18 and 22 months, but not at 10 and 14 months.

Gesell Social Schedule

Profile analysis results reject the null hypothesis of parallelism, $F(3, 30) = 4.99$, $p < .01$, indicating that there is a (group $\times$ age) interaction. There is a significant change in performance over time, $F(6, 60) = 43.89$, $p < .01$, when the experimental and control scores are considered together. Overall, the experimental and control means are different (Hotelling T^2: $p < .01$), but the univariate t-test results show that experimental versus control scores are significantly different ($p < .001$) only at the 22-month test interval, that is, there are no significant experimental versus control differences on the Gesell Social Schedule at 10, 14, or 18 months.

A summary of the analysis of the performance data for the Gesell Schedules indicates that the experimental and control regression curves are not parallel and that when the experimental and control scores are taken together, there is significant change in performance over time. These statistical conclusions confirm that the positive slope to the experimental curves (on all four schedules) is steeper than the increase for the four control curves. Overall, experimental versus control mean Gesell performance is different, but experimental versus control differences do not begin until 14 months on the Motor and Adaptive Schedules, until 18 months on the Language Schedule, and until 22 months on the Social Schedule. Thus, experimental versus control Gesell differences on the Motor and Adaptive Schedules precede experimental versus control differences on the Language and Social Schedules. The comparative course of each aspect of early development for the experimental and control groups can be seen when the means at each of the monthly testing sessions are derived as a deviation in months from the monthly norms. Table 4-3 lists the mean deviation from age growth norms on the four Gesell Schedules.

Table 4-3   Mean Deviation from Age Growth Norms for
Experimental, Control, and Low Risk Contrast Groups
on the Gesell Developmental Schedules

	Age (Months)				
	6	10	14	18	22
Motor					
Experimental	1.48	2.19	3.21	4.70	5.53
Control	0.41	2.48	1.22	0.12	0.56
Low Risk Contrast	2.33	1.50	1.86	4.40	4.26
Adaptive					
Experimental	0.58	1.97	3.03	3.50	4.41
Control	-0.39	1.22	1.03	-0.47	-1.23
Low Risk Contrast	1.48	0.91	0.86	2.91	3.00
Language					
Experimental	1.40	0.62	1.72	1.97	4.98
Control	0.90	-0.02	0.92	-1.32	-1.92
Low Risk Contrast	1.28	0.26	2.33	1.93	0.00
Personal-social					
Experimental	1.20	2.13	2.89	3.00	5.81
Control	-0.11	1.32	2.39	2.09	0.92
Low Risk Contrast	2.70	1.83	3.26	4.41	6.26
Performance Mean					
Experimental	1.17	1.73	2.71	3.29	5.18
Control	0.20	1.25	1.39	0.11	-0.42
Low Risk Contrast	1.93	1.15	2.25	3.43	3.60

It is apparent that the greater strength on the nonlanguage related schedules precedes the strengthening that occurs in the latter half of the second year of life in language and social skills and is perhaps more revealing of the benefits of the early infant program. Whether the divergence of the group would occur in a similar fashion had the infant program not begun as early as it had might be answered by inferring from a comparison of the differential in developmental advances apparent on the various schedules at different levels. In other words, early peformance gains are foundational strengths upon which subsequent development depends. The comparison with the control group is revealing in that it is at 14 months that the control group performance does not continue to advance as might be reasonably anticipated based on their 10 to 14 month language and personal-social performance. Neither language nor adaptive performance develops to the comparable performance levels of the experimental group — two particular advantages that were fundamental as represented in the infant curriculum.

In summary, the Gesell data are comparable for both groups at 10 months of age, but the lack of growth on the adaptive and language schedules by the control group contributes heavily to the decline in developmental performance after the 14-month session. The experimental group showed relative strength early in their performance on the motor and personal-social schedules. The control group's performance decline on the adaptive and language schedules together with the experimental group's growth puts the experimental group nearly 6 months ahead developmentally.

Low Risk Contrast Group Gesell Comparisons

The small sample size for the low risk contrast group requires caution in drawing conclusions. However, important information can be gained in comparisons with conservative interpretation.

The Gesell Schedules were administered to the low risk contrast group according to the children's birthdates at the 6-, 10-, 14-, 18-, and 22-month levels. As previously noted, our contact with families in the beginning was less than consistent. Only four children were assessed at the 6-month testing because we lost contact with three families, one child was past the testing age when contacted, and one child was sick. This situation improved by the 10-month testing, where contact was reestablished with two families, but one child was ill during this period and another child was out of town at the time. By 22 months, two additional families moved and were not replaced in the study. Table 4-2 lists the means and standard deviations of performance on the Gesell Schedules across the testing sessions. Performance Means were converted into DQs so that this early performance could be compared to development assessed through standardized measures of intelligence. Comparisons were made between the low risk contrast and experimental group DQ scores and the low risk contrast and control group DQ scores.

In general, it seems that the performance levels for the low risk contrast and control groups are similar at the 10- and 14-month Gesell Schedules. In those periods where significant differences were identified, the experimental group demonstrated superiority. Both the experimental and low risk contrast groups were consistently superior to the control group after the 10-month assessment.

The comparative performance of the three groups is more clearly demonstrated when mean scores are derived as deviations in months from monthly norms. Deviation scores for all three groups on each schedule are listed in Table 4-3. These scores demonstrate that the low risk contrast and experimental groups are consistently ahead of the age group norms for the Gesell

Schedules, while the control group falls below age group norms on the Adaptive and Language Schedules. The low risk contrast group also demonstrated a surprisingly slow growth pattern on the Language Schedule compared with the experimental group, especially at 22 months. The experimental group's substantial superiority on this schedule may be accounted for by the emphasis on language development in the intervention program.

By 22 months of age, the experimental group is well ahead of age group norms on all schedules and the low risk contrast group is ahead of age group norms on all but the Language Schedule. On the other hand, the control group is below age group norms on the Adaptive and Language Schedules and less than 1 month ahead of age group norms on the Motor and Personal-social Schedules.

The overall developmental progress of the three groups up to this point is most clearly demonstrated by their Performance Means, which are listed in Table 4-2. As can be seen, the low risk contrast group and the experimental group are consistently superior to the control group except at the 10-month assessment, where the control group Performance Mean is greater than the low risk contrast group Performance Mean. Figure 4-1 illustrates the deviation from age group norms of Performance Means for the three groups. The control group is never more than 1.39 months ahead of the age group norms and at 22 months is 0.42 months below age group norms. On the other hand, the low risk contrast and experimental groups are both well ahead of age group norms at each assessment period.

At 10 months of age, the mean MA levels for children in all three groups as measured by the Performance Mean Gesell Developmental Schedules were relatively similar and well above their chronological ages (see Table 4-4). The

Table 4-4   Mental Age Levels for Experimental, Control, and Low Risk
Contrast Children from 10 Through 72 Months of Age

Age in	Gesell			Stanford-Binet		
Months	E	C	LRC	E	C	LRC
10	11.73	11.25	11.15			
14	16.72	15.39	15.84			
18	21.16	18.10	21.41			
22	27.18	21.28	25.38			
24				29.89	23.08	26.23
30				37.07	28.30	33.94
36				45.46	33.72	40.37
42				52.62	40.01	47.57
48				60.48	45.95	56.78
54				56.59	50.43	57.78
60				70.76	55.60	64.58
66				79.74	60.43	71.56
72				85.85	62.56	78.30

MA level for experimental children was less than ½ month higher than the MA level for control children at this point. However, by 22 months of age there was a 5.90 month MA difference between these two groups, a difference that became progressively larger with increasing age. Experimental children maintained a relatively constant rate of development across the infancy period with the exception of a rise at 22 months of age that was due primarily to increased sophistication in skills measured by the Language Schedule of the Gesell. Low risk contrast children demonstrated a small but steady increase in the rate of development across infancy, which reflected better performance on all four Gesell schedules. The progressively larger delays in development with increasing age demonstrated by control children reflected slower development in all four areas of neuropsychologic functioning, but deficiencies in fine motor and adaptive functioning were the most substantial.

In summary, the performance of the low risk contrast and experimental groups is comparable and considerably in advance of the control group by 22 months of age. We believe this is a demonstration of the importance of the mother in creating a positive, supportive psychological microenvironment for the child that encourages intellectual curiosity. In the case of the experimental children, this microenvironment was supplied in the form of an intervention program designed to serve the same function as the microenvironment provided naturally by the high functioning, low risk contrast mothers. Because all children resided within a physically impoverished, low SES, depressed census tract of the same city, the cause of these performance differences seems to be attributable to factors other than poverty per se.

The low risk contrast children show a lack of language growth at 22 months, while the experimental children demonstrate a substantial surge in language performance at this age. We believe this accelerated performance by the experimental children is a strength resulting from the heavy emphasis on language skills in the intervention program, which later supports high performance on the Stanford-Binet test of intelligence. This instrument is rather sensitive to verbal performance and, as language gains by these children continued, their IQ scores reflected the dominance in this area. This accelerated language performance was also reflected on the various language tests that were used across the preschool years (see Chapter 6).

INTELLECTUAL DEVELOPMENT (24 TO 72 MONTHS)

Standardized measures of intelligence have been the traditional method of comparison between groups. They are, for the most part, the only consistent and continuous measures used between research laboratories and within longitudinal investigations of development. They are the major basis of comparison between our target children and the cohort from the previous generation (referred to as high risk contrast) that we sampled in our original survey. Recall that the expected intellectual development for the control group was predicted from survey information of mean Cattell and Binet IQ scores for a group of children whose mothers had (WAIS) IQs below 80. These data show a decline in mean IQ from 92.5 at 24 months to 66.4 for children of 14 years or more. This latter figure approximated their own mothers' mean IQ of 68 and provides support for the value of maternal IQ as a better predictor of a child's adolescent IQ than the child's own IQ at age 2. It should be noted that the mean IQ up to 36 months was within the normal range and that a major decline occurred between that time and shortly after entrance into school. From that data, the hypothesis for this investigation was developed, which asked whether intervention could prevent such a decline in a similar group.

Measured Intelligence to 72 Months

After the infancy period (at 24 months of age), we began to administer standardized tests of intelligence. These initially included some Cattell Tests of Infant Intelligence (Cattell, 1940) along with the Stanford-Binet ([L-M, 1960] which was continued throughout the preschool testing program). Between 24 and 48 months, intelligence tests were administered on a 3 month birthday schedule and at 48 months we also began to administer the WPPSI (and eventually the WISC) test. The WPPSI test was administered alternately with the Stanford-Binet until school entrance and the WISC IQ test was administered thereafter.

The majority of the early Stanford-Binet IQ tests were administered by a single person, who was employed by the Project for its duration but was involved in no other aspect of the program. After 48 months and until all children were in school, some testings were performed by testers independent of both the Project and the University. Once the children were in school, all testing was performed by independent testers. The IQ testing was scheduled according to the child's birthday, thereby permitting the cumulation of test data for all children approximately according to age. This schedule was maintained for all of the experimental, control, and low risk contrast group children until the 60-month mark. At approximately 60 months, the control and low risk contrast groups began to enter kindergarten and, because of scheduling difficulties, uniformity in testing by the birthday procedure had to be modified and tests were administered within 2 months (plus or minus) of the 60-, 66-, and 72-month age points. The children were tested at the preschool Center in a separate part of the building. This procedure continued until all of the children—experimental, control, and low risk contrast—entered public school kindergarten. Thereafter, children were tested at a neutral site (e.g., a rented motel suite, a clinical psychologist's office).

The mean IQ scores (Stanford-Binet, L-M) of the experimental and control groups from 24 to 72 months are presented in Table 4-1. The data prior to 24 months shown in Figure 4-2 illustrate the mean Gesell DQ scores discussed in the previous section and presented in Table 4-1. The data after 22 months illustrate the mean Stanford-Binet IQ scores up through 72 months. Data from the alternate WPPSI and the later WISC testings are reported in a later section. Table 4-1 and Figure 4-2 summarize the Stanford-Binet scores used as the data in the multivariate profile analysis.

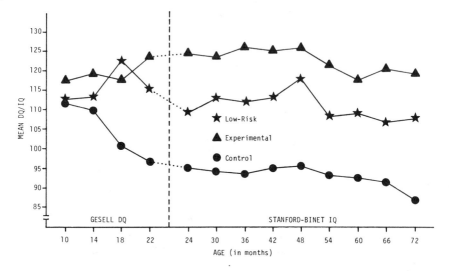

Figure 4-2. Mean Gesell DQ and Stanford-Binet IQ Scores for Low Risk, Experimental, and Control Groups for 10 Through 72 Months

The multivariate analysis of Stanford-Binet data indicated that the experimental and control group performances were essentially parallel, $F(8, 26)$ = 1.47, n.s., and the experimental group's mean level of performance was significantly superior, $F(9, 25) = 14.38$, $p < .01$, to the control group's mean level of performance over the 24 to 72 month period. Each group shows a significant change, $F(16, 52) = 2.94$, $p < .001$, across time in performance. Performance is relatively stable up to 48 months, but declines after this point. The major movement apart between the groups occurs by 2 years of age and the differences then stabilize. Actually, the estimate of intellectual development derived from the Gesell DQ is rather good. As can be seen, the difference between the 22-month Gesell DQ and the 24-month Stanford-Binet IQ is close to 1 point for each group (123.55 to 124.60 for experimental and 98.09 to 96.18 for control). The correlation between experimental children's 22-month Gesell DQ and 24-month Stanford-Binet IQ is $r = .56$ ($p < .02$) and for the control children it is $r = .71$ ($p < .01$).

In general, both groups attained IQ performance levels that were stable and maintained throughout the preschool program. At the first IQ testing at 24 months, there was a difference of more than 28 points between the experimental and control groups. This difference was maintained between the groups across the preschool program (mean difference is 29.50, SD = 2.22, range 25.27 to 32.60). At 24 months the experimental group's mean IQ was 124.60 (SD = 11.73) compared with the control mean of 96.18 (SD = 10.21), which compares to overall means of 122.80 and 93.29, respectively. The overall means are a reasonable estimate of the early preschool performance and a reflection of the differential between the experimental and control groups across this time period, for example, when the group means at 54 months (some 30 months from the first testing) are compared. The stability of performance for both groups, at their respective levels, is probably contributed to by the repeated testing across time under optimum conditions for all children. In fact, there is this same stability generally within individual performances within groups.

Test of Examiner Bias

Examiner bias in Stanford-Binet IQ scores was assessed by comparing scores obtained by the project examiner from the 48 through 72 month assessments with scores obtained during the same general period by independent examiners brought in on three separate occasions during the same period for this purpose. Separate Stanford-Binet general (GIQ) scores were derived for each child from assessments by the project examiner and assessments by the independent examiners. The correlation between the project and independent examiner GIQ scores was r = .96, although the mean project examiner GIQ scores for both experimental and control children were higher than the mean independent examiner GIQ scores (E-Project = 121.09, E-Independent = 114.10; C-Project = 92.04, C-Independent = 87.18). The GIQ difference between groups was 29.05 points for project examiner scores compared with 26.92 points for independent examiner scores.

LOW RISK CONTRAST GROUP MEASURED
INTELLIGENCE TO 72 MONTHS

The low risk contrast group children were tested in the same manner as the experimental and control group children, meaning they received testing on the same schedule and were tested past 48 months by independent testers who were unaware of their group assignment. Their testing was done during the preschool program by the same testers who tested the experimental and control group children.

Table 4-1 also lists the mean IQ and range of performance at each testing age for the low risk contrast group children on the Stanford-Binet from 24 through 72 months. As for the control group children, the 72-month score represents the last test before first grade and/or the performance score at the end of kindergarten. Contact with families and their children across this period was much more consistent than during the Gesell testing and the data set was relatively complete. Figure 4-2 includes the mean Gesell DQ and Stanford-Binet IQ scores for the low risk contrast group and is displayed in comparison to the experimental and control group children. The experimental group's performance was superior overall to the low risk contrast group's performance except at the 18-month testing, and both groups were superior to the control group on all testings after 10 months. Profile analysis comparisons were not made because of the small sample size of the low risk contrast group. They do, however, allow for meaningful comparisons if conservative.

The major movement apart for the three groups occurred before 2 years of age. During this period of early development the experimental group's performance increased slightly, most probably because of their involvement in the program, which emphasized cognitive skills. The low risk contrast group demonstrated an initial surge of development that peaked at 18 months. Then their performance leveled off and remained fairly stable except for another peak at 48 months. Some of this variability may reflect performance differences for one or two subjects in this relatively small group that disproportionately influence the group mean. The control group's performance begins to drop immediately during the Gesell assessment and continues to drop until the 30-month assessment. They experience a small recovery over the next three testings, but subsequently drop even further in performance. At the 72-month mark, the experimental children's average Stanford-Binet IQ score is 11.36 points higher than the average for the low risk contrast group and 32.35 points higher than the average for the control group.

The 22-month Gesell DQ performance mean for the low risk contrast group is not as good an estimate of the 24-month Stanford-Binet IQ as it was for the experimental and control groups, but this is influenced by missing data for the group at this point. The next three assessments bring the mean for the group closer to the range of scores achieved across the Gesell testing. The low risk contrast IQ performance at 24 months is a rather good estimate of performance from 54 through 72 months. In general the trends in Stanford-Binet IQ performance for the low risk contrast and experimental groups are quite similar, with a slow increase in performance, a peaking at 48 months, and a subsequent decline.

The drop in performance between the last Gesell testing and the first Stanford-Binet testing for the low risk contrast but not the experimental group may be related to differences in language development. The low risk contrast children demonstrated a lack of language development on the Gesell measure at 22 months; the Stanford-Binet instrument is particularly sensitive to verbal performance. The strength in language demonstrated by the experimental children on the Gesell testings is most likely responsible for their sustained performance across test instruments. The superiority of the experimental group's language skills during this period was also confirmed through more indepth language assessment, which is reported in a later chapter. It was most likely the intervention program's heavy emphasis on verbal interaction and the development of verbal skills that influenced the experimental group's superior verbal performance. Following the early surge in language growth by the experimental group, the low risk contrast and control groups demonstrated a similar but delayed growth in these skills. It seems that the same developmental pattern occurred, but that growth was accelerated for the experimental group.

Within Differences Among Groups

An examination of the distribution of IQ scores at each yearly developmental data point reveals substantial qualitative difference among groups. In Table 4-5, the percentage of scores at or greater than 1 standard deviation (i.e., <85) is presented for the experimental, control, and low risk contrast groups. The experimental group showed no scores below 85 and in fact only one child scored below 100 in IQ. By 72 months more than a third of the control group had scores below 85 and only three children ever scored over 100 with any consistency.

Table 4-5   Proportion of Experimental and Control Groups
with IQ Score <85

	Age (Months)				
	24	36	48	60	72
Experimental	0%	0%	0%	0%	0%
Control	6%	6%	11%	22%	39%
Low Risk Contrast	14%	12%	0%	0%	0%

A comparison of the distribution of IQ scores for the low risk contrast and experimental groups shows both have relatively similar low percentages of scores that are below average. Only one low risk contrast child scored below 85 before 42 months. That child, who incidentally was premature and ill most of the first 2 years, recovered slowly in performance and by 72 months scored 94 on the Stanford-Binet. At the time of entrance into first grade, no children in either the low risk contrast or experimental groups were functioning below 85 as measured by the Stanford-Binet and the Wechsler scales, while nearly 40% of the control group were below 85 IQ.

Mental Age Growth

The mean MA levels for children based on Gesell scores at 22 months of age and Stanford-Binet IQ scores at 24 months of age were about 6 months different and the correlation between these two sets of scores was $r = .85$. The MA performance difference between groups on the Stanford-Binet increased from 6.81 months at 24 months of age to 23.29 months at 72 months of age (see Table 4-4). The apparent increasing delay in intellectual development for control children is compared both with the norm group and with the rate of development for the experimental children. The MA difference increases steadily while the IQ difference remains relatively stable across this period, with an average IQ difference between groups of 29.50 points ($SD = 2.22$).

By comparison, the low risk contrast group mental age was about 2 to 3 months different — lower than experimental and higher than control — at the 22- and 24-month age levels. By 72 months of age, the low risk contrast group is about 1 1/2 years ahead of the control group and about 7 months behind the experimental group but 6 months ahead of expected age level. The control group is nearly a year behind the norm using this estimate of intellectual growth.

General IQ

We calculated a GIQ mean for the early IQ performance scores (24 through 42 months) and a late GIQ (48 through 72 months), a procedure suggested by McCall, Appelbaum, and Hogarty (1973) to derive a reasonable estimate of IQ performance over a series of longitudinal measures. In addition, the GIQ is less influenced by individual variation and can provide a better picture of the trend in intellectual performance and growth than single point estimates. In Table 4-6 the mean early and late GIQ scores and their correlations for all three groups are presented. The correlation between the early and late GIQ scores for the groups is rather good and in fact is as good or better a score to which the separate data points relate than do individual points relate to each other, that is, between the early and late GIQ periods. The late GIQ, mean of the 48 to 72 month Stanford-Binet scores, also was seen as a reasonable way of comparing Stanford-Binet performance to Wechsler test performance.

Table 4-6 Comparison of Early and Late Stanford-Binet GIQ
Performance for Experimental, Control, and Low Risk Contrast Groups

| | Early GIQ (24-42 mos.) | | Late GIQ (48-72 mos.) | | |
	Mean	SD	Mean	SD	
Experimental	124.0	9.5	121.4	5.4	$r = .70^*$
Control	94.8	8.7	91.8	10.8	$r = .84^*$
Low Risk Contrast	112.4	18.9	111.1	16.8	$r = .94^*$

$^*p < .05$

The early to late GIQ change for both the experimental and control groups is a decline on the order of 2 to 3 points. The early GIQ, however, is a more adequate reflection of performance during the period between 24 and 42 months than the late GIQ is of the events between 48 and 72 months. In particular the experimental and control groups reached a high in performance after the early GIQ period and from 48 to 72 months lost 6.76 and 8.83 points, respectively. The decline from this point coincides with a change in the testing procedures (viz., the alternation between Stanford-Binet and WPPSI testings and the use of independent testers for the majority of tests).

Actually, the decline for the experimental group occurred only during the first year of the change in testing (i.e., up to 60 months), while the decline continued for the control group from 60 to 72 months. This latter period represents the time of kindergarten for the control children. In other words, on the Stanford-Binet there was a loss among the control children of nearly 6 points after entering kindergarten, a loss contrary to the expectation of a gain because of the effect of schooling for such children. This was part of a declining trend that began at 48 months. We might also have anticipated this decline to continue for the experimental children as suggested by their 48- to 60-month performance, but it did not; in fact their mean IQ rose slightly during their final year in the preschool program.

The low risk contrast group maintained a fairly steady growth pattern about midway between the experimental and control groups. The general stability in performance can most likely be attributed to the effect of repeated testing and the optimum conditions developed for administration. In addition, the magnitude of the experimental group's performance, especially in comparison to the differential between the low risk contrast group and the control group, suggests some inflation because of the combining effects of the intense preschool training and the repeated testings. An attempt to gain a better estimate of these effects is afforded by performance comparisons among groups on other IQ tests (viz., WPPSI, WISC; discussed in the follow-up assessment chapter). The overall performance differential between the experimental and control groups, these possible testing artifacts effects withstanding, is a substantial demonstration of the general and positive influence of the early education program's influence on the intellectual development of children at risk for significant performance declines.

5
Learning and Performance

This chapter presents performance data on a series of problem solving tasks used to assess the learning characteristics of the experimental and control children during the preschool and early elementary school years. Results from a color-form matching task, a probability matching task, and an oddity discrimination task are described. These data represent an attempt on our part to develop broader information about the effect of the educational treatment program on the children's intellectual growth.

The significant differences in IQ test performance reported in the previous chapter do not adequately reveal the quality of the early difference in intellectual strength between the groups of treated and untreated children. As part of our overall scheme to examine the effect of the treatment program, we were concerned with determining to what extent the children would be able to gather developmentally meaningful information and sustain positive intellectual growth beyond the training situation. Because most, if not all, discussions of intellectual growth are dominated by references to IQ scores, the socio-psychological context from which individual children derive cognitive stimulation is essentially ignored and little information with utility for mounting psychoeducational reforms is revealed. For children who must endure what amounts to a psychoeducationally nonsupportive and impoverished home environment, it is crucial to nurture their ability to develop actively and independently the information needed to sustain cognitive growth. These learning data suggest that risk for atypical intellectual development results in part from a failure to develop the cognitive ability to actively manipulate one's personal learning environment.

Throughout the preschool phase of the treatment program and continuing into the early elementary years, three learning task paradigms were employed.

1. *Color-Form Matching Task*: This task provided information on the development of the subject's attention to color and form stimuli. In organizing and selecting information from competing stimuli, the child

can demonstrate a variety of strategies. The developmental speed and increasing sophistication with which an individual learns to organize stimuli may be seen as an early index of cognitive growth.

2. *Probability Match Task*: This task arranges reinforcement of a simple two-choice discrimination task so that events seem random while permitting observation of the development of strategy behavior and sensitivity to reinforcement contingencies. The subject's job — to maximize reinforcement — requires sensing the ratio schedule, which can be done through hypothesis testing. Younger children usually respond with primitive strategies such as perseverating to position, while bright and older children hypothesis test and come to appreciate the significative aspect of a stimulus as the means of finding problem solutions.

3. *Oddity Discrimination Task*: This task's paradigm filled a dual role by providing information on the role selective attention plays in the development of children's learning sets and enabling us to observe the growth of the child's appreciation of stimulus relations. The first case is a perceptual learning function that requires both organizational and categorization skills. In the second case this task reveals how such information is applied during problem solving behaviors.

Testing procedures were substantially uniform across both measures and years. The three learning measures were administered annually for 7 years beginning when the children were between 2 and 3 years of age. Each task was given individually in a relaxed and private atmosphere at the infant center in Milwaukee. The tester assigned to conduct each test session did not verbally reinforce specific responses. However, child motivation was encouraged by such general comments as "you are doing fine" or "this seems easy for you." Each child received a tangible reward (i.e., candy) at the end of each session.

During the course of our investigation, we became concerned that subtle differences in manipulanda, discriminanda, and presentation format could be influencing the children's performance. Three years into the research program, we changed from hand held to machine displayed presentations of the task stimuli in an effort to control for these methodological problems. The Wisconsin Learning Research Machine (Garber & Hagens, 1971) was designed and built specifically for this aspect of the assessment program. This apparatus included programmed learning paradigms, used visual displays, and automatically recorded all instrumental dependent measures.

The color-form, probability match, and oddity tasks were chosen because the paradigms themselves particularly suited our interest, which was to gain a measure of differential performance in achieving learning criteria between the treated and untreated children while simultaneously providing an opportunity to observe longitudinally the thinking processes of children. The three experimental paradigms selected afforded continuous measures across time and allowed observation of the response attributes that each task's discrimination learning paradigm required for proper solution. In other words, the children's responses in these particular learning paradigms enabled us to measure and evaluate response strategies while minimizing the importance of problem solutions as the major research goal.

We assumed that cognitive development is an ordered behavioral sequence, the developmental path of which could be observed experimentally as behavioral changes over time in discrimination response attributes. The three response attributes of attending, evaluating, and manipulating according to the demands and requisites of the stimuli sampled through the three learning measures certainly do not represent the limits of experimental concern in the area of discrimination learning ability. However, these three constructs do allow us to describe the quality and extent of differences in learning performance between the experimental and control groups. In addition, these constructs lent themselves to evaluations of interindividual differences over time in response patterns chosen as modes of problem solution.

DEVELOPING DISCRIMINATE ATTENTION TO STIMULI CUES

The color-form matching task was concerned with the pattern of the experimental and control children's attention to color and form stimuli across age. Within this task, color and form stimuli were seen as attentional cues characteristic of different perceptual dimensions. In order to maximize information input, children must learn to use various strategies, for example, as in the process of attention, when organizing and selecting information from among a group of competing stimuli. The developmental growth of the attentional process depends on both experience and a complex ontogenetic sequence of the sensory system. Performance on the color-form task provided an opportunity to examine the increasing developmental sophistication in the cognitive processing of exteroceptive stimulation.

The stimulus material for the color-form paradigm consisted of colored geometric forms (square, circle, and triangle; red, green, yellow, and blue). Each testing session consisted of 36 trials. Testing sessions were conducted at 1-year intervals between the chronological age periods of 30 and 102 months. On each trial, three stimuli were displayed to the child, who was then asked to match one of two stimuli to a third (the standard). One stimulus matched the standard with respect to color. The other matched the standard in form. A preference for a dimension, whether color or form, was indicated when the child's responses predominantly favored one dimension or the other. Specifically, a two-tailed binomial test (Conover, 1971) was employed to determine a cutoff ($p < .05$) for individual scores. All scores exceeding this cutoff point were interpreted as indicating that the child's responses were consistently toward one dimension. The order to stimulus cue presentation was randomized (Fellows, 1967) so that form or color preferences would be distinguishable from responses made along other, less nonsophisticated dimensions. The children could match consistently on one or the other dimension of color or form, but not if they responded simply to position (i.e., left or right). Position perseveration or alternation represent two nonsophisticated response modes that are typical of early developmental patterns.

The color-form paradigm is a forced choice task in which a response must be made on each trial. But it is only through a consistent application of an equivalence rule that one dimension or another could receive a significantly higher percentage of the responses. An inconsistent pattern of responses would be revealed by a roughly equal number of responses to both color and form stimuli.

We have used the construct of consistency in the application of equivalence rules to compare the performance across time of the experimental and control children. For each test interval, we computed the percentage of responses that each target child directed toward color and toward form stimuli. The highest percentage response to a dimension was used as the measure to analyze the experimental and control children's color-form performance over time. By averaging the highest percentage of responses made to each dimension at each test interval within each group, we in effect gave credit to the child who was using rules effectively, irrespective of a preference for color or form. Because inconsistent responding results in 50% responses to both color and to form stimuli, color-form scores range from 50% to 100% when computed in this manner. The group mean data are presented in Table 5-1 and displayed in Figure 5-1.

As can be seen in Figure 5-1, the experimental color-form preference was superior to that of their control counterparts. The experimental group mean percentage of highest responses to color or to form dimensional stimuli ranged from 75% to 93%. Ceiling effects for experimental performance are reflected in the general lack of slope to the experimental performance curve. The control children, on the other hand, began (at 30 months) by exhibiting an average of only 55% responses to color or form stimuli. But their group performance consistently improved (except at 54 months), so that mean percentage scores rose

Table 5-1 Group Mean Highest Percentage of Responses Made to
Either the Color or Form Dimensional Stimuli by the Experimental and
Control Children on the Color-Form Matching Task by Age

Age in Months	Experimental			Control		
	n	Mean	SD	n	Mean	SD
30	16	79.72	17.30	14	54.82	3.34
42	17	91.11	10.59	14	69.23	13.94
54	15	78.44	18.37	17	64.03	17.39
66	17	75.40	17.73	17	68.26	17.88
78	15	87.04	12.50	17	69.26	18.91
90	17	84.28	17.20	17	75.28	19.63
102	10	93.12	6.16	8	91.09	10.25

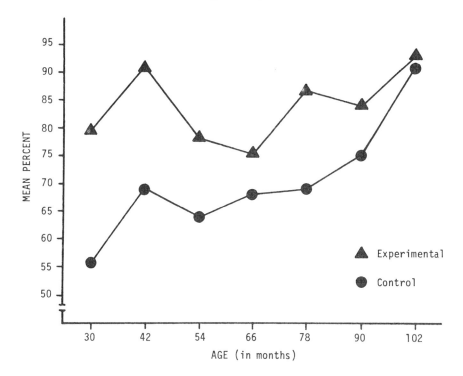

Figure 5-1. Group Mean Highest Percentage of Responses Made to Either Color or the Form Dimensional Stimuli by the Experimental and Control Children on the Color-Form Matching Task by Age

to 91% at 102 months. In other words, the experimental children exhibited sophisticated color-form preference performance at each of the seven test intervals, while the control youngsters changed over time from relatively unsophisticated (30 months) to relatively sophisticated (90 and 102 months) attention to color-form stimuli. The control children did not exhibit the degree of sophisticated color-form behavior shown by the experimental children as preschoolers (30 months) until after 2 years of elementary schooling (90 months). This finding can be viewed as an index of a developmental lag that may be characteristic of the control children's problem solving behavior during these early childhood years.

A multivariate profile analysis procedure (Timm, 1975) was used for statistical evaluation of the experimental and control children's color-form regression curves. The test of parallelism compared the slopes of the experimental and control regression curve segments for group movement between successive test intervals. The analysis of the children's color-form responses failed to reject the parallelism hypothesis, $F(5, 29) = 2.05, p > .10$. This statistic reflects the fact that both increases and decreases in scores between time points were parallel for the experimental and control groups, that is, the curve of each group rose or fell at the same time as the others. However, ceiling effects resulted in a limited range for experimental variation (about 15 points), while the control group overall raised their performance by about 40 points.

The profile analysis time hypothesis tests whether or not there were significant changes in performance between 30 and 102 months when the performance levels of both groups of children are taken together. The null hypothesis of no difference for the multivariate time analysis was rejected, $F(10, 50) = 3.29$, $p < .01$. We conclude that there was a significant effect with increased age (i.e., repeated measurement) for the children's color-form performance, especially for the control youngsters. Finally, effects of group designation were evaluated under the third hypothesis of the multivariate profile analysis. The null hypothesis that over all six test intervals there was no between group difference was rejected, $F(6, 28) = 11.19$, $p < .01$. We can conclude, therefore, that the experimental children's color-form performance was significantly superior to that of the control youngsters.

Examination of performance variations within tests and per child provide additional information about the development of color-form discrimination learning skills. Some children shifted preferences between years and some within session, but more to the point were the differences in response behavior (i.e., the style or strategy) employed. We evaluated individual performance in order to understand how the children went about the job of performing on this task.

The strength of the experimental youngsters' superior color-form performance lies primarily in the children's task behavior before their entrance into second grade (prior to 90 months). Post hoc comparisons of individual time points using Bonferroni-Dunn confidence intervals revealed that experimental versus control differences were not significant at 90 and 102 months. Over time, the experimental children exhibited rather stable color-form responding, beginning with dimensional responding that was consistent from the very earliest testing (30 months). The exception to this trend was seen at 66 months when there was a bimodal distribution of experimental color-form scores. In other words, for almost all testings most of the experimental children responded predominantly to a single dimension and the responses of each child clustered near his/her experimental peers.

Some of the within group performance shifts across time are revealed as intraindividual shifts among specific experimental and control children. These performance changes are attributable, perhaps, to within task administration pressures, such as boredom, fatigue, minor illness. In fact, some children switched preferences within session and verbally noted that they were quite aware of what they were doing. We found that another view of differential performance between groups, which is more individual specific, is revealed by looking at the percentages of children within each group who showed a preference rather than the mean group response to a dimension.

The experimental group shows a pattern of early strong dimensional preference, beginning at the earliest testing (30 months) and continuing through all test intervals. At every age period, at least 80% of the experimental group demonstrated preferences for either color or form stimuli. However, although the experimental children preferred form stimuli more often, there was no predominant preference over *all* testings for one dimensional category, whether form or color; nor was there a significant shift in dimensional preference across categories (e.g., from color to form preference) as the children matured.

In general, the control group's performance reflects a change from predominantly nondimensional to dimensional (either color or form) responding. Through the first three testings (30 to 54 months), nearly three-fifths of the control children did not demonstrate a dimensional preference. It was not until 66 months and after some kindergarten experience that a majority of the control children became dimensional responders. At that time, the control children exhibited a dominant preference (47%) toward color. By 102 months (third grade), five of the eight control youngsters tested exhibited form preference.

The analysis of the changes in the children's performances suggested that the tendency to show dimensional preference is more important than what dimension is preferred. It also suggested that preference is indeed influenced by such conditions as experience, namely, a highly structured preschool program and/or severe disadvantagement. In these data there was not a single continuum of preference across time for either group; rather there were considerable differences between individual children in the pattern of dimensional preference exhibited between the chronological ages of 30 and 102 months.

The control children's concomitantly lower performance on intelligence and language tests gave evidence of the complexity of the color-form matching task. This suggestion is supported by such evidence as given by Kagan and Lemkin (1961) that form attention is associated with higher mental test scores and by Farnham-Diggory and Gregg (1975) that form cues are difficult to extract. In other words, especially at the younger preschool ages, the color-form matching task is both a more complex task and more sensitive to early cognitive growth than its appearance as a relatively simple task suggests.

On the other hand, the experimental children were more consistent than the control youngsters in their application of equivalence rules. At least 80% of the experimental group exhibited a unidimensional preference through all seven test intervals, and the experimental percentages exceeded the control averages at every test interval. At 30 months, 13 of 14 control children perseverated. It was not until their completion of kindergarten (66 months) that even half of the control group exhibited a definite preference. And it was not until the end of third grade (102 months) that the control children as a group demonstrated the degree of preference (i.e., greater than 80% dimensional responders) that their experimental counterparts had demonstrated 6 years earlier at 30 months. Perseveration behavior has been observed in animals (Harlow, 1959), among both normal (Gholson, 1980) and retarded (Zeamon & House, 1963) children, and among low achieving college students (Bloom & Broder, 1950). In fact, failure to alter behavior across test trials (perseveration) is accepted where attention is drawn by the most salient stimulus features. Inhelder and Piaget (1958) argued that perseveration behavior is a manifestation of the child's logical immaturity. Osler and Shapiro (1964) implied that more salient cues and less reinforcement to incorrect responses could lead to a decrease in the incidence of perseveration. Further, as these data suggest, the ability to recognize more salient cues in order to differentiate incorrect from correct reinforcement varies according to particular levels of cognitive sophistication among the children being tested. At least initially, the control children apparently lacked the level of cognitive maturity necessary for consistent color-form responding.

Evidence of the individual child shifting within task behavior dimensions supported the notion that benefits to cognitive development accrued from the early environmental stimulation afforded the experimental group. Certainly an important factor in the experimental children's success at developing unidimensional preferences, as well as in the control children's lack of success, must be the differential in the quality of early experience for the two groups. In their review of perceptual learning development, Kidd and Rivoire (1966) suggested that very young children often show a preference for form in matching paradigms, then switch to color, and eventually switch back to form. We have reported these same shifts in the percentage of experimental color and form responders beginning at 54 and continuing at 78 months. It may be that this period of dimensional preference shifting is an indication that the children, as a group, are experimenting with alternative ways to respond. Therefore, their performances may reflect the benefits of both early and successive experiences with this task. For example, Gaines (1970) presented evidence: that color or form attention is a function of set, that selective attention can be changed by training a new response set, and that dimensional selections have an influence on other modes of perception, cognition, and learning. As Melkman and Deutsch (1977) suggested, it seems that shifts in stimulus preferences are developmental changes in the manner in which a child organizes the stimulus environment. In other words, an individual's sophistication with respect to both the orientation and maintenance aspects of the attentional process is related to cognitive maturation, that is attributable to some combination of both maturational and experiential factors.

To summarize the discussion up to this point, the color-form data suggest that the experimental and control children demonstrate similar rates of learning but at different levels and that the test of color-form matching becomes a less sensitive paradigm to developmental differences across this age period because the experimental and control groups do, in effect, come together. Therefore, the lack of rate differences is probably a reflection of restricted performance attributable to the nature of this matching paradigm. Level, then, is a better index of cognitive skill performance. Depending on the way learning is evaluated, this paradigm might not differentiate developmental performance adequately. However, although rate change is parallel, the level difference indicates there is an early critical component to successful cognitive performance.

Siegler (1976) argued that young children's perceptions are centered on certain characteristics of the stimulus configuration at the expense of other attending dimensions. In older children, perception and judgment become decentered and attention is paid to all characteristics in the configuration (Hale & Morgan, 1973). Mackworth and Bruner's (1966) work on eye fixation phenomena in children demonstrated that varying amounts of attention are needed as a function of the stimulus configuration and that attention to various dimensional aspects is modified both qualitatively and quantitatively with changes in developmental level.

Experience, then, should be viewed as an important parameter influencing learning performance. In part, the lack of early quality experience for the control children interfered with the maturation of appropriate learning habits and delayed changing over to more sophisticated performance styles. Thus, for these children, the early immature, learning styles were reinforced, prolonged, and even became antagonistic to cognitive growth. In the color-form task, the development of this antagonistic learning system was characterized by the delay in the cessation of perseverative response modes. Control youngsters demonstrated significantly advanced chronological ages before consistent unidimensional responding and consistent application of color-form equivalence rules were utilized. We have documented the extent of delay in the elimination of perseveration response modes for the control children. The question remains: At what cost to the child, in developmental terms, has this delay caused impairment in the control children's potential for future learning success?

RESPONSE STRATEGIES FOR PROBLEM SOLVING TASKS

The probability match task revealed additional evidence concerning the relationship of children's early experience to the development of their learning performance characteristics. Performance on this task is especially sensitive to the early development of strategy behavior, that is, the rules and/or plans in the decisionmaking process that individual children use to develop problem solutions. Choice of the solution is influenced by the need for the individual to strike a balance among three factors: the degrees of certainty that a solution can be reached, the solution speed or time required to solve the problem, and the degree of cognitive strain or exertion imposed by the plan employed (Bruner, Goodnow, & Austin, 1956). Longitudinally observed changes in strategy behavior can be usefully viewed as a reorganization of mental operations by the child that occurs only as he/she uses them (Kuhn, 1962), that is, experience begets reorganization. Thus, the growth of problem solving strategies is a complex, ontogenetic sequence that has developmental characteristics (Stevenson, 1970) and for which individual variation reveals differences in contrasting levels and maturity of intellectual development (Kagan & Kogan, 1970).

We used a two-choice probability task to examine the problem solving behavior of the experimental and control children at 1-year intervals over a 7-year period (CA range: 30 to 102 months). The stimuli were simple red and blue squares, simultaneously exposed to the children for 100 trials at each test session. The child was instructed simply to find the "correct" (i.e., reinforced) square. The correct square was reinforced with a chime. There was no negative reinforcement. The red square was reinforced in 33% of the trials, while the blue square was reinforced in 67% of the trials. Positions of the stimulus cards and reinforcements were randomized (Fellows, 1967) to mitigate against, for example, reinforcement of position perseveration or position alternation strategies.

Analysis of the data from the task used two performance measures: the number of correct responses and the number of response changes made to the stimulus dimensions of position and color. The number of correct responses represented the sum or reinforced responses, red or blue. A change score was computed for position and for color. A response change for position was indicated when a child altered his/her choice to a new position in response to information gained from previous outcomes. Position change scores were cumulatively added across successive trials. Similarly, the change score for the color dimension represents the number of times a child chose the blue stimulus after a previous selection of the red square and the number of times the red stimulus was selected following a choice of blue. A binomial probability was used to establish ($p < .05$) the cutoff for the number of response changes toward a particular color or position that exceeded chance levels, over 100 trials.

The multivariate profile analysis examined the question of whether there were any significant between and/or within group differences in the mean percentage of instances across trials for which the experimental and control children chose a reinforced stimulus. A profile analysis failed to reject ($p < .10$) that the experimental and control regression lines were parallel, that the correct responses of the children irrespective of group designation were equal across conditions (i.e., sequential task administrations), and that the mean percentage of correct probability match choices for both the experimental and control groups were similar between 66 and 90 months. In fact, for both the experimental and control groups the mean percentage of reinforced responses neither exceeded nor fell below chance levels (viz., 50%) by more than 4 percentage points for any chronological age period tested. In general, the probability match data revealed no significant differences in the amount of reinforcement gained with respect to developmental groupings specified by either high (experimental) versus low (control) cognitive experience or by young (66 months) versus older (90 months) chronological age designations.

Young children (CA: 3 or 4 years) usually attain, within the first 10 to 20 trials of the task, a level of performance that approaches the performance level for adults in the final phase of their task exposure. Thus, developmental hypotheses (e.g., Weir, 1967) argue that there should be no increase in the mean number of correct responses across trials for various age ranges studied. When we analyzed performance according to the initial and final selection rate of the correct response, the frequency counts for both groups at 30 and 42 months were consistent with chance level. This fact indicates that the children did not adopt a maximizing strategy, the only solution possible where reinforcement is randomly arranged. The absence of a maximizing strategy in both groups suggested that the children, irrespective of age and degree of cognitive experience, responded to position and were essentially insensitive to the differential reinforcement of the two stimulus dimensions on the task.

There were some differences between this study and Weir's (1967) that could account for the lack of maximizing. In Weir's study, responses to several levers were reinforced, with each lever having a different reinforcement value throughout the task. However, because the position of a lever did not vary, what Weir referred to as "maximization of reinforcement" was in fact a position reinforced response. This procedure confounded position with maximization as a strategy to be exhibited by young children.

Because our presentation of the two stimuli was randomized for the variable of position, in order for a child to maximize, he/she needed to systematically eliminate the irrelevant variable of position and respond in terms of the more salient task dimension of color. Once responding to the critical dimension had begun, discovery of the most frequently reinforced stimulus was possible. Identification of the more critical dimension in the present study demanded discernment between 67% reinforcement ratios and 33% chance levels. This task was perhaps too difficult for young children (CA $\leq$ 8 years) to actually solve.

We were able to study the development of the children's strategies over trials and in their search for correct task solution, that is, to observe the manner in which their response behavior changes as they develop a "mode of attack." Specifically, we assessed response change strategies exhibited by the children as a function of the differential reinforcement. This procedure, in effect, provides an opportunity to observe how children respond to outcome, which is positive and negative information fed back immediately to the subject upon each response choice and which can be used by the subject when selecting subsequent choices.

We compared the experimental and control groups' mean number of position response changes from the time the children were 30 months until they had completed the third grade of elementary school (102 months). Both groups increased their mean times of position response changes over time. The experimental mean rose from 14 to 68 between 30 and 102 months while the control mean changed from 9 to 65 over this same period. The fact that between the experimental and control groups only the mean number of position response changes occurring at 42 and 54 months are significantly different (p

< .05) suggested that the tendency among the experimental children to exhibit response changes occurred before school entry and that the lack of appropriate experience assumed for the control group interferes with the development of this process.

The finding that the number of position response changes increased over time led us to investigate further the nature of developmental changes in the strategy behaviors employed by the experimental and control youngsters. In particular, we examined the chronological speed with which the experimental and control children began to exhibit sophisticated adult modes of problem solving. This is actually a demonstration of the child's appreciation of the need to abandon a hypothesis when repeatedly disconfirmed, while at the same time returning to what are perceived to be more efficient maximizing strategies. Procedures to analyze this hypothesis testing behavior, termed win-stay:lose-shift, were reported by Moffitt and Coates (1969). A strategy was defined in terms of the child's patterning of successive responding over trials. "Winning" versus "losing" indicated that the child received or did not receive reinforcement as a result of an instrumental choice on a given trial, while "shifting" versus "staying" indicated the outcome of that choice (i.e., whether the child shifted or stayed with the same stimulus dimension on the succeeding trial.) The analysis paired a winning or losing choice with a staying or shifting outcome. Each response (n + 1) was scored as a stay or a shift based on the previous response (n). In other words, the child either "won" or "lost" on the (nth) response.

We used the Moffitt and Coates' procedure to compute four response strategy behaviors: (a) win-stay:lose-shift (WST:LSH), (b) win-stay:lose-stay (perseveration), (c) win-shift:lose-shift (alternation), and (d) win-shift:lose-stay (WSH:LST). Each strategy was computed separately for position and for color. Eight strategy scores were obtained for each child between the chronological ages of 30 and 102 months. Strategies were ranked with respect to the numerical value of responses and then averaged within group for each of the seven test administrations.

Win-stay versus win-shift and lose-stay versus lose-shift are contrasting aspects to the same response patterns. Together they become a sensitive index of the extent to which the child utilizes knowledge of the reinforcement outcomes of preceding trials in the hypothesis testing process while searching for solution to the task. These strategies are, in effect, specific demonstrations of the general ability to respond to reinforcement outcome. The win-stay:lose-shift hypothesis testing procedure demonstrates performance that responds to outcome and indicates a position or a color follower. A win-stay:lose-shift strategy leads much more quickly to the discernment of the reinforcement ratios built into the task trials.

It seemed to us that although there were no significant differences in reinforcement (or in the measure of performance success), there was considerable difference between groups in their use of strategies. While the control children's responses indicated that they were for the most part insensitive to the reinforcement contingencies, the experimental children's responses showed more dependence on the reinforcement outcome of the previous trial as information for subsequent responding. We compared the mean percentages of experimental and control children responding to reinforcement outcome across test intervals (Figure 5-2) and found that mean differences significantly favor ($p < .05$) the experimental children between the ages of 66 and 102 months. This fact suggests that experimental children grew to recognize the reinforcement contingencies of this task over time. They learned to adopt more sophisticated hypothesis testing behaviors than their control peers, that is, behaviors more likely to receive reinforcement. Note that more sophisticated hypothesis testing behaviors do not necessarily result in more reinforcement received; that is to say, there is a difference between an observed problem solving strategy and problem solving outcome. We were more interested in strategies and have determined that for this task the experimental group's strategy behavior was more sophisticated than the control group's strategy behavior.

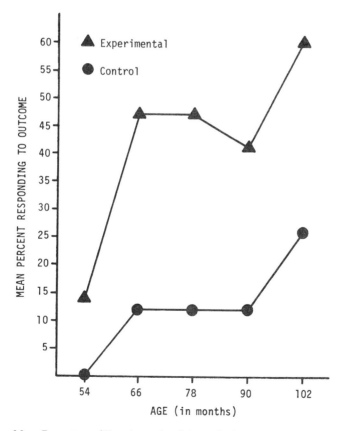

Figure 5-2. Mean Percentage of Experimental and Control Children Responding to Outcome on the Probability Match Task by Age

In general, data on the response patterns to positive reinforcement show that children from both the experimental and control groups exhibit, as preschoolers (54 months), dominant position perseveration response modes. Only four youngsters (one experimental color follower and two experimental and one control alternators) deviated from this group baseline trend of failure to change response strategy as a function of reinforcement outcome. However, between 47% and 60% of the experimental children tested between the end of kindergarten (66 months) and third grade (102 months) demonstrated significant color following or position following response modes. The control children showed far less inclination to develop sophisticated, outcome related response change strategies. In contrast, between the end of kindergarten and the third grade there were only two instances at each test interval, a control color follower and a control position follower (different control children were color and position followers at each test interval), where a significant instrumental choice response was made as a function of the reinforcement outcome on previous trials. Furthermore, 15 of the 17 experimental children exhibited first- or second-order change strategies (i.e., became color or position followers) at least once during the early elementary years (66 to 102 months), whereas only six of 18 children in the control group demonstrated this same level of appreciation for the information inherent in the reinforcement paradigm.

A nonparametric analysis of between group differences (Mann & Whitney, 1947) failed to reject the null hypothesis of no significant difference ($p > .10$) for the strategy rankings on both color and position dimensions at each yearly test interval between 30 and 102 months.

There are several possible explanations for the finding of no rank differences for strategy response modes between the experimental and control children on this task. First, there may be some difficulty in the Moffitt and Coates (1969) procedure for analyzing data from this task. Because, for example, win-stay:lose-shift scores and perseveration scores both use win-stay responses, a single response is, in fact, counted twice. Procedures that allow a single response to contribute to two strategy scores may mask some degree of individual differences in performance. For example, at 54 months, two experimental children exhibited the following position scores: 48 WST:LSH and 96 perseveration versus 56 WST:LSH and 17 perseveration. The large difference (96 vs. 17) between the two children in perseveration, the lower order strategy, is masked by some similarity (48 vs. 56) in win-stay:lose-shift strategy. Second, our finding of no group difference in rank order to strategies at least partially confirmed Moffitt and Coates' (1969) original findings. These authors reported no significant differences between low and high IQ groups for either the position or stimulus (read here for our task: color) win-stay:lose-shift strategy scores when reinforcement was at 66% (as it was in our task). There were IQ differences for WST:LSH position when reinforcement was 33% and for WST:LSH color at 100% reinforcement. But, as previously discussed, it may be that the difficulty the children experienced in discriminating between 50% (chance) and 67% (task specified) reinforcement ratios did, in fact, obscure performance differences in the sophistication with which the experimental and control children approached the probability match task.

The suggestion, therefore, in our analysis of between group rank differences to response strategy sophistication is that individual differences over time may act to confound demonstration of group performance sophistication. In other words, as we have done for the color-form task, we have concluded that it is necessary to view group differences within a developmental context. The need for such a research perspective was argued by McCall (1981) when he discussed issues of constancy versus change in child performance.

We have analyzed experimental and control probability match scores in an effort to discern any possible developmental patterns over time for the children's performance. A pattern might suggest that cognitive ability to respond at one level of sophistication needs to become sufficiently stable to permit successful maturation to the next higher order strategy. Some work by Bruner and colleagues (e.g., Bruner, Olver, & Greenfield, 1967) suggests that 2 years may represent an approximate interval for cognitive changes in problem solving ability.

Accordingly, we analyzed the experimental and control scores at 42, 66, and 90 months. As previously reported, at 42 months the experimental children made significantly more position response changes than the control youngsters and comparison at 66 months of the children's ability to respond to reinforcement outcome again revealed significant experimental superiority. Because there were no significant between group differences for a ranking of the eight strategy scores at 90 months, we separated the eight scores into their individual components, win-stay, win-shift, lose-stay, and lose-shift, for both color and position. This procedure provided useful information with which to profile the children's probability match performance. Specifically, the Mann and Whitney (1947) rank order test of each child's (both experimental and control) score for each of the four strategies within both stimulus dimensions showed significant differences in two areas: The experimental children exhibited significantly more ($p < .01$) position win-stay responses than the control youngsters, while control children significantly more often ($p < .01$) demonstrated position win-shift tendencies. There were no significant between group differences in the target children's exhibition of position lose-stay or lose-shift or of color win-stay, win-shift, lose-stay, or lose-shift strategies. There is therefore some support for our earlier speculation about the 2-year growth requirement of strategy modes by the end of second grade (90 months) performance. The absence of a demonstrated ability to shift or change nonreinforced stimulus choices should not imply that there can be no further developmental growth by either the experimental or control children toward the more sophisticated adult probability match response modes. However, whereas the experimental children maintained reinforced responses toward position but not toward the color stimulus dimensions, the control children seemed insensitive to the differential reinforcement of the two stimulus dimensions on the task even at 102 months.

In summary, the early probability match performance by the experimental children at about 3 years of age was characterized by response perseveration, but they soon learned to change their responses across trials (42 months), to differentially respond to reinforcement outcome (66 months), and to maintain the same response to the stimulus dimension of position when their preceding selection hypothesis was confirmed (90 months). Because the reinforcement ratios do not vary across chronological age, we interpreted these gains as a demonstration of the experimental children's maturing ability to order their problem solving environment.

On the other hand, by the end of third grade the control children demonstrated a gradual maturation of learning characteristics, but one that should prove antagonistic to their future cognitive growth. There were three learning characteristics revealed by the control group's performance on the probability match test: (a) the control children exhibited prolonged perseveration response modes that continued until the children entered public school (66 months), (b) they did not show interest in the provision or the nonprovision of reinforcement during problem solving, and (c) the control children, even as they were preparing to enter the fourth grade, failed to demonstrate any substantial enthusiasm for seeking out and finding solutions to the probability match task's reinforcement hierarchy. Whereas the experimental children exhibited increased ability to problem solve as they moved through elementary school, at 102 months the control group still failed to demonstrate even minimal evidence of the win-stay:lose-shift mode characteristic of adult problem solving behavior.

The lack of enthusiasm and apparent disinterest in approaching the problem solving task together with a general tendency to respond with the least sophisticated behavior patterns do not augur well for future cognitive growth of the control group children (Bloom & Broder, 1950). These learning characteristics are antagonistic to growth and are inherent in the learning styles the control children utilized as they attempted to organize the probability matching problem solving task.

THE ROLE OF PERCEPTUAL RECOGNITION IN IDENTITY DIFFERENCE PROBLEMS

We expanded our assessment of the role selection attention plays in the development of children's learning sets by considering the influence of perceptual learning abilities in an oddity discrimination paradigm. The act of perceptual learning initiates a differentiation process that requires both organizational and categorization skills. Not only are incoming stimuli organized into distinguishing sensory characteristics (e.g., figure ground, texture, tridimensionality), but also the shared characteristics themselves are abstracted into short and/or long term memory stores (Bruner & Potter, 1964). An increasing facility to interrelate stimulus cues is an indication of growth in the cognitive processes needed to organize the environment hierarchically. This developmental ability varies as a function of the child's degree of experience (Olver & Hornsby, 1967).

Relational learning includes finding solutions to discrimination problems that require differential appreciation of identity and difference cues. The instrumental choice is dependent upon the relation between the items in the stimulus display and the child must learn to respond correctly when specific elements of the display are replaced or their reward values reversed (House, Brown, & Scott, 1974). Therefore, a relevant developmental question for us concerned the role of perceptual learning in identity difference problems. We asked how the child's growing appreciation of stimulus relations, as indicated by an increasing facility to organize and categorize stimulus cues, would be applied in more sophisticated or extensive problem solving experiences.

We studied the children's learning performance on a three position oddity discrimination task. The oddity paradigm is a nonuniform stimulus display of an identity difference problem. The task presented the child was to choose the odd or discrepant stimulus from a horizontal array of three stimuli. Solution required the ability to determine similarities and differences among competing stimulus dimensions. Specifically, the child had to learn to respond to a difference relationship between the odd object and others of a set. By observing the child's responses across oddity trials, we hoped to reveal a particular stimulus selection process developmentally unique for each child at given developmental stages.

The oddity task consisted of 78 trials and was administered at 1-year intervals from the time the children were 30 months old until they had finished the third grade (102 months). Each oddity display contained three pictures of common objects such as trucks or chairs or bicycles. The child was instructed to find which of the three pictures was different. A candy reinforcer was provided, but only for correct choices. The position of the odd stimulus was randomized for all three positions.

There were basically four conceptual dimensions to the oddity instrument: color, form, number, and size. On each trial, one of these dimensions was relevant to task solution, one was irrelevant, and two were quiet (i.e., identical across pictures). For example, the following three items would constitute a typical oddity display: one large blue triangle, one medium blue triangle, and one small red triangle. Within this display, color is the relevant dimension, while size is an irrelevant cue, and number and form are quiet stimuli. A selection of the red triangle, therefore, would be rewarded.

All four stimulus dimensions appeared in every oddity trial, but each dimension was randomized to occur in the sequences as relevant, irrelevant, or quiet stimuli for problem solution. Each stimulus dimension was systematically varied across the 78 trials so that color, form, number, and size cues appeared as quiet, irrelevant, and relevant stimuli in a proportional number of trials. There were 13 subsets, or unique combinations of relevant with irrelevant cues, with each subset being presented six times. Thus, for the 18 trials in which color was the relevant dimension, there were six instances in which form was the irrelevant dimension, six trials for which number cues were irrelevant, and another six during which irrelevant size stimuli appeared. Beginning with the 42 month test session, the remaining six of the 78 oddity trials involved presentation of cues that required a function analysis for solution. For example, a baseball bat and a truck would be presented together with a ball. Because the ball and bat function together, the truck would be odd. We refer to trials requiring functional solution analysis as the *analytical conceptual dimension* in our oddity task.

The average number of reinforced responses (wins) across subcategories — the color, form, number, size, and analytical conceptual dimensions — constituted our primary index of the children's performance on the oddity task. The percentage of correct responses made to each of the five relational cues was computed and averaged for each child at each test interval. Thus, *average wins* differed from *total wins* because average wins weighted performance evenly across the five dimensional categories. Comparison of experimental group versus control group oddity task performance was based on an analysis of the children's group mean percentage of average win scores across the seven chronological age periods tested. The group mean performance data are presented in Table 5-2 and displayed in Figure 5-3.

Table 5-2   Means for Experimental and Control Groups for Children's Average Win Scores on the Oddity Task by Age

Age	*Experimental*			*Control*		
Months	*n*	*Mean*	*SD*	*n*	*Mean*	*SD*
30	6	47.09	2.75	10	35.39	6.37
42	16	49.84	13.20	14	36.09	6.68
54	17	51.42	10.55	17	34.28	5.86
66	17	44.15	13.92	16	35.68	9.56
78	15	58.47	12.32	17	45.32	10.49
90	17	61.01	13.19	17	52.78	11.64
102	10	64.79	9.07	8	62.12	3.62

As can be seen from Figure 5-3, the experimental children's oddity task performance was, in general, superior to that of the control youngsters. The experimental children began by exhibiting (at 30 months) a mean average win score of 47 points. Over time, the experimental average win score remained relatively constant through 54 months, fell slightly at 66 months, and then rose steadily until at 102 months the experimental children exhibited a mean average win score of 65 points. There was an 18-point rise in the experimental average win scores over time, with the sharpest increases occurring at the end of the children's first, second, and third years of elementary schooling (78 to 102 months). The control children began by exhibiting (at 30 months) a mean average win score ($X_C = 35$), which was 12 points below that exhibited by

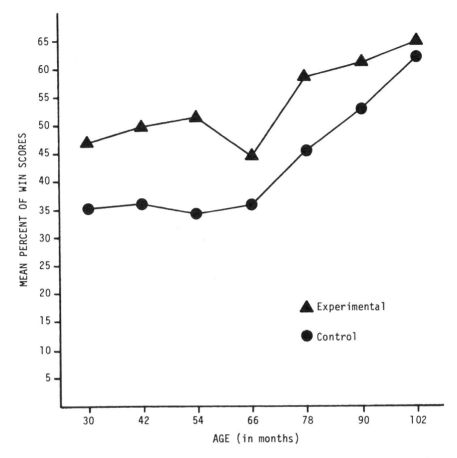

Figure 5-3. Comparison of the Experimental and Control Children's Mean Percentage of Win Scores on the Oddity Task by Age

their experimental counterparts. The control average win score remained relatively constant through 66 months, by which time these children had nearly completed kindergarten in the public schools. In fact, the control mean scores ranged from 34 to only 36 points between 30 and 66 months. As for the experimental children across first, second, and third grades (78 to 102 months), the control oddity performance also showed a steady rise in win scores. By 102 months, the control average win scores had risen 27 points over their performance of 6 years earlier.

The children's oddity performance was further evaluated by a multivariate profile analysis of the experimental versus control average win scores. The analysis failed to reject the null hypothesis of parallelism, $F(4, 30) = 1.01$, $p > .10$, thus suggesting that the interaction for group and age designation does not significantly contribute to group performance variation over time. The experimental and control regression curves are, in effect, parallel. The multivariate time hypothesis was rejected, $F(8, 60) = 8.67$, $p < .01$. We concluded that, over time, change in average win scores when experimental and control scores are considered together was significantly different. Finally, the null hypothesis that over all five test intervals there were no experimental versus control differences was rejected, $F(5, 29) = 10.45$, $p < .01$. We can conclude, therefore, that the overall experimental average win performance was superior to that of the control youngsters.

Each trial on the oddity task was complicated by the inclusion of one irrelevant and two quiet dimensions. Before making the differentiation between absolute and relative cue branches, the procedure required that the child determine which of five (not two) dimensions was critical for task solution. Successful performance demanded, in addition, the ability to analyze stimulus cues that changed from trial to trial and to make instrumental responses irrespective of outcome on the previous trial, while maintaining sustained attention for an extended test session. Although this made the children's task more difficult, the procedure provided us with the opportunity to investigate how response biases influence oddity performance, especially biases associated with either positional or dimensional preferences.

Comparison of the positional response biases exhibited by the experimental and control youngsters revealed few significant between or within group trends. There were roughly even distributions of choices to the left, center, and right display positions, which was expected under the condition of no group (between) or age (within) influences. The correct cue appeared equally in the left, center, and right positions. We examined the percentage of change responses (position shifts) to obtain an additional index of the children's appreciation that the correct response was not a function of position. The mean percentage of experimental shift responses never fell below the 60% level between 42 and 102 months. The mean percentage of control shift responses was below 60% at 42 months, but after the control children entered the public schools (completing kindergarten at 66 months), the mean percentage of control shift responses also never fell below the 60% level. There was about a 2-year difference in the experimental versus control children's understanding that the position of the correct stimulus cues changed across trials.

Among some control children during the preschool 30 to 54 month period, there was a tendency to perseverate by selecting the middle stimulus as odd, but as a group they did not make an inordinate percentage of responses to the center position. Also, the outcome on previous trials did not seem to influence subsequent choices for either group; position scores were roughly evenly divided between WST:LSH and WSH:LST strategies. Aside from the control performance at 42 months, group mean percentages of WST:LSH strategy scores were consistently at 50% levels ($\pm$ 4%). We concluded that a positional response bias did significantly confound the finding of experimental superiority on the oddity task. There remained significant between group differences in the youngsters' oddity performance after the control children entered kindergarten at 66 months.

Although our oddity task was complex and difficult for young children, we observed a developmental difference in ease of learning between the dimensional subcategories. We therefore analyzed the differential performance among the five stimulus subcategories across time. We used as a criterion for performance the age at which experimental and control children on the average correctly solved 50% or more of the color, form, number, size, or analytic oddity problems. We accepted 50% as an arbitrary level indicating "age of understanding" of the relational cues to a specific dimension. With the exception of 66 months when only 41% of the color-relevant items were solved correctly by the experimental children, once a group's mean percentage of correct responses within each of the five categories reached or exceeded 50%, the average percentage of solutions for neither the experimental nor the control youngsters fell below that chance level.

At 30 months, the experimental children demonstrated an understanding of color and form relational cues, while the number, size, and analytical categories did not begin to be appreciated until 78 months. The control children, on the other hand, first made 50% or more correct solutions of form cues at 78 months and of color and number stimuli at 90 months. The eight control children, tested at 102 months (the end of third grade), solved on the average 50% of the size and analytically relevant oddity displays.

It seems from these between group comparisons that differences in the ages of onset for adequate (50% solution rates) performance on the five oddity subtests favor the experimental children by at least 1 (for number relevant cues) and as many as 5 (for color relevant stimuli) years. The ability of the experimental children to appreciate, for example, form relevant oddity dimensions 4 years before their control counterparts certainly reflects a greater maturity in perceptual learning. There is therefore a developmentally related *ease of attending* first to color and form and then to number, size, and analytical relational cues. This finding is consistent with earlier reports (e.g., Huang, 1945).

The experimental and control children's differential appreciation of relevant stimulus cues, especially with respect to form dimensional preferences, seems to have influenced success on oddity performance. Although individual children changed dimensional preferences across successive test periods, the number of form preferrers within each group at each age interval remained relatively constant (eight to ten for the experimental group and three to six for the control group). Form preferrers, whether experimental or control children, exhibited higher average win scores than nonform preferrers within their own groups. This trend existed at all age intervals between 42 and 102 months for both groups, with the single exception of the control performance at 42 months. Moreover, this trend was especially clear during the preschool period (42 to 66 months) among the experimental children. For example, at 42 months there was a 13-point mean difference (56% vs. 43%) in the average win scores of experimental form and nonform preferrers.

Nonparametric analysis of between group rank differences (Mann & Whitney, 1947) revealed significant differences ($p < .05$) in the ordering of form and nonform scores. The higher average win scores for both experimental and control form preferrers underscore our earlier discussion regarding the development of attentional processes. Dimensional preferences can, in some situations, be response biases, but the observation of the maturation of these preferences can also index the development of the perceptual organizing process. It seems that the earlier such behavior occurs, the greater the facilitation of learning and performance on problem solving or discrimination tasks. It may be that their tendency to prefer form stimuli on the color-form task contributed to the superior performance of the experimental children on the oddity task.

Lipsitt and Serunian (1963) suggested that a correct response on six successive trials be used as a criterion to classify a child as a learner on the oddity task. Cross-sectional studies have found that a majority of young, nonretarded children do not exhibit six successive correct responses to oddity displays until they reach 5 or 6 years of age. For example, Hill (1965) reported that 10% of the 4-year-old children she tested reach criteria, while Croll (1970) found that only 13% of 4-year-olds were oddity learners. On the other hand, Neimark and Horn (1969) reported that a 2-year-old girl was able to solve oddity displays, but only after individualized inhome training. Gollin and Schadler (1972) suggested that by reducing the probability of reinforcement for positional response bias and by adding stimuli to the training arrays the salience of odd cues for preschoolers under the age of 5 can be increased. It might seem, then, that there is evidence of a critical age for oddity learning that is subject to the effects of training and experience, which can either facilitate or interfere with performance proficiency on an oddity test.

We found that once a child, experimental or control, was identified as an oddity learner, his or her performance did not fall below that level for learner designation, although there remained some variance in the children's responses across test sessions. Moreover, there were changes in the number of experimental versus control oddity learners over time. There were few control learners ($n = 3$) prior to 66 months. By the time they had completed third grade (102 months), seven of the eight older control children tested exhibited six successive correct instrumental choices to the oddity display. On the other hand, there is a different pattern of change for the experimental learners that suggests three stages for the experimental acquisition of the learner construct. At 42 months, there was only one experimental learner. Experimental performance between 54 and 78 months represented a second stage during which close to 50% of the experimental children met the learner criterion. The average age of onset for becoming an oddity learner was 5.4 years for the experimental group children, a finding consistent with the literature that reports that the majority of kindergarten and first grade children were able to learn oddity displays. As the children proceeded through school (78 to 102 months), there were steady increases in the number of experimental learners until, by the end of third grade, all of the experimental children tested ($n = 10$) made six successive correct oddity choices.

Although the group mean average win score declined at 66 months (end of kindergarten), the number of experimental learners increased. In part the decline is attributable to lower performance by several outlying experimental children with low scores. But the decline in average win scores may in part also reflect a cognitive transition period. That is, it may be a time during which the children are trying different strategies. This possibility is suggested by the fact that some individual scores are lower than at an earlier age. The percentage of experimental learners at 78 months compared with the percentages suggested by a composite regression line reported by House, Brown, and Scott (1974, p. 9) is below the percentage of learners found at this age in six cross-sectional studies (Brown, 1970; Brown & Lloyd, 1971; Gollin & Shirk, 1966; Lipsitt & Serunian, 1963; Penn, Sindberg, & Wolhueter, 1969; Porter, 1965). When we analyzed our data using the test items for which only color or form was relevant for solution, the percentage of experimental learners rose to 69% and the discrepancy between our results and the House, Brown, and Scott best fitting line was eliminated. The increase in the number of learners on color and form relevant displays supported the finding that performance is best and preferred on color and form stimuli.

In summary, we concluded: that the experimental oddity performance was significantly superior to that of the control children; that elementary school, especially the first, second, and third grades, promoted increases in the oddity performance of both groups of children; and that oddity performance gains were more pronounced for the control than for the experimental children because the preschool performance of the control youngsters was lower than their experimental counterparts'. With respect to this last point, on the oddity task as well as on the color-form and probability match tasks, there was an experimental versus control performance lag over time: The control children came to exhibit the same degree of discrimination learning performance sophistication that the experimental youngsters had exhibited at a much earlier developmental stage. On the oddity task, the control performance lag lasted at least 6 years (from 30 to 102 months). Moreover, and very unfortunately for the control children, the fact that experimental versus control mean average win score difference was reduced to 3 points at 102 months did not necessarily imply that experimental versus control oddity differences had disappeared, but only that differences were reduced for the oddity performance construct of average win scores.

As was the case for color-form performance, any performance construct for the oddity paradigm must take on developmental characteristics such that over time most if not all children will master the construct. But mastery of one developmental construct does not infer an end to unsophisticated discrimination learning performance, especially when additional, more developmentally advanced constructs are used. And it is because the detrimental influences of antagonistic learning styles accumulate across development that perseverative and unenthusiastic learning styles such as displayed by the control children bode poorly for these youngsters' potential for future intellectual growth.

CONCLUSION

We have reported in this chapter consistent findings across three discrimination learning tasks that the experimental children demonstrated more sophisticated early problem solving behaviors than did their control counterparts. The experimental group of children generally outperformed the control children in absolute performance levels, but more importantly revealed an earlier tendency to hypothesis test, to engage enthusiastically in the task, and to be sensitive to the reinforcement contingencies of the problem situation. The control group of children performed quite differently. Not only were their performance levels lower, but they tended to perseverative behavior, responding stereotypically, indicating by their responses that they were insensitive to the reinforcement feedback information and by their general behavior, which was unenthusiastic and even passive, that they were disinterested in engaging in the tasks.

We have suggested that such behavior on the part of control children is prototypic of the more rigid, unsophisticated trial-error behavior of older poorly-performing school age children (e.g., Bloom & Broder, 1950; Bresnahan & Shapiro, 1972; Osler & Fivel, 1961; Osler & Kofsky, 1966; Osler & Shapiro, 1964). Further, we have suggested that the problem solving performance of the control children revealed a learned system of behavior that is presently and ultimately antagonistic to the increasingly complex demands that will be presented to these children and will, therefore, induce performance failure (which will interfere with additional knowledge gathering and beget additional failure). However, in that we also suggest that it is a system of behavior learned from experience, it has the potential to be remediated and so to help the child to effect more successful performance.

From our observations, it seems that a major contributor to the failure of the untreated children was that they did not learn the value of how to get involved. The treated children's enthusiasm and success were clear indications of their having learned early how to learn. These data, especially when considered together with the language development assessments, suggest that lower performance of the control group children resulted in part from a lack of sustained knowledge growth with increasing age caused by an antagonistic learning system that interferes with the process of accumulating the kind of information specifically addressed in tests of intelligence. It is, on the other hand, a behavioral activity that the experimental children seem to have more eagerly and successfully pursued.

In the next chapter on language development, we report an increasing differential between the experimental and control group children in language test performance. By 6 years of age (school entry), the experimental group's language skills were in some cases 2 years ahead of the control group's. The importance of these two significant components of intellectual growth, cognitive and language skills, is revealed in a chapter on mother-child interaction. Our observations of the mother and child showed that the experimental mothers cooperated with their children, who acted as the educational engineers on problem solving tasks. It was the children's use of verbal prods and enthusiasm in ordering problem elements for solution that led to the significant differences in success between the experimental and control dyads.

The skills necessary for cognitive growth are acquired through learning, which also requires the acquisition of appropriate decision making rules (Hunt, 1961). These rules are integral to the process of learning how to learn (Estes, 1970; Stevenson, 1972) and enable an individual to better utilize his or her cognitive abilities. Decisionmaking rules are learned cognitive behaviors. They will help an individual systematically construct concepts from information gained about the properties of environmental phenomena (e.g., Klausmeier, Ghatala, & Frayer, 1974). Gagne (1970) described this phenomenon as a complex set of intellectual processes constructed in hierarchically ordered sequences. Gagne identified eight successive stages in this process, the ultimate completion of which is a requisite for the achievement of adult thought levels.

Scandura (1972) observed that each of Gagne's eight types of learning could be represented by a set or ordered pairs in which each stimulus is associated with a unique response. In turn, each proper stimulus-response (S-R) pairing can then be ordered within hierarchical families (Maltzman, 1967) that define all possible task solutions at an individual's command at the moment of decision. In this sense, using Guilford's (1967) terminology, thinking becomes a convergent narrowing of stimulus options followed by a divergent ordering of response possibilities. All the possible convergent-divergent formulations are themselves subordinated to structures (Maltzman terms them "compound habit family hierarchies") for response approaches or biases. Success in this dual ordering (i.e., successful thinking) is measured in terms of performance: Did the actual manipulation of S-R arrangements result in the elicitation of the correct response for problem solution? According to this conceptualization of higher order mental processing, we attempt to be consistent in our descriptive summary of the abilities that contribute to effective problem solving.

Implicit in this conceptualization is Bruner's (1967) notion that cognitive growth is a continuous process fundamental to the child's ability to intellectually represent what has been learned as he or she matures. The pivot (Vygotsky, 1962) for this representation is the child's progressive accumulation of these proficiencies, which go beyond the immediate situation and provide the capacity to test hypotheses that are remote in their time and space dimensions. We can monitor this maturation process by concentrating on skilled behaviors in the form of children's response patterns. In our learning research program, we have analyzed the experimental and control children's response patterns in terms of their attentional sensitivity to changes in discrimination stimuli.

Many variables have been demonstrated to influence stimulus selection, including: (a) culture (Doob, 1960; Serpell, 1966; Suchman, 1966), (b) physiological status (Doehring, 1960; Peeke & Stone, 1973a, 1973b; Stone, 1960; Suchman, 1966), (c) race and social class (Marcus, West, & Gaines, 1968; Trabasso, Stave, & Eichberg, 1969), (d) cognitive style and learning skills (Gaines, 1969), (e) the structural characteristics of the stimuli (Huang, 1945; Melkman & Deutsch, 1977; Tampieri, 1968), (f) the degree of abstractness in task demands (Gindes & Barten, 1977), etc. But, as Horowitz (1969) has argued, the nature of the interaction among these influences depends on both the nature and the level of development of the individual in his or her relationship to this environment.

Bradbury and Nelson (1974) argued that a child's preference is suspended between two sets of criteria: strategies needed to solve the problem (i.e., the cognitive analysis of the task) and preferences for responding (e.g., inclinations toward "novelty" or "position" response patterns). Brown and Campione (1981) suggested that dimensional selection on a preference test is determined both by a developmentally related dimensional preference hierarchy and by the nature of the cues on the competing dimensions. Dimensional dominance is therefore a function of the interaction between discriminability of the stimulus and the response bias of the subject, which in turn is a function of the developmental level of the child. Response tendencies are expected to be controlled as a child matures and behavior in problem solving tasks becomes directed toward solution.

The environmental forces that influence the cognitive skill development necessary for problem solving originate in an impoverished but unique sociopsychological milieu. Zimiles (1972) suggested that cognitive development be viewed as habits of behavior (e.g., patterns of curiosity, the tendency to ask questions, the inclination to seek and expect to find solutions to problems, and to persevere in working at a task). He argued that these habits set the parameters for the alternatives a given individual has to relate to both objects and people. These alternatives bear on the development of the intellectual life of that person, but do not themselves constitute the child's cognitive content. These habits of behavior are environmentally determined, that is, they originate in a unique sociopsychological milieu that pressures learning performance.

In our early discussion of the learning performance we examined how the acquisition of concepts proceeds through a learning and decisionmaking process in which children learn how to learn over time. Stevenson's (1970) argument was that experience with learning situations facilitates efficient learning of new problems. He listed the following factors as contributing to improved performance: the elimination of biases and other incorrect response tendencies, the development of appropriate observing responses and increased attention to relevant cues, modification of expectancies concerning the difficulty of the problem, and the acquisition of strategies for maximizing the information from each response. In this regard, Bruner's (Bruner, Olver, & Greenfield,

1967) concept of the development of the higher mental processes is that they develop in situations that offer the opportunity for the individual to work in the dimension of time. The problem is present, but the solution demands that the child look back to past experiences and relate them to future goals. Children in impoverished and restricted environments are beset by immediate demands that allow little opportunity for looking ahead while planning decisions. Such developmental experiences may be more conducive to learning behaviors that secure immediate solution. Such learning styles, over time, may become antagonistic to the solution that requires hypothesis testing and strategies because the solution is displaced in time.

It is our argument, therefore, that the control children's learning styles grew and developed in ways that were antagonistic to their future learning. We can identify at least three characteristics of the socialization process, typical of the inner city, that act as negative influences on the cognitive growth of the seriously disadvantaged child. These are: a low IQ and low verbal principal caretaker who does not (cannot) provide appropriate stimulation for cognitive growth and thus creates a sociopsychological milieu that encourages the development of systems of learning antagonistic to proper problem solving abilities; highly structured preschools and kindergartens that emphasize the convergent thinking abilities necessary (e.g., for rote learning, at the expense of the divergent sensitivity necessary for more sophisticated and mature problem solving response modes); and the lack of planning for between grade transition that limits the academic success of disadvantaged youngsters when the nature of school demands change (e.g., when divergent thinking skills become mandatory in the middle elementary grades).

It is because early learning performance is not etched in stone, but rather governed by basic principles of learning—reinforcement and extinction—that there is at once danger and hope. There is a danger that, if not reinforced, the early skills in problem solving such as those demonstrated by the experimental children can be lost if not appropriately required by the decisionmaking situations to which youngsters are exposed. On the other hand, if the notion of a learned antagonistic system of behavior inappropriate for problem solving is a viable assumption, then there is the hope that children such as those in the control group can unlearn the inappropriate skills and develop appropriate problem solving skills. In other words, if the strategies needed for future school success are not reinforced early, then other styles are learned in their place. But the early learning styles that facilitate academic proficiency can become extinguished if not properly nurtured.

The sociopsychological milieu is not passive. It acts to either help or hinder children's learning. It is therefore important for parents, teachers, and other adults who work with young, especially preschool, children to provide adequate reinforcement for those problem solving skills required for an adequate development of each individual child's potential for cognitive growth.

6
Assessment of Language Development

The primary purpose of the language assessment program was to evaluate the influence of the preschool educational program and family intervention on the general language development of the experimental children and control children. In addition to general language development, we were concerned with defining and testing the various areas of linguistic capability, each of which might exhibit a different pattern of growth. Central to this problem was the question of how development of linguistic ability — a complex and elusive process that does not lend itself easily to quantitative measures — was to be measured over a period of years and with a degree of quantitative accuracy that would permit detection and objective comparison of developmental differences between groups of subjects. The development of a satisfactory technique for measuring language ability in its several aspects, considered critical for language growth, thus became an important corollary to our main purpose, to assess language development using the treated and untreated youngsters.

Samples of free language production were collected from each child as young as 9 months; however, it was only at the age range of 18 to 21 months that intelligible speech was recorded for enough members of each group to warrant analysis. A middle aged black woman who resided in the area was hired and trained to engage each child in play and conversation and to tape-record each entire session. She was also trained to administer the experimental and standardized language tests. She was particularly effective in establishing rapport with all the children. All testing and sampling sessions took place at the Infant Education Center in Milwaukee. Uher reel tape recorders (Model 4400) were used for recording and transcribing the sessions. All recordings were transcribed, proofread, and analyzed by trained graduate students at our laboratory in Madison.

Once a child has gained some control over syntax, quantitative measures of his or her spontaneous language production gradually lose their effectiveness as indices of development. Therefore, in order to continue to evaluate differential language development, we administered language tests whose measures make it possible to compare levels of control, developmentally, over specific aspects of grammar. The use of a wide variety of tests designed to measure the children's ability to imitate, comprehend, and produce grammatical structures provided a broad basis for evaluating differential language development between groups. In addition, we hoped to gain from the successive replications of these tests not only collateral confirmation of the differential in IQ test performance but also data that would show patterns of language development as the children grew older.

At the age of 36 months, each child was given the first of several tests that would measure his/her control over a wide range of grammatical structures. Three of these tests — a grammatical comprehension and two morphology tests — were modifications of previously published tests (Bellugi-Klima, 1968; Berko, 1958). These were used for measuring comprehension and elicited morphemic production, respectively. Two additional production tests (Picture Morphology, Tests 1 and 2) and two imitation tests (Sentence Repetition Tests I and II) were developed in our language laboratory.

In summary, we utilized a wide range of tests covering specific aspects of performance and administered them at regular intervals to provide the information necessary for making comparative assessments of development. We regularly sampled the children's spontaneous language production from the onset of intelligible speech to the time of entry into public school and in addition scheduled regular administration of tests of comprehension, imitation, and production. These tests were either developed by our researchers or adapted from tests developed elsewhere. A complete schedule of the tests given and the language samples obtained from the two groups of subjects over a 5-year period is presented in Table 6-1.

FREE SPEECH ANALYSIS: GROSS FEATURE TABULATION

The analysis of spontaneous speech measures was most useful for determining the level of the children's linguistic development during the first stages of language acquisition. As a child grows older, his/her linguistic repertoire expands beyond what may reliably be represented by segments of free conversation; in other words, the definitiveness of free speech analysis as a measure of linguistic development declines. However, even during the later stages of acquisition, the information derived through this procedure remained valuable, particularly in supporting and clarifying findings from more rigidly controlled language tests.

Sessions lasting approximately 45 minutes and involving play and conversation between the child and the language examiner were conducted and recorded every 3 months when the children were 18 to 35 months old. As each child reached the age of 36 months, language tests were included in the sessions and the periods of free conversation were reduced to approximately 20 minutes. The recorded samples from children 18 to 35 months old were completely transcribed and analyzed; thereafter, only 15-minute portions of the samples were used.

The analysis of language samples was based on the following measures: (a) mean number of utterances, (b) percentage of multiword utterances, (c) percentage of repetitive utterances, (d) mean vocabulary per sample, (e) mean cumulative vocabulary, and (f) mean length of utterance expressed as mean number of morphemes per utterance. All tabulations were mathematically reduced to counts for 10-minute samples in order to facilitate comparison across all age levels. Table 6-2 summarizes the data obtained on these measures.

An utterance is defined as any discernible word or set of words between initial and terminal junctures (full stops). Among young children who are learning their first language, the amount of intelligible speech per unit of time is expected to increase as language facility develops. Once learning has taken place, sheer output of speech becomes an indicator of situational circumstances and/or of the child's talkativeness rather than of language development. This point appears to have been reached by both groups at about 54 months of age (Figure 6-1).

Repetition of adults' and other children's utterances constitutes one of the first processes of language learning (Brown & Bellugi, 1964). Repetitive utterances can therefore be expected to make up a substantial portion of young children's early speech; the onset of repetition may, in fact, be an indication of the age at which language learning actually begins.

This process gradually gives way to greater use of spontaneous utterances. Among children who have learned the language, as well as among adult speakers, repetitive utterances constitute a negligible portion of free speech. Figure 6-2 shows that by age 21 months, when sampling began, the experimental group was already making its fullest use of repetition, whereas the control group did not do so until the next age level of 24 months. After age 39 months, the experimental children's use of repetitive utterances dropped to below 3% for the remainder of the sampling period, while the control children continued to use repetitive utterances for more than 3% of their utterances until they were 63 months old.

A child's earliest utterances typically consist of single words. Learning to put words together is the first step in the development of syntax. In the course of acquiring a first language, a child reaches a point after which utterances comprising two or more words are used at a fairly consistent rate. The age at which this point is reached, taken in conjunction with other indicators, may be an index of the pace at which language development is taking place. The experimental children reached this point at about 42 months of age, whereas the control children's rate of multiword utterances did not stabilize until the age of 51 months at the earliest (Figure 6-2).

Table 6-1 Language Testings and Free Speech Sample Collections: Schedule of Tests, Ages, and Sample Sizes

LANGUAGE TESTS	18-21	22-24	25-27	28-30	31-33	36	39	42	45	48	51	54	57	60	63	66	69	72	75	78	81
Sentence Repetition																					
Test I E	—	—	—	—	—	16	19	19	19	19	18	18	18	16	—	—	—	—	—	—	—
Test I C	—	—	—	—	—	11	15	17	18	18	18	17	17	17	—	—	—	—	—	—	—
Test II E	—	—	—	—	—	—	—	—	—	—	—	—	—	17	16	15	17	16	—	—	—
Test II C	—	—	—	—	—	—	—	—	—	—	—	—	—	16	18	17	15	15	—	—	—
Grammatical Comprehension																					
E	—	—	—	—	—	15	17	17	17	17	17	17	17	17	17	17	—	—	—	—	—
C	—	—	—	—	—	15	17	18	18	18	18	18	18	18	17	17	—	—	—	—	—
Picture Morphology																					
Original Test E	—	—	—	—	—	—	9	—	17	—	17	—	16	—	17	—	—	—	—	—	—
Original Test C	—	—	—	—	—	—	15	—	18	—	18	—	15	—	18	—	—	—	—	—	—
Revised Test E	—	—	—	—	—	—	—	—	—	—	—	—	—	—	—	—	17	—	17	—	—
Revised Test C	—	—	—	—	—	—	—	—	—	—	—	—	—	—	—	—	16	—	15	—	—
Berko Morphology																					
Original Test E	—	—	—	—	—	—	—	—	—	—	17	—	17	—	16	—	—	—	—	—	—
Original Test C	—	—	—	—	—	—	—	—	—	—	16	—	18	—	17	—	—	—	—	—	—
Revised Test E	—	—	—	—	—	—	—	—	—	—	—	—	—	—	—	—	14	—	15	—	14
Revised Test C	—	—	—	—	—	—	—	—	—	—	—	—	—	—	—	—	15	—	15	—	12
Illinois Test of Psycho-linguistic Abilities																					
E	—	—	—	—	—	—	—	—	—	—	—	17	—	—	—	—	—	—	—	17	—
C	—	—	—	—	—	—	—	—	—	—	—	17	—	—	—	—	—	—	—	17	—
Free Speech Samples																					
45-Minute E	16	17	16	16	16	—	—	—	—	—	—	—	—	—	—	—	—	—	—	—	—
45-Minute C	8	13	13	15	16	—	—	—	—	—	—	—	—	—	—	—	—	—	—	—	—
15-Minute E	—	—	—	—	—	17	17	17	17	17	17	17	17	17	17	16	17	11	—	—	—
15-Minute C	—	—	—	—	—	17	18	17	18	18	18	18	18	18	17	18	17	14	—	—	—

Note: The numbers listed represent sample sizes for experimental (E) and control (C) groups participating in each testing sample session.

Table 6-2 Free Speech Measures: Summary

Age (Mos)	X̄ Total Utterances		% Repetitive Utterances		% Multi-word Utterances		X̄ Morphemes Per Utterance (MLU)		X̄ Vocabulary Per Sample		X̄ Cumulative Vocabulary	
	E	C	E	C	E	C	E	C	E	C	E	C
21	16.33	6.30	30.69	8.50	26.81	19.78	1.59	0.92	10.28	3.99	7.12	3.28
24	33.26	15.87	24.41	29.69	40.82	53.17	1.84	1.76	15.68	7.52	17.65	9.06
27	45.52	25.32	23.69	27.47	57.75	34.47	2.48	1.63	33.52	11.58	32.12	15.72
30	46.29	35.21	13.94	6.40	61.25	54.20	2.68	2.38	26.44	18.63	44.53	27.44
33	56.65	59.36	7.57	4.07	70.38	68.19	3.41	2.90	30.69	27.39	59.47	43.39
36	63.77	58.37	3.06	4.94	72.24	70.77	3.40	3.13	39.01	31.36	73.29	55.94
39	79.96	61.01	3.19	9.00	79.00	62.72	3.79	3.02	70.52	50.80	90.82	71.78
42	71.57	75.28	2.18	3.71	81.18	68.94	4.28	3.38	70.09	59.14	108.35	89.00
45	82.45	72.59	1.59	5.17	77.29	71.17	4.29	3.66	83.91	65.43	129.00	106.67
48	84.47	81.88	1.18	4.11	77.59	70.94	4.24	3.39	87.06	70.06	149.41	125.61
51	75.87	84.67	1.59	4.11	76.00	76.39	4.18	4.04	79.69	73.56	167.29	144.39
54	86.30	88.58	1.77	3.61	81.77	73.89	4.84	3.97	94.81	83.64	188.29	164.78
57	76.11	82.71	2.12	3.44	76.53	73.78	4.57	4.04	85.18	87.33	206.47	184.89
60	77.28	72.98	1.65	1.94	78.59	79.44	5.07	4.50	86.89	77.21	221.47	198.72
63	79.95	77.12	0.65	4.06	78.00	68.59	5.29	4.65	90.59	95.57	239.06	216.94
66	71.36	70.41	0.88	1.11	77.62	75.44	5.70	5.17	91.58	91.16	258.88	237.06
69	63.60	65.42	2.41	1.12	76.41	74.53	5.10	5.49	84.99	87.84	275.41	254.78
72	67.11	55.47	0.47	0.92	79.81	73.63	5.57	5.03	83.62	76.91	292.06	269.89

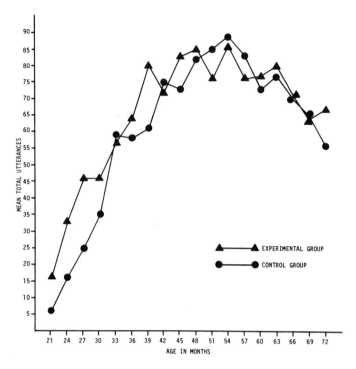

Figure 6-1. Mean Total Utterances from Free Speech Samples

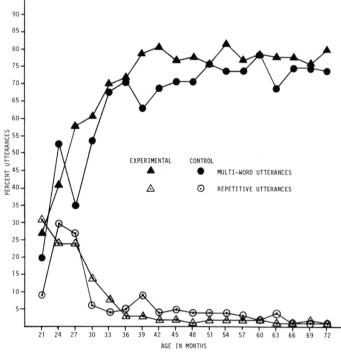

Figure 6-2. Percentage of Repetitive and Multiword Utterances from Free Speech Samples

The mean length of utterance is expressed in number of morphemes per utterance. The total number of morphemes in a sample is divided by the total
number of utterances in that sample to produce this measure. In our samples,
all lexical items and all inflectional endings were counted as morphemes. For
example, the word *cat* is a single morpheme, while *cats* is counted as two: *cat*
and the plural marker *s*. Irregular inflections were not counted and expressions such as *gonna* and *gotta* were given only one count each. The mean
length of a child's utterances (MLU) is a reflection of complexity and has been
widely used to indicate a child's stage of linguistic development (e.g., Bloom,
1970; Brown, 1973).

Differences in mean length of utterance are of necessity minute and do not
lend themselves well to conventional methods of analysis. A more informative method of presenting this important performance measure is to illustrate the progress of the two groups through the developmental stages as
signaled by the increase in MLU (Figure 6-3). Assignment of developmental
stages on the basis of MLU is an adaptation from Brown (1970), who suggested
that MLU stages might be a more revealing indication of the child's linguistic
capacity than chronological age. Scores from every two successive age levels
have been combined to show progress at 6-month intervals. It can readily be
seen that at virtually every stage the experimental children were younger than
the control children or were in the upper MLU range for that stage, or both. In

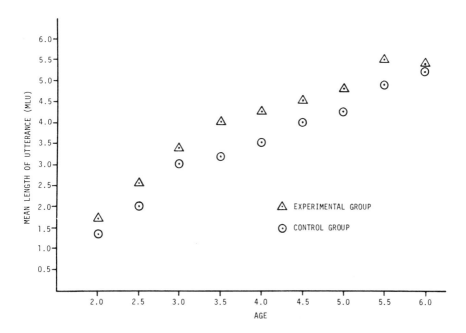

Figure 6-3. Mean Length of Utterance (MLU) at 6-Month Intervals, Distributed into Stages
(adapted from Brown, 1970)

other words, the experimental children not only reached the successive MLU stages earlier than the control children — sometimes by as much as a year as in the instance of Stage VI — but also progressed through these stages more rapidly.

Toward the end of the language sampling period, the MLUs of the two groups seemed to have reached comparable levels (Figure 6-3). Without additional data, it is not clear whether this pattern would have continued, but there is a strong likelihood that MLUs, like the other free speech measures, would reach a point after which it would no longer be indicative of language development. It is interesting to note, however, that when MLU counts are translated into developmental stages, the differences between experimental and control groups remain clear and consistent through virtually the entire length of the language sampling period.

The first occurrence of each word was counted as a vocabulary item. Inflection morphemes were disregarded; for example, *cat* and *cats* counted as one item. Proper names such as *Santa Claus* were counted as single items, as were compounds such as *shopping bag*. An exception was made for cases in which one of the parts of a compound was found to be productive. For example, if both *shopping bag* and *paper bag* occurred, *bag* counted as a vocabulary item, and so did both *shopping* and *paper*. This resulted in a count of three as opposed to the two that would result from counting only the compounds. This measure reflects the vocabulary range for a 10-minute sample.

This count differs from the mean vocabulary per sample in two major respects. First, only new items were added monthly to a master list for each child. Thus, words that tended to be used at every session (such as function words and the more common lexical items) were listed only once. Second, only those items that were produced spontaneously by a child were counted, thus eliminating any distortion that could be caused by the inclusion of such repetitive items as words from songs or nursery rhymes.

Perhaps more indicative of the child's actual vocabulary development is the rate of increase in the children's cumulative vocabulary. From age 30 months onward, the two groups had virtually identical rates of increase. In the period preceding 30 months, however, there was a sharp difference between the two groups, with the control group exhibiting very slow progress up to 27 months of age. What seems to have happened, then, is that although the control children recovered to achieve a comparable rate of increase after the 18 to 30 month period, their early lag behind the experimental group remained until after they were 60 months old. Their cumulative vocabulary count therefore remained approximately 3 months behind that of the experimental group.

The sampling of spontaneous speech during the earliest years of language acquisition necessitated the use of measures that seem to lose their sensitivity as the child's control over grammar increases. Such quantitative measures as total number of utterances, for example, when taken after a child has learned to construct sentences, have little significance beyond the fact of the child's talkativeness or reticence at the time of sampling. But during the first stages of

acquisition, when babbling is developing into language, the amount of intelligible speech is the prime indicator of the rate at which development is taking place. It is noteworthy that the greatest differences in total number of intelligible utterances and in mean vocabulary per sample between the two
groups appeared during this period (21 to 27 months), with the experimental
children producing significantly more utterances and using a significantly
larger lexicon per sample than did the control children. As Lenneberg (1967)
explains,

> Children between 18 and 36 months seem to have a tendency to run con-
> stantly through their repertoire of capacities. . . . The utterances of a child
> who is just beginning to speak (normally not much later than 30 months)
> may thus reflect the stages that his development of language capacity, par-
> ticularly understanding, have traversed, even though one may actually
> have taken place some 2 months before the other. By about 30 months,
> however, production soon becomes unreliable as an indicator of language
> capacities as is the case in the adult. (p. 286)

Our findings from the analysis of free speech samples generally support these
statements. However, we also observed differences in language production
patterns that continued well beyond the 30-month age limit set by Lenneberg.
The patterns for both percentage of repetitive utterances and percentage of
multiword utterances, for instance, were shown to differ in the two groups of
children until at least the age of 42 months. Moreover, our findings on one important measure — the mean length of utterance (MLU) — suggest a difference in
rate of development that distinguishes one group from the other through at
least the age of 66 months (Figure 6-4). These findings, especially when viewed
in the light of results from concurrent language tests, indicate that certain
measures used in the analysis of spontaneous or free language production may
continue to yield information on language development even beyond the point
at which language is presumed to have been acquired.

The data from free speech language analysis are most sensitive to intergroup
differences at the earlier month periods, revealing an initial language growth
by the experimental group far superior to the control. Quantitative measures
also suggested some interesting developmental trends. The first 8 to 12 months
of growth (between 18 and 30 months of age) seemed to be a critical period of
development for the experimental group or, conversely, a retarded period of
growth for the control group. Though the number of morphemes was highly
interrelated with total utterances, the fact that the experimental children produced a significantly larger number of unique vocabulary items and also used
utterances almost 50% longer than the control children gave added meaning to
the measure of gross numbers of morphemes. Indeed, this holds serious implications for the development of both linguistic and perceptual skills. An early
start at perceptual discrimination and labeling is, it seems, crucial to subsequent development of language skills.

134   6. Language Assessment

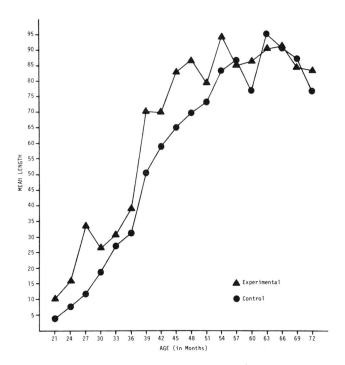

Figure 6-4. Free Speech: Mean Length of Utterance

These data indicate that free speech language analysis can be an effective method of delineating both quantitative and qualitative differences in treatment effects between experimental and control groups. Quantitative differences in the early months favored the experimental group. The qualitative differences suggested by four factors in the quantitative data — the number of repetitive utterances, the number of single-word utterances, the vocabulary range, and the mean number of morphemes per utterance — are supported by measures gained from the more structured language tests (e.g., sentence repetition and the ITPA) that also seek to establish developmental language patterns.

Thus, gross feature tabulation for the analysis of free speech samples is most sensitive to early language growth, when language behavior is more quantitative than qualitative. But as we shall see, even though the behavior of the experimental children beyond the 1½ to 2½ year age period was not shown by these measures to be quite as remarkable in comparison with the control children's, the differential in language development actually continued in an even more significant and sophisticated fashion in favor of the experimental group. It is difficult to know the true explanation of such behavior, but the implication is that if, as in other kinds of psychomotor development, the emergence of refined and developmentally sophisticated behavior is preceded by a period of intense practice on the part of the child, then the period between 18 and 30 months of age is of critical importance to future language development. It is in this early period that language tends to be used to react to situations and to comment on all observations with a demonstrative or identifying remark. Later, language tends to act upon the environment in attempts to initiate or appreciate the situation. These attempts introduce the abstract and more complex syntactic aspects of thought and language. This thesis is consistent with the treatment of thought and language by both Vygotsky and Piaget.

The parallelism test indicated comparable performance curves for the two groups. Differences between groups were significant ($p < .029$) only during the first two age levels tested (21 to 27 months), with the experimental children producing more intelligible utterances than the control group during that period. As is expected with this type of measure, the children in both groups produced significantly, $F(30, 38) = 4.21$, $p < .01$, more utterances as they grew older.

A significant, $F(15, 19) = 2.52$, $p < .05$, deviation from parallelism was shown by the two groups' performance scores on this measure. This difference in performance patterns occurred mainly in the first half of the sampling period. The overall difference between the two groups, according to the Hotelling T^2 statistic, was significant ($T^2 = 78.61$, $p = .023$), with the experimental children's percentage of repetitive utterances being the lower of the two. The percentage of such utterances would normally be expected to diminish significantly over time and did so for all of the children, $F(30, 38) = 3.73$, $p < .02$.

Parallelism was rejected on this measure, $F(15, 19) = 2.10$, $p < .10$. There was an overall difference in favor of the experimental group that approached significance (Hotelling $T^2 = 61.02$, $p = .068$). As with all other free speech measures, the increase in percentage of multiword utterances over time was significant, $F(30, 38) = 3.94$, $p < .01$, for all children.

The MLU performance patterns of the two groups were found to be parallel. Differences between the two groups were, on the whole, not significant. As they grew older, the children in both groups made significant progress on this measure, $F(30, 38) = 7.03$, $p < .01$.

The performance trends of the two groups on the vocabulary measure were found to be parallel. Although the Hotelling T^2 test showed no significant difference in overall performance between the two groups ($T^2 = 40.99$, $p = .245$), separate t tests indicated that the experimental children produced significantly ($p < .050$) more vocabulary items than the control children during the first three age levels sampled (24 to 30 months) as well as at the 39-, 45-, and 48-month levels. From age 51 months to the end of the sampling period, the two groups did not differ significantly in their use of vocabulary items. All children made significant, $F(30, 38) = 7.16$, $p < .01$, progress over time on this measure.

As in the measure of mean vocabulary per sample, the Hotelling T^2 test did not show any significant difference between the overall performance of the two groups ($T^2 = 21.92$, $p = .718$); however, separate t tests indicated that the experimental children maintained a significantly ($p < .05$) higher cumulative vocabulary than the control group from the first age level (24 months) through the 60-month level.

THE GRAMMATICAL COMPREHENSION TEST

The Grammatical Comprehension Test, a modified version of the test suggested by Bellugi-Klima (1968), consisted of 59 items arranged in 15 subtests[1], which in turn comprised 34 minimal contrasts that tested comprehension of the following structures:

1. Prepositions: *in/on/under* (1 subtest; 3 items)
2. Singular/plural nouns:
   a. Object position (1 subtest; 4 items)
   b. Subject position, with verbs in the present tense (1 subtest; 4 items)
3. Possessive noun markers (1 subtest; 4 items)
4. Can't/can (1 subtest):
   a. Used in statements (2 items)
   b. Used in *wh-* questions (2 items)
5. Conjunctions:
   a. *Or/and* (1 subtest; 4 items)
   b. *Either-or/neither-nor* (1 subtest; 4 items)
6. Negative affix *un-* (1 subtest; 4 items)
7. Adjectives (1 subtest):
   a. Size: *small/big* (2 items)
   b. Color: *purple, blue, green, red* (2 items)
8. Comparative (1 subtest):
   a. *Bigger/smaller* (2 items)
   b. *More* (2 items)
9. Joined comparatives (1 subtest):
   a. *Bigger and flatter* (1 item)
   b. *Smaller and rounder* (1 item)
10. Pronouns:
    a. *Him/himself* (1 subtest; 4 items)
    b. *Themselves/each other* (1 subtest; 4 items)
11. Active/passive (1 subtest; 4 items)
12. Embedded clauses (1 subtest; 6 items)

Each item consisted of an action that the child was asked to demonstrate using dolls, blocks, toy animals, or other objects that were made available during the test session. The entire test took from 25 to 30 minutes to administer.

At every age level tested, the performance of the two groups was evaluated on the basis of percentage of subtests correct, mean number of subtests ac-

---

[1]A 16th subtest (2 items), which contained two nonreversible passives, was discarded because the items could not be minimally contrasted.

quired, and mean number of contrasts acquired. A subtest was considered to have been correctly answered only when the child had given correct responses to *all* items within that subtest. Each subtest answered correctly represented, conservatively, a grammatical structure comprehended.

The point at which a child was considered to have acquired a subtest was the age level at which he or she began to demonstrate consistent comprehension of the structure being tested; that is, when all items in the subtest were answered correctly each time the child took the test. If, for example, a child gave correct responses to a subtest at every age level except at 42 months, the age of acquisition for that subtest was recorded as 45 months. The number of subtests acquired was recorded for each child and the mean calculated for each group at every age level tested.

In this test, a contrast was usually represented in a pair of sentences that differed from each other only in the specific feature being tested. Two contrasts generally constituted a subtest. Subtest V (*can't/can*), for example, consisted of the following:

Here is a ball and here is a jack. Look, I can roll the ball (demonstrate).
1. Show me the thing that can't roll.
2. Show me the thing that can roll.
Here is a pencil. We use it to write with. Here is a spoon. We use it to eat with.
3. Show me: What can't write?
4. Show me: What can write?

A child who responded correctly to all four questions was credited with two contrasts, or one subtest. He or she had to answer both items 1 and 2 or both items 3 and 4 to be given credit for one contrast. Correct responses to only items 1 and 4 or 2 and 3 were not counted. As was the case with subtests, a contrast was considered to have been acquired only when it was being answered correctly at every age level through the end of the testing period.

Observing the acquisition of contrasts provided additional information on the growth of the children's comprehension of grammatical structures because it demonstrated the process by which each structure was gradually mastered. For instance, both groups acquired the constrast *or/and* plus nouns much earlier than they did *or/and* plus adjectives. This will be discussed subsequently in greater detail.

Analysis of Results

SUBTESTS CORRECT

Deviation from parallel was significant, $F(20, 24) = 4.22$, $p < .01$, as was the overall difference between groups, $F(11, 23) = 9.94$, $p < .01$. Although all of the children improved their scores significantly (Hotelling $T^2 = 156.85$, $p = .000$) as they grew older, the difference between the two groups' rates of improvement was striking. For example, the experimental group's initial performance was not matched by the control group until 21 months later, at 57 months, and the level attained by the experimental children at 42 months was reached by the control children only at the end of the testing period, at 66 months (Figure 6-5).

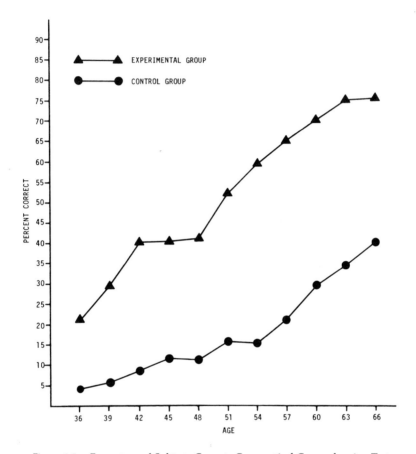

Figure 6-5.   Percentage of Subtests Correct: Grammatical Comprehension Test

SUBTESTS ACQUIRED

Deviation from parallel in the two groups' performance trends was significant, $F(10, 24) = 13.77$, $p < .01$. The experimental children acquired significantly (Hotelling $T^2 = 294.20$, $p = .000$) more subtests overall than the control group. The difference between groups at every age level was also significant ($p < .013$) in favor of the experimental group. On the whole, the children acquired significantly, $F(20, 48) = 16.54$, $p < .02$, more subtests as they grew older. The experimental children, however, gained significantly, $F(10, 33) = 30.65$, $p < .001$, more over time than did the children in the control group (Figure 6-6).

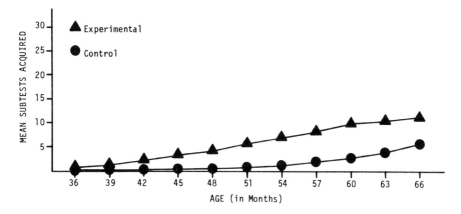

Figure 6-6. Grammatical Comprehension: Mean Subtests Acquired

CONTRASTS ACQUIRED

Deviation from parallel between the two groups was significant, $F(10, 24) =$ 8.82, $p < .01$. Overall differences between groups were significant (Hotelling $T^2 = 133.46$, $p = .000$) in favor of the experimental group, who by age 36 months had already acquired 3.5 contrasts, a figure not equaled by the control group until they were 51 months of age. By that age (51 months), the experimental children had demonstrated acquisition of 14.3 contrasts, a performance equaled by the control group only at 66 months. The experimental children were thus consistently ahead of their control counterparts by at least 15 months on this measure (Figure 6-7).

Acquisition Patterns

We compared the two groups' progress in the acquisition of specific grammatical structures (Table 6-3). Except for the embedded clauses subtest, which

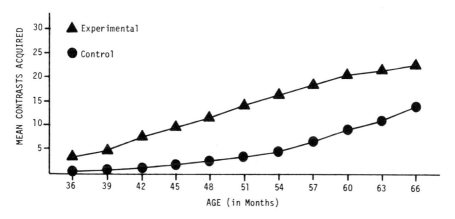

Figure 6-7. Grammatical Comprehension: Mean Contrasts Acquired

only one child comprehended partially, all the subtests were broken down into their component contrasting pairs. A contrast was considered to have been mastered or acquired by a group when at least 60% of that group had acquired it. When all contrasts comprising a subtest had been acquired in this manner by a group, acquisition of the complete subtest by that group was considered to have taken place.

Table 6-3   Grammatical Comprehension Test: Acquisition Patterns
(Structures acquired by at least 60% of each group; items in bold type
are complete subtests)

Experimental	Age (months)	Control
	36	
Possessive noun marker: *boy's daddy/daddy's boy* *Can't/can*: in statements	39	
Can't/can: in wh- Q *Or/and*: with nouns Prepositions: *in/under* *on/under*	42	
in/on	45	
Possessive noun marker: *mommy's girl/girl's mommy* Adjectives: Negative affix un-: *small/big* *covered/uncovered* *purple/blue, green/red* *piled/unpiled*	48	
Comparative: *more* Reflexive/reciprocal pronouns: **hit themselves/each other**	51	*Or/and*: with nouns

feed themselves/each other
Reflexive: *hits him/himself*
Singular/Plural Noun (Object):
  jack/jacks
Active/Passive: pushes/is pushed by
        chases/is chased by
	54	Possessive noun marker:
		  boy's daddy/daddy's boy

Or/and: with adjectives	57	Adjectives: *small/big* Comparative: *more*
Singular/Plural Noun (Object): *ball/balls* Joined Comparatives: *Smaller and rounder*	60	Prepositions: *in/under*

Comparative: *bigger/smaller*	63	Possessive noun marker:
		  mommy's girl/girl's mommy
		Negative affix un-:
		  covered/uncovered

Reflexive: *feeds him/himself*	66	***piled/unpiled*** *Or/and*: with adjectives **Active/Passive: pushes/is pushed by** **chases/is chased by**

Table 6-3 (continued)   (Structures not acquired; percentages of
acquisition at 66 months in parentheses; complete subtests in bold type)

Experimental	Control
	Adjectives: *purple/blue, green/red* (56)
	Prepositions: *on/under* (56)
	in/on (50)
	Reflexive/Reciprocal Pronouns:
	feed themselves/each other (50)
	hit themselves/each other (56)
	Reflexive Pronouns:
	feeds him/himself (50)
	hits him/himself (50)
	Singular/Plural Noun (Object):
	jack/jacks (44)
	ball/balls (50)
	Can't/can: in statements (44)
	in wh- Q (39)
	Comparative: *bigger/smaller* (28)
Joined Comparatives:	**Joined Comparatives:**
bigger and flatter (53)	*smaller and rounder* (22)
	bigger and flatter (6)
Singular/Plural Noun (Subject) + Verb:	**Singular/Plural Noun (Subject) + Verb:**
doll walks/dolls walk (53)	*doll walks/dolls walk* (22)
dolls jump/doll jumps (53)	*dolls jump/doll jumps* (11)
Either-or/Neither-nor:	*Either-or/Neither-nor:*
with nouns (29)	with nouns (11)
with adjectives (29)	with adjectives (11)
Embedded Clauses: Group I (0)	Embedded Clauses: Group I (0)
Group II (6)	Group II (0)

By the time they were 48 months old, the experimental children had acquired three of the 15 subtests: *can't/can*, the prepositions *in/on/under*, and the possessive marker. In addition to these three subtests, the distinction *or/and* with nouns was acquired at 42 months and the contrasts *small/big* and *covered/uncovered*, at 48 months. Between 51 and 60 months of age the experimental children completed acquisition of the subtests on adjectives, the negative affix, and *or/and*. They also acquired all of the contrasts for three new subtests (*themselves/each other*, active/passive, and singular/plural nouns), one contrast for the subtest on comparatives, one for the subtest on *him/himself*, and one for the subtest on joined comparatives. During the next 6 months, they completed the acquisition of *him/himself* and comparatives. The remaining contrast for joined comparatives was acquired by only 53% of the group and was therefore not included among their acquisitions.

In comparison, no structure was acquired during the first 12 months by the control group. In the following 12 months, five contrasts, but no complete subtests, were acquired. The contrasts were *or/and* with nouns, *boy's daddy/daddy's boy* (possessive noun marker), *small/big* (adjectives), more (comparative), and *in/under* (prepositions). Two subtests (possessive noun marker and *or/and*) were completed during the next 6 months. Also acquired during this period (63 to 66 months) were the complete subtests for the negative affix *un-* and for active/passive. Thus, the control group's total range of acquisition over the 30-month period consisted of only four complete subtests and three contrasts, in contrast to the experimental group's 11 complete subtests and one contrast.

The three subtests not acquired by the experimental group were the singular/plural subject plus verb, *either-or/neither-nor*, and embedded clauses. They also failed to reach criterion on the joined comparatives *bigger and flatter*. With the exception of the singular/plural subject plus verb distinction, these structures were the most complex in the test and were not expected to be acquired by the children until after 6 years of age.

While it was obvious that the experimental children had mastered the singular/plural distinction with nouns used as objects, they did not seem to comprehend the same distinction when nouns were used as sentence subjects and followed by inflected verbs. These results followed the pattern of previous studies. Owings (1972) obtained similar results with his subjects acquiring the singular/plural noun distinction at the age of 5 years and the singular/plural noun plus inflected verb distinction at 6 years. Carrow (1968) reported that her subjects understood singular subjects earlier than they did plural subjects. Breaking down the subtest into its component pairs, we found similar patterns: More children in each group responded correctly to the sentences with singular subjects than to those with plural ones. At the 66-month level, for instance, 100% of the experimental group and 76% of the control group responded correctly to "The doll jumps," whereas only 53% of the experimental group and 29% of the control group responded correctly to "The dolls jump."

Each group of children also seemed to encounter the same degree of relative difficulty among contrasts within other subtests. For example, each group acquired *or/and* with nouns 15 months earlier than *or/and* with adjectives. With the experimental group the ages of acquisition were 42 and 57 months, respectively, and with the control group, 51 and 66 months, respectively. *Boy's daddy/daddy's boy* was acquired at 39 months by the experimental group, 9 months earlier than *mommy's girl/girl's mommy*, which was acquired at 48 months. For the control group the ages of acquisition were 54 and 63 months, also 9 months apart. *Covered/uncovered* seemed only slightly easier than *piled/unpiled*, which both groups acquired only 3 months later (experimental, ages 48 and 51 months; control, ages 63 and 66 months). In each case the more difficult item seems to have required a more advanced vocabulary than the easier one. Thus the contrast *or/and* with adjectives required a knowledge of the words *red* and *blue*, although not necessarily the ability to distinguish between the colors they represent.

With a few exceptions such as *can't/can*, the order in which the grammatical structures tested were learned followed the same general pattern in the two groups. As Table 6-3 illustrates, however, the ages at which these structures were acquired were, without exception, earlier in the experimental group. The time lag between the groups ranged from 6 months (comparative *more*) to 18 months (*in/under*).

As the results of the Grammatical Comprehension Test demonstrate, there was a substantial difference in performance level between the two groups of children, both at any given age and over the complete 30-month.span of testing. The experimental children understood significantly more structures at each age level tested, acquired grammatical structures 6 to 18 months earlier than did the control children, and over the 30-month testing period acquired more than twice as many structures as the control children did. In terms of age of acquisition of specific structures, the experimental children performed on a level equal to or better than did the children tested by Carrow (1968) and Owings (1972), whereas the control children performed on a much lower level.

Comparison with Other Groups

In order to gain a wider perspective on the performance of the Milwaukee children on the Grammatical Comprehension Test, an effort was made to administer the same test to children within the same age range but from other localities and from families of different socioeconomic levels. Three groups were tested for this purpose: a middle-to-high SES group (white, $n = 18$, mean age 50 months) from Madison, Wisconsin; a low-to-middle SES group (white, $n = 18$, mean age 66.35 months) from Stoughton, Wisconsin; and a low-SES group (black, $n = 87$, subdivided into five age levels $= 42, 45, 48, 51$, and 54 months) from Chicago (viz., Head Start children). Comparisons between groups were made for similar age levels on the two measures previously found to be the most significant for evaluation: the number of subtests correct and the number of features acquired.

The results of this comparison study are reported in greater detail elsewhere (Reyes & Garber, 1976). In general, the best performance came from the Madison and the experimental groups, both of whom correctly completed significantly ($p < .001$) more subtests than the control and the Chicago groups at the age levels compared. The experimental children also had significantly ($p < .05$) higher scores than the Stoughton children who, in turn, had significantly ($p < .01$) higher scores than the control children. Between the control and the Chicago groups the differences were small at first but increased steadily until at 54 months the difference was significant ($p < .02$) in favor of the Chicago group.

On the acquisition of grammatical features,[2] the Madison children exhibited

---

[2]For this category, "acquisition" in the comparison group was defined as comprehension by at least 60% of the group for a *single* age level. More stringent requirements were applied to the Milwaukee children (see p. 137) in view of their repeated testing.

the best performance, showing comprehension of 11 of the 15 subtests at 51 months. Next were the experimental children, who by 51 months had acquired five subtests; by 63 months, ten subtests; and by 66 months, 11 subtests. The Stoughton children demonstrated acquisition of ten subtests at 66 months; the Chicago children, five subtests by 54 months. The lowest level performers were the control children, who had acquired no subtest by 51 months and only four subtests by 66 months.

It will be recalled that the Madison children comprised the only high SES group in this study. The Stoughton children, on the other hand, came from a low income area, but certainly not from the type of inner city neighborhoods from which the Chicago and Milwaukee groups were drawn. Furthermore, none of the other groups — not even the Chicago children — stood the statistical likelihood of becoming retarded that the experimental and control children did at the time of birth. Bearing these facts in mind, the performance of the experimental group on this language test was impressive. The difference in performance level between this group and the control group — a difference that is emphasized by the performances of the other groups tested — is a measure of the success of the educational program's emphasis on language skills.

SENTENCE REPETITION TEST I

Like the Grammatical Comprehension Test, the first Sentence Repetition Test was introduced when the children reached the age of 36 months. The primary purpose of this test was to compare the development of the experimental and control children's abilities to imitate sentences of varying degrees of complexity during their 4th and 5th years of life (i.e., 36 to 60 months). A secondary aim was to study the effectiveness of the test as a tool for measuring differential language development.

The test consisted of 34 sentences representing 16 clause types (Gleason, 1965) and their transformations.[3] The sentences varied in length from four to eight words and from five to 11 morphemes and ranged in complexity from kernels to double base transformations. Some of the transformations represented were the negative, yes/no interrogative, *wh-* interrogative, passive, and *do* transformations. The sentences were broken down into their component features (single words and markers) as an aid in analyzing responses to test items. These features and their frequency of occurrence can be found in Table 6-4.

The test was administered to the subjects at 3-month intervals (between 36 and 60 months of age) by our language tester. After several minutes of play

---

[3]The Sentence Repetition Test was originally devised by Peter Fries and modified by Richard Dever at the University of Wisconsin in 1967. A revision of the test, called Sentence Repetition II, was made by Reyes, who also developed the scoring procedures for both tests (see Reyes & Garber, 1971, for additional details).

Table 6-4 Mean Number of Whole Responses by Category

Age (Mos)	Group	n	I. Exact Repetition X̄	% of Items[a]	II. A. With transpositions Major X̄	%[b]	Minor X̄	%[b]	II. B. With omissions Major X̄	%[b]	Minor X̄	%[b]	II. C. With substitutions/additions Major X̄	%[b]	Minor X̄	%[b]	III. No Repetition X̄
36	E	16	9.00	27	0.25	1	1.25	5	7.50	30	12.13	52	4.44	19	5.06	22	0.75
	C	11	3.91	12	0.45	1	1.09	4	16.18	54	13.18	48	2.55	9	4.55	17	1.27
39	E	19	11.53	34	0.42	2	1.21	6	5.42	22	13.11	62	3.00	14	5.00	24	0.26
	C	15	5.47	16	1.07	4	1.40	5	12.93	44	13.47	50	5.67	20	5.07	19	0.73
42	E	19	15.37	46	0.16	1	0.79	4	3.16	16	10.79	60	3.05	17	5.11	30	0.00
	C	17	5.88	18	0.47	2	1.53	6	9.82	36	13.82	53	5.65	21	7.06	27	1.06
45	E	19	17.58	53	0.05	0.2	0.89	5	2.21	12	10.11	63	2.21	13	4.16	27	0.00
	C	18	7.06	21	0.67	2	1.44	5	7.50	27	14.11	53	5.89	22	6.83	27	0.83
48	E	19	18.74	56	0.05	0.3	0.68	5	1.26	7	10.32	70	1.63	9	5.05	33	0.00
	C	18	8.11	24	0.78	3	0.94	3	6.72	25	15.00	59	4.78	18	7.56	31	0.33
51	E	18	18.83	56	0.06	0.3	0.44	3	0.94	6	9.56	64	2.06	12	4.06	29	0.06
	C	18	9.39	28	0.22	1	0.83	3	5.33	21	14.22	59	5.28	21	6.11		0.39
54	E	18	21.39	63	0.11	1	0.50	4	0.72	5	8.22	67	1.67	10	3.39	29	0.00
	C	17	9.53	28	0.24	1	0.88	3	4.18	15	13.82	59	5.18	20	8.06	31	0.24
57	E	18	21.72	64	0.00	0	0.28	2	0.67	5	8.11	67	1.00	7	3.67	30	0.00
	C	17	11.07	34	0.06	0.3	1.29	5	2.94	12	13.18	60	4.00	16	8.00	37	0.00
60	E	16	20.94	62	0.06	0.2	0.69	5	0.31	2	8.63	66	0.88	6	4.38	34	0.00
	C	17	12.18	36	0.18	1	1.06	5	1.76	7	13.18	62	4.24	18	8.00	37	0.00

[a]Percentage of total number of items given
[b]Percentage of total number of imperfect repetitions

time in the testing room, the child was given the directions for the test ("I want to see if you can say what I say. Can you say this? Say 'Frank ran in the street,' " etc.). The sentences were delivered by the examiner somewhat more loudly and slowly than in ordinary conversational speech, but with normal intonation and stress patterns. Each sentence was repeated once if the child did not respond or if his or her response was inaudible. These steps were taken in order to minimize recall difficulty and such factors as inattentiveness and shyness on the part of the child. The test took from 10 to 15 minutes to administer. Each session was recorded on tape and later transcribed and scored by graduate students trained in linguistic analysis.

The responses were classified according to the following scale:

I.   Exact Repetition (allowing for minor articulatory distortions)
II. Imperfect Repetition
    A.   Responses containing transpositions
        1.   Major changes: extensive or nonpermissible transpositions
        2.   Minor changes: permissible transpositions (e.g., *Kathy* and *Mary* for *Mary* and *Kathy*)
    B.   Responses containing omissions
        1.   Major omissions
            a.   Clauses and phrases
            b.   Nouns and main verbs
        2.   Minor omissions
            a.   Words other than nouns and main verbs
            b.   Markers
    C.   Responses containing substitutions or additions (including transformations and other recodings)
        1.   Major substitutions/additions
            a.   Clauses and phrases
            b.   Nouns and main verbs
        2.   Minor substitutions/additions
            a.   Words other than nouns and main verbs
            b.   Markers
III. No Repetition (silence, babbling, talking about something else)

Responses in Categories I and III were counted only once. Responses that comprised imperfect repetitions were counted under any or all of subcategories IIA1, IIA2, IIB1, IIB2, IIC1, or IIC2, depending upon the nature of the error. For example, a single response containing a major omission, a major substitution, and a minor substitution was counted once under IIB1, once under IIC1, and once under IIC2. Within a single response, similar deviations were counted only once, regardless of frequency of occurrence. The percentage of imperfect responses that contained each level of each type of error was determined by dividing the number of responses under each subcategory by the total number of imperfect repetitions.

Responses in Category II (Imperfect Repetition) were further analyzed in order to determine the percentage of morphemes each child was able to repeat among the sentences that had been repeated imperfectly, the percentage of imperfect repetitions that preserved the underlying structures of the stimulus sentences, and the number and types of omissions. These omissions were classified into phrases (defined for the purposes of this study as groups of any two or more words), single words, and markers. Only words and markers omitted by themselves (i.e., not as part of a larger omitted segment) were included in the count for single word and marker omissions.

Types of Response

I. EXACT REPETITION
The experimental children produced significantly ($p < .001$) more exact repetitions than did the control children at every age level (Figure 6-8). Their overall advantage, as measured by the Hotelling T^2 statistic was also significant (Hotelling $T^2 = 85.85$, $p = .000$). Although all the children's scores improved significantly, $F(16, 52) = 14.235$, $p < .01$, over time, the difference between the two groups tended to increase with each age level. Deviation from parallel was significant, $F(8, 26) = 7.18$, $p < .01$.

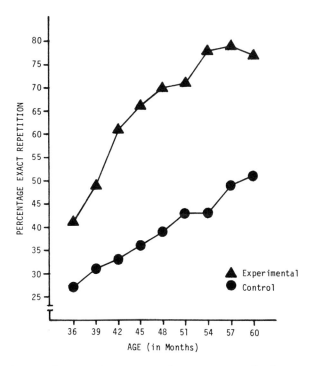

Figure 6-8.   Sentence Repetition I: Percentage of Exact Repetition for the Experimental and Control Children

By age 45 months, the majority of the experimental children were exactly repeating over 50% of the test sentences. At the 54-month level, all but two had scores over 50%. In contrast, almost all of the control subjects had scores of 50% or lower throughout the 2-year testing period: At 60 months, only three of these children scored above 50% and the majority still had scores of 40% or lower. There was no significant deviation in parallelism between experimental and control children. The experimental children demonstrated an overall advantage in percentage of structures preserved (Hotelling $T^2 = 28.53$, $p = .040$) and they produced significantly ($p < .002$) higher percentages of structures preserved scores at every age level. All children's scores also improved significantly, $F(16, 52) = 7.25$, $p < .01$, over time.

II. IMPERFECT REPETITION

The scores on the measures under this category have been converted into the percentages of imperfect repetitions they represent, that is, for each child, the number of responses under each level of each subcategory has been divided by the total number of imperfect repetitions made by that particular child. As previously noted, an imperfect response may contain more than one of the six types of errors under this scoring category. It is therefore possible for one type of error such as minor omission to be found in 100% of the imperfect repetitions, and for another type, such as major omission, to be found in 95% of the same responses. The two groups differed mainly in their performances on the major level of each measure under this category. Throughout the 2-year testing period, the control group responses consistently showed larger percentages of major level errors of any type than did those of the experimental group. Percentage scores on the minor level were generally comparable between the groups.

IIA. Responses with Transpositions. Transpositions on the major level were the least commonly found errors in either group: They occurred in no more than 2% of the imperfect responses of the experimental group and in no more than 4% of the control children's, at any age level. During the first year of testing, the control group tended to have significantly ($p < .05$ at 39, 45, and 48 months) more errors of this type than the experimental group. After the 48-month level, the performances of the two groups on this measure became comparable as the level of such errors became negligible.

On the minor level, the performance of the two groups was comparable throughout the 2-year period, errors of this type being found in 3% to 6% of the imperfect repetitions of each group. No trend was observable in the longitudinal performance of either group on this measure.

An examination of the responses that contained order changes showed that such errors clustered around double adjectives (e.g., the *big red* ball, a *new baby* brother, the *two little* boys) and conjoined words or phrases (e.g., *Mary and Kathy*, *dump trucks and garbage trucks*). Transposition of adjectives indicates that the rules for the sequence of adjectives have not been mastered. Transposition of conjoined words or phrases, on the other hand, may be attributed more to errors in immediate recall than to an incomplete grasp of ordering rules.

IIB. Responses with Omissions. The greatest and most consistent differences between the two groups under the imperfect repetition category were found in the percentage of responses with omissions on the major level. Errors of this type were found in significantly ($p < .05$) higher percentages in the control group than in the experimental group at all age levels.

The two groups' performances on this measure followed the same trends as for exact repetition: Although both groups showed improvement with age in terms of progressively smaller percentages of major omissions, the initial score for the experimental group was approximated by the control group only after 9 months of testing. Thereafter, the experimental group's performance was consistently a year in advance of the control group's (Figure 6-9). After the 48-month level, at least 44% of the experimental children no longer made any major level omissions, whereas over 50% of the control children still had major omissions in up to 30% of their imperfect repetitions even at 60 months (Figure 6-10).

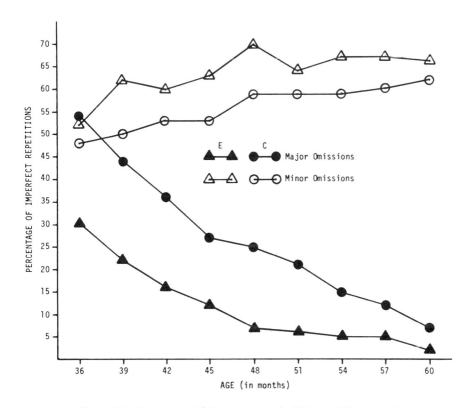

Figure 6-9. Responses with Omissions on the Major and Minor Levels

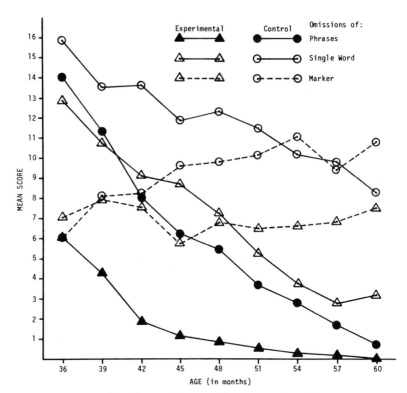

Figure 6-10.   Mean Number of Major (Phrase) and Minor (Single Word and Marker) Omissions Made by Experimental and Control Children

For both groups, minor omissions were the most common type of error throughout the 2-year testing period, constituting 52% to 70% of the imperfect responses among the experimental children and 48% to 62% among the control children. With the exception of the 39-month age level, when the experimental group had a significantly larger percentage than the control group ($p < .05$), the performances of the two groups were comparable on this measure.

On the average, the percentage of minor omissions among the control children tended to increase as they grew older. In the experimental group, the percentages on this measure from 39 months onward remained substantially the same.

IIC.   Responses with Substitutions/Additions.   Major substitutions/additions were found in 6% to 19% of the imperfect responses in the experimental group and in 9% to 22% of those of the control group. Consistent differences between the two groups emerged only after the 42-month level, with the experimental group making errors of this type in significantly smaller percentages ($p < .05$) than the control group. This was attributable in part to the fact that from 45 months onward an increasingly large number of experimental children had stopped making any errors of this type.

As with the two other measures under the imperfect repetition category, performances on the minor level of substitutions were comparable at all age levels between the two groups. Both groups tended to have errors of this type in larger percentages of their imperfect responses as they grew older.

III. No REPETITION

After 39 months, and with the exception of one child at the 51-month level, all the children in the experimental group attempted to repeat every sentence presented to them, while those in the control group continued not to repeat some sentences up to the 54-month level. Significantly ($p < .05$) more sentences were not repeated by the control children than by the experimental children at every level from 39 through 48 months. Thereafter, differences between the two groups were negligible.

Analysis of Imperfect Repetitions

All imperfect repetitions, irrespective of types of error, were further analyzed for the percentage of morphemes in the original sentences that were found in the imperfect responses and for the percentage of imperfect repetitions that preserved the underlying structures of the original sentences. The first was regarded as a predominantly quantitative measure—how much of the imperfectly repeated sentence was remembered and reproduced by the child, regardless of the presence or absence of structure in the response. The second was a qualitative measure and was regarded as an indication that the original sentence, although inaccurately reproduced, had been comprehended. These two measures can be taken as separate indicators of how closely the imperfect responses approximated the original test sentences.

PERCENTAGE OF MORPHEMES REPEATED

At every age level tested, a significantly ($p < .01$) larger percentage of morphemes was repeated by the experimental than by the control children (see Figure 6-11). This finding indicates that even when they had errors in their responses, the experimental children were giving quantitatively closer approximations of the test sentences than were the control children.

While both groups repeated larger portions of the test sentences as they grew older (Figure 6-11), the control group's best performance, at 60 months, was comparable only to the 42-month level performance of the experimental group. By the age of 45 months, all but one of the experimental children were repeating over 70% of the morphemes in the test sentences. At 57 and 60 months, all of them were doing so. In the control group, less than half surpassed the 70% mark before the 54-month level; at 60 months, four members of the group still had not done so.

PERCENTAGE OF STRUCTURES PRESERVED

Imperfect repetitions that retained the underlying structures of the test sentences were considered *structure preserving*. These included recodings into dialect, appropriate answers to questions, and omissions or substitutions of adjectives, markers, and most function words, including the various forms of the verb *be*. Although parallel performance trends were observed in the two

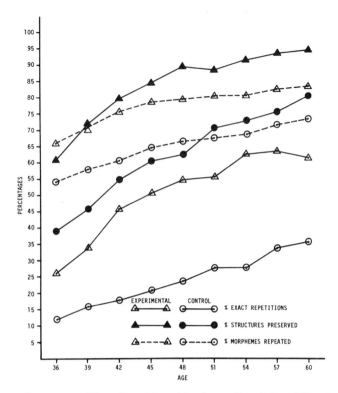

Figure 6-11. Percentages of Exact Repetitions, Morphemes Repeated, and Structures Preserved (Sentence Repetition Test)

groups, there was a significant, $F(9, 25) = 2.40$, $p < .04$, between group difference in overall performance in favor of the experimental group. Separate t tests indicated that at every age level the experimental children's imperfect responses had significantly ($p < .002$) greater percentages of structures preserved than did those of the control children. Over the 2-year testing period, the children in both groups preserved a significantly, $F(16, 52) = 7.24$, $p < .001$, greater percentage of structures in their imperfect responses. It took the control group 9 months, or four test sessions, to equal the experimental group's initial test score; another 9 months (from ages 45 to 54 months) to gain what the experimental children gained in 3 (from ages 36 to 39 months); and still another 6 months (from ages 54 to 60 months) to approximate the experimental children's scores at age 42 months.

Comparison of Morphemes Repeated, Structure Preserving Responses, and Exact Repetitions

The percentages of exact repetitions, morphemes repeated, and structures preserved have been the "positive" measures (as opposed to counts of errors) used in this study. In addition to their usefulness as individual indices of performance, these three measures taken together provide a comprehensive view of the groups' performances over the 2-year period (Figure 6-11). It may be noted that for each group the trends taken by the two measures for imperfect responses tended to follow the same pattern as did the trend for exact repetition. Each of these measures in fact exhibited substantial correlations with the percentage of exact repetitions. This finding suggests a close relationship between the child's ability to repeat stimulus sentences accurately and his or her ability either to repeat portions or to construct structurally acceptable equivalents of those items he or she has not accurately reproduced.

It will also be seen that at some time during the testing period each group reached a point at which the percentage of structures preserved equaled or surpassed the percentage of morphemes repeated. This point may be taken as an indication that the group had reduced their omission of those morphemes essential to the underlying structures of the test sentences. The experimental group reached this point at 39 months, whereas the control group did not do so until the 51-month level.

Analysis of Omissions

PHRASE OMISSIONS

Significantly ($p < .02$) fewer phrases (groups of any two or more words) were omitted by the experimental group than by the control group at every age level (see Table 6-5). Both groups omitted fewer phrases as they grew older; however, there was a difference of 9 to 12 months between the performances of the two groups on this measure. For instance, the experimental group's scores at 36, 42, and 48 months were not equaled by the control group until 45, 57, and 60 months, respectively.

SINGLE WORD OMISSIONS

With the exception of the 39-month level, significantly ($p < .05$) fewer single words were omitted at all age levels by the experimental group than by the control group (see Table 6-5). Both groups omitted fewer single words as they grew older despite the concurrent decrease in phrase omissions, which contributed to a raised count on this measure. As with phrase omissions, the control group's performance lagged behind that of the experimental group by approximately 9 to 12 months.

The definite article ("*The* two girls looked at a little house") accounted for the largest percentage of single word omissions in both groups at all age levels. Auxiliary verbs ("*Does* Mary have a sister?") made up the second largest percentage of word omissions; the copulative *be* ("All the children *are* in school") and qualifiers ("Joe threw the *big red* ball") came next.

MARKER OMISSIONS

The two groups omitted approximately the same number of markers at the first three age levels. From 45 months onward, the experimental group had significantly ($p < .02$) fewer omissions than the control group. The number of marker omissions remained substantially on the same level within each group from the 45-month level to the end of the testing period.

Table 6-5   Mean Phrase, Single-word, and Marker Omissions:
Sentence Repetition Test I

Omissions	Words & Markers: Frequency	36 mos. E	C	39 mos. E	C	42 mos. E	C	45 mos. E	C
Phrases		6.00	14.00	4.24	11.33	1.88	8.06	1.12	6.22
Single Words	201	12.85	15.82	10.76	13.53	9.12	13.65	8.71	11.89
Nouns	56	0.57	1.45	0.35	0.73	0.29	0.71	0.24	0.33
Personal pronouns	12	0.93	1.55	0.88	1.20	0.47	1.18	0.59	1.06
Main verbs (excluding be)	30	0.64	1.00	0.18	0.93	0.29	0.88	0.24	0.67
Auxiliary verbs	13	3.08	1.82	2.24	1.73	1.95	2.59	1.48	2.11
Be (copulative)	5	1.21	1.55	1.06	1.20	1.12	1.24	0.82	1.11
Qualifiers	38	1.29	1.64	1.71	2.27	0.88	1.94	0.53	1.44
Wh- and how	6	0.43	0.18	0.24	0.27	0.00	0.00	0.06	0.11
a/an	8	0.64	0.73	0.47	0.80	0.47	0.29	0.29	0.78
the, that	25	3.71	5.45	3.47	3.20	3.71	4.47	4.18	4.00
Prepositions & particles	6	0.07	0.00	0.06	0.07	0.00	0.18	0.06	0.17
Conjunctions	2	0.39	0.45	0.24	0.13	0.12	0.12	0.12	0.11
Markers	51	7.00	6.00	7.94	8.07	7.59	8.24	5.71	9.61
Progressive -ing	5	0.29	0.56	0.35	0.40	0.12	0.41	0.18	0.17
Past tense	18	2.43	2.00	3.18	3.00	2.53	2.35	2.06	3.50
Past participle	4	0.71	0.45	0.94	0.27	0.53	0.88	0.29	0.83
Third person -s	5	1.14	0.82	0.83	1.00	1.47	1.12	1.12	1.50
Plural	9	1.57	1.73	2.00	2.87	2.29	2.59	1.71	2.50
Comparative -er	1	0.36	0.36	0.35	0.20	0.29	0.29	0.18	0.25
Objective case	5	0.29	0.09	0.12	0.27	0.12	0.35	0.00	0.67
Be plural marker	4	0.21	0.00	0.18	0.07	0.35	0.18	0.12	0.22

The past tense, third person, and plural markers made up the largest percentages of the total marker omissions for each group. After the 42-month level, although the experimental group generally omitted fewer markers of any type than the control group, there seemed to be no pattern to the types of marker omissions made by either group.

The responses to the Sentence Repetition Test were analyzed in four progressively detailed stages. First, the number of correct responses was obtained; second, the imperfect repetitions were examined for the types of error present; third, these same imperfect repetitions were analyzed to determine how closely they approximated the test sentences; and fourth, the responses from which portions of the test sentences had been omitted were reexamined to determine what these omissions comprised.

The extensive analysis of inexact repetitions was undertaken in recognition of the possibility that a young child's ability to repeat sentences accurately

48 mos.		51 mos.		54 mos.		57 mos.		60 mos.	
E	C	E	C	E	C	E	C	E	C
0.82	5.44	0.50	3.67	0.24	2.76	0.12	1.65	0.00	0.70
7.29	12.33	5.24	11.50	3.71	10.18	2.77	9.82	3.19	8.29
0.18	0.28	0.00	0.67	0.12	0.29	0.06	0.18	0.00	0.24
0.24	1.17	0.35	0.50	0.06	0.29	0.12	0.41	0.19	0.47
0.06	0.67	0.12	0.28	0.00	0.24	0.06	0.18	0.06	0.29
1.06	2.50	1.29	2.89	0.82	2.71	0.53	2.59	0.44	1.94
0.53	1.22	0.53	1.06	0.53	1.00	0.47	0.94	0.19	0.59
0.77	1.33	0.29	1.44	0.24	1.00	0.29	1.00	0.38	1.12
0.06	0.28	0.24	0.17	0.06	0.35	0.06	0.35	0.06	0.24
0.53	0.56	0.06	0.56	0.18	0.29	0.12	0.88	0.06	0.53
3.82	3.89	2.35	3.56	1.47	3.47	1.06	3.18	1.75	2.65
0.00	0.22	9.99	9.17	0.00	0.06	0.00	0.12	0.00	0.06
0.06	0.22	0.12	0.22	0.00	0.24	0.00	0.00	0.00	0.06
6.82	9.83	6.47	10.17	6.59	11.06	6.82	9.41	7.50	10.82
0.06	0.11	0.12	0.11	0.00	0.06	0.12	0.41	0.00	0.06
2.00	3.83	2.12	3.83	2.41	4.47	2.47	3.59	2.38	3.94
0.82	0.89	0.65	0.89	0.71	1.18	0.65	1.29	0.69	1.24
1.94	1.94	1.47	1.94	1.88	2.06	2.41	2.00	2.25	2.18
1.65	2.11	1.47	2.11	1.12	2.18	1.18	1.41	1.56	2.29
0.24	0.22	0.18	0.50	0.06	0.35	0.00	0.29	0.00	0.18
0.00	0.61	0.00	0.17	0.06	0.18	0.00	0.00	0.00	0.06
0.12	0.11	0.35	0.28	0.35	0.65	0.06	0.41	0.25	0.88

may be evidence of extralinguistic rather than linguistic skills. Were the children who scored high on exact repetitions merely better at *parroting* than those who did not, or did they show any other evidence of greater linguistic ability, such as better comprehension of the test sentences?

A comparison of the errors made by the two groups of children would give some indication of their comparative awareness of the structures that they were attempting to imitate. For example, a child who omits only function words and markers from a test sentence and responds in telegraphic style is more likely to have understood the sentence than a child who deletes large chunks and items such as nouns and main verbs from the same sentence. One reason is that function words, such as articles and auxiliaries, not only are *low information* words, but also occupy unstressed positions in the sentence (Brown & Bellugi, 1964) and as such may not have been heard by the child (Slobin & Welsh, 1967). Another reason may be that the child's dialect pattern is interfering with his/her awareness of the structures in the test sentence. Thus, the frequent omission of the verb *be* in its various forms by both groups in the present study may be largely a reflection of the dialect spoken in the predominantly black neighborhoods in which the children have been raised. On the other hand, the omission of phrases and *high information* words cannot be explained by either of these reasons and could be regarded as more telling errors. The analysis of the types of error made by the two groups has shown that while they had about the same percentages of errors on the minor (or function word and marker) level, their percentages of major errors differed radically: The imperfect responses of the experimental group had consistently and significantly smaller percentages of omissions and substitutions on the clause, phrase, and lexical item levels.

A further indication of the difference in level of grammatical control between the two groups is the proportion of imperfect responses preserving the underlying structures of the stimulus sentences, as in the following examples:

Sentence No. 2:   Mary has a new baby brother.
Response: Mary got a new baby brother.
Sentence No. 10:   Dump trucks and garbage trucks are real big.
Responses: Dump trucks and garbage trucks they're real big. Dump trucks are real big and garbage trucks are real big.

Lenneberg (1967) saw this type of response as an indication that the sentence had been understood and so distinguished it from *parroting*, which produces mistakes that show a lack of insight into the grammatical structure and semantic content of the sentence. The following are examples of the latter type of response:

Sentence No. 19:   Is Jim running a long way?
Response: Jim long way?
Sentence No. 22:   Where is that dirty brown dog running?
Response: Dirty brown running.

As mentioned earlier, the experimental children consistently produced significantly larger percentages of structure preserving responses than did the control children. An interesting observation is that after the age of 36 months the percentage of such responses exceeded that of the morphemes they repeated (Figure 6-11). In contrast, the control children's percentage of repeated morphemes continued to exceed that of structures preserved until the 48-month level. This is indicative of the use each group made of the morphemes they did repeat: Those repeated by the experimental group after age 36 months were predominantly essential to the structures of the test sentences, while until age 48 months those repeated by the control group were not.

This raises the question of whether a child's ability to repeat linguistic structures accurately is an indication that he/she also comprehends and can spontaneously produce those structures. Slobin and Welsh (1967) seemed convinced that this is so and challenged earlier assertions that linguistic imitation is "a perceptual-motor skill not dependent on comprehension" (Fraser, Bellugi,

& Brown, 1963). In the present study, the numerous instances of responses that preserved the underlying structures of the test sentences demonstrate that the child does understand some sentences he/she is unable to repeat, whether because of interference from another dialect pattern or because the structure is too complex for him/her to reproduce verbatim. While it follows that the child understands some sentences he/she is able to repeat exactly, it cannot be assumed that his/her ability to repeat any sentence is proof of comprehension of that sentence. Hall and Turner (1971), for example, failed to find evidence of any relationship between correct imitation and comprehension of specific sentences.

The findings in the present study, however, indicate that children who repeat more sentences accurately also tend to produce more responses that demonstrate understanding of the underlying structures of those sentences they have failed to reproduce verbatim. These findings agree with those of Clay (1971), who noted that among four groups of children who performed differently in a sentence repetition test, the better performers in terms of exact repetitions also made fewer "unacceptable" or ungrammatical reductions and substitutions than acceptable ones, while the reverse was true among the poorer performers. The present study in fact shows a close correspondence between the number of sentences repeated exactly and the percentage of imperfect repetitions that preserved the underlying structures of the original sentences. It seems reasonable, therefore, to conclude that a child's performance on a sentence repetition test is a demonstration not only of "a perceptual-motor skill not dependent on comprehension" but also of the degree to which he/she understands and controls certain syntactic structures.

SENTENCE REPETITION TEST II

At 60 months both groups of children were given another repetition test, developed by Elena Reyes, and consisting of a completely new set of sentences. The object of this second testing was to determine whether the differences in performance level shown by the two groups on the first test would continue to be evident on another test of a similar type but comprising different structures. A corollary aim was to observe the influence of sentence length and syntactic complexity on performance. This necessitated revising the test design so that these two factors could be controlled to some extent.

The test consisted of 36 sentences controlled for syntactic complexity and sentence length. Syntactic complexity was determined by the number of transformational steps from the kernel sentence, by the compounding of one of the elements in the kernel sentence, and by the restructuring of the original sentence to incorporate an additional clause. Sentence length was determined by the number of words. Six sentence types were used to generate the 36 items in the test. Two of these consisted of six words each, two of seven words each, and two of eight words each. The number of words was held constant from kernel through its more complex reconstruction. Table 6-6 illustrates the test design.

Table 6-6   Sentence Repetition Test II Design

Sentence Length[a]	Sentence Group	Kernel Sentences	Number of Transformations 1	2	3	Sentences With Compounds	Two-Clause Sentences
			Levels of Complexity				
6	A	12	10	14	27	26	17
6	B	19	29	16	23	2	6
7	C	20	35	1	8	4	25
7	D	37	9	18	13	33	32
8	E	11	36	24	5	30	31
8	F	34	38	22	3	28	7

[a]Number of words

The numbers in the table (other than *Sentence Length*) refer to the item numbers in the test.[4] Each kernel (K) consisted of a simple sentence with an active verb and a qualifying prepositional phrase. Three of the verbs used in the kernel sentences were in the simple past tense (*laughed, built, sent*); one was present tense, third person singular (*chases*); one was in the be + ing, progressive form (*are coming*); and one was in a have + ed, or perfective form (*has painted*). From these kernels were generated one, two, and three step transformations (T1, T2, and T3), as well as sentences with compounds (C) and two clause sentences (2C). One step transformations consisted of passive constructions (2 full, 2 truncated) and yes/no questions (2 sentences). Sentences with two step transformations were yes/no questions with *do* (2), yes/no questions with passive constructions (2 full, 1 truncated), and a negative construction with *do*. Three step transformations comprised four *wh*-questions with *do* and two *wh*- questions with passive construction (1 full, 1 truncated). Of the sentences with compounds, two had compound subjects, two had compound verbs, and two had compound direct objects. Each of the two clause sentences consisted of one principal and one subordinate clause. Two of these clauses were nested, with deleted conjunctions; three were nonnested, with conjunctions; and one was nonnested, with the conjunction deleted. All of the sentences with compounds and with two clauses had verbs in the active voice.

The testing procedures followed that described earlier for the first Sentence Repetition Test. The test, which took about 25 minutes to administer, was

[4]Two practice sentences, given before the test, and two extra sentences (Nos. 15 and 21) within the test itself were not considered part of the design and were not included in the scoring and are therefore not shown here.

given at five age levels: 60, 63, 66, 69, and 72 months. Each test session was recorded on tape and scored by graduate students trained in linguistic analysis.

Scoring

A simplified form of the scoring system used in the first Sentence Repetition Test was applied to the present test. Each response was classified as Type 3, Type 2, or Type 1, according to the following scale:

Response Type	Description
3	Exact repetition
2	Inexact repetition; basic structure preserved
1	Inexact repetition; basic structure not preserved

In both categories of inexact repetition (Types 2 and 1), the errors may consist of omissions, additions, substitutions, transpositions, or combinations thereof. The difference lies in the extent to which these errors affect the structure of the stimulus sentence. In a Type 2 response, the errors do not result in any substantial alteration in the structure of the test sentence. There is therefore no positive indication of failure to understand the sentence. Recodings into a nonstandard dialect fall into this category; so do omissions of markers, such as those for the past tense and the third person singular, whether or not the rest of the sentence shows the influence of dialect. A Type 1 response, on the other hand, gives no indication that the sentence has been understood because the errors result in the extensive alteration or even in the destruction of the original structure.

Comparisons were made between the overall performances of the experimental and control groups in terms of percentages of total responses within each scoring category. Parallelism, group effects, and time effects were determined through Biomedical Computer Programs (BMDPs 11V profile analysis, 3D, and 2V). Also compared were the groups' responses to each of the complexity and length groupings. An additional within group analysis of performance on each of the complexity and length groups was also undertaken to determine what effect, if any, syntactic complexity and length had on the performance of each group. Use of these statistical programs required substitution of column means for missing observations and adjustment of the sample sizes to experimental = 17 and control = 18.

Table 6-7 summarizes the results of the repetition test according to sentence complexity. Table 6-8 presents the results according to sentence length. For ease in determining the proportions of the responses in the different categories, the mean scores have been converted into percentages.

Exact Repetition: Type 3 Responses

The performance trends of the two groups on this measure were found to be parallel. There was, however, a significant, $F(5, 29) = 5.37$, $p < .01$, overall

Table 6-7 Sentence Repetition Test II: Percentages of Responses in Each Category by Sentence Category

Age (Mos)	Response Category	Experimental							Control							Community Comparison Group						
		K	T_1	T_2	T_3	Cpd.	2C	X̄	K	T_1	T_2	T_3	Cpd.	2C	X̄	K	T_1	T_2	T_3	Cpd.	2C	X̄
60	3	55	50	45	54	37	22	44	28	28	28	23	15	11	22	68	55	55	65	55	48	58
	2	38	42	43	28	50	65	44	47	40	24	22	45	39	36	27	30	26	20	32	31	28
	1	7	8	13	18	13	14	12	24	32	47	56	40	50	42	5	15	19	14	13	21	15
	% Structures Preserved							80							50							75
63	3	57	49	56	55	38	21	46	28	29	25	23	23	12	23							
	2	39	44	33	33	51	66	44	54	45	39	29	53	51	45							
	1	4	6	12	13	11	14	10	19	26	36	49	24	37	32							
	% Structures Preserved							83							61							
66	3	64	47	56	57	39	21	47	28	24	35	33	27	17	27	69	58	57	64	49	36	56
	2	33	46	29	28	54	72	44	55	56	33	19	59	57	46	21	35	29	26	42	38	32
	1	3	7	15	15	7	7	9	17	21	32	49	14	26	26	10	7	14	10	10	26	13
	% Structures Preserved							85							67							75
69	3	66	64	75	71	45	31	59	40	36	36	40	30	26	35							
	2	29	32	19	25	51	63	36	48	49	30	25	50	49	42							
	1	5	4	6	4	4	6	5	12	15	34	35	20	25	24							
	% Structures Preserved							89							68							
72	3	66	58	56	69	43	31	54	45	40	52	40	26	22	38	54	63	57	60	48	38	53
	2	30	37	41	29	57	66	43	44	47	31	38	67	60	48	36	22	32	22	43	40	32
	1	4	5	3	2	0	3	3	10	12	17	22	7	18	14	10	15	12	18	8	22	14
	% Structures Preserved							94							80							72

Key to Response Categories: 3 = Exact repetition
2 = Sentence not repeated exactly but basic structure preserved

...gory by Sentence Length (Number of Words)

Age (Mos)	Response Category	Experimental				Control				Community Comparison Group			
		6 Words	7 Words	8 Words	X̄	6 Words	7 Words	8 Words	X̄	6 Words	7 Words	8 Words	X̄
60	3	57	44	31	44	32	23	13	22	64	58	51	58
	2	39	38	56	44	37	30	43	36	26	21	36	28
	1	5	18	14	12	32	48	45	42	10	22	14	15
% Structures Preserved					80				50				75
63	3	58	46	34	46	35	21	14	23				
	2	37	36	60	44	40	42	53	45				
	1	5	18	6	10	25	38	33	32				
% Structures Preserved					83				61				
66	3	62	50	31	47	32	34	17	27	62	50	55	56
	2	36	36	60	44	47	38	55	46	32	31	32	32
	1	3	15	9	9	22	29	29	26	6	20	13	13
% Structures Preserved					85				67				75
69	3	69	58	50	59	43	35	27	35				
	2	29	34	47	36	43	41	41	42				
	1	3	9	4	5	14	25	33	24				
% Structures Preserved					89				68				
72	3	63	59	40	54	50	35	29	38	65	46	49	53
	2	36	37	58	43	42	45	55	48	29	32	36	32
	1	2	5	2	3	8	20	16	14	6	22	15	14
% Structures Preserved					94				80				72

Key to Response Categories: 3 = Exact repetition
2 = Sentence not repeated exactly but basic structure preserved
1 = Sentence not repeated exactly; basic structure not preserved

difference in performance between the two groups in favor of the experimental group. Individual t-test comparisons showed significant ($p < .001$) differences in favor of the experimental group at each of the age levels tested. The children in each group improved their scores significantly, $F(8, 60) = 6.02$, $p < .01$, as they grew older. At no time, however, did the control group scores equal even the initial scores of the experimental group.

Deviation from parallelism was significant, $F(4, 30) = 3.22$, $p < .05$, by the two groups for the percentage of structures preserved. The experimental children preserved significantly (Hotelling $T^2 = 29.61$, $p = .002$) higher percentages of structures than did the control children. The difference between groups at every level was significant ($p < .002$) in favor of the experimental group. On the whole, the children preserved significantly, $F(8, 60) = 20.45$, $p < .01$, higher percentages of structures as they grew older. The experimental children, however, gained significantly, $F(4, 132) = 33.32$, $p < .001$, more on this measure over time than did the control children.

Inexact Repetition: Type 1 Responses

Of the responses that were classified as inexact repetitions, the first type, or Type 1, may be considered the poorest type of response because it contains errors that result in the destruction of the basic structure of the original sentence. Among the possible reasons behind responses of this type are lack of comprehension of the test sentence, unthinking imitation or parroting of the sounds in the sentence, or failure to remember what has been said. Group differences, determined through t tests, were significant ($p < .001$) on this measure at every age level tested in favor of the experimental group, who consistently made fewer responses in this category than did the control group. Although both groups made fewer Type 1 responses as they grew older, the control children at 72 months — the last age level tested — were still producing as many of these responses as the experimental children had at 60 months.

Inexact Repetition: Type 2 Responses

This category comprises inexact repetitions that did not alter the basic structure of the test sentences. The great majority of errors among responses in this category consisted of the omission of plural, third person singular, and past tense/past participle markers. Included in this category, therefore, are responses with errors attributable to the influence of black dialect, in which the use of such markers is optional. Other omissions were of the definite article and of the different forms of *be*.[5]

---

[5] In cases where the omission of *be* altered the sentence structure, as in passive structures, the responses were classified as Type 1. An example of this is the change from "I was laughed at this morning" (No. 10) to "I laughed at this morning."

PERCENTAGE OF TOTAL RESPONSES

Approximately equal percentages of the two groups' total responses were classified as Type 2 at each of the age levels tested. In no other category were such small differences observed between the two groups. The largest difference, 8 percentage points, was found at the 60-month level, at which the control group produced Type 2 responses amounting to 36% of total responses, as opposed to the experimental group's 44%. This is related to the large percentage of Type 1 responses in the control group at this age level. Differences at other age levels ranged from 1 to 6 percentage points.

PERCENTAGE OF IMPERFECT RESPONSES

Another means of expressing Type 2 responses is to show what percentage of the total number of imperfect repetitions they represent. This conversion was necessary in order to show the relationship between the two types of imperfect repetition and to have a measure that could be compared directly with the Structures Preserved measure used in the first Sentence Repetition Test.

Expressed as percentages of total inexact repetitions rather than of total responses, Type 2 responses ranged from 80% to 94% among the experimental children and from 50% to 80% among the control children. As was the case with Type 3 and Type 1 responses, there was a difference of 12 months — the entire length of the testing period — between the two groups on this measure.

Comparisons Within Groups: Sentence Complexity and Sentence Length

Figures 6-12 and 6-13 illustrate the relative difficulty of each complexity and length division for each group of children as measured by the number of percentage points each group scored above or below its own overall mean for a particular response category. Two response categories were used for this comparison: Type 3 (exact repetition) and Type 1 (inexact repetition; structure not preserved). The signs for Type 1 responses have been reversed; thus, for each type of response the farther above the zero line the score is marked, the better the performance of that group on the particular division as compared with its own overall mean in that response category. Each bar represents the average number of percentage points from the mean through the five age levels tested.

SENTENCE COMPLEXITY

As Figure 6-12 indicates, both groups encountered the same relative levels of difficulty of repetition among the different complexity divisions. Most difficult to repeat were sentences with two clauses (2C), followed by those with compounds (C). The other four divisions, consisting of kernel sentences and their successive transformations, were found by both groups to have approximately the same level of difficulty for exact repetitions, with one step transformations being slightly more difficult than the others.

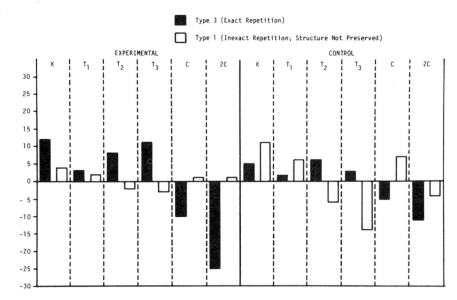

Figure 6-12.   Average Percentage Points from Group Means for Type 3 and Type 1 Responses According to Structural Complexity (Sentence Repetition Test II)

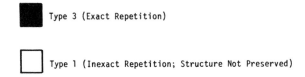

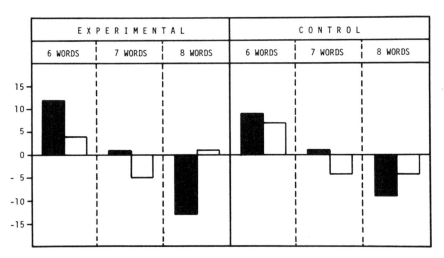

Figure 6-13.   Average Percentage Points from Group Means for Type 3 and Type 1 Responses According to Sentence Length (Sentence Repetition Test II)

Among Type 1 responses (inexact repetitions that do not preserve the basic structures of the test sentences), the pattern of distribution over the six sentence divisions was not as clear-cut as among exact repetitions. For each group, kernels tended to be easier to preserve as structures than any of the three transformations, and there seemed to be increasing levels of difficulty between successive transformational steps. These were trends not evident among exact repetitions.

Sentences with compounds also seemed to be easier to preserve than two clause sentences; however, the degree of difficulty presented by these two sentence types on this measure did not match that for exact repetition. As Figure 6-12 indicates, the most difficult structures to preserve were the two and three step transformations (two step transformations used combinations of either negative or question forms with either *do* or a passive verb form; three step transformations added *wh-* to these combinations). For the experimental children, there was no difference in degree of difficulty between sentences with compounds and two clause sentences.

SENTENCE LENGTH

In both groups, difficulty of repetition increased with length (Figure 6-13). Six word sentences were also found easier to preserve structurally than longer ones. This was not so, however, for seven and eight word sentences; in fact, the experimental children seemed to have more difficulty with seven word than with eight word sentences. An examination of the responses to individual sentences showed that the structure responsible for poor (Type 1) performance by both groups on seven word sentences was the verb form *have + -ed* (e.g., "He has painted most of the pictures"), which was used to generate the sentences in one of the seven word groups.

In general, however, the greatest differences in response patterns between the two groups were found mostly among sentences with combinations of questions or negatives with *do* or passive verb forms (T2) and among *wh-* sentences with these combinations. These sentences seemed especially difficult for the control children to comprehend, as may be deduced from their inability to repeat them in such a way as to retain their underlying structures.

Comparison with Other Children

For the purpose of obtaining some perspective on the experimental and control groups' performances, particularly in view of the influence of dialect observed in their responses, Sentence Repetition Test II was also administered to a group of children whose speech was presumably not subject to the same influence. These children, who were drawn from preschools in and around the Madison area, came from white families of undetermined socioeconomic levels. They were divided into the following groups:

61 months ($n = 14$, age range = 60–62 months, mean age = 61.07 months)
65 months ($n = 12$, age range = 63–68 months, mean age = 64.9 months)
71 months ($n = 10$, age range = 70–71 months, mean age = 70.5 months)

Each group was tested once. A white examiner, following the procedures used for testing the experimental and control children, administered the test. Results from these tests were compared with those from the nearest age levels (60, 66, and 72 months) of the experimental and control groups.

The number of Type 3 responses (exact repetitions) did not differ to a significant degree between the experimental and the white groups at any of the age levels compared. Like the experimental group, the white children had significantly ($p < .05$) greater percentages of exact repetitions than the control children at all age levels compared.

As expected, there were considerably fewer Type 2 responses among the white children than among either the experimental or the control children because errors in this type of response were generally attributable to dialect influence. At 60 months, for example, the white children's Type 2 responses made up only 28% of their total responses, versus 44% and 36% among the experimental and control children, respectively. At 66 and 72 months they had 32%, whereas the experimental children had 44% and 43% and the control group had 46% and 48%.

These Type 2 responses, however, represented approximately the same percentages of the total imperfect repetitions of the experimental and white groups at 60 and 66 months; and at 72 months, the experimental group's converted percentage was significantly ($p < .001$) higher than the white group's. This indicates that at this age level, there were more errors of the type that altered or destroyed the original structures among the white than among the experimental children. Also, as mentioned earlier, the experimental chidren had significantly ($p < .002$) higher percentages than the control children at every age level, while the white children's scores were significantly ($p < .01$) higher than the control children's only at 60 months. Their scores on this measure were comparable at the two other age levels tested.

These differences between the actual number of Type 2 responses and the percentage of imperfect repetitions they represent are attributable in part to the relatively large number of Type 1 responses from the white group at the three age levels (15%, 13%, and 14%) at 60, 66, and 71 months as compared with the experimental group's 12%, 9%, and 3%. The control group started out with a much higher percentage of Type 1 responses (42%), but at 72 months had the same percentage as the white group.

Despite the influence of black dialect on the Milwaukee children's test performance, therefore, the experimental children performed at the same level as did a contrast group of white children and, indeed, even outperformed them on at least one measure at one age level. The control children, on the other hand, performed on a level comparable with the white group on one measure at two age levels, but in general fared poorly in comparison with both their experimental counterparts and the white children.

The two sentence repetition tests seem to have been effective as instruments for comparing language development in two groups of children during the 4th, 5th, and 6th years of life. In a series of measures designed to provide checks on one another, the trends that have emerged follow a pattern that consistently differentiates between the performances of the two groups. Emphasizing this difference is the finding that the experimental children did at least as well on this test as children who came from other and apparently much less disadvantaged families.

TESTS OF MORPHOLOGY:
THE PICTURE MORPHOLOGY TEST AND
THE BERKO TEST OF MORPHOLOGY

The Picture Morphology Test was first given when the children reached the age of 36 to 39 months. This test, which was developed by our laboratory, was designed to elicit the production of inflectional morphemes through stimulus questions accompanied by illustrations of familiar objects. It was one of two tests administered for the purpose of measuring the development of the children's acquisition of the rules for generating inflectional morphemes.

The other test was the Berko Test of Morphology (Berko, 1958), which was first administered when the children were 48 to 51 months old. Berko's test used nonsense syllables that conformed to the rules for sound combinations in standard English in order to ensure that the child had internalized morphological rules, was able to generalize those rules to a new situation, and had not memorized an inflected form (e.g., *glass: glasses*) as a lexical item. Berko concluded that children do not treat words idiosyncratically, but rather in accordance with general morphological rules.

Other studies of the acquisition of inflectional morphology (Anisfield & Tucker, 1967; Bellamy & Bellamy, 1969; Graves & Koziol, 1971; Newfield & Schlanger, 1968; Solomon, 1972) that have used Berko type tests confirmed Berko's earlier findings that the pattern of acquisition is one of regularity and simplicity. Using a Berko type test, Natalicio and Natalicio (1971) found that for Spanish speaking children learning English as a second language, the pattern of acquisition of inflectional morphology was comparable to the pattern of acquisition for native speakers.

Both Berko (1958) and Miller and Ervin (1964) have noted that real words are easier for children to inflect than nonsense syllables. Two plausible explanations offered are that the child has stored some of the real words plus their terminal morphemes in memory as single lexical items and that when given a nonsense word the child must assimilate the unfamiliar item and then add the proper inflection. Our Picture Morphology Test (hereafter referred to as *PM*), which uses real words, was developed and administered to eliminate the confusion that may be caused by the use of nonsense words (see Dever & Gardner, 1970). By first giving this test and later the Berko, we could compare the results of the two tests.

The primary objective of this phase of our language assessment was to compare the development and acquisition of the inflectional allomorphs of standard English between the two groups of children in the Milwaukee Project and to determine how the intervention program affected that development and acquisition. Because our subjects were speakers of a nonstandard dialect that often deletes the majority of the morphemes tested, we suspected that their morphological production would not be the same as that of speakers of standard English. A comparison of the influence of dialect on the performance of the two groups was therefore included in our study.

The PM was first administered at the 36-month age level to each child and then at 6-month intervals thereafter. The Berko test was first administered at 48 months. Thereafter, the tests were given alternately, with each child receiving either a Berko or a PM at 3-month intervals. Beginning at 66 months, revised versions of the PM and Berko were administered alternately at 3-month intervals. Testing was discontinued near the end of the children's first year in public school, when each child had received at least two revised PMs and two revised Berkos.

Both tests were administered following Berko's original (1958) suggestions. In the Picture Morphology Test, the child was presented with colored pictures of animals and people; in the Berko, colored, cartoon-like figures of animals or people performing various actions were used. The PM tester followed the paradigm: "Here is a doll. Now we can see two _____." The paradigm for the Berko test was, "Here is a wug. Say 'wug.' Now there is another one. There are two of them. There are two _____." The subject was asked to repeat the nonsense word to ensure that he or she had perceived its phonemic components correctly; if the subject responded incorrectly, he/she was corrected and asked to repeat the stimulus words. The subject was not asked to repeat the stimulus items for the PM because it was assumed that real words would not cause perceptual confusion.

The Berko test consisted of 38 items and examined the same features as did Berko's original morphology test. The test explored a wide range of inflectional allomorphs: noun plurals, possessives (both singular and plural), the third person singular of the verb, the progressive form, the past tense, the comparative and superlative, the derived adjective agentive, and the diminutive and compound. Test items were added to elicit the /-s/ and /-z/ allomorphs of the third person singular present of the verb, the unmarked (third person plural) form of the verb, and irregular noun plurals. The PM was composed of 19 test items and was designed to elicit fewer inflectional allomorphs than the Berko test.

Two factors were considered in revising the Berko test. First, we wanted to simplify the test overall. This included eliminating ambiguous items such as diminutives and compounds for which there could be more than one correct response and the possessive plural where it was impossible to tell whether a response was a correct application of a morphological rule or simply a repetition of the stimulus item. The real word items were also eliminated because the PM had been specifically designed to test inflections of real words. Thus, the revised version of the Berko contained only nonsense words. Our second objective was to expand the range of morphological tasks provided by the test. This was accomplished by the addition of items involving back formation (producing an uninflected form when given an inflected form) and by using varied stimulus forms to elicit a given morpheme (such as producing the third person singular form when given either the progressive [-ing] form or the past tense).

The PM was revised to produce an item-by-item correspondence with the revised Berko, thus facilitating comparison of the two tests. It was felt, however, that some irregular forms should be retained as test items; therefore, we included in the revised PM four irregular forms in addition to the 42 items that were matched with those on the revised Berko.

All of the tests were administered and recorded by the Project's language examiner. The original PM and Berko took approximately 3 to 5 and 10 to 15 minutes, respectively, to administer; the revised PM and Berko each took between 15 and 20 minutes. All tests were transcribed and scored in the language laboratory by trained language researchers. A small number of test items (5% for the first two age periods, less than 1% thereafter) could not be scored because of recording difficulties or other technical problems. These items were not included in the analysis.

Four categories of response were established:

A = Expected morpheme
B = No morpheme
C = Overgeneralization
D = Irrelevancies and silence

It was decided to establish the above categories in order to determine and account for the influence of dialect factors (such as omission of the plural marker) as well as the pattern of overgeneralization of morphological rules that has been observed in young children (McNeill, 1970; Slobin, 1971).

Statistical tests for parallelism, group effects, and time effects, using the measure of percentage of expected morphemes, were conducted through the use of BMDPs. This required the substitution of column means for all missing observation points and adjustment of sample sizes to experimental = 17 and control = 18. The comparison data for the experimental and control groups on the PM and the Berko are presented in Table 6-9.

Picture Morphology Test

Parallel trends were found in the two groups on the measure tested (percentage of expected morphemes). Between groups there was a significant (Hotelling $T^2 = 48.33$, $p = .000$) difference in favor of the experimental group. Individual t tests showed that the experimental children had significantly ($p < .011$) higher scores than the control children at every age level tested. The children in both groups showed significant, $F(12, 56) = 15.63$, $p < .01$, improvement in their scores as they grew older. However, the control group's scores lagged behind the experimental group's by approximately a year.

Table 6-9 Mean Percentages of Responses in Four Categories of the Picture Morphology and Berko Morphology Tests

Picture Morphology

Age (Mos)	(A) Expected Morpheme		(B) No Morpheme		(C) Over-generalization		(D) Irrelevant Responses & Silence	
	E	C	E	C	E	C	E	C
Original Version								
36	28	12	54	44	4	1	13	43
42	34	21	56	49	5	5	5	20
48	37	24	50	55	6	4	6	16
54	43	28	49	56	6	7	2	9
60	46	29	48	61	5	5	1	6
Revised Version								
66	53	44	40	49	3	6	2	3
72	60	49	32	44	6	4	1	2

Berko Morphology

Age (Mos)	(A) Expected Morphemes		(B) No Morpheme		(C) Over-generalization		(D) Irrelevant Responses & Silence	
	E	C	E	C	E	C	E	C
Original Version								
51	21	17	71	57	1	1	6	24
57	26	17	66	56	1	1	3	15
63	27	19	70	69	1	2	1	10
Revised Version								
69	29	18	71	72	2	2	1	5
75	37	20	60	74	3	1	2	2
81	38	20	58	78	2	1	0	1

Berko Test of Morphology

As with the Picture Morphology Test, the overall difference between the two groups was significant (Hotelling T^2 = 50.95, p = .000) in favor of the experimental children. Individual t tests indicated comparable scores between the groups at 51 months and significant ($p < .037$) differences at each age level tested thereafter. The groups' performance trends deviated significantly, $F(5, 29)$ = 2.68, $p < .05$, from parallel. The overall time effect was significant, $F(10, 58)$ = 3.40, $p < .01$, as was the time x group interaction, $F(5, 165)$ = 4.04, $p < .002$. The control group's scores trailed behind those of the experimental group by at least 24 months.

Both groups did better on the PM than on the Berko. These results agree with those of other investigators (Berko, 1958; Brown, 1973; Miller & Ervin, 1964) who have found that children inflect real words sooner and more easily than nonsense syllables.

Part of our analysis consisted of an estimate of the order of acquisition for six morphemes on the PM (present progressive, possessive, plural, third person singular, regular past, and irregular past) and a comparison with the results obtained by Brown (1973). We also compared the two groups' performances on individual allomorphs of four morphemes (noun plural, possessive, third person singular, and irregular past) with those recorded in other studies (e.g., Anisfield & Tucker, 1967; Berko, 1958; Brown, 1973; Bryant & Anisfield, 1969). In addition, we analyzed our data on these same allomorphs on the basis of the final sounds of their stems, as suggested by Solomon (1972) and Brown (1973). Briefly stated, the three morphemes that were acquired earliest by both groups were the present progressive, possessive, and plural morphemes; the allomorphs found most difficult were the /id/ (past) allomorphs (see Table 6-10).

It was observed that certain stimulus forms, notably those ending with /iz/ or /id/ allomorphs, seemed to affect performance adversely on most item types. The one type of item not affected by these particular stimulus forms was back formation. On PM II (revised PM), both the experimental and control groups obtained uniformly high results on all items involving back formation, often scoring 100% correct on an item. Results on Berko II were also better than average. This indicates that the task of back formation is much easier than the other morphological tasks on the two tests and possibly that different psycholinguistic processes are involved. In the case of the PM, it is possible that back formation involves little more than recognition of a stem learned as a lexical item. The Berko results are more difficult to interpret. It would seem in this case, that mere recognition of the given morpheme is sufficient for correct performance as opposed to the ability to supply it where it is needed.

The majority of non-A responses fell into category B (no morphemes). According to the rules of black dialect, certain morphemes are optional; thus, to omit them is also correct. For instance, the absence of the plural morpheme and of -s verbal concord are both accepted in black dialect (Fasold, 1972).

Table 6-10 Order of Acquisition of Selected Features on the Picture Morphology Test

Tests	Age (Mos)	Experimental Group						Control Group					
		1 Progressive	2 Possessive	3 Plural	4 3rd Person Regular	5 Past Regular	6 Past Irregular	1 Progressive	2 Possessive	3 Plural	4 3rd Person Regular	5 Past Regular	6 Past Irregular
Original Version	39	66.7	38.9	37.5	5.6	0.0	—	60.0	3.3	7.3	—	0.0	0.0
	45	82.4	29.4	40.7	21.9	20.6	—	77.8	20.8	22.3	—	8.7	11.1
	51	88.2	29.4	50.5	29.4	18.8	—	83.3	22.9	33.7	—	11.1	11.4
	57	100.0	34.4	42.5	21.9	56.3	—	86.7	40.0	26.7	—	17.1	16.7
	63	94.1	50.0	40.0	38.2	38.2	—	77.8	25.0	24.4	—	20.0	19.4
		(1)	(2)	(5)	(2)	(2)	(0)	(1)	(2)	(5)	(0)	(2)	(2)
Revised Version	69	91.2	58.8	30.0	19.6	19.6	15.6	71.9	59.4	28.1	31.3	16.6	10.4
	75	97.1	76.5	51.5	31.6	31.6	20.6	86.7	70.0	41.0	33.3	23.3	17.8
		(2)	(2)	(4)	(6)	(6)	(2)	(2)	(2)	(4)	(2)	(6)	(3)

Note: Mean percentage of correct responses for each group at each age period on the Picture Morphology Test. The numbers in parentheses indicate the number of items that tested a particular morpheme.

Speakers of black English do use standard English plural allomorphs, but the use of plurals is not constrained, as it is for speakers of standard English. In other words, the speaker of standard English has no options outside the three plural allomorphs and irregular plural formations; not to mark the plural is considered incorrect. The speaker of black English, however, has the additional option of not marking the plural and still being correct within the context of that linguistic system. Many linguists who have studied black dialect (e.g., Dillard, 1972; Fasold, 1972; Labov, 1972) agree that there is a system of pluralization conforming to the standard English system and differing only in terms of the option to mark or not to mark the plural. The large percentage of "no morpheme" responses supports this view. Also, among standard English speakers age is a crucial variable in the development of morphemic production. Because of this optional rule in black dialect, however, production does not always increase consistently with age (for example, note the experimental group's performance on plurals in Table 6-10).

There is clearer evidence of morphological development from results on other test items. The overgeneralization of morphemic inflections to irregular items such as the past tense forms of *ring* and *run* indicates that the children not only have some concept that such endings change the meaning of a word, but also that they are able to use these endings productively. The experimental children tended to overgeneralize more often than did the control children on the irregular items of PM II; in many cases overgeneralizations occurred more frequently than B (no morphemes) responses.

Another index of the comparative range of the two groups' linguistic abilities might be their performance on those items that are not affected by dialect usage, such as adjective inflections (including the comparative and superlative), the progressive (-*ing*), and the agentive (-*er*) endings. These items comprised 21% and 32% of the unrevised PM and Berko, respectively, and 17% and 19% of the revised versions. We compared the two groups' scores on these items alone and on the remainder of the test, on the premise that differences in test performance caused mainly by a stronger influence of black dialect on one of the groups would show up as differences in the scores on dialect sensitive features alone. In other words, there would be little or no difference between the two groups' scores on the items not affected by dialect usage. We found this to be true, but only for the first three age levels on PM I and only for the first age level of Berko I. Moreover, as Figures 6-14 and 6-15 show, differences on the items not sensitive to dialect increased progressively after the first level on both tests. From 57 months onward, the experimental children had significantly (PM I, $p < .02$; PM II, $p < .01$; Berko I, $p < .01$; Berko II, $p < .05$) higher scores than the control children had on these items. The experimental children's scores on dialect sensitive items were also significantly higher than were the control children's at all age levels on PM I ($p < .02$) and Berko II ($p < .01$) and at the 75-month level of PM II.

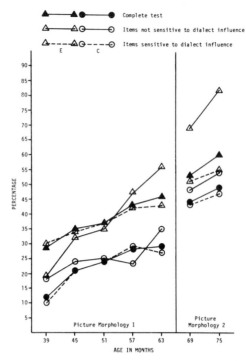

Figure 6-14.   Analysis of Correct Responses for Dialect Influence (Picture Morphology Test)

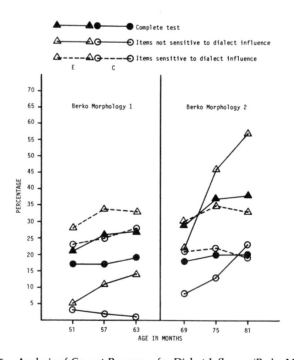

Figure 6-15.   Analysis of Correct Responses for Dialect Influence (Berko Morphology Test)

We interpreted these findings as suggesting that the experimental children's advantage over the control children on PM I may have been primarily attributable at first to a greater proficiency in standard English acquired before the test was first administered as a result of their preschool experience. Their continued advantage from age 57 months through all subsequent testings (including PM II and Berko II), however, seems to reflect a more advanced state of morphological development because differences were no longer limited to dialect sensitive items but extended to the other items as well. These latter items, furthermore, included features (e.g., adjective endings, including comparative and superlative) not expected to be acquired by children until later in their development (Donaldson & Wales, 1970). This, and not proficiency in standard English alone, may be the cause that underlies the early absence of significant differences between the two groups on these items. By the age of 57 months, however, it was clear that the experimental children's grasp of these features exceeded that of the control children to a significant degree.

Despite their generally higher scores on dialect sensitive items, the experimental children, like the control children, are speakers of black dialect. On Berko I, in fact, the experimental group had significantly ($p < .01$) higher scores than the control group had on items not affected by dialect (but not on dialect sensitive items). The same was true for the first testing (69 months) of PM II. These findings underscore the fact that the patterns of dialect usage are factors that must be considered when comparing the performance of experimental and control children with that of white middle class children on tests of standard English. It is not surprising, then, that not even the experimental group performed with the proficiency of standard English speakers (see Anisfield & Tucker, 1967; Berko, 1958) on testing instruments designed to elicit standard English inflectional allomorphs. Indeed, it would be unreasonable to conclude that these children are linguistically deficient on the basis of such a comparison.

It is unfortunate that existing tests of English morphology should, by their nature, lean so heavily toward the use of standard English inflections. Despite the limitations imposed by their dialect patterns, however, the experimental children demonstrated a superior degree of mastery of the rules for producing inflectional morphemes in comparison with their counterparts in the control group. Their level of performance was consistently higher and their progress greater and more steady on the complete test as well as on that portion of the test not subject to dialect influence. It seems safe to conclude, as on the repetition tests, that the factors underlying these differences are developmental and have more to do with a group of grammatical concepts than with patterns of dialect.

THE ILLINOIS TEST OF PSYCHOLINGUISTIC ABILITIES

The Illinois Test of Psycholinguistic Abilities (Kirk, McCarthy, & Kirk, 1968) was used to measure the linguistic abilities of the children in the program. Because the subtests of the ITPA provide a variety of language tasks, both verbal and nonverbal, the findings on individual subtests could be compared with those on other language tests used in the program.

The ITPA attempts to evaluate a child's encoding and decoding abilities by measuring linguistic behavior in terms of level or organization, psycholinguistic process, and channel of communication. The levels of organization are the representational and automatic. The former subsumes those processes that require a high degree of voluntary activity, while the latter includes the more habitual and mechanized processes of arranging and reproducing linguistic phenomena. There are three processes: the receptive (the ability to recognize and understand phenomena), the expressive (the ability to express concepts synthesized from that understanding), and the organizational (the ability to manipulate these concepts internally). Although it is theoretically possible to postulate many channels of communication, the ITPA restricts its observation to the auditory-vocal and visual-motor channels. The instrument is designed so that each subtest measures one process through one channel at one level of organization.

The ITPA was originally developed to assess linguistic abilities in children who were mentally retarded or had general learning disabilities. As Carroll (1972) observed in his review, however, the widest use of the ITPA has been the assessment of language development in lower class children from minority groups. One reason for this is that the ITPA is the only standardized measure intended to assess specific and different language abilities as opposed to a global verbal IQ. Because many preschool programs for the disadvantaged have focused on the development of language skills, the ITPA has been the logical choice. Despite its widespread use, however, the ITPA has been criticized on the grounds that the test as a whole may not have a marked correlation with the developmental skills basic to language usage and reading and that its subtests do not take into account the fact that responses may vary according to the subject's use of standard or nonstandard English. The first criticism is supported by a number of factor analytic studies that, however, fail to make sufficient use of other reference tests.

Nonetheless, studies of the construct validity of the ITPA (Hare, Hammill, & Bartel, 1973) have indicated that at least some of the subtests do identify separate psycholinguistic traits. In the study by Hare et al., six ITPA subtests were factor analyzed with parallel tasks equivalent to the subtests in all but one dimension of the theoretical model. The ITPA subtests loaded significantly on only one factor and were identifiable in terms of the theoretical model on level, process, and channel.

The hypothesis that the ITPA is weighted to favor speakers of standard English has been tested by Whitcraft (1971). On each of the ITPA subtests, Whitcraft compared the performance of subjects who spoke standard English with that of speakers of nonstandard English, notwithstanding the fact that both groups were of normal intelligence. Whitcraft's findings suggest that speakers of nonstandard English do poorly on the ITPA not because they are deficient in the linguistic abilities being tested but because they find it difficult to encode and decode in a dialect peripheral to their own.

In the ITPA's normative sample, the percentage of potential speakers of nonstandard English was small. Paraskevopoulos and Kirk (1969) reported that subjects for the normative group were chosen from average school classrooms. The communities included Bloomington, Danville, Decatur, and Urbana in Illinois, and Madison, Wisconsin. For these communities, the percentage of blacks and other speakers of nonstandard dialects is low, as compared with that for large cities where varieties of nonstandard English are spoken. Forty-two black children were included in the sample; however, because the standardization sample was drawn from middle range schools, none of which had black enrollments over 10%, these black subjects were more likely to be familiar with the standard English used by their peers in school than would subjects from predominantly black schools. This virtual exclusion of nonstandard dialect speakers from the normative sample may result in a weakness in the ITPA's evaluative power when it is used with subjects who speak nonstandard English.

We administered the ITPA to all of the children in the experimental and control groups. The test was administered to each child at about 4.5 years of age and again at about 6.5 years, when the children had been in the first grade for about 6 months. This retesting was decided upon as a result of the wide differences in performance between the two groups at 4.5 years and to see if the differences would remain constant once the children had entered public school and were exposed to standard English in public school.

We have used the ITPA, then, to provide a standardized measure of the effectiveness of an early educational intervention program on psycholinguistic development and to extend the test sample to speakers of nonstandard English.

Each subject took the ten major subtests of the ITPA described as follows:

1. *Auditory Reception* (AR: Representational-Reception-Auditory). This test measures the child's ability to determine the meaning of verbally presented material. The child responds with a "yes" or a "no" or even a shake or nod of the head to questions ranging from "Do dogs eat?" to "Do wingless birds soar?"

2. *Visual Reception* (VR: Representational-Reception-Visual). This test measures the child's ability to understand visually presented material. The child is shown a single stimulus picture and then is asked to select from among four response pictures the item closest in structural similarity to the item in the stimulus picture.

3. *Auditory-Vocal Association* (AVA: Representational-Association-Auditory). This test evaluates the child's ability to see relationships among concepts presented orally through a series of incomplete analogies such as "A dog has hair; a fish has _____."

4. *Visual-Motor Association* (VMA: Representational-Association-Visual). This test measures the child's ability to relate concepts visually presented to him/her. The child is shown a stimulus picture or, at

the test's upper level, two related stimulus pictures and is asked to find the one of four optional objects or relationships most closely related to the first. Examples include: hammer related to nail, circle and oval related to square and rectangle.

5. *Verbal Expression* (VE: Representational-Expression-Verbal). On this test, the child's ability to express his/her own concepts orally is measured. He/she is given several familiar objects (ball, envelope) and asked to "Tell me all about this." Scoring is based on the number of discrete, relevant, and approximately factual concepts the subject mentions.

6. *Manual Expression* (ME: Representational-Expression-Manual). This subtest gauges the ability to express concepts manually. The child is shown several pictures of common objects (coffee cup, telephone) and is asked to pantomime the action usually associated with the object.

7. *Grammatic Closure* (GC: Automatic-Closure-Grammatic). This tests the child's ability to handle the syntax and morphology of standard English. The child must complete statements like "Here is a dog; here are two _____." "The boy had two bananas. He gave one away; and he kept one for _____."

8. *Visual Closure* (VC: Automatic-Closure-Visual). This subtest evaluates the child's ability to discover partially concealed objects (e.g., dogs hidden in garbage cans and behind fences).

9. *Auditory Sequential Memory* (ASM: Automatic-Sequential Memory-Auditory). This tests the child's ability to reproduce a sequence of orally presented numbers.

10. *Visual Sequential Memory* (VSM: Automatic-Sequential Memory-Visual). This tests the child's ability to reproduce from memory a series of meaningful geometric figures presented on plastic chips.

The tests for Sound Blending and Auditory Closure are considered supplementary to the ITPA and were not administered as part of this project. The procedure for administration was followed exactly as given in the Examiner's Manual (Kirk, McCarthy, & Kirk, 1968). The same examiner administered the test to all subjects at both testing sessions.

For both the experimental and control groups, the following data were calculated:

1. *Mean Scaled Score* (MSS). Scaled scores for individuals are derived according to the tables in the Examiner's Manual by adjusting the raw scores of each of the subtests to eliminate age as a factor. The MSS for group data was derived by averaging the mean scaled scores of all subjects in a particular group.

2. *Psycholinguistic Age* (PLA). The individual PLA represents the level of overall linguistic skill attained by the child. Comparing PLA with the CA shows whether the child is above or below average. The group PLA was derived by averaging the individual PLAs for all members of the group.

3. *Psycholinguistic Quotient* (PLQ). The individual PLQ is derived by dividing the PLA by the CA and multiplying the results by 100. In terms of linguistic ability, the PLQ is comparable to an IQ. The PLQ for a group was derived by averaging the PLQs of the individuals within the group.

For each of the two testings, the two groups' performances were compared with the aid of BMDP 3D *t* test and T² statistic. A paired *t* test was used to compare the results of the two testings for each group. There were no missing observation points for this data set, but one control subject was not tested. Therefore, the analysis was completed with adjusted sample sizes of experimental = 17 and control = 17.

Table 6-11 presents the mean scores for the two groups on the two testings of the ITPA. In terms of PLA, the experimental group was 1 year and 4 months ahead of the control group on the first testing (ITPA 1) and 1 year and 2 months ahead on the second (ITPA 2). Overall comparisons on this measured showed a significant (Hotelling $T^2 = 86.02$, $p < .000$) difference in favor of the experimental group. Separate *t* tests also showed the experimental children significantly ($p < .000$) ahead of the control group on each of the two testings. On ITPA 1, the experimental children's PLA was 9 months ahead of their mean CA. In contrast, the mean PLA for the control group was 8 months behind their own CA on ITPA 1 and 9 months behind it on ITPA 2.

The experimental children had a mean PLQ of 114.02 on ITPA 1, 29 points above the control group's mean PLQ. On ITPA 2, the experimental group mean PLQ was 107.76, which was 20 points higher than the control group mean. Again, overall comparison showed a significant (Hotelling $T^2 = 89.06$, $p < .000$) difference, as did separate *t* tests ($p < .000$).

On each of the ten major subtests given, Hotelling T^2 comparisons showed a significant ($p < .000$) overall difference in favor of the experimental group. On the first testing the experimental children's mean scaled scores were significantly ($p < .000$) higher than the control group's on all subtests. These results held true for the second testing, with slightly smaller but also significant differences on the VC ($p < .001$), VSM ($p < .028$), and ASM ($p < .053$) subtests.

Both groups had generally lower scores on the second testing than on the first and performance levels decreased for both groups on approximately half of the subtests. Both groups had significantly ($p < .01$) lower scores on the VR and AR subtests, as well as on the VE and GC subtests (E, $p < .001$; C, $p < .05$) for the second testing. In addition, the score for the VC subtest, the total mean scaled score, and the mean PLQ decreased significantly ($p < .001$) for the experimental group. The one subtest on which the two groups showed significant ($p < .001$) improvement was the VSM. It should be noted, however, that the normative sample scored 36 for each subtest, with a standard deviation of 6.

Despite the marked drop in their scores, the experimental group still performed within the average range for each subtest on ITPA 2. The mean scores

Table 6-11 ITPA: Mean Scaled Scores, Psycholinguistic Ages (PLA), and Psycholinguistic Quotients (PLQ)

Group		Mean Age (Mos)	Subtests										Total MSS	PLA (Mos)	PLQ
			AR	VR	AVA	VA	VE	ME	GC	VC	ASM	VSM			
1	E	54	37.06	46.06	40.65	41.00	42.41	43.47	41.94	43.77	40.53	40.12	41.70	63.00	114.02
	C	54	29.06	37.88	29.53	31.88	34.71	38.59	29.06	31.88	33.12	29.71	32.54	46.47	84.75
2	E	76	37.18	40.24	36.41	38.94	37.12	42.94	32.77	37.59	38.88	42.47	38.45	82.29	107.76
	C	77	29.18	34.65	25.88	30.47	31.24	39.00	25.59	30.24	34.00	37.29	31.75	67.59	87.34

for the control group, on the other hand, fell below average on the AVA, AR, and GC subtests. Moreover, as pointed out earlier, the experimental group's performance remained significantly superior to the control group's across all of the subtests, even on this second testing.

In their extensive review of the ITPA literature, Sedlack and Weener (1973) observed that the AVA, GC, and AR subtests correlate most strongly with general mental ability and yield the highest predictive coefficients for academic achievement. In fact, they concluded that the combination of AVA and GC subtest scores is a better predictor of most academic criteria than any other combination of scores, perhaps even better than the total ITPA score. Sedlack and Weener also noted that the three subtests mentioned above distinguish more consistently than other subtests between good and poor readers, social classes, and white and nonwhite racial groups. As Figure 6-16 shows, it is on these three key subtests that the control children's score fell more than 1 standard deviation below the norm.

Severson and Guest (1970) reported several studies that indicate that disadvantaged black children show depressed scores on measures of the auditory channel on the ITPA except for the ASM subtest, on which they show unusually high scores. These observations are supported in a study by Cicirelli, Evans, and Schiller (1970), who examined ITPA performance patterns among Head Start pupils from several ethnic groups. In the present study, the scores of the control group on the auditory channel subtests were indeed among their lowest, especially on the second testing, when their scores on these subtests fell below the normal range (Figure 6-16). The scores of the experimental group on these subtests, although within the normal range, also tended to be among their lowest, especially on the second testing. However, neither group showed the exceptionally high scores on the ASM subtest that other researchers have reported (see Severson & Guest, 1970).

Some parallels may be noted between the results of the present study and those of Whitcraft (1971). For example, her first grade subjects who spoke standard English (SE) had a mean scaled score 6.7 points higher than those who spoke nonstandard English (NSE). This was the same margin of difference between the mean scaled scores of our experimental and control subjects on the second ITPA testing, given when the children were in the first grade. Also, the largest differences in scaled scores between the experimental and control groups were generally found on the same subtests on which Whitcraft's SE and NSE groups differed most. These subtests included AR, AVA, VMA, and GC. The smallest difference between Whitcraft's two language groups, as well as between our experimental and control groups, was on ME. These similarities may suggest that the main advantage of the experimental over the control group lies in the experimental children's greater proficiency in SE. The patterns of performance exhibited by the experimental group did not seem to resemble that of Whitcraft's speakers of SE; rather, it followed that of the NSE speakers. The main differences were the experimental group's higher scores on the AR,

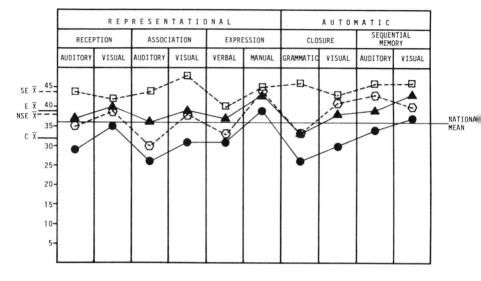

Figure 6-16.   Comparison of Mean Scaled Scores from ITPA 2 with Results from Whitcraft (1971)

AVA, and VE subtests. Figure 6-16 shows that, despite their lower scores on all subtests, the control children's performance pattern is quite similar to those of the experimental group and of Whitcraft's NSE group.

The single characteristic that differentiates the experimental group's performance patterns from those of the two other groups is that, with the exception of the GC subtest, all of the mean subtest scores of the experimental children are above the national average of 36. Their mean GC score is, however, still within the normal range. Among Whitcraft's NSE subjects, four subtest scores (AR, AVA, VE, and GC) are below the national mean but are still within the normal range. The control children, on the other hand, scored below the national mean on all but two subtests (ME and VSM). Of these scores, those for three subtests (AR, AVA, and GC) are below the normal range. It seems, then, that while the scores of all three groups—our two groups and Whitcraft's NSE—were adversely affected by the dialect they spoke, the fact that the control children performed at a level much lower than did the two other groups suggests a lower level of general language development not attributable to dialect usage alone.

Because of the problem of sampling for standardization, it is difficult to draw conclusions from the performance of disadvantaged speakers of NSE particularly on subtests involving the auditory-vocal channel. Low performance levels by these subjects in this area do not necessarily indicate cognitive or linguistic deficiencies because they could have resulted from an unfamiliarity with the vocabulary and syntax of SE. Dillard (1972), for instance, pointed out the inevitable variance in the production of SE inflectional allomorphs among speakers of black dialect. The GC subtest, which tests the child's ability to handle the syntax and morphology of SE is obviously the subtest most sensitive to differences in surface structure between SE and NSE. It is precisely on this subtest that both experimental and control groups scored their lowest during the second testing (ITPA 2). The substantial drop in the experimental children's scores on this subtest from the first to the second testing could be attributed in part to the influence of their peers in public school on their own language patterns (Labov, 1972; Natalicio & Natalicio, 1971).

Although the ITPA has been criticized for its accuracy in assessing the cognitive and linguistic abilities of NSE speakers, we hoped it could provide an estimate of the children's development to compare with the developmental norms of speakers of SE. It is clear from the data that the intervention program, which placed considerable emphasis on verbal expressive behavior, enabled the experimental children to perform as well as average middle class children on all subtests. Had the ITPA been standardized to include speakers of NSE, both groups might have obtained better scores. We do not believe, however, that the gap between the experimental and control groups would have diminished significantly.

OVERVIEW

From the age of 18 months until after they had entered the public school system, the children in both experimental and control groups were tested periodically on specific aspects of their language development. Evaluation began with quantitative measures of spontaneous language production and progressed to tests of receptive and expressive language, exemplified respectively by the Grammatical Comprehension and Sentence Repetition tests. Later tests consisted of elicited production of inflectional morphemes to test the children's internalization of the rules governing English morphology. Through regular replication of these tests, it was possible to compare not only the two groups' performance levels at any given age but also their progress in acquiring the structures that the different tests covered.

Whenever possible, comparisons were made between our subjects in both groups and children of approximately the same age from other environments. Despite the difficulties arising from the nature of our testing program — particularly the multiple retestings of our subjects — these comparisons provided a broader context in which to view the results of our own experimental testing. Our objective was to determine, however approximately, the standings of both the experimental and control groups with respect to the general population. Furthermore, because both groups of subjects were speakers of NSE, we were interested in finding out how we could "factor out" the influence of dialect on their performance. In this way we could determine whether the differences between the two groups could be attributed to greater language competence or simply to dialect patterns. For some of our tests, therefore, we developed measures that would not penalize the subjects for using constructions that could be identified with black dialect.

The impact of the intervention program on the language development of the experimental children can best be demonstrated by the data summarized in Table 6-12.

Diagonal lines have been drawn to underscore the consistency with which the two groups performed, relative to each other, on all the tests. As the summary table illustrates, it took the control children from 1 to 2 years to match the scores obtained by the experimental children. Differences tended to be greatest on the Grammatical Comprehension Test and smallest on the first version of the Berko.

The extent to which some of the experimental measures maintained their sensitivity to language growth was limited by the children's increasing age. Quantitative measures of spontaneous language production, in particular, seemed to decrease in sensititity as the children grew older. For example, after the age of 39 months, the two groups no longer showed consistent differences in mean number of utterances; and after reaching a plateau—roughly from 45 through 54 months for each group—scores tended to taper off, indicating that there no longer was any positive relationship between age and quantity of verbal output. Similarly, on such measures as percentage of structures preserved (Sentence Repetition), the experimental children obtained very high scores from the third testing onward; thus, little information regarding their improvement could be derived thereafter.

However, as illustrated by Figure 6-17, the mean difference between the two groups over all of the tests remained on a relatively consistent plane

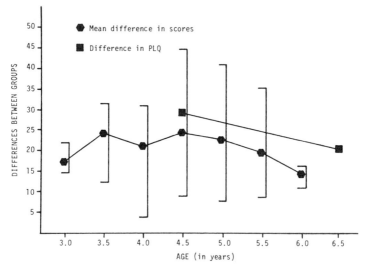

Figure 6-17. Overall Range of Differences and Mean Differences Between Experimental and Control Groups Across All Language Tests and Differences Between Groups on ITPA PLQ

Table 6-12 Summary of Performance Data for the Major Language Tests[a]

Age	Grammatical Comprehension				Sentence Repetition				Picture Morphology		Berko Morphology		ITPA PLQ	
	% Subtests Correct		Mean Contrasts Acquired		% Exact Repetitions		% Structures Preserved		% Items Correct		% Items Correct			
	E	C	E	C	E	C	E	C	E	C	E	C	E	C
3.0	21.33	4.07	3.47	0.28	26.21	11.72	60.58	38.81	27.89	11.73				
3.5	40.06	8.61	7.65	1.33	46.00	17.64	79.94	54.65	33.88	21.33				
4.0	41.18	11.22	11.71	2.78	55.12	24.00	90.12	62.72	36.65	24.11	20.65	16.57		
4.5	59.95	15.22	16.53	4.89	62.77	28.06	92.29	73.12	43.12	28.13	26.38	17.41	114.02	84.75
5.0[b,c]	70.53	29.61	20.65	9.28	61.81	35.82	95.25	80.59	45.88	28.50	27.25	19.29		
					43.82	22.19	79.71	49.88						
5.5	75.65	40.36	22.65	14.17	47.47	27.53	84.60	67.00	52.53	43.88	28.87	18.40		
6.0					52.50	36.87	94.44	79.87	60.24	49.13	36.79	20.33		
6.5											37.58	19.68	107.76	87.33

[a] Scores for the Grammatical Comprehension Test, ages 3–5, and Sentence Repetition Test I, ages 3–5, are averages of two testings within each 6-month interval.

[b] Sentence Repetition Test II was administered from age 5.

[c] Picture Morphology Test and Berko Test of Morphology were revised after age 5.

throughout the 3 ½ years of testing, reaching its highest levels from the ages of 3.5 through 4.5 years and tapering off slightly thereafter. To a lesser degree the two groups' MLU trends (Figure 6-17) also followed the same lines. It is this consistent performance differential, more than any single comparison of test results, that separated the two groups, supported the conclusions drawn separately from the individual tests, and suggested that there was indeed a difference between the experimental and control subjects in the developmental processes that affect language performance.

Comparisons with other groups, both black and white, have indicated that despite problems related to dialect use the experimental children generally performed on levels comparable to those of children from other environments who are presumed to be of normal intelligence. On the Grammatical Comprehension Test, for example, the experimental children demonstrated a grasp of grammatical structures that equaled that of white children from predominantly middle to high SES families and exceeded that of white and black children from low to middle SES families. On the ITPA, the experimental group's performance, while hampered by dialect influence, was also within the established normal range. The control children, on the other hand, consistently performed at levels lower than any of the comparison groups studied, including the low SES black groups.

Almost unavoidable in expressive language testing in English is the bias that favors speakers of SE. This has come about because certain features that are considered central to English grammar, such as the singular/plural distinction and some uses of the copulative verb *be*, are elements considered optional in many nonstandard dialects, including black dialect (Dillard, 1972; Labov, 1970). On the two Sentence Repetition tests, therefore, as well as on the original and revised versions of the PM and Berko tests, we devised alternative methods of scoring to enable us to compare the two groups' performance without relying too heavily on features regarded as optional in black dialect. On the Sentence Repetition tests, the *Structures Preserved* measure represents this alternative method. If the child repeated a stimulus sentence in his/her own words or using his/her own dialect patterns and without destroying the basic structure of the test sentence, he/she was given credit for having understood the sentence (although not for imitating it accurately). If the only factor causing the large differences between the exact repetition scores of the two groups had been the children's use of the dialect, therefore, their respective inaccurate repetitions would have shown approximately the same percentages of structures preserved. As the findings indicate, however, the experimental children understood a significantly ($p < .01$) greater percentage of those items than the control children did. It is apparent that the differences between the two groups, at least on this test, have much deeper roots than their use of dialect, and that other cognitive factors such as short term memory and comprehension of syntactic and semantic structures are involved.

On the morphology tests, our alternative scoring method consisted of examining the children's performance on those items that are not believed to be affected by dialect usage, such as adjective inflections, and the progressive (-*ing*) and agentive (-*er*) endings. Despite the fact that this category included features not expected to be acquired by children until later in their development, the experimental children's performance on these items in both the PM and Berko tests increasingly surpassed that of the control children from the second age level onward (Figures 6-14 and 6-15). As on the repetition tests, it seems that developmental skills, and not merely dialect usage, underlie the superior performance of the experimental group as compared with the control group.

We tried to interpret the results of our language testing as an index of the differential in language development attributable to treatment between the two groups of children and further to understand language growth in these two groups, the contribution of dialect usage notwithstanding. From our tape recordings of their conversational speech, we are certain that the experimental children, as well as the control children, do speak their dialect and did so perhaps to an even greater extent when they entered public school and were among other speakers of black dialect. The differences we have found lie rather in the rate at which they acquired concepts and relationships as expressed through syntactic structures. Our study was focused mainly on the children's acquisition of English morphology and syntax. We have not made comparisons of their ability to articulate the sounds of English, whether standard or nonstandard, except in connection with their production of intelligible language in the earlier part of our program and of inflectional endings in the tests of morphology. Where there was a possibility that test results could be influenced by dialect patterns, we devised alternative scoring systems in order to determine whether one group was being influenced more than the other. It is our belief that these were indeed differences brought about by the intervention program.

7
Mother-Child Interaction

In order to longitudinally assess the effects of the mother's and child's participation in the intervention program, we observed them in structured mother-child teaching situations. This aspect of the investigation sought to understand the nature of the mother-child interaction and what role it plays in the cognitive language development of the child. We examined the relationships among various aspects of the mother's attitude, language, and cognitive abilities, as well as her manner of interacting with her child. We made observations in the home, including personal interviews with the mother, and in addition we administered the Maternal Attitude Scale (MAS) and Social Reaction Inventory (Falender, 1969).

Essentially, we completed two replications of our observations of the mother and child in structured interaction sessions, separated in time by 2 years. All sessions were videotaped and rated later to provide several kinds of information including: the mother's performance on a learning task, how the mother and child interacted on a problem solving task, how the child performed on various tasks independently, and the nature of the language used by the mother in her communication with the child. These observations were conducted during the preschool years when the children were between 2½ and 3, and again between 4½ and 5. Interviews were given both in the home and at the preschool center for both the experimental and control families.

Our research amplified the Hess and Shipman (1965, 1968) findings by comparing the experimental dyads with the control dyads. We planned a series of studies to examine various aspects of the mother-child interaction. For these studies we conceptualized the child as being the center of an input-feedback system involving both the parent and extrafamilial stimulation (see Figure 7-1). The interaction between the mother and the child was conceptualized as a reciprocal feedback loop and suggested how both the amount of responsive behavior by the mother and her conceptual style contribute toward determining the nature of the interaction.

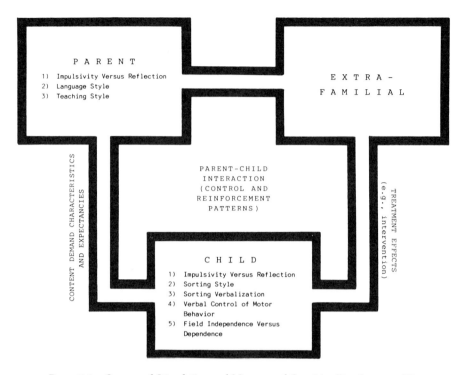

Figure 7-1. Sources of Stimulation and Measures of Cognitive Development: The
Conceptualization of the Components of the Mother-Child Interaction

There is little argument to the fact that there is a significant epidemiologic
association between family SES level and children's academic performance.
For example, Milner (1951) divided first graders into a high and a low group
on the basis of reading and language test scores. Her data indicated that social
class was a concomitantly distinguishing factor between the two groups. In
fact, only one low SES child was found among the high scorers and only one
middle SES child among the low scorers. Observing preschoolers, Mimbauer
and Miller (1970) also reported that middle SES preschool children were
superior to low SES children on a series of learning tasks. In addition, there
was a mean IQ difference between the groups of nearly 30 points in favor of
the middle SES children.

These and other studies, although providing evidence of the existence of
such differences between SES groups, provide little data on the nature of the
differences. The Milner (1951) study did, however, include a child and maternal interview containing questions related to the home environment. These
data revealed that the children in the high achievement group exhibited
significantly more responses that expressed appreciation of the time their
mothers spent in such activities as taking them places and reading to them.
Also, the children possessed at least several storybooks with which the parents

spent time reading to them. The relationship that Milner's study revealed between home variables and achievement pointed to the importance of process variables in the home environment for intellectual development.

Dave (1963) attempted to delineate the home environmental variables that are important for intellectual development. He reported a high positive correlation (.80) between six home environment variables and fourth graders' total scores on an achievement battery. These process characteristics were summarized as six variables of the home environment relevant to educational achievement: achievement pressure, language models in the home, academic guidance provided in the home, stimulation provided in the home to explore various aspects of the larger environment, intellectual interests and activity in the home, and work habits emphasized in the home. Dave's correlation of .80 stands in sharp contrast to much lower correlations (less than .50) obtained for the relationship of SES and school achievement, education of the parents, and father's occupational status. It seems from these data that what the parents do in the home is more important than the family's characteristics *per se*. A further implication of such data is that such variables as race, IQ, or SES might be better termed *surface variables* because they are not adequate measures for differentiating among families, and particularly for understanding how families that are low SES or defined as socioculturally unique influence their children's performance.

More detailed investigations (e.g., Bernstein, 1960; Hess & Shipman, 1965) have sought to understand how the interactional process influences language and cognitive development and how it varies with socioeconomic status. In addition to general differences in the mother-child interaction, there seemed to be patterns peculiar to SES levels. Bernstein (1960) differentiated two speech patterns used in social communication: restrictive and elaborative. The restrictive pattern consists of imperatives to command behavior without explanation or rationale. The elaborative speech pattern, on the other hand, includes causal and contextual relationships. These speech patterns were further investigated by Hess and Shipman (1965) and found to be used by mothers in interaction with their children. Mothers were also found to use different styles of control to regulate the child's behavior. The two types of speech patterns were related to three styles of behavior control: imperative-normative, subjective-emotional, and cognitive-rational.

Hess and Shipman (1968) found that middle class mothers tended to use the cognitive-rational control style more often in teaching their children, whereas lower class mothers tended to use imperatives. The use of imperatives to control and regulate behavior correlated with lower maternal intelligence and was related to a cognitive style that consists of relational grouping strategies, in which a stimulus obtains its meaning from its relation with other stimuli (e.g., doctor::nurse). The use of relational grouping suggests relatively low attention to external stimulus details, subjectivity, and a noncategorical style of thinking. This style of thinking, Hess and Shipman concluded, is engendered by the available information in lower class homes, that is, it lacks context and causal relationships, and the pattern of cognition that develops results in deficiencies for the children in various types of problem solving and conceptual behavior. Mothers with limited verbal skills tend to interact with their children in a more physical, less organized, and more punitive manner. Mothers with higher level skills use more sophisticated behavior in problem solving situations. They tend to offer verbal clues and give verbal prods while organizing the task to facilitate solution by the child. The low verbal mother is characterized by behavior using imperatives and restricted verbal communications, a behavior control system that more than likely has a general stultifying effect on problem solving behavior and other aspects of normal cognitive growth.

Hess and Shipman (1968) emphasized that a distinguishing feature of the different behavior control systems is the extent to which they allow displacement in time for problem solution. To the extent that this is inhibited by restrictive behavior control, there is a concomitant stultification of cognitive growth.

Bruner (1966) conceptualized cognitive growth in three stages, emphasizing development of symbolic representation as a continuous process beginning with relationships dependent upon motoric actions. As he/she moves toward the development of symbolic representation skills, the child is able to represent the world to him/herself through images or spatial schemes that are relatively independent of action. For Bruner, the role symbolic representation plays in the development of language and the higher levels of cognition is as the tool that enables a child to go beyond the immediacy of the problem to include past experience and future consequences in the problem solving situation. Bruner pointed out that such skills grow out of the early environmental experiences of the child's home and in interaction with significant others.

Hess and Shipman (1968) also found that a passive compliant attitude is induced in the child through this negative form of interaction, by weakening self-confidence and dampening motivation. As a result of a series of investigations using this experimental paradigm of a structured mother-child teaching session, Hess and Shipman (1967) found several specific maternal behaviors that affect the child's learning: Prompt maternal feedback is most necessary to the child's learning of the task, while task informing, engaging, and control behaviors are not; the greater the proportion of mothers' messages asking or telling their children to perform specific aspects of a task, the less likely they are to learn the task; more intelligent mothers use fewer physical commands; there is no correlation between maternal intelligence and propensity to use verbal commands or verbal questioning; and the use of questioning to evoke verbal information correlates with maternal intelligence and with the child's learning of the task. Using data from the same population, Brophy (1970) reported that only middle SES mothers consistently employed an initial orientation to the task, asking their children to focus their attention on the stimuli or giving pre-response instructions specifying appropriate verbal labels.

Additional experimental evidence supporting the importance of the mother's structuring of the cognitive environment of the infant and child can be obtained from a study by Wachs, Uzgiris, and Hunt (1967). They found significant differences favoring middle class infants in the use of objects as a means in foresighted behavior, in verbal facility, and in the attainment of object permanence, as compared with lower-class infants. Kagan (1968) reported that the number of changes in activity during free play periods made by lower class infants decreased between the ages of 8 and 13 months, while it increased during the same period for middle class infants. He hypothesized that lower class mothers may discourage exploratory behavior through nonresponse.

In addition to the importance of the content of the verbal exchange between mother and child, Zigler (1963) argued for the importance of the nature and contingencies of reinforcement utilized by the mother in affecting her child's behavior. He found that whereas information about the correctness of the problem was more effective for middle SES children, praise was more reinforcing for lower SES children. Brophy (1970) found that the degree of informational specificity in maternal teaching patterns is related to SES and the situation: Low SES mothers were more specific in postresponse than in preresponse feedback and more specific in correcting errors than in confirming correct responses. Low SES mothers were effective in correcting, suppressing, or eliminating undesired behavior, but they failed either to indicate the desired or appropriate response or to relate the essence of a task sufficiently to the context in which it occurred (i.e., to the goals or purpose of the task). A general conclusion from these data then is that the major difference between the class levels of the mothers was in their facility to attach meaning to situations and to structure relatively unstructured situations.

A more extensive investigation into the home environment by White (e.g., White & Watts, 1973) observed "A" versus "C" mothers and their children interacting within their normal home environment. "A" mothers tended to have intellectually more highly developed children than did the "C" mothers. By 30 to 33 months, "A" children spent a significantly greater amount of time with their mothers on more intellectual activities such as teaching, facilitation, and routine talk than did the "C" mothers and children. In addition, "A" mothers and children showed significantly more encouraging and initiating behaviors toward each other than did the "C" mother-child dyads. In contrast, the "C" mothers significantly outperformed "A" mothers in the amount of discouragement and failure in control they employed with their children. From these data the authors concluded that a dimension of encouragement-discouragement in the mother's behavior was most critical for 2-year-old children. During this age period, the "A" mother encouraged three times as many of her child's activities as she discouraged, while the "C" mother's discouragement of the child was twice as frequent as was her encouragement.

Wilton and Barbour (1978) employed White's observation scales to investigate the differences in activities and techniques used by mothers from families at risk for cultural-familial mental retardation (as well as contrast homes) while interacting with their older (30 to 46 months) and younger (12 to 27 months) children. The results supported White's findings. For the older but not the younger children, the high risk group interacted less with their mothers and participated in less highly intellectual activities than did the contrast group. The mothers of the older high risk children engaged in more discouragement of their children's activities than did the contrast group and engaged in less didactic teaching and less encouragement of their children's activities in general.

The nature of the mother-child interaction as characterized by Hess and Shipman's and White's analyses is consistent with Vygotsky's hypotheses concerning the development of language and cognition. Vygotsky (1962) hypothesized that speech becomes internalized thought. Luria (1961) further suggested that the degree to which this speech has been internalized can be indexed by the extent to which a child seeking help from adults makes use of this help, that is, how the child applies the results to his/her independent activity thereafter. It is then that the mother-child interaction determines the organization and quality of thought.

For us the Hess and Shipman procedure and data represented both a model for studying the early interaction between mother and child and a way to understand the important characteristics of the interactional process that might account for a child's success or failure in a variety of problem solving settings; for example, maternal education level (Streissguth & Bee, 1972), types of maternal control (Bee, Van Egeren, Streissguth, Nyman, & Leckie, 1969; Hess & Shipman, 1965), language codes used in interaction (Olim, Hess, & Shipman, 1967), and ratio of positive to negative feedback given by the mother to the child during interaction (Feshbach, 1973). The use of punishment or negative feedback, very specific directions, few questions, and few task orienting instructions were consistently associated with poor performance in the structured mother-child interaction teaching session; while specific reference to stimulus materials, introduction, requests for verbal response, and especially more praise and positive feedback were associated with facilitated task performance (Bee et al., 1969; Feshbach, 1973; Hess & Shipman, 1967). Their data point to the mother as the agent responsible for direction and change in the interaction and in effect the primary mediator of the environment for her children.

Every mother creates an environment for her child that is quite different from that created by other mothers, and this is so even though all may live in essentially the same physical environment. Indeed, because it is the nature of the early psychological environment created by the mother which significantly influences social, emotional, and cognitive development, then where the mother is of low IQ and low verbal skills the psychological environment tends to be impoverished and the children's cognitive development seriously restricted. The Hess and Shipman data (e.g., 1968) indicated that the way in which the mother combines linguistic and regulatory behavior in interaction with her child induces and shapes the information processing strategies and cognitive styles in the child and acts either to facilitate or to limit intellectual growth. We were therefore especially interested in observing how the interaction process between low SES, low IQ, low verbal skill mothers and their children would be affected as a result of their participation in an experimental treatment program.

The teaching session employed was structured to provide both mother and child an opportunity to influence the interaction. The major interest of these observations was to assess the effects of the extrafamilial stimulation upon the interaction of the experimental mother and her child in comparison with the nontreated control mother and child. It was of particular importance then to compare the patterning of both the maternal teaching style and the children's response style during the interaction sessions between the groups.

Two replications of our observation of structured mother-child interaction sessions (Study I, Study II) were conducted, separated in time by about 2 years and directed by Dr. Carol Falender. In the first series of observations, all children over 18 months of age ($n = 27$) from both experimental and control groups were included. The children were about 3 years of age. The second study began when the children were about 5 years of age. Each series of observations was videotaped and rated later by trained technicians to provide several kinds of information, including: how the mother performed on a learning task, how the mother and child interacted on a problem solving task, how the child performed independently on various tasks, and the nature of the language used by the mother in her communication with her child.

STUDY I

Our first study evaluated the quantity and quality of information transmitted in the teaching and interaction patterns of the experimental and control mother-child dyads. We examined the type of feedback (verbal or physical) between mother and child by observing the types of controls, reinforcements, and teaching methods employed by mother as well as child. The analysis of the information transmitted and shared in the dyad used the frequency counts of the types of responses made by either the mother or the child. Each of the behaviors was rated and grouped into one of 12 stimulus and 12 response categories (see Table 7-1).

In Study I, all experimental sessions were conducted in a specially prepared room in the preschool center. The testing room was equipped with a one-way mirror for videotaping and sound recording equipment, so that each session with each mother-child dyad could be recorded for later analyses. Prior to each session the mother and child were brought to the laboratory, seated at a table, and given an explanation of the tasks they were to perform. The experimenter then left the room and observed the mother and child through the one-way mirror. Each session consisted of a three part sequence of tasks.

Table 7-1   Behavioral Rating Scale Categories

Stimulus Behaviors	Response Behaviors
1. Informing teaching	1. Supplies verbal information
2. Positive verbal feedback	2. Answers question
3. Negative verbal feedback	3. Requests verbal information
4. Requesting verbal feedback	4. Positive verbal feedback
5. Control	5. Negative verbal feedback
6. Requesting physical feedback	6. Nonverbal response visual
7. Physical information-teaching, nonverbal	7. Manipulative nonverbal response
8. Positive physical feedback	8. Response to physical feedback, request
9. Negative physical feedback	9. Negative physical feedback
10. Ignores	10. Ignores
11. Passive nonteaching behavior task related	11. Task related physical nonperformance, passive
12. Nontask related behavior	12. Nontask related physical behavior

Each two events (mother-predicate, child-predicate) was considered one sequence: one stimulus, one response. Then Attneave's (1959) information theory analysis was applied.

Note: The scale was developed after Caldwell's (1969) categorization and rating system for naturalistic observations and was adapted to a structured situation along the lines of the Hess and Shipman (1965) scale. The scale was revised for Study II and adapted for computer analysis.

Task 1: Storytelling

First, the mother was asked to tell her child a story based upon the lion card of the Children's Apperception Test (Hess & Shipman, 1968). Sentence length, syntactic structure, content, and abstraction (proportion of abstract nouns and verbs in relation to the total number of nouns and verbs used) were taken as measures of the mother's language facility.

The information transmission analysis revealed that the experimental mother-child dyads shared more information than did the control dyads. The experimental dyads also had less "equivocation of transmission," that is, given a certain stimulus (maternal behavior) there was less uncertainty of the child's response. The children of both groups exhibited more general behaviors than did the mothers of either group, with no significant differences between the experimental and control children in general behavioral emission level.

Experimental mother-child dyads used significantly more verbal-verbal transmissions than did control dyads and significantly less physical-physical interactions than did the control dyads ($p < .01$). In addition, control dyads had more verbal-physical sequences in which the mother initiated verbally and the child responded physically (see Figure 7-2). The experimental dyads performed more of the opposite sequences: The mothers initiated a physical behavior, the child responded verbally. Finally, the control children and mothers initiated more "ignoring" behaviors that did the experimental children or their mothers.

Task 2: Block Sort and Etch-a-Sketch

Each mother was requested to teach her child to sort a number of blocks by both color and form and to copy three designs on a toy Etch-a-Sketch. The sorting task was the MAPS (Kagan, Moss, & Sigel, 1963), which required the mother to choose three figures from an array of 21 and give a reason for grouping the figures together. Each mother was requested to make seven independent groups of three figures for each of the 21 stimuli presented. This task was intended to reveal the mother's typical or preferred manner of grouping stimuli and the level of abstraction employed in perceiving and ordering objects. Responses were scored as descriptive part-whole, descriptive global, relational-contextual, and categorical-inferential. From this analysis the mother's categorization style could be compared to her child's preferred style.

Each mother learned the Block Sort task while her child played with a toy truck in a separate room with a second experimenter. The first experimenter

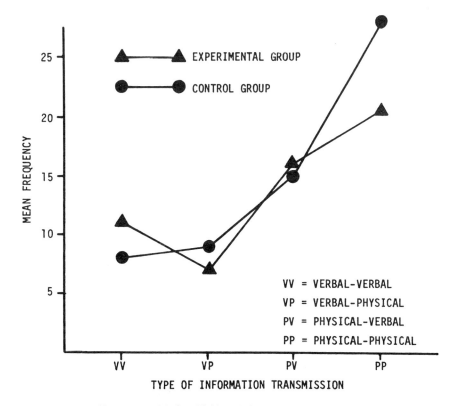

Figure 7-2. Mother-Child Verbal and Physical Interactions

instructed the mother to sort the blocks into four groups. Each mother was given as many trials as necessary to complete the sorting through trial and error with corrections given after each block was placed. When the mother had learned the task, she was given 15 minutes to teach it to her child.

For the next task a standard Etch-a-Sketch board was used. Both the mother and her child were instructed to draw a simple square on the Etch-a-Sketch board similar to one illustrated in a drawing. Each was to turn one knob. They were instructed to practice until satisfied and then call the experimenter to watch them draw it again.

A rating scale, adapted from Caldwell's computer compatible APPROACH coding (1969), translated each component behavior into a numerical code consisting of subject/predicate behavior units emphasizing verbal and physical behavioral action analysis, control and reinforcement contingencies, and teaching method.

The analyses for these two tasks were directed toward evaluating the amount and nature of information transmitted and shared between the mother and child. Each of the rated behaviors was grouped into one of 12 stimulus and 12 response categories (see Table 7-1). Each two events (mother-predicate, child-predicate) was considered one sequence: one stimulus, one response. Attneave's (1959) information theory analysis was then applied.

The experimental dyads were significantly ($p < .05$) more successful on the Block Sort than were the control dyads. Additional analyses were performed on the specific verbal and physical response behavior emitted during the Etch-a-Sketch and Block Sort tasks. On both tasks, experimental children exhibited a greater amount of verbal behaviors than did the control children, who enacted more physical behaviors (see Figure 7-3). In addition, the experimental

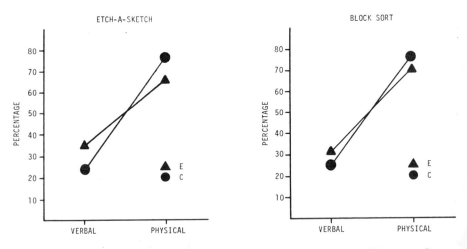

Figure 7-3.   The Percentage of Verbal and Physical Behavior as a Function of Treatment Group (Experimental and Control) and Task

children emitted more verbal behaviors than did the mothers of either group. No significant differences were evidenced between the two groups of mothers.

On the Etch-a-Sketch task, experimental females emitted more verbal behaviors than did any other group. Similarly, the control females exhibited more verbal behaviors than did control males, but the same number as experimental males (see Figure 7-4). Conversely, control males enacted the most physical behaviors during the Etch-a-Sketch task, followed by control females and experimental males. On Block Sorting, experimental males were the most verbal, followed by control and experimental females. And, conversely, control males exhibited the most physical behaviors, experimental males the least.

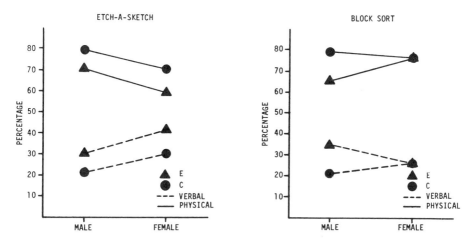

Figure 7-4. The Percentage of Verbal and Physical Behaviors as a Function of Sex, Group, and Task

The experimental children used fewer requests for verbal information and positive verbal feedback than did the control children on the Block Sort task, but a greater number of all verbal categories (except 4 and 5, unused by both groups) on the Etch-a-Sketch task. A greater number of experimental children supplied verbal information and answered questions than did control children during the Etch-a-Sketch task ($t = 1.92$, $p < .10$) and experimental children made more requests for verbal information and positive verbal reinforcement than during the Block Sorting task ($t = 2.41$, $p < .05$). In figure 7-5 we have illustrated for comparison purposes the categories used within and between the Block Sort and Etch-a-Sketch tasks.

Although there were no significant differences between maternal behaviors on either task, the experimental mothers required less time to complete the Block Sort task than did the control mothers and more time to complete the Etch-a-Sketch than did the control mothers.

The experimental children transmitted more information than did the control children, and both groups of children transmitted more information themselves, although not a significantly different amount, than did the mothers of

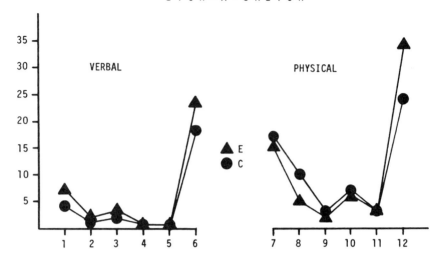

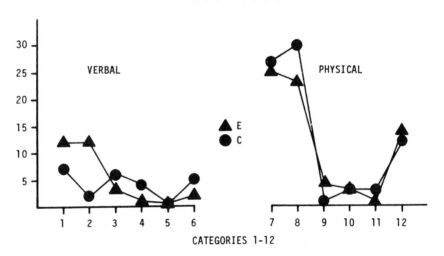

Figure 7-5. Types of Verbal and Physical Behaviors as a Function of Category, Treatment Group, and Task

either group. However, there was a greater amount of shared information between the experimental mothers and children than in the control dyads. Because there was no significant difference in the amount of information transmitted by the mothers, these data suggest that in the experimental dyad, it was the child's responses that were primarily responsible for the information communicated within the dyad and the greater amount of shared information found between the dyads. This difference is attributable in part to the better coordination (i.e., less equivocation of information) between the stimulus or maternal behavior and the response by the child. In other words, there was less uncertainty and a more stable response pattern between both maternal overt (verbal) and covert (physical) stimuli and the child's responses. Although the direction of the interaction seemed mainly to be from the mother to her child, it was actually her child who was manipulating the interaction.

The preschool program's stress on general language development, with emphasis directed particularly at the development of expressive verbal behavior, was reflected in the mother-child interaction results. It seemed that the increased verbal fluency and expressiveness of the experimental children may have prompted the mothers to be more expressive.

Hess and Shipman (1967) emphasized the importance of verbal information in a teaching situation and that it is the particular responsibility of the mother. They found that maternal IQ, the mother's type of questioning to evoke verbal information, and the child's task success to be positively related. However, in our study, it seemed that the experimental children themselves were the main force in supplying verbal information and in fact initiated verbal communication. In effect, they verbally oriented themselves in response to the mothers' covert stimulation. In contrast, when the control mothers verbally requested behaviors from their children, their responses were most often physical. In Hess and Shipman's (1967) research, a negative correlation was found between task success and direct demands for physical behavior (for a nonverbal response). The control children, on the other hand, did not initiate enough verbal interaction to guide sessions or to respond consistently to maternal behaviors.

Gordon (1969) observed that intervention programs, intended to change the behaviors of mothers toward their infants, had a stronger effect on mother-daughter dyads than on mother-son dyads. Our observations support Gordon. In this study, for example, female chidren were more verbal than male children on the Etch-a-Sketch. There is also some indication that mothers of experimental daughters in our sample were more verbal than mothers of control daughters.

A working hypothesis among some researchers has been that lower SES children do not experience the quality of parent-child interaction that occurs in middle class homes. In contrast to the lower SES mothers, middle class mothers employ considerable face-to-face vocalization and smiling; they reward their children's maturational progress and often enter into long periods of play with the child (Kagan, 1969). Assuming this to be a reliable description, what seems to be occurring in this situation is that the experimental child, because of his/her preschool experience, assumes the responsibility of the mother in the dyad. In other words, the children's attempts to structure the information transfer themselves guide the mothers in the teaching situation. This was made possible as a result of the experimental child's level of language development and ability to express him/herself verbally. There is also evidence that the mothers were beginning to respond in kind.

In summary, these data from our first study of mother-child interaction strongly suggested that the preschool program's emphasis on language development facilitated communication and the transfer of information in the mother-child dyad. In this situation, where the mother was of low IQ and low verbal skills, the experimental children were responsible for guiding the flow of information and providing most of the verbal information. The mothers of the two groups showed little difference during the teaching session but because of the experimental children's responses, there was more shared information in the experimental dyads.

STUDY II

In the replication study, conducted about 2 years after the first, the children were about 5 years of age. One obvious concern was to see whether evidence for the differential effect of preschool treatment continued. In this second study, we were particularly interested to see if the feedback phenomenon noted earlier from the experimental children to their mothers and back had increased. The first study revealed a dominant role of the experimental children in directing portions of the interaction with their mothers. And although significant maternal differences did not occur, there was some evidence to indicate a beginning effort by the experimental mothers to initiate verbal behaviors in addition to the behaviors evoked by their children's questioning. We hypothesized that the feedback effects observed earlier would be more generalized, both in the interaction session and in maternal behavior, as a function of the experimental children's exposure to the project's continuing emphasis on expressive language. Support for this phenomenon would be revealed by significant differences in the patterning of information between the groups such that there would be greater behavioral predictability in the experimental dyads than we found earlier.

We improved our methodology to more adequately evaluate the interaction between mother and child. There were 39 dyads including 21 experimental and 18 control pairs. This time all experimental sessions were conducted in a specially designed mobile laboratory parked near each child's house. As before, all sessions were videotaped through a one-way mirror using a Sony Rover unit and rated at a later time. In addition, only the Block Sort and Etch-a-Sketch tasks with the following modifications were used: (a) the Block Sort task was changed so that width and height were relevant dimensions and color and shape were irrelevant; (b) the mothers learned the Block Sort task to a criterion of two correct sorts before teaching it to their children; (c) the task score on the Block Sort task was based on the child's placement of additional blocks after the learning session as well as on the piles made during the session; (d) instructions were given to the mother and child together to draw a square on the Etch-a-Sketch; and (e) the rating scale was revised to reflect more directly the immediately relevant behaviors.

Procedures

Session I, Task 1: Block Sort

The materials were 21 wooden blocks varying in color (red, yellow, green, blue), shape (square, triangle, round), width (thick, thin), and height (tall, short). The blocks were to be sorted into four piles. First, all the tall, thin blocks; second, all the short, thin blocks; third, all the tall, thick blocks; and fourth, all the short, thick blocks. Color and shape were irrelevant dimensions.

Each mother learned the Block Sort task while her child played with a toy truck in a separate room with a second experimenter. The first experimenter gave the mother the following instructions:

"Here is a group of blocks that have different colors, shapes, heights, and widths. We would like you to teach *(child's name)* to sort them into four groups. We will practice first so you will understand how to sort. After you sort each block, I will tell you if you are correct. After you see how to sort the blocks, you can teach *(child's name)* how to sort. O.K. Here is the first block. Which other ones do you think go with this block?"

"(IF CORRECT) Yes, that's right. What others go with these? (IF WRONG) No, that block doesn't go in this pile. Try again."

After the first sorting the mother was directed to practice another time. If the categories were confused, practice was continued until two correct sortings without corrective feedback had occurred. At the completion of the learning the experimenter said:

"O.K. Now it is time for you to teach *(child's name)* to sort these blocks. You will be given 15 minutes to teach him/her. If you finish before I return, knock on the door. Then I'll come in and ask *(child's name)* to put three more blocks in the right piles to make sure he/she understands. So be sure to leave the blocks in piles when you are finished."

Either at the end of 15 minutes or when the child knocked on the door, the experimenter returned to the experimental room with three additional blocks not included in the original 21 blocks. The experimenter noted whether the piles on the table were correct and recorded this information. She then asked the child to place each of the three additional blocks in the correct piles. The child was given a placement score.

Session I, Task 2: Etch-a-Sketch

The standard Etch-a-Sketch board was used (one knob when turned makes a horizontal line, the other when turned makes a vertical line, and the board can be erased by shaking it upside down). With both the mother and her child in the experimental room, the experimenter brought in an Etch-a-Sketch board and said:

"Now you and *(child's name)* are to draw this square *(pointing to the picture of a drawn square)* on the Etch-a-Sketch board. Let *(child's name)* turn one knob; you turn the other knob. To erase, turn the board upside down like this *(demonstrate)* and shake it. Practice drawing the square until you are satisfied that you and *(child's name)* can draw it together. Then knock on that door and I'll come back to watch you both draw it together again."

When the child knocked, the experimenter returned to the room, asked the mother and child to draw the square again, and scored them on (a) correct square and (b) each turning one knob.

At the completion of these two mother and child tasks, the mother was taken to an adjoining room by one experimenter; her child remained in the room with the other experimenter. The mother was administered the Matching Familiar Figures Test (MFFT) (Kagan, Rosman, Day, Albert, & Phillips, 1964). The test was timed and errors recorded. At the same time, the second experimenter administered the Kansas Reflectivity-Impulsivity Scale (KRISP) (Wright, 1971) to her child, recording errors and time to respond.

SESSION II

During the second session, which occurred approximately 2 weeks after the interaction session, the experimenter administered two additional tasks to each child. The first was the Sigel Sorting Task (SST) (Sigel, 1971), a series of line drawings of stimulus forms of animals, people, and objects. The experimenter asked, "Which two go together and why?" The second task was the Children's Embedded Figures Test (CEFT) (Karp & Konstadt, 1963), which was administered according to the standardized instructions.

Rating Procedure and Analysis

As noted earlier, the replication effort used improved methodology. In particular we spent considerable time training coders for the observation, a necessity given the increasing complexity of behavior in these dyadic situations compared with those in Study I.

TRAINING OF CODERS

Coding was done by three students after they had obtained satisfactory interrater reliability on a series of training tapes. All students had had extensive experience in language transcription of tapes. Mastery of the interaction code entailed 12 to 15 hours of training involving discussion of categories, practice coding on a training tape, independent coding, and refining and clarifying categories on a second series of training tapes. Coding consisted of chains of behaviors by the mother, followed by her child, followed by the mother, etc. Reliability was determined by a ratio of observed behavioral units in common among the raters. Interrater reliability was established at an average of .91 for all ratings across the six categories. Reliabilities ranged from .79 (verbal negative feedback) to .99 (physical negative feedback).

Dependent variables

The coded sequences were first subjected to an information theory analysis (Attneave, 1959) to evaluate the patterning of information exchanged between the mother and her child. Three measures were derived from this analysis; namely, the amount of information transmitted by the mother and by her child, and the association or relatedness of the first two. If there were an equal probability of any behavior occurring following a given behavior by the other, there would be greatest uncertainty. That is, given a behavior by one member of the dyad, what is the certainty or the probability of the behavior by the other?

Teaching times varied; therefore, it was necessary to use percentages derived by dividing the number of behaviors in each category by the total number of behaviors that occurred. In addition percentages of each of the behaviors in the six categories were computed for mothers and for children in each group. These frequencies were evaluated in a multivariate analysis of variance (MANOVA) with chronological age of the child as a covariate.

Analysis

The MANOVA analysis was used to evaluate the amount and type of behaviors enacted by the mothers and children. Three major concerns of this evaluation were: evidence of program treatment effects, that is, a comparison of experimental versus control; evidence of a reciprocal feedback loop from child to mother, noted in our first series of observations a couple of years earlier; and evidence of the transmission trends, that is, the relationship between verbal questionings of the mother and her child. We were seeking evidence of an increased communication facility, developmentally related, that was "regulating" the interaction and response styles. This would be revealed in higher task scores, greater information correspondence, and more sophisticated correlate task performance as a function of the differential in experience and age.

This analysis considered group (experimental, control), sex (male, female), and age (old, young). Additionally, univariate analyses and *t* tests were used to evaluate some task scores and the amount of time required to learn the task.

Blocking for sex, as an additional variable of concern, was done in order to ascertain whether, as the literature has suggested, the sex of the child influences the type of interchange in the dyad. Two aspects of this concern are that, first, girls tend to be more verbal and boys more physical and, second, that the mother in turn would have as a result differing expectations for the kind of response, perhaps independent of any actual differences in rate. Gordon (1969), for example, reported that mother-daughter pairs may experience more reciprocal feedback effects than mother-son pairs. We also blocked for age because of the large age span associated with obvious differences in verbal ability and a difference in how mothers interact with younger and older children. The subject characteristics are reported in the following table (Table 7-2).

Table 7-2 Number and Mean Age of Children in Study II:
Mother-Child Observations

Group	n	Younger	n	Older
Experimental[a]				
Female	4	4.0	6	5.6
Male	7	4.2	4	5.7
Control				
Female	4	4.6	5	5.1
Male	4	4.6	4	5.2

[a]Four younger treated siblings are included.

REPORT AND INTERPRETATION OF RESULTS

The results were considered in three parts: (a) behavioral category frequency results considered as a function of whether task instructions were given to the mothers alone or to both the mother and child, (b) information theory analysis results, and (c) the correlate task scores.

Behavior Rating Analysis

The effect of the treatment program on the experimental dyads was revealed as significant by both quantitative and qualitative differences between the behaviors of the experimental and control groups. Table 7-3 lists the percentage of occurrence of behaviors of mothers and children by task and group. On the Block Sort task, in which only the mother received instructions, the experimental children emitted significantly more verbal information processing behaviors and more verbal and physical positive feedback, while the control children used significantly more physical information processing and more negative verbal and negative physical feedback. Similarly, on the Etch-a-Sketch, in which both mother and child received instructions, the experimental children used significantly more verbal information processing and more verbal and physical positive feedback and significantly less physical information processing than did control children. The experimental children received higher overall task scores on both measures than did the control children.

The differences that might be expected as a result of instructing either one or both members of a dyad were revealed not in the child behavior but in the maternal behavior. On the Block Sort tasks, where only the mother was instructed, no significant behavior differences were found between the experimental and control mothers. But as may be seen on the right side of Table

Table 7-3 Percentage Occurrence of Behaviors of Mothers and Children
by Task and Group

| | Block Sort | | | | | | Etch-A-Sketch | | | | | |
| | Mother | | | Child | | | Mother | | | Child | | |
Behavior Categories	E	C	F	E	C	F	E	C	F	E	C	F
1. Verbal information processing	.29	.27	.13	.31	.06	68.3***	.22	.19	.21	.25	.07	29.80**
2. Physical information processing	.35	.32	.35	.32	.60	69.4***	.44	.36	3.23	.62	.87	34.70***
3. Verbal positive feedback	.07	.06	.37	.15	.02	68.5***	.10	.04	4.29*	.08	.03	19.10**
4. Physical positive feedback	.03	.01	.15	.14	.08	58.4***	.09	.01	10.20**	.03	0	18.50**
5. Verbal negative feedback	.21	.21	.01	.08	.15	31.8**	.11	.28	15.53**	.01	.02	2.40
6. Physical negative feedback	.04	.05	.10	.03	.17	30.5**	.03	.10	22.70**	.01	.03	1.85

*p < .05
**p < .01
***p < .001

7-3, the experimental mothers used significantly more verbal and physical positive feedback on the Etch-a-Sketch task, when both mother and child were instructed, than did the control mothers. The control mothers used significantly more verbal and physical negative feedback on this task. Although there were no significant differences between the experimental and control mothers in the amount of verbal or physical information processing behaviors, analysis of the experimental mothers' verbal information processing behaviors on the Block Sort task, when only the mothers were given instruction, revealed that experimental mothers tended to supply verbal responses to informational requests (.15 of .29), while control mothers were making verbal requests for specific physical responses (.24 of .27).

The effect of instructions given to one or both members of the dyad is an important variable to consider, the confounding of task and sequence presentation notwithstanding. In the Block Sort task, considerable uncertainty is induced because the mothers have to compensate in their communication and by their teaching skills for what is gained when both members of a dyad are instructed, as in the Etch-a-Sketch task. However, although the mothers of both groups were comparable on Block Sort where uncertainty was high, the experimental mothers on the Etch-a-Sketch task were able to be more positive, less negative, and less physically controlling. In fact, it seemed that the experimental mothers were imitating the positive feedback behaviors of their verbal children. The control mothers, on the other hand, used considerable verbal requests for physical responses and spent a lot of time in demonstration with no verbalization. These data are similar to those reported by Bee et al. (1969) for mothers with low performing children. The control mothers were in some ways forced to use physical control behaviors in response to their children's physically disruptive and inattentive behaviors.

Information Theory Analysis

The information theory analysis revealed that the experimental mother-child dyads developed a greater association of mother-child behaviors on both tasks than did the control dyads and indicated a greater association of mother-child behavior in the experimental group than in the control group. That is, given a certain behavior by the mother, there was greater certainty of the behavior of the child in the experimental dyad on both tasks (Block Sort: $F = 5.13$, $p < .05$; Etch-a-Sketch: $F = 8.57$, $p < .01$). On the Etch-a-Sketch task, the control mothers transmitted a significantly greater amount of information ($F = 10.98$, $p < .01$).

Significant male/female distinctions were also indicated. Mothers of females used more verbal information processing behaviors than did mothers of males. On the Etch-a-Sketch task, mothers of males used significantly more negative verbal, $F(1, 28) = 4.28$, $p < .05$, and negative physical, $F(1, 28) = 10.19$, $p < .01$, feedback. There was more physical blocking and physical assault by mothers of males than by mothers of females.

Mothers also acted differently as a function of the age of the child. There was more use of physical blocking and assault by mothers of younger children during both tasks. Mothers of older children used more verbal encouragement during Block Sort than did mothers of younger children.

The older more verbal experimental children, as might be expected, transmitted more information than did any other group on the Etch-a-Sketch task. These data provide evidence that the experimental child directed the information flow. For example, although on the Block Sort task only the mother was given instructions, the experimental children asked significantly more questions and enacted more verbal behaviors than did the control chilren and in effect obtained the instructions from her (see Figure 7-6). The experimental mothers show a corresponding acquiesence to this solicitation by responding to requests with more verbal cues for manipulation and sorting than did the control mothers. It seemed that while the control mothers directed the Block Sort task, the experimental children's questioning prods of their mothers in effect resulted in the children directing the interaction. This role of the experimental children was more clearly seen on the Etch-a-Sketch task where both mothers and the children were given the task instructions (see Figure 7-7). Again, as in the Block Sort task, the control dyad mothers directed the task,

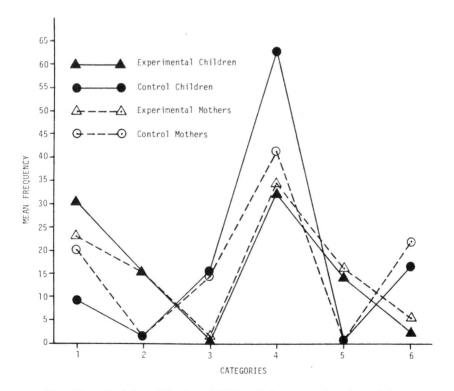

Figure 7-6. Block Sort: Behaviors of Children in Experimental vs. Control Groups

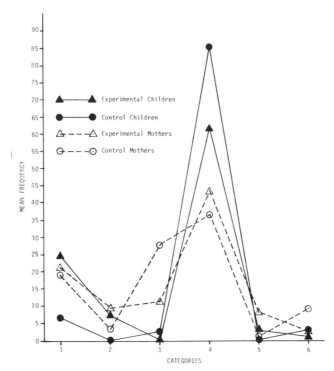

Figure 7-7. Etch-A-Sketch: Behaviors of Children in Experimental vs. Control Groups

resulting in a greater amount of information being transmitted by them than by the experimental mothers. In the experimental dyads the children, and particularly the older experimental children, guided the interaction and transmitted more information than did any other group. The experimental children utilized more verbal orienting and informing behavior as well as commands; and the older experimental children used more positive verbal feedback in contrast to the control children who enacted more physical behaviors. On this task, the direction of teaching seemed to be from the children to their mothers, at least in the experimental dyads.

These results also indicated an increased efficiency of communication in the teaching situation between the experimental children and their mothers. The experimental dyads' high task scores can be attributed to the children, who assumed responsibility for the communication of information by providing task structure in the form of questions and praise to their mothers. In contrast, there were fewer consistent or cooperative responses in the control dyads. Although the control mothers attempted to direct the session, they seemed to lose sight of the goal, namely, the sorting categories they had learned. Neither group of mothers utilized verbal labels for the Block Sort groupings. However, the experimental children were able to abstract the categories through their mothers' active sorting, while the control children were not.

Thus, these data indicated that the feedback effects evidenced in the earlier mother-child interaction study had become more pronounced as a function of the 2 additional years of stimulation and maturation. The coordination of maternal and child information was more closely associated for the experimental dyads than for the control on both tasks, suggesting continued development of the stable response patterns observed in the earlier study. These results are also consistent with other investigations, which report that the low SES, low IQ mother is unable to structure a learning situation, but is adept at suppression of undesirable behaviors (Bee et al., 1969; Hess & Shipman, 1965; Schoggen & Schoggen, 1976; White & Watts, 1973; Wilton & Barbour, 1978). Indeed, we found that the majority of the control mothers' verbal commands were for specific physical responses from their children such as "Put that one here." They also spent much time in demonstration (performing the task for the child) with no verbalization. These physical suggestions gave the child little opportunity to practice the task and lacked reference to the final goal, which was to sort the blocks and verbally label them by the categories they had just learned.

Throughout the tasks the experimental children took an active directing approach to the instruction. They asked more questions, emitted more verbal orienting and conforming behaviors, and made more positive verbal feedback statements than did the control children. The control children, in contrast, could be characterized as passive negative learners. They emitted significantly more physical blocking behaviors than did the experimental children. In addition, association between the control children's and mothers' behaviors was much lower than for the experimental mothers and children.

These results give support to the hypothesis that physical proximity is not the critical determinant in the development of the mother-child interaction. There was a high association of behavior between experimental children and their mothers, even though they had been separated for many of their waking hours since the age of 6 months, in contrast to the control children, who presumably spent a great deal of time with their mothers. The lack of face-to-face interaction with adults, the low value placed on verbal interaction, and the rewarding of passive behaviors have been identified as more characteristic of low SES homes and, more specifically, homes where the primary caretaker is of low IQ and low verbal skills. These data support the notion that the *quality* of interaction, such as the spontaneity and responsiveness of the participants, is a more significant influence on the cognitive development of the child than *intensity*.

There is an important additional consideration to be derived from this notion of quality versus intensity (e.g., amount of time) that has implications for understanding how low IQ, low verbal skill mothers may inadvertently but negatively influence the social and cognitive development of their young children. Physical separation of the child from the mother to attend preschool may, by reducing the amount of interaction between mother and child in the low SES home, also reduce the negative quality of the interaction, for example, a feature Hess and Shipman's (1965) data suggested, the form of imperatives used by the mother to control her child and limit interaction. A primarily negative form of interaction carried out extensively over many years may considerably limit cognitive growth, as seen in the control children's behaviors.

Because of this unusual negative learning milieu, there develops, in my opinion, not simply a lack of cognitive growth, but rather, an antagonistic cognitive system that interferes with performance and encourages the child to develop an unmotivated passive style of interaction with his/her environment. The data on the Etch-a-Sketch task revealed significantly more negative feedback, verbal and physical, enacted by the control mothers than by experimental mothers. The reduced amount of time on the one hand reduces the exposure of the child to negative quality interactions but it may also be, as speculation permits, that the behavior of the experimental children, learned through positive interactions, effectively neutralizes the tendency of the mother toward restrictive or inhibitory interactions. In other words, although there remains in the mother the desire to reduce behavior or limit the interaction, the experimental child "manipulates" her and draws her into the interaction as a positive partner.

These results from the mother-child interaction sessions therefore provide evidence that changes induced in the child by an extrafamilial educational treatment program have the additional results of inducing changes in the mother's behavior during interaction with her child. The results obtained during the mother-child interaction sessions indicated that the greater amount of information transmitted in the experimental dyads, as compared with the control dyads, was primarily a function of the quality of the experimental child's verbal behavior. The experimental children supplied more information verbally and initiated more verbal communication than children in the control dyads. In fact children in the experimental dyads took responsibility for building the flow of information—providing most of the verbal information and direction. The mothers of both groups evidenced minimal differences in their teaching ability during the interaction sessions. However, in the experimental dyads the children structured the interaction session either by their questioning or by teaching their mothers. As a result, a developmentally more sophisticated interaction pattern developed between the experimental children and their mothers, which contributed to faster and more successful problem completion.

Although considerable speculation centering upon the most efficient change method in early childhood education continues, these results suggest that stimulation of the child and the mother can provide generalized effects, whether through modeling, reinforcement, or attitude change. Furthermore, the generalized effect of such changes must occur over time appropriate to the changing needs of the child and family. Gordon (1969) reported not only changes similar to those reported here, but also significant behavior changes in the mothers' participation in community affairs and attendance at night school, and a general increase in their academic and social status.

Our observations suggest the beginning of some of these changes in these families, who are typically regarded as a most difficult population to change.

Cognitive Style: Correlate Tasks

The purpose of these assessments was to ascertain the effect of longitudinal intervention on the development of the children's cognitive styles and self-perceptions. We made assessments of conceptual tempo, sorting skills, field independence-dependence, and self-concept. A child's cognitive style and self-concept substantially influence the behavior strategies he/she employs in problem solving tasks. Substantial differences in the use of strategies have been noted for children as a function of their family SES.

At the completion of mother-child interaction observations in Study I, the mother and child were taken to separate rooms and administered measures of conceptual tempo. The maternal measure was the Matching Familiar Figures Test (MFFT) (Kagan, 1965) and the child's was the Kansas Reflection-Impulsivity Scale for Preschoolers (KRISP) (Wright, 1971). Similarly, 2 years later at the conclusion of the mother-child interaction observation in Study II, both mother and child were administered the MFFT.

In each study, at a second session approximately 2 weeks after the interaction session, the child was administered two additional tasks: the Sigel Sorting Task (SST) (Sigel, 1971) and the Children's Embedded Figures Test (CEFT) (Karp & Konstadt, 1963).

Child Measures

MEASURE OF CONCEPTUAL TEMPO

The KRISP is a modification of the MFFT adapted for preschool children. The drawings are simpler, but the measurements are the same as on the MFFT: number of errors and time to first responses (by which the responder can be characterized as *impulsive* or *reflective*).

Conceptual tempo is defined as the time a subject takes to consider alternative solutions and the number of errors made before choosing the correct stimulus in a situation of high response uncertainty. Styles of responding are categorized along a dimension of impulsive versus reflective responding. *Impulsive* refers to subjects who respond quickly with a large number of errors on a measure, while the *reflective* responder requires long response times and has a low error score on a test series.

Previous research indicates that reflective children usually outperform impulsive children on academically related tasks. Specifically, reflective children (those characterized by slow decisions and accurate responses) tend to make fewer word recognition errors and fewer reasoning errors (Kagan, Pearson, & Welch, 1966), to perform more complex activities in the preschool (Welsh, 1975), to have longer attention spans, to be less hyperactive (Ault, Crawford, & Jeffrey, 1972), and in general to be at a lower risk for learning problems than impulsives. The impulsivity-reflectivity dimension has been related to problem solving (Kogan, 1976), reading skills (Kagan, 1965), inductive reasoning

(Kagan et al., 1966), and preschool behavior (Welch, 1974), with reflective children generally outperforming the more impulsive children.

Minimal attention has been given to the relation between maternal and child conceptual tempo. Campbell (1973) described particular patterns of maternal behavior during interaction and reported significant differences in maternal behavior as a function of the child's conceptual tempo. Reflective children had mothers who were more involved in task solution and expressed higher expectations for achievement of their children than did mothers of impulsive children. Mothers of impulsive boys tended to focus attention on one aspect of the task, to make more suggestions about impulse control, and to give somewhat more negative feedback.

A limited number of studies have been conducted investigating the effects of training on conceptual tempo (Debus, 1970; Kagan et al., 1966; Siegelman, 1969). Such training efforts have been only partially successful. For example, Siegelman attempted to train impulsive children to be reflective by reinforcing a delay period before the response. He found that this was not sufficient and suggested that it may be necessary to train scanning and attention deployment searching techniques during the delay period. Feuerstein, Rand, Hoffman, and Miller (1980), working with mildly handicapped adolescents, have had success in modifying problem solving related behaviors such as conceptual tempo. Modification of these basic problem solving approaches, which influence learning styles across various activities, requires further investigation.

Results from the administration of the KRISP to the experimental and control children indicated that the experimental group responded at a level developmentally more sophisticated than the control group's. On the KRISP the experimental children had significantly ($p < .01$) fewer errors than the control children had. The time to first response did not significantly differentiate the groups (all older experimental children were classified as reflective). It seemed that the KRISP may have been too easy for the older experimental children, as they obtained both uniformly low errors and low response times. These results, however, are compatible with the Messer (1976) critical analysis of the MFFT in that differences in errors rather than time seemed to be the critical factor in distinguishing the two groups.

On the MFFT no significant differences for either time or errors were noted between the experimental and control mothers. The mean time to first response for mothers in the experimental group was 12.7 seconds (range 5.22 to 22.9) and for control mothers 15.85 (range 4.1 to 36.3). For the experimental mothers, the mean number of errors was 12.61 (range 0 to 23.8) and for the control mothers 14.6 (range 5 to 25+).

Two years later, when the children were about 5 years old, the MFFT was administered to all of the children, but not to the mothers. No between group differences on this task for either errors or time were noted. When the children from each group were classified as impulsive or reflective, no differences in the numbers in each group were evident. Correlational analysis conducted on the previous KRISP data and MFFT data for the children revealed no significant correlation between the measures derived from these separate instruments for any group or subgroup of the sample.

MEASURE OF CONCEPTUAL STYLE

The manner in which children sort or group a number of unrelated items is one way of evaluating how they perceive and order their environment. Using a series of pictures modified from the Sigel Conceptual Sorting Task (Kagan et al., 1963), each child was asked to place two pictures together (out of three) and tell why they go together. The children's reasons were described in three categories:

1. *Descriptive responses* are those in which some physical aspect (color, shape, size) of the pictures is chosen (e.g., they both have stems, both are round).
2. *Relational responses* indicate a common relationship between the two pictures chosen and require little analysis of the stimulus array (e.g., doctor and nurse, husband and wife).
3. *Inferential categorical responses* require an abstraction and the greatest amount of analysis of the stimulus display (e.g., they are both fruits).

Descriptive and relational responses are considered more concrete in nature and require less processing and organizational skills than do the categorical responses. Low SES mothers tend to use relational groupings, which indicates low attention to external stimulus detail and subjectivity. Implusive mothers tend to use relational categories more frequently than reflective mothers do.

The test provided a measure of the conceptual style, presumed to have been affected by the mother and/or caretaker who shaped the child's environment and the child's emerging perceptions. Hess and Shipman (1965) postulated that a mother who uses a relational grouping strategy is likely to have a child who uses the same. However, in their sample, the 4-year-old children whose mothers used relational categories tended to lack any consistent cognitive style or grouping. For children, the measure distinguishes between those who group perceptions according to surface characteristics or perceived relationships and those who engage in analysis or abstraction of the stimulus display. For example, some children would look at pictures of an apple and a pear and say, "They both have stems" (a descriptive response). Others would categorize and say, "They are fruits." Others might say, "They both lay on the table" (relational). The relational response requires the least analysis of the stimulus array. This measure therefore provided additional information concerning the child's analysis of stimulus materials, scanning strategies, and general problem solving strategies.

The experimental children utilized sortings based upon categorization and description, both strategies requiring analysis of the stimulus display. In contrast, the control children had difficulty verbalizing the type of sorting they had chosen and tended to use strictly relational sorts based upon the least amount of stimulus analysis. The results from the control children are compatible with findings that children of low IQ mothers often use relational groupings or are unable to label sortings at all (Hess & Shipman, 1965).

MEASURE OF FIELD INDEPENDENCE-DEPENDENCE

The Children's Embedded Figures Test (CEFT) by Karp and Konstadt (1963) consists of two standard shapes (a tent and a house) embedded in a series of colored drawings and is a measure of field dependence-independence. The child must find the shape in the drawing. There is an initial training series preceding the test.

Field independence-dependence is a general style of responding that children use to respond to external cues in their environment. The CEFT is designed to measure this style of responding in preschool children. Field independence, or the ability of an individual to separate a figure from the ground in which it is embedded, is distinguished from field dependence, the inverse. Field dependency is viewed as a feminine trait, or present in males in families where the father is absent or distant. Field dependent subjects are reported as dependent in their interpersonal relations, suggestible, conforming, and likely to rely on others for guidance and support (Witkin, Dyk, Faterson, Goodenough, & Karp, 1962).

Field independence-dependence is defined not only in terms of the ability to separate figure from ground, but also as the ability to orient oneself in space with conflicting visual cues (Witkin et al., 1962). Thus, this measure gives information about the types of cues the child is sensitive to: whether they are internal (self-generated) or external (from the environment).

The experimental children as a group were more field independent — able to find significantly more embedded figures in the stimulus displays (XE = 5.26 v XC = 2.88, $p < .01$). This was further evidence of increased perceptual sophistication on a measure that is correlated with other aspects of personality development (Witkin et al., 1962). Field dependence is associated with passivity and dependence in interpersonal relationships. A field independent individual is able to ignore certain misleading environmental cues and analyze the environmental input efficiently. This finding coincides with the findings for the differential performance of the two groups of children on the learning tasks.

SUMMARY

Children in the experimental group responded at a developmentally more sophisticated level on these three measures of cognitive style than did the control children. The experimental children utilized sortings based upon categorization and description, both strategies involving analysis of the stimulus display. In contrast, the control children had difficulty verbalizing the type of sorting they had chosen and tended to use strictly relational sorts, based upon the least amount of stimulus analysis. In general, the experimental children analyzed the stimulus array in a more thorough manner than did the control children. This is generally consistent with the children's performance on the other learning tasks.

Perception of Self

In order to obtain information on how children perceive themselves, measures of self-concept and sex role development were administered to them.

Sex role development

Although there are many interpretations of sex role development and its relation to the child's cognitive development, Kohlberg (1968) has described the process as simultaneous and interrelated. As children grow older, they develop increasingly rigid conceptions of sex role and preference. Peer pressure and pressure exerted by parents, siblings, and teachers usually force the child to conform to sex role stereotypes. A number of studies have reported that lower SES children not only tend to develop more rigid sex role stereotyping but do so at an earlier age than do their middle class counterparts. In this study, we predicted that there would be more sex typed preference responding among the experimental children and particularly among the boys.

We had some clues upon which to base this prediction of sex role development. Interpreting physical aggression as a male activity, as many of the scales do, we had early evidence of sex role differences when we observed the experimental and control group children together in playground activity. The experimental children tended to be more verbal than physical in their aggression and the boys exhibited more physical aggression than did the girls (Falender, 1969). Some evidence also exists suggesting that as children become more sophisticated, that is, after they adopt their sex role identity, they begin to widen their range of acceptable possible behaviors in play with opposite sex children.

Two versions of the "It" toy preference test (Falender, 1969) were administered to the children. The data indicated that older experimental children, both boys and girls, and the younger experimental boys responded with strong sex preferences ($p < .001$). No older experimental boys and only one younger boy chose a toy that the test labeled "female." In contrast, the control children exhibited less rigid toy preferences. However, there was a tendency for the boys to be more adherent to sex role stereotype in toy preferences. On dress preferences there was a significant difference in masculine choices by sex of child across group ($p < .001$).

In dramatic contrast to these results are the data from the standard administration of the test. When the instructions were "Which toy would 'It' prefer?" there was an overwhelming tendency for both sexes of the experimental group to choose male toys and for the control children to choose about half female and half male typed toys. There were no significant differences by sex of the child, across group, in choice of masculine toys for "It." These results confirm anecdotal and research evidence that children perceive "It" to be male. When asked for their own preferences, females' toy and dress choices were very different.

Looking at the preferences between groups on the "self" administration, there is strong adherence to sex appropriate choices among members of both groups. There is the possibility that there has been some modification of the stereotypes prompted by women's liberation discussions of nonsexist childrearing and teaching, or there may be some questions of validity of the "It" scale and the concept utilization of how certain toys and dress should be associated with a certain sex. There is clear evidence from this study, however, that given the sex preference categorizations, both groups of children associate certain behaviors with certain sexes. For boys, with increasing age, sex role preferences become more definite. For girls, especially girls in the experimental group, there was a developmental trend to expand toy preferences to include some typically masculine choices.

These data are consistent with Kohlberg's (1968) conceptualization that children experiment with their "boyness" or "girlness" after acquiring the label and gradually develop choices and preferences they feel comfortable with themselves. The experimental group seemed to have comfortably adopted their sex roles and, in the case of the older children, have broadened their ranges of behavior to integrate typically male and female behaviors. This behavior is generally associated with older children at a higher stage of cognitive development. There is, in addition, some evidence of the effect of peer group pressure upon the development of the boys' behavior by their choice of same sex playmates.

SELF-CONCEPT

Although the measurement of self-concept tends to precipitate argument, it is agreed that the concept of self is an important index of the child's adjustment. Verbal report procedures used with older children are not adequate with less verbal young children. Gresham (1981) reviewed the literature regarding normal and atypical development of children's social and interpersonal skills. In several studies, preschool children's personal attitudes were used to successfully discriminate those self-confident children whose school performance was superior to youngsters who lacked an age appropriate self-concept.

It was hypothesized that the experimental children, having high rates of success in their school environment and receiving praise for their intellectual development, would have high self-concepts. Results, however, revealed no significant differences between groups and were only suggestive based on the sex × group interaction, which approached significance. The fact that there was no difference between groups in self-concept may reflect the satisfaction of all of the children within their cultural milieu. However, once the children enter elementary school, self-concept differences may emerge.

Maternal Attitude

A large part of a mother's attitude toward her children stems from her own general outlook on life and her belief in her ability to control events in her own life and surroundings. Typically, research has described lower SES subjects as feeling unable to control their environment (e.g., Battle & Rotter, 1963; Coleman, 1966) and seeing themselves as "powerless, helpless, and over- whelmed" by their children (Minuchin, Montalvo, Guerney, Rosman, & Schumer, 1967). Such feelings of helplessness are associated with an *external locus of control* which reflects the belief that events are largely determined by fate or chance, as opposed to an *internal locus of control*, reflecting the belief that individuals themselves are capable of controlling life events. In our assess- ment of maternal attitudes, we included a study of locus of control among our experimental and control mothers.

Low SES mothers, who generally feel externally controlled, may believe that they have little influence on the development of their children (Tulkin, 1970). However, Gordon (1969) reported a shift from external to internal ori- entation among low SES mothers who had participated in his home stimula- tion program. His intensive program had evidently caused a restructuring of the mother's attitude as a result of her child's success as well as of her increased self-esteem and feelings of hope. We administered an adaptation of the Social Reaction Inventory (Gordon, 1969) to the mothers in the experimental and control groups. The questionnaire consists of 40 sentences in 20 pairs and was administered orally to the mother at home. The mother was asked to choose the one sentence of the pair with which she agreed. One sentence is intended as a reflection of choice and one a reflection of chance.

Differences between groups were significant ($p < .05$) both on the number of *choice* responses, or consequences felt to be under the control of the in- dividual, and on the number of *chance* responses, or consequences felt to be the result of fate or chance (Table 7-4). The experimental mothers showed a greater tendency toward an internal locus of control and therefore had a greater feeling of self-confidence and control over their lives.

Table 7-4   Locus of Control for Experimental and Control Group
Mothers

	n	Experimental	Control	F
Choice statements	17	11.2	6.1	6.13*
Chance statements	18	5.8	12.3	6.96*

df = 33, *$p < .05$

MATERNAL ATTITUDE SCALE (MAS)

A measure of the mothers' childrearing attitudes was provided by the Maternal Attitude Scale (Cohler, Weiss, & Grunebaum, 1970), which was ad- ministered orally to all of the mothers in the mothers' homes. All of the home interviews were conducted by an interviewer of the same racial background as each mother. The MAS measures the mother's attitude on five factors that are related to issues that must be "negotiated" (Sander, 1965) between mother and child during the child's first years of life. Tulkin and Cohler (1973) have developed the following five second order orthogonal or independent factors from the MAS test items:

I. *Inappropriate control of the child's aggressive impulses.* Inappropriate control reflects the mother's attitude that children's impulses cannot be channeled into socially appropriate behavior but must be inhibited completely.

II. *Discouragement versus encouragement of reciprocity.* Reciprocity reflects the attitude that infants can communicate and seek social interaction with their mothers, and that the mothers can understand and respond.

III. *Appropriate versus inappropriate closeness.* Attitudes involving appropriate closeness suggest that a mother does not view her baby as a narcissistic extension of the self and does not seek to attain through the baby gratifications that have been missing in her own life.

IV. *Acceptance versus denial of emotional complexity in childrearing.* Acceptance involves a mother's recognition that motherhood is sometimes more work than pleasure and that mothers do not always know what is best for their children.

V. *Comfort versus discomfort in perceiving and meeting the baby's (physical) needs.* Comfort implies that mothers feel they understand what babies want and provide for their babies' needs.

Previous attitude scales have been criticized for manifesting a variety of problems (Becker & Krug, 1965), including the ease of confusing an attitude or belief regarding the desirability of a particular behavior with the behavior itself. The emphasis of such instruments is usually on what subjects think and not on what they feel. The MAS was designed to counter these objections. Therefore, for our purposes, this scale represented a means of assessing attitudes against which we could corroborate actual behavior observed in structured mother-child interactions. The adaptation and degree of responsiveness of both the mother and the child are the essential indicators for determining the congruence of the mother's appraisal of her child's demands.

Differences approached significance ($.10 < p > .05$) between the two groups on two factors: The attitude of the experimental mothers reflected more appropriate closeness with their children and more acceptance of the emotional complexities of childrearing than did those of the control mothers. A near significant group × sex interaction on the dimensions of discouraging reciprocity was also observed, with more experimental mothers of girls and more control mothers of boys expressing attitudes that encouraged reciprocity.

Although it is generally believed that maternal childrearing attitudes are indicative of a mother's behavior toward her child, there has been little empirical evidence of (viz., significant correlations) how closely expressed attitudes relate to actual behavior. One exception is the study by Tulkin and Cohler

(1973), which used the MAS and found significant correlations between child-rearing attitudes and overt maternal behavior among middle SES mothers but not among low SES mothers.

We correlated the five MAS categories with the 12 behavior rating and information categories for both the Block Sort and Etch-a-Sketch tasks for both the experimental and control dyads.

Experimental Dyads. On the Block Sort task, mothers who believed in appropriate controls were more likely to engage in verbal informing behaviors ($p < .01$) and were less likely to engage in prolonged nontask oriented physical behaviors ($p < .05$). On the Etch-a-Sketch task, mothers who endorsed statements reflecting a belief in appropriate controls were more likely to utilize positive verbal reinforcement and verbal teaching and informing behaviors as well as verbal control for no reason, or for the reason of normative rules conduct ($p < .05$). These mothers also were less likely to demonstrate or physically point out. Also, on the Etch-a-Sketch task, mothers who endorsed statements reflecting a belief in discouraging reciprocity tended to use physical blocking and physical assault.

The association between the encouragement of reciprocity (Factor II) and information association was significant ($p < .05$) on the Etch-a-Sketch task. Also on the Etch-a-Sketch, mothers with more adaptive attitudes on the MAS factor of appropriate closeness (Factor III) achieved significantly more information association ($p < .05$), that is, greater predictability of a given mother or child behavior.

There was a less clear cut association between the acceptance of complexity in childrearing (Factor IV) and mother-child interaction behaviors. Acceptance of complexity in childrearing is negatively associated with verbal informing, verbal requests for physical behavior, and controlling for no reason given. Mothers with more adaptive attitudes on the MAS factor of comfort in their ability to perceive needs of the child (Factor V) used fewer control behaviors with no reason given and more task unrelated behavior ($p < .01$).

Control Dyads. On the Block Sort test, the attitude of inappropriate control of aggressive impulses for control dyads was positively correlated with verbal encouragement and control behaviors with a reason given. There was a negative correlation between discouraging reciprocity (Factor II) and enacting control behaviors with no reason given. Control mothers with more adaptive attitudes on the MAS factor of appropriate closeness (Factor III) engaged in less task related, extraneous activity and supplied less verbal feedback. Mothers who endorsed statements reflecting a belief in reciprocity were less likely to use verbal correction or orientation ($p < .05$) on the Etch-a-Sketch and less likely to verbally request physical feedback on the Block Sort. They did tend to encourage verbally, demonstrate, and use physical blocking. Mothers who expressed attitudes of comfort in perceiving their children's needs (Factor V) tended to encourage verbally and tended not to control without a reason given ($p < .05$) on the Etch-a-Sketch task.

From these observations of the mother-child interaction, we found differences in overt maternal behavior between the experimental and control mothers when their children averaged 5 years of age and a significant relationship between maternal attitude and childrearing behavior. Specifically, on the Etch-a-Sketch task experimental mothers were more positive, less negative, and less physically controlling than were control mothers. On both tasks, there was greater behavioral predictability between mother and children in the experimental group. On the MAS there were significant differences between the two groups on two factors: appropriate closeness and acceptance of complexity in childrearing. Both groups of mothers endorsed MAS items in the direction of overrestrictiveness, but this was especially true for the control mothers. The experimental mothers felt more uncertain than the control mothers about the best ways of caring for a child, but indicated more appropriate closeness.

The correlation between the MAS and observations on the 12 mother-child interaction categories indicated that, among experimental mothers, attitudes reflecting appropriate closeness and encouragement of reciprocity (i.e., that infants can communicate and that mothers can understand and respond) were significantly correlated with greater information association or behavioral predictability between mother and child. Mothers in this group whose attitudes reflected appropriate control were more likely to engage in verbal informing behavior, to use positive verbal reinforcement, and to use verbal control without any reason given. They were also less likely to engage in task related physical behavior. Those who expressed a belief in discouraging reciprocity tended to use physical blocking and physical assault.

In contrast, relationships between the control mothers' expressed attitudes and their behavior in interaction with their children were low and were generally not in predicted directions. Tulkin and Cohler (1973) explained their similar finding among low SES mothers in terms of these mothers' feelings of powerlessness toward their children. Thus, while a mother might endorse attitudes reflecting a belief in reciprocity, she may be less likely to act on her beliefs because she feels she can have little influence over her child. She may desire extensive interaction with her child, but may feel there is nothing she can do to encourage it.

The congruence between the experimental mothers' attitudes and behavior, on the other hand, resembles the finding for Tulkin and Cohler's (1973) middle class population. The effects of treatment, either direct or indirect, seemed to have influenced the experimental mothers. From the mother-child dyads we had evidence of feedback from the experimental children to their mothers. On the MAS the experimental mothers expressed beliefs that were more adaptive than those of their control counterparts. These findings suggest that an aspect of the treatment effect took the form of moving the relationship closer between mothers' attitudes toward childrearing and their actual practice.

SUMMARY

In summary, then, we found that the experimental dyads transmitted more information during structured mother-child interaction sessions than did the control dyads, and this was seen as a function of the quality of the experimental child's verbal behavior. The experimental children supplied more information verbally and initiated more verbal communication than did children in the control dyads. The children in the experimental dyads took responsibility for guiding the flow of information and providing most of the verbal information and direction. The mothers in both dyads indicated little differences in their teaching ability during the testing session. However, in the experimental dyads the children structured the interaction session either by their questioning or by teaching the mother. As a result, a developmentally more sophisticated reciprocal feedback system seemed to have developed between the experimental children and their mothers, which contributed to faster and more successful problem completion. Thus, the intensive stimulation program undergone by the experimental children has benefited both the experimental child and the experimental mother by broadening their verbal and expressive behavioral repertoire.

The experimental children performed at a consistently more advanced developmental level on all three of the cognitive style tasks than did the control children. The experimental children evidenced more reflective responding on the KRISP by emitting fewer errors than did the control children. On a conceptual sorting task the experimental children utilized sorting based upon categorization and description, both strategies requiring analysis of the stimulus display. In contrast, the control children had difficulty verbalizing the type of sorting they had chosen and tended to use strictly relational sorts, based upon the least amount of stimulus analysis. On a field independent-dependent measure, the experimental children were more field independent (able to find more embedded figures in the stimulus displays), than were the control children. The assessment of perception of self did not differentiate between the groups of children.

8
Follow-Up Assessment of Development

Assessment of intelligence began prior to school entry and continued through the middle school years for both experimental and control children. This assessment used the Wechsler series, including first the WPPSI (Wechsler, 1967) through 72 months and subsequently the WISC (Wechsler, 1949). This test series was begun prior to preschool termination when the children were 48 months of age and continued as the measure for following the children's performance through school. The Wechsler series as reported here was administered in part by different independent (outside the University) testing teams using blind testing procedures. For those test administrations the family coordinator would pick up each child at home and bring him or her to a neutral testing site (usually a hotel suite) a few miles from home where the child was received by uninformed (as to the experimental or control status of the children) test personnel. The child was assigned a code number and the tester was given only the child's first name.

WPPSI assessments, which correspond with Stanford-Binet assessments at 48, 60, and 72 months of age, are summarized in Table 8-1. The mental age (MA) difference between the experimental and control children over the 48 through 60 month period was lower for WPPSI scores than for Stanford-Binet scores (see Table 8-2). At 72 months of age there was an MA difference of 15.41 months on the WPPSI, compared with an MA difference of 23.29 months on the Stanford-Binet. The discrepancy in performance on the WPPSI and Stanford-Binet was not equal for experimental and control children: The average discrepancy between the WPPSI full scale IQ scores and the Stanford-Binet IQ scores across the three assessments was 9.81 IQ points for the experimental children and 7.05 IQ points for the control children. The MA differences and differences in the rate of general intellectual development were smaller for WPPSI assessments than for Stanford-Binet assessments. A best estimate of the difference between groups during the 48 through 72 month age period could be based on average performance on these two instruments. In this case, using such an average, the MA difference between groups increased from 14.11 months to 19.35 months across this period.

Correlations between the Stanford-Binet and WPPSI IQ scores were $r = .95$ at 48 months, $r = .91$ at 60 months, and $r = .82$ at 72 months of age, and the correlation between the Stanford-Binet and WPPSI GIQ scores (averaged performance) across these three points was $r = .96$. These discrepancies are consistent with those reported by others (Flynn, 1984; Sattler, 1982), but higher than the average correlation of $r = .80$ identified in 47 comparison studies (Jensen, 1982).

The mean full scale WPPSI IQ dropped slightly for experimental children while the mean for control children fluctuated but remained relatively unchanged across the three assessments. Low risk contrast children maintained a consistent WPPSI IQ level slightly lower than that for experimental children but equal to the general population mean. The average WPPSI difference between experimental and control children from 48 through 72 months of age was 25.88 points $(SD = 3.90)$ and experimental scores were an average of 9.82 points $(SD = 2.61)$ higher than scores for low risk contrast children. When all Stanford-Binet and WPPSI assessments across the 24 through 72 months period were considered together, the average difference between experimental and control children was 28.59 points $(SD = 3.00)$ and experimental scores were an average of 11.39 points $(SD = 2.54)$ higher than scores for low risk contrast children.

Profile analysis of WPPSI IQ scores (Full Scale) indicated there was a marginally significant, $F(2, 32) = 2.78$, $p < .10$, group × age interaction for experimental and control scores. Separate analyses for the individual groups indicated the drop in experimental WPPSI scores from 48 through 72 months of age was significant, $F(2, 15) = 3.93$, $p < .05$, but there was no change in control scores. Experimental children had significantly, $F(3, 31) = 27.97$, $p < .001$, higher WPPSI full scale IQ scores across the 48 through 72 month age period. There was no change in the rate of verbal IQ development for either group, but there was a parallel and significant decline, $F(4, 64) = 3.57$, $p < .05$, in the performance measure for both groups, although mainly for the experimental group.

FOLLOW-UP STABILITY OF MEASURED INTELLIGENCE

A psychologist tested all children at some time during each year according to a schedule arranged by convenience. Test scores corresponding most closely to 84, 96, 108, and 120 months of age were grouped for comparison. Descriptive statistics for WISC full scale, verbal, and performance IQ scores are summarized in Table 8-3 and illustrated along with WPPSI test performance in Figure 8-1. The mean full scale WISC IQ at 84 months of age was approximately 6 points lower than the 72 month full scale WPPSI IQ for both experimental

Table 8-1   WPPSI Full Scale, Verbal, and Performance IQ Scores for Experimental, Control, and Low Risk Contrast Children

Group Age (Mos)	Full Scale				Verbal				Performance			
	M	SD	Range	n	M	SD	Range	n	M	SD	Range	n
Experimental												
48	113.94	8.54	96.00-129.00	17	112.24	9.00	94.00-125.00	17	113.29	8.80	97.00-129.00	17
60	110.41	6.84	97.00-121.00	17	111.00	4.80	100.00-117.00	17	108.24	9.51	95.00-127.00	17
72	109.00	6.37	99.00-122.00	16	109.06	5.84	100.00-120.00	16	107.44	8.16	95.00-127.00	16
Control												
48	85.44	12.40	63.00-115.00	18	84.28	11.39	67.00-111.00	18	89.50	13.04	66.00-116.00	18
60	82.67	11.28	64.00-107.00	18	83.94	12.13	65.00-114.00	18	84.39	10.15	69.00-100.00	18
72	87.60	9.88	64.00-109.00	15	89.73	10.51	66.00-114.00	15	87.60	9.48	69.00-101.00	15
Low Risk Contrast												
48	101.38	12.81	80.00-117.00	8	102.50	10.57	84.00-117.00	8	100.13	15.38	77.00-115.00	8
60	100.88	11.36	80.00-116.00	8	104.25	8.65	87.00-115.00	8	97.13	14.71	76.00-115.00	8
72	101.63	13.53	88.00-123.00	8	103.50	10.14	91.00-119.00	8	100.25	14.69	84.00-123.00	8

Table 8-2 Mean MA Scores for Experimental, Control, and Low Risk
Contrast Groups Derived from the WPPSI and WISC IQ Tests

Age	WPPSI			WISC		
(Mos)	E	C	LRC	E	C	LRC
48	54.69	41.01	48.66			
60	66.25	49.60	60.53			
72	78.48	63.07	73.17			
84				86.47	67.85	86.10
96				98.88	79.23	95.84
108				110.80	90.58	110.52
120				125.02	103.55	122.80

and control children. The difference between groups on the WISC at 84
months was 22.17 IQ points, which is similar to the 21.40 difference between
the groups on the last WPPSI assessment. The MA difference between experimental and control groups on the WISC at 84 months of age was 18.62
months, which compares to the MA difference of 15.41 months on the WPPSI
at 72 months of age (see Table 8-2)

Experimental and low risk contrast children maintained relatively stable
WISC IQ levels through 120 months of age, with an average IQ difference between the two groups of 19.81. The IQ level for control children rose steadily,

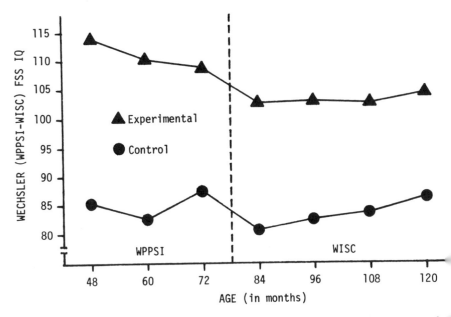

Figure 8-1. Means of Experimental and Control Groups' FSS IQs for 48 Through 120 Months

Table 8-3 WISC Full Scale, Verbal, and Performance IQ Scores for Experimental, Control, and Low Risk Contrast Children

Group Age (Mos)	Full Scale				Verbal				Performance			
	M	SD	Range	n	M	SD	Range	n	M	SD	Range	n
Experimental												
84	102.94	10.97	83.00-123.00	17	102.06	11.10	82.00-123.00	17	103.53	11.11	86.00-124.00	17
96	103.00	11.48	88.00-132.00	17	101.29	8.34	89.00-118.00	17	105.47	15.39	80.00-142.00	17
108	102.59	12.03	89.00-129.00	17	98.82	8.84	84.00-113.00	17	106.47	16.37	83.00-143.00	17
120	104.18	11.53	93.00-138.00	17	101.71	7.84	90.00-123.00	17	105.94	15.31	82.00-147.00	17
Control												
84	80.77	8.73	65.00- 93.00	17	81.82	7.20	69.00- 94.00	17	82.71	11.66	64.00-106.00	17
96	82.53	9.58	63.00-103.00	15	81.67	7.19	69.00-101.00	15	85.60	10.25	64.00-106.00	15
108	83.87	11.06	72.00-107.00	15	82.13	10.16	67.00-104.00	15	88.87	12.13	67.00-113.00	15
120	86.29	10.12	72.00-106.00	17	84.24	9.44	71.00-105.00	17	90.94	11.90	75.00-120.00	17
Low Risk Contrast												
84	102.50	12.96	91.00-125.00	8	102.50	12.12	90.00-120.00	8	101.63	14.18	86.00-129.00	8
96	99.83	10.70	86.00-112.00	6	99.83	12.77	79.00-114.00	6	100.17	10.46	85.00-111.00	6
108	102.33	12.37	86.00-121.00	6	102.33	14.14	90.00-129.00	6	101.50	11.04	85.00-118.00	6
120	102.33	7.87	89.00-111.00	6	101.00	7.59	94.00-114.00	6	103.50	10.48	86.00-115.00	6

reducing the difference between experimental and control children by 4.3 IQ points. The difference between groups at 120 months is nearly 18 IQ points. While the IQ difference between experimental and control children decreased after the 84 month assessment, the MA difference between these two groups increased from 18.62 months to over 21.47 months across the next 3 years (see Table 8-3). Therefore, the early delay in neuropsychologic and intellectual development evidenced by control children's performance during infancy and early childhood was followed by delays in intellectual development through the early school years.

Profile analysis of WISC full scale scores indicated that performance was parallel between 84 and 120 months. There was no significant change in scores over time, but the experimental full scale WISC scores were significantly, $F(4, 30) = 11.54$, $p < .01$, higher than control scores across the 84 through 120 month period. Bonferroni-Dunn confidence intervals ($p = .05$) for group differences at 84, 96, 108, and 120 months did not include zero, indicating that there were significant differences between the groups at each of these three points.

Between 48 and 72 months, the ages of the first WPPSI testing and final WPPSI testing prior to public school first grade, the experimental group changed in IQ from a mean of 113.94 ($SD = 8.54$) on the WPPSI to a mean of 109.0 ($SD = 6.16$) on the WPPSI, nearly a 5 point decline in about 2 years' time. The control group, on the other hand, changed from a mean of 85.44 ($SD = 12.40$) at 48 months, to a mean of 87.60 ($SD = 9.00$) at 72 months, an increase of more than 2 points. The control group actually declined from the 48-month age mark nearly 3 points to the 60-month age mark, which was the final testing prior to public school kindergarten entry. Therefore, the 72 months' mean of 87.60 is a nearly 5 point increase from the 82.67 ($SD = 11.28$) at 60 months (after 1 year of school). However, after the first year of school the control group declined over 6 points in WISC IQ to a mean of 80.77 ($SD = 8.47$), compared with an approximately 6 point decline in WISC IQ for the experimental group to a mean of 102.94 ($SD = 10.97$). From this point the experimental group remained fairly stable through the fourth grade (X = 104.18, $SD = 11.53$), while the control group showed a gradual increase of about 5.5 points through the fourth grade (X = 86.29, $SD = 9.81$).

The strength of the developmental difference in performance between the experimental and control groups once in school was indicated not only by measured IQ, but particularly by end of first grade language and learning data that gave us additional information relative to the intellectual strengths of the experimental and control children. For example, the language data completed up through the first grade, including the ITPA, showed a continued differential development in favor of the experimental children on several aspects of psycholinguistic development. In fact, completed language data up to first grade entrance showed the experimental children having a 1 to 2 year performance advantage over the control children. Second, the follow-up of the development of the children's learning performance skills was consistent with preschool levels and showed a continued differential superiority for the experimental group over the control group on tests that had been administered from 2 years of age on. It was not until the control children had completed 2 to 3 years of elementary schooling that the lag between experimental and control performance disappeared (as measured by the differential in the learning performance constructs described in the learning chapter).

At the end of the fourth year of school, the experimental children's performance continued to be superior to that of the control group of children. At that point in time 60% of the control children scored 85 or below in IQ, compared with none in the experimental group. In Figure 8-2 we have illustrated the percentage of children scoring 85 or below on the Stanford-Binet from 24 to 72 months and on the WISC from 84 to 120 months. This reflects the changing quality within each group across time.

Because at most of the time points there were outliers in both the experimental and control groups, it was important to plot individual profiles. For WPPSI-WISC full scale (FS) data, the children who had scored high at the first data point remained high in the experimental group and the children who had scored low remained low in the control group. The data can be reanalyzed, either by removing them and subjecting the rest of the data to profile analysis

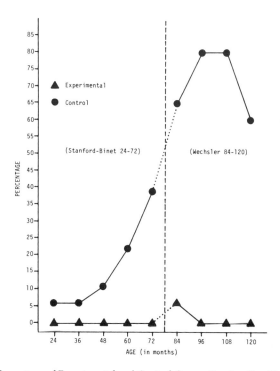

Figure 8-2.   Percentage of Experimental and Control Groups Scoring One Standard Deviation or More Below IQ Test Mean for 24 Through 120 Months

or by adjusting for the initial score of each individual over the rest of the time points by subtracting or covarying the scores. The correlation matrix (see Table 8-4) at least partially confirms this analysis. The correlation matrix reveals only positive entries, a finding that fails to contradict the assertion that a high score at one test interval would result in a similarly high score at subsequent test periods. Conversely, low scores seem to result in subsequent exhibitions of low scores. There is a drop in correlation for both the experimental and control groups between 72 and 84 months. This period marked the transition for the experimental children from treatment to first grade (as well as from the WPPSI to the WISC). The drop in FS correlation between these two test periods may be attributable either to the change from WPPSI to WISC IQ forms or to some developmental phenomenon related to this transition period. I will comment on different (experimental vs. control) developmental trends for Wechsler verbal and performance scales (i.e., the subtests for FS scores) later in this chapter.

When making interpretations of intellectual development based on IQ test data, social scientists learn to consider the various methodologic precautions involved in generating such data, including who administers the test, in what

Table 8-4 Correlation Matrices for Experimental and Control Group WPPSI/WISC (Combined) – FSS IQs for 48 through 120 Months

Months	48	60	72	84	96	108	120
				Experimental Group			
48	8.54						
60	.67	6.84					
72	.60	.44	6.37				
84	.51	.51	.32	10.97			
96	.61	.64	.61	.58	11.48		
108	.53	.35	.52	.55	.77	12.03	
120	.59	.45	.54	.52	.75	.73	11.53
Mean	113.94	110.41	109.00	102.94	103.00	102.59	104.18
				Control Group			
48	12.40						
60	.83	11.28					
72	.79	.55	9.88				
84	.65	.62	.19	8.47			
96	.43	.61	.09	.68	8.70		
108	.42	.46	.34	.53	.71	10.04	
120	.45	.53	.40	.49	.73	.88	9.81
Mean	85.44	82.67	87.60	80.77	82.53	83.87	86.29

kind of situation, and the nature of the group being tested. The bulk of the data reported in the literature presents two major problems as a reference source for this research. First, it is mainly cross-sectional and/or group data for which the complement changes between testings. It is, therefore, difficult for the literature to reveal the extent to which individual differences influence or change with such performance across time. Second, notwithstanding the problem of cross-sectional interpretations from the literature, is the fact that across many years the IQ test instrument used changes and so even within individual comparisons are confounded with between test differences. We commented earlier, for example, that changes from WPPSI to WISC forms of the Wechsler IQ test may have confounded the correlation analysis between 72 and 84 months. Even when the test may be the same, there is still the problem that within individual comparisons between tests may be confounded by the differences in the sensitivity of the test to the various developmentally related intellectual skills.

To some extent, these problems are minimized by longitudinal data derived from an intact sample across a sufficient time span so that the various influences of, for example, time, situation, test sensitivity, and individual nuances in performances either stabilize or reveal themselves in some pattern of consistent performance about which we can reliably make some interpretational comment. The data in this study must be interpreted with the above mentioned precautions in mind. But there was still clearly reflected a consistent differential movement in experimental versus control performance across time. Certainly, the efficacy of the preschool education and maternal rehabilitation program on the intellectual development of the experimental group of children was clearly demonstrated by these data. However, there are some additional points of interest about these data that should be commented upon.

The movement of test performance levels across such factors as the alternation of tests (viz., Stanford-Binet and WPPSI), comparisons across tests (WPPSI to WISC), and across unique experiences (viz., entry into school) are important concerns because each holds implications for understanding changes in test performance. For example, Dearborn and Rothney (1941) reported a significant retest gain and then drop in test performance when a second test was alternated with one administered earlier. The comparability of WPPSI to WISC performance has also been commented on and suggests no reasons for performance to be comparable on each for an individual (Sattler, 1982).

In addition to these several factors, it is important to consider the differences between the target group, in this case black and disadvantaged, and the national groups upon which the tests were normed. Also of considerable importance is what effect the changing social milieu on successive generations has had as a factor requiring that the norms be revised. Thorndike (1978), for example, suggested that there is a natural decrement in Binet performance between 5 and 9 years of age of nearly 5 points for the population as a whole. If, however, significant performance differences between treated subjects on the order of 3 or 4 points are considered important, surely a 5 point unaccounted shift should be of serious concern. But without longitudinal data on a qualified subject sample for which the integrity of the constituency is protected over time, it is quite difficult to understand the meaning of such small point differences because of the possible influences of unaccounted for individual variation and differences in tests. For example, McCall, Appelbaum, and Hogarty (1973) suggested that changes in IQ performance of a full deviation or even two are not uncommon for some portion of the population over time.

Thus, in our search for understanding of the nature of the differences between the experimental and control groups, we have attempted to examine these differences with a caution that presumes a measure of caprice due to individual, situational, and test factors, that can operate to hearten or dishearten the researcher whose hopes or anticipations are restricted to one or two assessments in time. For these data, a consistent mean difference of better than a standard deviation provided adequate evidence to the difference in performance between the experimental and control groups resulting from the treatment intervention and as well provided an indication of potential for such group differential to be maintained over time.

In summary, the experimental group's performance showed some decline prior to school entry: 5 points on WPPSI FS scores and a 6 point decline from the WPPSI FS to the WISC FS scores after 1 year of school. On the WISC FS itself after 4 years of school, there was a slight increase. There were several reasons, perhaps, to account for the decline prior to school entry, as we noted above, although there were no changes within the actual treatment program. However, the fact that during this preschool period, 48 to 72 months, WPPSI testing was alternated with Stanford-Binet testings and administered by independent testing teams may have contributed to the decrease (e.g., Anastasi, 1958). Testing from 84 months and beyond was entirely by independent teams who used the WISC and no similar decline was found.

For the control group, in summary, there was a loss in IQ performance prior to public school that was regained after kindergarten only to be lost again after first grade. Some spurt in performance after the initial school experience is typical for seriously disadvantaged children and is comparable to the increase seen in our original survey data for children of low IQ mothers (see Figure 8-1). However, the loss by the control group is nearly recovered by the end of the fourth grade. The 7 point loss in performance level between the WPPSI and WISC tests was comparable to the experimental group's performance, and the control group essentially recouped that loss by the end of the fourth grade.

The control children experienced similar changes in test procedure, but did not show a comparable preschool to school decline and did, it seemed, benefit from their school experience. The differential between the groups at the end of fourth grade remained on the order of 20 points. The intervention of school seemed to support the performance of the control group, at least at their level—for example, compare the control mean IQ of 85.44 at 48 months to their mean IQ of 86.29 at 120 months (less than a 1 point gain). The experimental children lost nearly 10 points during that same period (113.94 at 48 months to 104.18 at 120 months), although half of that loss occurred prior to public school entry and for the other half explanation is confounded by a shift in tests. One possible explanation for the stabilized performance in both groups could be the expansion of the special services program in the Milwaukee Public Schools, although this is a tenuous explanation in light of the poor achievement test performance in school by both groups.

THE "ARTIFICIAL" INFLUENCE OF INTERVENTION

The supplementary stimulation program for experimental children created an environment that cannot be considered simply a reallocation of natural variations in intellectual stimulation. Based on the results of the early cross-sectional study, low risk contrast children were assumed to be receiving adequate stimulation naturally within their homes to support normal rates of cognitive development even though they lived in the same disadvantaged neighborhoods as did the experimental and control children. It is possible to estimate the extent of the additional or artificial influence on the rate of neuropsychologic and intellectual development that results from the intervention program by comparing the DQ and IQ levels of the experimental group with the DQ and IQ levels of the low risk contrast group.

Experimental DQ scores were slightly higher than low risk contrast DQ scores across the infancy period. There was a mean difference between the experimental and low risk contrast groups of 4.91 points $(SD = 3.87)$, with the major difference occurring at 22 months of age. This latter score difference resulted from the relatively high performance on the language schedule by the experimental children, which probably reflected the effect of the program's considerable emphasis on verbal stimulation.

The average difference between these two groups across all Stanford-Binet assessments was 11.91 IQ points $(SD = 2.43)$, and across all WPPSI assessments was 9.80 IQ points $(SD = 2.61)$. To the extent that the Stanford-Binet is a more verbally loaded test than the WPPSI is, the larger difference for Stanford-Binet scores may also be a reflection of the program's emphasis on verbal stimulation and adult interactions with the children. The average difference between the experimental and low risk contrast groups across all Stanford-Binet and WPPSI assessments was 11.39 IQ points $(SD = 2.54)$, perhaps a reasonable best estimate of the additional effect of intervention on the level of intellectual development during early childhood and the preschool years. In contrast, but by the same reasoning, there was an average difference between low risk children and control children across these same assessments of 17.27 IQ points $(SD = 3.41)$ and a MA difference of 19 months, which could be a reasonably good estimate of the real delay in intellectual development for the control children, delay that can be attributed to the natural variation in the level of intellectual stimulation provided by mothers with a considerably lower level of intelligence (but living in the same neighborhood). Once the intervention program was over, the difference between experimental and low risk contrast children diminished. The average difference between these two groups on WISC assessments collected over 7 years was only 1.45 IQ points ($SD = 1.75$). Therefore, by this line of reasoning, the WISC IQ level for experimental children could be a reasonable estimate of their "true intellectual level," separate from any artificial effect attributable to the intensity of the intervention.

VERBAL IQ AND PERFORMANCE IQ

Both the WPPSI and WISC IQ tests provide separate IQs for verbal and performance skills. The Verbal Scales (VS) are more highly structured than the Performance Scales (PS) and are considered to reflect information at hand. The Performance Scales are thought to reflect the ability to solve problems upon meeting new situations (see Tables 8-1 and 8-3).

WPPSI verbal IQ scores dropped slightly for experimental children but rose for control children, resulting in a significant, $F(2, 32) = 3.63$, $p < .05$, group × age interaction for these scores. Separate analyses of verbal scores for each group indicated that the change in scores over time was not significant for either group. In contrast, there was a parallel and significant, $F(4, 64) = 3.57$, $p < .05$, drop in WPPSI performance IQ scores for experimental and control children across the 48 through 72 month period. Experimental children scored significantly higher than control children did on both the verbal, $F(3, 31) = 26.37$, $p < .001$, and the performance, $F(3, 31) = 20.03$, $p < .001$, subtests of the WPPSI. Both verbal and performance IQ scores for low risk contrast children were lower than those for experimental children, but they were comparable to the mean for the general population.

Profile analyses of WISC verbal and performance subscale IQ scores indicated that performance was parallel for verbal and performance scores across time. Analyses of WISC verbal and performance scores for the two groups indicated no significant change over time. Experimental children scored significantly higher than did control children on both the verbal, $F(4, 30) = 18.06$, $p < .01$, and the performance, $F(4, 30) = 7.55$, $p < .01$, subscales of the WISC over this period. One tailed Bonferroni-Dunn confidence intervals ($p = .05$) for group differences on verbal and performance scores from 84 through 120 months did not include zero, indicating that experimental scores were significantly higher than each mean control score across this time period.

Tables 8-1 and 8-3 also list the mean Wechsler Verbal IQ (VIQ) and Performance IQ (PIQ) for the low risk contrast group at each testing age. VIQ performance dominates PIQ performance for the low risk contrast children through the first year of school just as it does for the experimental children. The experimental group is consistently slightly superior to the low risk contrast group on PIQ while their VIQ scores are quite similar. Both the low risk contrast and experimental groups are consistently superior to the control group on both VIQ and PIQ subscales.

Thus, these separate analyses confirm that the experimental group is significantly superior on both the WPPSI and WISC for the VS and PS scores. These subscale performance data are revealed to have an over time pattern of intellectual performance that is rather different for the groups prior to school but becomes similar once the children are in school. Between 72 and 84 months, there is an FS performance decline of about 6 points for both the experimental and control groups. It is the decline in preschool WPPSI performance by the experimental group in comparison with the control group that contributes to the significant difference in the developmental patterns between these two groups. Performance on the WISC during the first four grades of school of both groups is essentially similar. Actually, there is improvement for both groups on the WISC test, although it is more pronounced for the control group. There is no real improvement in VS scores over time. For the experimental and control groups, it is PS performance that shows the improvement, and why this is so remains speculative. Such a finding would be, according to Sattler (1974), a reflection of the use of accumulated knowledge. In any event, interpretation of the VS and PS performance differential between groups is more understandable than differences within groups, that is, it could be attributable to a continuation of the benefit of the preschool educational treatment program for the experimental children.

Wechsler (1949) suggested that there may be some diagnostic significance when the difference between VIQ and PIQ is of a certain magnitude (10 to 15 points) in a particular direction. The discrepancy between mean VIQ and PIQ within a group reaches a maximum of 7.56 for the experimental group at 108 months (PIQ > VIQ) and 6.74 maximum (PIQ > VIQ) at 108 months for the control group (although in some individual cases this discrepancy is on the order of 20 or more points). In the preschool years the experimental group's VS performance was superior to their PS performance and was also a better reflection of the Full Scale IQ. The control group, rather interestingly, shows higher VS than PS performance only at the end of kindergarten. The experimental group's VS performance is superior to their PS performance but then shifts after entering school, where as we have noted the pattern of performance is similar, though at very different levels, to the performance of the control group. The control group consistently shows higher PIQs then VIQs from 48 to 120 months (except at the 72 month mark).

Vernon (1969) suggested that intelligence tests give a better estimate of potential than do other measures of achievement. But the greater usefulness of an intelligence test lies in its ability to predict "educability or trainability because of its greater generality, and because it samples the reasoning capacities developed outside school which the child should be able to apply in school, e.g., to new subjects" (p. 27). In this light, these data allow as a possible interpretation for the discrepancy between PS and VS performance that the potential for learning continues at a more substantial level outside the school situation (i.e., as indicated by the PIQ). The question remains then, as to whether with proper home and school education this potential could be reflected in higher VS performance or even in a change in the differential of the VS to PS positions in level, for both the experimental and control group children. Additionally, Vernon's suggestion that IQ predicts educability indicates that a higher learning potential exists even for the control group children.

One additional speculation rests on what might be a nonapparent benefit that accrues to the IQ scale performance of urban children as compared with those children in rural settings. It might well be expected that comparable children under similar treatment conditions but in a different setting, rural versus urban, might show not only lower IQ scale performance but also PIQ lowered again by the less complex experiential factors in a rural setting that might otherwise contribute to the extra-school performance learning that sustains (or lifts) the IQ of low SES urban children (Lehmann, 1959). In most research on the efficacy of compensatory education for disadvantaged black and white children, insufficient attention is given to the sociocultural implications of differences between rural and urban settings for intellectual development — yet this differential has been fairly well documented (Heber, Dever, & Conry, 1968).

Therefore, one interpretation might regard the higher performance on the PS relative to the VS as an indication of extra-school (or environmental) learning, while the lower VS performance may result from two factors. One factor we believe is inadequate attention to language skill development in the schools, which in turn combines with the breakdown of sophisticated language skills because of the influence of peers on street language development (Labov, 1967). In other words, not only does the educational program of the public schools work inadequately on language skill development (include reading here), but that problem is exacerbated by the influence of peers. The effect of this latter factor might be reflected, albeit in quite an opposite way perhaps, in the elevated performance on the PS. But it is certain, elaborate interpretional commentary aside, that the fairly sophisticated language development attained by the experimental group, partly reflected in the strength of the VIQ prior to school and partly by the level of reading upon entering school, is not being maintained (supported) as the children move through their postintervention public schooling.

The comparatively low FS IQ performance of the controls is reflected by their VS IQ, but not by the higher PS IQ. The VS and FS IQ scores may not reflect the individual child's ability but rather the inadequacy of the school and home environments in fostering the appropriate verbally based skills needed to perform successfully. In this light, the control children's higher PS IQ performance (higher than FS) might well indicate potential that is being interfered with by the lack of appropriate language and verbal skills, the critical tools with which to work in the world of school.

Indeed, as we have suggested before, the lower performance of the control children that contributed to the discrepancy in Stanford-Binet assessments between the experimental and control groups should not be taken simply as an irreversibly deteriorated performance, but rather as an index of significant delay; that is, there remains a potential for responsiveness and a potential to learn and perform successfully under the proper educational and environmental conditions. In the preschool period, the experimental children's language performance was extremely strong and VS performance was higher then PS performance and also a good reflection of the overall IQ. As the influence of the strong verbal environment of the preschool gave way to the influences of the environment, namely peers, the experimental children's pattern of performance seemed more similar to the control children's. Note that preschool (72 months) and third grade (108 months) PS IQs were quite comparable (107.44 vs. 106.47), whereas the VIQs at these same ages showed a difference of over 10 points (109.06 vs. 98.82). In other words, it could be argued that declining IQ is most directly the result of a deterioration in language skill development, a responsibility of both school and home that neither adequately assumes.

In Figure 8-3, we have presented the data in bar graph form to show the proportion of the group for whom VS performance was superior to PS performance, as well as the proportions of VIQ = PIQ and PIQ > VIQ. Actually, both groups in this comparison were quite comparable, with the experimental group showing a slight strength in the proportion of VIQ > PIQ, but one that is also achieved by the control group after their kindergarten experience. This increased superiority within group was maintained for the control children, but decreased for the experimental children as both groups moved through first grade. From first grade through fourth grade, the shift continued to a greater proportion of PIQ > VIQ performers, although at a slower rate for the experimental group. It is actually a most provocative observation that, although there is a difference in IQ levels (nearly 20 points), the pattern of performance within groups with respect to PS and VS performance is parallel.

The comparability of performance levels for the low risk contrast and experimental groups provided support for the efficacy of an early intervention strategy to prevent mild or cultural-familial retardation in at risk families. The experimental children, although they were the offspring of low IQ inner city dwelling mothers, were functioning within the normal range of intellectual functioning. Their performance was comparable to that of the low risk contrast children born into families with high (>100) levels of maternal IQ, and the performance of both of these groups was significantly superior to that of the control group, who received no treatment. The control group was functioning nearly 20 points below normal and had a 60% rate of below 85 IQ scores.

These data on the differential in performance over time between groups indicate that it is possible to reduce the effects of environmental factors

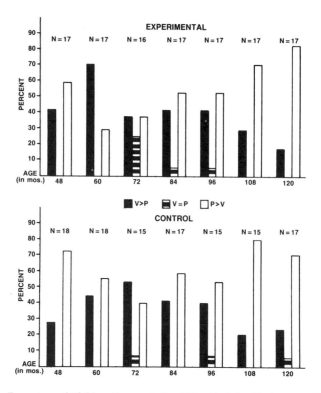

Figure 8-3. Percentage of Children Demonstrating Either Verbal or Performance Dominance on Wechsler IQ Tests for the Experimental and Control Groups Across Age

contributing to high levels of risk by mitigating negative environmental experiences. The level of performance for the experimental children is impressive, although the decline in IQ scores over the 48 through 84 month period should be further investigated. We have asked whether the consistent performance of the low risk contrast group is a more realistic reflection of the experimental group's performance than is their own early performance (48 through 72 months). If this is true, it suggests that their early performance levels were elevated by the intensity of training in the preschool program, and that this elevated performance diminished when the children entered the less intense school setting. In addition to possible effects of quite different environments and experiences, the discrepancy between preschool and school performance for the experimental children also indicates the sensitivity of measures of IQ and the plasticity of behavior requisite for IQ performance within a relatively short period. These factors require further investigation and are significant for planning future intervention.

General IQ (GIQ)

In their 1973 monograph, McCall, Appelbaum, and Hogarty pointed out the importance of distinguishing between a subject's average IQ over several assessments and the single IQ assessment. The importance lies in the difference between this general IQ as a best estimate of IQ performance and the single point estimate, which may often merely be an inflection in a sequence of assessments that may or may not reflect general intellectual performance. In the case of an inflection that is a rather extreme estimate of IQ, this fact might be revealed only by examining the IQ patterning in the sequence of assessments. For the intellectual development of a single individual and even for a group pattern of IQ development, there are somewhat strong inflections that may not be fairly reflected in single point estimates.

We have examined the relationship of the General IQ (GIQ) to the single estimate for both groups and in a later section have detailed individual performance so that differences in individual IQ performance profiles can be seen. There are several points of inflection in the Wechsler performance illustrated in Figure 8-1.

1. For the experimental group there are the following:
   a. A high point at the 48-month mark, where the WPPSI was first administered.
   b. The change between the 72-month and 84-month marks where the WPPSI gave way to the WISC.
   c. The 84-month mark, which suggests a leveling off point.
2. For the control group there are the following:
   a. The gain in IQ through kindergarten, from 60 to 72 months.
   b. The loss through first grade as the WPPSI at 72 months gave way to the WISC at 84 months.
   c. The gradual recovery of that loss from 84 months through 120 months.

In Table 8-5 we have presented the means for both IQ estimates: the single point 72-month and 120-month IQs and the preschool and school GIQs.

Table 8-5 Comparison of Preschool (WPPSI) and School (WISC) Period Wechsler Point IQ Measures and General IQ Measures for Experimental and Control Groups

Age Period	Experimental				Control			
	Mean	SD	Range	n	Mean	SD	Range	n
Preschool								
72-mo IQ	109.00	6.37	(99.00-122.00)	16	87.60	9.88	(64.00-109.00)	15
WPPSI GIQ	111.28	6.26	(100.00-122.67)	17	84.82	10.37	(65.00-110.33)	18
School								
120-mo IQ	104.18	11.53	(93.00-138.00)	17	86.29	10.12	(72.00-106.00)	17
WISC GIQ	103.18	9.88	(91.75-131.00)	17	82.77	8.73	(69.25-102.25)	18

Note. GIQ means are based on GIQs calculated for each child using only actual scores. No substituted data were used in these calculations.

In Table 8-6 the correlation matrix is presented for the preschool IQ at 72 months and the school IQ at 120 months in comparison with the GIQs for the preschool period (WPPSI) and the school period (WISC). These data reveal first that the preschool GIQ and the school GIQ are significantly ($p < .05$) correlated to their respective single point assessments at 72 and 120 months for both the experimental and control groups. Furthermore, the GIQ tends to relate more strongly to either the 72- or 120-month single estimates than they do to each other. The preschool GIQ is a better predictor of IQ at 120 months than is the 72 month IQ, for both groups. For the experimental group these correlations are all significant, while for the control group, all are significant with the exception of the 72-month preschool IQ performance's relationship to either 120-month IQ or the school GIQ. For both groups the preschool and school GIQs are significantly ($p < .05$) related ($r_E = .70$ and $r_C = .62$). The higher GIQ correlations reflect the reduced variability found in related single assessments and support the argument that a single age point IQ estimate can be an inflection that is not a good estimate of present or future intellectual development.

We examined the top and lower half of each group to consider the independence of profile variability from IQ level. On an individual basis not all children showed sizable inflections across time and some in fact remained stable throughout, even across, the WPPSI-WISC transition. For the experimental

Table 8-6 Correlations between Preschool and School Wechsler Point
IQ Measures and General IQ Measures for Experimental
and Control Groups

	Preschool Period (WPPSI)		School Period (WISC)	
	72-Month IQ	WPPSI GIQ	120-Month IQ	WISC GIQ
72-Month IQ				
Experimental				
Control				
WPPSI GIQ				
Experimental	.76*			
Control	.80*			
120-Month IQ				
Experimental	.54*	.69*		
Control	.40	.47*		
WISC GIQ				
Experimental	.58*	.70*	.87*	
Control	.35	.62*	.86*	

*$p < .05$

group the higher performances (median rank and above) were 9.9 points higher (115.94 vs. 106.04) and lost only 7 points across time as compared with a 9.35 point loss for the lower ranked IQ children. The rank order correlation for both the experimental and control groups between preschool and school were significant ($p < .01$) $rs = .72$ and .67 (respectively), indicating again that there was not much movement within group between ages.

The control group, however, showed a different rate of change. The lower rank GIQs averaged 77.76 and decreased to 76.34 on the school GIQ, while the upper rank IQs averaged 91.89 and declined about 3 points across time (to 89.19). Therefore, while the upper rank IQs increased their difference over the lower rank IQs in the experimental group (9.90 points to 12.25 points), the upper and lower ranks' difference in the control group decreased (from 14.13 to 12.85) because of the loss of the upper rank children in IQ level. Although the loss by the upper ranks between groups was comparable, the range of scores was quite different. For the experimental group the range is 111.67–122.67 (x = 115.94) and for the upper control group rank it is 83.33–110.33 (x =91.89), which do not overlap. The lower rank experimental IQ ranged from 100.00–110.67, closer to the control group high rank but still very different because, for instance, only one child's preschool GIQ was over 100 in the control higher rank IQs, while all of the experimental preschool GIQs in the lower rank are over 100.

We made these same comparisons for the low risk contrast group using only the children who were tested at 120 months. This analysis gave us an additional estimate of the representativeness of the $n = 6$ sample to the $n = 8$ sample, which included two higher scoring subjects, and a check on the appropriateness of using extrapolation procedures to gain point estimates of IQ where a test was missing. The correlation matrices for the comparisons are presented in Tables 8-7 and 8-8.

In the matrix for $n = 6$, the correlation coefficients are somewhat lower than in the $n = 8$ matrix, although the ordinal relationship of the coefficients is essentially the same. The mean performance levels are also somewhat reduced here, but again they remain essentially comparable. In terms of our question about the reduced sample, it can be seen that the early and late GIQs are significantly related and are better estimates of preschool to school performance levels than are the 72- to 120-month single point measures. Furthermore, the strength of the relationship and the comparability of the means in the $n = 6$ and $n = 8$ matrices are indicative of the representativeness of the reduced sample as an estimate of low risk contrast performance (even without the two higher scoring children, who were missing test data at 120 months).

One additional comparison made was a consideration of the relationship between GIQ measures on the earlier Stanford-Binet tests and the subsequent low risk contrast test performance. In Table 8-9 we have presented the Stanford-Binet and Wechsler GIQ means and the correlation coefficients from the comparisons.

Table 8-7   Correlation Coefficients for Comparisons of 72-Month and
120-Month Single Point IQ Performance Levels to Early and Late GIQ
Scores for the "Reduced" Low Risk Contrast Group

	72 mos.	120 mos.	Early GIQ	Late GIQ
	(WPPSI)	(WISC)	(WPPSI)	(WISC)
72 mos.	Mean = 96.50			
(WPPSI)	SD = 10.80			
120 mos.	r = .61*	Mean = 102.33		
(WISC)		SD = 7.90		
Early GIQ	r = .88*	r = .65*	Mean = 96.90	
(WPPSI)			SD = 10.00	
Late GIQ	r = .89*	r = .75*	r = .82*	Mean = 100.57
(WISC)				SD = 8.50

Note. Two subjects with missing WISC scores were eliminated making the sample size $n = 6$.
*$p < .01$

Table 8-8   Correlation Coefficients for Comparisons of 72-Month and
120-Month Single Point IQ Performance Levels to Early and Late GIQ
Scores for the Low Risk Contrast Group

	72 mos.	120 mos.	Early GIQ	Late GIQ
	(WPPSI)	(WISC)	(WPPSI)	(WISC)
72 mos.	Mean = 101.63			
(WPPSI)	SD = 13.53			
120 mos.	r = .82*	Mean = 102.33		
(WISC)		SD = 6.65		
Early GIQ	r = .94*	r = .82*	Mean = 101.33	
(WPPSI)			SD = 12.00	
Late GIQ	r = .94*	r = .90*	r = .90*	Mean = 104.68
(WISC)				SD = 11.33

Note. Sample size adjusted to $n = 8$. Single WISC scores obtained for two subjects were used to estimate 120-month performance and Late GIQ performance.
*$p < .01$

Table 8-9 Comparison of Stanford-Binet, WPPSI, and WISC GIQ
Scores for the Low Risk Contrast Group

Test	Early S-B GIQ	Late S-B GIQ	WPPSI GIQ	WISC GIQ
Early S-B GIQ	Mean = 112.38 SD = 18.87			
Late S-B GIQ	$r = .94^*$	Mean = 111.05 SD = 16.82		
WPPSI GIQ	$r = .96^*$	$r = .90^*$	Mean = 101.33 SD = 12.00	
WISC GIQ	$r = .87^*$	$r = .94^*$	$r = .90^*$	Mean = 104.68 SD = 11.33

Note. Sample size adjusted to $n = 8$ and missing data substituted through interpolation from scores for each individual.
$^*p < .01$

This matrix reveals high significant correlation coefficients for comparisons of the Stanford-Binet, WPPSI, and WISC GIQ scores. Even the early Stanford-Binet GIQ shows a high significant correlation to the late WISC GIQ. The GIQ for low risk contrast children is a rather good estimate on both tests across this entire early developmental period and shows higher correlations than those revealed for either the experimental or control groups.

In Table 8-10 we have presented the mean Stanford-Binet and Wechsler GIQs for all three groups for comparison. This comparison of Stanford-Binet and Wechsler GIQ means provides some interesting observations on the performance of the three unique groups across three different periods of time (24 to 48, 48 to 72, and 84 to 120 months). The Stanford-Binet GIQ does not reveal any particular differences in performance change across the preschool periods. The low risk contrast group performance continues to be the most stable, losing little more than 1 IQ point. The differences in performance level between the groups also remains substantially the same from early to late. The late Stanford-Binet GIQ, of course, coincides with the early WPPSI GIQ (both at 48 to 72 months) and reveals about a 10-point difference between the low risk contrast and experimental groups, and only about 7 points difference from the control group. This 10-point difference for the low risk contrast and experimental groups between Stanford-Binet (L-M) and the WPPSI is consistent with reports in the literature for disadvantaged children at these IQ perfor-

Table 8-10   Comparison of Stanford-Binet and Wechsler GIQ
Performance Scores for the Experimental, Control, and Low Risk
Contrast Groups

| | Stanford-Binet | | | | Wechsler | | | |
| | Early GIQ | | Late GIQ | | Early GIQ | | Late GIQ | |
Group	Mean	SD	Mean	SD	Mean	SD	Mean	SD
Experimental (n = 17)	124.0	9.5	121.4	5.4	111.3	6.3	103.2	9.9
Control (n = 18)	94.8	8.7	91.8	10.8	84.8	10.4	82.8	8.7
Low Risk Contrast (n = 8)	112.4	18.9	111.1	16.8	101.3	12.0	104.7	11.3

mance levels. The control group performance, although considerably lower overall, shows a mean level discrepancy of the same order.

As we have previously discussed, the discrepancy between the early and late Wechsler GIQs was the largest for the experimental group, but this discrepancy reflected the change in treatment, that is, the removal of the preschool program between the early and late GIQ periods. The GIQ change for the low risk contrast and control groups was on the same order (+3.4 and −2.1, respectively), although in different directions. We noted earlier that after a slight decline, the control children seemed to be gaining support from their school experience and as indicated here were generally maintaining their performance level, although it was low. However, when comparisons of low risk contrast and control children were made, the low risk contrast group seemed to be more stable in its later performance as compared with its earlier levels, while the control group's performance declined slightly.

The comparability of late Wechsler GIQ performances of the experimental and low risk contrast groups perhaps has implications for overall experimental group performance. The earlier experimental group performance was quite high in comparison to both the low risk contrast and the control group, but this level was not an objective of treatment, considering that the hypothesis entertained normal intellectual growth. The implication that normal intellectual growth was achieved but masked by the exaggerated performance on the IQ test during the preschool training period was suggested by the comparability of the low risk contrast and experimental groups' late Wechsler GIQ performance levels.

In summary, the correlation matrix indicates that the untreated low risk contrast and control groups show more consistent, more highly correlated intellectual performance across these various age periods, while the treated experimental group shows less consistent, less highly correlated performance as they move out of the treatment phase into schools. However, this eventually translates into a school performance level that stabilizes and becomes comparable to the untreated low risk contrast children even while they remain superior to the control group.

Control Children and the Preschool Experience

With the advent of major social welfare programs in the 1960s, including, but not only, Head Start, many daycare and preschool programs became available to the disadvantaged. A number of control children attended one or another of these programs, an experience that we did nothing to influence nor, by the same token, were we able fully to monitor. We therefore knew only by the mothers' reports whether their children were in such programs and otherwise received no further information about the programs or how much time was spent in them. Seven of the 18 children in the control target group attended one of these programs for about 1 year in the year prior to kindergarten. The Stanford-Binet mean GIQ of the attending group was 91.7 (SD = 13.8), compared with a mean GIQ of 91.4 (SD = 9.1) for the 11 children who did not attend any such program. Their school GIQ (mean WISC) was 81.9 (SD = 10.7), compared with a mean GIQ of 83.3 (SD = 7.8). Such programs do not seem to have made a difference in the intellectual development of those seven children who received some preschool experience, based on comparison with the rest of the group.

Inter- and Intraindividual IQ Performance Variation

IQ CHANGE BY GROUP

In examining individual intellectual performance there are several characteristics, including present level of performance, general level (average across age), and the pattern of development. McCall et al. (1973) reported an average change for middle class children of 28.5 points between 2½ and 17 years of age; more than 14% show a 40 or more point shift. Furthermore, they concluded that the outside environment is as potent an influence for changing IQ as is the family environment. Certainly no less should be true, and probably more so, for low SES children from families of low IQ mothers. Because we have noted significant individual variation within groups as well as between groups, we were especially concerned with examining inter- and intraindividual variations in IQ performance as well as the present performance levels.

As previously discussed, the correlation of WPPSI FS performance between 48 and 72 months for the experimental and control groups was .60 and .79, respectively (significant at $p < .05$), and the 48- to 120-month WPPSI to WISC correlation was .59 and .45, respectively, for both groups (significant at $p < .05$). However, the correlation coefficient was independent of the means of the distributions and therefore did not reveal the nature or extent of the individual variation across time. The general WPPSI-WISC FS performance of the groups can be best described as a significant linear trend ($p = .000$). The quadratic trend was influenced greatly by across time changes in WPPSI FS performance for the experimental children. The linear but not the quadratic trend to experimental and control regression curves was significantly different, but again mainly because of the preschool performance change of the experimental group. Certainly, not all of the children showed performances similar to the decrease (or negative slope) in the experimental group's WPPSI FS performance over time. In fact, some of the children remained very stable and others' performance increased over time. Of course, for all of the children there were the effects of school entrance to consider as an influence on their performance as well as, in a few cases, abrupt or traumatic events because of some significant change in home life. Otherwise the direction of FS IQ change in portions of the experimental and control groups was comparable from 60 to 72 months (over 40% increase) and from 72 to 84 months (over 20% increase); however, 81% of the control children (compared with 47% of the experimental children) showed an increase between first and fourth grades.

As we noted previously, once school began, both groups showed, generally, PIQ superior to the VIQ. The discrepancy between the PIQ and VIQ was for a majority of the children rather small (see bar graph, Figure 8-3), but in some instances it was very large. Where the discrepancy was very large (20 or more points), it was for those children who were the highest scorers in their groups. Furthermore, for these four children (all boys) there was a similar pattern once they entered school—their IQ performance increased. In one case, a strong IQ performer in the control group was lost to us for a time and so the pattern of performance was not as clear, although it seemed that PIQ > VIQ and there was an improvement in his performance once school began. For our part, we found no obvious explanation other than that the more intellectually competent disadvantaged children did manage to find advantage in their early school experience that was evidently not found by the other lower performers in their respective groups to a similar extent. However, it is important to note again in this regard that school seemed to have effectively discontinued the decline in IQ performance for the control group and had a similarly positive influence on the experimental group.

IQ CHANGE BY SEX

There was for both groups an even, or nearly so, distribution of boys and girls at this time: The experimental group included nine boys and eight girls and the control group had nine boys and nine girls.

Males have been reported to be more likely than females to show an increased IQ (e.g., Bayley, 1968) and, for poor black children (Roberts, Crump, Dickerson, & Horton, 1965), boys were less likely to show the general group decline than were girls. For the experimental group the girls lost an average of 10 points from the end of preschool (72 months) to the end of fourth grade (120 months), whereas the experimental boys averaged only a 1-point loss across the same time (see Table 8-11). For both girls and boys the bulk of the loss occurred between 72 and 84 months, 8.2 and 5, respectively. Therefore, allowing that the 72 to 84 month losses were somewhat comparable, these data show that the boys not only are less likely to show the general group decline but, in fact, gained an average of 4 points in school (84 to 120 months), while the girls lost an average of 1.8 points. For the control group across the same time period, 72 to 100 months, the boys gained 1.2 points while the girls lost 1.1 points. The boys gained less (3.1 points) than the girls (5.8 points) between 84 and 120 months, but the bulk of the difference was attributable to the greater loss in IQ performance for the girls (6.9 points) between 72 and 84 months than for the boys (–1.9 points). The control group data might be better estimated as a change from 60 months, not 72 months, when they began public school. After 1 year of kindergarten, the girls in the control group showed an average 8.6 gain, compared with no (0) average change for the boys. However, for the control girls most of this gain was lost in first grade (–6.9 points).

In summary, it seems that for both groups the school experience was similar: The boys showed less decline as they proceeded through school and in fact increased once into school. The school experience did seem initially to favor the control girls, but this advantage dissipated in first grade and was recouped only somewhat as the girls proceeded through the early grades.

Relationship of Experimental and Control Children and Maternal IQ

The original criteria for a family's selection included a maternal IQ of less than 75 on the WAIS, after the initial screening variable of 6 or below on the verbal subtest. We have examined the relationship of these maternal entry scores with the children's general preschool and school IQ levels. There are several problems inherent in comparisons of this kind, including the correlation of *young* children's IQs with *adult* parents' IQs, the changing nature of the

Table 8-11 Mean Change in FSS Wechsler IQ Performance by Sex for Both Experimental and Control Children from Preschool Through Fourth Grade

Group	n	Age (Months)			
		60–72	72–84	84–120	72–120
Experimental					
Boys	9	–1.9	–5.0	+4.0	–1.0
Girls	8	0.0	–8.2	–1.8	–10.0
Control					
Boys	9	0.0	–1.9	+3.1	+1.2
Girls	9	+8.6	–6.9	+5.8	–1.1

environment (for both groups) of low SES black children and its effects on IQ stability, and of course the restrictive criterion of < 75 IQ for the population sample.

Comparisons of mother-child IQ were made using the child's general level IQ for preschool and for school. In other words, we compared the average preschool IQ (48, 60, and 72 months) and also the average school IQ (84, 96, 108 and 120 months). The general preschool IQ level was the average of WPPSI scores and the school general IQ level was the average of WISC scores.

We determined the relationship of the maternal IQ (MIQ) to the child's IQ for both the initial MIQ and the follow-up MIQ nearly 8 years later. We compared MIQ with the child's general IQ (GIQ) as we considered that a more reliable estimate of IQ performance than the single 72-month or follow-up 120-month IQ measure. In Table 8-12 we have presented the correlation of MIQ with both the single preschool (72 months) and fourth grade (120 months) GIQ as well as the general preschool and general school GIQ.

Table 8-12 Relationship of Children's Preschool and School Wechsler Age Point IQ Measures and General IQ Measures to Mothers' IQ on Early and Late Tests

Age Period	MIQ-Early		MIQ-Late	
	Experimental	Control	Experimental	Control
Preschool Period				
72-Month IQ	−.20	.25	−.30	.30
WPPSI GIQ	−.10	.21	−.19	.26
School Period				
120-Month IQ	.33	.33	.38	.29
WISC GIQ	.26	.15	.24	.12

Note: Missing data at 72 and 120 months for children were substituted through interpolation from scores achieved at other testing months. One experimental mother's late test score was substituted using the group mean.

In Table 8-12 the correlations are low and nonsignificant, although a change in relationships is evident from preschool to school testing. During the preschool period experimental children who scored relatively high within their group had mothers who scored relatively low within their group, resulting in negative correlations for the 72-month point measure of IQ and the WPPSI GIQ for comparisons with both early and late measures of MIQ. However, during the school period the relative position of these children within their group was positively correlated, although nonsignificantly, with the relative position of their mothers within their group. On the other hand, the relative position of control children within their group was positively correlated, although nonsignificantly, at both the preschool and school testings with both the early and late measures of MIQ.

At this point no conclusive explanation can be made of the change in relationship between the relative positions of the experimental children and their
mothers from the preschool to the school period. It is, however, possible to
speculate that children coming from homes where the MIQ level was the
lowest benefited the most from the enriched intervention environment, but
upon entering the less stimulating school program, their enhanced performance stabilized without compensatory extramural support. It should be noted
that the relationships between children's relative positions and mothers' relative positions within their groups were comparable for the experimental and
control groups for the school period.

We extended our earlier analysis of the upper and lower half of each group
defined by children's GIQ levels by comparing the average MIQ level for high
and low groups (see Table 8-13). No differences are apparent between the
average MIQ levels for the upper and lower halves of the groups defined by
children's GIQ levels.

Table 8-13   Comparison of Average Maternal IQ Levels (Early and
Late) for High and Low Scoring Children Within the Experimental and
Control Groups

	Experimental		Control	
Test	MIQ-Early	MIQ-Late	MIQ-Early	MIQ-Late
WPPSI				
High	68.89	71.40	66.22	71.67
Low	67.25	74.00	73.88	79.63
WISC				
High	70.44	74.07	66.22	72.56
Low	65.50	71.00	65.67	69.89

We also compared the MIQ performance obtained from the initial WAIS
test for the mothers in the low risk contrast group to their children's GIQ performance on the Stanford-Binet and Wechsler series (WPPSI and WISC). The
MIQ scores in this discussion include only seven mothers for whom we have
IQ test performance scores for their children. The two others include one
mother who was lost before testing began and a second mother who was lost
before the end of the Gesell testing period. The mean MIQ of these seven
mothers was 111.6 ($SD = 3.8$; range: 106–118). Table 8-14 presents the correlation coefficients for the MIQ comparisons of these seven mothers to their
eight children across what are essentially three developmental periods (24
months to 48 months, 48 months to 72 months, and 72 months to 120 months,
with the late Stanford-Binet GIQ period overlapping the early Wechsler
WPPSI GIQ period). The correlation coefficients are low and not significant
across all periods.

Table 8-14   Correlation Coefficients of Maternal IQ Comparisons to
Their Child's GIQ on Early and Late Stanford-Binet and Wechsler Tests
for the Low Risk Contrast Group

Maternal IQ	Early S-B GIQ	Late S-B GIQ	WPPSI GIQ	Wechsler GIQ
Mean = 111.6 SD = 3.8 Range = (106–118) n = 7	-.15	-.01	-.01	.20

Two characteristics of these data are worth noting. First, there is at least a trend toward a positive and perhaps stronger relationship in IQ performance across time between mother and child and, second, the middle developmental period performance assessments on the Stanford-Binet and WPPSI relate poorly but equally well to the MIQ.

We retested low risk contrast mothers nearly 8 years later. Two mothers not retested included one mother who moved out of state and a second who refused to continue with the assessment program after her child had finished first grade.

The data showed no significant correlations, although they were stronger than for the larger sample, which included two high scoring children who scored much higher in fact than their MIQ. The data revealed no consistent pattern between either the mothers' pre- or post-IQ and this group of children's GIQ performance levels across the three developmental periods. The low risk contrast group mother-child IQ comparisons were on the same order of relationship during this early stage of life as were the IQ performance comparisons for the experimental and control groups, except for a stronger relationship on the Wechsler GIQs.

The conclusion remains that for low risk contrast children early IQ performance is, according to these data, a better predictor of later developmental performance on IQ tests than is their mothers' IQ. In comparison with the experimental and control groups, the direction and order of these relationships were the same. GIQ measures of IQ performance related at least as well or better than single point estimates to each other for all children between different development periods, and better, although weakly, to MIQ. For all of the children (experimental, control, and low risk contrast), their own early IQ performances on the Stanford-Binet and Wechsler tests were better predictors of performance in subsequent development periods than were their mothers' IQ performances. This was perhaps an indication of the intrusive effects of these children's unusual environment on their intellectual development.

These data are quite interesting in that they do not support the contention by Erlenmeyer-Kimling and Jarvik (1963) that one should expect an IQ correlation between mother and child of about .50. For several comparisons of maternal and child performance they are close, but in general the correlations are much lower than .50. For the experimental children the treatment program has changed the order of their IQ test performance, and even the direction with respect to the MIQ, but the untreated control group correlations are similarly low. Perhaps for these mothers there is a problem in effecting a good test performance because of their southern rural experience and the cultural problems inherent in performing on these kinds of tests. Perhaps this factor is also related to the change in performance levels seen for all children during these periods of time. In any event, we can only speculate when accounting for the discrepancy these data show in the mother-child IQ comparisons. The performance of the low risk contrast mothers, considering their different school experience, is somewhat stronger, certainly comes closer to the .50 estimate, and offers some support for this interpretation. Obviously, a more conclusive basis for such inferences must wait upon the adult performance comparisons of these children to their mothers.

DISCUSSION

For both groups, IQ performance is relatively stable with even a slight increase in IQ as they move through school. The GIQ seems to be a better estimate for prediction of the GIQ at 120 months than is the actual performance at that time. However, this might be expected to change as the children continue to develop.

For the most part stability of the IQ across time has been a consistent assumption implicit in the use of IQ tests not only to predict for future educational placement of individuals, but also as a basis for the development of most preventive early intervention procedures. For example, because it is assumed that early and late IQs are highly related, it is further assumed that increased early IQ performance will be sustained subsequent to treatment. However, most research of this type has ignored or overlooked substantial individual differences, which include significant changes in the IQ distribution through the major developmental periods (e.g., Goulet, 1973; Johannesson, 1974; McCall et al., 1973).

For the moment, let us examine briefly the Berkeley Growth Study to consider the implications, longitudinally, of its IQ data for the subjects in our sample. The Berkeley Growth Study (Hunt & Eichorn, 1972; Jones & Bayley, 1941; Jones et al., 1971) is one of the most systematic longitudinal studies dealing with general intellectual growth. A sample of normal children from white, English speaking, and above average SES families was selected. The children were given repeated testings from 1928, when the study began, which were continued through childhood. The test-retest correlations of tests (Wechsler) administered at different ages and compared with IQ performance at 17 or 18 months improved with age after 18 months, but it was not until the 5 to 7 age period that a relatively high degree of predictability was obtained. The mean IQ for several administrations between 5 and 7, that is, tests administered at the very beginning of the formal school experience, better predicted IQ performance at the end of high school. But as Brody and Brody (1976) pointed out, the sample from the Berkeley study was limited in generalizability because it was a biased sample. However, it is perhaps in its bias that its implications are most instructive.

One could conclude from the results of the Berkeley study that a consistently positive environment fosters intellectual growth and provides for higher early to late correlation. Because the seriously disadvantaged black child with a low IQ mother does not have a positively fostering environment from early school through adolescence, both in terms of the home and the school, it is most difficult to use the preschool intellectual performance of advantaged white children as an appropriate and/or adequate basis for predicting either school or adult IQ levels for these black children. At least in part because of the continuation of an impoverished home environment and the lack of extra-familial compensatory educational and rehabilitation programming and an educational system that could more adequately serve their educational needs, the nonwhite and/or seriously disadvantaged child is continuously threatened with significant negative influences on his/her intellectual performance through to maturity.

Intellectual growth is not constant throughout the growth period. Rather, it is more reasonable to assume that the structure of intellectual abilities both determines and is determined by learning. Therefore, when intellectual performance is measured under optimal, or at least traditional circumstances, then the expectation for highly correlated adult performance must assume the existence of such optimal conditions throughout the growth period. In other words, what one learns is determined not only by what is made available to learn and what has been learned but also by how one learns. And how one learns is a mix of abilities, learned strategies, and motivation. Because it must be assumed that this situation is less than optimal for the seriously disadvantaged, the probability of successful academic performance by such a child is accordingly reduced.

9
Analysis of the Children's Performance in School

As all of the experimental and control children entered the first grade in the Milwaukee Public Schools, the preschool program closed. Follow-up evaluations of the target children were begun, mainly for the purpose of monitoring the target children's intellectual performance, but included observations of their academic achievement as well as their general school adjustment. Coupled with these data on the children, additional information was collected on the type of school programs available to the children, as well as school district modifications such as busing and expansion of special education services. The target children entered school as many significant changes were taking place educationally on national, state, and local levels.

Our analysis of the children's performance focused on the elementary grades, the time during which they must acquire the basic knowledge needed to be successful in school and ultimately to function as adults in our society. Reading literacy levels, for example, are expected to be acquired by the sixth grade. And, in perhaps an equally critical developmental domain, 10-year-old children are expected to have made substantial progress in developing the social competency necessary for dealing with their world. The child's school achievement level can also be used (e.g., Bock, Stebbins, & Proper, 1977) as a means of estimating any residual benefits from early intervention efforts, other possible influences on development notwithstanding.

The task of follow-up evaluation was quite difficult. Some of the difficulty we anticipated because of the problems we experienced at the beginning of the program in maintaining family contacts. We were fortunate that our attrition rate over 10 years of the study had been less than 20% of our target families. After several experiences with losing contact with families, we learned to develop more intimate knowledge of the target families' friends and relatives in order to help maintain contacts. These tracking procedures were especially important in our attempts to follow the control families, because contact here had been less frequent than with the experimental children and parents. When regular programming ended at the time of school entrance, our follow-up evaluations were again subject to many of the logistical problems (e.g., attrition because of family mobility or temporary absence because of illness) with which longitudinal research in general is fraught.

As the children moved through the elementary grades, we used the records of the Milwaukee Public Schools as a source of help in finding "lost" families. We used the Freedom of Information Act ruling, which on the basis of signed, parental release forms granted us access to cumulative school records. Records were sometimes incomplete because report cards, standardized test results, and special class placements had been either lost or misfiled because of transfers between schools. Some children changed schools several times during the elementary grades and they were less likely to have full and accurate school records. The Milwaukee Public School System has made considerable effort, based on our observations, to collect and organize information on its students.

SCHOOL PLACEMENTS

In the Milwaukee Public School System, kindergarten is a half-day optional program. When children in the experimental group became old enough to enter kindergarten, we discussed with each family the option of attending public kindergarten or continuing the children's preschool program. The parents agreed, considering the children's exceptional progress, that it was important to consolidate gains by maintaining the educational program, especially the reading program. Thus, the children in the experimental group remained in the educational program until they were ready to enter first grade, while the control children entered kindergarten as they came of age. With respect to the control group families, no influence or attempt to influence any portion of the lives of the control children was made, especially regarding school-type placement. For example, by the mothers' report, seven control children attended some kind of preschool before they entered kindergarten. All of the control children entered public school at the appropriate age.

Upon first grade entrance, all of the experimental children were able to read at a readiness level or better. We were concerned that this initial and most important of academic skills have a fair chance to grow. In order to accomplish this we decided to avoid the obviously poor schools that predominated in the children's neighborhoods. We therefore examined published fourth grade achievement performance for each school in order to choose the schools closest to the children's neighborhoods that reported performance levels comparable to the citywide median.

The Milwaukee Public School System's open door registration policy permitted children to attend any school within the city limits so long as space was available and transportation could be provided. Considering the tested achievement and IQ levels of the experimental youngsters, it was considered important that these children attend schools that had mean achievement score distributions for the fourth grade that were not considerably below the national and citywide averages.

Within the city of Milwaukee, for the 1970–71 school year, there were 118 elementary schools, which varied in the average academic performance levels their pupils achieved each year. Table 9-1 compares nationwide and citywide fourth grade achievement averages on the Iowa Tests of Basic Skills with the average performance of fourth grade students from two subsets of city schools, namely, the seven local neighborhood schools that the experimental children entering first grade should have attended and the two selected nearby schools that the first group of children did enter. By comparison it becomes apparent that there is a considerable discrepancy among the nationwide, citywide, and seven local school averages. The distribution of performance categories indicates that performance declines as we move from the national distribution to the city distribution to the neighborhood schools distribution. The percentage of children whose composite Iowa achievement scores are below average rises from 23% (nationwide) to 40% (citywide) to 64% (the seven neighborhood inner city schools).

Table 9-1 Profiles of the Nationwide and Citywide Averages As Well As the Performance Within Seven Local Neighborhood Schools and Two Selected Nearby Schools for Fourth Grade Students on the Iowa Test of Basic Skills[a]

Profiles	Reading AV		Math AV		Composite AV	
Nationwide	54		54		54	
	+23	−23	+23	−23	+23	−23
Citywide	53		50		48	
	+9	−38	+16	−34	+12	−40
7 Neighborhood schools[b]	43		42		33	
	+2	−55	+5	−53	+3	−64
2 Nearby schools[c]	51		56		55	
	+12	−37	+18	−26	+12	−33

[a]Reference: Milwaukee Public Schools (1972).
[b]The seven local neighborhood schools refer to the seven elementary schools that the initial group of nine experimental children were originally scheduled to attend during first grade.
[c]The two selected nearby schools refer to the two elementary schools that the initial group of nine experimental children actually did attend during first grade.

Because it was not possible to control for class or teacher placement and because it was felt to be in the best interests of the children, the public schools were given only Reading Readiness scores with no background data on the children. However, the information was discovered independently by a school psychologist for the Milwaukee Public Schools, who was able to identify the experimental children and who then informed their teachers. In addition, it became obvious that the children had had previous schooling.

Although the two schools were racially integrated, the populations were not stable. The proportion of the black population in the two schools was increasing as more white families moved from the inner city to the neighboring areas.

SUMMER SCHOOL TUTORIAL PROGRAM

The summer following first grade we invited the experimental children to attend a 6-week half-day summer tutorial program. Instruction emphasized reading and mathematics. This program was held at our Education Center in Milwaukee and was staffed by three certified teachers. It was hoped that this program would minimize any detrimental effects of summer between first and second grades. This one summer tutorial program was our only direct educational intervention with the experimental children after they graduated from our preschool.

Each child in this special half-day summer program was picked up at home at 12:30 p.m. and returned at 4:30 p.m. From 1:00 until 4:00 p.m., the children generally participated in the following four educational periods:

1:00–1:45 Small Group Reading
1:45–2:00 Free Time
2:00–2:30 Individualized Reading
2:30–2:45 Snack
2:45–3:15 Small Group Arithmetic
3:15–4:00 Individualized Arithmetic Projects

The actual program was kept as flexible as possible in order to allow the teachers to respond to the needs of each child. The materials used in the reading program included the same basal series each child had used in first grade, along with other reading games and projects. The math curriculum followed the text used by all Milwaukee Public Schools.

In planning for the enrollment of the second group of experimental children into first grade, we visited each appropriate neighborhood school to try to select schools sufficiently adaptable to be able to meet the needs of children entering first grade who could read as a result of their participation in a preschool program. In addition, as a result of an earlier meeting with school officials, we established a line of communication to the Milwaukee Public Schools Central Administration. They helped us to identify schools receptive to early childhood programs and schools that had more innovative programs (e.g., one school allowed first graders who could read at higher levels to take reading with higher grades).

When the next group of children entered first grade (accompanied by their mothers), they handed in a letter from us along with the appropriate registration forms. This letter, addressed to the principal, informed him or her that the child had been enrolled in a University of Wisconsin sponsored preschool program and that the school could obtain from us the child's Metropolitan Achievement Test scores. Beyond this, no further information regarding the nature of the program or the child's participation in it was offered to the school. These letters were placed in the children's cumulative school folders.

Five of the initial group of children entering first grade were returned to their immediate neighborhood schools, three remained in the transfer schools at their parents' request, and one child who had been placed in a foster home transferred to an appropriate school nearer home. The control children entering first grade remained in their home schools and moved into second grade.

Among the second group of experimental children entering first grade, after individual conferences with each family four were entered into their neighborhood schools. Because for two of these children their appropriate schools were at the lowest end of the Milwaukee Public School academic spectrum, we chose with their parents to have them attend the next closest school to their homes. The second control group moved from kindergarten into first grade.

The set of four schools that the second group of experimental children attended in first grade was, overall, representative of citywide averages for the administrative variables, but slightly below the city's mean achievement levels. For example, although mean class sizes were comparable (30.7 vs. 31.4), 56% of the fourth grade students in these six schools were below average performers on the Iowa battery versus 40% below average citywide. The eight schools that the control children entered were comparable in both their achievement levels and administrative makeup to the schools their experimental counterparts entered that same year. All of the schools that either an experimental or a control child attended were primarily black (76%) in their racial makeup.

The second school year was essentially uneventful. Only one child out of both groups did not adjust satisfactorily. This child was the experimental child who, as was previously noted, was placed in a permanent foster home when his family disintegrated and the mother was declared legally unfit to care for her children. When the child became too disruptive in school and could not be kept in the regular class, he was transferred by the Milwaukee Department of Social Services to a private residential facility.

ASSESSMENT OF SCHOOL PERFORMANCE

Our follow-up of the target families included both inventories of the home environment and evaluations (i.e., academic, intellectual, and health measures) of the children's development during the early elementary grades. During the summer before school entry, each experimental and control child was administered an IQ test and a series of learning and language tests. IQ tests were administered by an independent testing team. As the children continued through school, we continued to update our assessment data, concentrating in particular on their intellectual development and achievement test performance. However, once the intervention program had ended and all children from both groups were entered in school, the logistics of administering assessments became much more complex and the number of measures had to be reduced. The information we have collected attempts a characterization of the differential progress made by the experimental children and their families after the direct intervention effort ended in comparison with progress made by the control children and their families.

School Deadlines

An assessment of school readiness was made for each experimental and control child before he/she entered school, using the Metropolitan Readiness Battery (Form A) and the Primer Battery (Form B). In the spring of the year prior to their entrance into first grade, each experimental child was given both batteries, while the control children were administerd the Readiness Battery at the end of kindergarten by the public schools.

The correlation between percentile scores on the Metropolitan Readiness Battery (Form A) collected prior to school entry and measures of intelligence at 72 months of age was $r = .76$ for Stanford-Binet IQ scores and $r = .71$ for WPPSI IQ scores. Only three control children scored at or above average (over the 33rd percentile), but all experimental children scored above the 50th percentile. The mean readiness percentiles were 75.94 ($SD = 12.28$) for experimental children, 29.60 ($SD = 24.87$) for control children, and 58.80 ($SD = 36.31$) for low risk contrast children. Table 9-2 profiles the number and percentage of experimental and control children scoring superior, high normal, average, low normal, and low on the Metropolitan Readiness Test (MRT) prior to first grade.

Table 9-2 Number and Percentage of Experimental and Control Children Scoring Superior, High Normal, Average, Low Normal, and Low on the Metropolitan Readiness Test Given Prior to First Grade

Readiness Status	Letter Rating	Percentile Rank Range	Experimental n	Experimental %	Control n	Control %
Superior	A	92–99+	3	18%	0	0
High Normal	B	69–91	10	59%	2	13%
Average	C	31–67	4	24%	2	13%
Low Normal	D	7–29	0	0	9	60%
Low	E	1–6	0	0	2	13%
n			17		15	

Because 13 of 17 experimental children received either an A or B letter rating, and because 11 of 15 control children received a D or E readiness grade, we expected the experimental children would prove better prepared than their control counterparts to meet the challenges of first grade. Readiness scores on the MRT are supposed to be predictive of future academic achievement levels (Hildreth, Griffiths, & McGauvran, 1969). The 1964–65 U.S. Office of Education's *Cooperative Research Program in First Grade Reading Instruction* (Bond & Dykstra, 1967) examined the academic performance of 9,497 pupils who took the MRT Battery (Form A, 1965 Revision) in early October and parts of the Stanford Achievement Test (Primary I Battery) the following May. Table 9-3 lists expectancies for the relationship between MRT scores and Stanford Battery scores and suggests that pupils at the A or B readiness levels (percentile scores above 68) tend to have spring grade equivalents from 2 to 14 months (2.0 to 3.2) above Stanford subtest norms. On the other hand, the most likely grade equivalents for pupils at the D or E readiness levels (percentile scores below 30) fall between 3 and 7 months (1.5 to 1.1) below the norm of 1.8 for the six Stanford subtests.

Metropolitan Achievement Assessment Procedure

Each spring following the children's completion of their first, second, third, and fourth years of elementary schooling, the Metropolitan Achievement Test (MRT) appropriate to the grade just completed was administered. The test

Table 9-3   Median Stanford Grade Equivalent in May for Pupils at Each Metropolitan Readiness Level for the Previous October, as Found for the 9,497 First Grade Participants in the 1964–65 USOE Cooperative Research Program in First Grade Reading Instruction (Bond & Dykstra, 1967) Who Took Both Tests

Metropolitan Readiness			Median Stanford Grade Equivalent						
Score Range[a]	Percentile Rank Range	Letter Rating	Word Read.	Para. Mean.	Vocab	Spell	Word Study Skill	Arith[b]	# of Cases[b]
77–102	92–99+	A	2.5	2.6	2.9	2.6	3.2	2.6	749
64–76	69–91	B	2.1	2.0	2.5	2.2	2.4	2.2	2,253
45–63	31–67	C	1.7	1.7	2.0	1.8	1.9	1.8	3,678
24–44	7–29	D	1.5	1.5	1.5	1.5	1.5	1.5	2,223
0–24	1–6	E	1.3	1.4	1.4	1.1	1.2	1.2	594
Correlation with Readiness[c]			.63	.60	.63	.64	.57	.67	9,497

[a]Total score, Form A or Form B.
[b]Arithmetic test was taken by only 6,561 pupils; it was not part of the research study. Number of cases for readiness levels A, B, C, D, and E were 621, 1,747, 2,624, 1,301, and 268, respectively.
[c]Computed from raw scores on both tests.

consists of the Primary I Battery (Grade 1), the Primary II Battery (Grade 2), and the Elementary Batteries (Grades 3 and 4). The batteries are made up of a series of nationally normed exams in several forms with acceptable $(.84 < r < .96)$ reliability coefficients. Along with the MRT, these exams provide a continuous test battery for the first nine grades in school from kindergarten through junior high.

The Milwaukee Public School System had incorporated MAT exams into their citywide testing program, which aided in data collection across this 4-year period. Our primary concern was the progress of the children in Total Reading and Total Math, but we were also interested in progress in the individual subtest areas. Because several subtests are not included in the Primary I Battery, the number of time points varies across subtest areas. The Word Analysis subtest is contained in the Primary I and Primary II Batteries, but is replaced by a Language subtest in the Elementary Battery. To facilitate analysis of these subscales, we statistically combined Word Analysis and Language subtest data across the 4 years.

The analysis of the MAT data compared academic growth for the two groups across the first 4 years of school. Conversion tables were used to derive standard scores that express the results for each subtest area (e.g., Word Knowledge) for all batteries and all forms on a single, common scale. In these assessments we were interested in how much progress they were making rather than their actual grade placement. At the end of the fourth year, these children were given the Elementary Battery (Form F) as were all other students in the schools. The standard scores were converted into percentile and grade equivalent scores based on the fact that the children were completing their fourth year of school rather than the fact that they were in the third grade. This difference would not have affected conversion to grade equivalents but was an important consideration for conversion to percentile scores. Tables 9-4 and 9-5 list percentile and grade equivalent scores, respectively, for experimental and control group MAT performance across the first 4 years of school.

Percentile and grade equivalent scores are simple transformations of standard scores. However, performance levels for several children were so low that their standard scores could not be found on the conversion table. It was not possible to give these children negative scores, so they were given a score of zero for a percentile rank. This created an artificial floor level that inflated the average for the group percentile scores. The control group scores are found predominately at the lower quarter of the conversion table, where percentile and grade equivalent scores are depressed in relation to standard scores. It is necessary therefore, to use caution in comparing group performance levels on percentile ranks. With this in mind, it is still apparent from Table 9-5 that the experimental group was superior in performance on reading related tests across the 4 years and on math related tests for the first 3 years.

While the mean readiness percentile for experimental children at the end of intervention predicted that they would do above average academically, their

Table 9-4 Mean Percentile Scores for Experimental and Control Groups on the Metropolitan Achievement Tests for the First 4 Years of School

MAT	Experimental				Control			
	1	2	3	4	1	2	3	4
Composite Scores								
Total Reading	48.71	30.82	25.06	19.00	31.53	14.72	15.62	8.82
Total Math	33.51	26.65	22.65	10.63	17.75	10.63	10.43	9.39
Subtest Scores								
Word Knowledge	48.82	35.59	28.29	21.71	28.24	16.25	16.78	10.70
Reading	48.94	27.59	22.53	17.75	38.88	15.01	17.41	7.50
Word Analysis	44.53	35.32	22.35	15.06	19.71	10.58	14.71	9.62
Spelling		33.41	31.38	23.98		11.96	16.38	17.31
Math Computation		25.35	31.21	18.28		14.24	17.93	12.79
Math Concepts		28.59	25.59	11.81		11.08	12.15	15.08
Math Problem Solving		32.59	16.53	9.79		15.26	10.88	10.19

Table 9-5 Mean Grade Equivalent Scores for Experimental and Control Groups on the Metropolitan Achievement Tests for the First 4 Years of School

MAT	Experimental				Control			
	1	2	3	4	1	2	3	4
Composite Scores								
Total Reading	1.88	2.35	2.69	3.19	1.60	1.95	2.33	2.51
Total Math	1.63	2.33	2.88	3.07	1.31	1.86	2.39	3.09
Subtest Scores								
Word Knowledge	2.01	2.50	2.85	3.43	1.52	2.00	2.50	2.74
Word Analysis	1.73	2.52	2.78	3.10	1.23	1.67	2.42	2.69
Reading	1.81	2.13	2.49	3.00	1.60	1.95	2.33	2.51
Spelling		2.40	2.88	3.52		1.73	2.27	3.05
Math Computation		2.27	3.31	3.68		1.94	2.84	3.30
Math Concepts		2.38	2.92	2.91		1.82	2.32	3.16
Math Problem Solving		2.50	2.56	2.83		2.02	2.31	2.96

mean MAT Total Reading percentile score at the end of the first year of school was only 48.71. The mean readiness percentile was substantially lower for control children but predicted their MAT Total Reading Level of 31.53 at the end of the first year of school much more accurately. The low risk contrast group's readiness percentile also predicted their first year MAT Total Reading percentile level of 57.36 quite accurately. Readiness percentiles were less predictive for MAT Total Mathematics levels for all three groups, with experimental, control, and low risk contrast children scoring 42.43, 11.85, and 18.22, respectively, below the level predicted by the preschool measure.

Although standard scores increased significantly ($p < .01$) for both groups over the 4 years of schooling, percentile ranks decreased for both groups over the same period. This indicates that although their performance levels increased significantly in relationship to where they began, they did not make progress as fast as did the children who comprised the norm group used to standardize the MAT Batteries. The deterioration in percentile ranks is quite marked and was unanticipated, especially for the experimental group, which had a mean readiness percentile of 75.94 on the MRT just before entering school. Comparisons of grade equivalent scores at the end of the first year of school (Table 9-5) with expectancies based on readiness scores (Tables 9-2 and 9-3) indicate that the deterioration in performance began in the first year of school and was probably more severe for experimental than for control children.

To further analyze the nature of the children's progress from grade to grade, we computed mean gains in months for grade equivalent scores on the MAT Batteries (Table 9-6) for each group. Each group made less than 2 years' progress from the end of the first year to the end of the fourth year, and neither group exhibited a 1-year gain in performance between any two school grades except for the experimental group's progress on Mathematics Computation between the second and third year. Overall, smaller gains were made in Total Reading than Total Math. The experimental group made more progress in Total Reading than did the control group, but less progress in Total Math, although they were superior on Mathematics Computation. This suggests that Mathematics Concepts and Mathematics Problem Solving were particularly weak areas for the experimental group, while Word Knowledge and Reading were particularly weak areas for the control group.

We investigated the progress of the children through their first 4 years of school further by computing the percentage of children in each group who performed above average, average, and below average on Total Reading, Total Math, and each MAT subtest each year. These percentages are based on stanine scores and are presented in Table 9-7. The expected distribution (Durost, Bixler, Wrightstone, Prescott, & Balow, 1971) for the percentage of children scoring in each of these groups is approximately 25%, 50%, and 25%, respectively.

Table 9-6   Gains in MAT Grade Equivalent Levels Between the 1st-2nd,
2nd-3rd, and 3rd-4th Years of School for the Experimental
and Control Groups

MAT	Experimental				Control			
	1–2	2–3	3–4	Total Gain	1–2	2–3	3–4	Total Gain
Composite Scores								
Total Reading	.47	.34	.50	1.31	.35	.38	.18	.91
Total Math	.70	.55	.19	1.44	.55	.53	.70	1.78
Subtest Scores								
Word Knowledge	.49	.35	.58	1.42	.48	.50	.24	1.22
Reading	.32	.36	.51	1.19	.18	.47	.00	.65
Word Analysis/Language	.79	.26	.32	1.37	.44	.75	.27	1.46
Spelling		.48	.64	1.12		.54	.78	1.32
Math Computation		1.04	.37	1.41		.90	.46	1.36
Math Concepts		.54	–.01	.53		.50	.84	1.34
Math Problem Solving		.06	.27	.33		.29	.65	.94

It seems that the schools were comparatively more successful at promoting reading than mathematics skills over the 4-year period for both groups. The experimental group distribution of stanine scores was superior to the distribution for the control group, although neither group approximated the expected distribution after the first year. The experimental group finished the first year of school with an overall performance somewhat similar to the expected distribution and gradually shifted in performance to average and below average levels as the children progressed through the next 3 years of school. On the other hand, no control children ever scored in the above average range of performance and after the first year less than 30% of these children performed within the average range for either Total Reading or Total Math.

After the first year of school, the experimental children demonstrated a relative weakness in Total Math compared with Total Reading. Performance decreased in both areas over the next year, but Total Reading performance demonstrated a more dramatic decrease and the two areas were at equal levels by the end of the second year. Over the next year, Total Reading performance remained relatively stable although no experimental children continued to perform above average. Total Math performance shifted slightly to the average range during the third year. By the end of the fourth year, Total Reading performance made a significant shift from the average to the below average range, and Total Math performance made an even more dramatic shift downward, with only 12% of the group remaining in the average range.

Table 9-7 Distribution by Percentage of Experimental and Control
Children's Performance Levels on the Metropolitan Achievement Test
Across the First 4 Years of School

Experimental

MAT	1 +	1 0	1 −	2 +	2 0	2 −	3 +	3 0	3 −	4 +	4 0	4 −
Composite Scores												
Total Reading	.47	.29	.24	.06	.41	.53	0	.41	.59	0	.24	.76
Total Math	.06	.29	.65	.06	.53	.41	0	.53	.47	0	.12	.88
Subscale Scores												
Word Knowledge	.47	.24	.29	.06	.53	.41	.06	.29	.65	0	.24	.76
Reading	.53	.24	.24	.41	.53	.06	.29	0	.71	.24	0	.76
Word Analysis/Language	.47	.29	.24	.47	.41	.12	0	.41	.59	0	.18	.82
Spelling				.41	.53	.06	.18	.53	.29	.35	.06	.59
Math Computation	.53	.24	.06	.59	.06	.53	.41	.53	.06	.12		.82
Math Concepts				.53	.47	0	.53	.47	0	.24		.76
Math Problem Solving	.06	.65	.29	.06	.23	.76	0	.12	.88			

Control

MAT	1 +	1 0	1 −	2 +	2 0	2 −	3 +	3 0	3 −	4 +	4 0	4 −
Composite Scores												
Total Reading	.71	0	.29	.29	0	.71	.24	0	.76	.12	0	.88
Total Math	.41	0	.59	.12	0	.88	.24	0	.76	.12	0	.88
Subscale Scores												
Word Knowledge	.59	0	.41	.29	0	.71	.24	0	.76	.12	0	.88
Reading	.88	0	.12	.24	0	.76	.24	0	.76	.12	0	.88
Word Analysis/Language	.53	0	.47	.18	0	.82	.18	0	.82	.12	0	.88
Spelling				.12		.80	.24		.94	.35		.88
Math Computation				.18	0	.82	.24	0	.76	.18	0	.82
Math Concepts				.12	0	.88	.18	0	.82	.29	0	.71
Math Problem Solving	.18	0	.80	.06	0	.94	.12	0	.88			

Control children finished the first year with no members of the group in the above average range but 71% in the average range for Total Reading and 41% in the average range for Total Math performance. Over the next year, performance levels in both Total Reading and Total Math areas dropped drastically, and although they fluctuated slightly over the next 2 years, they never increased substantially enough to place 25% of the group in the average range of performance. Although there is a decrease in Total Math performance in the last year, it is not as dramatic as the decrease demonstrated by experimental children for the same period.

The distributions of performance levels for each group across the first 4 years of school clearly reveal that children in both groups were performing poorly in school, and that their performance became progressively worse as they continued their education. At the end of the fourth year, at least 13 of the experimental group and 15 of the control group had to be considered below average achievers on both Total Reading and Total Math when compared with the national norms. With few exceptions, percentile scores for children after completion of the fourth year of school were below the percentile scores they achieved after the first year of school.

Intelligence as measured by standardized IQ tests has been found to be highly predictive of academic performance within the general population (Sattler, 1973). If measured intelligence is considered an ability level or potential for achievement, it should be highly correlated with measures of academic achievement as the children progress through school. In order to investigate this relationship, we correlated MAT Total Reading and Total Math performance levels with WISC Full Scale IQ scores at the end of each year.

The concurrent validity of WISC IQ scores and MAT Total Reading scores ranged from $r = .48$ to $r = .70$ and averaged $r = .60$ across the first 4 years of school. The predictive validity of first grade WISC IQ scores for fourth grade MAT Total Reading scores ($r = .68$) was comparable with the concurrent validity of IQ and MAT scores at the end of first grade ($r = .67$) and the end of the fourth grade ($r = .70$). As is typically found, first grade MAT scores predicted fourth grade MAT scores slightly better ($r = .76$).

Despite the fact that experimental and low risk contrast children maintained a consistent IQ level at the mean for the WISC and contrast children evidenced a slight rise in IQ, all children experienced substantial declines in achievement percentiles across the first 4 years of school. Experimental, control, and low risk contrast children demonstrated drops of 29.71, 22.71, and 28.46 percentile points, respectively, for Total Reading and 22.88, 8.37, and 34.78 percentile points, respectively, for Total Mathematics. The relatively small drop in Total Mathematics percentile scores for control children resulted from their "bottoming out" on the assessment instrument. Statistical comparisons indicated Total Mathematics percentile scores were significantly, $F(4, 28) = 3.86$, $p < .05$, higher for experimental children than for control children, but there was no difference between the Total Reading percentile levels for these two groups across the first 4 years of school.

The experimental children entered school with relatively high IQ scores and scored average or above average on the MAT schedules after the first year. In contrast, the control children entered school with relatively low IQ scores and scored average or below average on the MAT schedules. As they progressed through school, MAT performance levels for both groups dropped while their IQ scores remained relatively stable. Therefore, the experimental children started school as average achievers relative to their potential as measured by IQ and by the end of the fourth year had to be considered underachievers, using the same criterion. The control children started school as overachievers relative to their assessed potential and by the end of the fourth year were considered average achievers using this criterion.

In summary, both groups declined in performance over the 4-year period, but the brighter experimental children lost more because their decrease in performance relative to their potential made them underachievers. The control children also declined in performance, but in contrast remained within average ranges of achievement relative to their potential. Correlations between WISC Full Scale IQ scores and MAT standard scores over the 4-year period support the conclusion that, above and beyond ability level or potential as measured by IQ tests, other factors contributed significantly to declines in academic performance observed over the first 4 years of school.

COMPARISON OF LOW RISK CHILDREN'S
PERFORMANCE IN SCHOOL

In order to make follow-up comparisons of performance for the low risk contrast group, MAT scores were collected at the end of each year of school just as they were for the experimental and control children. Our main concern was with the progress by the children on the composite scores of Total Reading and Total Math. Unfortunately, the data collected for the low risk contrast group are limited. The sample of children in this group was relatively small (LRC = 8) compared with the experimental (n = 17) and control (n = 18) groups, and the children were not equally tested across the 4-year period. This made comparisons of performance levels difficult, but we believe that meaningful information was gained by conservative comparisons of overall group performances and by consideration of individual performance variation within the low risk contrast group.

Table 9-8 lists percentile scores and grade equivalent scores for the three groups across the 4 years of school and Table 9-9 lists gain scores for these measures across the same period. On Total Reading, the average gain for each of the three groups across 4 years of school is less than one-third year for each year in school. The average gain in Total Math is less than one-half year for each year in school.

The low risk contrast and experimental groups' performance curves for Total Reading are both higher than the control group's performance and seem

Table 9-8 Mean Total Reading and Total Math Percentile Scores and Grade Equivalent Scores for the Experimental, Control, and Low Risk Contrast Groups for the First 4 Years of School

	Year 1		Year 2		Year 3		Year 4	
Group	P	GE	P	GE	P	GE	P	GE
Total Reading								
Experimental	48.71	1.88	30.82	2.35	25.06	2.69	19.00	3.19
Control	31.53	1.60	14.72	1.95	15.62	2.33	8.82	2.51
Low Risk Contrast	57.36	2.20	32.63	2.35	47.17	3.48	28.90	3.40
Total Math								
Experimental	33.51	1.63	26.65	2.33	22.65	2.88	10.63	3.07
Control	17.75	1.31	10.63	1.86	10.43	2.39	9.39	3.09
Low Risk Contrast	40.58	1.80	22.85	2.08	24.75	2.83	5.78	2.71

Table 9-9 Gains in MAT Percentile and Grade Equivalent Levels Between the 1st-2nd, 2nd-3rd, and 3rd-4th Years of School for the Experimental, Control, and Low Risk Contrast Groups

	Total Reading		Total Math	
Group	Percentile Score Gain	Grade Equivalent Gain	Percentile Score Gain	Grade Equivalent Gain
Year 1-2				
Experimental	−17.89	0.47	−6.86	0.70
Control	−16.81	0.35	−7.12	0.55
Low Risk Contrast	−24.73	0.15	−17.73	0.28
Year 2-3				
Experimental	−5.76	0.34	−4.00	0.55
Control	−0.90	0.38	−0.20	0.53
Low Risk Contrast	14.54	1.13	1.90	0.75
Year 3-4				
Experimental	−6.06	0.50	−12.02	0.19
Control	−6.80	0.18	−1.04	0.70
Low Risk Contrast	−18.27	−0.08	−18.97	−0.09
Total				
Experimental	−29.71	1.31	−22.88	1.44
Control	−24.51	0.91	−8.36	1.78
Low Risk Contrast	−28.46	1.20	−34.80	0.94

to be essentially equal except for a jump in low risk contrast scores after the third year of school. A review of individual performance within the group reveals that one child's (#42) performance increased 30 points from the end of the second year to the end of the third year. The average increase for the rest of the children assessed was approximately 10 points. This same pattern is observed in the subtests contributing to the composite Total Reading score. This and the fact that the child's score decreased 35 points on the next testing indicate that one child's score artificially inflated the group mean after the third year of school.

There were no significant differences in performance levels between the low risk contrast and experimental groups for Total Reading or Total Math except for the third year assessment of Total Reading ($p = .032$). For these comparisons the Bonferroni intervals procedure was used to adjust t-test p values for the effects of multiple analyses of the data (Timm, 1975, p. 165). The low risk contrast group mean was inflated at this point by the performance of one child whose performance dropped closer to the rest of the group on the next testing. A review of subtest results also reveals that there was a significant difference in group performance for the third year assessment for Word Knowledge ($p = .087$), Word Analysis/Language ($p = .027$), and Reading ($p = .021$). However, these differences also reflect the inflated low risk contrast mean influenced by this child's performance.

Comparisons between the low risk contrast and control groups on the composite Total Reading scores indicate that the low risk contrast group was superior to the control group after each year, but significant ($p = .001$) differences between the two groups were identified only for the third year. Again, this may be attributed to the inflated group mean resulting from the performance of Subject #42 at this point. On the composite Total Math scores, the low risk contrast group failed to make progress during the fourth year and was surpassed by the control group on the fourth year testing. The low risk contrast and control groups' performance curves were not significantly different for Total Math.

In general, it can be seen that performance levels for the experimental group on Total Reading and Total Math were equal to or superior to performance levels for the low risk (or "normal") contrast group. Both groups remained generally superior to the control group through the first 4 years of school.

SPECIAL EDUCATION SERVICES

During the 1970s, the Milwaukee Public School System experienced major and significant changes in its administrative guidelines and its program planning procedures. In particular, during this time the city of Milwaukee simultaneously attempted both to expand special and exceptional education services and to comply with the order to desegregate their public schools. These changes were especially important because of their influence on the day-to-day working of individual classrooms and schools across the city.

School administrators indicated that during the late 1960s and early 1970s many new and innovative programs, particularly Title I programs, had been implemented for the elementary grades. In addition, federal and state laws (e.g., Wisconsin Chapter 89; Wisconsin Statute Chapter 115, subchapter IV; Federal P.L. 94-142) mandated the expansion of special and exceptional education services by the mid-1970s, the time during which the target children entered the public school system. The stated goal of these expanded programs was to provide effective and efficient diagnostic and placement procedures to meet the needs of handicapped children. Multidisciplinary teams (M-teams) were established to diagnose disability areas and to recommend placement within 12 separate service categories (e.g., autistic, educable mentally retarded, visually handicapped). These expanded special and exceptional education services have in fact substantially increased the number of children being served. School officials reported that during the 1977–78 school year 9,827 children with exceptional educational needs were served. They estimated at the time that this figure would increase by approximately 2,000 students in subsequent school years.

The expansion of special education services is important in that it can represent increases in the programming options teachers have as they attempt to individualize instruction. For example, a Title I teacher could be used to give a slow reading child the one-on-one instruction he or she needs to keep pace with class peers. Placement in a classroom for the learning disabled could be used to provide the structure that another child might need before he/she will be able to master particular subjects. Unfortunately, however, there is no administrative guarantee that all, or even most, special service referrals will result in better quality instruction. The lack of specific and real differences between special and regular education instruction (Dunn, 1968) only exacerbates this problem.

The general academic adjustment of experimental and control children was assessed in terms of the number of children in each group who repeated a grade and the number of children who received special or exceptional education assistance. The Milwaukee Public School System had a no-fail policy for the first 3 years of school during the early 1970s. Special or exceptional assistance was provided when needed, but children were not held back. If they continued to experience enough difficulty by the end of the third year, however, they were placed in *extended primary* classes for the fourth year. A larger number of control children than experimental children received special or exceptional educational assistance each year, usually in the areas of language skill training or reading, and all but two of the eight low risk contrast children also received such assistance. Although the average achievement level had declined dramatically for children in both groups and there was no difference between groups in terms of MAT reading scores, twice as many control children as experimental children were placed in extended primary classes for their fourth year in school.

Table 9-10 profiles the number of experimental and control children receiving special and/or exceptional education services consideration during the first

4 years of their elementary schooling. In particular, we have listed M-team referrals, exceptional class placements (only 2 of the 12 options were utilized), instances of supplemental classroom services and summer school tutoring as reported in the children's cumulative school folders, and the number of children in each group who repeated a grade.

Table 9-10   Number of Experimental and Control Children Repeating a Grade and Number Receiving Special or Exceptional Educational Assistance During the First 4 Years of Elementary Schooling

| | Experimental | | | | Control | | | |
| | Year | | | | Year | | | |
Assistance	1	2	3	4	1	2	3	4
Children Repeating Grades	0	0	0	5	0	0	0	10
Children Receiving Assistance	1	1	8	7	7	8	7	16
Types of Assistance								
M-Team Referrals	0	0	2	0	0	0	2	1
Behavior Disabilities Class	0	0	1	1	0	0	1	0
Learning Disabilities Class	0	0	0	0	0	0	1	1
Diagnostic Teacher	0	0	0	0	0	1	0	0
Title I Reading	0	0	5	3	1	2	5	9
Title I Mathematics	0	0	1	2	0	1	3	1
Title I Language	0	0	0	0	5	5	0	0
Title VII Reading	0	0	0	0	0	0	0	9
Sensory-Motor Reading	0	0	1	0	0	1	2	0
Required Summer School	1	1	1	1	2	0	0	0
Total Instances of Assistance[a]	1	1	11	7	8	10	14	21

[a]Some children received more than one type of assistance during a school year making the total instances of assistance greater than the number of children receiving assistance for some grades.

Two trends are important when we consider the number of target children who received exceptional education assistance. First, the control children, in comparison with their experimental counterparts, were diagnosed more immediately upon school entrance as being in need of special help. At the end of grades 1 and 2, one experimental child each year attended summer school. Thus, there were only two instances of experimental children receiving supplemental educational services during the children's first 2 years of elementary schooling. In contrast, 8 and 10 control children in the first and second grades, respectively, received some special service consideration. In fact, 44% of the control group ($n = 8$) were referred during kindergarten for special assistance. One attended an Easter Seal Developmental Center, three were placed in a self-contained, special education kindergarten, and four received Title I language instruction. In particular, special language tutoring was continued during the first and second grades when five control children (28%) were enrolled in a Title I language program.

Second, it is important to understand that changes from one year to the next in the availability of services within given schools are confounded by between grade trends. Not all Milwaukee Public Schools, for example, had Title I programs and some that did have the program restricted it to certain classes or grades. Thus, the reduction in Title I language services for the control children in grades 3 and 4 (no children were referred) does not necessarily imply an improvement in the children's language skills. Rather, it merely states that the group as a whole did not receive this type of special assistance.

These confounding factors notwithstanding, the number of services children from both groups received as they moved through the school system did not seem to increase. The proportional instances of assistance given (i.e., the number of instances divided by the group n) steadily rose from .06 to .71 for the experimental children and from .44 to 1.67 for the control group between the first and fourth grades.

In addition to the expansion of exceptional education services, the Milwaukee School System underwent administrative changes when, in 1975, the Federal Court ordered that one third of the public schools (53) would have to have a "minority racial balance" of 25% to 45% by September 30, 1976. By 1977, two thirds of the schools, and by 1978 all of the schools, had to have this balance. The Milwaukee School Board adopted a desegregation plan based on voluntary integration in combination with educational incentives. As a result, in September of 1976 the Milwaukee Public Schools initiated a unique integration plan that established alternatives to the regular educational program in elementary, junior high, and high schools throughout the city.

As part of the integration plan, Milwaukee's schools were divided into three zones, each zone having 35,000 children from kindergarten through twelfth grade. Each zone, in turn, was divided into four racially balanced leagues of two elementary schools each. Each league included approximately 5,000 elementary pupils. Within each zone, four schools were chosen as specialty schools. In order for a child to attend a specialty school, the parents had to request the transfer and there had to be room for a child of that race. All of the specialty schools were racially balanced.

The specialty schools included:

1. *Fundamental school* with emphasis on basic skills in reading, mathematics, and English, required homework, and strictly enforced rules of discipline.
2. *Multiunit individually guided education (IGE) schools* that included 120 to 150 multiaged pupils grouped in a variety of instructional patterns, including small group instruction, large group instruction, and independent study.
3. *Open education school* that was flexible, nongraded, and multiaged, and where the students initiated or selected learning activities and evaluated their own work.

4. *Continuous progress school*, an upgraded school with flexible multi-aged groups where the instructional groupings were based on a pupil's needs and interests and the student advanced at his/her own rate.

In addition to the four specialty schools in each zone, there were three citywide specialty schools that parents could apply to for admission for their children. These included:

1. *Teacher pupil learning center school*, where individualized instruction was provided based on needs identified by diagnostic procedures. Each student's progress was carefully monitored and parents were involved in the school.
2. *Montessori school*, which included children up to 8 years and used Montessori's self-correcting, sequential learning materials.
3. *Gifted and talented schools*, where students in the fourth to sixth grades were selected by their local schools and presented with a challenging curriculum, periodic evaluation, and early preparation for higher education.

Students whose local schools had become specialty schools had to apply for enrollment in that school or be bused to a different school. During the summer of 1976, the city of Milwaukee mounted an extensive publicity campaign to explain the integration plan to its citizens. It was our experience that much of the prepared material was not easily understood by parents with limited reading ability (e.g., the target parents of the Milwaukee study). This no doubt limited the ability of some disadvantaged families to take advantage of the specialized educational opportunities.

One child, an experimental fourth grader, attended a specialty school that was also his local school but became an open education school. Although both the staff of the public school and the parent coordinator encouraged the mother to sign the papers to permit him to stay at this school, the mother refused to register him; yet she did not want him to be bused. Fortunately, the school decided to pick him as one of the local minority group children who could attend to maintain racial balance. The lack of understanding on the part of this experimental mother was not uncommon among target families. Rather than choose a school based on the needs of their children, parents left the school placement to the schools or to chance.

REPORT CARDS AND TEACHER RATED
READING LEVELS

Two other sources of data help characterize the child's school performance: the children's report cards and their grade-by-grade reading levels rated and reported by the classroom teachers.

Report cards in the Milwaukee School System provided a general assessment, from the school's point of view, of pupils' behavioral and academic adjustments. Also included in school evaluation of students were graded profiles for reading, mathematics, and language and the number of times target children were either tardy or absent during each school year. The report card format also specified that evaluations be made of the children's personal and social growth, but these grades were often left blank and so were not included in our analysis. The classroom teachers entered into each student's cumulative school folders periodic ratings of reading levels and progress based on the reading series the child had completed. The basal series was indexed from 1 (*Readiness*) to 12 (*Independent*), depending on the text's degree of reading difficulty. The date at which a child's reading group moved from one basal reading level to the next was recorded in the child's folder. This information was used to compile end of grade profiles on the target children's instructional reading levels. We sampled report cards and reading levels for 10 experimental and 10 control children at the end of each of the first four grades of elementary schooling.

With respect to the target children's reading levels, we found that the control group's average levels were 3.8 (first grade), 6.5 (second grade), 7.5 (third grade), and 9.5 (fourth grade), whereas the experimental group's mean levels were 5.0, 7.7, 8.9, and 10.4 for the first, second, third, and fourth grades, respectively. The experimental average reading levels were consistently ahead of the control children's, but not significantly so. There was a steady increase, from one year to the next, in the average levels achieved by each group. However, neither group's mean performance for the end of any grade was comparable to expected performance standards. For example, by the end of first grade, children in the Milwaukee system are expected to have completed basal texts rated at Level 7 (hard first). But, with the exception of one experimental boy who scored at Level 8, none of the target children was rated higher than Level 6 at the end of first grade. These mean reading levels as reported by the Milwaukee Public Schools were not consistent with, and in fact are below, the reading achievement levels obtained from the end of grade Metropolitan Achievement Test batteries.

Target children, across the first four grades of school, were typical of other Milwaukee elementary pupils in both the number of times they were tardy and the number of times they were absent from schools within a given school year. There were a few instances of target children whose home situation interfered with their school participation. For example, one experimental boy, whose family was unable to provide the clothing he needed to attend school regularly, was frequently absent (i.e., 34 to 45 days each year) until a social worker intervened at the beginning of the school year and provided the clothes he needed to wear to school. But these and similar instances were exceptions. In general, target children attended school on all but 10 to 15 days each school year (the city mean) and were reported tardy, on the average, only once every 2 months.

When we considered report card subject areas, we found that the predominant grade, by far, for reading, mathematics, and language was a C (average) among both groups of children at all four grades. Because a single grade was essentially being given to all children each year, there was no difference in the mean experimental and control performance in the three subject areas for which we have compiled data.

And, finally, to the limited extent that class conduct and deportment can be determined from report cards, the experimental children were seen by their teachers as more active and less compliant than the control youngsters. The experimental children played and worked well with others and shared ideas well, but their basic school deportment, as noted on report cards, was said to be in need of control. There were, of course, exceptions to this trend among the experimental youngsters, with some evaluated as respectful and hard workers and there were also instances in which control children were specifically rated as behavior problems.

The interpretation of these data has been minimized because it is incomplete. The extent to which report cards and information on reading levels were missing made it difficult to adequately compute between group comparisons. Furthermore, we lacked information on general class performance. Report card and reading level data are difficult to interpret without knowledge of the standard to which the school, and especially the teacher, makes reference for their judgments concerning school performance and behavior. For example, one limitation in assessing reading achievement by reading level is the tendency of some teachers to keep the whole class at one level to avoid the problems of teaching children at varied levels. In part, this tendency is indicated by the teacher's assessment of whether or not the child is acquiring the needed reading skills. There were nine sample children (two experimental and seven control) whose report cards indicated they were reading preprimer basals (Level 3) at the end of first grade. By that time children typically are expected to have completed at least Level 7 (hard first). But in only two cases (both control children) did the teacher indicate by a letter grade of D (needs to improve) that the children's reading skills were insufficient. Yet the data from the Metropolitan testing would argue that the target children, especially the experimental group, read at a higher level than indicated by the children's report cards. Such conflicting data make interpretation difficult. So although we have included these school reports in order to add to the picture of the target children's progress through school, we relied primarily on our own measures for interpretation of the children's development during these early school years.

Comparison of School Achievement and Wechsler IQ

There is a confounding of the factors responsible for performance in early school: the individual, the "carried-with" effects of treatment, and the effectiveness of the public school's elementary education program. Individual performance is measured by IQ level and the "carried-with" effect of treatment is the performance differential between the mean IQs of the experimental and control groups. The measure of social competency suggested by Zigler and

Trickett (1978) is far less an objective measure of important school related behavior competencies than are either the IQ or achievement performance — although social competency ultimately is just as critical in importance. In fact, reports of early education programs have shown an unusually high number of behavior problems, even as in our own follow-up findings, for preschool treated children. Therefore, social behavior notwithstanding, the efficacy of preschool treatment is not simply an all-or-none argument where either the treated children are or are not intellectually superior to an untreated control. Efficacy instead must be a continuing reflection relative both to the children's own skills and to the environmental opportunities available to them. There are considerable difficulties for even the most gifted of the disadvantaged as they move into and through the elementary school environment of large American inner city schools. The low level of academic performance in the experimental and control attended inner city schools suggested that the academic environment was a depressing influence on the experimental and control children's achievement performance through grade four.

A most relevant question then is to what extent MAT performance reflects a child's ability to achieve early school competencies. We could argue that MAT scores themselves are not so much a reflection of the child's ability to achieve as a reflection of an inadequacy on the part of the academic environment to motivate the child to realize this academic potential. Several authors (Egeland, DiNello, & Carr, 1970; Mussen, Dean, & Rosenberg, 1952) have discussed the comparative validity of the Wechsler Intelligence Scale for Children (WISC) and the Metropolitan Achievement Batteries. These authors generally agreed with Sattler (1973) that the WISC IQ is usefully related to scores on academic achievement tests for a variety of child groupings. This may be true, but the WISC IQ is a measure of potential and may not be an immediate reflection of school performance in poor academic settings. The children's WISC FS scores are an indication of individual potential and may be quite discrepant from MAT performance levels for children in deprived environments. In other words, even with an apparent adequacy of educational resources (e.g., desks, books, and teachers), the schools attended by children in this study failed to translate the academic potential of these children into the higher achievement levels of which the children seemed capable.

The experimental and control children's acquisition of school knowledge can be viewed as part of a larger acculturation process. This process, through its various components of home, friends, and school, acts to define the quality of the child's development of habits of learning (Zimiles, 1972). In our description of the entering performance differences between experimental and control children at the time of first grade entry, we presumed that the experimental children's base learning potential was adequate and superior to that of the control children. That is, the experimental children's entering school performance, as measured by our preschool series of intelligence, language, and discrimination learning tests, was well within normal (average and above) ranges and should have functioned to facilitate successful school achievement. Moreover, we posited that the control children, in contrast to their experimental peers, were developing, prior to school entrance, learning habits that were to be antagonistic to future successful academic performance. We have applied this notion of learning environment interaction to the analysis of the children's school achievement performance in an effort to interpret the progression across grade changes in terms of the interaction for each child among habits of learning, the quality of their classroom stimulations, and the demand performance requisites of the school system.

In our earlier discussions about the nature of the interaction between mother and child from these families (Hess & Shipman, 1965), we described the developmental processes that may pressure some children from poor families to acquire learning styles and dispositions toward authority that are maladaptive for later experiences in the classroom. Bee et al. (1969) discussed social class variation in maternal teaching strategies and speech patterns. And at least two studies, one by Kohn (1963), which examined white working class mothers, and a follow-up report by Hess (1970), which focused on black mothers from four different social status levels, suggested that SES related differences in maternal teaching behaviors are translated into between class differences in mothers' definitions of the role their children should fulfill when they enter school. Hess, in particular, argued that when preparing preschoolers for first grade entrance middle class mothers have a more "noninstruction orientation," emphasizing effect and preparation, while lower class mothers are more school relevant in their instructions, stressing obedience and achievement.

These authors suggested that there is a kind of conditioned control carried with the child from his/her at home training that influences attitude toward and behavior during the first days at school. This conditioned control could become manifest as adaptive reductions in a child's responses to classroom stimulation and it has been suggested that such inhibition deficits (Denny, 1964; Heal & Johnson, 1970) can be arranged (within both classical conditioning and discrimination learning paradigms) to expose basic intelligence deficits among the mildly retarded.

Rist (1970) and Pederson, Faucher, and Eaton (1978) argued that schools help reinforce the class structure of society. Rist, for example, showed that a child's placement in first grade reading groups reflects a social class composition rather than ability groupings and that these social class groupings persist at least through the first several years of elementary schooling. Most importantly, though, is the point that there is a pattern of behavior that teachers direct toward these social class groups that can become a more powerful negative influence on the child's later achievement than his/her ability. We think that it is reasonable to assume that the inhibiting and depressing motivational experiences of early development interact with the austerity of some elementary school programs. Therefore, public school curricula, with their emphasis on formal and convergent training in the primary grades, and the tendency of inner city schools to emphasize behavior control act to reinforce and consolidate the antagonistic learning system that characterizes the overall early school performance of the mildly retarded.

Our assessment was sensitive to this type of analysis for several reasons. First, we had compiled baseline measures on the experimental and control children's learning behavior prior to school entrance in an effort to determine how the children progress to the more sophisticated achievement levels and how they build upon these same learning strengths and weaknesses (Gagne, 1970). These data allowed us to estimate the achievement potential of each youngster before he or she entered the first grade. There remain large discrepancies among the nationwide, citywide, and sample school averages, which actually emphasize the extent of underachievement typical of the classroom performance of the students in the sample (inner city) schools.

There are differences in schools and classrooms and obviously across the individual children. School influences can reinforce and consolidate antagonistic learning styles, but they vary as they are filtered down differentially within individual classrooms and are, additionally, mediated according to specific teacher-child interactions. We have used achievement performance profiles, information published by the Milwaukee Public Schools on the 36 sample schools, to estimate the end product quality of third and fifth grade instruction within each school, and thus to measure the extent of similarity (or dissimilarity) between the target child's achievement growth and that of his/her school peers. Taken together, this information afforded us the opportunity to gauge the extent to which particular schools exert stimulus pressure (both positive and negative) on the performance of individual students and to observe the progress toward achievement growth that each child made in acquiring the knowledge items on the school curriculum. This helped to place in perspective target group performance patterns with respect to the national, Milwaukee city, and sample school achievement averages for elementary aged students.

No test is valid for all purposes and in all situations and any study of test validity is germane to only a few of the possible uses or inferences from the test scores (French & Michael, 1966). Specifically, we are concerned about the increased questioning of the construct validity of the Metropolitan Series. Such questions center around the degree to which the Metropolitan is an adequate measure of achievement performance that can withstand socioeconomic, race, ethnic, and intelligence variation. For example, Hodges (1978) states that although the 50th percentile represents the MAT norm, the average level for children from poor families is the 20th percentile, or about one grade level below the norm. Becker (1977) reported that when considering the Metropolitan performance for graduates of Project Follow Through among the eight major sponsors (excluding Direct Instruction) the median falls at the 24th percentile for Total Reading, at the 16th percentile for Total Mathematics, at the 28th percentile for Spelling, and at the 20th percentile for Language. Our own analysis of the Language subtest on the MAT elementary Form F Battery showed several incidences of usage examples (e.g., "you is," "Don't that boy know") that were acceptable for a black dialect but were incorrect under standard English rules. Such mixing of dialects would depress the language performance of black youngsters. This conclusion is consistent with the finding of Eagle and Harris (1969), who documented significant (SES × MAT) interactions and argued that failure to account for these interactions will result in a masking of pupil performance. And finally, Mitchell (1967) suggested that although the Primary I Battery has adequate predictive validity for both white and black children, there were differences in the variability (i.e., comparing the range of standard deviations) between the two racial groups. Taylor and Crandell (1962) found similar differences in the range of scores when the children were divided by IQ scores (>110, 91–110, <90). This lack of variability for low IQ and black children is an indication of possible floor effects (i.e., homogenizing the truncated range of minority group performance by giving minimum scores to all test participants), which could skew performance interpretations.

SUMMARY

Most of the children in all three groups were enrolled in schools in their immediate neighborhoods and, although they often transferred, they generally remained within a limited group of schools located in the core area of the city. The average achievement level on the Iowa Test of Basic Skills for all fourth graders in these schools was compared with the average achievement level for all fourth graders in Milwaukee schools and the national standardization sample of fourth graders (Milwaukee Public Schools, 1972). The general achievement level for all Milwaukee fourth graders was below the level for the national sample, and the achievement level for fourth graders from the small group of core area schools attended by children in this investigation was even lower. The decline in MAT percentile scores for children in the experimental, control, and low risk contrast groups mirrored the profile of differences between the average achievement levels for the national sample, all Milwaukee fourth graders, and fourth graders enrolled in the core area schools.

Why the experimental children's school performance levels slowly but consistently declined across the first four elementary grades while IQ performance was maintained is not clear. We speculated along several lines of thought. The schools the target children attended had average school performance scores lower than the Milwaukee citywide average and schools on the national average. School administrative variables such as pupil-teacher ratio, pupil-aide ratio, and years of teaching experience were also examined, revealing some differences in comparison to other Milwaukee city schools but no differences substantial enough to explain the significant academic declines. No consistent curriculum differences were noted.

10
Family Risk and Child's Intellectual Development

This investigation tested the hypothesis that a major risk factor for low and declining IQ performance for children born into disadvantaged families is the low IQ, low verbal skilled mother. By mitigating the negative effects of the early impoverished social and psychological daily microenvironment presumably created by the low functioning mother through an intervention program, we found that these children have abilities that are masked by a behavioral system nurtured within this setting, which is antagonistic to cognitive and intellectual development. The negative effects of this behavioral system are exacerbated by experiential demands in settings beyond the control of the children, but perhaps not beyond their abilities.

This intervention program interrupted the development of the antagonistic behavioral system and provided the treated children with the opportunity to demonstrate their natural abilities. By encouraging the development of cognitive, language, and social skills in children, and by simultaneously providing social, academic, and vocational rehabilitation for the low functioning mothers, the serious declines in IQ performance typical for this group were prevented and the treated children entered public school demonstrating normal intellectual development.

The identification of mental subnormality by IQ test usually occurs coincidentally with increasing evidence for school failure, at least for those children who have mild mental handicaps. This coincidence of events causes confusion as to why either event occurs. The phenomenon has been attributed in some quarters simply to a social bias, that is, that the increasing incidence of identified mental retardation is disproportionate among the low SES population and therefore is an index of a condition largely determined by the imposition of middle class standards and values by schools biased against the poor and minority groups. It is further argued that the prevalence figures, derived through IQ test identification of mental subnormality, are inflated estimates of true retardation because such tests are unfairly biased against cultural minority groups.

The fact that the prevalence figures fall away sharply after adolescence is attributed to the ability of these same people to adjust to society — although not to school. In other words, many persons are "mentally retarded" only through the school years and make an adequate adjustment to the environment upon termination of schooling. They then become "nonretarded." Of course, an alternative interpretation to this social-cultural environmentalist argument sees these same data as additional justification for hereditary factors as the major determinant of intellectual performance, that is, that the poor are by definition inadequately endowed to be intellectually successful. Again, it is the unfortunate coincidence of a number of perhaps only epidemiologically related factors derived during the school years and beyond that has permitted this confusion in the search for the etiologic origin of mild mental retardation.

The intention, as Birch et al. (1970) pointed out, to develop sensitive and efficient methods for identifying potentially inadequate or mentally subnormal children early in life — especially well in advance of school failure — is to avoid the social and personal cost of identifying that child only after he or she manifests incompetence in school. Early identification should thereby provide two possibilities: preventing the development of intellectual incompetency by understanding the source or origin of the influence on such performance, and enabling more effective and prospective planning for children's special educational training to be undertaken.

In the first case, children's intellectual performance is dependent upon certain cognitive and language tools; needs in these areas identified early could be addressed preventively rather than by remediation. In the second case, early needs can be planned for educationally by closely coordinating preschool and elementary school programs. In either case the early identification of such children through family factors provides a basis for a parent curriculum to support the educational programming by the schools. Using a child's poor IQ performance or academic failure in school as the basis for educational treatment often requires assumptions about the causes of such poor performance and leads to remedial treatment predicated on apparent need rather than to programming that understands educational process.

FAMILY RISK AND THE FALLACY OF POPULATION BASE RATES

The general approach to identifying a population sample for the study of risk factors in mild mental retardation is to focus on the common socioeconomic indices of poverty. In some cases with the added criterion of low IQ, it was hoped that together low SES and low IQ could be used as entry variables and thereby provide an opportunity to gain insight into the family process. It is the family process that holds the key to understanding the developmental experience of young children. However, as has been pointed out (Garber, 1975; Light & Smith, 1969; Shipman, 1976), these variables do not directly measure either the amount or the quality of the developmental experience for the child in the home. As Shipman (1976) suggests, the greater influences on the developing child are not what the family is (status) or its physical environs (situation), but what the family creates as a psychological environment and does therein in interaction (process). It is in the analysis of the process variations of the target families that we can hope to understand what and how background and environmental variables influence the cognitive and language development of young children and the related early education program.

Typically, researchers have looked carefully at such maternal variables as mother's education, IQ, and occupation in order to determine the differential status of the children postintervention. But because these indices often inappropriately assume constancy of meaning within and across groups (Light & Smith, 1969), they tell us little about the quality of the developmental experience. As Tulkin (1968) pointed out, because within a given SES level there is a range of home environments "controlling for social class does not even equate experiential patterns among various populations" (p. 335). Therefore, predictions of developmental outcomes based on SES indices are often extremely tenuous.

Where the mother is of low IQ, it has been assumed that she can create only an impoverished psychological environment and cannot counter the negative and oppressive influences of severe disadvantagement. Although this is true for some mothers with low IQ, it is important to dispel such overgeneralizations. Some can, with help, intervene in their own families' lives so that their children, unlike other families similarly disposed, do not succumb to the ills of severe socioeconomic disadvantagement. This is a particularly important analysis because one major aspect of research aimed at understanding the prevention of mental retardation has implications for the distribution and allocation of a society's resources. Typically, the distribution is determined by what are gross demographic population features epidemiologically associated with low performance. However, these features are not measures of process and therefore cannot but fail to determine the needs of individual families and thereby, of course, the treatment approach appropriate to the families' rehabilitation.

Shipman, McKee, and Bridgeman (1976) reported that much of the variability in the way mothers relate to their children is independent of the SES level of the family. As Shipman et al. (1976) noted, "at best, less than 13% of the variance in any of these process variables can be explained by any one of the status or situational variables" (p. 87). That the correlations among status and situational variables were relatively high in this study demonstrated that these are surface measure variables and do not adequately reflect family process. Consistent with Shipman et al. (1976), the general low magnitude of these correlations suggests that much of the variation in family attitudes and behaviors is independent of variation in family status. Shipman et al. (1976) also concluded, on the basis of their analysis of the relationship among status, situational, and process variables (e.g., maternal attitudes and behaviors), that low income people are not a homogeneous group and that "the notion of a homogeneous 'culture of poverty' is a myth" (p. 95).

Therefore, the most logical point at which to begin to examine the characteristics for a successful family intervention program as a means of improving a child's intellectual performance is to determine which family variables have the greatest impact on the child's cognitive development in individual families. The typical measure of the efficacy of such programs has been simply the intellectual development of the target children. However, efficacy cannot be readily measured unless selection and the dependent measures selected as performance variables are unconfounded. The selective process would require statistical approximations of the risk factor of a family for mental retardation, which in turn would use the IQ measure to confirm assumptions based on stereotype. In other words, because the estimate of risk relies on what may be rather superficial evaluations such as SES and IQ, the evidence for differentiating among kinds of intervention needed by apparently similar families, on the one hand, and for ascertaining the potential for deriving and sustaining benefits from intervention across time, on the other hand, may be lost or masked because the rather more significant component of a family's life, the interactional process, is not evaluated.

The design of this study considered an analysis of IQ measures adequate to differentiate between children and their families in order to understand in what manner the efficacy of the intervention is influenced by either the child or the family. Considerable individual variation between early and late IQ measures (e.g., McCall et al., 1973) and other within group sources of variation, together with a need to know more of the nature of intellectual development, make it imperative that analysis of treatment effect not remain at the gross level of group performance. We tried several ways of separating children both in the experimental group and in the control group to determine whether their patterns of performance were a reflection of family quality. At first we concerned ourselves with those children in the experimental group and those in the control group whose IQ developmental trend was opposite to the rest of their group. In other words, in the experimental group some children showed a declining trend in IQ performance with increasing age in spite of the intervention program, while some control children showed increased or sustained normal IQ performance even without the benefit of the enriched educational preschool program. (These data are detailed in the section on individual child and family reports.) This analysis failed to differentiate significantly between children and their families and led us to use the family risk status (namely the mother's and father's personal characteristics) as a possible way to understand the efficacy of the program.

We were sure from our own observations that many families, although sharing the criteria for selection such as low IQ, low verbal skills, low socioeconomic and educational levels, and poor residential areas, were nevertheless quite different in family process. We hypothesized, therefore, that there should be differences in how the children from such families would sustain the benefits from early programs. For example, even in our experimental group of families, there is a range of cases from total family disruption to situations in which the family process approximates the stereotype of the middle class family (Kagan, 1968).

We assessed all of the families on a high risk index derived from several in current use. Included were assessments of the mother and home in addition to SES and IQ, for example, low maternal IQ (<75), age of mother at target child's birth ($<20>35$), number of children (>4), poor home environment or inability to manage home (including marital status), literacy (<4 or >4 to <8), spacing of children (<12, 12–18, 19–24 months), space before target child (<18 months), number of younger siblings (>3) by school age.

There is obviously some arbitrariness to the values one can assign to each risk factor and there is also some argument as to whether they are all indeed separate or separable items. And there is some problem in the validity of some of the items – notably, educational status. These problems notwithstanding, we tried to separate families according to level of risk. That is, assuming that all members of both the experimental and control groups were high risk, we asked whether some families were of a lower high risk status and whether this would be reflected in the ability of their children to maintain IQ performance postintervention. We assigned risk values to each family and separated them according to above and below average. We then separated the children by family risk level and averaged GIQ performance. Again, notwithstanding the nature of the measure and the problem of justifying the assignment of value, there seemed to be about a 12-point difference in preschool GIQ between the low high risk families and the high high risk families in both the experimental and control groups (see Table 10-1). In the experimental group, the low high risk group has a mean of 117.8 as compared with 106 for the high high risk group on the WISC. In the control group, the difference is about 12 points, from 92 to 79.8.

Table 10-1   Mean WPPSI-WISC and Stanford-Binet GIQ Levels as a
Function of Higher and Lower Risk Status

Age Period	Experimental			Control		
	Low	High/Low	High	Low	High/Low	High
Wechsler GIQ						
Preschool	117.8	109.0	106.0	92.0	82.6	79.8
School	110.5	99.2	98.1	85.4	82.3	80.5
Stanford-Binet GIQ						
Preschool	124.9	121.8	117.9	100.1	89.4	86.2

From preschool to postintervention GIQ performance, those children from the highest risk families also had as a group a lower mean GIQ performance. The lower risk experimental children changed 7.3 IQ points from preschool to postintervention and the higher risk experimental children lost nearly 8 points in IQ score. The difference of 12 points in mean GIQ was maintained, and the decline for both low and high was comparable. The pre- to post-GIQ change was not as clear, understandably, in the control group where the shifts were −6.6 and +.7 points, respectively, for the low and high children. The lower risk children were about 5 points superior to the higher risk children. The difference is made somewhat clearer when the six high children are more closely examined. Two of the six rose sharply between preschool and postintervention and at 120 months averaged 98, while the other four averaged 75.3. In both groups, it seems that the efficacy of the intervention effort (as efficacy is measured by the performance of the children), is the quality of home environment that exists throughout and persists beyond intervention. The word *persist* is meant to refer to the negative aspects of the home that remained although masked during intervention, to effect downward pressure on performance after intervention was terminated.

A similar comparison was made between the low and high risk families on the basis of their Stanford-Binet (preschool) GIQs. In the Stanford-Binet data prior to intervention termination, the same trend holds. For the experimental group the difference between the low and high risk groups is 7 points, but for the control group the difference is nearly 14 points.

This analysis is not conclusive and although the difference between the low and high risk groups is significant ($p < .05$) within the experimental groups, both preschool and postintervention, there remain some discrepancies—for example, the two children in the high risk control group who deviated most in postintervention GIQ performance from the other children in that group. Similarly, in the high low group there were discrepancies in performance that were not clearly low or high. For both the experimental and control groups, the high low group tended to follow the trend of decreasing mean GIQ as we moved from lower to higher risk. However, assignment of low, high, or low high did not seem to predict IQ level, as there were children who were both higher and lower in GIQ than in the other two groups. The strength of the difference, discrepancies notwithstanding, emphasizes the influence of the home on the intellectual growth of the child. Assignment of risk levels through more detailed screening procedures would reduce the false negatives and positives and improve the effectiveness and efficiency of therapeutic preventive programming based on risk screening. The improvement of screening procedures attempting to ascertain risk level depends on more careful analysis of families in order to weigh the influence of family characteristics, which are part of the family process, on the growth of their children.

We separated families according to low or high level on several of the risk variables. These date are presented in Table 10-2. The *n* is sometimes very small and the complement of families changes. In other words, the separation

Table 10-2 Comparison of Children's GIQs within Group on Individual Risk Factors

| | Experimental | | | | | | | | | | Control | | | | | | | | | |
| | Low | | | | | High | | | | | Low | | | | | High | | | | |
Risk	n	Pre	SD	Post	SD	n	Pre	SD	Post	SD	n	Pre	SD	Post	SD	n	Pre	SD	Post	SD
# Children																					
3–4	6	111.5	8.7	111.5	15.9						9	84.6	14.0	82.4	8.6					
5+						11	108.3	4.9	101.1	6.0						9	85.0	5.6	83.1	9.5
Literacy																					
> 4th grade	10	110.1	7.3	102.6	11.6						8	87.8	12.4	84.4	7.5					
< 4th grade						6ª	111.8	6.8	101.8	5.7						10	81.9	8.6	81.4	9.9
Spacing to Target Child																					
> 18 months	8	115.8	4.9	107.2	11.5						11	82.9	10.1	82.9	9.9					
< 18 months						9	107.2	4.5	99.5	6.8						7	87.7	10.8	82.4	7.5
Mother's Age at Target Child's Birth																					
21–34	13	111.5	6.1	103.5	10.8						11	82.9	10.1	84.0	10.1					
20–35						4	110.3	7.9	101.9	7.1						7	81.3	14.4	80.7	6.2
Sibling in Special Class																					
No	12	111.4	6.1	100.8	6.6						8	89.8	12.4	86.5	9.8					
Yes						4	114.8	5.6	108.1	15.6						10	80.8	6.5	79.7	6.9
Quality of Home																					
Good	14	112.4	6.1	103.4	10.0						16	87.0	8.6	83.6	8.9					
Poor						3	106.0	5.6	98.3	2.3						2	67.3	3.2	75.7	1.9
Maternal IQ																					
>70	12	110.6	7.1	105.0	10.9						11	86.7	11.3	84.2	10.7					
<70						5	112.8	3.8	98.6	4.6						7	81.7	8.4	80.5	4.2

ª One mother refused to take the WRAT.

of families into low, high low, and high risk groups is not consistently reflected when the individual risk variables are considered separately. Although it would be most convenient to find some one variable that would differentiate among these families for those at the highest risk, it is the compounding of factors that acts to precipitate crises and disrupts families. There are, however, in these individual risk factors some discernible trends or patterns.

For low SES families there is a tendency for IQ to decrease with increasing family size. For the experimental group, there was about a 3-point advantage for the children from smaller families and, more importantly, the GIQ did not decrease across time. This was not evident for the low scoring control group. The factor of maternal literacy did not seem to make a difference in the preschool and postintervention GIQs for the experimental children. There was a preschool GIQ difference, which was somewhat maintained into school. Spacing to target child, as indicated by the number of months to the birth of the target child from the birth of the next oldest sibling, had a strong effect in the experimental group, and one for which the differential was maintained across the preschool to postintervention GIQ measures. There was no effect for this risk variable apparent in the control families.

The variable of age of mother at her child's birth seemed to have some effect but only in the control group. The risk variable of siblings in special class, tied originally to the definition of cultural-familial retardation, related to the control group's preschool and postintervention GIQs more clearly than to the experimental group's. In the experimental group, two of the families had children among the highest scorers, while two others were among the lower scorers. This is perhaps a reflection of the problems associated with special class placements (i.e., whether it is for educational or behavioral problems). The quality of home variable was in the expected direction of influence for both experimental and control children. It was most clear in the control group where the poorest quality homes yielded two of the three lowest scoring children. An additional risk variable assigned similarly for all children in both groups was maternal IQ; however, we separated children within groups according to MIQs above and below 70 on the follow-up maternal WAIS. There was some benefit across time to the children with above IQ 70 mothers, for both groups.

This discussion has been mainly to suggest some of the variation that exists within this seemingly homogeneous group. With the exception of the risk variable *sibling in special class*, the effect of being on the low risk side of these seven variables is realized in higher GIQs across time. This also holds true for the control group children (except for the variable of *number of children in the family*). We have not submitted these variations to statistical analysis because of changing and small *n*s, but the overall trend is rather instructive in two ways: that being on the lower end of high risk is an advantage and that individual risk variables compound to influence IQ negatively (recall that for both groups low risk preschool and postintervention GIQs are higher than for the high risk group). For children to be at either a lower or higher risk level of the high risk scale is no guarantee of their IQ performance levels, as there are indeed children who are both higher and lower within their risk group. If we accept the trend that higher levels of risk on variables known not to enhance growth, then we could postulate that, for example, those children at high risk levels with IQs higher than children at lower risk levels on similar variables might at those lower levels achieve higher IQ performances. In other words, high risk prevention is not intended to prevent just low IQs but also IQs lower than they otherwise have to be.

The delineation of characteristics of individuals and/or of their families indicating they are at very high risk for disruptive or calamitous crises to their life process is therefore fundamental to the question of preventing mental retardation.

It is of greatest concern because the sensitivity of the selection procedure used by prevention studies must insure that risk status is not casually assigned. Indeed, the final measure of the efficacy of a therapeutic intervention, as in any treatment, requires a sensitive baseline from which to depart. If the treatment is applied to a nonresponsive situation, then little or no movement can be expected. It is possible, for example, to presume as Clarke (1973) did, that there are three groups from which the to-be-treated sample can be drawn from the larger population. These three groups are not readily discernible because of the tendency to believe that the high risk group is homogeneous, for which further support is often taken from the several superficial characteristics obvious to the casual observer held in common by the members of these groups. Nonetheless, the three groups are: those for whom the treatment is appropriate and the results successful, namely, prevention of low intellectual performance; those for whom the treatment is not necessarily inappropriate but actually not entirely necessary because their intellectual performance is in the normal range and destined to remain so; and those for whom the treatment is not appropriate because their intellectual performance is normal and low and destined to remain so. Therefore, of these three groups, we have assumed that without some program of psychoeducational therapy as in most intervention studies the normal course of development for the first group would be threatened.

However, it has not been made clear by most prevention efforts that therapeutic intervention is expected to be successful with only a portion of its target population. A major distraction to the interested observer of a target population of the seriously disadvantaged is the obvious economic and physical depression in which they live. In addition, the disadvantaged include racial, cultural, and ethnic minority groups and have obvious characteristics that identify them as members of that minority group that, together with their abject environment, supports the altogether casual observation that all members of the group are alike and the notion that with proper treatment, all can be moved into the average or better range. Unfortunately, this is impossible at present. What rather was the objective of this intervention was the prevention of mental retardation in those individuals who were identified from among a target population to be at high risk for intellectual retardation with increasing age. Risk, however, is based in probability and suggests proportional outcomes. That is to say, there will remain after the selective identification procedure some individuals for whom low intellectual performance is inevitable and some who are quite normal. We will, hopefully, learn to screen out these individuals and make educational interventions of this kind both more effective and more efficient. Therefore, as screening procedures for assessing risk factors continue to improve and become more sensitive, this sensitivity will increase the probability that those at high risk selected for preventive programming can and will be successfully treated. Then we will not miss individuals who can benefit and we will not include those for whom another kind of intervention is more appropriate.

The direct implications of this selection procedure are twofold, that it is ineffective to include those who cannot benefit in a particular specialized program of educational therapy and grossly inefficient to include those who need not participate. There is neither the manpower nor the money available, to say nothing of the untold human suffering that is caused when false hopes are raised.

When the selection procedure for this study was developed, our extensive epidemiologic survey of a seriously disadvantaged population revealed that, beyond the obvious physical depression of low SES, there were identifiable families who were responsible at a greater rate for children with low IQs. We have hopefully begun to move from looking at high risk for mental retardation as simply a factor of poverty or disadvantagement to the finding that there is within the physically impoverished environment of disadvantagement a unique impoverished psychological environment created in seriously disadvantaged families where the mother is of low IQ and poor verbal skills. We believe that now we have come a step further in that those variables of SES and IQ may be insufficient for screening without those variables that evaluate the characteristics of family process. This argument does not dismiss low SES as an important initial screening variable for the high risk families trapped by poverty which continually exacerbates even the most ordinary problems and creates threats to life. And it does not dismiss low intelligence, which has further helped to trap some families in their impoverished surroundings. But such variables alone do not reveal the tendency and/or the ability for a family to respond successfully to a program of rehabilitation therapy, including intense psychoeducational programming of the children.

COMPARISONS OF DEVELOPMENT FOR SIBLING AND CONTRAST SAMPLES

During the course of this investigation, an attempt was made to sample intellectual development in other children from the target experimental and control families and from low and high risk contrast populations. At least two major efforts over the years were made to test all siblings in each family from infants to adults. This was logistically extremely difficult to accomplish because of the geographic dispersion of family members so widely distributed in age and because individual differences in personal and social activities made scheduling testing sessions nearly impossible. In addition we included in the experimental treatment program, after the first assignment of 20 children, five subsequently born siblings from five different families. These data were not included in earlier data presentations of experimental versus control comparisons. We thought it might be possible to gain from these various data sets an estimate of possible diffusion effects attributable to the intervention program with the target child and mother. Examination of these data actually proved rather informative both in estimating possible within family diffusion effects and in providing a basis for overall comparisons between the experimental and control target groups and the original survey sample of a high risk contrast group.

Thus, in addition to the experimental and control target children, we present comparison data for the small group of five experimental siblings who were entered late into the experimental program, the untreated siblings of the experimental and control families, the low risk contrast target children and their siblings, and the original high and low risk contrast sample developed during the original survey of the Milwaukee inner city census tracts. In all, there are nine samples and although they are uneven in terms of methodology used to develop the data (i.e., cross-sectional vs. longitudinal, differences in tests, etc.), they are instructive when conservative comparisons are made. These data provide both an estimate of the benefit diffusing to other family members attributable to treatment and a graphic illustration of the intervention's marked effect on the intellectual development of target children in comparison to untreated control and contrast groups over time.

Intellectual Development of Treated Experimental Siblings

Subsequent to the selection and placement of the original sample of children, we began to include the next born sibling. Through this procedure five additional children were enrolled in the infant education program. This aspect of the program was discontinued because it became logistically impractical for us to manage. These five children, each the younger sibling of an experimental target child, were in effect the youngest children in the program. These children proceeded through the same educational program as their immediately older siblings did and were assessed on the same basis as well. The Gesell data described earlier did not include these younger siblings.

The Gesell Developmental Schedules were administered to these five younger siblings at the ages of 6, 10, 14, 18, and 22 months. Their older siblings, who had preceded them through the infant program, were on the average nearly 20 months older. Four of the older children (ranges: 16 to 26 months) were mobile and talking at the birth of the younger sibling; one of them was only 12 months older.

The performance of the younger and older siblings was essentially comparable through the 14-month testing session and generally similar to the previously described performance of the experimental group. Whereas there was fairly rapid acceleration after the 14-month age point for the older experimental siblings in comparison with the experimental group mean, the younger experimental siblings declined slightly with respect to their own earlier performance at 18 months before rising at the 22-month mark. This becomes more apparent when the performance mean is derived as deviation scores from the developmental norm (see Table 10-3).

Table 10-3   Average Deviations from Age Group Norms for
Experimental Group, Older Sibling, and Younger Sibling Performance
Mean Scores for 6 Through 22 Months

	Age (Months)				
Group	6	10	14	18	22
Experimental Group	1.17	1.73	2.71	3.29	5.18
Older Siblings	2.20	1.38	1.95	4.50	6.45
Younger Siblings	1.43	1.23	2.18	1.73	2.75

These data reveal that the monthly growth rate at 18 and 22 months for the older siblings was more than twice that for the younger children. The younger siblings at 22 months were nearly 3 months ahead of the norm, but the older siblings were more than 6 months ahead. One possibility is that the older siblings benefited more directly from the mother's simultaneous participation in the maternal rehabilitation program (during part of which time, incidentally, she was pregnant), which was either ongoing or nearly over as these older children moved through the accelerated performance period and which acted together with the actual infant stimulation program. The experimental group's mean performance level is perhaps also a reflection of the effect of an overlap of the maternal rehabilitation program with the infant program.

The younger experimental siblings were tested from 24 months to 72 months with the Stanford-Binet (L-M) on the same schedule as were the other target children. The mean DQ and IQ performances for both the younger and older siblings are illustrated in Figure 10-1, which also includes the overall experimental group mean for comparison purposes.

There are at least two interesting features of these data. First, the older siblings dominated the growth performance measures on the Gesell Schedules and up to 30 months on the Stanford-Binet, but the younger siblings came to dominate their older siblings across nearly the entire preschool period, although performance for both siblings was quite similar. In fact at the upper ages, from 42 to 66 months, during the more formal portion of the curriculum (e.g., the reading program), the younger siblings were superior to the overall group mean. Second, their performance fell sharply at 72 months of age. Their older siblings were generally below the group mean, as were their younger siblings, but did not show the same drop in performance at the 72 month mark. These upper ages of the preschool program are particularly interesting in comparisons of the younger and older experimental siblings because the younger siblings entered kindergarten whereas their older siblings had remained in the preschool program. The performance measure drop at 72 months or at the end of public school kindergarten for the younger siblings did not occur for the older siblings who stayed in the preschool program nor for the experimental group overall. (Beginning at 48 months, only four siblings are included because one family moved.)

In Figure 10-1, data are illustrated to indicate more clearly differences between these sibling subgroups. For the younger siblings, there is, as in their Stanford-Binet performance, a drop in their WPPSI performance from 60 to 72 months, while their older siblings also show a decline in their WPPSI performance consistent with the overall experimental group performance but one not seen in their Stanford-Binet performance. Thus, in all of these comparisons, for the experimental older siblings and for the other experimental target children who stayed in the experimental program instead of attending the public school kindergarten, there is a similar trend toward declining WPPSI IQ scores continuous from 48 months to 72 months. The older siblings are similarly below the overall experimental group mean on the WPPSI, as they were on the Stanford-Binet. However, what does seem different is the rate at which the groups recover from this decline, and they all essentially do — sooner or later. In other words, particularly for the experimental younger and older sibling comparison, there is a suggestion that the effect of public school kindergarten is relatively positive. It has acted to facilitate the adjustment of the younger siblings to school so that they already begin to improve and stabilize their intellectual performance in first grade, at the end of which their IQ (Full Scale) performance increases. The older siblings, on the other hand, do not begin to change IQ (Full Scale) performance until the end of third grade, at which time their mean IQ (Full Scale) performance shows an increase.

Figure 10-2 presents the performance curve of the control group in order to provide additional comparative support for the interpretation of the positive effect of kindergarten. The control group's performance is not as clearly supportive of this argument because the pattern of performance prior to kindergarten through the fourth grade is different, but then again so was the group's early developmental experience. The control group performance declines from 48 months to 60 months and then shows a sharp rise after their kindergarten experience, only to decline through first grade. However, they begin to recover during the second grade; by 96 months, and certainly 108 months, they are at or above their 60-month IQ performance level. At each age subsequent to 84 months, they show a gain, indicating recovery from their post first grade low, which the older experimental siblings also show, although their recovery begins a year later.

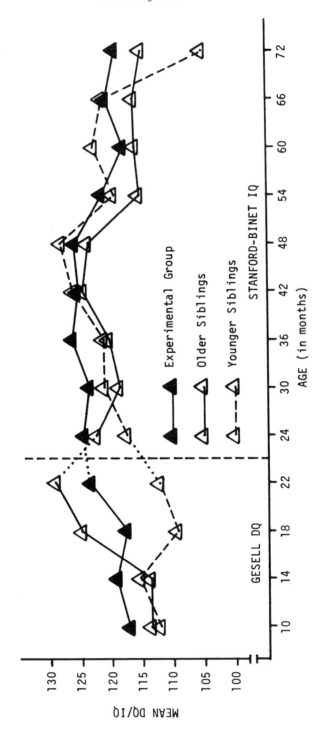

Figure 10-1.   Mean Experimental Group, Older Sibling, and Younger Sibling Gesell DQ/Stanford-Binet IQ Performance for 6 Through 72 Months

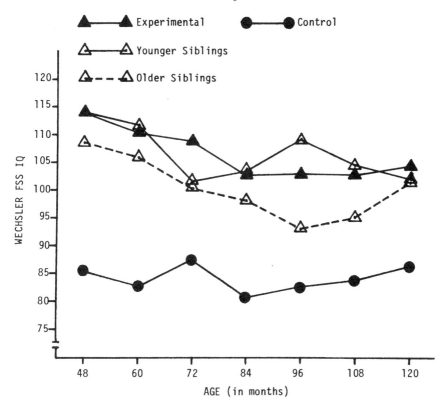

Figure 10-2. Comparison of Experimental Older and Younger Siblings on the Wechsler IQ Tests

In the experimental group, preschool experience seemed to raise IQ levels in a special way, but these early performance gains were negatively affected by the transition and concomitant adjustment to school with the less structured kindergarten and/or first grade experience. What is important might be termed a contrast effect of experience, that is, how one set of experiences affects another with which it contrasts. For the control children, early experience was very different from that of experimental youngsters because it was less enriched, and there is a marked contrast between this experience and kindergarten, which seemed to elevate their performance at 72 months. Although this was only a momentary elevation and their performance declined after the kindergarten experience, this elevated performance was in sharp contrast to the general trend of their performance. However, once the adjustment to school was made, with the contribution of the kindergarten experience, the improvement in performance attributable to school began.

Low risk contrast group children might be seen as somewhat comparable to the younger experimental sibling group in terms of their developmental experience. Presumably they both had positive and supportive preschool experiences and both entered school with kindergarten experience. Care must be used in interpreting the meaning of these curves because they are based on the performance of relatively few children (LRC = 8, YESib = 4), and stability of the group mean is somewhat strained because of the variability in performance of several children. The low risk contrast group performance can be said to be comparable to the younger experimental sibling group performance after the 72-month testing. In general, the younger experimental siblings improved in performance after the decline at 72 months, and although the low risk contrast children's performance did not fade in kindergarten, there was a comparable improvement in performance after 72 months. The older experimental siblings who did not have kindergarten experience did not begin recovery until third grade, and the experimental group did not show its highest school performance level until fourth grade.

Within the limitations of these data, there is some support for the suggestion that kindergarten experience is important for getting about the business of adjusting to school, which is slowed by the continuation of the preschool intervention. The critical evolving qualitative components of intellectual development, including social skills, language, and problem solving, are in need of support prior to kindergarten, but kindergarten experience may facilitate the development of social competencies appropriate to and necessary for future school adjustment (see Zigler & Trickett, 1978).

Combined Experimental Siblings

The analysis of the experimental group's performance does not include the younger siblings' performance in experimental group means. Only in the following table (Table 10-4) have we combined the performance of the younger siblings with the overall experimental group performance means.

Table 10-4 Comparison of Mean Wechsler IQ Performance for the
Extended Experimental Group (Experimental Children and Siblings) and
the Limited Experimental Group

Age (Months)	Extended Experimental		Limited Experimental	
	n	Mean	n	Mean
48	21	113.90	17	113.94
60	21	110.66	17	110.41
72	20	107.55	16	109.00
84	21	103.05	17	102.94
96	21	104.19	17	103.00
108	21	102.95	17	102.59
120	21	103.72	17	104.18

There is relatively little difference in the overall experimental mean, with some decrease at 72 months because of the younger experimental siblings and a slight increase into the school years because of the younger siblings' gains beyond first grade.

Nontarget Siblings of Both Experimental and Control Target Children

Beginning around the time the initial selection of families for the study was made and over the next 8 years, while we had close contact with the families, we tried to test all of the siblings in both the experimental and control families. This testing was performed by various independent testing teams from the Milwaukee area. These teams were from the Milwaukee Public School, private agencies, and two universities in Milwaukee (University of Wisconsin-Milwaukee and Marquette University). Testing was done in the families' homes. The testers were not told to which group the family belonged. The task of accumulating the sample of siblings was made especially difficult, even beyond the complicated logistics of testing so many individuals across a wide age range in many locations, because of problems with identifying all of the immediate members of an individual household and also because appointments were often not kept, especially by busy teenagers.

In Figure 10-3, we have illustrated the mean course of intellectual development for the siblings of both the experimental and control target children combined in comparison to the mean performance of the high risk contrast group derived from the original survey data. In general, the curves are similar in that both decline, with an increasing percentage of below 80 IQ scores. The drop is greater in the contrast group curve, with a greater number of below 80 IQ scores. Considering that there is a difference of more than 10 years between the testings, the comparability of these two groups' performance is rather good, suggesting that the phenomenon of declining IQ performance with increasing age in siblings from families with low IQ mothers is reliable.

In Table 10-5, the siblings group and contrast group mean IQ performances and incidence of scores below 80 are compared across increasing age periods. The general trend in IQ performance for the sibling offspring of low (<75) IQ disadvantaged mothers holds in that there is a mean IQ performance decline with increasing age and there is an increasing percentage of 80 or below IQ scores.

In Figure 10-4, the intellectual performance of the experimental and control siblings has been separately illustrated for comparison. The siblings of the control target children show a performance comparable to that of the siblings of the experimental target children up until the 84-month mark, with both groups declining slightly. However, at the 84-month mark the control group begins to decline from a mean of 87.2 to a mean of 74 at 168 months and beyond. The experimental siblings, on the other hand, discontinue the decline from the higher infancy level of 90.2 at 84 months, where their mean is 86.8, and maintain a fairly stable performance level to 168 months, where the mean is 86.1 The mean performance data are presented in Table 10-6 for comparison of the

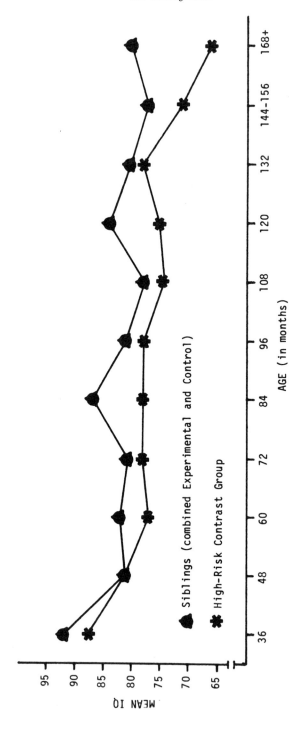

Figure 10-3.   Comparison of IQ Performance for Untreated Siblings and a High Risk Contrast Group

Table 10-5   IQ Performance Means and Incidence of Low (< 80)
Performance for Experimental and Control Siblings (Combined) and a
High Risk Contrast Group

Age		Siblings			Contrast	
	n	Mean IQ	% <80	n	Mean IQ	% <80
3-5	83	83.5	34%	86	85.5	22%
6-8	72	83.5	33%	77	78.2	57%
9-11	68	81.5	43%	53	76.0	62%
12+	67	79.9	49%	54	70.0	87%

two groups of siblings, along with the change in incidence of 80 or below IQ scores with increasing age.

As we moved out on the age dimension, the frequencies became smaller and individual performances tended to distort the mean at the higher ages; therefore, we began to group scores beyond 132 months. Percentages of IQ scores < 80 are also shown for combined age groupings, as was done in the illustration of experimental and control sibling performance in Figure 10-4 in order to represent more fairly the frequency counts between groups across the age categories.

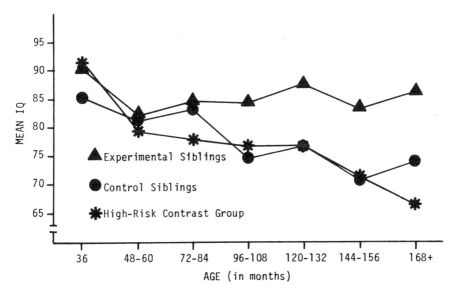

Figure 10-4.   Mean IQ Performance Levels for the Experimental and Control Siblings Compared to Performance for High Risk Contrast Sample

By separating the experimental and control siblings, a rather sizable difference in performance can be seen beyond the 84-month mark, as well as a substantial difference in the quality of the performance distribution. In the latter case, this difference is revealed by the higher incidence of IQ scores below 80 in the control sibling population than in the experimental sibling population. In fact, the incidence of IQ scores below 80 for the control siblings is generally twice that for the experimental group siblings. If we again compare the performance curve for the experimental and control siblings to the original contrast group across time, it can be seen that the control siblings coincide in their declining IQ performance with the original contrast group, and the comparison of the incidence of IQ scores < 80 is also quite similar. Therefore, the performance of the sibling offspring of mothers with IQs below 80, illustrated in Figure 10-4 as the contrast group performance, is repeated and demonstrated to be a reliable phenomenon by the comparative performance of the sibling offspring of the control families where the mother is below 75 in IQ.

The marked difference in performance for experimental sibling offspring after 84 months of age suggests diffusion from the maternal rehabilitation program's benefits into the family. The exact nature of the benefit or the mechanism for its diffusion is not revealed by any measure we made with the families. Anecdotal observations on family behavior at family-school gatherings, such as parent coffee hours, suggest that there was a growing involvement with the program as time went by. In fact, a small graduation ceremony for the first children leaving the program to enter school was attended by over 200 people, a number out of proportion to the nine children who were graduating. It would have been possible, however, only by continuous measurement of each nontarget sibling throughout the course of the preschool

Table 10-6   Experimental and Control Sibling[a] Mean IQ Performance
with Increasing Age

Age (Mos)	Experimental				Control			
	n	Mean IQ	SD	% <80	n	Mean IQ	SD	% <80
≤ 36	16	90.2	8.0	12.5%	6	85.2	15.5	17%
48	17	84.1	14.3	35%	15	78.2	16.2	48%
60	17	80.2	12.2		12	84.2	18.2	
72	11	82.7	11.7	32%	10	79.1	11.4	30%
84	14	86.8	9.5		13	87.2	17.4	
96	13	87.8	8.4	31%	11	74.6	15.6	62%
108	16	80.9	10.5		10	74.6	23.6	
120	9	87.4	12.5	20%	9	80.7	15.2	65%
132	16	87.7	13.7		8	72.9	12.3	
144-156	19	83.3	9.4	42%	11	70.8	12.3	73%
168 +	21	86.1	9.5	29%	16	74.0	15.9	69%

[a]These sibling data include no target children from either experimental or control group.

program and beyond to have provided a baseline from which we could have judged more conclusively whether the large discrepancy between sibling IQ performance was in fact the byproduct of a diffusion of the intervention program to nontarget family members.

Low Risk Contrast Siblings

We tested the siblings of the low risk contrast children over the same period of time and in the same manner as we tested the nonparticipating siblings of the experimental and control groups. This testing was also conducted by the same independent testing teams uninformed as to the families' group assignment. The mean IQ performance levels for the low risk contrast sibling group are presented in Table 10-7.

Table 10-7 Mean Full Scale IQ Performance Levels for the Low Risk Contrast Sibling Group for 48 Through 168 Months

Age (Mos)	Mean	SD	n
48-60	91.4	10.9	8
72-84	108.1	17.8	7
96-108	93.0	15.1	9
120-132	93.4	6.0	8
144-156	97.0	9.1	4
168	98.0	17.9	6

The siblings of the low risk contrast sample were comparable in performance to the original low risk contrast sample. Performance remained very stable for the group between preschool and adolescence, with the exception of increased mean performance at school entry age. Performance was on average in the normal range.

Comparison of Target Children by Ordinal Position

An additional source of information by which the possibility for diffusion could be established more reliably was change in IQ performance of siblings ordinally closest to the target child. Two assumptions we made were that the discontinuation of the declining IQ performance observed in the siblings of the experimental group children around age 84 months, but not seen for the contrast group or the nontarget control siblings, would begin prior to the 84-month mark and that the effects of diffusion would be strongest nearest the target child. Therefore, we used the experimental child and the control child to plot the mean IQ performance of their siblings according to their ordinal position to the target child. To be sure, this is only a way of gaining an estimate of the force of the target child as the possible source for the diffusion of the intervention program effect. Sixteen target children in each group had siblings that were younger and/or older. The mean IQ of these children is presented in Table 10-8.

The difference between younger and first older ordinally positioned siblings' mean IQ performance is 10.3 IQ points for the control group and 5.8 IQ points for the experimental group. This is suggestive, complications of adjusting for age, sex, and other methodological problems of IQ testing notwithstanding, that the difference is the result of the experimental target child's effect on the next older sibling and that that effect is to reduce or to slow the IQ decline. Again, the mechanism for this diffusion effect from the child and the relationship of the mother to nontarget siblings is not apparent.

We carried the mean IQ performance curve for the ordinal position of siblings out to the fourth and older position. These data are illustrated in Figure 10-5. The mean at each ordinal position as well as the median have been presented for comparison purposes. Essentially, the two groups are quite similar at the younger position and the median scores are equal. The percentage of IQ scores <80 is also about the same. As the transition across the target child's position is made, the rate of loss is very different between groups. This differential can be seen in Figure 10-5 and is revealed as a slower rate in decline for the experimental group, which at the transition from younger to first older is nearly 5 points for the experimental family siblings but translates into about a 17-point difference at the oldest position. In other words, it seems that there is a slowing effect on the rate of decline effected by the experimental target child, which brakes the declining IQ of older siblings beginning with the next oldest. The decline for the control siblings begins at the younger position and continues through the control target child and the subsequent ordinal

Table 10-8   Mean IQ Performance of Siblings Identified by Ordinal
            Position Relative to Target Children

Group		Younger Siblings		1st Older	2nd Older	3rd Older	4th Older
Experimental	X	90.4		84.6	85.6	79.5	85.0
Siblings	Median	(87.8)		(89.5)	(84.1)	(79.3)	(85.5)
	n	13	Target Child	17	16	11	19
	≤80	8%		29%	31%	58%	37%
Control	X	92.5		82.2	78.2	74.4	68.7
Siblings	Median	(87.8)		(82.5)	(76.7)	(71.8)	(70.0)
	n	10		15	10	8	13
	≤80	10%		40%	60%	63%	77%

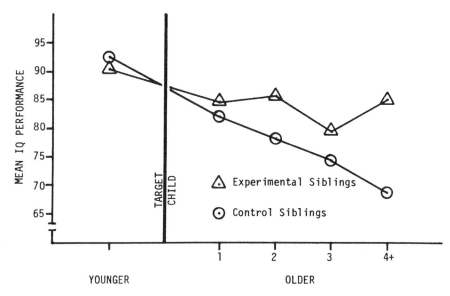

Figure 10-5. Mean IQ Performance of Siblings Identified by Ordinal Position Relative to Target Child

positions unabated. At the fourth older position, the mean IQ of the siblings (68.7) approximates the mean maternal IQ for these families at entry to the program (66.5). Also, the distribution of IQs is different from the first older position and beyond, with a considerably greater incidence of IQ scores <80.

In Figure 10-6, we have illustrated the change in deviation of the mean IQ at each ordinal position from the mean IQ of the family. To be sure, this is confounded with IQ level, but it is clear that there is a rather marked difference in the movement of individual family members' performance levels across these ordinal positions. In other words, after the major drop in IQ between the younger and first older position, the experimental families show about a point or so change, suggesting an evenness of the diffused effect across the family, whereas the control group deviation from the family mean declines rapidly to negative levels. An additional analysis of family IQ performance considers IQ as a function of family size (Table 10-9). As noted previously, IQ declines with increasing family size.

The data in Table 10-9 do not, of course, include the IQs of any of the target children. These data suggest that the experimental program's greatest effect is for the smallest families, but that there is benefit for even larger families, as we compare the experimental and control means at five or more children. This latter finding would seem to suggest an increased awareness by the mother of her familial responsibilities, attributable to the maternal rehabilitation program, in a way that has been effective in offsetting an expected decline in mean family IQ performance with increasing family size. This decline is, however, found in the control families.

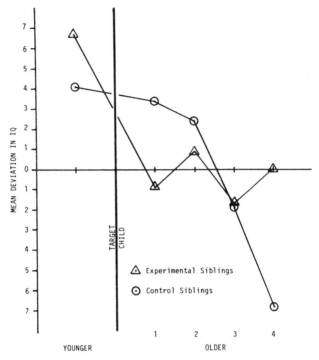

Figure 10-6.   Sibling Deviation from Family Mean IQ by Ordinal Position Relative to Target Child

Again, a sequential measurement of the sibling IQ performance levels on a time line coincident with various phases of the experimental program would have provided a more sensitive baseline from which to judge whether there is an effect of the experimental program diffusing from the mother and the target child. There is, however, on the basis of our other assessments initially no reason to expect the sizable post 84-month difference between experimental and control siblings. The families' (mothers' and general family) characteristics were, on all measures, not significantly different. A conclusive demonstration of diffusion would be instructive as to the cost-benefit implications of future

Table 10-9   Mean Family IQ as a Function of Family Size

		Family Size					
Group		2	3	4	5	6	7+
Experimental	X	99.0	86.0	83.6	79.3	84.0	85.5
Control	X	90.5	80.5	84.3	73.5	79.6	77.6

programs for disadvantaged families. These data suggest at least the necessity to include, in the evaluation schema of future similar investigations, assessment of nontarget family members and psychoanthropologic observations of family functioning as well. Such an effort would be rewarded by providing information on possible additional sources of disruption of a family rehabilitation effort, that is, where adolescents not targeted may distract from the thrust of therapy toward a parent and/or a younger child.

EXPERIMENTAL AND CONTROL GROUP
PERFORMANCE BEYOND 120 MONTHS

When intervention ceased, the children were tested once each year for the first 4 years. Independent psychologists were employed to test children en masse, arranged for logistical convenience rather than at age levels, and test scores corresponding closest to 84, 96, 108, and 120 months of age were grouped for comparison (see Table 8-3).

After the children were IQ tested at the 120-month level, however, it became even more difficult to test them on a regular yearly basis. We did manage to retest the children at around 12 and 14 years of age, again using the WISC for consistency.

In the following table (see Table 10-10), the IQ performances for the experimental, control, and low risk contrast groups are presented. From these data it seems that the experimental and low risk contrast children have maintained a normal (GIQ = 100) level of intellectual performance, while the control children have continued to rise to a mean of 90.65 (GIQ). In comparison, the low risk contrast group shows a slight decline (GIQ = 98.5) to a level slightly below the experimental group's and nearly 8 points superior to the control group's. These data represent IQ measures for nearly 85% of the children who were considered members of original experimental and control families.

Profile analyses indicated that there was no change in WISC Full Scale IQ scores for experimental children and that their IQ level from 84 through 168 months of age was significantly higher than the IQ level for control children. Profile analyses of all WISC IQ scores indicated that there was a significant group × age interaction, $F(5, 29) = 4.00$, $p < .01$, for the rate of general intellectual development. There was no change in the rate of development for experimental children across the 84 through 168 month follow-up period, but there was a steady increase in the rate of development for control children over this period that was significant, $F(5, 13) = 3.81$, $p < .05$. There was a parallel and significant increase, $F(10, 58) = 2.81$, $p < .05$, for both groups in the rate of development as assessed by performance measures of intelligence, but experimental children experienced a significant, $F(5, 12) = 12.55$, $p < .001$, decline in the rate of development as assessed by verbal measures of intelligence. The rate of development for experimental children was significantly

Table 10-10 WISC Full Scale, Verbal, and Performance IQ Scores for
Experimental, Control, and Low Risk Contrast Children

| Group | Full Scale | | | | Verbal | | | | Performance | | | |
Age (Mos)	M	SD	Range	n	M	SD	Range	n	M	SD	Range	n
Experimental												
144	98.94	11.76	82.00-124.00	17	91.00	8.76	81.00-109.00	17	107.29	16.88	85.00-135.00	17
168	101.06	10.91	87.00-125.00	16	93.19	7.18	84.00-104.00	16	109.06	15.06	92.00-143.00	16
Control												
144	89.18	12.31	71.00-112.00	17	86.00	9.27	65.00-101.00	17	94.71	16.32	75.00-122.00	17
168	91.13	11.93	67.00-112.00	16	85.38	10.38	65.00-106.00	16	99.13	13.38	75.00-121.00	16
Low Risk Contrast												
144	99.60	14.26	88.00-121.00	5	95.00	12.29	82.00-108.00	5	105.20	15.74	93.00-132.00	5
168	97.40	6.80	88.00-104.00	5	96.00	4.90	92.00-104.00	5	103.40	8.62	92.00-115.00	5

higher than the rate of development for control children in terms of performance, $F(6, 28) = 5.72$, $p < .001$, verbal, $F(6, 28) = 18.43$, $p < .001$, and general measures of intelligence, $F(6, 28) = 10.60$, $p < .001$, across this follow-up period, but Bonferroni-Dunn confidence intervals for assessments at 144 and 168 months of age were slightly below zero, indicating that the differences of 9.76 and 9.93 IQ points between groups at these individual comparison points only approached significance.

Although the experimental children as a group maintained a normal IQ level and were superior to the control group, their school behavior was poor and quite similar to the control children's deportment in school. Almost without exception, reports of lags in performance and discrepancies between potential and achievement were accompanied by reports of difficulties in attention span and motivation and/or attitude problems. As the children grew older, there were psychological reports of increasing conduct problems and absenteeism, which reflect negative attitudes toward school. Poor self-concept, unmet needs of support, and a concern for nurturance were frequently emphasized in these reports. Several of these children were no longer living with their natural mothers: At least one was placed in a foster home, another was in a residential setting for emotionally disturbed children, and one child was placed with an aunt by the social welfare services because of reports of child abuse. Over one third of the files included referrals to social welfare agencies to provide underwear, socks, winter coats, and other basic clothing items so that the child could continue to attend school. One can only speculate on how such deprivation influences the child's general self-concept and expectations and how these in turn affect his or her performance in academic areas. Individual reports on each child's behavior are presented in Chapter 11.

COMPARISONS OF INTELLECTUAL DEVELOPMENT

In Figure 10-7, we have illustrated the course of intellectual development for all nine of the groups for which we have made IQ assessments, including the low risk contrast siblings and low risk contrast target children, the experimental sibling group, the control sibling group, as well as the experimental and control target groups. These data afford comparisons to the performance of the original survey low and high risk contrast groups. When comparing performance levels for these groups, it must be remembered that assessments for untreated siblings and contrast groups were cross-sectional, while assessments for the experimental, experimental younger siblings, control, and low risk contrast target groups were longitudinal measures, developed at successive and consecutive intervals. This illustration demonstrates the range of difference between groups of untreated children from disadvantaged backgrounds where the IQ level of the mother varied. But even more so, comparison of mean IQ levels for these nine groups clearly reveals the difference in performance for

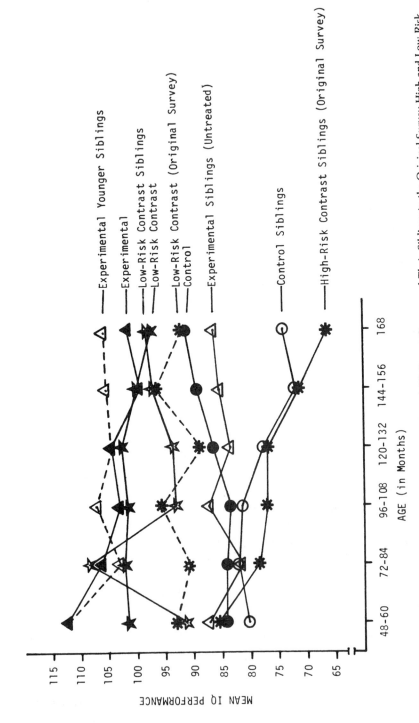

Figure 10-7. Comparison of IQ Performance with Increasing Age of All Target Groups and Their Siblings to the Original Survey High and Low Risk Contrast Groups

children from microenvironments that are considered conducive to intellectual development and those hypothesized to be deleterious for intellectual development. The offspring of the high risk, low IQ control families followed the trend of declining IQ performance with increasing age demonstrated by the original high risk contrast group. Although demonstrating considerably lower mean intellectual performance growth as they developed (compared with their treated older siblings), the siblings of the experimental group were nearly 10 points higher in performance than the control siblings at maturity. The performance levels of siblings of the low risk contrast children were quite comparable to the earlier low risk contrast sample's developmental level. The low risk contrast children's performance was somewhat higher, considering that most of their mothers had IQs over 100, while the original survey contrast group extended down to 80. The scores for the low risk contrast group were also above all other cohort sample means, including their own siblings'. Some of the difference in favor of the low risk contrast children is probably attributable to benefits accruing from the repeated testing for this group as compared with the single or infrequent testing of their siblings.

We noted in our discussions of the epidemiology of high risk populations that one characteristic was the increasing incidence of below 80 IQs with increasing age at a rate quite a bit higher than for the offspring of higher IQ low risk mothers. In Table 10-11, we compare the rate of below 80 IQs with increasing age for the high and low risk populations.

From Table 10-11 it can be seen that the incidence of low IQ (< 80) has been dramatically reduced in the experimental group as compared with the control group. The experimental group seems most similar to the low risk contrast group and to the low risk contrast sibling group, followed by the experimental siblings and the control target group. The control siblings and the high risk contrast groups are most alike. The control group has a lower rate of decline than the control siblings or the high risk contrast group. Some of the discrepancies, as we compare these various groups, are attributable to benefits that accrue to IQ performance because of repeated testing over time. The

Table 10-11   Percentage of 80 or Below IQs with Increasing Age for All
Groups Compared

Group	Age (in Months)				
	48	72	96-108	120	144+
Experimental	0	0	0	0	0
Control	33%	12.5%	33%	35%	41%
Low Risk Contrast (Target)	12.5%	12.5%	0	0	0
Experimental Siblings (Untreated)	35%	32%	31%	20%	35%
Control Siblings	48%	30%	62%	65%	71%
Low Risk Contrast Siblings	0	0	11%	0	10%
High Risk Contrast (Survey)	11%	56%	63%	63%	87%

stability in performance attributable to that effect is apparent in the case of the control and low risk contrast groups as well as for the experimental group. The table also points out the discrepancies that will occur in longitudinal data obtained by repeated sequential testing on a single cohort as compared with a similar population from which cohorts are selected cross-sectionally for testing over time. Obviously, the most dramatic comparison remains the experimental group children to the four high risk groups (experimental siblings-untreated, control, control siblings, and contrast) because the experimental group's performance has been maintained in the normal range and remains above the other groups in mean IQ performance, and because there is no indication of below 80 IQ functioning through 14 years of age and 9 years of schooling.

SUMMARY

In summary, we believe these comparisons provide additional support for the effects of the microenvironment created by the mother, who most directly influences cognitive development for children. The experimental group in this study was provided with an intensive intervention program assumed to be similar to the microenvironment provided naturally by mothers with high IQs (>100), even though they also live within a generally disadvantaged setting.

The comparability of IQ measures across the preschool and early school years for the low risk contrast and experimental groups supports our basic premise that mild retardation can be prevented by offsetting the negative influences of the microenvironment created by the low IQ, low verbal skilled mother. The performance of both groups across this period was in marked contrast to performance levels for the control children who resided in the same general geographic setting, but grew up in microenvironments created by low functioning mothers. It is these children who are most likely to demonstrate the dramatic declines in intellectual performance previously believed to be characteristic of the majority of children from deprived environments.

11
The Children and Their Families

In this chapter we have drawn together anecdotal information and individual performance data for the children and the families who participated in this project. The purpose of this information is to complement the data obtained by formal assessment procedures (e.g., standardized tests, experimental learning and language tests, and mother-child observations) that have been presented primarily as group data. The child and family histories described here were based on interviews; reports from teachers, psychologists, and social workers; and informal observation. This type of information describes family characteristics, patterns, and functioning (which are typically not revealed by other more formal measures) and thus increases the ability to gain some insight as to the character and substance of these families. These anecdotal descriptions are intended to provide an appreciation of the heterogeneity of these families and, as well, to reveal their strengths despite the numerous adverse influences that pervaded their lives.

The family environment constitutes a powerful influence against which all other environmental influences become secondary. Stereotypes have been developed that negatively characterize the black family, the hispanic family, the native-American family, and little therefore has been said about either the strengths or the considerable heterogeneity of differences among these families. The stereotype characterization has often been unfairly narrow and demeaning and suggests implicitly that limitations in the performance of these children are understandable. This state of affairs is at once insidious and untrue. The limits to successful performance are complex and not explained away by socioeconomic differences. Intrafamilial factors, which developmentally influence the quality of the learning experiences of the child, may have been either inadequate and/or inappropriate for the challenges he or she is to face in the world at large. In effect, a closer examination of the characteristics of each child's family is as important as the assessment of the individual child. To whatever extent an educational program matched to an individual will be effective, that program will require the reasonable ability of the family to extend the educational program into the home.

The black family in most recent descriptions has had its weaknesses and problems featured, and yet it is the family that is perhaps the very mechanism that has aided blacks through historically hard times by providing love, companionship, self-esteem, and a refuge from the outside world. Therefore, although most attention has focused on the social pathology of the black family, there is far more evidence that points to its strengths. Understanding the processes in family functioning, especially as they impact on developing educational programs for the culturally different black child, is a critical factor, although seriously underdeveloped. In large cultural groups, we tend to underestimate both the extent and significance of the diversity within the group, explaining behavior by the more obvious features that distinguish between groups.

Socioeconomic status has traditionally been used to explain child performance, whether successful or unsuccessful. When research responds to the stereotypes of social class, little regard is shown for the differential processes within and between families of similar SES, the process by which the family mediates development of its children. Indeed, SES has been confirmed repeatedly as the significant predictor of a child's academic success (Coleman et al., 1966). Yet, there is a disconcerting factor in that the low SES subpopulation groups contain, and may even have trapped, excess numbers of minority or culturally different children. What we have is the fact that SES predicts well the failure of culturally different children because, as Cole and Bruner (1971) suggested, "the yardstick of success is the middle class, the power of which renders cultural differences into deficits." The academic failure of such groups should not confirm the failure of some sort of homogeneous lower class group, but rather to confirm that this group is quite *different* from the group upon which the development of most assessment instruments has been predicated. It is a signal that a prescriptive educational program is needed.

The following brief anecdotal family histories will, I hope, serve to illustrate the diversity of family functioning among the study families and thereby demonstrate the lie of the insidious stereotype. The names of the individual family members are fictitious. The majority of the information was collected when we had closest contact with the families. Follow-up interviews, occasional visits, and telephone calls were sources of information about the family that combined with public school information about the children to provide a sense of the children's and families' growth beyond the preschool program. The information has been limited because of space and because every effort was made to represent a family fairly and not simply to chronicle what we knew about them.

EXPERIMENTAL GROUP CHILDREN

Beth
Family Characteristics

	Year of Birth	Highest Grade Completed	# Children Own Family	Age at Birth First Child	Age at Birth Target Child	1967 WAIS IQ (FS)	1974 WAIS (FS)	1974 WRAT Reading Grade
Mother	1934	9	10	24	32	59	62	2.6
Father	1935				33			

Children		Sex	Year of Birth	1974 Tested IQ	1974 WRAT Reading Grade	1974 Actual Grade	Public School Placement
	1	M	1957	78	3.9	9.4	EMR
	2	M	1961	72	3.5	7.4	
	3	M	1962	73	4.6	6.4	
Target	4	F	1966	99	2.9	2.4	
	5	M	1971	87			
	6	F	1973				

Beth, the fourth of six children, was born when her mother was 32 years old. Six months after her birth, her parents separated. No father was present in the household after that time, although two more children were born within the next 7 years. The children were reared by the mother with the help of her relatives, who lived in the neighborhood. Financial support was largely through food stamps, welfare payments, Title 19, and the mother's earnings as a part time cleaning person.

Beth's mother was the third of 10 children. A ninth grader when she dropped out of school, she had a second grade reading level. Her Full Scale WAIS IQ, which was 59 at the beginning of the program, rose only to 62, 8 years later. When she came to Milwaukee from her native Arkansas at the age of 20, she had never had a paying job. Her only employment since then was as a cleaning person. Despite these handicapping circumstances, she was one of the most loving and supportive mothers in the program. The family home, though in need of repairs, was clean and adequately furnished. Many photographs of the children were in view; when the children were in school, bookcases filled with books appeared in the home.

As a young child at the Center, Beth, with her lively sense of humor, was outstanding and popular among her peers. Notwithstanding a slight eye defect that required corrective lenses, she became an excellent reader and displayed a retentive memory. Because her mother could not read, Beth learned to listen carefully to the notices that the Center usually sent home to the parents. She would then relate the message to her mother, word for word.

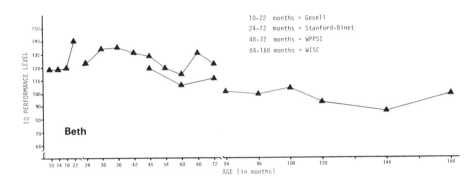

Beth's Stanford-Binet IQ from age 24 to 72 months ranged from 114 to 135, with an average GIQ of 122.9. For the greater part of this 4 year period, her scores were on or above the mean for her own group.

On the Wechsler tests, Beth's Full Scale IQ, which had ranged from 106 to 119 (GIQ 112) during her preschool years, dropped to a range of 86 to 104 (GIQ 97) after she entered public school. These scores, however, were still above the control group mean and were considerably higher than the tested IQs (72 to 78) of her older siblings.

Beth entered public school with good skills in reading, the area in which she was to do her best work in the next 4 years. Cooperative primary tests given in the second grade placed her within the average range, on both national and citywide bases, in cognitive abilities. In comparison with other students in the city, she placed within the upper average range in reading and within the middle average range in word analysis and mathematics, but was rated below average in listening.

On the Metropolitan Achievement Tests, Beth's scores on the Total Reading, Language, and Total Math subtests placed her on or above grade level during her first 3 years in school. After her third year her performance was slightly below grade level in Total Reading and Language and a year below her grade level in Total Math. Beth maintained her MAT scores at near average range in the seventh and tenth grades.

In public school Beth received generally average grades, with some unsatisfactory marks in areas of language and arithmetic during second and third grades. Although her teachers spoke with approval of her reading ability, their other comments from second grade on revealed problems of adjustment on Beth's part. On her third grade report card, for instance, was the following note: "Very sassy – doesn't want discipline – talks back. Disrespectful." In an evaluation of Beth's progress conducted when she was in fourth grade, a school psychologist noted that while teachers had commented on Beth's "expressions of temper," her name had also been placed on the list of children who were considered to be of superior ability within her school. The psychologist rated Beth's intellectual ability as average and described her self-concept and contact with reality as adequate. The report added that while Beth was probably "able to stand up for her rights physically and verbally in altercations with her peers," she was somewhat dependent upon adult figures and needed regular nurturing and attention from her teachers in order to maintain a consistent level of academic success.

In the middle school years, Beth got into trouble several times because of her behavior. She received six deportment records for fighting, using bad language, and refusing to follow directions.

Bonnie
Family Characteristics

	Year of Birth	Highest Grade Completed	# Children Own Family	Age at Birth First Child	Age at Birth Target Child	1967 WAIS IQ (FS)	1974 WAIS (FS)	1974 WRAT Reading Grade
Mother	1946	6	7	17	22	52	53	k.8
Father	1943	10	3	20	25			

Children		Sex	Year of Birth	1974 Tested IQ	1974 WRAT Reading Grade	1974 Actual Grade	Public School Placement
	1	M	1963	59	1.9	4.4	EMR
	2	M	1964	83	2.5	4.4	
	3	F	1966	76	1.3	2.4	EMR
Target	4	F	1968	111	1.2	k.4	
	5	M	1972	94			

Bonnie's mother was one of seven children. She and her husband were both in their late teens when they left Arkansas for Wisconsin. At the age of 17 she had the first of her five children. She was 22 when Bonnie, her fourth, was born. After 6 years of public school, Bonnie's mother remained virtually illiterate, with a WRAT reading level below the first grade. Her Full Scale WAIS IQ was 52 at the original testing and 53 at the retest, 6 years later. Through the vocational program she secured full time employment as a nurse's aide. Her husband, who had gone as far as the 10th grade in school, worked intermittently as a bartender. In 1976 he died of a liver disease. Shortly afterward, Bonnie's mother became ill and stopped working. The family went on welfare at that time.

Bonnie, an active, articulate child, was close to her family, especially to her father, who used to come to visit her in school. She was often seen making gifts to bring home to him. Throughout her preschool years at the Infant Center, Bonnie performed exceptionally well on all her language tests, often scoring well above her own (experimental) group's mean, particularly on the Sentence Repetition Test. On the two testings of the ITPA, her PLQ was 118.1 at 54 months and 110.8 at 78 months, 4 and 3 points, respectively, above the experimental group mean and over 20 points above the control group average PLQ.

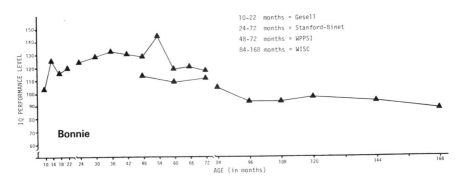

Over 4 years of testing, Bonnie's Stanford-Binet IQ ranged from 117 to 144, with an average (GIQ) of 125.4. Throughout the 4-year period, her scores remained on or above the average for her group.

On the Wechsler tests, Bonnie's Full Scale IQ, which had been close to her group's average from her fourth to her seventh year, dropped to well below that average in the last five testings, ranging from 87 at age 14 years to 96 at age 10. These scores, however, were in marked contrast to the tested IQs not only of her mother but also of her older siblings, all three of whom were doing poorly in school and reading far below their respective grade levels. Her elder sister and an elder brother were assigned to special classes for the educable mentally retarded.

During her first 2 years in public school, Bonnie did well in all academic areas. Her grades were satisfactory and her performance on the Metropolitan Achievement Test was within the average range. She seemed, however, to have some difficulty with social and behavioral adjustment. She was described by her first grade teacher as being disrespectful to adults and peers, given to fighting and outbursts of temper, and lacking respect for the belongings of others. Another teacher speculated that much of Bonnie's misbehavior was prompted by her older sister, who dominated her. After the second grade her behavior was reported to have improved, although she continued to be inattentive in class and to get into occasional fights on the playground. By this time her academic performance had fallen below grade level in all areas, including reading, previously one of her favorite activities. On the Metropolitan Achievement Test taken at the end of third grade, her performance had also fallen below her grade level. Although her teacher recommended that she be retained in Extended Primary, the school psychologist advised otherwise on the grounds that Bonnie's lowered achievement was more likely attributable to her attendance problem, her attitude, and her inattentiveness in the classroom than her inability to do the work. She was then transferred to a multiunit, individually guided education school, where she seemed to make fair progress in her academic and personal development. Bonnie maintained her achievement levels in the MAT when tested in grades seven and ten. However, she continued to have difficulty in peer relationships

Bonnie lived with her mother, her father's mother, her three brothers, and her sister in a rented five-room apartment. Her mother, sickly since her husband died, stopped working. She felt that Bonnie was doing well in school and was getting along well with others. Bonnie, she said, whined a lot at home and "wants to be the baby;" she always spoke of her father and of the things he let her do when he was alive. But, she added, "Bonnie is not a real bad kid."

Brad

Byron

Family Characteristics

		Year of Birth	Highest Grade Completed	# Children Own Family	Age at Birth First Child	Age at Birth Target Child	1967 WAIS IQ (FS)	1974 WAIS (FS)	1974 WRAT Reading Grade
Mother		1943	8	8	18	23	59	Moved	
Father		1933	11	9		33		Moved	

		Sex	Year of Birth	1974 Tested IQ	1974 WRAT Reading Grade	1974 Actual Grade	Public School Placement
Children							
	1	M	1961	89(1970)		Moved	
	2	F	1962			Moved	
Target	3	M	1966			Moved	
Target	4	M	1968			Moved	
	5	F	1971			Moved	
	6	F	1974			Moved	

Brad's mother was born in Mississippi but moved to New Orleans, where she worked intermittently as a beauty parlor attendant. She was married at the age of 17 and had her first child at 18. An eighth grader when she dropped out of school, she had a WAIS IQ of 59. She and her husband separated after the birth of her second child. In 1966 she moved to Milwaukee with her eldest son and started living with Brad's father, a police officer. They had four children, of whom Brad was the eldest. Byron, who was born 2 years later, was also enrolled in the Infant Center. The children's father, 10 years older than their mother, lived with the family in a well kept, upper floor apartment and was the family's sole means of support. In 1971 the family moved to Louisiana, where Brad entered public kindergarten and Byron was placed in a daycare center.

Brad had a greater inclination than his brother toward language activities. He was fond of listening to stories and was an eager participant in reading readiness games. Often he would surprise his teachers with long, coherent, logical sentences. During the time for free choice activities, Brad preferred books and quiet games while his younger brother amused himself with toy trucks.

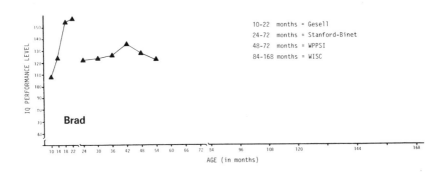

Throughout the time he was at the Center, Brad's Stanford-Binet IQ kept pace with that of his group. The sole exception was at age 42 months, when his score was 135.5, exceeding his (experimental) group's mean by almost 10 points.

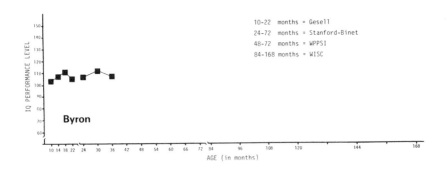

Byron was tested only three times. His scores on these occasions were well below the mean for his group but were at least 10 points above that of the control group.

Christopher
Family Characteristics

	Year of Birth	Highest Grade Completed	# Children Own Family	Age at Birth First Child	Age at Birth Target Child	1967 WAIS IQ (FS)	1974 WAIS (FS)	1974 WRAT Reading Grade
Mother	1936	10	4	18	31	68	77	6.6
Father								

Children	Sex	Year of Birth	1974 Tested IQ	1974 WRAT Reading Grade	1974 Actual Grade	Public School Placement
1	M	1954	91(1969)			Moved
2	M	1957	78(1969)		EMR	Moved
Target 3	M	1967	125	1.9	1.4	

Christopher's mother was born in Mississippi, the second of four children. She married at the age of 17 and had the first of her three living sons at 18. Her husband, the father of her two eldest sons, was killed at home when the children were 6 and 3 years old. She moved to Milwaukee 5 years later. Christopher was born when she was 31 years old. Although Christopher's father saw his son regularly for about 5 years, he never lived with the family. He left the state when Christopher was 5 years old and corresponded with him only sporadically. The mother, who suffered periods of ill health, worked on and off in nursing homes and factories. Supplementing her earnings were AFDC and social security payments.

One of the few literate mothers in the project, Christopher's mother had a sixth grade reading level and a tenth grade education. Her Full Scale WAIS IQ, which was 68 at the time of the initial survey, rose to 77 at retest, 8 years later. She seemed to be an anxious, unhappy person, beset by illnesses, worries, and problems. Both of her older sons, who had witnessed their father's violent death, developed emotional problems and on several occasions threatened her and Christopher with bodily harm. One of them spent much time in detention homes and mental institutions. His mother feared that Christopher would grow up to be like his half-brothers.

Christopher lived alone with his mother for several years, sharing a bedroom with her in their three-room rented house. Even when he was a small child, his mother used to discuss her problems and fears with him. Perhaps because of this, Christopher developed a very close relationship with his mother. Even as a young child, he was concerned about her health and was more considerate about her needs than was usual for children of his age.

At the Infant Education Center, Christopher was a serious child who quickly showed an aptitude for mathematics and problem solving activities. During this time, he became an able reader and showed an exceptional memory. At the age of 5, for instance, he could remember the birthday and street address of every child in the Center.

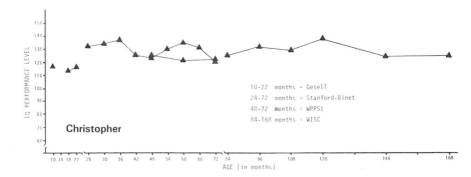

Christopher had a Stanford-Binet IQ that ranged, over 4 years, from 120 to 137, with an average (GIQ) of 127.8. With few exceptions, his scores were considerably higher than the average for his group.

Wechsler IQ tests from ages 4 through 14 showed a Full Scale IQ range of 121 to 138, consistently higher than the average for the experimental group and as much as 50 points higher than the control group average.

Evaluations made by his grade school teachers and the results of standardized achievement tests from first to fourth grade indicate that Christopher's academic performance was completely satisfactory. Grades of "Outstanding" were predominant in his first grade final report card, and he placed in the high to above average categories on the three subtests of the Cooperative Primary Tests.

On the Metropolitan Achievement Tests, Christopher's performance in all areas was consistently at or above his actual grade level. The results from these tests placed him (in relation to national norms) within upper and above average categories on the different subtests, with the exception of computation. On this subtest, he performed on the high level, with a national percentile ranking of 96.

During the second and third grades, Christopher seemed to develop problems with his work habits and his relations with his peers. His teachers observed that he did not complete his assignments on time and did not get along well with other children. His third grade teacher's remark that Christopher wanted "to have his own way about most things" and did not "respect the rights of others" was restated in a somewhat different light by a school psychologist, who noted that "(Christopher's) curiosity and high level of self-confidence could possibly bring (him) into conflict with others." The same psychologist, evaluating Christopher at the end of the third grade, also described him as a "well motivated, well adjusted child" whose academic achievement was above grade expectancy in all areas and was commensurate with his intellectual functioning.

In the open school to which Christopher went after completing third grade, he was described as bright but often seemingly unmotivated. He had also lost some of his self-confidence and seemed to the school psychologist "a somewhat sad youngster who has some concerns regarding his ability to be successful in his environment." A psychological evaluation conducted on Christopher during the fourth grade indicated that although his intellectual abilities ranged from high average to superior, his achievement was only within the average range in relation to his age group. The school psychologist suggested that emotional concerns might be interfering with his motivation in school, and thus with his academic performance. Toward the end of the year, however, Christopher's teacher reported an improvement in his attitude and further commented that Christopher was reading above grade level, was an eager and able participant in his math group, and was demonstrating in his written work "an absolutely *fantastic* imagination, and excellent grammar and storytelling skills." It seemed, then, that Christopher responded well to the atmosphere of the open classroom.

Christopher made considerable progress in grades five through ten, receiving good reports. This was also reflected in his maintaining the same level of performance on the Metropolitan Achievement Tests, with average scores in Reading and above average scores in Math.

Cindy
Family Characteristics

Cindy was the youngest of four children. Her father, who died in an industrial accident when she was 2, had a ninth grade education and had been an assembly worker in Mississippi for 7 years before coming to Wisconsin. In Milwaukee he obtained a better paying job as a foundry worker, a position he kept until the time of his death 5 years later.

Cindy's mother, also from Mississippi, was the fifth of 11 children. When she married Cindy's father, she was 19 years old and had already had one

	Year of Birth	Highest Grade Completed	# Children Own Family	Age at Birth First Child	Age at Birth Target Child	1967 WAIS IQ (FS)	1974 WAIS (FS)	1974 WRAT Reading Grade
Mother	1940	11	11	18	26	65	64	2.8
Father	1933	9		25	33			

		Sex	Year of Birth	1974 Tested IQ	1974 WRAT Reading Grade	1974 Actual Grade	Public School Placement
Children							
	1	M	1958	83	4.4	9.4	
	2	F	1960	79	6.0	7.4	
	3	M	1962	85	3.9	5.4	
Target	4	F	1966	105	2.1	2.4	

child. She had Cindy when she was 26. Although she completed the 11th grade, her reading level was below the third grade. Her Full Scale WAIS was 65 at the time of the initial survey and 64 at retesting, 7 years later. Until she came to Wisconsin to join her husband, 2 years before Cindy's birth, she had never had a paid job. Her first position was as a laundry attendant. For a year she worked full time at this job, which paid her $44 a week. At her next position, as electric wire assembler, she earned $180 per week.

During the period of the study, the family moved three times, from a house, to an apartment, and again to a house. These home were always well kept and clean. Books, mainly bible stories and children's literature, were in evidence. All members of the family, including Cindy's father, were very cooperative and courteous toward our research staff.

At the preschool, Cindy was alert, quick, and popular with the teachers as well as with her peers. Aside from having to wear glasses to strengthen weak eye muscles, she had no serious physical or medical problems.

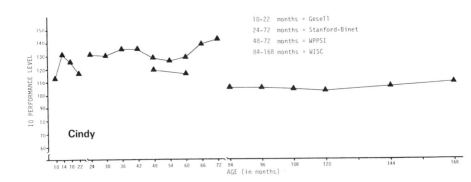

On the Stanford-Binet, Cindy's IQ ranged from 126 to 142, with an average of 132.8, over 4 years of testing. At 72 months, shortly before she entered public school, her IQ was 23 points higher than the average for her own group, and 55 points higher than the control group average.

Cindy's Full Scale IQ on the Wechsler tests followed the pattern for her group, although her actual scores were generally slightly higher than the group average. Her lowest score (102, obtained at age 10) was still 16 points above the corresponding mean score for the control group.

When she entered public school, Cindy's tested IQ (Stanford-Binet) was 129; on her Metropolitan Reading Readiness Test, she obtained a rating of A and a ranking in the 98th percentile. As a result of adjustment problems, however, her classroom performance in the first grade was not satisfactory. A student teacher who observed her class attributed her poor performance to the disorganized conditions in the classroom and to the unsympathetic attitude of Cindy's teacher who, for instance, insisted on calling her by her other given name, despite requests from Cindy's former teachers and from Cindy herself that she be called by the name to which she had been accustomed.

Although she ended her first year in public school with grades of D in one or more areas of reading, language, and arithmetic, Cindy's scores on standardized achievement tests indicated that she was achieving on her grade level in reading and language and well above her grade level in arithmetic.

Cindy's Metropolitan Achievement Tests showed a generally satisfactory performance on Total Reading at the end of the fourth grade. Her scores on Language and Total Math, while on grade level for first through third grades, showed a serious drop at the end of fourth grade. However, on the Peabody Individual Achievement Test that Cindy took in fourth grade during a psychological evaluation, her performance in all areas except Math placed her on a high third grade to middle fourth grade level; her Math performance was on a 6.7 grade level.

From the results of standardized tests, as well as from her school records, it is evident that Cindy overcame the difficulties of her first year in school. In the elementary school years, she was well liked by her teachers and her peers. She was described by her teachers as "an extremely pleasant girl who is well accepted by her peers," and by the school psychologist as "a happy, well adjusted girl who recognizes and accepts the limitations of the family socioeconomic status but is capable of seeing herself as in individual whose aspirations may be more ambitious than those of her siblings." Her progress continued to be promising during the middle school years. Her achievement scores on the Metropolitan Achievement Test in seventh and tenth grades were about average in Reading and above average in Math.

Gloria
Family Characteristics

	Year of Birth	Highest Grade Completed	# Children Own Family	Age at Birth First Child	Age at Birth Target Child	1967 WAIS IQ (FS)	1974 WAIS (FS)	1974 WRAT Reading Grade
Mother	1942	10	5	18	24	71	80	4.8
Father	1932	6	6		34			

Children		Sex	Year of Birth	1974 Tested IQ	1974 WRAT Reading Grade	1974 Actual Grade	Public School Placement
	1	M	1960	80	6.2	7.4	
	2	F	1962	73	4.5	6.4	
	3	F	1963	90	5.0	5.4	
	4	M	1964	79	2.3	4.4	
	5	F	1965	86	1.7	2.4	
Target	6	F	1967	111	1.8	1.4	
	7	M	1972	90			
	8	M	1975				

Gloria came from a large, two parent family. Her mother, who came to Milwaukee from Arkansas when she was 25 years old, already had three children of her own when she married Gloria's father. She and Gloria's father had five children, of whom Gloria was the third. The family lived in a nine-room house.

Gloria's mother had completed the tenth grade. Her WRAT reading grade was 4.8. At the beginning of the project, her Full Scale WAIS IQ was 72; at retest, after 7 years, it was 80. A good seamstress, she sometimes took in sewing to supplement the family income. She had some training in power sewing, although she did not finish the training course. She was a pleasant person who, together with her husband, provided a stable and loving home for the family.

Gloria's father, 10 years older than his wife, came to Milwaukee from Mississippi at the age of 16. Although his formal education stopped at the sixth grade, he had little trouble finding and holding employment. He had a $125-a-week job as a machine operator in a tannery until he lost his hand in a job accident. When he resumed work, it was as a maintenance person for the same company.

Gloria was a somewhat shy but friendly and well liked child who showed special ability in the arts at an early age. At the Infant Center she often produced colorful and intricately designed pictures that impressed her peers and the teachers.

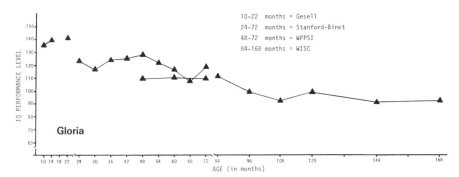

Gloria's Stanford-Binet IQ ranged from 107 to 128 over 4 years of preschool testing. Although her scores declined steadily from 128 at 48 months to 107 at 66 months, her last Stanford-Binet testing at 72 months rose again to 118.

Gloria's Full Scale IQ, which remained stable between 109 and 111 from ages 4 through 7, underwent a decline during her second grade in public school. From age 8 through the last testing session at age 14, Gloria's WISC Full Scale IQ ranged from 91 to 99, below the average level for her group but still above control group averages for the same period.

Throughout her first 4 years in public school, Gloria earned satisfactory grades and commendatory remarks from her teachers, who praised her working habits and pleasant relationships with her peers. In the fourth grade she earned above average marks in language arts and in her response to art experiences.

Reading seemed to be a more difficult area for her, despite her having started out as a good reader. Her relative weakness in this area was apparent in her Metropolitan Achievement Test scores. Gloria started out a year above her grade level in Total Reading but did not show any progress in the next 2 years. Thus, despite some progress in her fourth year, her achievement scores in Total Reading were still approximately a year below expectancy for that grade. Her best performance was in Total Math, where she consistently scored above her group's average from first grade through fourth.

In a psychological evaluation conducted during third grade, Gloria's intellectual functioning was estimated to be within the high average range. Her strongest areas of achievement were in spelling and math and her weakest was in reading comprehension. Although her achievement was considered below her intellectual capability, no serious problems were noted. Thus far, Gloria's academic and social progress in school was satisfactory.

Gloria's performance on the Metropolitan Achievement Tests dropped below average in Reading when tested in the seventh grade. Her scores in Math were maintained in the seventh grade but dropped below average in the tenth grade. Although involved in a fight with another girl at 15 years of age, she received good reports from her teachers, who reported no discipline problems in the classroom.

Harriet
Family Characteristics

	Year of Birth	Highest Grade Completed	# Children Own Family	Age at Birth First Child	Age at Birth Target Child	1967 WAIS IQ (FS)	1974 WAIS (FS)	1974 WRAT Reading Grade
Mother	1934	10	10	19	33	75	R^a	R^a
Father	1930	6	4	23	37			

Children		Sex	Year of Birth	1974 Tested IQ	1974 WRAT Reading Grade	1974 Actual Grade	Public School Placement	
	1	M	1953	68(1966)			EMR	Moved
	2	F	1956	86(1969)				Moved
	3	M	1957	74(1969)			EMR	Moved
	4	M	1959	85	4.6	9.4		
	5	M	1960	76	1.8	7.4	EMR	
	6	F	1962	104	5.5	6.4		
Target	7	F	1967	123	4.1	1.4		

^{a}R = Refused

Harriet's parents were born in Georgia. They were married soon after their arrival in Milwaukee. When the first of their seven children was born, Harriet's mother was 19 years old and her husband was 23. Harriet, the youngest, was born 14 years later. After several years of marital conflict, the parents separated. Harriet was 4 years old at the time. Her mother then started working full time as a nurse's aide at a nursing home. Supplementing her $82.50 weekly salary were child support and Title 19 payments.

Aside from the problems accompanying the parents' separation, there were others involving some of the older children. Of Harriet's four brothers, three needed placement in special classes for the mentally retarded. Two of these three brothers were arrested for various offenses and were assigned to vocational rehabilitation programs.

Harriet, born prematurely, was small for her age. At the Infant Center, she was a frail, quiet child who rarely joined the other children in group games, preferring to watch from the sidelines until a quieter activity was initiated. However, when phonics and reading readiness activities were introduced, she responded with excitement and animation, surprising her teachers with the speed at which she learned to read.

Harriet's Stanford-Binet IQ, tested at various times over a period of 4 years, ranged from a high of 135.5 at 24 months to a low of 114 at 66 months, with an average (GIQ) of 120.6. With the exception of her 60- and 66-month scores, Harriet's IQ level was equal to or above the average for her group.

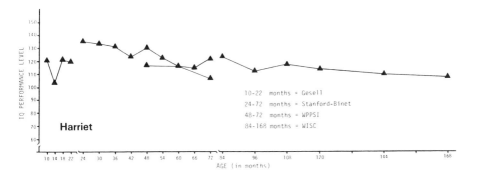

Harriet's IQ level, as reflected by her Full Scale scores on the Wechsler tests, remained high in comparison with that of her own group. On the WPPSI, taken before she entered public school, her Full Scale IQ ranged from 106 to 116, with an average (GIQ) of 113. From the first through eighth grades her WISC Full Scale IQ ranged from 107 to 123, with an average (GIQ) of 114.

Harriet's Metropolitan Achievement Test scores parallel findings by the school psychologist. With the exception of Total Reading, Harriet's fourth grade scores were depressed, although they remained above her own group's average. In contrast, her Total Reading score indicated that she was achieving well above grade level in that area.

Unlike her siblings, Harriet made excellent progress in public school, despite her noticeably frequent absences. Through her first 3 years in school, particularly, she elicited unqualified praise from her teachers, not only for her ability in reading—her strongest area—but also for her performance in all other subjects and her popularity with her peers. A psychological study conducted during third grade showed "indications that she has superior potentials" and recommended her evaluation for possible superior class placement. The same study, however, found "suggestions of some fears and anxieties . . . related to interaction at home with an older brother, and in the immediate neighborhood" and stated that although Harriet seemed fairly well adjusted, the possible negative influences of her environment were cause for concern. Apparently these problems started to surface, for although she continued to be a good student, her fourth grade teacher commented that Harriet "has not seemed to be herself lately." A psychological study, conducted in the fourth grade, showed a drop in her overall achievement level and an increasing "concern regarding her own safety in her home environment. She (was) fearful of physical harm from her brothers or others, while her mother (was) out of the house."

Harriet recovered from her early setback in the fourth grade, as indicated by her scores in the Metropolitan Achievement Test, which were above average in both Reading and Math in the seventh and tenth grades. She received several suspension notices for school absence in the tenth grade and was reported to have become pregnant at age 16, before graduating.

Helen
Family Characteristics

	Year of Birth	Highest Grade Completed	# Children Own Family	Age at Birth First Child	Age at Birth Target Child	1967 WAIS IQ (FS)	1974 WAIS (FS)	1974 WRAT Reading Grade
Mother	1921	11	17	21	45	74	74	4.8
Father	1921	7	11	21	45			

		Sex	Year of Birth	1974 Tested IQ	1974 WRAT Reading Grade	1974 Actual Grade	Public School Placement
Children							
	1	F	1942				Moved
	2	M	1944				Moved
	3	F	1945				Moved
	4	M	1947				Moved
	5	M	1954	89(1969)			Moved
	6	F	1955	88	12.2	12+	
	7	F	1956	88	7.7	11.4	
	8	M	1957	80	2.8	10.4	
	9	M	1959	72	4.4	9.4	
	10	F	1959	99	8.7	9.4	
	11	F	1961	81	3.9	7.4	
Target	12	F	1966	106	3.5	2.4	

Helen was the youngest of 12 living children in a close knit, stable family. Helen's parents, both 45 years old when she was born, had been married 11 years when they moved to Milwaukee from Louisiana. Both parents were from large families themselves: Helen's mother was the seventh of 17 children, and her father, the eldest of 11.

Both of Helen's parents worked full time: Her father was a crane operator and her mother cooked for a nursing home. Helen's father dropped out of school after seventh grade. Her mother had gone a little further, up to the eleventh grade. However, her reading level remained slightly below the fifth grade.

Despite its size and the fact that both parents were working full time, Helen's family was one of the happiest in the program. From the outset the family was described by interviewers as extremely cooperative and the children as "bright and well behaved." The mother's concern for her children was evident in her comments regarding their health, their problems, and their interests. Although she said that she did not "have time to even read the Bible," she and her husband were active in church and lodge activities.

Throughout her 6 years with the Infant Center Education Program, Helen was a happy, secure child, full of laughter and enthusiasm. She was liked by everyone around her and was regarded as a leader by the other children. In all her undertakings, such as learning to read, Helen's progress was closely followed and strongly supported by her family, who regarded her as special and who attended every meeting and open house to find out how she was doing.

In the 4 years prior to her entrance into public school, Helen's Stanford-Binet IQ ranged from 110 to 132.5. She obtained her highest scores from age 36 through 48 months and her lowest from 48 through 72 months.

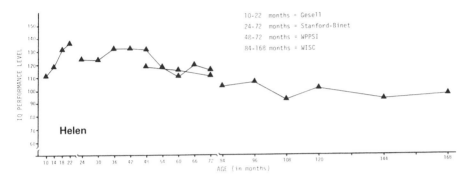

On the Wechsler tests, Helen's Full Scale IQ declined from 118 on the first WPPSI test at 48 months to 92 on the postthird grade WISC testing at 108 months. As of the last test (at 168 months), however, her Full Scale IQ rose to 96. Although her IQ performance in comparison with her own group was erratic beginning with her entry into public school, it continued to be well above the mean performance level of the control group.

In public school, Helen continued to be popular among her peers and with her teachers, who described her as a very good student and a pleasure to have in class. A recurring complaint, however, was that Helen was too talkative and stubborn.

On the Metropolitan Achievement Tests, Helen generally obtained scores on or above grade level during her first 2 years in school. During the third grade, her performance continued on grade level for Total Reading and Total Math, but started to decline for the Language subtest. By fourth grade, Helen's performance on all three subtests had fallen below grade level, although she continued to keep up with her own group on Total Reading and Total Math.

The Peabody Individual Achievement Test, which Helen took during a psychological evaluation in fourth grade, indicated that she was achieving at and above grade level expectancies in Math and Reading Recognition, but showed achievement lags ranging from 7 months in Reading Comprehension to 1 year in Spelling.

Helen was further described by the school psychologist who evaluated her as a rational, optimistic child whose "social sensitivity, friendliness, and congeniality has caused her to be appreciated in the school situation by adults and well liked by peers."

Helen's performance on the Metropolitan Achievement Tests was about average in Reading and Math when tested in the seventh and tenth grades. She was described by her teachers as having "good potential." At 17 years of age, she became pregnant but continued in regular school, although her grades dropped slightly.

Herbert
Family Characteristics

	Year of Birth	Highest Grade Completed	# Children Own Family	Age at Birth First Child	Age at Birth Target Child	1967 WAIS IQ (FS)	1974 WAIS (FS)	1974 WRAT Reading Grade
Mother	1944			21	23	62	Moved	
Father	1937			28	30		Moved	

		Sex	Year of Birth	1974 Tested IQ	1974 WRAT Reading Grade	1974 Actual Grade	Public School Placement
Children							
	1	F	1965	103(1969)			Moved
	2	M	1966				Moved
Target	3	M	1967				Moved
	4	F					Moved

Herbert was the third of four children. His mother was 21 years old when she had her first child and 23 when she had Herbert. Her WAIS IQ was 62 in 1967, at the time of the first testing. There was no record of her having been employed in Milwaukee. By the time Herbert was 2, his parents were having severe marital problems. As a result of a physical attack by her husband, Herbert's mother left Milwaukee with her children and returned to her mother's home in Arkansas. Because she was reluctant to remove her child from the Infant Center, arrangements were made for Herbert to live temporarily with another family in the project. After 2 months, however, his father intervened. Herbert then lived with his father for a month, while continuing to attend the Infant Center during the day. At the end of the month, Herbert's mother moved him back to Arkansas because she did not want him to see his father. Eventually the parents were divorced. The family officially left the Family Rehabilitation Program in 1970 when Herbert was 3½ years old.

During his infancy, Herbert was an unhappy child, often crying and whining for no apparent medical or physical reason. When he was about 15 months old, the staff after several meetings decided to place him temporarily with the older children, who were then between 2½ and 3 years of age. The older children's attention and behavior had a positive effect on him. When he returned to his own group 6 months later, he had learned many activities appropriate for an older child and subsequently became a leader among the younger children.

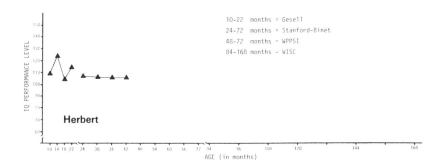

With its range of 105 to 106.5, Herbert's IQ from age 24 to 42 months seemed fairly stable. While it was approximately 17 to 21 points lower than his group's mean IQ, it remained at least 10 points above the control group's mean through each of the four testings available.

Jerry
Jessica
Family Characteristics

Jerry lived with his parents, his younger sister Jessica, who was also enrolled at the Infant Education Center, and a younger brother. The eldest of the children, their half-sister, was a victim of a drowning accident. The family lived in a house described by Center staff members as "beautiful, well furnished, and spotless."

Jerry's mother was born in Mississippi, the second of six children. She had a child when she was 16 years old, dropped out of school after eleventh grade, and moved to Milwaukee, where she married Jerry's father. For some time she worked at the checkout counter of a laundry, where she was paid $60 a week for 45 to 50 hours of work. She then operated a filling machine in a brewery.

The three younger children's father, a fork lift operator, was 10 years older than their mother. When he moved to Milwaukee from Tennessee, he was 19

	Year of Birth	Highest Grade Completed	# Children Own Family	Age at Birth First Child	Age at Birth Target Child	1967 WAIS IQ (FS)	1974 WAIS (FS)	1974 WRAT Reading Grade
Mother	1946	11	6	16	21	62	78	5
Father	1936	10	6		31			

Children		Sex	Year of Birth	1974 Tested IQ	1974 WRAT Reading Grade	1974 Actual Grade	Public School Placement
	1	F	1962	108	12.9	6.4	
Target	2	M	1967	112	2.9	1.4	
Target	3	F	1968	104	1.4	k.4	
	4	M	1974				

years old and had completed the tenth grade of school. Heart trouble kept him out of work for some time, during which he received disability payments. No other benefits were collected by the family.

By all accounts, the family was a pleasant one, although the children's father was described by Center staff as overly protective and somewhat difficult to know. He was, for instance, reluctant to let his children go on field trips but would not communicate with the teachers himself. The children's mother, a more outgoing person, was cooperative and enthusiastic about attending open house, conferences, and parties at the Center.

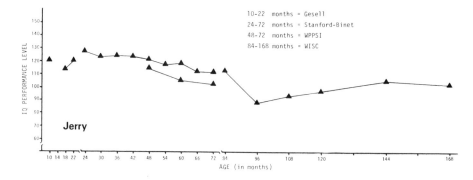

Jerry's Stanford-Binet IQ started out at 127 and declined to 111 over the 4 years of testing. From age 24 months through 60 months his scores were generally on or slightly (2 to 5 points) below the experimental group mean. In the last two testings his scores dropped further (8 to 9 points) below the group average, although they remained at least 20 points above the control group mean.

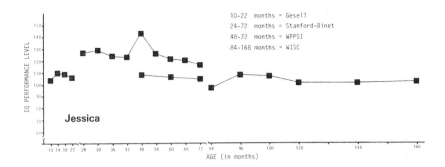

Jessica's Stanford-Binet IQ was, with one exception, close to the mean for her group. The exception was at 48 months, when her score was 143, or 17 points above the mean. In general, however, her scores also tended to decline over the 4 years of testing.

Jerry's Full Scale IQ was generally below the average for his group. After rising to 112 at age 84 months, a year after school entrance, Jerry's score dropped to 88, its lowest level. In the following 6 years, it rose to 102.

From the age of 48 months through 84 months, Jessica's Full Scale IQ ranged from 97 to 107 and remained below the group average. After the age of 96 months, however, she scored above or very slightly below the mean for her group.

Both Jerry and Jessica demonstrated achievement as measured by the MAT generally above the average level for their group. Jerry, in particular, obtained very high scores in Reading and Language. No fourth grade scores were available for Jerry; however, his third grade scores showed achievement on his grade level in all three areas.

Jessica's MAT scores were slightly lower than her brother's. On all three subtests, however, she had third grade scores above those of her own group and at or above her actual grade level.

Despite their success on the achievement tests, Jerry and Jessica did not obtain good grades in school. Jerry was noted by his teachers to be a good reader. However, his teachers complained of his unwillingness to exert effort and of his talkativeness. A psychologist, further noting his uncooperativeness and his "insolent manner," described Jerry as "quite immature."

Jessica's teachers also complained that she worked "only when she pleases" and talked too much. Both children received grades of C and D and were referred for screening for facilitative psychoeducational therapy by their classroom teachers. In both cases, however, the school psychologist considered their development as age appropriate and recommended "no other intervention outside the good teaching practices of the professional educator" for the two children.

In the seventh grade, Jerry's score in the Metropolitan Achievement Test dropped below average in Reading but improved in Math. He was described by his teachers as an average student who could do better if he applied himself. In the tenth grade, he received suspension notices for tardiness

Jessica's performance on the Metropolitan Achievement Test was variable. Her scores in Reading dropped in the fifth grade but rose in the middle years, although they remained below average. Her Math scores continued to be low. She was considered to be a good worker and an average student. She received a few notices for tardiness.

Joan
Family Characteristics

	Year of Birth	Highest Grade Completed	#Children Own Family	Age at Birth First Child	Age at Birth Target Child	1967 WAIS IQ (FS)	1974 WAIS (FS)	1974 WRAT Reading Grade
Mother	1943	10	18	21	23	71	72	2.4
Father	1936	11	4	28	30			

Children		Sex	Year of Birth	1974 Tested IQ	1974 WRAT Reading Grade	1974 Actual Grade	Public School Placement
	1	M	1964	81	2.9	4.4	
	2	F	1965	95	1.6	3.4	
Target	3	F	1966	99	1.6	2.4	
	4	F	1969	83			
	5	F	1970	88			
	6	F	1972	102			
	7	M	1974				

Joan lived with her parents and her six brothers and sisters in a 10-room house. Her father, a hardworking, ambitious person who expressed much concern regarding the discipline and education of his children, worked about 50 hours a week at a factory and as a steward for a labor union. He reported earning over $17,000 a year. Joan's mother did not have any outside employment aside from working briefly as a nurse's aide. Despite a tenth grade education, she read only at a second grade level. Her WAIS IQ was 71 at first testing, 72 at retest. Herself one of 18 children, she bore eight children within a span of 11 years. The last child died 3 months after birth.

The family home during Joan's infancy was overcrowded and disorganized. The teacher from the Infant Center who first visited the home reported a noise level so high that Joan's crying could not be heard. Joan's parents, who were having severe marital problems at the time, frequently had fights that required police intervention. When there was trouble at home, Joan would come to the Center sullen, uncommunicative, and physically aggressive. Her favorite activity was to play house, acting out the roles of her parents. Unfortunately, she also adopted her parents' and siblings' reaction to frustration and anger, lashing out at whomever was near her. Because she frequently started fights with the other children, they excluded her from their games. Her moodiness also kept her from participating in organized activities with other children; often she chose to exclude herself, sitting with arms folded and glaring at the others. Although she found group work difficult, Joan was able to focus her attention and to learn when working with a teacher on a one-to-one basis.

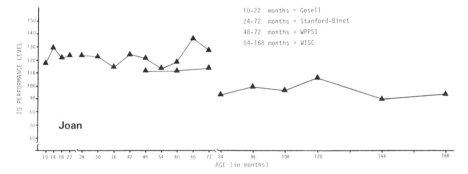

Over 4 years of testing, Joan showed a Stanford-Binet IQ that ranged from 113 to 136, obtaining her highest scores just before she entered public school. Before age 66 months, her IQ level was generally below that of her group, although substantially above that of the control group.

In public school, Joan exhibited the same traits she had shown while at the Center. A psychological study conducted in her third grade mentioned that in the classroom during the previous year Joan "was very hyperactive, could not work independently, had a short attention span, was easily distracted, disobeyed her teacher and those in authority many times, fought verbally and physically much of the time and in general was not making the social, academic, or psychological growth that was expected of her." Her school records indicated, however, that she was receiving satisfactory grades in the basic academic areas, and that it was her school related behavior that her teachers regarded as unacceptable, as demonstrated by the many check marks she received in this area.

Joan's Full Scale IQ (WPPSI/WISC) exhibited a drop during her first 3 years in public school, from her preschool levels of 111 to 113 to a range of 93 to 99. At age 10, her score rose to 106; however, as of the last testing at age 14, her score was 93.

Joan's school achievement, as shown on the Metropolitan Achievement Tests, was consistently behind that of her own group. On the Total Reading and Language subtests her performance pattern followed that of the control group more closely than that of her own group. Her performance was poorest on Total Math, where she lagged behind her grade by 2 full years.

Despite her poor performance, Joan apparently liked school, "as she seemed to see it as an escape from the home authority and also a place where she could control her environment rather than her environment controlling her," the school psychologist reported. Evaluated again in fourth grade, Joan was described as "a child of low average intellectual capability whose academic achievement lagged because of lack of continued environmental and school en-couragement, a lack of feelings of self-confidence and self-worth, and other anxieties and fears." The report went on to say that Joan's achievement lag was "more reflective of inattentiveness to instruction, inappropriate attitudes and behavior, and a poor self-image than her lack of ability to learn." Joan's psychological evaluation conducted when she was 14 years old reported that she was making slow progress. Soon after this report, she became pregnant.

Joseph
Josh
Family Characteristics

	Year of Birth	Highest Grade Completed	# Children Own Family	Age at Birth First Child	Age at Birth Target Child	1967 WAIS IQ (FS)	1974 WAIS (FS)	1974 WRAT Reading Grade
Mother	1950	10	10	16	16	75	80	6.2
Father	1945	9	17	21	21			

Children		Sex	Year of Birth	1974 Tested IQ	1974 WRAT Reading Grade	1974 Actual Grade	Public School Placement
Target	1	M	1966	88	1.6	2.4	
Target	2	M	1969	111	k.6	k.4	
	3	F	1970				
	4	F	1971				

Joseph's mother, one of the youngest in the study, was 16 years old when he was born. In WRAT reading grade level (6.2) and WAIS IQ (75 at first testing, 90 at retest), she ranked higher than most of the mothers in the project. She and her husband were both from Louisiana and both from very large families:

she was the seventh of 10 children, and he was the sixth of 17. They were married and moved to Milwaukee when she was 15 years old and he was 20. In the next 5 years, they had five children of whom Joseph was the eldest. The second child died of pneumonia a few months after birth. The third child, named Josh, was also enrolled in the Infant Education Program. He was 3 years younger than Joseph. The two boys had two younger sisters.

The children's mother, who at various times worked as a maid and as a cook's assistant, had attended school through the tenth grade. Their father, who had gone as far as the ninth grade, worked at the Infant Education Center as a janitor. At the start of the program, each parent had several hobbies and interests, such as reading, swimming, and membership in church groups; the children's mother played pool and their father played the piano and worked out regularly at the Salvation Army gymnasium. Both parents were described by survey workers as very pleasant and cooperative, and their living quarters as very clean. Joseph, then the only child, was well fed, well clothed, and apparently well loved.

Within a few years, however, the parents' behavior changed radically. Joseph was often harshly punished by both parents for breaking rules they were constantly revising. Joseph's mother bragged to his teachers about the way she used her whip on her child. At the Center, Joseph began to have screaming fits whenever he could not get what he wanted; as his mother became more erratic in her behavior toward him, he became more uncontrollable. By the time Joseph was 5, his parents were fighting violently with each other and with their children. He was often left alone to care for his younger brother Josh and his two younger sisters and was beaten if the younger children were hurt in any way. Their father would in turn leave, putting Joseph in charge. On three such occasions, fires were set on mattresses, causing damage to the furniture. Joseph was said to have set the fires. By the time of the third fire the children's parents had separated; their mother, who was suffering from several ailments, including a heart murmur, a kidney disorder, and depression, was in and out of hospitals and obviously could not handle her own problems, much less those of her children. The three eldest children were showing obvious signs of emotional disturbance. In school, Joseph was so disruptive that he frequently had to be bodily removed from the classroom. At home he behaved sadistically toward his younger siblings, once "branding" Josh on the chest with a heated potato masher. Josh soon demonstrated the same low tolerance for frustration, fascination with violence, and disruptive behavior that his older brother did. After the third fire, the three older children were placed in the custody of the Department of Public Welfare and placed in separate foster homes. Both Joseph and Josh were in and out of different foster homes and residential treatment centers.

This family represented the most inadequate home environment among all of the families in the program. The violence and unpredictability at home had obvious effects on both Joseph and Josh, who were unable to continue in regular school despite their intelligence.

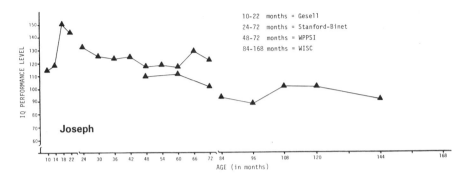

Through the entire period of Stanford-Binet testing (24 to 72 months), Joseph's IQ, with its range of 116 to 132, closely followed the average IQ for his group. There was, however, a declining trend in his scores, which started from 132 at 24 months and reached a low of 116 to 118 during the three successive testings between 48 and 60 months.

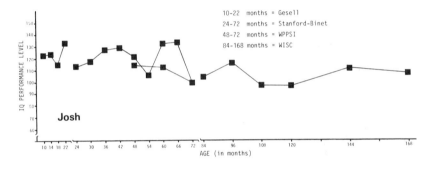

Josh's early Stanford-Binet scores were below his group's average; after his 48th month, however, they became quite erratic, gaining as many as 27 and losing as many as 34 points between testings. His IQ level reached its lowest point at 72 months, when it dropped from 133 – its highest point – to 99.

On the WPPSI/WISC tests Joseph's Full Scale IQ dropped rapidly from 111 at 60 months to a low of 88 at 96 months, his postsecond grade testing. From that point on, his scores ranged from 91 to 101.

As on the Stanford-Binet and some of the language tests, Josh's showing on the Wechsler tests was erratic. After a decline from 114 to 99 over the 2 years preceding his public school entrance, Josh's Full Scale IQ ranged from 116 to 96, with a score of 107 on his last test at 168 months.

With the exception of the Language subtest, all MAT scores for Joseph indicated achievement well below the average for his group. On Total Reading Joseph's scores were depressed after the second grade, coinciding with his transfer to an ungraded school. On Total Math his scores remained on the second grade level during the last 3 years of testing. Joseph's best achievement level after the second grade was in Language, where his last two test scores placed him on a third grade level, above the average for his group.

MAT results for Josh were available only for his first 2 years in school. On the Total Reading and Language subtests, Josh's scores, though consistent with his grade level, placed him behind his group by approximately half a year. On the Total Math subtest Josh showed no progress between first and second grades in school.

A report made when Joseph was in a residential treatment center stated, according to his teacher, that he was "continuing to move steadily in all areas of his academics." He continued, however, to have difficulty in dealing with frustrations and anxieties and constantly depended upon adults for guidance in both his work and behavior. The report continued, "if the controls and structures are not there, (Joseph becomes) bossy, loud, and aggressive."

His brother Josh also had severe emotional problems, described in part by a psychiatrist as based upon "fright, cumulative rage, and a tremendous state of limbo with regard to where he belongs." In the day school to which he had previously been assigned, he frightened the other children and later even the staff with his physical threats, and so was isolated from the rest of the children as much as possible. Finally, the attending psychologist decided that his emotional state had deteriorated to the point of necessitating 24-hour care and recommended his placement "in a 24-hour structured therapeutic milieu that can directly meet his needs of dependency and protection."

A psychological evaluation conducted when Joseph was 16 and Josh was 13 concluded that both children had "high levels of anxiety, excessive fears, and disturbed interpersonal relationships." Joseph's IQ then tested at 91 (Verbal 92, Performance 100), while Josh's was 82 (Verbal 80, Performance 104). At that time, they were both in ED programs. It seems that the extremely inadequate home environment in which both these brothers had to live had devastating and apparently irreversible effects, impeding development to their full potential.

Justin
Family Characteristics

Justin was the fourth of six living children in a single parent household. His mother, one of 12 children, came to Milwaukee from Mississippi as a child of 8. She attended a special class ("C") for the educable mentally retarded in the Milwaukee Public Schools, where she finished the ninth grade before dropping out. Her Full Scale WAIS IQ was 73 on the first testing and 78 at retest after 7 years. She read at a first grade level.

	Year of Birth	Highest Grade Completed	# Children Own Family	Age at Birth First Child	Age at Birth Target Child	1967 WAIS IQ (FS)	1974 WAIS (FS)	1974 WRAT Reading Grade
Mother	1944	9	12	19	24	73	78	1.5
Father								

Children		Sex	Year of Birth	1974 Tested IQ	1974 WRAT Reading Grade	1974 Actual Grade	Public School Placement
	1	M	1963	72	2.9	4.4	EMR
	2	F	1964	68	0.6	3.4	
	3	F	1966	83	0.6	1.4	EMR
Target	4	M	1968	107	1.7	1.4	
	5	F	1972	85			
	6	F	1975				

Although she seemed to love her children, Justin's mother was unable to provide an adequate home for them. The only mother in the Vocational Training Project to fail all of its courses, she made brief attempts to word as a nurse's aide, but was not able to hold a job. She was, however, an expert pool player and spent much time shooting pool in neighborhood bars, leaving the children to fend for themselves. The house was often cold, dirty, and disorganized; the children often went to school hungry, inadequately clothed, and unwashed. At least six social service agencies were known to have tried to help Justin's mother manage her household, all to little or no avail. Her children—two of whom were assigned to special classes for the educable mentally retarded —rarely went to school. One of them was enrolled a year late.

While at the Center, Justin frequently arrived hungry and in need of a bath. He became used to being fed, clothed, and washed at the Center; at times he himself would request his teachers to give him a bath.

More immature than his peers and a late talker, Justin required much individual attention in his early years. Possibly because of the nurturing he received at the Center but not at home, he loved coming to the Center and would eagerly wait for the car to pick him up.

With a Stanford-Binet IQ that ranged from 91 to 117 over 4 years of testing, Justin was one of the poorer performers in his group; in fact, his scores for the first two testings were closer to those of the control group. His performance, however, improved steadily until it reached its peak (117) at 54 months. After this point his scores declined. At school age (72 months) his IQ was 103.

Justin's performance on the Wechsler tests was erratic. His preschool Full Scale IQ rose from 96 to 107 over a 2-year period; after entering public school,

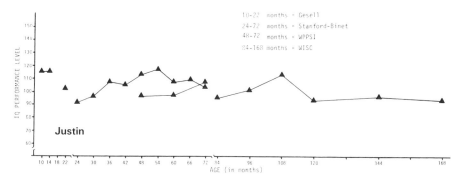

it dropped to 95 and in the next 2 years rose again to 113, considerably above the experimental group average. The last testing, at age 14, showed a drop back to 93, the lowest Justin ever scored on this test.

Public school was difficult for Justin. Although his general intellectual functioning was estimated to be in the average range, his reading and spelling skills were far below his actual grade level.

After first grade, the only subtest of the Metropolitan Achievement Test that showed grade level performance on his part was Language (second grade). Even on this subtest, however, Justin's subsequent performance was below his grade level.

Justin also demonstrated emotional and behavior problems. He seemed unable to get along with his peers and his teachers and was often the subject of disciplinary action, ranging from being sent home (for fighting) to suspension (for "continually disrupting the class"). His teachers described him as moody, easily frustrated, and irresponsible, and observed that he frequently seemed upset by events in his home. His mother complained about the difficulty of taking care of her children without a husband at home. The effects of Justin's inadequate home environment were noted in his psychological evaluations, which indicated that Justin had a very poor self-image and needs for adult nurturance and support that were not met.

Justin's MAT scores in the seventh grade were extremely low. He received several suspension notices for bad language and excessive truancy. It seems that his behavior hindered his performance.

Marty
Family Characteristics

Both of Marty's parents were high school graduates. His father also completed a course in upholstering. Marty's father came to Milwaukee from Texas

	Year of Birth	Highest Grade Completed	# Children Own Family	Age at Birth First Child	Age at Birth Target Child	1967 WAIS IQ (FS)	1974 WAIS (FS)	1974 WRAT Reading Grade
Mother	1946	12	5	20	20	68	76	2.6
Father	1945	14		21	21			

	Sex	Year of Birth	1974 Tested IQ	1974 WRAT Reading Grade	1974 Actual Grade	Public School Placement
Children						
Target 1	M	1966	123	1.6	2.4	

at the age of 19. At the time of the 1966 survey, he had been employed for
some time as a wringer in a tannery. He was 21 years old and his wife was 20
when Marty, their only child, was born. Two years later they separated and
Marty's mother took over the responsibility of supporting herself and her son.

Despite having finished high school, Marty's mother read only at the second
grade level. Her Full Scale WAIS IQ was 68 at the initial testing and 76 at retest
after 7 years. Before her marriage she had worked as a salesperson earning
$1.25 an hour. After the separation she started full time janitorial work at a
machine factory, where she earned $160 per week. A warm and loving
mother, she did not seem to find it difficult to work and at the same time provide excellent care for her son, often practicing with him the skills he was learning at the Center. Eventually she remarried, but separated from her second
husband.

Marty was the only child in the program with no brothers or sisters. He was
unusually large for his age, standing four feet seven inches tall by the time he
was 6 years old. Because of his exceptional size and strength, his teachers at the
Center often found it necessary to curb his exuberance when he played with
the other children, to ensure that he did not accidentally harm them.

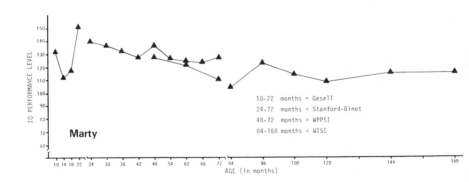

Marty's Stanford-Binet IQ was consistently above the mean for his group. From 2 to 6 years of age, it ranged from 123 to 139, with an average (GIQ) of 127.3. When he entered public school, Marty had an IQ of 127.

On the Wechsler tests, Marty exhibited a Full Scale IQ considerably above the experimental group mean on most of the testings. Starting from 127 at 48 months, his scores declined steadily over the next 3 years until at age 7, a year after he entered public school, it was 104, about the same as the group mean. After a rise to 123 the next year, his scores dropped to 108 at age 10. He regained some of the drop, showing a score of 115 at both 12 and 14 years of age.

While at the Center, Marty excelled in verbal problem solving activities and mathematics, but had some difficulty with visual discrimination and alphabet recognition. Although a check showed no medical problems, this difficulty seemed to persist and contributed to Marty's problems in public school.

Except for Total Math, Marty's scores on the MAT subtests placed him closer to the control group mean than to that of his own group. His performance in Reading and Language was more than 1 and ½ years below his grade level. In Total Math, a relatively strong field for Marty, his fourth grade performance dropped slightly below the second grade level.

Marty, it was observed, loved to draw and if left alone would do this to the exclusion of other academic activities. This may be another reason why, despite his high IQ, he had great difficulty with classroom work.

In addition to his academic difficulties, Marty experienced emotional and behavior problems severe enough to warrant his placement in an exceptional education program. He was suspended from school several times because of aggressive behavior toward his teachers and other children. His teachers complained that Marty was disrespectful, called his teachers and his classmates names, constantly talked and wandered around the room, and became sullen and withdrawn when reprimanded. His large size and physical maturity also added to Marty's problems of adjustment. Marty, according to his teachers, was "clumsy and avoided physical activities on the playground during noon hour and recess." He lacked friends because the other children were afraid of him, and he was accused in turn of bullying other children.

As of age 10, Marty was enrolled in a program for the emotionally disturbed and he continued to have difficulty controlling his behavior. Throughout the middle school years, he received several suspension notices for disruptive behavior, using bad language, and assaulting a teacher.

Peter
Family Characteristics

Peter was the youngest of three children. His mother was 16 years old when she came to Wisconsin from Tennessee, and 18 when she had her first child.

	Year of Birth	Highest Grade Completed	# Children Own Family	Age at Birth First Child	Age at Birth Target Child	1967 WAIS IQ (FS)	1974 WAIS (FS)	1974 WRAT Reading Grade
Mother	1934	11	10	18	24	74	81	4.8
Father								

Children		Sex	Year of Birth	1974 Tested IQ	1974 WRAT Reading Grade	1974 Actual Grade	Public School Placement
	1	F	1961	84	4.2	7.4	
	2	M	1963	91	3.8	5.4	
Target	3	M	1967	104	1.7	1.4	

She was 24 years old and unmarried when Peter was born. For about 12 years after the birth of her first child, she and her children were on welfare. She subsequently obtained full time employment, earning $600 a month as a cook in a hospital. She later married a machinist who also worked full time and earned the same salary; however, her husband apparently did not live at home. Like many of the mothers in the Project, Peter's mother came from a large family: she was the fourth of 10 children. She had an eleventh grade education but had a reading level that did not quite come up to the fifth grade. Her Full Scale WAIS IQ, 74 at the initial test, rose to 81. She was a quiet woman who rarely spoke about herself but was concerned about her children and attended most of the activities at the Infant Education Center.

Peter, born prematurely, at first tended to move and speak in a way that seemed younger than was appropriate for his age. It was later noticed that his behavior was even more immature when his mother was around. One of his habits, for instance, was to place in his mouth anything he found. This habit was discovered to be the cause of an elevated lead level in Peter's system. With the help of the parent coordinator, Peter's mother was able to correct this habit as well as to change her own behavior toward her son.

From age 24 to 72 months, Peter's Stanford-Binet IQ ranged from 137.5 to 104 (GIQ = 121.8), with a downward trend after the age of 48 months. His score reached its lowest point (104) at 72 months, just before he entered public school.

On the Wechsler tests Peter's scores from age 48 through 84 months showed the same downward trend (129 to 104) as did his Stanford-Binet IQ. From age 84 months, however, Peter's Full Scale IQ rose steadily. On the last testing, at age 168 months, he demonstrated a Full Scale IQ of 119, almost 15 points above the mean for his group.

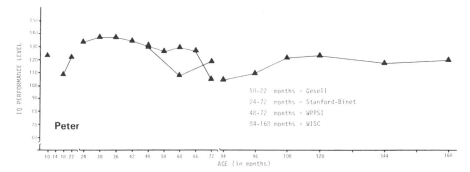

Peter's Metropolitan Achievement Test scores indicated achievement below his grade level in Language and Total Math in third grade, with improvement in fourth grade. On the Total Reading subtest, Peter's performance was on grade level during his first 3 years in school but slightly below it during his fourth year. It was, however, average for his group.

Despite his high IQ scores and despite signs of improvement in his achievement tests, Peter's adjustment to public school was not satisfactory. His teachers complained of his inattentiveness and lack of motivation, and his consequent inability to finish his assignments. A psychological evaluation report on Peter during third grade stated that while his intellectual functioning and academic achievement were average for his age and grade placement, these were lowered somewhat by emotional factors. Peter apparently had little self-confidence and an accompanying low level of aspiration. Although he reportedly enjoyed reading, Peter's generally apathetic attitude toward school prompted a multidisciplinary team to recommend his enrollment in a psychoeducational therapy program.

Peter did very poorly on the Metropolitan Achievement Test in the fifth grade. However, when he was tested in the seventh grade, his scores had improved to near average in Reading and to average in Math. His behavior continued to be problematic and he received several suspension notices for fighting and absences from school.

Richard
Family Characteristics

Richard belonged to a large and upwardly mobile family. The sixth of eight children, he was born a year after his family arrived in Milwaukee from Mississippi. Both of his parents also came from large families: His father had nine brothers and sisters and his mother had 12. In Mississippi both parents

	Year of Birth	Highest Grade Completed	# Children Own Family	Age at Birth First Child	Age at Birth Target Child	1967 WAIS IQ (FS)	1974 WAIS (FS)	1974 WRAT Reading Grade
Mother	1942	11	13	15	24	66	64	5.8
Father	1936	9	10	21	30			

Children		Sex	Year of Birth	1974 Tested IQ	1974 WRAT Reading Grade	1974 Actual Grade	Public School Placement
	1	M	1957	93	8.5	10.4	
	2	M	1959	103	14.1	9.4	
	3	F	1961	85	2.8	6.4	
	4	F	1963	83	5.2	5.4	
	5	F	1964	72	3.9	4.4	
Target	6	M	1966	105	2.0	2.4	
	7	M	1971	103			
	8	M	1975				

worked on farms, Richard's mother as a cotton picker earning $3.00 daily for 8 hours of work, and his father as a $5-a-day farm hand. Their situation improved considerably once they were in Milwaukee. Richard's mother, with an eleventh grade education, completed the vocational training program for the project mothers and obtained work as a nurse's aide. She had worked for over 8 years and earned $680 a month. Her husband, who had gone only as far as ninth grade, found employment as a metal grinder at $200 a week. His reported monthly salary was $1,200. The family lived in a relatively large and well furnished house.

Richard's mother had a Full Scale WAIS IQ of 66 at the start of the survey and 64 upon retest after 7 years. Her reading level was just below the sixth grade. She was a pleasant woman who showed much interest in her son's activities and academic progress. She kept a scrapbook of Richard's participation in the Infant Educational Stimulation Program and said that Richard "seemed to be real smart when he went to the Center."

Richard's Stanford-Binet IQ, which ranged between 122.5 and 133.5 and was above his group's mean IQ from age 24 through 54 months, dropped below the group average to a range of 114 to 117 during the next three testings. His average IQ over the 4 years of Stanford-Binet testing was 120.3.

The Wechsler tests record differences in Richard's Full Scale IQ before he entered public school, during his first 2 years in school, and during the following 6 years. His preschool scores ranged from 113 to 119; in the 2 years after

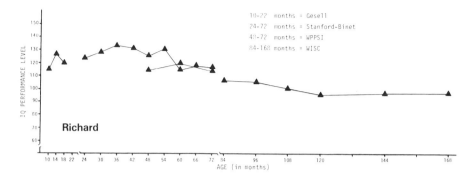

entering public school, his Full Scale IQ dropped to 105 to 106. His score at ages 12 and 14 was 96, which was below his group's average and indicated a loss of 9 IQ points since testing at 8 years of age.

Richard was admitted to first grade 3 months before his sixth birthday. At that time, a social worker who visited the family observed that the family's emotional and financial stability, its sustained interest in education, and the availability of older siblings for academic assistance would support Richard's early admission if it was so recommended by the school psychologist. With a warning that Richard seemed to be "of only average intelligence" and might therefore "find himself in a very competitive academic situation with slightly older children," the school psychologist permitted Richard's early enrollment.

The transition to public school seemed to have been difficult emotionally for Richard. Although at the Infant Center he had been a quiet child who enjoyed all learning activities, his primary school teachers complained of his talkativeness, aggressiveness, and fits of temper. He received reprimands and suspensions for being "sarcastic and uncooperative," refusing to obey, and fighting. His behavior apparently affected his academic success: His teachers all reported that he was "very able to do good work," but that he was "easily distracted and needed to be the center of attention." A psychological evaluation conducted on Richard while he was in Extended Primary indicated average intellectual abilities but a full year's lag in academic achievement.

These findings were supported by Richard's performance on the Metropolitan Achievement Tests, which showed serious lags in Total Reading and Language during the third and fourth years of school, and in Total Math during the fourth year.

The school psychologist recommended "teacher presence, encouragement and direction on a personal basis," because Richard "responds to attention and encouragement, (but) needs prodding at times in order to project himself."

Richard made great strides in Math in the middle school years. His MAT scores improved from very low to average in the seventh and tenth grades. His Reading score improved in the seventh grade but dropped again in the tenth grade.

Sam
Sarah
Family Characteristics

	Year of Birth	Highest Grade Completed	# Children Own Family	Age at Birth First Child	Age at Birth Target Child	1967 WAIS IQ (FS)	1974 WAIS (FS)	1974 WRAT Reading Grade
Mother	1942	10	8	18	24	69	77	5.8
Father	1932	12	3	28	34			

Children		Sex	Year of Birth	1974 Tested IQ	1974 WRAT Reading Grade	1974 Actual Grade	Public School Placement
	1	M	1960	98	7.9	8.4	
	2	F	1962	70	3.0	5.4	
	3	M	1964	80	2.5	4.4	
	4	M	1965	88	1.2	2.4	
Target	5	M	1966	94	1.6	2.4	
Target	6	F	1968	122	1.3	k.4	
	7	F	1970	94			
	8	F	1971	88			
	9	F	1973				

Sam and his younger sister Sarah, who also participated in the Infant Education Program, were the fifth and sixth of nine children, all born within a 16-year period. Their parents were born in Arkansas and moved to Milwaukee 5 years after their marriage. Their father, a disabled veteran, was a pastor who drew no salary for his work. A high school graduate with 9 months of barber school, he became a machinist and was a construction worker when he had to quit work because of asthma and heart trouble. The family then subsisted on disability compensation and welfare benefits.

The children's mother went to school through the tenth grade. Her reading level was slightly below the sixth grade; her WAIS Full Scale IQ, which was 69 at initial testing, was 77 at retest. She had never been employed; however, she did some sewing at home. Although the impressions gathered from the first survey indicated a crowded, seemingly unmanageable household, these conditions did not seem to have adversely affected either Sam or Sarah. Soft spoken and cheerful, they got along well with the other children at the Center and seemed to enjoy all types of activity.

Throughout the 4 years of preschool testing, Sam's Stanford-Binet IQ was considerably lower than his younger sister's. Between the ages of 30 and 48 months his scores rose from 106 to 132. After a drop back to 105 at 54 months, they assumed a similar rising trend in the next 1½ years, reaching 123 at age 72 months.

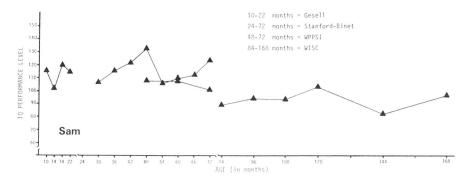

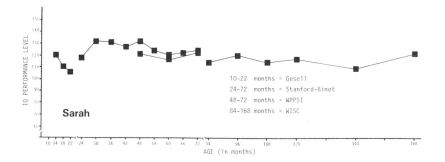

After the first testing, Sarah's Stanford-Binet IQ was consistently above the mean for her group, following the mean for her group very closely from 54 to 66 months. At 72 months when she entered public school, her IQ was 124.

As on the Stanford-Binet test, Sam's scores on the Wechsler tests were often far below those of his group. After his entrance into public school, his Full Scale IQ dropped from 100 at 72 months to 89 a year later. At age 10, his score rose to 103; however, it dropped to 96 as of the last testing at age 14.

Sarah's Full Scale IQ, with its range of 114 to 122, remained well above the experimental group mean over the 11 years of Wechsler testing. As of the last test (at 168 months, or 14 years of age), it was 121 (20 points above the group's mean).

Sam did fairly well in school, although his teachers commented on his slow progress in arithmetic. On his Metropolitan Achievement Tests, however, Sam did better on Total Math than on the Total Reading and Language subtests. On Total Math he surpassed his group during the last 2 years, although he remained half a year below his actual grade level. His MAT performance on Total Reading and Language, though more than half a year below his grade level, was above his group's average in his fourth year. During his first 3 years, however, his scores on both subtests placed him closer to the control group than to his own.

Judging from her teachers' comments and her MAT scores, Sarah seemed to be doing better in school than her brother. On the Language and Total Math subtests of the MAT, her scores placed her consistently above her grade level.

On Total Reading during her third year in school, her MAT score dropped to set her back by half a year. No fourth grade MAT scores were reported for Sarah.

Both Sam and Sarah were described by their teachers as friendly and cooperative; Sarah, in particular, was often complimented by her teachers for her attitude toward school and her ability to get along with her peers. Both children were described by school psychologists as slow responders on tasks, but also as task oriented and well motivated. One problem associated with them was the frequency of their absences. This had also been a problem at the Infant Center, when their father used to keep them from school because he felt that their clothing was inadequate. Although this problem was resolved by parent coordinators at the Center, the meagerness of family resources — or the father's attitude toward it — apparently continued to affect the children's school attendance. Records indicate that the children were not able to join field trips because they could not pay for the trips or were absent because of lack of presentable clothing, despite the efforts of school social workers to provide clothes and assurances by teachers that the children could join the trips without expense.

Sam's MAT scores dropped into the low range in both Reading and Math in the seventh and tenth grades. On the other hand, Sarah's performance in Math improved, with her scores moving from the average range in the fifth grade to well above average in the seventh and tenth grades. Her Reading scores did not improve, remaining in the low range. She continued to receive good reports from her teachers as a "cooperative child."

Susan
Family Characteristics

Susan's parents were born in Louisiana. Both went to school until the ninth grade. Susan's mother, 7 years younger than her husband, was 17 years old when she had the first of her eight children. She was 32 years old when Susan, her youngest, was born. Through the maternal vocational program, Susan's mother, whose WAIS IQ was 68, found employment as a hospital aide. Susan's father, however, was unable to find work and, when Susan was 4, the family moved back to Louisiana.

Coming from a warm, loving, and stable family, Susan was herself goodnatured and warm, often the first to notice and the first to comfort any child who was unhappy. Because of this she was popular with the other children and was greatly missed. After her family left, Susan stayed on in Milwaukee for a while, living with her initial infant teacher. Two months later she joined her family in Louisiana.

	Year of Birth	Highest Grade Completed	# Children Own Family	Age at Birth First Child	Age at Birth Target Child	1967 WAIS IQ (FS)	1974 WAIS (FS)	1974 WRAT Reading Grade
Mother	1935	9	11	17	32	68	Moved	
Father	1928	9	6	24	39		Moved	

Children		Sex	Year of Birth	1974 Tested IQ	1974 WRAT Reading Grade	1974 Actual Grade	Public School Placement
	1	F	1952	70(1969)		Moved	
	2	M	1953	85(1969)		Moved	
	3	F	1954	96(1969)		Moved	
	4	F	1957	78(1969)		Moved	
	5	F	1959	85(1969)		Moved	
	6	F	1963	95(1969)		Moved	
	7	M	1965	62(1969)		Moved	
Target	8	F	1967			Moved	

Susan's Stanford-Binet IQ, which ranged from 123 to 130 over 2 years of testing, was average for her group but was never less than 20 points above the control group average for the same age level.

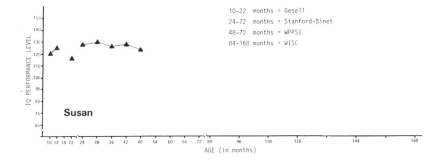

Tammy
Family Characteristics

Tammy's family consisted of her father, her mother, and seven children of whom she was the youngest. Both of her parents were born in Mississippi;

	Year of Birth	Highest Grade Completed	# Children Own Family	Age at Birth First Child	Age at Birth Target Child	1967 WAIS IQ (FS)	1974 WAIS (FS)	1974 WRAT Reading Grade
Mother	1935	10	6	20	30	63	68	4.8
Father	1936	10	9	19	29			

		Sex	Year of Birth	1974 Tested IQ	1974 WRAT Reading Grade	1974 Actual Grade	Public School Placement
Children							
	1	F	1955	80(1969)			Moved
	2	M	1956	99	6.6	11.4	
	3	M	1958	93	7.1	10.4	
	4	M	1960	83	4.6	7.4	
	5	F	1963	98	4.8	6.4	
	6	M	1965	83	2.7	4.4	
Target	7	F	1966	96	1.9	2.4	

both dropped out of school after the tenth grade. Four years after their eldest child was born, Tammy's father, then 23 years old, came to Milwaukee. By this time they already had three children and were expecting a fourth. After the birth of the fourth child, Tammy's mother joined her husband in Milwaukee. For some years they received AFDC payments, until both parents found work that gave them enough income to support their growing family. Tammy's mother worked as a janitor in a hospital, where she earned $400 a month. Tammy's father, a hard working man who had been a butcher and a construction worker, found work in a brewery that paid him $310 a week. He was working 8 hours daily, 7 days a week as a truck driver for this brewery and earned $25,000 a year. The family lived in a well furnished, nine-room house.

Despite the family's economic stability, difficulties with household organization and rearing the children were observed. At the time of the initial survey, the family lived in a cottage described as being "in disarray." Tammy's mother, whose WAIS Full Scale IQ at the time was 63 (68 at retest in 1974) and whose reading grade was 4.8, showed signs of a warm relationship with her children, but gave the interviewer the impression of having "given up on the possibility of giving them individual attention."

There were indications that Tammy—a quiet, shy child who frequently played by herself—was not receiving much attention at home. She often had accidents: Once she was seriously burned by hot water falling from a stove, at another time she cut her foot badly on a tin can but did not tell anyone about it until she began limping noticeably. She often came to the Center with her hair uncombed and her clothes crumpled and was so self-conscious about it that the teachers took it upon themselves to straighten out her clothes and comb her hair before letting the other children see her.

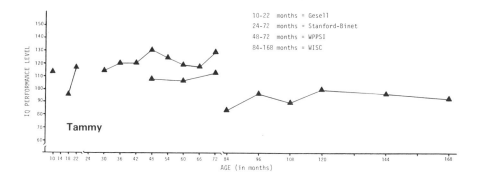

Tammy's Stanford-Binet IQ ranged from 114 to 130, with a mean of 123.4, over 3½ years of testing. Although her first three scores (range = 114 to 120.5) were below the corresponding means for her group, they were at least 20 points above those of the control group. By age 48 months she started to show an IQ that equalled or surpassed the experimental group mean in all but one instance. At school age, her IQ was 128, as compared with the group mean of 119.2.

Prior to school entry Tammy's Full Scale IQ on the Wechsler tests ranged from 106 to 112. After her first year in public school this dropped to 83, only 2 points above the control group mean for that testing. In later testings, however, her scores rose to a level somewhat closer to that of her own group.

In public school Tammy continued to be as quiet and shy as she had been at the Infant Center. Her teachers noted this and praised her pleasantness and sense of responsibility. However, Tammy's grades were not good. She received Ds in the areas of reading, language, and arithmetic, notably in third grade and in the Extended Primary grade to which she was assigned in her fourth year of school.

Although Tammy's performance on the three subtests of the MAT was on grade level during first and second grades, it was consistently below her own group's average. During her third and fourth years in public school, her achievement in all areas fell below grade level, with lags ranging from ½ year (Total Math, third grade) to 2 years (Total Math, fourth grade). In general, Tammy's performance on the MAT was closer to the control group's average than to that of her own group.

As assessed by the psychologist who evaluated her during her fourth year (Extended Primary) in school, Tammy's intellectual functioning was in the high average range; however, with the exception of spelling, she was academically "2 to 3 years behind age expectation" in all areas. (It is interesting to note that spelling was the one area in which Tammy consistently received Ds.) Tammy apparently also saw herself as "depressed, dependent and weak," and perceived the environment as "threatening and full of obstacles." She felt she was not actively liked by other children and saw her home as a source of personal safety and protection.

Tammy's MAT scores remained low when she was tested in the seventh grade. When she was in the eleventh grade, she became pregnant and, after delivery, kept the baby.

Wally
Wilbur
Family Characteristics

	Year of Birth	Highest Grade Completed	# Children Own Family	Age at Birth First Child	Age at Birth Target Child	1967 WAIS IQ (FS)	1974 WAIS (FS)	1974 WRAT Reading Grade
Mother	1947	11	9	18	20	73	78	6.3
Father								

Children		Sex	Year of Birth	1974 Tested IQ	1974 WRAT Reading Grade	1974 Actual Grade	Public School Placement
	1	F	1965	89	2.2	3.4	
	2	M	1966	87	1.8	2.4	
Target	3	M	1967	99	1.7	1.4	
Target	4	M	1969	113			
	5	M	1971	94			
	6	F	1973				

Wally and Wilbur, the third and fourth of six children, lived with their mother, their younger brother and sister, and their older half-sister and half-brother in a six-room house. Although their parents were separated for several years, the household was described by Center workers as well managed and happy, with the children taking care of one another when their mother was not at home. The mother, who had gone to school through the eleventh grade, had a sixth grade reading level and a WAIS IQ that was 73 at first testing and 78 at retest. She was 19 years old and had had two children when she moved to Milwaukee from Louisiana. Wally was born a year later and Wilbur 2 years afterward. Her first job after completing the vocational training course was as an aide in a home for the elderly. She also worked 3 hours a day as a school crossing guard. Supplementing her earnings of $200 a month were food stamps as well as welfare and Title 19 payments.

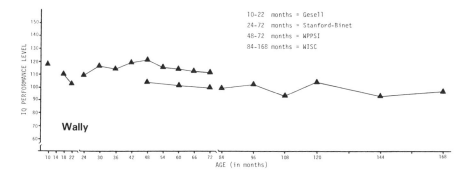

Wally's Stanford-Binet IQ was consistently lower than his group's average through the 4 years of preschool testing. After rising from 109 at 24 months to 121 at 48 months, his scores declined steadily during the next 2 years. At the time he entered school, his IQ was 111.

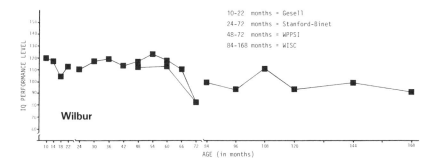

From age 24 months through 54 months, Wilbur, like his brother, had scores below the experimental group average. His IQ range during this period was 110.4 to 123. From 54 months through 72 months, his scores assumed a different pattern, first rising to the level of the group, then dropping sharply to a point below the control group mean. Between age 66 months and 72 months, Wilbur's IQ dropped from 110 to 82, a loss of 28 points.

As on the Stanford-Binet, Wally's performance on the Wechsler tests was generally below his group's average. There was a slight but steady decline in his Full Scale IQ from 48 months through 84 months, from 104 to 99. He scored 104 again at 120 months and then dropped to 93 at 144 months and rose slightly to 96 at 168 months.

Wilbur's Full Scale IQ was generally below the experimental group mean. As on the Stanford-Binet, Wilbur's score dropped abruptly between age 60 months and 72 months — in this case, losing 31 points. His later tests showed relative improvement, although his scores remained below the group mean.

Reading was Wally's best MAT subtest. In his fourth (Extended Primary) year his score placed him ½ year above his group's average level, although still ½ year below the fourth grade level. His performance in Language dropped in his third and fourth years to below the control group mean. On Total Math he experienced a similar decline in his third year but improved in his fourth, at least to the average level reached by the two groups, which was 1 year below actual grade level.

Wilbur did quite well on the MAT. On all three subtests, his performance was consistently above his actual grade level. His best showing was on the Language subtest, where his scores placed him more than 1 year above his grade level in his first 3 years in school. During these 3 years he also performed above grade level on Total Reading and on or above grade level on Total Math.

Wally was a quiet, generally passive boy who moved and acted slowly. At the Infant Education Center his teachers were at first concerned because he often finished his projects long after the other children. However, when they observed that his usual approach to problems was unhurried and methodical, they allowed him to work at his own pace. Unfortunately, his grade school teachers did not seem to have given him this same allowance. Despite a school psychologist's observation that he was "thoughtfully responsive" and "responded excellently to acceptance and encouragement, but seems to have a natural tendency to be slow and cautious when making verbal responses," his teachers repeatedly complained of his "laziness" and slowness; these, in fact, were major contributors to Wally's grades of D in reading and arithmetic and to his placement in Extended Primary. Possibly Wally had already reacted adversely to these complaints, because one of his teachers commented that he "hurried through his math and is doing very poorly."

Wilbur was also quiet and cautious. The youngest child at the Infant Center, he was a great favorite with the teachers and the other children. Perhaps because of this, there was a short period at the beginning of first grade during which Wilbur was extremely disruptive and aggressive in the classroom. However, he soon made the adjustment to the classroom and settled down to become, in his teacher's words, "a nice little boy, a pleasure to have in class."

In the tenth grade, Wally received several suspension notices for truancy and for an incident involving starting a fire in a trash basket. His brother Wilbur maintained his earlier promise, testing at the average level in the seventh grade on the MAT Reading and Math subtests.

CONTROL GROUP CHILDREN

Arlene
Family Characteristics

	Year of Birth	Highest Grade Completed	# Children Own Family	Age at Birth First Child	Age at Birth Target Child	1967 WAIS IQ (FS)	1974 WAIS (FS)	1974 WRAT Reading Grade
Mother	1947	12	12	18	20	66	72	4.8
Father	1944							

		Sex	Year of Birth	1974 Tested IQ	1974 WRAT Reading Grade	1974 Actual Grade	Public School Placement
Children							
Target	1	F	1967	66			
	2	M	1969				
	3	F	1971				
	4						
	5						

Arlene's mother first came to Milwaukee when she was 19 years old. She had Arlene a year later and two more children in the next 4 years. During this period, she was apparently unemployed and separated from Arlene's father: The family had been on welfare for several years and no male had been consistently present at home. From time to time she and her children would move to her mother's home in Georgia and then return to Wisconsin. She married and had two more children after Arlene had entered public school.

A high school graduate, Arlene's mother had a WRAT reading grade of 4.8. Her WAIS Full Scale IQ was 66 at the start of the project and 72 at retest after 7 years. She was described by a school social worker as "a warm, friendly lady who is interested in the health and welfare of her five children." The family home was a well kept two-bedroom upper flat.

Arlene was described by her mother as a "bright, happy, quiet" child who got along well with her siblings and her many friends and who was helpful around the home. As a young child, she seemed somewhat sickly and was hospitalized for anemia.

Starting from 98.2 at age 2, Arlene's Stanford-Binet IQ dropped steadily over the next 3 years to a low of 76 at age 5. By age 6, however, her score rose to 86, which was the average for her group.

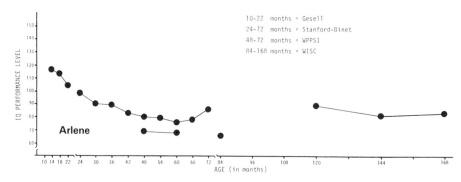

On the Wechsler tests from the ages of 4 to 7 years, Arlene obtained very low scores, even in relation to her own group, with a Full Scale IQ that ranged from 66 to 69. As of the last testing at age 14 years, however, her score had risen to 83, just 3 points below her own group's mean IQ.

Arlene seemed to have gone twice through her first grade of school, first while she was in Georgia and again when she returned to Milwaukee. Despite a persistent stuttering problem serious enough to require supplemental speech and language programming, Arlene did well in school, both academically and socially. She received grades of Outstanding or Satisfactory in all subject areas, and her teachers rated her work as on or above her grade level.

Arlene's Metropolitan Achievement Test scores in the fourth year in school indicate she was achieving on a mid-third grade level on Total Reading and Total Math and on her grade level on Language. On all three subtests, her performance for that year was well above the averages for her own group as well as the experimental group.

Aside from her mother's supportive attitude, mentioned earlier, it was also evident that Arlene's friendly, pleasant disposition contributed to her success in school. Her teachers praised her attitude and work habits and described her as "well behaved and well liked by all her peers" and as "a very good worker who does all her assignments very promptly." In her third grade teacher's words, "Your daughter is one to be proud of."

Arlene maintained her achievement level in Math, as indicated by her scores in the MAT conducted in the tenth grade. She was enrolled in a Speech and Language Disabilities Program and, although she slipped in Reading, a psychological evaluation done at age 16 showed she had made significant progress in reducing speech avoidance. She still, however, had intermittent speech dysfunction.

Craig
Family Characteristics

Craig's parents were both born in Arkansas and both had lived in Milwaukee since they were children. Both went to school in Milwaukee, his mother up to the twelfth grade and his father to the eleventh. Craig, the eldest

	Year of Birth	Highest Grade Completed	# Children Own Family	Age at Birth First Child	Age at Birth Target Child	1967 WAIS IQ (FS)	1974 WAIS (FS)	1974 WRAT Reading Grade
Mother	1945	12	9	22	22	74	77	5.6
Father	1947	11	8	20	20			

		Sex	Year of Birth	1974 Tested IQ	1974 WRAT Reading Grade	1974 Actual Grade	Public School Placement
Children							
Target	1	M	1967	75	1.2	1.4	
	2	F	1969	107			
	3	M	1970				

of the three children, was born when they were 22 and 20 years old, respectively. They separated when Craig was 4 years old and were divorced 4 years later.

Craig's mother had a WAIS IQ of 74 at the start of the project and 77 at retest after 7 years. Her WRAT reading grade was 5.6. At various times she worked as a waitress, a hospital aide, and a dietary aide, receiving partial AFDC and medical assistance payments and food stamps. The apartment in which she lived with her three children was clean and adequately furnished.

From the start of the project, Craig's mother was somewhat apathetic and wary of school and social service agencies. Her attitude was possibly worsened by her experience with a hospital where her youngest daughter had been tested for a heart condition. During the tests, the child had undergone heart catheterization; a subsequent infection resulted in the child's loss of her fingers and toes. A social worker who visited the home described the attitude of Craig's mother as "rather unrealistic" in relation to her children's problems. At the age of 4, for instance, her youngest child had not started to talk and had just learned to walk; yet she stated that there was nothing wrong with the child and that she expected her to enter kindergarten the following year. She had the same attitude toward Craig's school problems, believing that he would grow out of them.

Craig was a shy, soft spoken, rather unresponsive boy, described by both his mother and his teacher as a "loner" who had few friends and spent a lot of time alone watching television. He was aggressive toward his two sisters and often fought with them.

Craig's Stanford-Binet IQ, which ranged from a high of 98.2 at 24 months to a low of 76 at 72 months, was below his own group's average for the greater part of the 4-year testing period. He obtained his lowest scores at 66 and 72 months, when his IQ dropped to 6 and 11 points below the corresponding control group means.

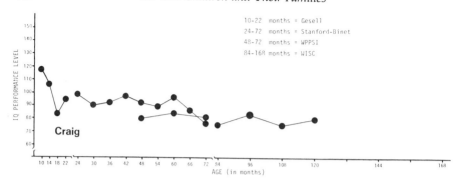

On the Wechsler tests, as on the Stanford-Binet, Craig's performance was below his own group's average for the greater part of the 11-year period of testing. His Full Scale IQ, which ranged from 80 to 84 before he entered school, dropped to a range of 75 to 83 beginning with school entry.

Metropolitan Achievement Tests indicated that after the first grade, Craig made little progress in Language and Total Math. In these subtests he was performing below his own group average, falling to 2 years below grade expectancy by his fourth year in school. Although his scores were relatively better on the Reading subtest, where he was on grade level during his first 2 years, his fourth year (Extended Primary) performance was 1½ years below grade level and below his own group average.

From the time he entered school, Craig had learning problems. In first grade, he was referred for psychological study because of his "poor verbal skills, short attention span, and immaturity." A neurological examination revealed no evidence of previous central nervous system damage or of any chronic progressive disease of the nervous system. The examining physician concluded that Craig was neurologically immature but had potential for learning. Craig was also enrolled in the ESEA Title I Language Program and a sensorimotor training program. During the next 3 years, Craig was the subject of several multidisciplinary team studies that indicated a low average to borderline intelligence, visual-motor difficulties, and delays in receptive and expressive vocabulary and in auditory memory for sentences. In addition, he impressed the examiners as "a rather emotionally isolated child" who had "much difficulty in dealing with his emotions." Craig's mother, while aware of her son's learning difficulties, seemed to be opposed to exceptional education programming. According to her, she had also been slow in school, had been in a "special class," and had not been helped by it. She further believed that Craig would outgrow his school problems.

Craig did not, however, outgrow his emotional and learning problems. A psychological evaluation conducted when he was 12 years old recommended placement in a program for the emotionally disturbed. He received many suspensions (approximately 60) for refusing to work, assaulting students, and stealing.

Christine
Family Characteristics

	Year of Birth	Highest Grade Completed	# Children Own Family	Age at Birth First Child	Age at Birth Target Child	1967 WAIS IQ (FS)	1974 WAIS (FS)	1974 WRAT Reading Grade
Mother	1945	9	3	12	22	71	78	5.4
Father	1930	10	4		37			

Children		Sex	Year of Birth	1974 Tested IQ	1974 WRAT Reading Grade	1974 Actual Grade	Public School Placement
	1	M	1957	105	6.3	11.4	
	2	M	1961	80	3.3	6.4	
	3	M	1962	79	6.1	5.4	
	4	M	1965	89	2.2	4.4	
Target	5	F	1967	74	1.3	1.4	
	6	M	1969	94			
	7	M	1972				

Christine was the fifth of seven children and the only daughter in a closely knit, two parent family. Although neither of her parents had had more than 10 years of school, both had steady jobs: Her father, who worked at night in a factory, earned $1,000 monthly; her mother earned $530 monthly as a cook in a daycare center. The family came to Milwaukee from Arkansas shortly after Christine's birth. Her mother, who read at a mid-fifth grade level, had a WAIS Full Scale IQ of 72 at the time of the survey and 78 at retest. She was 12 years old when she had her first child; by the time she was 20, she had had three more. She was 22 years old and her husband was 37 when Christine was born. The family lived in a clean, well furnished apartment.

Because she was the only girl in a large family, Christine was "spoiled and babied," according to her public school teachers. She was a shy, quiet girl who was cautious with strangers.

Christine's Stanford-Binet IQ was, on the whole, lower than was average for her group. Ranging from 83 to 97.7 over the 4-year testing period, it exceeded the group mean only twice during that period. At school age (72 months), her IQ was 87, which was also the mean IQ for her group.

On the Wechsler tests, Christine's performance in relation to her group paralleled that on the Stanford-Binet from 48 through 72 months, with scores on or above the group average. After her first year in public school, her Full Scale IQ, which ranged from 82 to 91, dropped to 74. Although her scores subsequently improved, ranging from 80 to 95 during the next 7 years, her last

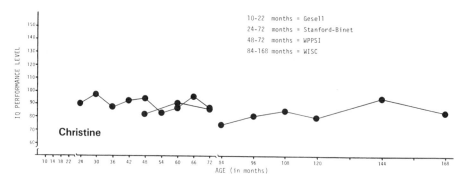

score, at age 14, was 2 points below the control group mean and 20 points below the mean for the experimental group.

Christine's achievement in Total Math, as measured by the Metropolitan Achievement Test, was on grade level from first to third grades and almost on grade level during her year in Extended Primary. She did not do as well on the two other subtests: On Total Reading she had progressed only slightly since her second grade testing and was more than 1 year below her grade level. In Language, she showed no improvement over her first grade score during the next 2 years. She did better in her fourth year; however, her language achievement was still 1 year below her grade level.

During her first years in public school, Christine was described as a "very quiet, sweet girl" by her teachers, who also noted that she was easily distracted and therefore could not finish her work. Like three of her older brothers, she had difficulties with reading and was placed in Extended Primary, where she seemed to make good progress. Frequent absences were a problem during Christine's second year in school: Apparently, the family had just moved and Christine was afraid to go to school alone. Although her parents promised to arrange for one of Christine's brothers to accompany her to school, her attendance continued to be poor. Two years later, when she was 9 years old, Christine was raped and had to be hospitalized. Despite these circumstances, Christine continued with school and began to show some progress.

When tested on the Metropolitan Achievement Tests in seventh and tenth grades, Christine's scores showed that she had maintained her performance levels in Reading and Math.

Elmer
Family Characteristics

The youngest of six children, Elmer was also the only son in this two parent family. His parents had been married 7 years when they came to Milwaukee from Arkansas. Elmer was born a year later. His father, who had dropped out

	Year of Birth	Highest Grade Completed	# Children Own Family	Age at Birth First Child	Age at Birth Target Child	1967 WAIS IQ (FS)	1974 WAIS (FS)	1974 WRAT Reading Grade
Mother	1941	9	12	16	26	66	72	2.4
Father	1936	10	7	21	31			

Children		Sex	Year of Birth	1974 Tested IQ	1974 WRAT Reading Grade	1974 Actual Grade	Public School Placement
	1	F	1957	78	4.2	9.4	
	2	F	1959	63	2.4	8.4	EMR
	3	F	1961	65	2.8	6.4	EMR
	4	F	1962	69	2.7	5.4	
	5	F	1965	81	1.2	2.4	EMR
Target	6	M	1967	85	1.2	1.4	

of school after the tenth grade, had been a $60-a-week forklift operator before coming to Milwaukee to work as a molder in a foundry. He was earning $125 a week when he became ill and had to stop working. To supplement the family's Title 19 income and her husband's disability payments, Elmer's mother started working full time as a housekeeper in a nursing home while her husband took a training course in electronics. Later, however, she became ill and quit her job. The family received disability, welfare, and Title 19 payments.

Elmer's mother, who went through the ninth grade of school, read at a second grade level. Her WAIS Full Scale IQ, 66 at first testing, was 72 at retest after 7 years. The second of 12 children, she had had a child of her own before she was 16. She was married at the age of 18 and had Elmer when she was 26 years old.

The family, including the two eldest daughters, who were working and had children, lived in a 10-room house, described as "slightly disorganized" and in need of repair. Of Elmer's five sisters, three went to special classes for the educable mentally retarded.

On the Stanford-Binet test Elmer's scores were below the average for his group at all age levels except 66 months, when he equalled the group mean of 93. His IQ, which ranged from 85 to 94 from age 24 through 66 months, dropped to 76, its lowest point, at 72 months, the end of the period of Stanford-Binet preschool testing.

On the Wechsler tests, Elmer showed marked improvement after his entrance into public school. From a preschool range of 80 to 86, slightly below his own group's average, his Full Scale IQ rose steadily above the group mean. At the last testing (age 14 years), Elmer's IQ was 100, 14 points above the mean for his group and 4 points below that of the experimental group.

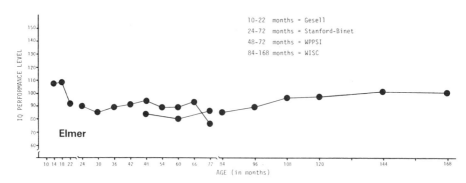

Elmer, a very quiet, gentle boy who liked to paint, was hospitalized briefly before his entrance into public school because of a high lead level in his system. He had no behavior related problems in school and was described by his teachers as a polite child who "is cooperative and nearly always tries to do his best."

The Metropolitan Achievement Test indicated varied trends in Elmer's school achievement: On the Total Math subtest his performance matched his group average, although this average was below grade level for the third and fourth grades. His scores in language, while quite low during second grade, rose during third and Extended Primary grades to a level above the average for both groups. His fourth year Extended Primary score nevertheless remained below his grade level. Elmer's performance was poorest in Total Reading, where it dropped to almost 2 years below grade level in his third and fourth year testings.

Because of his courteous and pleasant demeanor, Elmer was well liked by his teachers. They continued to remark, however, on Elmer's poor reading achievement. Elmer, who in kindergarten had been in an ESEA Title I Language Development Program, was placed in Extended Primary after third grade. At the same time he received special help from the Reading Center, where he was described as making good progress and showing "commendable initiative and enthusiasm."

Elmer's progress in the middle school years was good. His scores on the Math subtest of the MAT, conducted in the seventh and tenth grades, improved, although his Reading scores dropped slightly. Other than one suspension notice for fighting, he was a well behaved student.

Faye

Family Characteristics

Faye's parents had been married 8 years when they moved to Milwaukee from Mississippi, where her father had been a $50-a-week farm hand. The following year Faye, the sixth of their eight children, was born. Twins — a boy

	Year of Birth	Highest Grade Completed	# Children Own Family	Age at Birth First Child	Age at Birth Target Child	1967 WAIS IQ (FS)	1974 WAIS (FS)	1974 WRAT Reading Grade
Mother	1938	10	12	20	28	69	80	3.5
Father	1939	5	5	21	29			

Children		Sex	Year of Birth	1974 Tested IQ		1974 WRAT Reading Grade	1974 Actual Grade	Public School Placement
	1	M	1958	65		1.7	8.4	EMR
	2	F	1960	76		2.4	8.4	EMR
	3	F	1961	85		4.4	6.4	
	4	M	1963	85		1.5	5.4	
	5	F	1964	82		1.7	4.4	
Target	6	F	1966	84		1.9	2.4	Head Start (1 year)
	7	M	1971	89				
	8	F	1971	92				

and a girl—were born 5 years later. Faye's father, the only wage earner in the family, first worked in a tannery and eventually became a construction worker. This job, while paying as much as $235 a week, was seasonal; during the winter the family would go on welfare to supplement his unemployment compensation and the children's Title 19 assistance.

Faye's mother never worked outside the home. She completed the tenth grade of school—5 years more than her husband had—but had a third grade reading level. Her Full Scale WAIS IQ, 69 at the start of the study, was 80 when she was retested after 7 years. She was a pleasant, friendly woman who cooperated well with the research staff.

The original family dwelling, a five-room apartment, was described as poorly ventilated, poorly lighted, dirty, and in need of repair. The family moved to another place in the city, and home conditions improved.

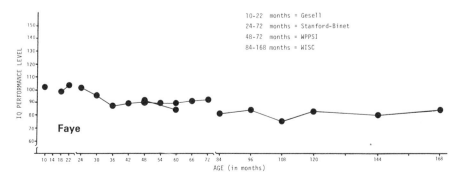

Over a large part of the 4-year Stanford-Binet testing period, Faye's IQ was below the control group average. From 101.4 at age 24 months, her score dropped sharply to 87 within a year. From age 42 through 72 months she continued to have scores between 89 and 92.

Faye's Wechsler test scores showed a declining trend. Her Full Scale IQ, which was 91 when she was 48 months old, dropped by degrees to 75 when she was 9 years old. Her last WISC test, taken at age 14 years, showed a rise to 84, still 2 points below the control group average and 20 points below that of the experimental group.

Faye, who had a year of Head Start before entering public school, on the whole kept pace with her group. Like her group, however, she remained at a mid-second grade level in Total Reading achievement through third and fourth grade in school and was 1 year below grade level in Language. On the Total Math subtest she made little improvement from the third to the fourth grade, scoring at the mid-second grade level on both testings.

As a young child, Faye was shy and often uncommunicative. She had an allergy that often caused her to break out into a rash. During these times she was irritable and difficult to test. At other times, however, she seemed calm and happy. This was noted by her primary school teachers, who also described her as hard working and cooperative. Apparently Faye became more outgoing as she grew older: Her third and fourth grade teachers complained that she "has become a talker" and "talks too much."

Faye's performance on the Metropolitan Achievement Test showed considerable variation over the middle school years. Her score in Reading improved when she was tested in the seventh grade, but slipped back again in the ninth grade. Her performance in Math remained low throughout. Beginning in the ninth grade, several of her teachers reported tardiness and she received suspension notices for not working and for disrupting the class.

Grace
Family Characteristics

Grace lived with her parents and three sisters in an attractive, well furnished house owned by her family. She was the youngest of six children, the two eldest of whom were her mother's children by a previous marriage. Both of her parents were born in Arkansas, each the seventh of eight children.

Grace's parents worked full time. Her mother, who dropped out of school after tenth grade, had a reading level just below the sixth grade. In this, as well as in IQ (73 at initial testing, 81 on retest), she ranked higher than most of the mothers in her group. She married her first husband when she was 18 years old and had her first child at 19. Two years later she came to Milwaukee and

	Year of Birth	Highest Grade Completed	# Children Own Family	Age at Birth First Child	Age at Birth Target Child	1967 WAIS IQ (FS)	1974 WAIS (FS)	1974 WRAT Reading Grade
Mother	1929	10	8	19	39	73	81	5.8
Father	1931	5	8	30	37			

Children		Sex	Year of Birth	1974 Tested IQ	1974 WRAT Reading Grade	1974 Actual Grade	Public School Placement
	1	M	1948				Moved
	2	F	1951				Moved
	3	F	1961	67	2.2	7.4	EMR
	4	F	1963	75	3.3	5.4	
	5	F	1966	92	1.6	2.4	
Target	6	F	1968	84		k.4	

shortly thereafter was divorced. After 7 years she remarried. She was 39 years old when Grace was born. For short periods she worked as a packer in a supply company and as an orderly, finally securing fulltime housekeeping work in a hospital. Her last reported earnings were $100 a week. She was interested in sewing and crocheting and started several times to take vocational courses in sewing and millinery, but did not complete any of them. She was a friendly person, affectionate toward her children and cordial to the Center staff.

During the first survey, Grace's mother expressed concern about the fact that her husband "didn't get too high in school." He had quit school after the fifth grade and started working when he was about 14 years old. He, however, tried to improve his reading and writing skills through a vocational course. He had come to Milwaukee when he was 19 and earned $140 weekly as a steel grinder in a factory.

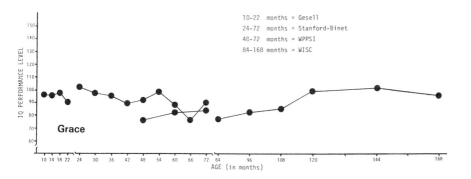

Grace's Stanford-Binet IQ, which started out at 102 when she was 24 months old, followed a generally declining pattern until age 66 months, when it reached 76, well below her group's average. Her next testing (at 72 months), however, placed her once more on her group's mean level.

Grace's Full Scale IQ, as measured by the Wechsler tests, was lower than the average for her own group from the ages of 48 through 84 months (range: 76 to 84). From the age of 96 months (8 years), however, she obtained higher scores. Her score of 95 at 168 months placed her only 9 points below the experimental mean and 9 points above the mean for her own group.

On the three MAT subtests, Grace's scores started out on grade level but did not increase appreciably during her second year in public school. On Language and Total Reading, but not on Total Math, Grace's scores rose during her third year to bring her performance closer to her grade level, but were depressed again during her fourth year in school. The reverse was true for her Total Math scores: While they remained low from the second to the third grade, her fourth grade scores were high enough to bring her within ½ year of the expected level for her actual grade.

As an infant, Grace was described by the testing staff as "ornery" and "hard to handle." Her quick temper was also noted by her teachers in public school, where she was described as more interested in crafts than in academic areas. Grace joined the school orchestra and participated in art projects, but like her sisters she had a difficult time learning to read.

Grace repeated the fifth grade. Over the middle school years, she continued to be an underachiever because, according to her teachers, she had poor study skills and experienced difficulty in following directions.

Hal
Family Characteristics

Hal's parents were born in Mississippi and came to Milwaukee when they were in their teens. His mother, one of ten children, completed a vocational training course in dress alteration in addition to 11 years of public school. For a while she worked in garment factories, cutting sweaters and making hats; but after being laid off twice she took a job as a part time cleaning person for state office buildings. She earned $75 a week. Her WAIS IQ was 70 at the time of the first survey and 72 at retest after 8 years. She read on a mid-fifth grade level.

Hal's father, 12 years older than his wife, dropped out of school after the eighth grade and worked as a laborer and as a shipping clerk in Mississippi. At 19 he moved to Milwaukee to work in a tannery. At this job, which he held for over 25 years, he earned $130 a week.

	Year of Birth	Highest Grade Completed	# Children Own Family	Age at Birth First Child	Age at Birth Target Child	1967 WAIS IQ (FS)	1974 WAIS (FS)	1974 WRAT Reading Grade
Mother	1945	11	10	19	22	70	72	5.6
Father	1933	8			34			

		Sex	Year of Birth	1974 Tested IQ	1974 WRAT Reading Grade	1974 Actual Grade	Public School Placement
Children	1	F	1964	100	2.9	4.2	
Target	2	M	1967	93	1.6	1.4	
	3	M	1968				
	4	M	1972				

Although Hal's parents were described initially as very cooperative and willing to participate in the program, his mother was very protective of Hal during the early part of the program and was one of the last mothers to trust the research staff. As an infant, Hal was also distrustful of strangers and until he came to know the examiner was one of the most difficult control children to test. Except on the learning tests, however, Hal proved to be one of the best performers in the control group. He also adjusted readily to public school and obtained higher achievement scores than most of the children in both groups.

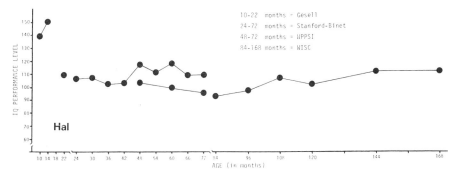

Hal had one of the highest IQ ranges of his group. His Stanford-Binet IQ, which ranged from 101.5 to 117 over 4 years of testing, was never less than 8 points above the average for his group. At only one point, however, did it approach the experimental group average.

Throughout the 11 years of Wechsler testing, Hal's Full Scale IQ was at least 7 points higher than the mean for his group. Although it showed a declining trend (103 to 93) from age 48 months through 84 months, it rose (range: 97 to 112) to above the average level of the experimental group. Hal demonstrated one of the best performances on the Metropolitan Achievement Test, exceeding the average for the experimental as well as his own group. His scores on all three subtests placed him on or above grade level throughout his first 4 years in school.

Hal attended a Fundamental School and responded to its requirements in a very satisfactory manner. He was described as "very well adjusted to school and learning," as a cooperative, independent worker, and as an excellent student. His grades consisted mainly of As and Bs.

In the seventh and tenth grades, Hal's performance on the Metropolitan Achievement Test continued to reflect the promise of the early years, with scores well above average in both Reading and Math. He received consistently good reports from his teachers and was described by them as a "high achiever."

Hank
Family Characteristics

	Year of Birth	Highest Grade Completed	# Children Own Family	Age at Birth First Child	Age at Birth Target Child	1967 WAIS IQ (FS)	1974 WAIS (FS)	1974 WRAT Reading Grade
Mother	1942	4		16	24	49	54	1.1
Father	1933	8		19	27			

Children		Sex	Year of Birth	1974 Tested IQ	1974 WRAT Reading Grade	1974 Actual Grade	Public School Placement
	1	F	1958	61	4.2	9.4	EMR
	2	M	1961	75	4.4	8.4	
	3	M	1962	77	3.3	6.4	
	4	M	1963	87	3.1	5.4	
	5	F	1965	88	4.1	3.4	
Target	6	M	1966	85	1.5	2.4	
	7	M	1968	92			

Hank was the sixth of seven children. Until the year before his birth, his family lived in Mississippi, where his father worked as a filling station attendant and his mother as a field hand. His mother, who quit school after fourth grade, picked cotton and hoed fields for a living. She married Hank's father and had her first child when she was 16 years old and her husband was 19. Seven years later they moved to Milwaukee, where Hank's father found work, first as a car jockey, then as a security guard. He earned $108 a week. Hank's mother worked for about 3 years as a housekeeper in a nursing home, but left her job because of poor health. At this time she and her husband separated. She and her children then started receiving welfare payments and food stamps.

Survey workers described the family as pleasant, friendly, and cooperative. Although the family home at the time of the survey was shabbily furnished and had no playthings for the children, the children were, in one examiner's words, "well behaved and well loved." Hank's mother was eager to participate in the program because she wanted her children to "have a better education." She herself could barely read, and her WAIS IQ of 49 (54 at retest) was one of the lowest in the program.

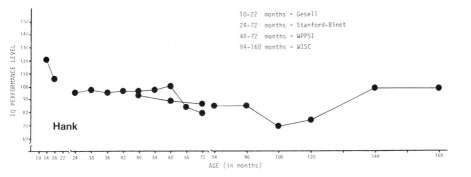

Hank's Stanford-Binet IQ, which ranged from 95 to 97 from age 24 months to 54 months, declined from 100 to 79 from the ages of 60 through 72 months.

Hank's Full Scale IQ, which declined gradually from 93 at 48 months to 85 at 84 and 96 months, dropped abruptly to 69 the following year. After scoring 74 at 120 months, his score rose 24 points to 98 at 144 and 168 months.

Throughout his first 4 years in public school, Hank performed not only below his own grade level but also below the average for his own group on all three MAT subtests. His best achievement scores (Total Math) indicated a lag of about 1 year. He was, however, about 3 years below grade level in Language and Total Reading achievement.

Hank did not do well in public school. A sensorimotor training program that he attended while in special kindergarten did not correct visual motor deficits, detected during psychological screening, including poor eye-hand coordination, reversals of letters and numbers, and poor reading readiness. He was then enrolled in a Title I language development program, where he showed some progress.

Additional problems were noted in school. Hank's clothing, for instance, was not adequate. Social workers several times explained the ESEA clothing program to his mother and assisted her in obtaining clothes for the children. An older brother had behavioral difficulties and was assigned to a Treatment Center. After third grade, Hank was given Extended Primary placement, where he had difficulties in reading and spelling.

Hank's score on the Metropolitan Achievement Test in the seventh grade showed little improvement in performance. From the tenth grade on, he received several suspension notices for tardiness and for frequent absences.

Ike
Family Characteristics

	Year of Birth	Highest Grade Completed	# Children Own Family	Age at Birth First Child	Age at Birth Target Child	1967 WAIS IQ (FS)	1974 WAIS (FS)	1974 WRAT Reading Grade
Mother	1940	9		18	27	72	Moved	
Father	1939	8		19	28		Moved	

Children		Sex	Year of Birth	1974 Tested IQ	1974 WRAT Reading Grade	1974 Actual Grade	Public School Placement
	1	F	1958				EMR (1966) Moved
	2	F	1961				Moved
	3	F	1962				Moved
	4	M	1964				Moved
Target	5	M	1967				Moved

Ike's mother, a ninth grader when she dropped out of school, was 27 years old when Ike was born. Her WAIS IQ was 72. She and her husband, together with their four children, had just moved to Milwaukee from Chicago, where she was a $60-a-week factory worker. Her husband, who was a self-employed handyman in Chicago, found fulltime employment in Milwaukee as a construction worker. One year older than his wife, he had had 8 years of school.

At the time of the survey, both parents expressed great interest in the intervention project. They were especially concerned about their eldest daughter, then 8 years old, who had been placed in a special (EMR) class. As Ike's mother described her, "she listen and understand but won't tell the teacher what she know." Shortly after becoming participants in the study, however, the family moved and efforts to reestablish contact with them failed.

Jennie
Family Characteristics

	Year of Birth	Highest Grade Completed	# Children Own Family	Age at Birth First Child	Age at Birth Target Child	1967 WAIS IQ (FS)	1974 WAIS (FS)	1974 WRAT Reading Grade
Mother	1944	12		17	23	68	72	3.2
Father	1946	11			21			

Children		Sex	Year of Birth	1974 Tested IQ	1974 WRAT Reading Grade	1974 Actual Grade	Public School Placement
	1	F	1961	46	2.0	6.4	EMR
	2	F	1963	51	1.5	5.4	EMR
	3	M	1964	78	1.6	4.4	
	4	M	1965	53	0.2	3.4	TMR
Target	5	F	1967	65	k.9	1.4	Head Start (1 year)

Jennie was the youngest of five living children, all born within a period of 6 years. The eldest daughter, Jennie's half-sister, was born when her mother was 17, and had two young children of her own. Jennie's parents were divorced and her mother remarried. The family, including the eldest daughter and her children, lived in a seven-room house. The house was described by Center staff as scantily furnished, noisy, and disorganized.

Both of Jennie's natural parents were born and raised in Wisconsin. Her mother, whose Full Scale IQ was 68 (72 at retest after 7 years), had completed the twelfth grade of school but read on a third grade level. Aside from babysitting jobs and a short period of working as a hotel maid before her first marriage, she had not worked outside the home. Jennie's father, who was a mechanic in a garage, had gone as far as the eleventh grade. During the 6 years of the program, he did not have a steady job and the family subsisted on AFDC and Title 19 payments. The family lived with Jennie's maternal grandmother, together with the grandmother's three daughters and two sons. Most of the time either Jennie's father or her mother was out of town or in jail, and Jennie's grandmother had to look after Jennie and her brothers and sisters. However, because she also had her own children and most of the rest of her 21 grandchildren to look after, she was unable to maintain a clean environment or provide adequate food and clothing for the children.

Soon after Jennie's parents were divorced, her mother married a machinist who was employed full time and earned $200 a week. The family then moved into its own house, where conditions improved, but not substantially. Social workers reported a history of abuse of Jennie and her siblings by the stepfather. On two occasions, the children were placed under the custody of the county Department of Public Welfare. All of the children seemed to have problems. A brother and a sister were epileptic, a condition described by the attending physician as inherited from their father. Another brother was hit by a car and suffered brain damage. He was placed in residential treatment and only came home on weekends. Jennie's two eldest sisters were in special EMR classes. Jennie's mother was often in trouble with the police and was arrested for "cutting a woman's throat."

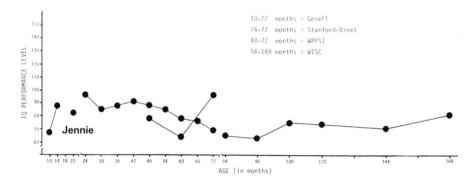

Jennie had one of the lowest IQs in the control group. Her Stanford-Binet IQ, which started out at 96 (the average for her group), began its decline at age 42 months and continued to the end of the Stanford-Binet testing at age 72 months, when it reached its lowest point of 69.

On the Wechsler tests Jennie showed one of the poorest Full Scale IQ ranges: With the exception of age 72 months, when she obtained a score of 96, Jennie consistently performed below her group's mean level. Again with the exception of age 72 months, her Full Scale IQ from 48 through 168 months ranged from 63 to 81. Since entering public school, her best score was 81 at 168 months (14 years).

On Total Reading, Jennie's poorest subtest on the MAT, her scores remained on approximately the mid-first grade level throughout her first 4 years in public school. Her performance on the Language subtest was only slightly better. On Total Math Jennie demonstrated better progress: Her fourth year score, although 1 year below her grade level, was average in relation to both her own group and the experimental group.

Jennie, like her siblings, attended school very irregularly. Her parents seemed to have made no effort to correct this problem. Jennie did poorly in school and did not seem to get along well with her peers. Her mother commented on her behavior at home as "smart mouth" and said Jennie's teachers described her as "mean."

Jennie's MAT scores in Reading dropped from average to below average when tested in the seventh and tenth grades. She maintained her score in Math in the seventh grade, but it dropped into the low range in the tenth grade. Her deportment record included some notices for fighting and tardiness.

Maggie
Family Characteristics

	Year of Birth	Highest Grade Completed	# Children Own Family	Age at Birth First Child	Age at Birth Target Child	1967 WAIS IQ (FS)	1974 WAIS (FS)	1974 WRAT Reading Grade
Mother	1926	4	11	24	41	59	69	2.2
Father	1922							

Children	Sex	Year of Birth	1974 Tested IQ	1974 WRAT Reading Grade	1974 Actual Grade	Public School Placement
1	M	1950				Moved
2	M	1951				EMR
3	M	1953	67(1969)			Moved
4	F	1956	83	2.4	11.4	Moved
Target 5	F	1967	87	k.5	1.4	

Maggie, the youngest of five living children, was born when her parents were in their 40s. Her siblings, who were 11 and 17 years her senior, no longer lived at home. The year before Maggie was born the family had moved to Milwaukee from Mississippi, where her parents had been farm workers. Her father, who worked as a machine cleaner in a foundry, was about 4 years older than his wife. Maggie's mother did not know how much education her husband had had, but according to her, "he don't have too much learning."

Maggie's mother came from a family of 11 children. She knew how old she was but could not seem to remember the dates on which she was born and married. Her Full Scale WAIS IQ was 59 on the first testing and 69 on the second, 6 years later. She reported the extent of her education as either 3 or 5 years; however, with her second grade reading level, she could barely read or write. At the start of the program she made the following comment on her children's and her own reading problems:

> None read too good, but the girl (the next youngest, then 11) reads better than any of them. I have them trying to read at home and the teachers tell me I can't read too good myself. But I didn't go to school or get no learning. I can hardly teach them, because I don't know how.

A nervous, sickly person, Maggie's mother was in and out of the hospital for various illnesses. In addition to having undergone surgery for gallstones and treatment for high blood pressure, back trouble, "female problems," and "nerves," she also complained that:

at times I can't see too good and I can't think too well. My remembrance is
awfully short. Sometime my sight seem to leave me. I can hardly get no
glasses. I don't have money.

Because of her health problems, she was unable to work outside the home
or attend to the household. Maggie's father used to do much of the housework
and also taught the children to cook and clean house. He sometimes came to
the Center to talk about family problems with some staff members. When
Maggie was 4 years old, her father left home and the family received help
through government programs, including welfare, food stamps, and Title 19.

Maggie lived in a six-room house with her mother, two teenage foster
sisters, and the young child of one of her foster sisters. The house was clean
but in great need of repair.

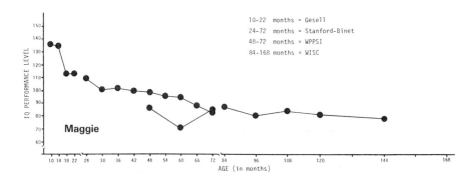

Maggie's Stanford-Binet IQ scores indicated a progressive decline from 109
at age 24 months to 82 at age 72 months. By 66 months her IQ, which was
higher than the control group average, had fallen 4 points below the mean. At
72 months she lost another 6 IQ points and thereafter remained below the corresponding mean for her group.

With the exception of a score of 70 at 60 months and 78 at 144 months,
Maggie's Full Scale IQ, with a range of 80 to 86, was within 1 to 6 points of the
control group average.

On the Total Reading subtest, Maggie's scores were slightly below the
average level for her group. Her Language subtest performance, however, was
erratic, with most of her scores considerably below her group's average. Her
Total Math scores, while close to her own group's average for the first 3 years,
dropped off during Maggie's fourth year in school. All of Maggie's fourth
grade scores showed her to be about 2 years below her grade level in achievement.

Maggie was a friendly child who cooperated well with and was liked by her
peers as well as her teachers. However, she did very poorly in academics and
was enrolled in exceptional education programs for learning disabilities and
for speech and language development. An older sibling was also enrolled at
one time in a special class for the educable mentally retarded.

In the middle school years, Maggie continued in a learning disabilities program, while her participation in the speech and language program was discontinued. When evaluated in the ninth grade, she was functioning at a mid-fourth grade level in reading and general information and a low fourth grade level in math. In spelling she functioned at a low third grade level.

Nathan
Family Characteristics

	Year of Birth	Highest Grade Completed	# Children Own Family	Age at Birth First Child	Age at Birth Target Child	1967 WAIS IQ (FS)	1974 WAIS (FS)	1974 WRAT Reading Grade
Mother	1932	4	6	15	35	52	58	k.4
Father	1932	6	2		35			

Children		Sex	Year of Birth	1974 Tested IQ	1974 WRAT Reading Grade	1974 Actual Grade	Public School Placement
	1	M	1947				Moved
	2	F	1954	62	4.6	12+	EMR
	3	F	1956	45	0.2		TMR
	4	M	1958	76	2.6	8.4	
	5	F	1960	88	2.8	7.4	EMR
	6	M	1962	69	2.0	6.4	
	7	M	1964	73	2.1	4.4	
Target	8	M	1967	84	1.4	1.4	

Nathan was the youngest of eight living children. Of the 14 children born in his family, five died soon after birth and one was killed in an accident. Nathan's mother, who had her first child when she was 15, married Nathan's father when they were both 17 years old. They moved from Mississippi to Milwaukee when they were 35 years old, the year Nathan was born. Here Nathan's father worked as a crane operator and his mother as a housekeeper in a nursing home. Together they earned about $9,000 a year. The family lived in a well kept ten-room house until Nathan was 8 years old, when his parents were divorced. His mother continued working, with welfare payments supplementing her earnings.

Neither of Nathan's parents went to school for very long: His father dropped out after the sixth grade and his mother after the fourth. His mother's WAIS IQ scores — 52 at first testing and 58 at retest — were among the lowest in the project and her reading grade level (kindergarten) was the lowest. All of Nathan's siblings also had exceptionally low reading levels. Two of his sisters were in special EMR classes, another sister was in a special TMR class.

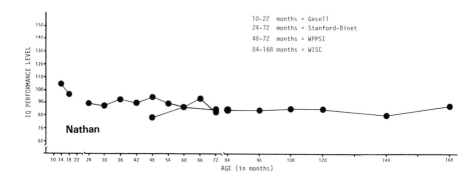

Nathan's Stanford-Binet IQ, which was generally below the average for his group, ranged from 82 to 94 over the 4-year testing period, with its lowest point at 72 months, immediately prior to his entrance into public school.

Starting out at 78, well below his group's average, Nathan's Full Scale IQ on the Wechsler tests rose and remained steady over the next 10 years, with its range of 80 to 87.

On the Metropolitan Achievement Tests, Nathan's best showing was in Total Math, where his scores for the first, second, and fourth grades were above his grade level. In particular, his fourth grade performance on this subtest was in advance of both his and the experimental group's by over 1½ years. On Total Reading his scores approximated grade level during his first 3 years but dropped back in his fourth grade to 2 years below grade expectancy. His performance on the Language subtest was poor in second and third grades but improved somewhat, although still 1½ years below his own grade level, in fourth grade.

Because Nathan was quiet and unaggressive, he seemed to have pleased his public school teachers more than his quicker peers in either group. In the lower and middle primary grades, his problems consisted mainly of his inability to pay attention in class; otherwise he was described as a "very sweet boy." Third grade was particularly successful, with his teacher describing him as "a very dependable, sweet child" whose behavior was excellent and who was "a pleasure to have in the classroom." Although his grades in all subjects suffered an abrupt drop in the fourth grade, where he was reading on a second grade level, he was promoted to the fifth grade at the end of the school year.

On testings conducted in the seventh and tenth grades, Nathan's MAT scores remained consistently low in Reading, while his scores in Math remained above average. His teachers described him as "slow, but hard working."

Oliver
Family Characteristics

	Year of Birth	Highest Grade Completed	# Children Own Family	Age at Birth First Child	Age at Birth Target Child	1967 WAIS IQ (FS)	1974 WAIS (FS)	1974 WRAT Reading Grade
Mother	1934	7	7	29	33	71	72	k.6
Father	1926	8		37	41			

		Sex	Year of Birth	1974 Tested IQ	1974 WRAT Reading Grade	1974 Actual Grade	Public School Placement
Children							
	1	F	1963	93	2.7	4.4	
	2	M	1965	104	2.3	3.4	
Target	3	M	1967	96	1.4	1.4	Head Start (½ year)
	4	F	1968	70			
	5	F	1969	92			

Oliver's parents had been sharecroppers in Tennessee before they moved to Milwaukee in search of better work. At the time his mother was 32 years old and his father was 40. They had been married 15 years and had two living children. In the next 3 years, three more children — Oliver and two daughters — were born. Oliver's parents separated when he was 4 years old.

Oliver's father, who had an eighth grade education, was a laborer in a foundry. He maintained contact with his family despite the separation. Oliver's mother was overweight and sickly. She suffered from high blood pressure and diabetes and, aside from a brief period when she ironed shirts for a laundry, did not feel well enough to work outside the home after her arrival in Milwaukee. Although she had completed the seventh grade, she read on a kindergarten level. Her WAIS IQ was 71 at the original testing and 72 at retest. Before their separation, Oliver's parents seemed unable to maintain a clean and organized household and were once referred to as "drinkers and bums" by their landlord. Conditions improved for the family after the separation. Oliver's mother and the children received welfare payments and other forms of aid and moved from their old apartment to a house. Although the house was still described by staff members as disorganized, with "many relatives in and out of the house," Oliver's mother was reported to be "trying hard to improve things for her family."

Oliver's Stanford-Binet IQ range of 98 to 112.5 was one of the highest in his group. His scores were highest from age 36 months through 48 months and thereafter declined to his initial level of 98. On all testings his scores exceeded the corresponding means for his group, although they were still considerably lower than the experimental group mean.

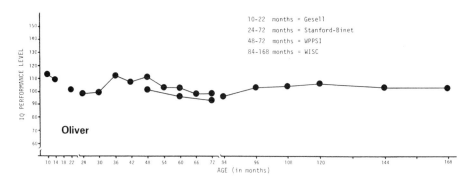

After an initial decline from 101 at 48 months to 93 at 72 months, Oliver's Full Scale IQ on the Wechsler tests rose to a range of 103 to 106 from the age of 96 months (8 years) through 168 months (14 years). The last two scores were 4 and 2 points higher than the corresponding experimental group means.

Oliver's school achievement, as measured by the MAT, was generally closer to the experimental group trend than to that of his own group; in fact, in his fourth year in school, his performance on all of these subtests exceeded that of the average experimental child by 1 year in Total Reading and ½ year in Language and Total Math. In terms of grade expectations, however, he was still ½ year behind on the last two subtests.

Oliver attended Head Start for ½ year before entering public school. A bright, lively child who was interested in athletics—his mother said he had received a trophy for basketball—Oliver also did fairly well academically in his first 4 years in school. His teachers, however, complained about his talkativeness and his lack of seriousness in his attitude toward classwork. One teacher quoted Oliver as saying he did not care about his grades; another wrote that Oliver "could be a good pupil if someone would get after him."

When tested in the seventh grade, Oliver maintained his scores on the Metropolitan Achievement Tests in the average range in both Reading and Math. However, his scores dropped into the low range when tested in the tenth grade. He also received several suspension notices for talking in class and disruptive behavior.

Pam
Family Characteristics

Pam lived with her parents and two brothers in a clean, well furnished house. Her parents, both from Georgia, moved to Milwaukee 4 years after they were married. Pam's father earned from $480 to $525 weekly as a foreman

	Year of Birth	Highest Grade Completed	# Children Own Family	Age at Birth First Child	Age at Birth Target Child	1967 WAIS IQ (FS)	1974 WAIS (FS)	1974 WRAT Reading Grade
Mother	1946	9	11	20	21	64	68	4.4
Father	1935		6	31	32			

Children		Sex	Year of Birth	1974 Tested IQ	1974 WRAT Reading Grade	1974 Actual Grade	Public School Placement
	1	M	1966	99	1.2	1.4	
Target	2	F	1967	86	1.2	1.4	Head Start (1 year)
	3	M	1977				

in a construction company. With his salary and the additional earnings brought in by his wife from part time babysitting jobs, the family was able to buy a house in a relatively good neighborhood.

Pam's mother was a pleasant woman who was described by her children's public school teachers as very cooperative and concerned with her children's progress in school. She dropped out of school after the ninth grade and read on a fourth grade level. Her Full Scale WAIS IQ, 64 at first testing, was 68 at retest after 7 years. She was 16 years old when she married Pam's father, who was 11 years older. Her first child was born when she was 20 and Pam was born less than 1 year later. A third child was born when Pam was 10.

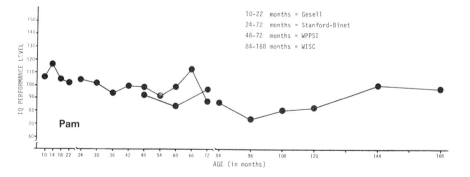

Pam's Stanford-Binet IQ, which ranged from 87 to 112, was generally on or above the average level for her group. She obtained her highest score (112) when she was 66 months old and her lowest score (87) when she was 72 months old.

11. The Children and Their Families

Before she entered school, Pam's Full Scale IQ on the Wechsler tests had a range of 83 to 96. In the first 2 years of school her IQ underwent a rapid decline, reaching its lowest point of 73 at age 96 months. Since then her Full Scale IQ rose once more; at last testing (168 months) it was 97, 7 points above her own group's average and 4 points below the experimental group mean for the same age.

Consistently behind her own group on the Total Reading and Total Math subtests of the MAT, Pam in fourth (Extended Primary) grade was about 2 years below her actual grade level on these two subtests. While she obtained better scores in Language, her performance on this subtest still placed her 1 year below her actual grade. Pam's MAT scores were in the low range when tested in the seventh and tenth grades, with her Total Math score dropping very low in the tenth grade.

Pam was an outgoing but rather sickly child who often complained of "not feeling well" at school. Before she was 5, she was hospitalized for meningitis. She also had a heart murmur that required medical attention. Before entering public school, she attended Head Start for 1 year. She was described as well behaved and cooperative by her teachers, but her academic progress was slow.

Paul
Family Characteristics

	Year of Birth	Highest Grade Completed	# Children Own Family	Age at Birth First Child	Age at Birth Target Child	1967 WAIS IQ (FS)	1974 WAIS (FS)	1974 WRAT Reading Grade
Mother	1947	12		19	20	71	83	6.8
Father		12						

	Sex	Year of Birth	1974 Tested IQ	1974 WRAT Reading Grade	1974 Actual Grade	Public School Placement
Children						
1	F	1966	92(1970)			
Target 2	M	1967	86			

The younger of two children, Paul was born when his mother was 20 years old. Soon after his birth, his parents separated. When he was 5 years old, Paul and his sister were sent to live with their maternal grandmother in Louisiana, where they stayed for 2 years. The family then moved out of the city and back again several times.

Little was known of Paul's father besides his being born in Wisconsin and completing the twelfth grade. Paul's mother, who had also completed the twelfth grade, had the highest reading grade level (6.8) of all the mothers in the program. Although her original WAIS IQ was 71, her retest score 6½ years later was 83, again the highest among all the mothers. Paul, unlike most of the control children, was enrolled in a nursery school before entering kindergarten.

As a young child, Paul was alert and easy to work with and was one of the better test performers in the control group. He had a Stanford-Binet IQ range that placed him closer to the experimental group than to his own group. His lowest score, at 24 months, was 105 and his highest was 123 at 48 months.

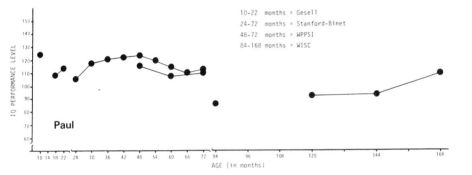

On the Wechsler tests Paul's Full Scale IQ equalled the experimental group mean from age 48 to 72 months. After his entry into public school, his score dropped to 86, which was closer to, although higher than, the control group mean for that age (84 months). Except for two missing scores (at 96 and 108 months), his scores rose steadily to a final score of 109 at 168 months, which was 8 points above the corresponding experimental mean score.

The irregularity of Paul's presence in the city did not permit administration of the MAT over consecutive years. From the scanty data available, it seemed that Paul's best achievement performance was in Total Math, where in third grade he performed on grade level. In contrast, his reading achievement for the same grade was only equal to the mean for his own group, which was ½ year below actual grade level.

Paul seemed to have some adjustment problems in public school. Although he was described by his teachers as enthusiastic and motivated, he also seemed to be quite aggressive. He was suspended from school several times because of fighting with other children and "making threatening, disrespectful comments" to a teacher. In a teacher's words, Paul "has high social reasoning, a concern for justice, and leadership ability" and "when (he) feels or sees injustice he barges in head and fists first." These problems impeded Paul's academic progress as well.

Paul's scores on the MAT dropped to the low range in both Reading and Math when tested in the seventh grade. His school attendance in the eighth grade was very unsatisfactory and he received several suspension notices. An alternative program was recommended for him when he was in the eleventh grade.

Penny
Family Characteristics

	Year of Birth	Highest Grade Completed	# Children Own Family	Age at Birth First Child	Age at Birth Target Child	1967 WAIS IQ (FS)	1974 WAIS (FS)	1974 WRAT Reading Grade
Mother	1940	8		18	27	71	Moved	
Father								

Children	Sex	Year of Birth	1974 Tested IQ	1974 WRAT Reading Grade	1974 Actual Grade	Public School Placement
1	M	1958				Moved
Target 2	F	1967				Moved

Penny's mother stopped going to school after the eighth grade. Two years before Penny was born, she and her husband separated and she moved to Milwaukee with her son, then 8 years old. With her earnings of $1.15 an hour as a shortorder cook, she supported herself, her son, and Penny. She had a WAIS IQ of 71.

Penny was described by Center workers as "happy and well cared for," and her mother as having a "decent, good attitude toward a difficult life." Shortly before enrollment in the project, the family moved and efforts on the part of the Center to reestablish contact were unsuccessful.

Ted
Family Characteristics

Ted was the younger of two children. His sister, 2 years older, was placed in a special EMR class. His mother, who grew up in Wisconsin and was also in a

	Year of Birth	Highest Grade Completed	# Children Own Family	Age at Birth First Child	Age at Birth Target Child	1967 WAIS IQ (FS)	1974 WAIS (FS)	1974 WRAT Reading Grade
Mother	1947		3	18	20	61	66	2.6
Father	1944		14	21	23			

		Sex	Year of Birth	1974 Tested IQ	1974 WRAT Reading Grade	1974 Actual Grade	Public School Placement
Children							
	1	F	1965	57	1.4	2.4	EMR
Target	2	M	1967		1.2	k.4	

special EMR class, had a second grade reading level and a Full Scale WAIS IQ that was 61 at first testing and 66 at retest. Ted's father, born in Arkansas, was one of 14 children. Neither parent was working: Ted's mother received social security payments; the children and their father received welfare payments and food stamps.

Living conditions at the family home were described by staff members as squalid and miserable. Ted's father, an alcoholic, frequently subjected his wife to ridicule and physical abuse. As an infant, Ted was often left alone in his bed or on the floor during all night drinking parties. Because of their parents' inability to meet their basic health, nourishment, and emotional needs, Ted and his sister were removed from their parents' home and placed in foster homes by the Department of Public Welfare. Ted was 3 years old at the time. After 2 years he was returned to his parents' home but was kept under the supervision of the Department of Public Welfare for another 2 years. The family was also helped in its homemaking and financial affairs by the Jewish Vocational Services.

Ted's Stanford-Binet IQ scores were among the lowest in the project. After the first and lowest score of 64, his IQ range remained between 74.9 and 80.5,

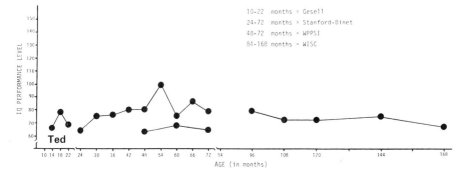

with two exceptions. These exceptions occurred at age 54 months, when he scored 99, and at age 66 months, when his score was 86.

Ted's preschool Wechsler tests indicated a Full Scale range of 63 to 68. After his entry into public school his scores improved, reaching a high of 79 at age 96 months (8 years). On his last testing (168 months), however, his Full Scale IQ dropped to 67.

From the first through the third grade, Ted's MAT scores on the Language and Total Math subtests indicated achievement equal to or above the mean for his group. His third grade Total Math score in fact exceeded the experimental group mean. In fourth (Extended Primary) grade, however, his scores dropped to almost 1 year below those of the children in his group and almost 2 years below his actual grade. His Total Reading scores were on grade level and average for his group during his first 2 years in school; however, he did not make any progress in the next 2 years. His fourth year performance on this subtest was lower than average for both groups and 2 years below his grade level.

Ted and his sister were not being properly attended to. Ted came to school dirty and inadequately clothed. Once he was sent home because his clothes had not been changed for some time and smelled strongly of urine. Ted was an extremely withdrawn and passive boy who seldom talked to his peers. He was referred for supportive services by his teacher because of his poor self-concept, his lack of friendship at school, and his weak academic skills. A psychologist's report stated that while Ted did not seem truly retarded, placement in a program for the educable mentally retarded could prove very beneficial for him, because he needed "much attention, extra help, and personal contact . . . (and) much success experience to help him develop a sense of adequacy."

In the sixth grade, Ted was reported as not making progress. A psychological evaluation found he was extremely withdrawn, especially with peers, and recommended he be placed in a program for the emotionally disturbed.

Wendy
Family Characteristics

Wendy was the only child in this two-parent household. Her three half-brothers, her father's children by a previous marriage, did not live at home. Wendy's mother earned $73 a week as a fish packer in a food processing plant. Before moving to Milwaukee, she worked in Mississippi for 4 years as a full time cleaning woman in a school at a salary of $20 a week. A high school graduate, she read on a fourth grade level. Her WAIS IQ was 65 at first testing and 66 at retest. She was 25 years old when she married Wendy's father and 26 when Wendy was born.

	Year of Birth	Highest Grade Completed	# Children Own Family	Age at Birth First Child	Age at Birth Target Child	1967 WAIS IQ (FS)	1974 WAIS (FS)	1974 WRAT	Reading Grade
Mother	1940	12	3	26	26	65	66	4.8	
Father	1930	12	4	36	36				

		Sex	Year of Birth	1974 Tested IQ	1974 WRAT Reading Grade	1974 Actual Grade	Public School Placement
Children							
Target	1	F	1966	83	2.0	2.4	

Wendy's father, 10 years older than his wife, was in Milwaukee for some time before he met Wendy's mother. At the time he had a full time job at a foundry and also worked evenings and weekends at a filling station. Eventually he obtained a $220-a-week position with a large assembly plant as a welder. The family lived in a very clean and well kept home. Although Wendy's parents were described by Center workers as very friendly and cooperative, Wendy's father was not consistent in giving the research staff permission to examine Wendy's school records. As a result, our knowledge of Wendy's progress in school was sketchy at best.

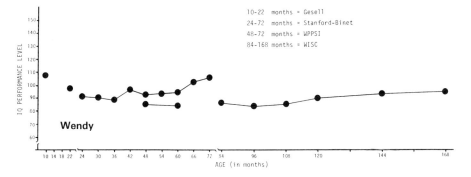

Wendy's Stanford-Binet IQ, which was several points below the control group mean during the first year of testing, rose to match her group's average in the next 2 years, eventually surpassing it by as much as 18 points. Her scores from the ages of 24 through 36 months ranged from 88 to 91. In the next four testings her IQ ranged from 92 to 96, and in the final two tests she had scores of 102 and 105.

Wendy maintained a fairly even performance level on the Wechsler intelligence tests, with a Full Scale IQ range of 83 to 86 from the age of 48 months through 108 months. Her last test, at 168 months, showed a rise to 94. These scores were on or above the average for her own group.

Wendy's achievement, as measured by the MAT, was generally better than that of the others in her group, although slightly behind that of the experimental children. Like the average child in each group, she performed on grade level during her first 2 years but started falling behind in her third year. Overall, her scores for the fourth grade indicated achievement slightly over 1 year below her grade level, with Language as her poorest subtest.

From the few school records available, it seemed that Wendy did fairly well in school. She apparently had some academic difficulty during fourth grade, when her teacher commented on her "lack of basic skills" in all areas. She was, however, promoted to the fifth grade and made satisfactory progress in all subjects.

Wilma
Family Characteristics

	Year of Birth	Highest Grade Completed	# Children Own Family	Age at Birth First Child	Age at Birth Target Child	1967 WAIS IQ (FS)	1974 WAIS (FS)	1974 WRAT Reading Grade
Mother	1940	8	15	17	27	65	67	3.2
Father	1937	10	7		30			

Children		Sex	Year of Birth	1974 Tested IQ	1974 WRAT Reading Grade	1974 Actual Grade	Public School Placement
	1	F	1957	86	6.5	10.4	
	2	F	1959	99	16.2	9.4	
	3	M	1961	83	2.4	6.4	
	4	F	1963	94	5.7	5.4	
	5	M	1965	95	2.1	3.4	
Target	6	F	1967	75	1.0	1.4	

Wilma, a lively, rather aggressive child who, as a Center staff member once observed, liked to "snap her fingers and twist and bump and grind," was the youngest of six children. Her parents separated a few years after her birth and her mother remarried.

Wilma's stepfather was a welder who earned $180 a week. Her mother had a $95-a-week job as a laundry worker. An eighth grader when she dropped out of school, Wilma's mother read on a third grade level and had a WAIS IQ of 65 (67 at retest). She was 20 years old and had already had two of her six children when she married Wilma's father. She had Wilma when she was 27 years old.

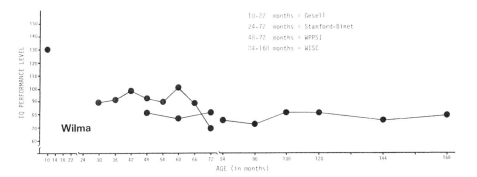

On all but two of the Stanford-Binet testings Wilma's scores were below the mean for her group. Her score at age 72 months (69) was especially low. She obtained her highest scores, 98 and 100, at 42 and 60 months.

On the Wechsler tests, Wilma's Full Scale IQ, with its range of 72 to 81, was consistently lower than the mean for her group. She obtained her lowest score of 72 during her second year in school.

Like the rest of her group, Wilma seemed to be at least 1 year below actual grade level in school achievement as measured by the MAT. As was generally true of her group, her poorest performance was on Total Reading and her best on Total Math. In addition, Wilma surpassed her group's average performance on the Language subtest for the fourth grade.

Progress was slow in public school for Wilma, according to her teachers, who described her as a slow learner and a poor reader. Her aggressiveness contributed to her problems. A referral for psychological and school social work services, submitted when she was in the second grade, contained this description of Wilma:

> Very aggressive. Often threatens other children. Continual rule breaker. Doesn't like corrections and becomes belligerent. Slow learner. L4 (Easy Primer) reader.

When tested in the seventh grade, Wilma's MAT scores were average in Math and below average in Reading. On the whole, she was doing reasonably well in school.

Woody
Family Characteristics

	Year of Birth	Highest Grade Completed	#Children Own Family	Age at Birth First Child	Age at Birth Target Child	1967 WAIS IQ (FS)	1974 WAIS (FS)	1974 WRAT Reading Grade
Mother	1947	9	13	18	20	73	75	2.8
Father	1947				20			

		Sex	Year of Birth	1974 Tested IQ	1974 WRAT Reading Grade	1974 Actual Grade	Public School Placement
Children							
	1	F	1965	69	0.7	2.4	Special class all day
Target	2	M	1967	72	0.8	k.4	
	3	M	1970				

Woody was born when both of his parents were 20 years old. He had an older half-sister who was in a special EMR class and a younger brother. Woody's mother was born in Mississippi, the fourth of 13 children. Although she had completed the ninth grade, she read on a level slightly below the third grade. Her WAIS IQ at initial testing was 73; at retest 6½ years later it was 75. She was 18 years old when she had her first child. The following year she moved to Milwaukee, where she married Woody's father. They separated when Woody was 2 years old. Woody's mother was unemployed and the family was supported through welfare and AFDC payments and food stamps.

As a young child, Woody was an extremely quiet boy who would not talk to teachers; consequently, it was difficult to assess his early language performance.

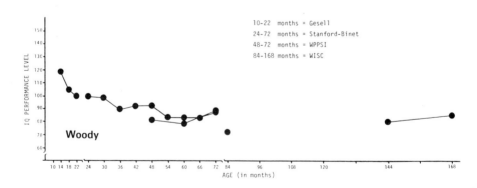

Woody's Stanford-Binet declined, in stages from 98.9 at 24 months to a range of 88.5 to 92 from 36 to 48 months, to 83 from 54 through 66 months. On his last Stanford-Binet testing (at 72 months), however, his IQ rose to 87, equalling the group mean.

On the Wechsler tests Woody's Full Scale IQ ranged from 78 to 88 from 48 through 72 months. After his entrance into public school, he took the test only three times. His scores ranged from 72 (at 84 months) to 85 (at 168 months), which was 6 points below the average for his group.

The available MAT scores showed Woody as consistently behind his own group on the Total Reading and Language subtests and on the same level as his group on Total Math, at least during the first and fourth grades. On this subtest he, like the average child in the project, was 1 year behind his actual grade level.

Before going on to the first grade, Woody went to special kindergarten where he participated in a language development program. Despite this added help, he had a great deal of difficulty in first grade, especially in reading. Woody's family moved and his school records were unavailable to us.

LOW RISK CONTRAST CHILDREN

The low risk contrast group originally consisted of ten children who, like those in the experimental and control groups, belonged to black families who lived in Milwaukee's inner core, but whose mothers had WAIS Full Scale IQs over 100. Early in the program, we lost contact with two families who moved out of state. Of the remaining eight children, two were brothers. Although still another family moved out of the state before the conclusion of the program, we were able to maintain contact with the parents and to test their child occasionally.

The seven mothers who remained with the program were 23 to 32 years old at the start of the study and had IQs that ranged from 106 to 118. Six of them were married, two of whom became divorced. Unlike the high risk mothers, all of the mothers in this group had at least a high school education when they entered the program, one had a junior college degree (AA), and at least three others had had from 1 to 3 years of college, vocational or in-service training courses. Five were employed outside the home, mainly in government offices, with monthly salaries that ranged from approximately $543 to $1,030.

Although most of the mothers in this group were eager to cooperate with us in the study, our contact with them was necessarily minimal, in some cases not going beyond the testing of the children. The following account, which includes family background and observations on the children's test performance, is therefore brief and general.

Bess was the eighth of nine children in a two-parent family. Her mother, who had a WRAT reading grade of 14.4 and had 2 years of college course work in sociology, earned $987 monthly as a job specialist, a position she said her college training enabled her to obtain. Bess' mother had a WAIS IQ of 106 initially and 109 at retest. Bess' father, a self-employed house painter, earned approximately $200 a week. The family received Title 19 aid for the children over 6 years. Six of the nine children in the family lived with their parents in their eight-room house.

Gabriel was an only child when his parents joined the program. His mother, who was a third year university student, was a broadcaster for a local TV station. When he was about 4 years old, he and his parents moved to Pennsylvania, where his sister was born the following year. The family then periodically returned to Milwaukee. On each of these visits, Gabriel's mother made it a point to get in touch with the Center staff so that Gabriel could be tested. An outgoing and articulate woman who seemed to be very much involved with her children, she listed her occupation as "full time housewife and mother." Her WAIS Full Scale IQ was 109. Gabriel's father, who had a degree in Business Management in addition to a BA, earned over $25,000 annually as Community Relations Director for a TV station in Pittsburgh. The family owned a seven-room townhouse condominium.

Mary and her sister, who was a year older, lived in a four-room apartment with their mother. Their parents were divorced when Mary was 8 years old, and the family received aid for several years through food stamps, welfare checks, and Title 19. Mary's mother, who had a WAIS IQ of 108 (110 at initial testing 7 years earlier), held an Associate in Arts degree but was unemployed. She was an emergency room technician, a student position that terminated when she graduated. She was hospitalized for a nervous breakdown and was in therapy for some time. She seemed bitter about being unable to find a job despite her education and said her college degree had not helped her in any way.

Robert lived with his mother and three half-siblings in a three-bedroom apartment. Another half-sister was married and lived in her own apartment. The older children were Robert's mother's children from a previous marriage. Robert's mother and father were not married, but paternity was legally established and Robert saw his father frequently. Both of Robert's parents were high school graduates. His mother's initial IQ of 109 dropped to 103 at retest. She had a reading grade of 8.3. Throughout Robert's childhood, his mother worked at various jobs, including typist and cashier. Her last position was as a teletype operator.

Tanya was the youngest of six children in what was reported as a highly intelligent family with strong sociopolitical commitments. Her mother had a WAIS IQ of 113. Her father taught at a college in the city. Although her parents were cooperative about allowing Tanya to be tested as a young child, they were concerned about her privacy and set an age limit beyond which they refused to allow further testing or release any information about their child. Consequently our knowledge of Tanya — the brightest of the children in the study — did not go beyond first grade in public school.

Warren and his younger brother Weldon lived with their parents and three older siblings in a well furnished eight-room house. A stepbrother and a stepsister, both older, did not live at home. Both of their parents were employed full time: Their father earned $1,200 monthly as a "cutter" and their mother worked for the county as a financial assistant at a monthly salary of $1,030. Aside from her full time employment, the children's mother also did part time work with a tax preparation company. At the start of the study her WAIS Full Scale IQ was 114; at retest it was 104. She had a WRAT reading grade level of 13.5. In addition to her high school education, she had completed a training course in tax preparation.

Whitney was an only child. His parents were divorced, and Whitney and his mother moved from their house into a two-bedroom apartment. Whitney's mother, who had a WAIS IQ of 118 (both testings) and a reading grade of 12.6, joined the Center staff as a paraprofessional teacher at the start of the project and later became the parent coordinator. She participated in seminars and received on-the-job training in preparation for her work. After termination of the project, she did clerical work in government agencies and was with the State Veterans Administration as a records clerk. She was actively involved in church and PTA activities.

Bess
Family Characteristics

	Year of Birth	*Highest Grade Completed*	*# Children Own Family*	*Age at Birth First Child*	*Age at Birth Target Child*	*1967 WAIS IQ (FS)*	*1974 WAIS (FS)*	*1974 WRAT Reading Grade*
Mother	1939	12 +	3	19	26	106	109	14.4
Father	1939	12	4	19	26			

		Sex	*Year of Birth*	*1974 Tested IQ*	*1974 WRAT Reading Grade*	*1974 Actual Grade*	*Public School Placement*
Children							
	1	M	1958	88			
	2	F	1959				
	3	M	1960	91			
	4	M	1962				
	5	M	1963				
	6	M	1965				
	7	F	1965				
Target	8	F	1968	93			
	9	M	1971	88			

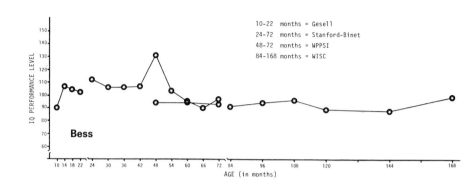

Gabriel
Family Characteristics

	Year of Birth	Highest Grade Completed	# Children Own Family	Age at Birth First Child	Age at Birth Target Child	1967 WAIS IQ (FS)	1974 WAIS (FS)	1974 WRAT Reading Grade
Mother	1944	12 + 3	2	22	22	109		
Father	1944	12 + 5	2					

		Sex	Year of Birth	1974 Tested IQ	1974 WRAT Reading Grade	1974 Actual Grade	Public School Placement
Children							
Target	1	M	1967	109			
	2	F	1973				

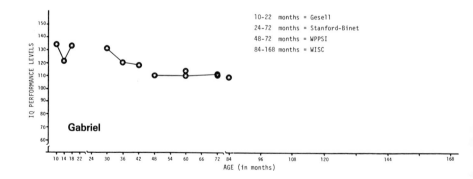

Mary
Family Characteristics

	Year of Birth	Highest Grade Completed	# Children Own Family	Age at Birth First Child	Age at Birth Target Child	1967 WAIS IQ (FS)	1974 WAIS (FS)	1974 WRAT Reading Grade
Mother	1940	12+1	3	26	27	110	108	
Father								

Children		Sex	Year of Birth	1974 Tested IQ	1974 WRAT Reading Grade	1974 Actual Grade	Public School Placement
	1	F	1966				
Target	2	F	1967	117			

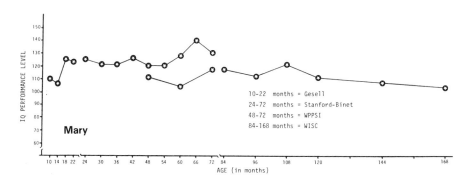

Mary

10-22 months = Gesell
24-72 months = Stanford-Binet
48-72 months = WPPSI
84-168 months = WISC

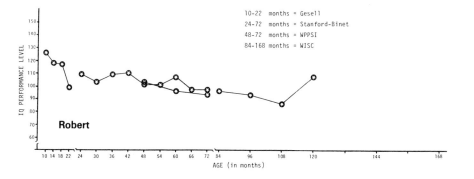

Robert

10-22 months = Gesell
24-72 months = Stanford-Binet
48-72 months = WPPSI
84-168 months = WISC

Robert
Family Characteristics

	Year of Birth	Highest Grade Completed	# Children Own Family	Age at Birth First Child	Age at Birth Target Child	1967 WAIS IQ (FS)	1974 WAIS (FS)	1974 WRAT Reading Grade
Mother	1934	12		22	33	109	103	8.3
Father	1931	12+3			36			

	Sex	Year of Birth	1974 Tested IQ	1974 WRAT Reading Grade	1974 Actual Grade	Public School Placement
Children						
1	F	1956				
2	M	1957	105			
3	F	1959	117			
4	M	1961	109			
Target 5	M	1967	96			

Tanya
Family Characteristics

	Year of Birth	Highest Grade Completed	# Children Own Family	Age at Birth First Child	Age at Birth Target Child	1967 WAIS IQ (FS)	1974 WAIS (FS)	1974 WRAT Reading Grade
Mother	1940	12+2	4	20	27	113		
Father	1939	12+3	5	21	28			

	Sex	Year of Birth	1974 Tested IQ	1974 WRAT Reading Grade	1974 Actual Grade	Public School Placement
Children						
1	F	1960				
2	F	1961				
3	F	1963				
4	F	1964				
5	F	1966				
Target 6	F	1967	125			

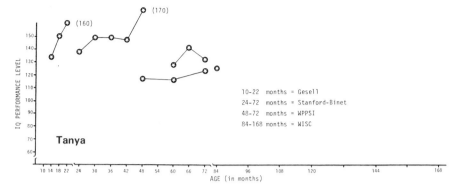

```
10-22  months = Gesell
24-72  months = Stanford-Binet
48-72  months = WPPSI
84-168 months = WISC
```

Tanya

AGE (in months)

Warren
Weldon
Family Characteristics

	Year of Birth	Highest Grade Completed	# Children Own Family	Age at Birth First Child	Age at Birth Target Child	1967 WAIS IQ (FS)	1974 WAIS (FS)	1974 WRAT Reading Grade
Mother	1943	12 +	5	17	23	114	104	13.5
Father	1942	8	10	18	24			

Children		Sex	Year of Birth	1974 Tested IQ	1974 WRAT Reading Grade	1974 Actual Grade	Public School Placement
	1	M	1960	95(1973)			
	2	F	1961	89(1973)			
	3	M	1964	88(1973)			
Target	4	M	1966	112			
Target	5	M	1967	93			

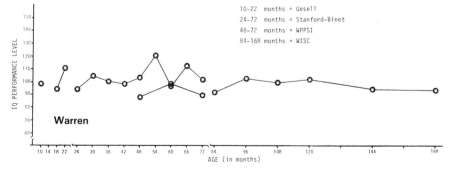

```
10-22  months = Gesell
24-72  months = Stanford-Binet
48-72  months = WPPSI
84-168 months = WISC
```

Warren

AGE (in months)

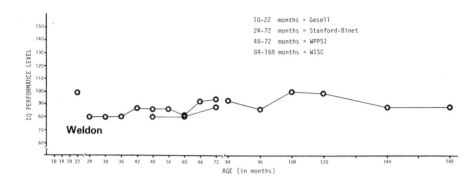

10-22 months = Gesell
24-72 months = Stanford-Binet
48-72 months = WPPSI
84-168 months = WISC

Weldon

Whitney
Family Characteristics

	Year of Birth	Highest Grade Completed	# Children Own Family	Age at Birth First Child	Age at Birth Target Child	1967 WAIS IQ (FS)	1974 WAIS (FS)	1974 WRAT Reading Grade
Mother	1942	12 +		24	24	118	118	12.6
Father								

	Sex	Year of Birth	1974 Tested IQ	1974 WRAT Reading Grade	1974 Actual Grade	Public School Placement
Children						
Target 1	M	1966	102			

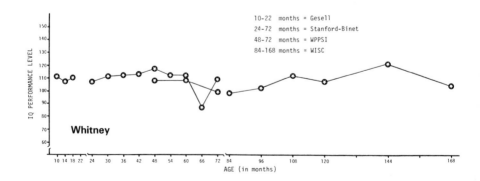

10-22 months = Gesell
24-72 months = Stanford-Binet
48-72 months = WPPSI
84-168 months = WISC

Whitney

IQ

On the average, the children in this group demonstrated IQs that ranged from 107 to 118 on the Stanford-Binet and from 97 to 103 on the Wechsler tests. These scores were from 8 to 13 points lower than the corresponding mean scores for the experimental children on the Stanford-Binet and WPPSI, but were very close to the experimental group mean on the WISC. Of these children, the two whose scores generally equalled or surpassed the experimental children's scores were Tanya and Mary. Tanya's IQ, which ranged from 128 to 170 on the Stanford-Binet and from 116 to 125 on the Wechsler tests, was the highest among all the children in the study. Mary's Stanford-Binet ranged from 120 to 125 from age 24 through 48 months and from 117 to 140 from age 54 through 72 months. On the WPPSI/WISC her Full Scale IQ from 72 months onward ranged from 103 to 121.

With one exception, the other children in this low risk group had Stanford-Binet IQs lower than those of the experimental children but higher than those of the control group. The one exception was Warren, whose scores did not equal the control group mean until he was 66 months old.

On the WPPSI/WISC tests, the low risk contrast children improved their scores on the whole while in public school, approaching or exceeding the experimental group mean by the time they reached the third grade. An exception was Bess, whose Full Scale IQ at 144 months was 88, 1 point below the control group mean.

School Achievement (MAT)

Of the six children for whom MAT results were available, three (Bess, Mary, and Whitney) had scores that indicated achievement at or above grade level, and three (Robert, Warren, and Weldon) showed scores that placed their achievement below their actual grade level. The three children who did well on the MAT obtained their highest grades on the Total Reading and Language subtests. By the end of the fourth grade, Whitney and Mary had Total Reading scores placing them 2 years and 1 year, respectively, above their grade levels and Language scores 1 year above grade level. In Total Math each of them scored ½ year below their actual grade. Bess, for whom fourth year scores were not available, placed on the mid-third grade level on all three subtests. Bess, Mary, and Whitney then showed a drop in MAT scores to grade level on Total Reading and Total Math when tested in the seventh and tenth grades.

The three children whose MAT results show below grade level achievement had scores generally on or below the control group average. Warren's fourth grade scores on all three subtests were at a mid-second grade level; his brother, Weldon, had much lower fourth grade scores (mid-first grade) on Total Reading and Total Math, but was only 1 year behind in Language. However, he achieved grade level scores when tested in the tenth grade in both Total Reading and Total Math. Robert, like Warren, had mid-second grade scores on his fourth year MAT.

School Adjustment

Like the children in the experimental and control groups, the low risk contrast children had varying degrees of success in public school. Of the eight children in this group, the only two about whom there were no reported difficulties in academic or social adjustment were Gabriel, whose family moved out of the state, and Tanya, whose progress her parents did not permit us to follow. Gabriel's mother reported that he was doing very well in school. The Comprehensive Test of Basic Skills, which Gabriel took in the third grade, placed him on or above the national average in all areas. His best performance was on Mathematics Concepts, where he placed in the 89th percentile. Tanya's first grade teacher described her as a "very strong student in all subjects—a pleasure to have in the classroom."

Among the remaining six children, Mary had the best reports from her teachers. From kindergarten through Upper Primary she was described as a very good student with excellent language skills who "talked too much at times." Her fourth grade teacher, while noting her "good work," also observed that she was "moody." At about this time, her mother requested psychiatric services for her. This was the only indication that Mary was going through some emotional difficulties, there being no further mention of it either from her mother or from her fifth grade teacher, who said only that she "needs work in self-control" and "must learn to take direction from adults." Mary had average to excellent grades in all areas, particularly in reading and language, and apparently did not need any special educational programming.

The only other child not placed in any special program was Weldon. According to his teachers, he added much to class discussion because he spoke well and had an excellent vocabulary; however, he was also described as an "attention-getting child" who needed close supervision and did not make use of his ability. He had several disciplinary reports—including two suspensions—for fighting, bad language, and uncooperative behavior, and was given an Extended Primary placement despite grades of Cs in all his Upper Primary subjects.

The four other low risk children had special help in one form or another. Three of these children (Bess, Robert, and Warren) received help for academic difficulties, and one (Whitney) was in a psychoeducational program because of emotional problems.

Although she did well on the MAT, Bess was found by the Title I Supportive Services Team to have academic deficits of 1 to 2 years and was enrolled in a remedial program to improve sensorimotor and cognitive skills during fourth grade. Her teacher described her as "quiet, conscientious, shy with peers . . . introverted."

In his first year in public school, Robert was observed to have problems learning to read and was referred to a multidisciplinary team the next year when he continued to have academic difficulties. Although he was seen by the team as "a happy boy with adequate self-concept and an outgoing personality" who "showed no evidence of emotional disturbance," he was also found to be "lagging nearly 3 years below expectancy for a child of his age, intelligence, and experience." The team concluded that while his emotional, social, and physical needs were adequately met by his parents and extended family, he was "deprived in other areas, such as being read to, which helps to develop reading-readiness skills," and therefore recommended Robert's placement in a speech and language disabilities program.

Warren had had a severe and permanent hearing loss in his right ear since birth, but it was not officially diagnosed until he was 9 years old and in third grade in public school. An earlier referral for psychological service, made while Warren was in kindergarten, stated that Warren did "not appear to be learning in the classroom, a small group, or even in a 1:1 relation," but that his vision, hearing, and physical health seemed normal and was "not felt to be the cause of (his) inability to remember basic skills or follow simple directions." He had particular difficulty with reading and language. After his hearing problem was detected, Warren was assigned to a speech and language disabilities program. Although he was described as "not a discipline problem," Warren, like his brother, was the subject of numerous disciplinary reports, for such reasons as fighting and "speaking disrespectfully to his teacher."

During Whitney's first 2 years in school, he was described as a very capable student who enjoyed school and was cooperative and well liked. Toward the end of second grade, however, his teacher, while still praising his academic work, complained that he was "very talkative, very sassy, and disrespectful." As his behavior began to affect his grades, he was enrolled in psychoeducational therapy at his mother's request. His grades improved and he completed more of his school assignments. All of Whitney's teachers stated that he had good academic potential, but that his learning was hampered by his aggressiveness and lack of self-control.

12
Epilogue: Commentary

The etiology of cultural-familial mental retardation remains a complex puzzle, but it is clear from two decades of early intervention research that early intellectual development is not fixed, is mutable, and can be modified by manipulating experience. The Milwaukee study results suggest that the environment is not effectively mediated by the low IQ, low verbal skilled mother and that the impoverished psychosocial early microenvironment in the home she creates is a major factor associated with her offspring's declining IQ performance. Through early intervention, this effect can be mitigated, thus preventing IQ declines.

In each developmental period, however, subsequent to infancy (0 to 3 years), although it is possible to maintain normal IQs, it also seems that this can be accomplished only with increasing difficulty. To the extent that this is true, it suggests most simply that there are limits to the performance benefits we can expect from an early intervention treatment. The question that remains is what causes these limits, that is to say, of course, in addition to ability. For example, there is probably some limit to performance transfer across developmental periods when children are trained on tasks within one developmental age period for a narrow set of aptitudes (viz., for IQ tests). The limit is not the aptitudes per se but the extent to which they relate to cognitive skills required for successful performance in addition to success on IQ tests, particularly information gathering and processing skills. In addition, because performance transfer of aptitudes is dependent on the nature of the home support system as well as school, there are limits to performance transfer between developmental phases due to retardation of skill development induced by social and emotional pressures in the home (Garber, 1982). Induced retardation limits the development of information gathering and processing skills. The retardation is induced by the psychosocial characteristics of the home microenvironment which actively interfere with the development of learning mechanisms necessary for intellectual growth. As a result, markers of early performance only appear adequate as predictors of future performance, but in fact belie a weakness in cognitive skills necessary for more sophisticated sets of demands that occur in successive developmental periods. Evidence for the induction of retarded behavior may be founded in reports of iatrogenic retardation (Kearsley & Zelazo, 1975), early differences in maternal handling of infants (Thoman, 1981), and the passive compliant syndrome in Hess and Shipman's thesis (Hess & Shipman, 1968). Early problem solving strategies such as trial and error or early social behavior such as timidity can be seen as early preschool age prototypes of behavior that remain relatively unchanged to interfere with performance as the child grows. This would certainly not explain all limits to intellectual growth, but the implications of the sociobehavioral support system is an as yet inadequately explored component of the process of intellectual development of children, especially those with unique developmental experiences.

There should also be considered the misleading effect of the fallacy that underlies the hope for transfer of intervention benefits to occur between the successive phases of development. That hope relates to the understanding of earlier intervention studies, such as the Skeels' study (Skeels, 1966), having demonstrated an innoculation effect. That is, that once early intervention has fostered normal IQ performance, it innoculates a child for life against all ills and that early performance benefits would not only be maintained but also would translate into school and adult success. As Clarke and Clarke (1976) pointed out, Skeels' postintervention phase of development was in effect another phase in which subjects experienced the positive environment of their adoptive homes. The value of this kind of intervention for school performance is additionally suggested in several other investigations: the study of the school performance differential of separated twins reported by Schiff, Duyme, Dumaret, Stewart, Tomkiewicz, and Feingold (1978); the study of the school performance of transracially adopted twins reported by Scarr and Weinberg (1978); and the study among children in the social housing experiment in Warsaw reported by Firkowska, Ostrowska, Sokolowska, Stein, Susser, and Wald (1978). In each of these studies school success was identified as behaviors related to family social status and the concatenation of appropriate support variables that follow the children beyond the preschool experience. It seems therefore that although it is possible to achieve improved intellectual performance or prevent expected declines in IQ test performance in children at risk for mental retardation, considerable questions remain as to the nature of intellectual growth and the mechanisms responsible for effecting growth and/or its limits. That understanding is fundamental if we are to be able not only to encourage intellectual performance across a wide range of experiences, but also to be able to effect the maintenance of performance benefits over time that result from intervention treatments.

DELINEATING THE ROLE OF MATERNAL
MEDIATION

Throughout the investigation, we were impressed with the vast array of influences that operate on the at risk family and their children. Although many of these influences may be experienced in common by other and perhaps more fortunate families, it was the unique interaction and intensity of these influences that acted to overwhelm certain families and put their children's future development at risk. The prospect for the social sciences being more effective in preventing deteriorating intellectual performance within the general disadvantaged populations of children, or for that matter for children in general, depends on delineating these influences and the mechanisms by which they operate on cognitive development. This information in turn is basic to the development of a psychoeducational technology effective in preventing poor intellectual performance.

Although the low and relatively narrow range of maternal IQ used as a criterion for this study presumed a relatively narrow range of general behaviors, it was apparent from our observations over the years that there were considerable differences among both the experimental and control families. We could see that some mothers did not seem to care and that some mothers cared very much and that there were homes in which there was no father and homes in which there were fathers who cared very much. These facts suggest that IQ, like SES, is a summary variable by which we can infer only in a preliminary way the nature of the psychosocial stimulation provided in the home microenvironment. Although family interviews and home observations were made, the kind of psychoanthropologic observations that now seem necessary to specify the mechanisms that influence intellectual development and to determine the significance of the differences that may exist among these mothers and their families unfortunately was not done.

The findings of the Milwaukee cross-sectional study and the longitudinal investigation supported the basic hypothesis that the most important environmental influence on cognitive development is the intimate interaction that takes place between the individual child and the parent or primary caregiver who mediates the environment for the child (Carew, 1980; Clark-Stewart, 1973; Feuerstein, 1979; Hunt, 1961; Jensen, 1968; Papousek & Papousek, 1982; Scarr, 1981; Vygotsky, 1962). It is also evident that this influence is of particular importance during infancy, when the child is most dependent on the primary caregiver. The experience of being reared by a primary caregiver who is retarded cannot be considered a *social deprivation* because it is not socially patterned and is not a defining characteristic of class, even though it may occur within lower SES groups with greater frequency than within other social groups (Deutsch, 1973; Jensen, 1968). The association between such experience and significant delays in cognitive development may cut across such classifications. This association should not be interpreted as evidence against the heritability of intelligence, but rather should be considered an indication of the extent to which natural variations in experience can influence the rate of cognitive development within a given genetic reaction range.

Often overlooked in Hunt's (1961) argument on the importance of early experience for cognitive development is his discussion of a reaction range for development, which is a product of inheritance. His theory postulated that individual variation in growth landmarks was evidence of this reaction change and could be viewed as "an inverse index of the capacity of various kinds of child-environment interaction to foster intellectual development" within these limits. Within this model, experience may fulfill what Gottlieb (1976) referred to as a "facilitating function," serving either to accelerate or to retard the rate of continuous transformations in the organizations or structures of intelligence through the processes of assimilation and accommodation.

If a retarded mother is incapable of adequately mediating the early experiences of her infant, realization of genotypic potential will be limited and the infant's performance level will be substantially retarded (Scarr, 1981). Future research must be designed to identify the specific processes through which the intimate interaction between infants and their primary caregivers serves either to hamper or to foster cognitive development.

In effect, although a higher probability for offspring IQ decline is indicated by low maternal IQ, the likelihood of treatment benefit may have a different probability level more closely specified by individual maternal (or other family) behaviors not adequately revealed by IQ test scores. This suggestion finds additional support in Shipman, McKee, and Bridgeman's (1976) report of a follow-up examination of Head Start data for child and program success factors. Their analysis indicated that the maternal child interaction process was poorly predicted by family status and situational variables, which at best explain less than 13% of the variance (p. 163). Such findings emphasize the need for future research to delineate more specific categories for individual variation in experimental designs attempting to identify the etiologic factors associated with cultural-familial mental retardation. Concentration on general indices of poverty or IQ scores in intervention research has distracted us from an adequate consideration of other influences among poor families such as parent attitudes and the lack of adequate role models for achievement (Hess, 1981). Obviously, the effectiveness of treatment strategies predicated on either general population descriptors or general developmental functions will be compromised by the extent of unaccounted variation within group because of factors not addressed by the treatment (e.g., intrafamilial differences in family functioning).

INDIVIDUAL PERFORMANCE AND POPULATION BASE RATES

The results of this investigation highlight the potential importance of refining the concept of risk as a strategy to help resolve the etiology of delay in cognitive development. To this end, it is imperative that empirically verified indices of risk be developed to replace broad demographic variables such as SES or minority group membership in order to limit the variability within populations for study. The association between the experiences of being reared by a primary caregiver who is retarded and significant delays in cognitive development identified in this prospective investigation is a step toward providing both a more precise index of risk than poverty and an indication of which process variables should be addressed by future research.

A more precise definition of risk within a framework of general systems theory formulated through an analysis of interaction outcomes has been offered by the North Carolina group (MacPhee, Ramey, & Yeates, 1984; Ramey & Haskins, 1981). Their major emphasis, however, remains on identifying broad SES differences and environmental conditions that influence responses to treatment rather than natural variations in experience associated with differences in the rate of intellectual development. Ramey and Haskins (1981), for example, questioned the value of the traditional psychological approach of studying individual differences in intellectual development and recommended that efforts be concentrated on the more global differences within which children develop. In effect, this not only dismisses a paradigmatic role for genetics to play in investigations of intellectual development but would further encourage polarized research in less fruitful directions, as in efforts at present critically characterized as excessively environmental.

Differences in outcome among early intervention studies, particularly those with apparently similar treatments, have not been easily reconciled in part because of the concentration on such global subject selection characteristics as SES level or low IQ and, as well, the tendency in such studies to invoke obvious differences in standards of living as both a measure of deprivation and an explanation for cultural-familial mental retardation or general delays in development.

The predictive validity enjoyed by the epidemiologic correlate SES occurs because it is a summary variable. Such variables mask individual variations within group that are perhaps more likely to be important to questions of treatment efficacy than is suggested by demographic variations between groups. The primary reliance on SES as a blocking variable in experimental designs investigating intellectual development tends to mislead us to the view that there is a general depression of intellectual performance for children in poverty and even, at least for some observers, to presume as Tulkin (1972) noted that a causal relationship exists. This view is further reinforced by assuming that the declining developmental function is an adequate description of IQ performance of low SES children. In actuality, it reveals neither the incidence of low IQ scores nor the factors that influence individual performance. As Appelbaum and McCall (1983) correctly pointed out, it must be determined empirically how well the developmental function of a group relates to the stability of individual differences. For the most part, this has not been possible because generally described samples have been the rule. Therefore, questions about the mutability of intelligence and the permanence of mental retardation cannot be appropriately addressed by intervention efforts in general because such questions presume incorrectly that the epidemologic association between low SES and low IQ justifies a general population base rate from which individual differences can be predicted.

SUBJECT SELECTION AND TREATMENT EFFECTS

The notion that early environmental action is global in nature leads to the assumption that children are at significant risk for delays in intellectual development simply because they came from low income or minority group homes (Wachs, 1984). In fact, almost without exception, compensatory education programs have concentrated on global and obvious environmental differences rather than on individual differences within subgroups. The findings of the early cross-sectional investigation in Milwaukee, for example, suggested that many of the children selected for preschool compensatory education studies may not have been retarded or at significant risk for delays in cognitive development. In the survey of inner city residents in Milwaukee (Heber, Dever, & Conry, 1968) to which Jensen (1969) referred, considerable variability in infant IQ performance was clearly demonstrated for the disadvantaged community of families at large as well as for the children in the pool of highest risk families (identified by mothers with IQ scores below 80) targeted as subjects for the subsequent intervention study. Although there was an excess incidence of low IQ scores for this population, the survey data did not demonstrate a uniformly depressed IQ effect that would indicate generally poor heritability for the so-called poverty environment. Rather, the disproportionate incidence of low IQ scores was found predominantly in families where the maternal IQ was below 80. Moreover, even such infants, when able to interact with verbally facile adults and engage in a variety of educationally stimulating experiences, as a group, maintained average or better IQ performance.

When stimulating experiences are given in a positive fostering environment, they seem to encourage successful social and cognitive performance and enhance a good endowment or mitigate the negative effects of poor heritability. Even given a primacy status for nature, it remains in function contingent upon the relative effects of the nurturing experience and its limits remain open to empirical test.

In contrast to most programs, the Milwaukee Project longitudinal investigation attempted to include only that subsample of infants born within the poverty area most seriously at risk for significant delays in cognitive development, which the cross-sectional study indicated should be limited to infants with mothers who were retarded. When children who are not at risk for delays are included in studies of environmental influences on the rate of cognitive development, the average difference between treated and untreated children can be substantially reduced. The mean IQ level for heterogeneous groups of untreated children does not accurately reflect the possible negative influence of inadequate experience, nor, therefore, does the mean IQ level for heterogeneous groups of treated children accurately reflect the possibility of preventing or ameliorating delays in cognitive development.

Early criticisms, most especially by Jensen (1969), condemning the potential of preschool experiences to offset the negative effects of heritability were both premature and unwarranted, considering the limits of the various efforts upon which the criticisms were based. The current generation of intervention studies, including the Milwaukee Project, were spawned during America's era of revitalization of consciousness for the plight of the disadvantaged. Most of the intervention studies (e.g., Gray, Klaus, & Ramsey, 1981; Schweinhart & Weikart, 1981) were ameliorative rather than preventive and concentrated on raising IQ levels. There is no question about the importance of these studies either as efforts to alleviate the negative effects of poverty or as to their efficacy in demonstrating the mutability of phenotypic intellectual functioning in general. However, although these many and varied programs are often cited as providing a unitary test of the social deprivation hypothesis and as preventive strategies for mental retardation (see Clarke & Clarke, 1977), they are actually more limited. In part the confusion relates to the time to which most of the present generation of preschool studies trace their origin. It was not only a time of revitalized consciousness for the disadvantaged (a sociopolitical concern), but also a time coincident with a new view of the malleability of intellectual performance.

The majority of the early intervention programs, namely, those included in the Lazar et al. (1982) report of the Consortium, were designed for the general purpose of preparing socially and economically deprived children for a successful school experience. They are inappropriately regarded as prevention studies (Ramey & Bryant, 1982) because they were directed at ameliorating low IQ performance as an objective intermediate to the goals of improving school achievement among the poor (Horowitz & Paden, 1973) and, ultimately, adult success (Keniston & Carnegie Council, 1977). Although subject samples included many children with low IQ scores, the studies are more limited in answering the questions of prevention of mental retardation than they seem because subject selection was based primarily on broad demographic variables related to poverty (Deutsch, 1973; Henderson, 1981) and the range of variability that exists within subclasses of the population was not accounted for (Appelbaum & McCall, 1983).

Most of the children in these studies cannot be considered mentally retarded because the average IQ scores of these subjects never fell below 80 (Zigler & Cascione, 1977). The measures of parent and sibling intelligence, the criterion factors in identification of cultural-familial mental retardation (Grossman, 1983; Heber, 1961), were rarely considered. Although correlations between SES and IQ level and academic achievement are relatively high, broad measures of SES account for less than 25% of the variance in these factors (Geismar & La Sorte, 1964; Pavenstedt, 1965). They do not reflect differences between poor but stable working families and poor but disorganized multiproblem families (the latter being the families more likely to contribute disproportionately to the relatively high level of mild retardation in low SES groups). As a result, the tendency to view disadvantaged children as homogeneous may have obscured important individual differences related to the etiology of intellectual deficits and, ultimately, to questions of intervention efficacy. Therefore, the value of the support Jensen (1969) derived for the concept of heritability from his survey of compensatory programming for children was compromised because it was a judgment of the general effort and was inappropriate. Early intervention studies should be compared for subject characteristics, treatment intensity, and purpose, because therein lie differences substantial enough to limit interpretations of data and to require admonitions of program failure or success to be more closely qualified. Without detailed information about subject samples, there are serious limits on any attempt to make valid inferences about population base rates that in effect compromise any general evaluation of efficacy.

The Milwaukee Project is most similar to a group of prevention studies that included children who were not already reduced in IQ performance at treatment onset. However, in comparison with other prevention studies, only the Carolina Abecedarian Program (Ramey & Haskins, 1981) was comparable to the Milwaukee Project because of its emphasis on subject selection and program intensity (for a review, see Ramey & Bryant, 1982). In both the Milwaukee and Abecedarian programs, subject selection went beyond other prevention programs' criterion of general poverty and developed a maternal risk factor: the higher the risk factor, the more likely the child is to be identified as mentally retarded in school. In addition, both the Milwaukee and Carolina studies attempted to test the hypothesis that early intervention could prevent declines in IQ performance and enable the children to maintain a mean normal group performance level by school age.

The major similarity of treatment strategy aside, several substantial differences remain. A most crucial difference is the nature of the selection procedure. The Milwaukee study established low maternal IQ of less than 75 (FS WAIS) as the entry criterion for normal newborns while the Abecedarian first selected poor families and then mothers with low IQ. There is nearly a full standard deviation difference between the mean of the lower IQ Milwaukee mothers and the higher mean IQ for mothers in the Abecedarian study. The resultant control on the homogeneity of the population can, as was noted earlier, help to account for the extent of difference between the treated and untreated groups in the Milwaukee study as compared with the Abecedarian. Control of the genotypic influence by the limited IQ range of the Milwaukee mothers also provides a better estimate of the role of experiential factors in mild cultural-familial retardation than does the low but more open selection criterion of maternal IQ used in the Abecedarian program. What implications the differences in sample and procedural variables hold for the interpretation of the efficacy of preventive intervention strategies for the at risk probably are considerable if the hoped for level of effectiveness is not to be compromised by unaccounted and unaddressed treatment needs of the children and families involved.

Future investigations of the influence of experience on the rate of cognitive development must account for individual differences within groups or at least reduce the variability within groups being compared. This requires selection of homogeneous populations of children using empirically verified indices of risk for delays rather than broad demographic variables such as SES. It should be recognized, however, that risk is a probability statement, and that even within relatively homogeneous populations there will be individual variations in development. For example, IQ scores for several experimental children in this investigation were relatively low compared with scores for the rest of the treatment group, indicating that the treatment was not as effective for them as for the other children. In contrast, two control children consistently scored at or slightly above the population mean and above some of the experimental group children even though they were at significant risk for delays and remained at home with their retarded mothers. If the influence of variations in experience is to be adequately assessed, such individual differences would not be considered outliers but would become the central concern for future investigations.

If we view early educational interventions in the development of at risk and disadvantaged children as an investment, then we must do more to protect that investment over the long term. As Zigler and Cascione (1977) have suggested, programs appropriate to different periods of the lifespan are needed. Coordination of these programs will provide the greatest benefit to children and particularly those whose development is at risk. In addition, for research to be helpful in this process, it must continue to identify the mediating variables between less broadly defined population characteristics (e.g., than SES) and summary constructs (such as IQ) in order to provide an understanding of which aspect of the environment should be addressed through social programs and which through educational programs and for whom each program is most likely to be effective.

COMMENTARY

Americans have long believed that hard work and talent will ultimately lead to success for each individual. Unfortunately, the myth of equal opportunities denies that "the circumstances of birth — and in particular the social and economic position into which a child is born — have much effect in determining where the individual ends up in life" (Keniston & Carnegie Council, 1977, p. 39). These factors also seem to be related to most of the differences that are observed among children in school performance, IQ scores, years of schooling actually completed, and even which schools were attended. For over two decades, concerned citizens in the United States have recognized inequalities of condition and have built program after program to establish equal status for the poor, minorities, and individuals with handicapping conditions. Unfortunately, most of these programs have not been based on the individual needs of children and their families but rather have directed efforts toward reforming, uplifting, changing, and educating the so-called "excluded" by strategies based on the broader social aspects of the problem.

The chief means used to correct inequalities ". . . was a brilliant American invention: universal, free, compulsory public education. This 'solution' was especially important for children and families because it gave children a central role in achieving the national ideal" (Keniston & Carnegie Council, 1977, p. 41). By broadening that concept to include education for *all* children, early intervention preschool programs were designed to prepare children in severely deprived areas for the school experience. Through extensive child care service and compensatory academic programming, educators and psychologists hoped to help the disadvantaged match the school performance of their age peers. Clarke (1973) contended that the programs were generally too short and too nonacademic, had no provisions for follow-up, and treated children mainly for their poverty and not for their developmental needs. I have proposed that the latter, that is, the presumption that the deprived population subgroup is homogeneous, is the fundamental flaw in intervention methodology.

It was argued that all children in deprived environments will be retarded without help and that social deprivation was the fundamental cause. Thus, it was theorized that if opportunity were equalized for all Americans, all children would be able to take advantage of opportunities offered as compensation for disadvantagement and that these opportunities would outweigh the negative influence of factors related to accidents of birth that are essentially maintained throughout their life. However, not all individuals who are poor need or are able to respond to equitably distributed compensatory educational and social programs. We have, I believe, not been cautious enough about relying upon such easily observed and easily measured surface variables as poverty in defining at risk populations. Such variables reflect only the grossest estimate of the life process of individual members of these subgroups. Obviously, in light of cost-benefit priorities, the first order of concern must be to reduce the incidence of low IQ and other developmental problems. But, if we are to effectively address this problem, we must identify specific risk factors predictive of declines in IQ performance so that we can address the source of the problem through treatment programs that are prevention oriented.

Although the results of the preschool evaluation of the Consortium (Lazar & Darlington, 1978; Palmer & Anderson, 1981), which showed higher performance levels and lower rates of special class placement, are regarded as having adequately rejoined Jensen's (1969) condemnation of the value of such programs, both are remiss in their casual attention to subject population characteristics. Failure to specify subject characteristics makes selection, assignment, and treatment coordination difficult and further clouds the issue of the efficacy of such programs. The ultimate benefits of either preventive or remedial treatment fall away as the individual nature of child and family problems that dispose these children to be at serious risk for abnormal development is not addressed by general programs. Therefore, measures of the efficacy of such extensive educational programs have been compromised by methodologic concerns regarding coordination of subject and treatment. The goal must be to develop treatments matched to the needs of individuals; then their ability to respond can be observed and any negative influences that might effect a discrepancy between potential and performance can also be ascertained and their effects mitigated.

Children from disadvantaged, at risk families have generally responded favorably and in a fairly similar fashion to preschool programs, but considerable differences have been found in how the benefits from such programs are sustained, which probably relates to how well such programs have compensated for deprivation in other areas of their lives. These differences persist because many families, although sharing common key indicator variables such as income and socioeconomic level, educational level of parents, general residential similarities, school facilities, etc., are quite different in the more fundamental family processes that characterize how they mediate the environment for their children. Situations range from families verging on total disruption and disintegration to a level of stability characterized by the stereotype of the well adjusted middle class family. Therefore, a more thorough understanding of differences among individual disadvantaged families is necessary in order to identify the extent to which families are capable of mediating and extending the educational process of preschool and school into the home and to identify which families may need extended support from outside sources to accomplish this goal.

The study of IQ test performance, the predominant data base in the discussions of intervention efficacy, increasingly seems to be best considered as parallel to the line of research investigating success in school and life. There are tempting parallels between IQ test performance and performance in life that are attributable to similarities in behavior patterns, but these must be empirically justified beyond epidemiologic relationships to qualify as indices of etiology. Occasionally, these lines of research do cross; however, they are not uniformly overlapping such that performance in one situation (viz., the IQ test) is predictive of performance in the other situation (viz., life). Epidemiologic data are fraught with apparent relationships that can provide a basis for social policy that dangerously tempts a servitude to ideologies trading on conveniences of time and/or the comfort of politics au courant rather than on social policy predicated on guides derived from programs of long term systematic research. Moreover, adequate societal alternatives to compensatory programs of educational and social care for the disadvantaged and at risk child cannot be forthcoming simply from IQ testing, but will require continued attempts to fashion treatment programs coordinated with subject selection qualifications that will help move children toward citizenship. The psychoeducational technology basic to prescribing effective educational programs, which Jensen (1969, 1980) appropriately argued for, requires a broader assessment protocol than the IQ test. Such a protocol should assess talents in addition to those measured by IQ tests, talents perhaps more closely associated with success in life.

Alternate treatment models for the development of individual skills and abilities should be viewed within a developmental model that recognizes the tremendous range of individual variation all along the normal (50 to 150) scale of intelligence estimates. At any moment in one's life, an inspired, encouraging mother or a cooperative sibling or a concerned grandparent or a supportive teacher can reinforce a behavior system appropriate to the academic demands of school or to the technological requisites of an industrial society. How these factors act and interact constitute a major source of influence on the developmental performance of maturing children.

Our ability to disrupt the development of antagonistic learning systems through preventive educational techniques cannot be confined to ecological treatments that are age restricted or to teach-the-task fading manipulations, for which cognitive generalizability is questionable. We will have to learn more about the developmental nature of induced antagonistic learning tendencies among the disadvantaged, in particular, to examine the nature of intrafamilial habits of learning.

Treatments, if they are to be effective, must be directly administered on a prescriptive basis to individual families. Determining the level of service needs for a family can be evaluated as risk relative to a child's suffering from induced mental retardation (Garber, 1982). Such a risk model has three basic components (Garber & McInerney, 1982). The first component involves establishing the family risk level and includes both the status variables (e.g., SES level, number of children) and the process variables (e.g., quality of home environment, parental attitude) that provide the overall framework within which the potential of offspring for impaired performance may be observed. This is the first step of a screening process for targeting children at risk.

The characteristics of the child represent the second, not the first, risk component. All youngsters place demands on their caretakers. Handicapped children are not always those with obvious developmental delays; nevertheless, they may make unanswerable demands on their families. For those who have more obvious early delays, family risk status will interact with the degree to which the child is intellectually impaired.

Systems risk is the third component of this risk model and is represented by those school and community variables with the potential to increase a child's risk for mental retardation (MacMillan et al., 1980) and include such school system factors as selection procedures, program options, and placement alternatives.

Each of the three risk components (family, child, and school) interacts and plays against the other two to influence variations in children's developmental performance. These components of our risk model become educationally important when they are used to characterize the environment within which each child is asked to learn. Appreciation of these risk characteristics and the nature of their influence on development offer the possibility for offsetting disability through prevention or remediation of those deleterious effects that are presented to the child.

The objective of the search for those sociobehavioral factors that act to inhibit intellectual development is not simply to catalog what does and does not happen cognitively for selected groups of children who mainly have in common low IQ test scores. Rather, it is an attempt to determine the origins of the cognitive behavior by which, ultimately, it is hoped will be revealed possible mechanisms for affecting intelligence. Temperament and genetic constitution, nourishment, opportunity to learn, encouragement, good eyesight and hearing, and loving and rational parents will all interact to some extent. Some may dominate others in their influence. But the concern we all must have is as to how this entire system can be manipulated on behalf of each child to facilitate his/her individual ability so that potential will be realized and so that maximum contribution to society, whatever its extent, will be made.

References

Adams, J. (1973). Adaptive behavior and measured intelligence in the classification of mental retardation. *American Journal of Mental Deficiency, 78*(1), 77-81.

Adams, J., McIntosh, E. I., & Weade, B. L. (1973). Ethnic background, measured intelligence, and adaptive behavior scores in mentally retarded children. *American Journal of Mental Deficiency, 78*, 1-6.

Anastasi, A. (1958). Heredity, environment, and the question "How?" *Psychological Review, 65*(4), 197-208.

Anisfield, M., & Tucker, R. C. (1967). English pluralization rules of six-year old children. *Child Development, 39*, 1201-1217.

Appelbaum, M. I., & McCall, R. B. (1983). Design and analysis in developmental psychology. In P. H. Mussen (Ed.), *Handbook of child psychology: Vol. I. History, theory, and methods.* New York: Wiley.

Asher, E. J. (1935). The inadequacy of current intelligence tests for testing Kentucky mountain children. *Journal of Genetic Psychology, 46*, 480-486.

Attneave, F. (1959). *Applications of information theory to psychology.* New York: Holt.

Ault, R. L., Crawford, D. E., & Jeffrey, W. E. (1972). Visual scanning strategies of reflective, impulsive, fast-accurate, and slow-accurate children on the MFF test. *Child Development, 43*, 1412-1417.

Ausubel, D. (1964). How reversible are the cognitive and motivational effects of cultural deprivation? Implications for teaching the culturally deprived child. *Urban Education, 1*(1), 16-38.

Baltes, P. B., & Nesselroade, J. R. (1973). The developmental analysis of individual differences on multiple measures. In J. Nesselroade & H. Reese (Eds.), *Life-span developmental psychology.* New York: Academic Press.

Bamman, M. A. (Ed.). (1969). *The Kaleidoscope Readers* (Teacher Edition). San Francisco: Field Education Publishers.

Battle, E., & Rotter, J. B. (1963). Children's feelings of personal control as related to social class and ethnic group. *Journal of Personality, 31*, 482-490.

Bayley, N. (1968). Cognition in aging. In K. W. Schaie (Ed.), *Theory and methods of research on aging.* Morgantown: West Virginia University Library.

Becker, J. (1977). A learning analysis of the development of peer oriented behavior in nine-month-old infants. *Developmental Psychology, 13*, 481-491.

Becker, W., & Krug, R. (1965). The parent attitude research instrument: A research review. *Child Development, 36*, 329-365.

Bee, H. L., Van Egeren, L. F., Streissguth, A. P., Nyman, B. A., & Leckie, M. S. (1969). Social class differences in maternal teaching strategies and speech patterns. *Developmental Psychology, 1*, 726-734.

417

Beilin, H. (1975). *Studies in the cognitive basis of language development*. New York: Academic Press.

Bellamy, M. M., & Bellamy, S. E. (1969). The acquisition of morphological inflections by children four to ten. *Language Learning, 19*, 199–211.

Bellugi-Klima, U. (1968). *Evaluating the young child's language competence*. Paper available through National Laboratory on Early Childhood Education, ERIC.

Bereiter, C. (1972). An academic preschool for disadvantaged children: Conclusions from evaluation studies. In J.C. Stanley (Ed.), *Preschool programs for the disadvantaged: Five experimental approaches to early childhood education*. Baltimore: Johns Hopkins University Press.

Bereiter, C., & Engelmann, S. (1966). *Teaching disadvantaged children in the preschool*. Englewood Cliffs, NJ: Prentice-Hall.

Bereiter, C., Osborne, J., Engelmann, S., & Reidford, P. A. (1965). An academically oriented preschool for culturally deprived children. In F. M. Hechinger (Ed.), *Preschool education today*. New York: Doubleday.

Berko, J. (1958). The child's learning of English morphology. *Word, 14*, 150–177.

Bernstein, B. (1960). Language and social class. *British Journal of Psychology, 11*, 271–276.

Bing, E. (1963). Effect of childrearing practices on development of differential cognitive abilities. *Child Development, 34*, 631–648

Birch, H. G., Richardson, S. A., Baird, D., Horobin, G., & Illsley, R. (1970). *Mental subnormality in the community: A clinical and epidemiological study*. Baltimore: Williams & Wilkins.

Bloom, B. S. (1964). *Stability and change in human characteristics*. New York: Wiley.

Bloom, B. S., & Broder, L. (1950). *Problem-solving processes of college students*. Chicago: University of Chicago Press.

Bloom, L. (1970). *Language development: Form and function in emerging grammar*. Cambridge: MIT Press.

Bock, G., Stebbins, L. B., & Proper, E. C. (1977). *Education as experimentation: A planned variation model: Vol. IV-B. Effects of follow through models*. Cambridge: ABT Associates

Bond, G. L., & Dykstra, R. (1967). *Final report no. X-001*. Coordinating Center for First Grade Reading Instruction Programs.

Bower, E. M., & Lambert, N. M. (1962). *A process for in-school screening of children with emotional handicaps*. Princeton: Educational Testing Service.

Bradbury, H., & Nelson, T. M. (1974). Transitivity and the patterns of children's preferences. *Developmental Psychology, 10*, 55–64

Bradley, R. H., & Caldwell, B. M. (1984). 174 children: A study of the relationship between home environment and cognitive development during the first 5 years. In A. W. Gottfried (Ed.), *Home environment and early cognitive development: Longitudinal research*. Orlando: Academic Press.

Braine, M. D. S., Heimer, C. B., Wortis, H., & Freedman, A. M. (1966). Factors associated with impairment of the early development of prematures. *Monographs of the Society for Research in Child Development, 31*(4, Serial No. 106).

Bresnahan, J. L., & Shaprio, M. M. (1972). Learning strategies in children from different socioeconomic levels. In H. W. Reese (Ed.), *Advances in child development and behavior*. New York: Academic Press.

Brody, G. H., & Brody, J. A. (1976). Vicarious language instructions with bilingual children through self-modeling. *Contemporary Educational Psychology, 1*, 138–145.

Bronfenbrenner, U. (1975). Is early intervention effective? In G. Guttentag & E. Streuning (Eds.), *Handbook of evaluation research* (Vol. 2). Beverly Hills: Sage.

Brophy, J. E. (1970). Mothers as teachers of their own preschool children: The influences of socioeconomic status and task structures on teaching specificity. *Child Development, 41*, 79–94.

Brown, A. L. (1970). Subject and experimental variables in the oddity learning of normal and retarded children. *American Journal of Mental Deficiency, 75*, 142–151.

Brown, A. L. (1973). Judgments of recency for long sequences of pictures: The absence of a developmental trend. *Journal of Experimental Child Psychology, 15,* 475–480.

Brown, A. L., & Campione, J. C. (1981). Inducing flexible thinking: A problem of access. In M. Friedman, J. P. Das, & N. O'Connor (Eds.), *Intelligence and learning.* New York: Plenum.

Brown, A. L., & Lloyd, B. B. (1971). Criteria of success in a developmental study of oddity learning. *British Journal of Psychology, 62,* 21–26.

Brown, R. (1958). *Words and things.* New York: Free Press.

Brown, R. W., & Bellugi, U. (1964). Three processes in the child's acquisition of syntax. *Harvard Educational Review, 34,* 133–151.

Brown, R. W., Fraser, C., & Bellugi, U. (1964). Explorations in grammar evaluation. In U. Bellugi & R. W. Brown (Eds.), *The acquisition of language. Monographs of the Society for Research in Child Development, 29*(Serial No. 92), 79–92.

Bruner, J. S. (1966). *Toward a theory of instruction.* New York: W. W. Norton.

Bruner, J. S. (1967). On cognitive growth, I and II. In J. S. Bruner, R. R. Olver, & P. M. Greenfield (Eds.), *Studies in cognitive growth.* New York: Wiley.

Bruner, J. S., Goodnow, J., & Austin, G. (1956). *A study of thinking.* New York: Wiley.

Bruner, J. S., Olver, R. R., & Greenfield, P. M. (Eds.). (1967). *Studies in cognitive growth.* New York: Wiley.

Bruner, J. S., & Potter, M. C. (1964). Interference in visual recognition. *Science, 144,* 424–425.

Bryant, B., & Anisfield, M. (1969) Feedback versus no-feedback in testing children's knowledge of English pluralization rules. *Journal of Experimental Child Psychology, 8,* 250–255.

Buros, O. K. (Ed.). (1972). *The seventh mental measurement yearbook.* Highland Park, NJ: Gryphon Press.

Caldwell, B. M. (1969). The new "approach" to behavioral ecology. In J. P. Hill (Ed.), *Minnesota Symposia on Child Psychology.* Minneapolis: University of Minnesota Press.

Campbell, S. B. (1973). Mother-child interaction in reflective, impulsive, and hyperactive children. *Development Psychology, 8,* 341–349.

Carew, J. V. (1980). Experience and the development of intelligence in young children at home and in day care. *Monographs of the Society for Research in Child Development, 45*(6–7, Serial No. 187).

Carroll, J. B. (1972). Review of the Illinois Test of Psycholinguistic Abilities. In O. K. Buros, (Ed.), *The seventh mental measurement yearbook.* Highland Park, NJ: Gryphon Press.

Carrow, S. M. A. (1968). The development of auditory comprehension of language structures in children. *Journal of Speech and Hearing Disorders, 33,* 99–111.

Caruso, D. R., Taylor, J. J., & Detterman, D. K. (1982). Intelligence research and intelligent policy. In D. K. Detterman & R. J. Sternberg (Eds.), *How and how much can intelligence be increased.* Norwood, NJ: ABLEX.

Cattell, P. (1940). *The measurement of infants and young children.* New York: Psychological Corporation.

Cicirelli, V. G. (1969). *The impact of Head Start: An evaluation of the effects of Head Start on children's cognitive and affective development.* Washington, DC: National Bureau of Standards, Institute for Applied Technology.

Cicirelli, V. G., Evans, J. W., & Schiller, J. S. (1970). The impact of Head Start: A reply to the report analysis. *Harvard Educational Review, 40,* 105–129.

Clarke, A. D. B. (1973). The prevention of subcultural subnormality: Problems and prospects. *British Journal of Mental Subnormality, 19* (Part 1, No. 36), 7–20.

Clarke, A. D. B., & Clarke, A. M. (1975). *Recent advances in the study of subnormality: A miniature textbook.* London: National Association for Mental Health.

Clarke, A. D. B., & Clarke, A. M. (1977). Prospects for prevention and amelioration of mental retardation: A guest editorial. *American Journal of Mental Deficiency, 81*(6), 523–533.

Clarke, A. M., & Clarke, A. D. B. (1974). *Mental deficiency: The changing outlook* (3rd ed.). New York: Free Press.

Clarke, A. M., & Clarke, A. D. B. (1976). Problems in comparing the effects of environmental change at different ages. In H. McGurk (Ed.), *Ecological factors in human development.* Amsterdam: North-Holland.

Clarke-Stewart, K. A. (1973). Interactions between mothers and their young children: Characteristics and consequences. *Monographs of the Society for Research in Child Development, 38*(6-7, Serrial No. 153).

Clausen, J. A. (1967). Mental deficiency: Development of a concept. *American Journal of Mental Deficiency, 71,* 727-745.

Clay, M. M. (1971). Sentence repetition: Elicited imitation of a controlled set of syntactic structures by four language groups. *Monographs of the Society for Research in Child Development, 36*(3, Serial No. 143).

Cohler, B., Weiss, J., & Grunebaum, H. (1970). Child-care attitudes and emotional disturbance among mothers of young children. *Genetic Psychology Monographs, 82,* 3-47.

Cole, M., & Bruner, J. S. (1971). Cultural differences and inferences about psychological processes. *American Psychologist, 26,* 867-876.

Cole, M., Gay, J., Glick, J. A., & Sharp, D. W. (1974). *The cultural context of learning and thought.* New York: Wiley.

Coleman, H. M. (1968). Visual perception and reading dysfunction. *Journal of Learning Disabilities, 1,* 116-123.

Coleman, J. S. (1966). *Equality of educational opportunity.* Washington, DC: U.S. Office of Education.

Comptroller General of the United States. (1976). *Training educators for the handicapped: A need to redirect federal programs.* Report to Congress.

Conant, J. B. (1961). *Slums and suburbs.* New York: McGraw-Hill.

Condry, S. (1983). History and background of preschool intervention programs and the Consortium for Longitudinal Studies, *As the twig is bent . . . Lasting effects of preschool programs.* Hillsdale, NJ: Lawrence Erlbaum.

Conover, W. J. (1971). *Practical nonparametric statistics.* New York: Wiley.

The Consortium for Longitudinal Studies. (1983). *As the twig is bent . . . Lasting effects of preschool programs.* Hillsdale, NJ: Lawrence Erlbaum.

Cook, T. D., & Campbell, D. T. (1979). *Quasi-experimentation: Design and analysis issues for field settings.* Chicago: Rand McNally.

Crandall, V. C., & Battle, E. S. (1970). The antecedents and adult correlates of academic and intellectual achievement effort. In J. P. Hill (Ed.), *Minnesota Symposia on Child Psychology* (Vol. 4). Minneapolis: University of Minnesota Press.

Crandall, V. J., Katkovsky, W., & Preston, A. (1960). A conceptual formulation for some research on children's achievement behavior. *Child Development, 31,* 787-797.

Crandall, V. J., Katkovsky, W., & Preston, A. (1962). Motivational and ability determinants of young children's achievement behavior. *Child Development, 33,* 643-661.

Crano, W. D., Kenny, D. A., & Campbell, D. T. (1972). Does intelligence cause achievement? A cross-lagged panel analysis. *Journal of Educational Psychology, 63,* 258-275.

Croll, W. L. (1970). Response strategies in the oddity discrimination of preschool children. *Journal of Experimental Child Psychology, 9,* 187-192.

Dave, R. H. (1963). *The identification and measurement of environmental process variables related to educational achievement.* Unpublished doctoral dissertation, University of Chicago.

Davis, A., & Eells, K. W. (1953). *Davis-Eells Games: Davis-Eells test of general intelligence or problem-solving ability, Manual.* Yonkers-on-Hudson, NY: World Book.

Davis, K. (1947). Final note on a case of extreme isolation. *American Journal of Sociology, 52,* 432-437.

Dearborn, W. F., & Rothney, J. W. M. (1941). *Predicting the child's development.* Cambridge: Sci-Art.

Debus, R. L. (1970). Effects of brief observations of model behavior on conceptual tempo of impulsive children. *Developmental Psychology, 2*(1), 22–32.

deLacy, P. R. (1970). A cross-cultural study of classification skills in Australia. *Journal of Cross-Cultural Psychology, 1*, 293–304.

deLacy, P. R. (1971a). Classificatory ability and verbal intelligence among high-contact aboriginal and low socio-economic white Australian children. *Journal of Cross-Cultural Psychology, 2*, 393–396.

deLacy, P. R. (1971b). Verbal intelligence, operational thinking and environment in part-aboriginal children. *Australian Journal of Psychology, 23*, 145–149.

DeLemos, M. M. (1969). The development of conservation in aboriginal children. *International Journal of Psychology, 4*, 255–269.

Denenberg, V. H. (1964). Critical periods, stimulus input, and emotional reactivity: A theory of infantile stimulation. *Psychological Review, 71*, 335–351.

Denny, M. R. (1964). Research in learning and performance. In H. Stevens & R. Heber (Eds.), *Mental retardation: A review of research.* Chicago: University of Chicago Press.

Deutsch, C. P. (1973). Social class and child development. In B. Caldwell & R. Riccuiti (Eds.), *Review of child development research* (Vol. 3). Chicago: University of Chicago Press.

Deutsch, M. (1966). Facilitating development in the preschool child: Social and psychological perspectives. In F. M. Hechinger (Ed.), *Preschool education today.* Garden City, NJ: Doubleday.

Deutsch, M. (1967). *The disadvantaged child.* New York: Basic Books.

Deutsch, M., & Brown, R. (1964). Social influences in negro-white intelligence differences. *Journal of Social Issues, 20*, 24–35.

Dever, R. B., & Gardner, W. I. (1970). Performance of normal and retarded boys on Berko's Test of Morphology. *Language and Speech, 13*, 162–181.

Dillard, J. L. (1972). *Black English.* New York: Random House.

Dixon, W. J. (Ed.). (1983). *BMDP statistical software.* Berkeley: University of California Press.

Doehring, D. G. (1960). Color-form attitudes of deaf children. *Journal of Speech and Hearing Research, 3*, 252–248.

Donaldson, M., & Wales, R. (1970). On the acquisition of some relational terms. In J. R. Hayes (Ed.), *Cognition and the development of language.* New York: Wiley.

Doob, L. W. (1960). *Becoming more civilized: A psychological exploration.* New Haven: Yale University Press.

Dunn, L. M. (1968). Special education for the mildly retarded—Is much of it justifiable? *Exceptional Children, 35*(1), 5–24.

Durost, W. N., Bixler, H. H., Wrightstone, J. W., Prescott, G. A., & Balow, I. H. (1970). *Metropolitan Achievement Tests* (Primary I, Primary II, Elementary—Form F). New York: Harcourt, Brace, Jovanovich.

Durost, W. N., Bixler, H. H., Wrightstone, J. W., Prescott, G. A., & Balow, I. H. (1971). *Metropolitan Achievement Tests* (Primer—Form F). New York: Harcourt, Brace, Jovanovich.

Durrell, D., & Murphy, H. A. (1964). *Speech to print phonics.* New York: Harcourt, Brace, & World.

Eells, K., Davis, A., Havighurst, R. J., Herrick, V. E., & Tyler, R. (1951). *Intelligence and cultural differences.* Chicago: University of Chicago Press.

Egeland, B., DiNello, M., & Carr, D. L. (1970). The relationship of intelligence, visual-motor, psycholinguistic and reading-readiness skills with achievement. *Educational and Psychological Measurement, 30*, 451–458.

Ellis, N. R., & Cavalier, A. R. (1982). Research perspectives in mental retardation. In E. Zigler & D. Balla (Eds.), *Mental retardation: The developmental-difference controversy.* Hillsdale, NJ: Lawrence Erlbaum.

Erlenmeyer-Kimling, L., & Jarvik, L. F. (1963). Genetics and intelligence: A review. *Science, 142*, 1477–1479.

Estes, W. K. (1970). *Learning theory and mental development.* New York: Academic Press.

Falender, C. (1969). *Aggression in the young child.* Unpublished master's thesis, University of Wisconsin-Madison.

Farnham-Diggory, S., & Gregg, L. W. (1975). Color, form, and function as dimensions of natural classification: Developmental changes in eye movements, reaction time, and response strategies. *Child Development, 46*, 101–114.

Fasold, R. W. (1972). *Tense marking in black English: A linguistic and social analysis.* Urban Language Series, Center for Applied Linguistics.

Fellows, B. J. (1967). Chance stimulus sequences for discrimination tasks. *Psychological Bulletin, 67*, 87–92.

Feshbach, N. D. (1973). Cross-cultural studies of teaching styles in four-year-olds and their mothers. In A. E. Pick (Ed.), *Minnesota Symposia on Child Psychology* (Vol. 7). Minneapolis: University of Minnesota Press.

Feuerstein, R. (1979). *The dyamic assessment of retarded performers: The learning potential assessment device, theory, instruments, and techniques.* Baltimore: University Park Press.

Feuerstein, R., Rand, Y., Hoffman, M. B., & Miller, R. (1980). *Instrumental enrichment: An intervention program for cognitive modifiability.* Baltimore: University Park Press.

Firkowska, A., Ostrowska, A., Sokolowska, M., Stein, Z., Susser, M., & Wald, I. (1978). Cognitive development and social policy: The contribution of parental occupation and education to mental performance in 11-year-olds in Warsaw. *Science, 200*, 1357–1362.

Fisher, R. A. (1949). *Design of experiments* (5th ed.). Edinburgh: Oliver & Boyd Ltd.

Flynn, J. R. (1984). The mean IQ of Americans: Massive gains 1932 to 1978. *Psychological Bulletin, 95*(1), 29–51.

Fraser, C., Bellugi, U., & Brown, R. (1963). Control of grammar in imitation, comprehension, and production. *Journal of Verbal Learning and Verbal Behavior, 2*, 121–135.

French, J. W., & Michael, W. B. (1966). *Standards for educational and psychological tests and manuals.* Washington, DC: American Psychological Association.

Gagne, R. M. (1970). *The conditions of learning.* New York: Holt, Rinehart, & Winston.

Gaines, R. (1969). The discriminability of form among young children. *Journal of Experimental Child Psychology, 8*, 418–431.

Gaines, R. (1970). Children's selective attention to stimuli: Stage or set? *Child Development, 41*, 970–991.

Garber, H. L. (1975). Intervention in infancy: A developmental approach. In M. J. Begab & S. Richardson (Eds.), *The mentally retarded and society.* Baltimore: University Park Press.

Garber, H. L. (1976). Preventing mental retardation through family rehabilitation. In *TADS infant education monograph.* Chapel Hill, NC: Technical Assistance Development System.

Garber, H. L. (1982). Preventing the induction of risk-relative sociocultural mental retardation. In *Mental retardation* (Proceedings of the symposium Mental Retardation from a Neurobiological and Sociocultural Point of View, Lund, Sweden). Goteborg, Sweden: CIBA-GEIGY.

Garber, H. L., & Hagens, J. (1971). *Wisconsin Learning Research Machine.* Madison: University of Wisconsin Rehabilitation Research and Training Center (unpublished technical report).

Garber, H. L., & McInerney, M. (1982). Sociobehavioral factors in mental retardation. In P. T. Cegelka & H. J. Prehm (Eds.), *Mental retardation: From categories to people.* Columbus, OH: Merrill.

Geismar, L. L., & La Sorte, M. A. (1964). *Understanding the multi-problem family.* New York: Association Press.

Gesell, A., & Amatruda, C. S. (1947). *Developmental diagnosis: Normal and abnormal child development* (2nd ed.). New York: Harper & Row.

Gholson, B. (1980). *The cognitive-developmental basis of human learning: Studies in hypothesis testing.* New York: Academic Press.

Gholson, B., & Beilin, H. (1979). A developmental model of human learning. In H. W. Reese & L. P. Lipsitt (Eds.), *Advances in child development and behavior* (Vol. 13). New York: Academic Press.

Gindes, M., & Barten, S. (1977). The development of equivalence rules for visual configuration. *Journal of Experimental Child Psychology, 24,* 11–23.

Gleason, H. A., Jr. (1965). *Linguistics and English grammar.* New York: Holt, Rinehart, & Winston.

Golden, M., & Birns, B. (1976). Social class and infant intelligence. In M. Lewis (Ed.), *Origins of intelligence.* New York: Plenum.

Goldstein, H. (1979). *The design and analysis of longitudinal studies: Their role in the measurement of change.* London: Academic Press.

Gollin, E. S. (1981). Development and plasticity. In E. S. Gollin (Ed.), *Developmental plasticity: Behavioral and biological aspects of variations in development.* New York: Academic Press.

Gollin, E. S., & Schadler, M. (1972). Relational learning and transfer in young children. *Journal of Experimental Child Psychology, 14,* 219–232.

Gollin, E. S., & Shirk, E. J. (1966). A developmental study of oddity problem learning in young children. *Child Development, 37,* 213–217.

Gordon, H. (1923). *Mental and scholastic tests among retarded children.* Great Britain: Board of Education.

Gordon, I. (1969). *Early childhood stimulation through parent education.* Final report to the Children's Bureau, Social Rehabilitation Service, Department of Health, Education, and Welfare, PHS R-306, Washington, DC.

Gottfried, A. W. (1984). Home environment and early cognitive development: Integration, meta-analyses, and conclusions. In A. W. Gottfried (Ed.), *Home environment and cognitive development: Longitudinal research.* Orlando: Academic Press.

Gottlieb, G. (1976). Conceptions of prenatal development. *Psychological Review, 83,* 215–234.

Goulet, L. R. (1973). The interfaces of acquisition: Models and methods for studying the active, developing organism. In J. R. Nesselroade & H. W. Reese (Eds.), *Life-span developmental psychology: Methodological issues.* New York: Academic Press.

Graves, M. F., & Koziol, S. (1971). Noun plural development in primary grade children. *Child Development, 42,* 1165–1173.

Gray, S. W., & Klaus, R. A. (1965). An experimental program for culturally deprived children. *Child Development, 36,* 887–898.

Gray, S. W., & Klaus, R. A. (1970). The early training project: The seventh-year report. *Child Development, 41,* 909–924.

Gray, S. W., Klaus, R. A., & Ramsey, B. K. (1981). Participants in the Early Training Project: 1962–1977. In M. J. Begab, H. C. Haywood, & H. L. Garber (Eds.), *Psychosocial influences in retarded performance: Vol. II. Strategies for improving competence* Baltimore: University Park Press.

Gresham, F. M. (1981). Social skills training with handicapped children: A review. *Review of Educational Research, 51*(8), 139–176.

Grossman, H. (1973). *Manual on terminology and classification in mental retardation.* Washington, DC: American Association on Mental Deficiency.

Grossman, H. J. (Ed.). (1977). *Manual on terminology and classification in mental retardation.* Washington, DC: American Association on Mental Deficiency.

Grossman, H. J. (Ed.). (1983). *Classification in mental retardation.* Washington, DC: American Association on Mental Deficiency.

Guilford, J. P. (1967). *The nature of human intelligence.* New York: McGraw-Hill.

Hale, G. A., & Morgan, J. S. (1973). Developmental trends in children's component selection. *Journal of Experimental Child Psychology, 15,* 302–314.

Hall, V. C., & Turner, R. R. (1971). Comparison of imitation and comprehension scores between two lower-class groups and the effects of two warm-up conditions on imitation of the same groups. *Child Development, 42,* 1735–1750.

Hare, B. A., Hammill, D. D., & Bartel, N. R. (1973). Construct validity of selected subtests of the ITPA. *Exceptional Children, 40,* 13–20.

Harlow, H. F. (1959). Learning set and error factor theory. In S. Koch (Ed.), *Psychology: A study of a science* (Vol. 2). New York: McGraw-Hill.

Havighurst, R. J., & Janke, L. L. (1944). Relations between ability and social status in a Mid-Western community. I. Ten-year-old children. *Journal of Educational Psychology, 35,* 357–368.

Hayden, A. H., & Haring, N. G. (1976). Early intervention for high risk infants and young children: Programs for Down's Syndrome children. In T. D. Tjossem (Ed.), *Intervention strategies for high risk infants and young children.* Baltimore: University Park Press.

Heal, L. W., & Johnson, J. T., Jr. (1970). Inhibition deficits in retardate learning and attention. In N. R. Ellis (Ed.), *International review of research in mental retardation* (Vol. 4). New York: Academic Press.

Heber, R. F. (1961). A manual on terminology and classification in mental retardation. *American Journal of Mental Deficiency* (Monograph Supplement), *65.*

Heber, R. (1970). *Epidemiology of mental retardation.* Chicago: Thomas Company.

Heber, R. F., Dever, R. B., & Conry, J. (1968). The influence of environmental and genetic variables on intellectual development. In H. J. Prehm, L. A. Hamerlynck, & J. E. Crossen (Eds.), *Behavioral research in mental retardation.* Eugene: University of Oregon Press.

Henderson, R. W. (1981). Home environment and intellectual performance. In R. W. Henderson (Ed.), *Parent-child interaction: Theory, research, and prospects.* New York: Academic Press.

Henderson, R. W. (1982). Personal and social causation in the school context. In J. Worell (Ed.), *Psychological development in the elementary years.* New York: Academic Pres.

Herrnstein, R. (1971). IQ. *Atlantic Monthly, 228,* 44–64.

Hess, R. D. (1970). Social class and ethnic influences on socialization. In P. H. Mussen (Ed.), *Carmichael's manual of child psychology.* New York: Wiley.

Hess, R. D. (1981). Approaches to the measurement and interpretation of parent-child interaction. In R. W. Henderson (Ed.), *Parent-child interaction: Theory, research, and prospects.* New York: Academic Press.

Hess, R. D., & Shipman, V. (1965). Early experiences and socialization of cognitive modes in children. *Child Development, 36,* 869–886.

Hess, R. D., & Shipman, V. C. (1967). Cognitive elements in maternal behavior. In J. P. Hill (Ed.), *Minnesota Symposia on Child Psychology* (Vol. 1). Minneapolis: University of Minnesota Press.

Hess, R. D., & Shipman, V. C. (1968). Maternal influences upon early learning: The cognitive environments of urban, pre-school children. In R. D. Hess & R. M. Bear (Eds.), *Early education.* Chicago: Aldine.

Hieronymus, A. N. (1951). Study of social class motivation: Relationships between anxiety for education and certain socio-economic and intellectual variables. *Journal of Educational Psychology, 42,* 193–205.

Hildreth, G. H., Griffiths, N. L., & McGauvran, M. E. (1969). *Metropolitan Readiness Tests.* New York: Harcourt, Brace, and Co.

Hill, S. D. (1965). The performance of young children on three discrimination-learning tasks. *Child Development, 36,* 425–435.

Hilton, T. L., & Patrick, C. (1970). Cross-sectional versus longitudinal data: An empirical comparison of mean differences in academic growth. *Journal of Educational Measurement, 7(1),* 15–24.

Hodges, W. L. (1978). The worth of the follow through experience. *Harvard Educational Review, 48(2),* 186–192.

Horowitz, F. D. (1969). Learning, developmental research, and individual differences. In L. P. Lipsitt & H. W. Reese (Eds.), *Advances in child development and behavior* (Vol. 4). New York: Academic Press.

Horowitz, F. D., & Paden, L. Y. (1973). The effect of environmental intervention programs. In B. Caldwell & H. Riccuiti (Eds.), *Review of child developmental research* (Vol. III). Chicago: University of Chicago Press.

House, B. J., Brown, A. L., & Scott, M. S. (1974). Children's discrimination learning based on identity or difference. In H. W. Reese (Ed.), *Advances in child development and behavior* (Vol. 9). New York: Academic Press.

Huang, I. (1945). Abstraction of form and color in children as a function of the stimulus objects. *Journal of Genetic Psychology, 66*, 59-62.

Hunt, J. McV. (1961). *Intelligence and experience.* New York: Ronald Press.

Hunt, J. McV. (1964). The psychological basis for using preschool enrichment as an antidote for cultural deprivation. *Merrill-Palmer Quarterly, 10*, 209-248.

Hunt, J. McV. (1968). Environment, development, and scholastic achievement. In M. Deutsch, I. Katz, & A. R. Jensen (Eds.), *Social class, race, and psychological development.* New York: Holt, Rinehart, & Winston.

Hunt, J. McV., & Eichorn, D. H. (1972). Maternal and child behaviors: A review of data from the Berkeley growth study. *Seminars in Psychiatry, 4*(4).

Huston-Stein, A., & Baltes, P. B. (1976). Theory and method in life-span development psychology: Implications for child development. In H. W. Reese & L. P. Lipsitt (Eds.), *Advances in child development and behavior* (Vol. 11). New York: Academic Press.

Hyde, D. M. (1969). An investigation of Piaget's theories of the development of the concept of number (as reported in DeLemos). *International Journal of Psychology, 4*, 255-269.

Inhelder, B., & Piaget, J. (1958). *The growth of logical thinking from childhood to adolescence.* New York: Basic Books.

Jensen, A. R. (1968). Social class and verbal learning. In M. Deutsch, I. Katz, & A. R. Jensen (Eds.), *Social class, race, and psychological development.* New York: Holt, Rinehart, & Winston.

Jensen, A. R. (1969). How much can we boost IQ and scholastic achievement? *Harvard Educational Review, 39*, 1-123.

Jensen, A. R. (1973). *Educability and group differences.* New York: Harper & Row.

Jensen, A. R. (1980). *Bias in mental testing.* New York: Free Press.

Jensen, A. R. (1981). Raising the IQ: The Ramey and Haskins study. *Intelligence, 5*, 29-40.

Jensen, A. R. (1982). The chronometry of intelligence. In R. J. Sternberg (Ed.), *Advances in the psychology of human intelligence* (Vol. 1). Hillsdale, NJ: Lawrence Erlbaum.

Johannesson, A. (1974). Aggressive behavior among school children related to maternal practices in early childhood. In J. deWit & W. W. Hartup (Eds.), *Determinants and origins of aggressive behavior.* The Hague: Mouton.

Jones, H. E. (1954). The environment and mental development. In L. Carmichael (Ed.), *Handbook of child psychology.* New York: Wiley.

Jones, H. E., & Bayley, N. (1941). The Berkeley Growth Study. *Child Development, 12*, 167-173.

Jones, M. C., Bayley, N., MacFarlane, J. W., & Honzik, M. P. (1971). *The course of human development.* Waltham, MA: Xerox College Publishing.

Kagan, J. (1965). Impulsive and reflective children: Significance of conceptual tempo. In J. D. Krumboltz (Ed.), *Learning and the educational process.* Chicago: Rand McNally.

Kagan, J. (1968). On cultural deprivation. In D. Glass (Ed.), *Proceedings of the Conference on Biology and Behavior.* New York: Rockefeller University Press.

Kagan, J. (1969). On the meaning of behavior: Illustrations from the infant. *Child Development, 40*, 1121-1134.

Kagan, J., & Kogan, N. (1970). Individual variation in cognitive processes. In P. H. Mussen (Ed.), *Carmichael's manual of child psychology* (Vol. 1). New York: Wiley.

Kagan, J., & Lemkin, J. (1961). Form, color, and size in children's conceptual behavior. *Child Development, 32*, 25-28.

Kagan, J., & Moss, H. A. (1962). *Birth to maturity.* New York: Wiley.

Kagan, J., & Moss, H. A., & Sigel, I. E. (1963). Psychological significance of styles of conceptualization. In J. C. Wright & J. Kagan (Eds.), *Basic cognitive processes in children. Monographs of the Society for Research in Child Development, 28*(2, Series No. 86).

Kagan, J., Pearson, L., & Welch, L. (1966). Conceptual impulsivity and inductive reasoning. *Child Development, 37*, 583-594.

Kagan, J., Rosman, B. L., Day, D., Albert, J., & Phillips, W. (1964). Information processing in the child: Significance of analytic and reflective attitudes. *Psychological Monographs, 78*(1, Whole No. 578).

Karnes, M. B. (1972). *Structured cognitive approach for educating young children: Report of a successful program*. Storrs: University of Connecticut, National Leadership Institute, Teacher Education/Early Childhood Technical Paper.

Karnes, M. B. (1973). Evaluation and implications of research with young handicapped and low-income children. In J. C. Stanley (Ed.), *Compensatory education for children ages two to eight: Recent studies of educational intervention*. Baltimore: Johns Hopkins University Press.

Karnes, M. B., Hodgins, A. S., Stoneburner, R. L., Studley, W. M., & Teska, J. A. (1968). Effects of a highly structured program of language development on intellectual functioning and psycholinguistic development of culturally disadvantaged three-year-olds. *Journal of Special Education, 2*, 405–412.

Karnes, M. B., Studley, W. M., Wright, W. R., & Hodgins, A. S. (1968). An approach to working with mothers of disadvantaged preschool children. *Merrill-Palmer Quarterly, 14*, 174–184.

Karnes, M. B., Teska, J. A., Wollersheim, J. P., Stoneburner, R. L., & Hodgins, A. S. (1968). An evaluation of two preschool programs for disadvantaged children: A traditional and highly structured experimental preschool. *Exceptional Children, 34*, 667–676.

Karp, S. A., & Konstadt, N. L. (1963). *Manual for the Children's Embedded Figures Test*. Baltimore: Authors (5900 Greenspring Ave., 21209).

Kearsley, R. B., & Zelazo, P. R. (1975). *Intellectual assessment during infancy and early childhood*. Paper presented at a meeting of the New England Pediatric Society, Boston.

Keniston, K., & The Carnegie Council on Children. (1977). *All our children: The American family under pressure*. New York: Harcourt, Brace, Jovanovich.

Kennedy, W., Van de Riet, V., & White, J. (1963). A normative sample of intelligence and achievement of Negro elementary school children in the southeastern United States. *Monographs of the Society for Research in Child Development, 28*(6).

Kidd, A. H., & Rivoire, J. H. (Eds.). (1966). *Perceptual development in children*. New York: International Universities Press.

Kirk, S. A. (1958). *Early education of the mentally retarded*. Urbana: University of Illinois Press.

Kirk, S. A., McCarthy, J. J., & Kirk, W. D. (1968). *Examiner's manual: Illinois Test of Psycholinguistic Abilities*. Urbana: University of Illinois Press.

Klaus, R. A., & Gray, S. W. (1968). The Early Training Project for disadvantaged children: A report after five years. *Monographs of the Society for Research in Child Development, 33*(4, Serial No. 120).

Klausmeier, H. J., Ghatala, E. S., & Frayer, D. A. (1974). *Conceptual learning and development: A cognitive view*. New York: Academic Press.

Knobloch, H., & Pasamanick, B. (Eds.). (1974). *Gesell and Amatruda's developmental diagnosis: The evaluation and management of normal and abnormal neuropsychologic development in infancy and early childhood* (3rd ed.). Hagerstown, MD: Harper & Row.

Kogan, N. (1976). *Cognitive styles in infancy and early childhood*. Hillsdale, NJ: Lawrence Erlbaum.

Kohlberg, L. (1968). Early education: A cognitive developmental view. *Child Development, 39*, 1013–1062.

Kohn, M. L. (1963). Social class and parent-child relationships: An interpretation. *American Journal of Sociology, 68*, 471–480.

Kuhn, T. S. (1962). *The structure of scientific revolutions*. Chicago: University of Chicago Press.

Kushlick, A. (1961). Subnormality in Salford. In M. W. Susser & A. Kushlick (Eds.), *A report on the mental health services of the city of Salford for the year 1960*. Salford, England: Salford Health Department.

Kushlick, A. (1964). *The prevalence of recognised mental subnormality of I.Q. under 50 among children in the south of England, with reference to the demand for places for residential care*. Paper presented to the International Copenhagen Conference on the Scientific Study of Mental Retardation, Copenhagen.

Labov, W. (1967). Some sources of reading problems for Negro speakers of nonstandard English. In A. Fraser (Ed.), *New directions in elementary English*. Champaign, IL: National Council of Teachers of English.

Labov, W. (1970). The study of language in its social context. *Stadium Generale, 23,* 30–87.

Labov, W. (1972). *Language in the inner city: Studies in the black English vernacular.* Philadelphia: University of Pennsylvania Press.

Lavin, D. E. (1965). *The prediction of academic performance.* New York: Wiley (Science Editions).

Lawton, D. (1968). *Social class, language and education.* London: Routledge & Kegan Paul.

Lazar, I., & Darlington, R. B. (1978). *Lasting effects after preschool.* Final Report, HEW Grant 90C-1311 to the Education Commission of the States, Cornell University, Ithaca, New York.

Lazar, I., Darlington, R. B., Murray, H., Royce, J., & Snipper, A. (1982). Lasting effects of early education: A report from the Consortium for Longitudinal Studies. *Monographs of the Society for Research in Child Development, 47*(2–3, Serial No. 195).

Lazerson, M. (1972). The historical antecedents of early childhood education. In I. J. Gordon (Ed.), *Early childhood education.* Chicago: University of Chicago Press.

Lehmann, I. J. (1959). Rural-urban differences in intelligence. *Journal of Educational Research, 53,* 62–68.

Lemkau, P. V., & Imre, P. D. (1966). *Preliminary results of a field epidemiologic study.* Paper presented at the Scientific Symposium for the Dedication of the Joseph P. Kennedy, Jr., Memorial Laboratories.

Lenneberg, E. H. (1967). *Biological foundations of language.* New York: Wiley.

Lewis, O. (1966). *La vida.* New York: Knopf.

Light, R. M., & Smith, P. V. (1969). Social allocation models of intelligence: A methodological inquiry. *Harvard Educational Review, 39,* 484–510.

Lipsitt, L. P., & Serunian, S. A. (1963). Oddity-problem learning in young children. *Child Development, 34,* 201–206.

Luria, A. R. (1961). *The role of speech in the regulation of normal and abnormal behavior.* New York: Pergamon Press.

Mackworth, N. H., & Bruner, J. S. (1966). *Selecting visual information during recognition by adults and children.* Unpublished manuscript, Harvard Center for Cognitive Studies.

MacMillan, D., Meyers, C., & Morrison, G. (1980). System-identification of mildly mentally retarded children: Implications for interpreting and conducting research. *American Journal of Mental Deficiency, 85,* 108–115.

MacPhee, D., Ramey, C. T., & Yeates, K. O. (1984). Home environment and early cognitive development: Implications for intervention. In A. W. Gottfried (Ed.), *Home environment and early cognitive development: Longitudinal research.* Orlando: Academic Press.

Maltzman, I. (1967). Individual differences in "attention": The orienting reflex. In R. Gagne (Ed.), *Learning and individual differences.* Columbus, OH: Merrill.

Mann, H. B., & Whitney, D. R. (1947). On a test of whether one of two random variables is stochastically larger than the other. *Annals of Mathematical Statistics, 18,* 50–60.

Marcus, M., West, K., & Gaines, R. (1960). *Color-form preference in young children of lower socioeconomic status and its relation to cognitive style.* Paper presented at Brain Behavior Research Center Seminar, Sonoma State Hospital, Eldridge, CA.

McCall, R. B. (1976). Toward an epigenetic conception of mental development in the first three years of life. In M. Lewis (Ed.), *Origins of intelligence.* New York: Plenum.

McCall, R. B. (1981). Nature-nurture and the two realms of development: A proposed integration with respect to mental development. *Child Development, 52,* 1–12.

McCall, R. B., Appelbaum, M., & Hogarty, P. (1973). Developmental changes in mental performance. *Monographs of the Society for Research in Child Development, 38*(Serial No. 150).

McNeill, D. (1970). *The acquisition of language.* New York: Harper & Row.

McNemar, Q. (1940). A critical examination of the University of Iowa studies of environmental influences upon the IQ. *Psychological Bulletin, 37,* 63–92.

Melkman, R., & Deutsch, C. (1977). Memory functioning as related to developmental changes in bases of organization. *Journal of Experimental Child Psychology, 23,* 84–97.

Mercer, J. R. (1972). Who is normal? Two perspectives on mild mental retardation. In E. Jaco (Ed.), *Patients, physicians and illness.* New York: Free Press.

Mercer, J. R. (1973). *Labeling the mentally retarded: Clinical and social system perspectives on mental retardation.* Berkeley: University of California Press.

Messer, S. (1976). Reflection-impulsivity: A review. *Psychological Bulletin, 83,* 1026–1052.

Miller, W., & Ervin, S. (1964). The development of grammar in child language. In U. Bellugi & R. W. Brown (Eds.), *The acquisition of language. Monographs of the Society for Research in Child Development, 29*(Serial No. 92), 9–34.

Milner, E. (1951). A study of the relationship between reading readiness in grade one school children and patterns of parent-child interaction. *Child Development, 22,* 95–112.

Milwaukee Public Schools. (1972). *School profiles: Citywide testing program school year 1970–1971.* Milwaukee: Department of Educational Research and Program Assessment, Division of Long-Range Development.

Mimbauer, C., & Miller, J. (1970). Socioeconomic background and cognitive functioning in preschool children. *Child Development, 41,* 471–480.

Minuchin, S., Montalvo, B., Guerney, B. G., Jr., Rosman, B. L., & Schumer, F. (1967). *Families of the slums: An exploration of their structure and treatment.* New York: Basic Books.

Mitchell, B. C. (1967). Predictive validity of the Metropolitan Readiness Tests and the Murphy-Durrell Reading Readiness Analysis for white and Negro pupils. *Educational and Psychological Measurement, 27,* 1047–1054.

Moffitt, A. R., & Coates, B. (1969). Problem-solving strategies and performance of severely retarded children. *American Journal of Mental Deficiency, 73,* 774–778.

Moltz, H. (1960). Imprinting: Empirical basis and theoretical significance. *Psychological Bulletin, 57.*

Morrison, D. F. (1976). *Multivariate statistical methods* (2nd ed.). New York: McGraw-Hill.

Mussen, P. H., Dean, S., & Rosenberg, M. (1952). Some further evidence on the validity of the WISC. *Journal of Consulting Psychology, 16,* 410–411.

Natalicio, D. S., & Natalicio, L. F. S. (1971). A comparative study of English pluralization by native and non-native English speakers. *Child Development, 42,* 1302–1306.

Neimark, E. D., & Horn, M. (1969). Development of discrimination and oddity learning set in a two year old girl. *Psychonomic Science, 17,* 108–109.

Newfield, M. U., & Schlanger, B. B. (1968). The acquisition of English morphology by normal and educable mentally retarded children. *Journal of Speech and Hearing Research, 11,* 693–706.

Nichols, R. C. (1981). Origins, nature and determinants of intellectual development. In M. J. Begab, H. C. Haywood, & H. L. Garber (Eds.), *Psychosocial influences in retarded performance: Vol I. Issues and theories in development.* Baltimore: University Park Press.

Olim, E. G., Hess, R. D., & Shipman, V. C. (1967). Role of mothers' language styles in mediating their preschool children's cognitive development. *School Review, 75,* 414–424.

Olver, R. R., & Hornsby, J. R. (1967). On equivalence. In J. S. Bruner, R. R. Olver, & P. M. Greenfield (Eds.), *Studies in cognitive growth: A collaboration at the Center for Cognitive Studies.* New York: Wiley.

Osler, S. F., & Fivel, M. W. (1961). Concept attainment: I. The role of age and intelligence in concept attainment by induction. *Journal of Experimental Psychology, 62,* 1–8.

Osler, S. F., & Kofsky, E. (1966). Structure and strategy in concept learning. *Journal of Experimental Child Psychology, 4,* 198–209.

Osler, S. F., & Shapiro, S. L. (1964). Studies in concept attainment: IV. The role of partial reinforcement as a function of age and intelligence. *Journal of Experimental Psychology, 35,* 623–633.

Owings, N. O. (1972). *Internal reliability and item analysis of the Miller-Yoder Test of Grammatical Comprehension.* Unpublished master's thesis, University of Wisconsin-Madison.

Palmer, F. H., & Andersen, L. W. (1981). Early intervention treatments that have been tried, documented, and assessed. In M. J. Begab, H. C. Haywood, & H. L. Garber (Eds.), *Psychosocial influences in retarded performance: Vol. II. Strategies for improving competence.* Baltimore: University Park Press.

Papousek, H., & Papousek, M. (1982). Infant-adult social interactions: Their origins, dimensions, and failures. In T. M. Field, A. Huston, H. C. Quay, L. Troll, & G. E. Finley (Eds.), *Review of human development.* New York: Wiley.

Paraskevopoulos, J. N., & Kirk, S. A. (1969). *The development and psychometric characteristics of the Revised Illinois Test of Psycholinguistic Abilities.* Urbana: University of Illinois Press.

Pavenstedt, E. (1965). A comparison of the child rearing environment of upper-lower and very low-lower class families. *American Journal of Orthopsychiatry, 35,* 89–98.

Pederson, E., Faucher, T. A., & Eaton, W. W. (1978). A new perspective on the effects of first-grade teachers on children's subsequent adult status. *Harvard Educational Review, 48*(1), 1–31.

Peeke, S. C., & Stone, G. C. (1973a). *Focal and peripheral processing of color and form.* San Francisco: Langley Porter (mimeo).

Peeke, S. C., & Stone, G. C. (1973b). *Parallel processing of redundant and non-redundant stimuli in two tasks.* San Francisco: Langley Porter (mimeo).

Peisach, E. C. (1965). Children's comprehension of teacher and peer speech. *Child Development, 36,* 467–480.

Penn, N. E., Sindberg, R. M., & Wolhueter, M. J. (1969). The oddity concept in severely retarded children. *Child Development, 40,* 154–161.

Peters, C. C., & McElwee, A. R. (1944). Improving functioning intelligence by analytical training in nursery school. *Elementary School Journal, 45,* 213–219.

Platt, W. D., & Blodgett, F. M. (1973). *Evaluation of health and physical growth of children in a special education project.* Milwaukee: Children's Hospital, unpublished manuscript.

Porter, P. T. (1965). *A developmental study of three-position form-oddity learning in young children.* Unpublished master's thesis, University of South Dakota.

Price-Williams, D. R. (1961). A study concerning concepts of conservation of quantities among primitive children. *Acta Psychologica, 18,* 297–305.

Ramey, C. T., & Bryant, D. (1982). Evidence for primary prevention of developmental retardation. *Journal of the Division of Early Childhood, 5,* 73–78.

Ramey, C. T., Collier, A. M., Sparling, J. J., Loda, F. A., Campbell, F. A., Ingram, D. L., & Finkelstein, N. W. (1976). The Carolina Abecedarian Project: A longitudinal and multidisciplinary approach to the prevention of developmental retardation. In R. D. Tjossem (Ed.), *Intervention strategies for high risk infants and young children.* Baltimore: University Park Press.

Ramey, C. T., & Haskins, R. (1981). The causes and treatment of school failure: Insights from the Carolina Abecedarian Project. In M. J. Begab, H. C. Haywood, & H. L. Garber (Eds.), *Psychosocial influences in retarded performance: Vol. II. Strategies for improving competence.* Baltimore: University Park Press.

Ramey, C. T., & Smith, B. (1977). Assessing the intellectual consequences of early intervention with high-risk infants. *American Journal of Mental Deficiency, 81,* 318–324.

Ramey, C. T., Sparling, J. J., Bryant, D., & Wasik, B. (1982). Primary prevention of developmental retardation during infancy. *Prevention in Human Services, 1,* 61–83.

Reed, E. W., & Reed, S. C. (1965). *Mental retardation: A family study.* Philadelphia: Saunders.

Reyes, E. V., & Garber, H. L. (1971). Measurement of language development. In *Rehabilitation of families at risk for mental retardation: A progress report.* Madison: University of Wisconsin Rehabilitation Research and Training Center (unpublished technical report).

Reyes, E. V., & Garber, H. L. (1976). *Developmental differences in language as measured by a sentence repetition test.* Unpublished paper appended to progress report, Rehabilitation Research and Training Center in Mental Retardation, University of Wisconsin-Madison.

Rheingold, H. L. (1956). The modification of social responsiveness in institutional babies. *Monographs of the Society for Research in Child Development, 21*(2).

Rist, R. C. (1970). Student social class and teacher expectations: The self-fulfilling prophecy in ghetto education. *Harvard Educational Review, 40,* 411–451.

Robbins, R. C., Mercer, J. R., & Meyers, C. E. (1967). The school as a selecting-labeling system. *Journal of School Psychology, 5*(4), 270–279.

Roberts, S. O., Crump, E. P., Dickerson, A. E., & Horton, C. P. (1965). *Longitudinal performance of Negro American children at 5 and 10 years on the Stanford-Binet.* Paper presented at the meeting of the American Psychological Association, Chicago.

Rockwitz, M. (1968). *How to prepare for the high school equivalency examination.* Woodbury, NY: Barron & Company.

Rogosa, D. R. (1979). Causal models in longitudinal research: Rationale, formulation, and interpretation. In J. R. Nesselroade & P. B. Baltes (Eds.), *Longitudinal research in human development: Design and analysis*. New York: Academic Press.

Rosenzweig, M. R. (1966). Environmental complexity, cerebral change and behavior. *American Psychologist, 21*, 321–322.

Rotter, J. B. (1966). Generalized expectancies for internal versus external control of reinforcement. *Psychological Monographs, 80*(1, Whole No. 609).

Sander, L. W. (1965). The longitudinal course of early mother-child interaction. In B. M. Foss (Ed.), *Determinants of infant behavior*, III. London: Methuen.

Sattler, J. M. (1973). Intelligence testing of ethnic-minority group and culturally disadvantaged children. In L. Mann & D. A. Sabatino (Eds.), *The first review of special education* (Vol. 2). Philadelphia: JSE Press.

Sattler, J. M. (1974). *Assessment of children's intelligence*. Philadelphia: Saunders.

Sattler, J. M. (1982). *Assessment of children's intelligence and special abilities* (2nd ed.). Boston: Allyn & Bacon.

Scandura, J. M. (1972). *Theory in structural learning*. New York: Gordon & Breach.

Scarr, S. (1981). *Race, social class, and individual differences in I.Q.* Hillsdale, NJ: Lawrence Erlbaum.

Scarr, S., & Weinberg, R. A. (1978). The influence of "family background" on intellectual attainment. *American Sociological Review, 43*, 674–692.

Scarr-Salapatek, S. (1971). Unknowns in the IQ equation. *Science, 174*, 1223–1228.

Schaefer, E. S. (1975). Factors that impede the process of socialization. In M. J. Begab & S. A. Richardson (Eds.), *The mentally retarded and society: A social science perspective*. Baltimore: University Park Press.

Schiff, M., Duyme, M., Dumaret, A., Stewart, J., Tomkiewicz, S., & Feingold, J. (1978). Intellectual status of working-class children adopted early into upper-middle-class families. *Science, 200*, 1503–1504.

Schoggen, M., & Schoggen, P. (1976). Environmental forces in the home lives of three-year-old children in three population subgroups. *JSAS Catalog of Selected Documents in Psychology, 6*, ms. #1178.

Schweinhart, L. J., & Weikart, D. P. (1981). Perry preschool effects nine years later: What do they mean? In M. J. Begab, H. C. Haywood, & H. L. Garber (Eds.), *Psychological influences in retarded performance: Vol. II. Strategies for improving competence*. Baltimore: University Park Press.

Sedlak, R. A., & Weener, P. (1973). Review of research on the Illinois Test of Psycholinguistic Abilities. In L. Mann & D. A. Sabatino (Eds.), *The first review of special education* (Vol. 1). Philadelphia: JSE Press.

Serpell, R. (1966). Selective attention in matching from sample by children. *Reports*, University of Zambia.

Severson, R. A., & Guest, K. E. (1970). Toward the standardized assessment of disadvantaged children. In F. Williams (Ed.), *Language and poverty: Perspectives on a theme*. Chicago: Markham.

Sherman, M., & Key, C. B. (1932). The intelligence of isolated mountain children. *Child Development, 3*, 279–290.

Shipman, V. C. (1976). *Notable early characteristics of high and low achieving black low-SES children*, PR-76-21. In the series Disadvantaged Children and Their First School Experiences: ETS-Head Start Longitudinal Study. Princeton: Educational Testing Service.

Shipman, V. C., McKee, D., & Bridgeman, B. (1976). *Disadvantaged children and their first school experiences: Stability and change in family status, situational, and process variables and their relationship to children's cognitive performance* (PR-75-78). Prepared under Grant H-8256, Department of Health, Education, and Welfare. Princeton: Educational Testing Service.

Siegelman, E. (1969). Reflective and impulsive observing behavior. *Child Development, 40*, 1213–1222.

Siegler, R. S. (1976). Three aspects of cognitive development. *Cognitive Psychology, 8*, 481–520.

Sigel, I. E. (1971). Language of the disadvantaged: The distancing hypothesis. In C. S. Lavatelli (Ed.), *Language training in early childhood education*. Urbana: University of Illinois Press.

Sigel, I. E., Anderson, L. M., & Shapiro, H. (1966). *Categorization behavior of lower- and middle-class Negro preschool children: Differences in dealing with representation of familiar objects*. Detroit: Merrill-Palmer Institute (mimeo).

Simonton, I. B. (Ed.). (1967). *Bank Street Readers* (Bank Street College of Education). New York: Macmillan.

Skeels, H. M. (1966). Adult status of children with contrasting early life experiences: A follow-up study. *Monographs of the Society for Research in Child Development, 31*(Serial No. 105).

Skeels, H. M., & Dye, H. B. (1939). A study of the effects of differential stimulation on mentally retarded children. *Proceedings of the American Association on Mental Deficiency, 44*, 114–136.

Skeels, H. M., & Fillmore, E. A. (1937). The mental development of children from underprivileged homes. *Journal of Genetic Psychology, 50*, 427–439.

Skeels, H. M., Updegraff, R., Wellman, B. L., & Williams, H. M. (1938). A study of environmental stimulation: An orphanage preschool project. *University of Iowa Study on Child Welfare, 15*(4).

Skodak, M. (1938). Children in foster homes. *University of Iowa Study on Child Welfare, 15*(4), 191.

Slobin, D. I. (1971). Developmental psycholinguistics. In W. O. Dingwall (Ed.), *A survey of linguistic science*. College Park: Linguistics Program, University of Maryland.

Slobin, D. I., & Welsh, C. A. (1967). *Elicited information as a research tool in developmental psycholinguistics*. Reproduced by Educational Resources Information Center.

Snow, C. E. (1972). Mother's speech to children learning language. *Child Development, 43*, 549–565.

Solomon, D. (1982). Theory and research on children's achievement. In J. Worell (Ed.), *Psychological development in the elementary years*. New York: Academic Press.

Solomon, M. (1972). Stem endings and the acquisition of inflections. *Language Learning, 22*, 43–50.

Stauffer, R. (1970). *The language experience approach to the teaching of reading*. New York: Harper & Row.

Stein, Z., Susser, M., & Saenger, G. (1976). Mental retardation in a national population of young men in the Netherlands: Prevalence of severe mental retardation (I), Prevalence of mild mental retardation (II). *American Journal of Epidemiology, 104*(2), 159–169.

Stevenson, H. W. (1970). Learning in children. In P. H. Mussen (Ed.), *Carmichael's manual of child psychology* (Vol. 1) (3rd ed.). New York: Wiley.

Stevenson, H. W. (1972). *Children's learning*. New York: Appleton-Century-Crofts.

Stevenson, H. W., Parker, T., Wilkinson, A., Hegion, A., & Fish, E. (1976). Longitudinal study of individual differences in cognitive development and scholastic achievement. *Journal of Educational Psychology, 68*, 377–400.

Stodolsky, S. S., & Lesser, G. (1967). Learning patterns in the disadvantaged. *Harvard Educational Review, 37*, 546–593.

Stone, M. (1960). Models for choice reaction time. *Psychometrika, 26*, 251–260.

Streissguth, A., & Bee, H. L. (1972). Mother-child interactions and cognitive development in children. *Young Children*, 154–173.

Suchman, R. G. (1966). Cultural differences in children's color and form preferences. *Journal of Social Psychology, 70*, 3–10.

Tampieri, G. (1968). La preferenza forme-colore nella percezione viva infantile. *Archivio di Psicologia, Neurologia, e Psichiatria, 29*(2), 159–199.

Tarjan, G., Wright, S. W., Eyman, R. K., & Keeran, C. V. (1973). Natural history of mental retardation: Some aspects of epidemiology. *American Journal of Mental Deficiency, 77*, 369–379.

Terman, L. M., assisted by B. T. Baldwin, E. Bronson, J. C. De Voss, F. Fuller, F. L. Goodenough, T. L. Kelly, M. Lima, H. Marshall, A. S. Raubenheimer, G. M. Ruch, R. L. Willoughby, J. B.

Wyman, & D. H. Yates. (1925). *Genetic studies of genius: Vol. I. Mental and physical traits of a thousand gifted children*. Stanford, CA: Stanford University Press.

Terman, L. M. & Merrill, M. A. (1960). *Stanford-Binet Intelligence Scale: Manual for the third revision Form L-M*. Boston: Houghton Mifflin.

Terrell, G., Jr., Durkin, K., & Wiesley, M. (1959). Social class and the nature of the incentive in discrimination learning. *Journal of Abnormal and Social Psychology, 59*, 270–272.

Thoman, E. B. (1981). Early communication as the prelude to later adaptive behavior. In M. J. Begab, H. C. Haywood, & H. L. Garber (Eds.), *Psychosocial Influences in retarded performance: Vol. II. Strategies for improving performance*. Baltimore: University Park Press.

Thorndike, R. (1978). Causation of Binet IQ decrements. *Journal of Educational Measurement, 15*, 197–202.

Timm, N. H. (1975). *Multivariate analysis with applications in education and psychology*. Monterey, CA: Brooks/Cole.

Tizard, J. (1974). Ecological studies of malnutrition: Problems and methods. In J. Cravioto, L. Hambraeus, & B. Vahlquist (Eds.), *Early malnutrition and mental development*. Symposia of the Swedish Nutrition Foundation (No. XII). Stockholm: Almquist & Wiksell.

Trabasso, T., Stave, M., & Eichberg, R. (1969). Attitude preference and discrimination shifts in young children. *Journal of Experimental Child Psychology, 8*, 195–209.

Tulkin, S. R. (1968). Race, class, family, and school achievement. *Journal of Personality and Social Psychology, 9*(1), 31–37.

Tulkin, S. R. (1970). *Mother-infant interaction the first year of life: An inquiry into the influences of social class*. Unpublished doctoral dissertation, Harvard University.

Tulkin, S. R. (1972). An analysis of the concept of cultural deprivation. *Developmental Psychology, 6*(2), 326–339.

Tulkin, S. R., & Cohler, B. (1973). Childrearing attitudes and mother-child interaction in the first year of life. *Merrill-Palmer Quarterly, 19*, 95–106.

Vernon, P. (1969). *Intelligence and cultural environment*. London: Methuen.

Vernon, P. E. (1979). *Intelligence: Heredity and environment*. San Francisco: W. H. Freeman & Company

Vygotsky, L. S. (1962). *Thought and language*. (E. Hanfmann & G. Vakar, Trans.). Cambridge: MIT Press.

Wachs, T. D. (1984). Proximal experience and early cognitive-intellectual development: The social environment. In A. W. Gottfried (Ed.), *Home environment and early cognitive development: Longitudinal research*. Orlando: Academic Press.

Wachs, T. D., Uzgiris, I. C., & Hunt, J. McV. (1967). *Cognitive development in infants of different age levels and from different environmental backgrounds*. Paper presented to the Society for Research in Child Development, New York.

Watson, E. H., & Lowry, G. H. (1967). *Growth and development of children*. Chicago: Year Book Medical Publishers.

Wechsler, D. (1949). *Manual for the Wechsler Intelligence Scale for Children*. New York: Psychological Corp.

Wechsler, D. (1955). *Manual for the Wechsler Adult Intelligence Scale*. New York: Psychological Corp.

Wechsler, D. (1967). *Manual for the Wechsler Preschool and Primary Scale of Intelligence*. New York: Psychological Corp.

Weikart, D. P. (1971). *Early childhood special education for intellectually subnormal and/or culturally different children*. Paper presented for the National Leadership Institute in Early Childhood Development, Washington, DC.

Weikart, D. P. (1972). Relationship of curriculum, teaching, and learning in preschool education. In J. C. Stanley (Ed.), *Preschool programs from the disadvantaged: Five experimental approaches to early childhood experience*. Baltimore: Johns Hopkins University Press.

Weikart, D. P., Bond, J. T., & McNeil, J. T. (1978). The Ypsilanti Perry Preschool Project: Preschool years and longitudinal results through fourth grade. *Monographs of the High/Scope Educational Research Foundation*, No. 3.

References 433

Weikart, D. P., & Lambie, D. Z. (1968). Preschool intervention through a home teaching program. In J. Hellmuth (Ed.), *Disadvantaged child* (Vol II). New York: Brunner/Mazel.
Weikart, D. P., & Lambie, D. Z. (1970). Early enrichment in infants. In V. H. Dennenberg (Ed.), *Education of the infant and young child*. London: Academic Press.
Weikart, D. P., & Wiegerink, R. (1968). Initial results of a comparative preschool curriculum project. *Proceedings of the 76th Annual Convention of the American Psychological Association, 3*, 597–598.
Weir, M. W. (1967). Children's behavior in probabilistic tasks. In W. W. Hartup & N. L. Smothergill (Eds.), *The young child*. Washington, DC: National Association for the Education of Young Children.
Weisz, J. R., Yeates, K. O., & Zigler, E. (1982). Piagetian evidence and the developmental-difference controversy. In E. Zigler & D. Balla (Eds.), *Mental retardation: The development-difference controversy*. Hillsdale, NJ: Lawrence Erlbaum.
Welch, M. J. (1974). Infants' visual attention to varying degrees of novelty. *Child Development, 45*(2), 344–350.
Wellman, B. L. (1938). The intelligence of preschool children as measured by the Merrill-Palmer scale of performance tests. *University of Iowa Studies in Child Welfare, 15*(3).
Wellman, B. L. (1940). Iowa studies on the effect of schooling. *Yearbook National Sociological Studies in Education, 39*, 377–399.
Wellman, B. L., Skeels, H. M., & Skodak, M. (1940). Review of McNemar's critical examination of Iowa studies. *Psychological Bulletin, 37*, 93–111.
Welsh, G. S. (1975). *Creativity and intelligence: A personality approach*. Chapel Hill: Institute for Research in the Social Sciences, University of North Carolina.
Werner, E. E., Bierman, J. M., & French, F. E. (1971). *The children of Kauai: A longitudinal study from the prenatal to age ten*. Honolulu: University Press of Hawaii.
Werner, E., & Smith, R. (1977). *Kauai's children come of age*. Honolulu: University Press of Hawaii.
Whitcraft, C. J. (1971). *Levels of generative syntax and linguistic performance of young children from standard and non-standard English language environments*. Unpublished doctoral dissertation, University of Texas, Austin.
White, B. L., & Watts, J. C. (1973). *Experience and environment: Vol. I. Major influences on the development of the young child*. Englewood Cliffs, NJ: Prentice-Hall.
Williams, M. L., & Scarr, S. (1971). Effects of short-term intervention on performance in low-birth weight, disadvantaged children. *Pediatrics, 47*, 289–298.
Wilton, K., & Barbour, A. (1978). Mother-child interaction in high-risk and socioeconomic status. *Child Development, 49*, 1136–1145.
Wisconsin Research and Development Center for Cognitive Learning. (1970). *Pre-reading skills program* (Kit). Chicago: Encyclopedia Britannica Educational Corp.
Witkin, H. A., Dyk, R., Faterson, H., Goodenough, D., & Karp, S. (1962). *Psychological differentiation*. New York: Wiley.
Wooley, H. T. (1925). The validity of standards of mental measurement in young childhood. *School & Society, 21*, 476–482.
Wright, J. C. (1971). *Kansas Reflection-Impulsivity Scale for Preschoolers (KRISP)*. St. Louis: Central Midwest Regional Educational Laboratory.
Wright, J. C., & Kagan, J. (Eds.). (1973). *Basic cognitive processes in children: Report of the Second Conference sponsored by the Committee on Intellective Processes Research of the Social Science Research Council*. Chicago: University of Chicago Press.
Zeamon, D., & House, B. J. (1963). The role of attention in retardate discrimination learning. In N. R. Ellis (Ed.), *Handbook of mental deficiency*. New York: McGraw-Hill.
Zigler, E. F. (1963). Rigidity and social reinforcement effects in the performance of institutionalized and non-institutionalized normal and retarded children. *Journal of Personality, 31*, 258–270.
Zigler, E. F. (1967). Familial mental retardation: A continuing dilemma. *Science, 155*, 292–298.
Zigler, E. F. (1969). Developmental versus difference theories of mental retardation and the problem of motivation. *American Journal of Mental Deficiency, 73*, 536–556.

References

Zigler, E. F., & Balla, D. (Eds.). (1982). *Mental retardation: The developmental-difference controversy*. Hillsdale, NJ: Lawrence Erlbaum.

Zigler, E. F., Balla, D., & Hodapp, R. (1984). On the definition and classification of mental retardation. *American Journal of Mental Deficiency, 89*(3), 215–230.

Zigler, E. F., & Cascione, R. (1977). Head Start has little to do with mental retardation: A reply to Clarke and Clarke. *American Journal of Mental Deficiency, 82,* 246–249.

Zigler, E. F., & de Labry, J. (1962). Concept switching in middle-class, lower-class, and retarded children. *Journal of Abnormal and Social Psychology, 65,* 267–273.

Zigler, E. F., & Trickett, P. K. (1978). IQ, social competence, and evaluation of early childhood intervention programs. *American Psychologist, 33,* 789–798.

Zigler, E. F., & Valentine, J. (Eds.). (1979). *Project Head Start: A legacy of the War on Poverty.* New York: Free Press.

Zimiles, H. (1972). An analysis of methodological barriers to cognitive assessment of preschool children. In F. Monks, W. Hartup, & J. deWitt (Eds.), *Determinants of behavior development.* New York: Academic Press.